THE PHILOSOPHY OF
ST. THOMAS AQUINAS

THE PHILOSOPHY OF ST. THOMAS AQUINAS

by

Hans Meyer

Translated by

Rev. Frederic Eckhoff

B. HERDER BOOK CO.

15 & 17 SOUTH BROADWAY, ST. LOUIS, MO.

AND

33 QUEEN SQUARE, LONDON, W. C.

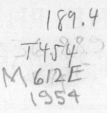

CONTENTS

Part I

ST. THOMAS AND THE THIRTEENTH CENTURY

CHAPTER   PAGE

  I.   HISTORICAL INFLUENCES 3
         1. Introduction 3
         2. Aristotle 5
         3. The Arabians 13
         4. The Jewish philosophers 17
         5. St. Thomas and Platonism 19
         6. The Influence of the Fathers and the early Scholastics   23

  II.   ST. THOMAS' CONTRIBUTION TO PHILOSOPHY 26
         1. Tradition and originality 27
         2. Aristotle and Christianity 35
         3. The Aristotelian basis of science 40
         4. Philosophy and theology 41

  III.   ST. THOMAS THE MAN 50

Part II

THE STRUCTURE OF REALITY

SECTION I

THE STRUCTURE OF INDIVIDUAL THINGS

  IV.   MATTER AND FORM 59
         1. Derivation and definition 59
         2. The relation between matter and form 65
         3. Evaluation of the theory of matter and form . . . 67
         4. Matter as the principle of individuation 72

  V.   ESSENCE AND EXISTENCE; THE PROBLEM OF UNIVERSALS . 81
         1. The essence of things 81
         2. The problem of universals 83

CHAPTER   PAGE

3. The kinds of essences and their properties 86
4. The existence of things 87
5. The relation between essence and existence . . . 89

VI. SUBSTANCE AND ACCIDENT 97
1. The kinds of substance 97
2. Substance and accidents 101
3. The categories 106
4. Quantity 108
5. Quality 110
6. Relations 114
7. Action and passion 118
8. The category of place 119
9. The category of time 120
10. Criticism 124

VII. THE CONCEPT OF BEING AND ITS ATTRIBUTES . . . 127

A. THE ANALOGY OF BEING

1. The concept of analogy 128
2. The kinds of analogy 129
3. The meaning of analogy 132

B. THE TRANSCENDENTALS

1. The individual transcendentals 134
2. The properties of the transcendentals 136
3. The philosophical importance of the transcendentals 136

SECTION II

THE HIERARCHY OF THE FORMS OF BEING

VIII. CORPOREAL THINGS 141

IX. THE LIVING BEINGS ON EARTH 146
1. The soul 146
2. The unity of the soul 149
3. The soul and its powers 151

X. THE DIFFERENT GRADES OF LIFE 154

XI. THE ANIMAL 159
1. The sense faculties 159
2. The sensitive appetite 164

CHAPTER   PAGE

            3. Instinct 168
            4. Summary 169

    XII. MAN; THE UNITY OF BODY AND SOUL 173
            1. The unity of the substantial form 173
            2. The soul's dependence on the body 176
            3. The subsistence of the human soul 177
            4. The individuality of the human soul 180

    XIII. MAN'S EQUIPMENT 182
            1. Man's bodily equipment 182
            2. Man's sensitive equipment 184
            3. The spiritual equipment 185
                a) The cognitive faculty 186
                b) The will 192
                c) Man's social and religious aptitudes . . . 200

    XIV. THE HUMAN PERSON 204
            1. The unity of the human person 204
            2. The substantial differences among human persons 206
            3. The difference between man and woman . . . 207
            4. The moving principle in the life of a personality . 209

    XV.   MAN'S METAPHYSICAL AND RELIGIOUS POSITION . . . 211

    XVI. THE HEAVENLY BODIES 219

    XVII. THE CREATED PURE SPIRITS 221
            1. The existence of the spirit world 221
            2. The nature of pure spirits 222
            3. The activities of pure spirits 225

    XVIII. GOD 233
            1. The formation of the concept of God 233
            2. The positive idea of God 236
            3. The analogical knowledge of God 238
            4. The theology of the two summas 242

                        SECTION III

                ORIGIN AND CORRUPTION OF THINGS

    XIX. BECOMING AND CHANGE OF THINGS 250

    XX.   BECOMING AND CAUSALITY 256
            1. Fundamental principles of causality 264

CHAPTER

PAGE

2. God and secondary causes 268

XXI. THE IDEA OF CREATION 271
1. The origin of the universe according to the Greeks 271
2. The concept of creation 274
3. Creation and time 278

XXII. THE ORIGIN AND PASSING OF THE UNIVERSE 281
1. Simultaneous or successive creation 281
2. The process of preservation 284

SECTION IV

ORDER IN THE UNIVERSE

XXIII. THE CONCEPT OF ORDER BEFORE THE TIME OF ST. THOMAS 294

XXIV. ORDER 298
1. God the Author of order 300
2. Order in the universe 301
a) Order and the individual 302
b) Order in the hierarchy of forms 304
c) Order in becoming and in the activity of things 305
d) Order and the universe 307

XXV. SENSE PERCEPTION 313
1. The order of knowledge 313
2. The objects of the senses 315
3. The nature of sense perception 317
4. The structure of the acts of perception 324

XXVI. INTELLECTUAL KNOWLEDGE 326
1. The object of intellectual knowledge 326
2. The intellect's knowledge of essences 329
3. The essential contents of things 334
4. The knowledge of the individual 342
5. Self-knowledge 345

XXVII. THE KNOWLEDGE OF TRUTH 351
1. The depositary of truth 351
2. The depositary of logical truth 353
3. Ontological truth and its connection with the concept
of God 356
4. The eternity and unchangeableness of truth . . 358

CONTENTS

CHAPTER   PAGE

XXVIII. THE ORDER AMONG SCIENCES 360
1. The division of sciences 360
a) Logic 361
c) The practical sciences 365
d) History 365
2. Methods 366

XXIX. MORALITY AND ITS RELATION TO BEING 368
1. Absolute being and absolute value 370
2. Moral values 372
3. The order of the reason and the order of the will 378
4. The order of good and the order of purposes . . 383

XXX. VIRTUE AND ORDER 388
1. The definition of virtue 388
2. Division of virtues 390
3. Virtue and the practical reason 399
4. Synteresis 400
5. The subject of the virtues 410
6. The rank of the virtues 411

XXXI. MAN'S SOCIAL NATURE AND THE NATURE OF SOCIETY . 417
1. Man's social nature 419
2. Grades of the community and the state 423
3. The nature of the civil community 433

XXXII. THE INDIVIDUAL AND THE COMMUNITY 438
1. The individual as an organic member of the community 440
2. The position of the individual in the community 445
3. Church and state 449

XXXIII. THE ETERNAL LAW 455
1. The concept of law 456
2. The eternal law 459

XXXIV. NATURAL LAW 464
1. The concept of natural law 464
2. The content of the natural law 468

XXXV. NATURAL RIGHTS 474
1. The right to physical existence 474
2. The right to property 475

CHAPTER   PAGE

3. The right of physical freedom 479
4. The right to work 485
5. The right to marry 486
6. The rights of man as a spiritual person 487
7. The natural rights of communities 491
8. The unchangeable natural law 493

XXXVI. HUMAN LAW AND DIVINE LAW 500
1. Positive human law 500
2. The divine law 506
3. Conclusion 510

XXXVII. THE ORDER OF SALVATION 512

XXXVIII. COMMENTARY 516
1. The objections 519
2. The force of the objections 521
3. The Thomistic view of the universe 526

XXXIX. PHILOSOPHY AFTER ST. THOMAS 543

APPENDIX. THE WRITINGS OF ST. THOMAS 549

INDEX 555

PART I

ST. THOMAS AND THE THIRTEENTH CENTURY

CHAPTER I

HISTORICAL INFLUENCES

1. **Introduction.** The altarpiece of St. Catherine's Church in Pisa represents the triumph of St. Thomas Aquinas. Illuminated by rays of heavenly light coming from Moses and St. Paul and the four Evangelists, St. Thomas is seated in the foreground with the *Summa contra Gentes* open on his knees. At one side stands Plato, at the other side Aristotle, and at his feet lies the defeated Averroes with his commentary on Aristotle.

In this picture the artist represents a significant chapter in the history of philosophy. He pictures the combination of the leaders of Greek philosophy and their doctrines with the Christian Gospel and St. Thomas' defeat of a false form of that combination which was irreconcilable with Christianity. The Christian religion, arising in the Hellenistic era and coming to full development amid the culture of antiquity, was no philosophy. Its Founder did not command His disciples to teach His doctrine in the schools of philosophy. His message of salvation was founded on divine authority. Throughout His life, in word and action, He referred to the mission that had been entrusted to Him by His heavenly Father. Nevertheless there are psychological and historical reasons for the approach of Greek philosophy and the Christian religion toward each other and for their subsequent union. The Pauline writings, it is true, frequently condemn the vanity of pagan philosophy, but St. Paul himself makes use of Stoic concepts that were in current usage, and in the prologue of St. John's Gospel the most widely accepted concept of Hellenism, the concept of the logos, enters the service of Christianity in order to make the person of Jesus more intelligible to the educated classes of the time. Later, too, the writings of some of the Fathers of the Church express distaste and opposition to pagan philosophy. But, while Ter-

3

tullian calls the philosophy of Plato "the storehouse of heretics," he despoils the systems of Plato and the Stoics to such an extent that he himself becomes a heretic by introducing philosophical ideas that were irreconcilable with Christianity.

In the patristic era the union of philosophy and the Christian religion, the reconciliation of reason and faith, were accepted as facts and their relationship was demonstrated by sound reasoning. Before their conversion to Christianity many Fathers of the Church had been educated in the pagan schools of rhetoric and philosophy, and even those who were of Christian parentage had absorbed the treasures of ancient culture. The profane knowledge of the world and of man was united in one and the same person with the Christian teaching and, like their prototype Philo, the Fathers were all the more unwilling to sacrifice the findings of profane knowledge when they began to realize that philosophy was useful in defending the faith and in developing an integrated and logical structure of theological doctrine. Christianity was being attacked as unreasonable. To meet the attacks of the enemies of Christianity they had to use scientific weapons, dialectics, and the current terms and concepts that had been developed by Greek philosophy.

Christianity is based on a theistic and teleological philosophy. The teachings of pagan philosophy were seen to have a close relationship with the doctrines of Christianity and sometimes they were even in agreement with the tenets of the Christian religion. Thus philosophy was found to be a suitable instrument for apologetics, and philosophical speculation was valuable for obtaining a deeper understanding of the contents of Christian teaching and for developing a system of theology. Greek philosophy thus became associated with Christian teaching as its friend and helper. Origen was the first to give Exodus 11:2 an allegorical interpretation, in which philosophy was compared to the silver and golden vessels and garments of the Egyptians which the Israelites had appropriated for the ornamentation of their temple. Indeed, one history of philosophy was intent on demonstrating the providential significance of Greek philosophy. Truth had already come into the world before Christ and was to be found in the enlightened spirits of Greek philosophy; the Logos, who revealed Himself fully in Christ, was to be found in embryo in Heraclitus, Anaxagoras, Socrates, Plato, Aristotle, and the Stoics, and others like them. Greek philosophy was considered the "teacher preparing the way for

Christianity" (Clement of Alexandria) and "the anteroom of Christianity" (Origen and St. Augustine). Everything that was true and that agreed with Christianity was to be taken over and used in the defense of the faith and for the development of a Christian philosophy. St. Augustine represents the highest point in this movement and is at the same time the writer most esteemed in the Middle Ages.

When intellectual activity was once more resumed after the chaos of the migration of nations and when scientific labors were again undertaken under the leadership of St. Augustine's writings, Scholasticism was faced with the great problem of faith and science, of reason and supernatural revelation with its many minor questions. All the master minds and the eminent schools, men of conspicuous mental stature and the most famous schools, vied with one another to find a satisfactory solution for the problem. The philosophy of the Carolingian period, the Neoplatonist John Scotus Eriugena, the dialecticians and their opponents, St. Anselm of Canterbury and Abelard, St. Bernard of Clairvaux and Peter Lombard, the schools of St. Victor and Chartres, indicate the different stages and the opposing views in the long attempt to reach a solution. About the turn of the thirteenth century this philosophical tradition, which had been nourished by the teachings of Plato and St. Augustine, was halted by a new intellectual movement in the direction of Aristotelianism. The basic problem, however, remained the same, although the thinkers of the thirteenth century now strove to evolve a complete philosophical and theological system in the form of a commentary on the *Sentences* and the *Theological Summa*.

Several methods may be used in attempting a comprehensive statement of the philosophy of a great thinker, but frequently no one method alone will enable us to grasp the essence of his system. Several methods must be used to obtain a comprehensive knowledge of an extensive and important philosophical system. Because of the receptive character of Scholasticism, especially in the thirteenth century, and because of its high regard for tradition and authority, we shall consider the thinkers and philosophical movements to which St. Thomas was indebted. But this method is by no means the only one or the most important.

2. **Aristotle.** Thomism has been called a synthesis of Aristotle and St. Augustine. These two great minds are the pillars of the Thomistic system. But this statement does not include all the historical influ-

ences and intellectual tendencies that form the background for St. Thomas' system. To understand completely the historical roots of Thomism and the nexus of problems that it claims to solve, we must go farther afield.

For St. Thomas, Aristotle was indeed the greatest thinker of all times. Early Scholasticism knew Aristotle only as a logician. Of the works composing the *Organon,* it knew only those on the categories and on judgment; these it knew in Boethius' translation. The complete *Organon* did not become known until the second half of the twelfth century through the translations and commentaries written by Jacob of Venice, Peter Abelard, Thierry of Chartres, and Otto von Freising. Even the authors of summas who wrote about 1200 were unacquainted with Aristotle's works except his writings on logic. Scholasticism reached its highest development in the thirteenth century when the complete writings of Aristotle became known. When St. Thomas was born in Neapolitan Roccasecca in 1226 or 1227, the movement toward Aristotle was fully developed. From Spain had come Syrian, Arabian, and Latin translations of the writings of Aristotle, Latin translations of Arabian commentaries, and original Arabian works. A group of translators, including Johannes Hispanus, Dominicus Gundissalinus, Gerhard of Cremona, and Michael Scotus, at the court of Archbishop Raymond of Toledo were active in disseminating the works of Aristotle. Besides this, a school of translators in Sicily had rendered certain Greek writings of Aristotle into Latin. This new philosophical material was first received by the faculty of arts of the University of Paris about 1200. In 1210 and 1215, by ecclesiastical prohibition the faculty of arts was forbidden to use Aristotle's works on the natural sciences and metaphysics; only the logical and ethical writings were permitted to be used. Pope Gregory IX, in 1231, commissioned William of Auxerre to examine critically the writings on the natural sciences and to purge them of teachings irreconcilable with the Church's doctrines so that he might permit the use of expurgated editions for the schools. As in the case of similar prohibitions of the Popes, notably in 1241 and 1263, these restrictions had no practical effect. The works of Aristotle were known to Alfredus Anglicus, William of Auxerre, the Parisian chancellor Philip of Greve, William of Auvergne, Roland of Cremona (the first Dominican professor at the University of

Paris) and by three Franciscans, namely, Thomas of York, Alexander of Hales, and St. Bonaventure.

Although excerpts and *florilegia* of Aristotle's works were in circulation, the principal sources were the translated writings of Aristotle himself. About 1255 all the known works of Aristotle were being studied in the faculty of arts. On leaving Monte Cassino, where he had been brought by his parents when he was five years old, St. Thomas went to the *studium generale* in Naples, founded in 1224 by Frederick II. Here he studied for seven years under Peter of Hibernia, an enthusiastic follower of the growing Aristotelian movement, who introduced him to Aristotle's scientific and metaphysical writings. Thus in his youthful years Thomas became acquainted with the mind of the great Greek. The Aristotelian influence was increased when, after his entrance into the Dominican Order, Thomas became a pupil of St. Albert the Great in Cologne.

St. Albert was responsible for the acceptance of Aristotle by the University of Paris and he was the first to recognize the value of the Aristotelian writings for Christian thought and culture. By collecting the works of Aristotle and by assimilating them into the treasures of Christian thought, he initiated the movement of Christian Aristotelianism. While the traditional Augustinian tendency remained dominant with the heads of the Franciscan Order (Alexander of Hales, John of Rupella, and St. Bonaventure) and with the older Dominicans (Roland of Cremona, Richard Fishacre, and Hugh of St. Cher), St. Albert marks the beginning of the Aristotelian era in the Dominican Order. Already in his commentary on the *Sentences* and in his *Summa de creaturis,* composed in 1250, because of which he was recognized as an authority in philosophical matters at Paris, St. Albert's extensive knowledge of Aristotle is evident. He was not disturbed by the prohibitions issued against the study of Aristotle. In the universality of his mind he sought to transmit the complete Aristotle to the Christian Middle Ages and he wrote his books on the natural sciences for his confreres that they might have a thorough knowledge of nature and a correct understanding of Aristotle.[1]

St. Albert clearly expressed himself with regard to his position toward Aristotle. The accusation that he was merely an imitator of

[1] *Phys.,* I, 1, 1.

Aristotle is entirely unfounded. He confesses that he is indebted to Aristotle because Aristotle excelled all others in logic, the natural sciences, metaphysics, and ethics.[2]"In matters of faith and morals St. Augustine is to be accepted rather than the Philosopher. But if we are speaking of medicine, I place more confidence in Galen and Hippocrates; if we are dealing with the nature of things, I trust Aristotle more than any other scientist."[3] The expert in any field has a right to be heard, and St. Albert's words are to be understood in this sense. No one can reach the heights of philosophical knowledge without knowing Plato and Aristotle.[4] Whenever Aristotle is in error or contradicts himself, and St. Albert says, *multum erravit,* Aristotle is to be rejected;[5] whenever his views are inadequate, they are to be complemented. The Stagirite's authority is rejected not only when his views run counter to Christian teaching; Albert exercises his critical faculty even in matters of profane science, going farther than Aristotle and often supplementing Aristotle's teaching with his own observations on plants and animals. His appreciation of the scientific contributions of Aristotle may be gathered from the fact that, like Cicero, he regarded the basis of authority as the weakest kind of proof and valued Aristotle according to the reasons adduced.[6] Yet he praises Aristotle as the *princeps philosophorum* and the *archidoctor philosophiae,* and with the Arabians he calls him the *regula veritatis,* and like Averroes he is of the opinion that in Aristotle the human mind has reached its highest point.[7]

What St. Albert had begun was continued in purer form by his disciple St. Thomas. His reasoning is more uniform and systematic than is generally admitted, yet it is true that in St. Albert's system the teaching of Aristotle, the Neoplatonic-Arabian concepts, and the traditional Augustinian theology remain unassimilated. St. Thomas, on the other hand, from the beginning followed the more consistent line of Aristotelian thought and is avowedly the Christian Aristotelian. St. Thomas accepts not only Aristotle's *Organon* but also Aristotle's teaching on the relation between logic and ontology, on being and knowledge, his natural philosophy, metaphysics, psychol-

---

[2] *De praedicam.,* I, 1; II, 2; *Eth.,* I, 1, 7.

[3] *In II Sent.,* 13, 2.

[4] *Met.,* I, 5, 15.

[5] *Summa theol.,* IIa IIae, q. 1, a. 4.

[6] *Perih.,* I, 1, 1; *Met.,* IV, 3, 2; *Summa theol.,* Ia, q. 1, a. 5.

[7] *Phys.,* VIII, 1, 11.

ogy, ethics, political science, the Aristotelian concept of philosophy and science, and the Aristotelian division of the sciences. He appropriates entire groups of proofs and observations from Aristotle and he is the first to incorporate the entire Nicomachean Ethics in the *Secunda secundae* of the *Theological Summa;* thus he goes much farther than St. Albert. He enters completely into the spirit of Aristotle's attitude to this earth of ours. From Aristotle he learned the orientation to created things and to real relations as well as the insight into the importance of a thorough methodology proportionate to the subject matter. It is an Aristotelian trait to argue from the properties of things, *ex propriis argumentari.*[8] We find in St. Thomas' works even beginnings of the historical genetic method, which did not, however, develop very far because of Scholasticism's lack of appreciation for historical thinking.[9] In the two summas and especially in the *Quaestiones disputatae* and the *Commentary on Aristotle,* St. Thomas adopted Aristotle's view about the need of clear definitions of philosophical terms, of an a priori analysis of being, of a clear statement of the problem and of the difficulties, for attaining a comprehensive knowledge of the subject matter.

It was no mere coincidence that the son of the Count of Aquino was attracted from his earliest years to the philosophy of Aristotle. Of St. Albert's many pupils, only St. Thomas came completely under the influence of the Aristotelian element; Ulrich of Strassburg inclined to Neoplatonism and Hugh of Strassburg remained loyal to the traditional Augustinian tendency. "A countryside," someone has remarked, "always produces inhabitants that resemble itself." St. Thomas is indeed the child of the Neapolitan countryside; the purity and clarity of its atmosphere and the openness of its horizon find happy expression in St. Thomas' thought. He was drawn by a natural affinity to the Stagirite's realism, his organic picture of the universe, and his rule of the golden mean. St. Thomas admired the structure of Aristotle's cosmos, erected from the wealth of reality, and the essential structure of being evident in the whole.[10] Thus Aristotle becomes St. Thomas' leader, his philosopher. The *robur auctoritatis Aristotelis* is the weapon he carries into the academic arena. Again and again we find the phrases, *contra philosophum, contra intenti-*

---

[8] *In II Sent.*, 1, 4.
[9] *De verit.*, XI, 1; *De spir. creat.*, X ad 8; *De malo*, XVI, 1; *De subst. sep.*, 7.
[10] *In I Phys.*, 15; *In II de coel.*, 17; *In III Met.*, 11.

onem Aristotelis, and *contra veritatem* used in his argumentation as synonymous.[11] But St. Thomas does not rely on authority alone. Like Boethius and St. Albert, he considers the proof from authority the weakest kind of argument. The factual proof is the most important, and he follows Aristotle because reason and truth are on his side.[12] The fact that other great minds have arrived at the same conclusions is, however, a corroborative proof.

St. Thomas possessed an excellent knowledge of Aristotle's writings and was able to quote him with masterly ease and precision. Already in his earliest writings, *De ente et essentia* and the *Commentary on the Sentences,* composed between 1254 and 1256, he refers repeatedly to Aristotle's fundamental teachings, extracts the latent conclusions within them, and incorporates entire parts of the Aristotelian system into his own philosophy. In the *Commentary on the Sentences,* Aristotle is quoted a hundred times in each book, and this practice continues in the *Quaestiones disputatae,* the *Quaestiones quodlibetales,* and even in the *Compendium of Theology.* St. Thomas even takes objections from Aristotle, for the most part precisely to refute them, and to show the harmony between his own teaching and that of Aristotle. Quotations from Aristotle find their way also into the commentary on the Sermon on the Mount, into the *Contra impugnantes Dei cultum et religionem,* and frequently quotations from other sources are given an Aristotelian turn.

At this point it would be well to consider the much discussed question about the value and originality of St. Thomas' commentaries on the writings of Aristotle.[13] St. Thomas did not write commentaries on all of Aristotle's works although he was acquainted with all of them and made diligent use of them. But just as St. Albert's paraphrases and the commentaries of the members of the faculty of arts went beyond their scope, so St. Thomas' writings on Aristotle are more than a mere commentary. This is evident from the fact that he often corrects his philosophical masters and rejects their conclusions. The mere commentator amplifies the thought of the text without allowing his own critical views to enter into the matter. In a sense, however, these writings of St. Thomas are commentaries since it is his intention to state objectively the contents of Aristotle's

---

[11] *Contra Gent.,* II, 61; *De pot.,* III, 12.

[12] *Summa theol.,* Ia, q. 1, a. 8 ad 2.

[13] The commentary on Aristotle was written between 1268 and 1272.

thought.[14] St. Thomas is indeed an excellent commentator since he based his studies on Latin translations of the Greek texts. Even St. Albert had recognized that these translations were superior to the Latin translations of the Arabic.[15] St. Thomas insisted on good translations [16] and ordered translations to be made for his purposes. Thus good Latin translations, especially those by his brother in religion, William of Moerbeke, were made at his request, *rogatu Thomae*. St. Thomas made comparisons between the different translations and he possessed sufficient knowledge of Greek to test the correctness of certain terms and expressions and, whenever his knowledge was insufficient, he consulted other scholars.[17] He made use of the commentaries of Boethius, Alexander, Amonius, Themistius, and Simplicius to throw more light on the thought of Aristotle.

From the viewpoint of philology and criticism his method is beyond reproach. In the prologue of his commentaries he announces the contents of the work and determines its position in Aristotle's system and its connection with the other works of the Philosopher. In the commentary proper he states the plan of the work, dividing it into books, lessons, and smaller divisions until he arrives at the separate thoughts. St. Thomas uses the analytical method, dissolving the whole work into the thought elements, in order, of course, to integrate them again and show their relation to the whole. Sometimes he even discovers a plan where none really exists. He always insists on an exact interpretation of the text and on an explanation of the context *ne esset alicui occasio errandi*.[18] When Aristotle proposes a problem for solution and neglects to carry out his intention in the course of the work, St. Thomas mentions it as the reason why later followers of Aristotle adopted divergent interpretations.[19]

Not only those teachings in the Aristotelian commentaries which are also found in St. Thomas' original works are to be considered Thomistic; these commentaries in their entirety are a part of his system. They are in reality philosophical textbooks with an Aristotelian background. St. Thomas readily acknowledges his debt to Aristotle. Aristotelian logic, ontology, natural philosophy, are all parts of a

---

[14] *In I Perih.*, 8; *In VI Phys.*, 5.
[15] *De an.*, I, 1, 4; *Met.*, V, 2, 5.
[16] *In V Phys.*, 10.
[17] *In I Perih.*, 10; *In III Met.*, 8; *In V Met.*, 5; *Contra Gent.*, III, 73.
[18] *De spir. creat.*, X ad 3.
[19] *De an.*, 16.

whole; whoever is acquainted with their fundamental truths can hardly refuse to accept them. It was not as an independent investigator that St. Thomas came upon Aristotle, but rather it was through Aristotle that he was introduced to the detailed problems of philosophy. Hence he discussed important epistemological, ontological, psychological, and ethical problems in these commentaries.[20]

At no time, however, is St. Thomas a blind follower of Aristotle. He is the Aristotelian indeed when he expands Aristotle's system, when he supports Aristotle's conclusions with his own reasoning, and when he applies Aristotle's ethical teachings to the social and political conditions of his own time. On the other hand, St. Thomas has his own method of systematizing, he borrows Aristotle's terminology for concepts of his own, he interprets Aristotle as saying more than he really does, and often he corrects or completes Aristotle's thought. Little importance is to be attached to St. Thomas' failure to interpret his master correctly in some minor questions, but it is well to note that in some important matters he does not penetrate to the original meaning. Thus he views Aristotle's theology with Christian eyes, placing an Augustinian interpretation on Aristotle. He does not always interpret St. Augustine in an Aristotelian manner, as is often supposed. Furthermore, he is unaware that Aristotle's concept of the *nus* in human personality is unacceptable to the Christian concept.

St. Thomas is not lacking in a critical attitude toward Aristotle; even with respect to Aristotle's criticism he shows himself a critic and concludes that Aristotle refutes Plato *non quantum ad intentionem Platonis, sed quantum ad sonum verborum ejus.*[21] He differs with Aristotle on various topics. Thus in questions of physics[22] he opposes Aristotle and adheres to the astronomers of his time, or he supports Aristotle for reasons of his own.[23] Above all he opposes the idea of the eternity of the world and the consequent eternity of motion, of time, and of the human race.[24] He does not agree with Aristotle's teaching about pure spirits[25] and replaces the Aristotelian teaching on

[20] *In II Eth. Nic.,* 8; *In V Eth. Nic.,* 9; *In VI Eth. Nic.,* 1.
[21] *In I de an.,* 8.
[22] *In II de coel.,* 10.
[23] *Ibid.,* 8.
[24] *In VIII Phys.,* 2; *In III Pol.,* 12.
[25] *Summa theol.,* Ia, q.50, a.3.

providence with the Christian view.[26] But what is most important
is that St. Thomas completes Aristotle's system both in form and
content. Especially in the fields of theology, anthropology, theodicy,
ethics, political science, the origin of ideas, and immortality is the
Christian complement noteworthy, inasmuch as the happiness of the
next life is considered together with earthly happiness, the supernatural virtues together with the natural, the individual and the state
are studied in relation to their supernatural end. Sometimes St.
Thomas is content with a slight correction while at other times he
makes a substantial change by filling an Aristotelian concept with
a Christian content. In general St. Thomas remains conscious of the
great abyss separating Christian thought from that of Aristotle,[27] but
his interpretation is predominantly favorable.

3. The Arabians. Whoever wishes to understand the perfecting of
the Thomistic system, particularly in its elimination of Aristotelian
Neoplatonic corruptions and in its development of individual doctrines, cannot neglect to study the relationship of St. Thomas to the
Arabians, the philosophers of Islam. Greek philosophy was diligently
studied in Syria where the Nestorian Christians of the schools of
Edessa and Nisibis and of the philosophical medical school of Gondechapur based their philosophical inquiries on Aristotle. With them
were associated the Monophysites of the schools of Resaina (Ras el-
'Ain) and Kinnesrin (Chalcis). But in addition to the logic of Aristotle the philosophy of Neoplatonism also found acceptance among
the Syrians. After the destruction of the school of Edessa the Nestorians of Syria fled to Persia; and after the subjugation of Syria and
Persia by the Arabs, the Syrian Christians made the treasures of
Greek learning known to the Moslems through their translations of
Greek and Syrian works into Arabic. Besides philosophical works,
mathematical and medical writings were also translated from the
Greek. In the cultural world of Islam, Greek learning was highly
regarded, and Aristotle in the garb of Neoplatonism was considered
pre-eminent. The ultimate problem was the reconciliation of Greek
philosophy and the religion of the Koran, an undertaking that led
to differences and intellectual strife within Islam as did similar attempts in Judaism and Christianity.

---

[26] *In VI Met.*, 3.
[27] *Summa theol.*, IIa IIae, q. 161, a. 1 ad 5.

In Oriental philosophy, Kindi was the first Aristotelian; Al Farabi (d. A.D. 950), the logician and metaphysician, was known as the second Aristotle. Avicenna (980–1037), the third Aristotelian, who was also a physician and theologian, excelled all the rest. His philosophical encyclopedia, which laid down a canon of conduct for physicians, gained him great renown among his contemporaries, and by his attempt to reconcile Aristotelian philosophy with the Koran he gave rise to a considerable movement among the theologians. The differences between science and faith assume notable proportions in the writings of Algazel (1038–1111) who, because of his inclination to mysticism, sought to repress philosophical rationalism in favor of orthodox theology and merited the wrath of Averroes by his work *Destructio philosophorum*. In western Islam, in Spain, neither Avempace nor Abubacer attained the stature of Averroes (1126–98) who together with Avicenna exercised conspicuous influence on Christian Scholasticism both by his commentaries on Aristotle and by his original writings. Averroes' Arabian commentators and disciples became known to the Western world at the same time as Aristotle himself; first the writings of Avicenna came to hand and then the writings of Averroes in translations by Michael Scotus.

St. Albert, the universalist, had known and evaluated the entire philosophy of the Arabians.[28] His detailed reports on the Arabians are even today an important source for the study of Arabian philosophy. And since Avicenna, like St. Albert, was inclined to the study of the natural sciences, he exercised a profound influence on the German Dominicans. St. Thomas' relationship to the philosophers of Islam is manifold. In part his philosophy was under the positive influence of the Arabians, and in part it shows the negative influence of opposition to their teaching. Among the Arabians he beheld the very undertaking to which he was dedicating his life's work: the merging of Aristotelian philosophy and a great religion into one harmonious whole. In Averroes, moreover, he found a model for his own commentaries on Aristotle. While St. Albert, in the form and content of his work, was indebted to Avicenna whose paraphrastic style he imitated, the purer Aristotelians followed Averroes. The labors of Averroes were continually directed toward a knowledge of the true Aristotle and for this purpose he tried to obtain an exact interpretation of the Philosopher's teachings through a division of his works

[28] *In II Sent.*, 13, 2.

and a suitable arrangement of their contents. Like St. Thomas after him, he sought to discover the *intentio Aristotelis*. Even though St. Thomas may have known the method of literal exegesis from his scriptural studies, the influence of Averroes is here undeniable. Averroes excelled St. Thomas in the extent of his reading; in his critical attitude toward the Greek, Arabian, and Jewish philosophers of earlier times he is comparable to Aristotle himself. St. Thomas, on the other hand, avoids the tedious and verbose style of Averroes and, because he had a better text available, he was able to approach closer to the *intentio Aristotelis*.

An analytical study of the sources used by St. Thomas establishes with certainty that he began the study of Aristotle and of the Arabian philosophers at the same time. In his early work *De ente et essentia,* in which he undertook a threefold task, namely, (a) the determination of the meaning of being and existence, (b) the metaphysical relation between being and existence in the various grades of being, and (c) their relation to logical concepts, St. Thomas drew from Aristotle and Boethius, but especially from Averroes and Avicenna. This work, we may note, does not bear the marks of genius, and it may be a consolation for beginners in philosophy to know that it shows signs of being a youthful effort despite the facility St. Thomas reveals in his arrangement of the subject matter and in his synthetic grasp of the problems. In the same way, his *Commentary on the Sentences* shows the influence of the Arabian philosophers; externally this influence is noted from the fact that in the first book Avicenna and Averroes are quoted almost a hundred times. Some of these citations are merely ornamental, but the majority of them have a bearing on the matter. St. Thomas, of course, does not always agree, but more often than not he accepts the contribution of the Arabians. In logic,[29] in the fundamental principles of ontology,[30] in questions of psychology,[31] and in natural philosophy[32] he appeals to them. At times he makes use of Aristotelian doctrines which have been strengthened by the authority of the Arabian philosophers, and at times he accepts Neoplatonic teachings or developments of Aristotle's conclusions.

[29] *In I Sent.,* 19, 4, 2; 17, 1, 5 ad 4.
[30] *Ibid.,* 3, 4, 1.
[31] *Ibid.,* 2, 1, 3.
[32] *Ibid.,* 8, 3, 3 ad 3.

Whenever the teachings of the Arabians, such as those about creation, the ultimate end of man, and the dependence of the human
will on the heavenly bodies, are not in accord with the Christian
faith, St. Thomas rejects them.[33] In the first book of the *Commentary on the Sentences* he rejects the Arabian teaching about the
knowledge of God and the procession of things from God.[34] He
also differs in certain epistemological questions.[35] Apparently St.
Thomas has no preference among the great Arabian philosophers;
he makes use of Avicenna and Averroes as suits his purpose. His
departure from the teachings of the Arabians is more noticeable in
the philosophical *Summa* (1259–64) and in the theological *Summa*.[36]
In the fundamental questions of philosophy he differs radically, as
also in the *Quaestiones de potentia, de spiritibus creatis,* and *de
anima,* where he was obliged to reject the psychological errors.[37] By
the nature of things he also had to oppose the Arabian teaching on
intelligence in the *De substantiis.*

Later on St. Thomas vehemently opposed Averroes, since Averroistic Aristotelianism found eminent supporters in Siger of Brabant
and Boethius of Dacia.[38] In their hands philosophy threatened to
eliminate the teachings of faith in the solution of fundamental problems and proposed a series of antichristian teachings. Arrayed against
this movement we find the Franciscan theologians (Alexander of
Hales, St. Bonaventure, Thomas of York, William de la Mare, John
Peckham, Matthew ab Aquasparta, Richard of Mediavilla, Bartholo-
mew of Bologna, and especially Raymond Lullus), the masters from
among the secular clergy (Gerhard of Abbatisvilla and Henry of
Ghent), and the lights of the Dominican order (St. Albert and St.
Thomas). In 1256 St. Albert wrote his *De unitate intellectus contra
Averroistas* and gave expression to his views in this matter also in
his *De quindecim problematibus* written at the behest of Aegidius
of Lessines. Likewise the work *De erroribus philosophorum,* a collection of propositions from Aristotle and certain Jewish and Arabian philosophers opposed to Christianity, erroneously ascribed to
the Augustinian Aegidius of Rome, was of Dominican authorship.

---

[33] *De verit.,* V, 9, 10; VI, 6.
[34] *In I Sent.,* 24, 1, 3.
[35] *De verit.,* II, 5; VIII, 11; X, 2.
[36] *Ibid.,* I, 1, 2, 5, 9; II, 2, 4, 9 f.
[37] *De pot.,* I, 2 ad 2.
[38] Cf. Mandonnet, *Siger de Brabant et l'averroisme latin au XIIIe siècle.*

When St. Thomas, during his second sojourn in Paris (1268–72), became aware of the fatal errors of Latin Averroism and of its influence on youthful thinkers, he felt himself obliged to oppose these heretics strenuously. Since Aristotle was held in such high regard, he thought it his most urgent duty to expose the false interpretation which Averroes had given Aristotle. St. Thomas had made his studies of Aristotle with the help of much better texts and was therefore convinced of the errors of Averroes. In his work *De unitate intellectus* (1270), he accuses the Arabian of a malicious interpretation of Aristotle's writings (*perverse exponit*), of a malicious presentation of the teachings of Themistius and Theophrastus (*perverse refert sententiam Themistii et Theophrasti de intellectu possibili et agente*), and he calls him the corrupter of peripatetic philosophy (*non tam fuit Peripateticus quam Peripateticae philosophiae depravator*). He accuses the Averroists of corrupting youth and calls on them to take an open stand, assuring them that they will find him and other friends of truth ready for combat. In his commentary on Aristotle's *Physics,* St. Thomas asserts that Averroes' comments on this book are often entirely false and that if anyone were to follow him the result would be confusion and disorder and, further, that the reasoning of Averroes is often frivolous and his conclusions laughable. In the commentaries on Aristotle's *Metaphysics* and on *De coelo* we find similar violent castigations.

Thus beside the positive influence of the Arabians we find this sharp disagreement throughout Thomistic writings. The principal errors which St. Thomas opposes in his earliest writings are the doctrine of an eternal world, the limitation of divine providence, monism in the concept of the human soul with the consequent denial of the soul's immortality, and the determination of the human will under the influence of the heavenly bodies. In addition he points out errors in epistemology. Ethical errors and the false teaching about man's last end appear only in a succeeding phase of Averroism and are refuted by later leaders of Christian Scholasticism. Thus the successful refutation of Averroism marks an important stage in the life work of St. Thomas, and this chapter in the history of medieval thought often was made the subject of artistic representation.

4. **The Jewish philosophers.** Another source which must not be lost sight of is the philosophy of Judaism, which continued always under the influence of the philosophy of Islam. In the beginning it

was subject to the religious philosophy of the Islamic Kalam, and later it came under the influence of Arabian Neoplatonism and Aristotelianism. The Aristotelian movement among the Jews began in the middle of the twelfth century and reached its height in the person of Moses Maimonides (1135–1204), who became famous as a writer on medicine, a codifier of the laws of religion, and principally through his great work on the philosophy of religion, *Guide for the Perplexed* (*Moreh Nebuhim*). Relying on Al Farabi and Avicenna, Maimonides tried to solve the great problem of faith and science by his attempt to reconcile the teachings of the Jewish religion and Aristotelian philosophy.

Maimonides was considered an authority in the Middle Ages. Even William of Auvergne and Alexander of Hales quoted him; St. Albert made an exact study of the *Guide for the Perplexed* and favored Maimonides' teaching about creation and his discussion of divination. To say that without Maimonides there would have been no St. Albert and no St. Thomas, is gross exaggeration, but his authority had real influence in the Middle Ages. In the Hellenistic period, Philo of Alexandria formulated the Judaeo-Alexandrine religious philosophy as an attempt to bring the revealed religion of Judaism into harmony with Greek philosophy. In this attempt Philo preferred those systems and doctrines that seemed to have some relation to the revealed religion of the Jews and were reconcilable with it. What Philo had done from the standpoint of Judaism, the Fathers of the Church did for Christianity. They labored for the same end, made use of the same systems and methods. We find an analogous process taking place in the Middle Ages. What Maimonides was doing for Judaism by bringing Aristotelian philosophy into harmony with it, St. Thomas was doing for the Christian faith. Thus alongside Jewish Aristotelianism we find Christian Aristotelianism. Like St. Thomas, Maimonides placed great emphasis on reason and knowledge; indeed, for him knowledge was man's greatest perfection which made him like to God. He taught that faith should be built on a rational foundation, and in his opinion no one excelled Aristotle in earthly knowledge. Besides knowledge, which should not be cultivated for itself alone, Maimonides pointed out the necessity of revelation partly for the instruction of the people and partly to serve as a criterion for the scholar. Between faith and knowledge there is no contradiction since both are founded in God. Thus St.

Thomas found in Maimonides' *Guide for the Perplexed* many teachings that belonged to the Christian tradition.

To his study of Aristotelian philosophy and Arabian literature, St. Thomas joined the study of Jewish literature. We find evidences of the influence of the *Moreh* already in the first book of the *Commentary on the Sentences,* but the Thomistic system as a whole and in its detail is entirely different from the *Moreh*. Maimonides at no time even attempted that mighty synthesis which St. Thomas had proposed for himself. From Jewish sources, St. Thomas accepts the five reasons for the necessity of revelation and faith,[39] and the fundamental idea of sacrifice as well as certain prescriptions pertaining to sacrifices.[40] In his explanation of the ceremonial laws and in his treatment of the Old Law in general, he is clearly influenced by the *Moreh*. St. Thomas agrees as often as he rejects in theodicy; he follows Maimonides in rejecting occasionalism, but disagrees with him in his teaching about the angels.[41] In treating of the origin of the world St. Thomas accepts the material presented by Maimonides, but he draws his own conclusions. So also, in explaining the narrative of creation, and in his teaching about providence and the end of the world, St. Thomas disagrees with the Jewish philosopher and corrects him.[42] Even in the chapter on prophecy, where it was thought St. Thomas was entirely dependent on Maimonides, we find that he is original in his division and in his explanation of the preparation for prophecy.[43]

5. St. Thomas and Platonism. Aristotle was St. Thomas' guide in this world but not in the next world; Aristotle helped him build up this world from below and classify it, but did not show him how to interpret it from above. In spite of the polemics that range through all of Aristotle's writings against the Platonists in the fundamental questions of epistemology, psychology, and ethics, the great philosophical synthesis of St. Thomas was completed by means of principles drawn from Platonism, Neoplatonism, and the philosophical teachings of St. Augustine. Pictorial representations of St. Thomas and his intellectual triumph rightly picture him together with Plato and Aristotle, since he made use of the hierarchically

---

[39] *In III Sent.,* 24, 1, 3.
[40] *In IV Sent.,* 40, 1, 4; 42, 2, 2; *Summa theol.,* Ia IIae, q. 102, a. 1–4.
[41] *Contra Gent.,* II, 97.
[42] *In I Sent.,* 39, 2, 2.
[43] *De verit.,* XII, 1–4; *Summa theol.,* IIa IIae, q. 171–74.

constructed cosmos of Aristotle and the eternal ideas of Platonic Augustinianism.[44]

It is erroneous to say that St. Thomas knew none of the works of Plato, although only in his later years is there any evidence of his acquaintance with them. In his commentary *De coelo* he often refers to Plato's *Timaeus* and he quotes from *Phaedo*.[45] In the same commentary he refers to the work *De deo Socratis* written by the Platonist Apulejus of Madaura, and also to the Στοιχείωσις θεολογική (*Institutio theologica*) of the Neoplatonist Proclus which was translated into Latin by William of Moerbeke in 1268.[46] He derived his knowledge of the Platonic idea from the writings of Aristotle, and together with Aristotle he condemned this autonomous world of ideas, but he did not reject the ideas as such. Correctly explained and interpreted, he said, they are "very true," and in accord with the Christian revelation.[47] In general, St. Thomas derived his knowledge of Platonism from Neoplatonic sources without apparently being aware of the changes that had taken place in the interval between Plato and Plotinus.

The influence of St. Augustine is paramount in the works of St. Thomas. During the period of early Scholasticism, St. Augustine was regarded as the supreme authority among the Fathers of the Church in theological questions, and as the inexhaustible source of all theological knowledge and wisdom. St. Anselm's writings are filled with the spirit of Augustinianism, and we find the same spirit of thought in Abelard, Peter Lombard, the Victorines, and the school of Chartres.[48] This high opinion of St. Augustine was unchanged in the heyday of Scholasticism, not only among the older masters of the Dominican and Franciscan orders and of the secular clergy at the University of Paris, but also among those who were beginning to adopt Aristotle as the basis of their speculations. St. Albert, who taught that the Scriptures, the dogmas of the Church, and tradition were the ultimate in theological principles, placed St. Augustine above Aristotle in theology, and declares that it is *impium* to differ with him in matters of faith and morals. St. Augustine's judgment is so decisive in St. Thomas' opinion that he ventures the statement,

[44] Cf. Huit in *Revue Thomiste*, 1911.
[45] Cf. *Prooemium, In II de coel.*, 21.
[46] *In II de coel.*, 13.
[47] *De div. nom., prol.;* chaps. 7 and 9.
[48] Cf. Grabmann, *Geschichte der scholastischen Methode.*

"Augustine says it is so, therefore it is true" (*Hoc dicit Augustinus in littera, ergo ita est*).[49] For him none of the Fathers of the Church are comparable to St. Augustine as representative of Catholic tradition. As a philosopher, St. Augustine bears the impress of the Neoplatonism of Plotinus and thus stands on different intellectual ground from St. Thomas the Aristotelian. This, however, does not prevent Aquinas from drawing heavily on St. Augustine's thought in the formulation of his teachings about God, creation, ideas, the preservation and government of the universe, miracles, the nature and origin of evil, and the idea of order. In treating of the human soul as an image of God and of its immateriality, St. Thomas uses the reasoning of the Bishop of Hippo; he accepts the natural laws developed by the Stoics which St. Augustine had received from Cicero. From the *City of God* he takes his cue in questions of the philosophy of history and many historical facts. In those instances where the two men are divided on principle, St. Thomas does not permit an open break; in his efforts toward reconciliation he softens the teaching of St. Augustine or interprets it extravagantly according to his own viewpoint.

One of the chief sources of Neoplatonism for the later Scholastics was pseudo-Dionysius the Areopagite, especially in four of his writings: *On the Divine Names, On the Heavenly Hierarchy, On the Ecclesiastical Hierarchy,* and *On Mystical Theology.* Ten letters attributed to the same author were highly respected in Christian literature, and the authority and genuineness of these letters were the subjects of literary contention for centuries. Today it is agreed that these works were composed between 485 and 515, and that the author made use of the Greek Fathers and the Neoplatonists, especially Proclus, although he seems to have been careful to conceal his sources. At the behest of Charles the Bald, John Scotus Eriugena translated these writings into Latin, and thus they were placed at the disposal of the Scholastics. It was only because their author was thought to be that Dionysius who was a disciple of the apostles, and thus endowed with the authority of apostolic times, that even St. Thomas found satisfaction in these compositions with their arbitrary exegesis, their twisted and obscure phraseology, their pseudo-mysticism, their artificial hermeneutics, and their distorted allegorical and mystical interpretations. St. Thomas was aware of their

[49] *In III Sent.,* d.39, 6; *Summa theol.,* IIa IIae, q.14, a.84.

strange, obscure style, but he sought to excuse it; he recognized that
the terminology was Platonic, but he did not realize that the author
was an adept in obscurity. St. Thomas remarks that often a single
word is given where a detailed explanation is called for, while at
other times there is a *multiplicatio verborum quae superflua videan-
tur*.[50] Durantel [51] has counted 1702 citations of pseudo-Dionysius in
the Thomistic writings, taken from all the works except the second,
third, and sixth letters. While St. Albert wrote commentaries on all
the works of pseudo-Dionysius (unfortunately the most important,
De divinis nominibus, is not in print), St. Thomas commented only
on *De divinis nominibus*. St. Thomas parted company with Dionysius in theodicy and in regard to teachings about ideas and creation,
but he agrees with Dionysius' opinions about spirits and readily
quotes him in mystical and ascetical matters.[52] We may judge the
measure of reverence accorded Dionysius from the fact that Dante
places him in paradise next to Boethius, St. Albert, and St. Thomas
himself.

Another source of Neoplatonism was the *Liber de causis*,[53] erroneously attributed to Aristotle. In his youthful years St. Thomas
thought the book to be from Aristotle's pen, but later he realized
that it was an excerpt from the Στοιχείωσις θεολογική of the Neoplatonist Proclus. The book was available to the Middle Ages in the
translation made by Gerhard of Cremona. Like St. Albert, St.
Thomas wrote a commentary (after 1270) on this work, and the
Neoplatonic parts of his teaching on causality are derived from it.

The Neoplatonic elements in his teachings about the virtues are
taken from Macrobius, who was also an important source for St.
Albert.

Next in importance to St. Augustine for the early Scholastics was
Boethius (d. 525). Besides translating works on logic, he transmitted
the metaphysical principles of Aristotle and thus exerted an Aristotelian influence on Scholasticism before the thirteenth century.
The Scholastics also learned from him the art of writing commentaries, as well as the method of dissolving a text into its component
parts, discovering its leading thought, and referring it to the whole.

---

[50] *De malo.*, XVI, 1 ad 3.
[51] Cf. Durantel, *Saint Thomas et le Pseudo-Denis,* 1919.
[52] *De subst. sep.*, chap. 16.
[53] Cf. Bardenhewer, *Die pseudo-aristotelische Schrift über das reine Gute,* 1882.

Both St. Albert and St. Thomas made use of his commentary *De interpretatione.* His work *De consolatione philosophiae* was a treasure house of definitions and first principles; his theological works were models for applying philosophical concepts and principles to the teachings of faith, and for the creation of a speculative theology. St. Thomas wrote commentaries on *Librum Boetii de hebdomadibus* and on *Librum Boetii de Trinitate,* the latter being written about 1257, during his first teaching engagement in Paris.

6. **The influence of the Fathers and the early Scholastics.** Almost all the Fathers of the Church, both Latin and Greek, are to be found among the many authorities quoted by St. Thomas. The Greek Fathers were made available to St. Thomas by means of Latin translations, and also through glossaries and *florilegia.* Unlike St. Albert, St. Thomas had not read all the Fathers whom he quotes; St. Albert's literary acquaintance was much more extensive. The authority of the Fathers of the Church in theological questions is of great weight for St. Thomas, except in those that border on philosophy. If one of the Fathers draws from a philosopher, his opinion is of no more weight than that of the philosopher whom he is quoting.[54] In explaining the narrative of creation, St. Thomas differs with St. Augustine, St. Basil, and St. Gregory of Nyssa. He is more often at variance than in agreement with Origen. St. John Damascene, a compiler of the late patristic period and much quoted by Alexander of Hales, St. Bonaventure, and St. Albert, is also frequently cited by St. Thomas. In psychology, especially in his explanation of the passions, St. Thomas makes frequent use of Nemesius, whose doctrines were made known to him by St. John Damascene. St. Isidore, the archbishop of Seville, was the author of a work called *Etymologia,* whose twenty volumes afforded a rich source of material for all the sciences. His three books on the Sentences paved the way for similar commentaries by later authors, and provided later philosophers with many definitions. St. Gregory the Great is often quoted as an authority on practical ecclesiastical affairs, and as the guardian of the morals of the people. Recent literary researches have shown that St. Thomas also made use of St. Cyril of Alexandria and the Greek councils, and that he recognized the value of the Greek *Catenae.*

The important figures of early Scholasticism also had their in-

---

[54] *In II Sent.,* 14, 1, 2 ad 1.

fluence on St. Thomas. Prominent among these were St. Anselm, whose motto, *"credo ut intelligam,"* St. Thomas sought to realize in his own life; Peter Lombard, whose books on the Sentences he made the foundation of his lectures in Paris; and Hugh of St. Victor, who, coming from Germany, had gained considerable fame as a teacher at the Augustinian monastery in Paris owing to his philosophical and theological speculations, as well as his moral and mystical teachings.

It need not be pointed out that St. Thomas came under the influence of the Scholastics of his own time. The Parisian theologians of the transition period, Praepositinus of Cremona and William of Auxerre, the author of a commentary on the *Sentences,* are often quoted by name, while other contemporaries are introduced as *quidam* and *alii.* St. Thomas was aware of the methods, tendencies, and systems that were in vogue among the faculties of arts, as well as those preferred by the Franciscans and the secular clergy. From the *Summa* of Alexander of Hales he learned better methods, and he was well informed about the contents of St. Bonaventure's lectures.

The closest relationship existed between St. Thomas and St. Albert the Great. It is well known that St. Thomas was taken captive by his brothers who were opposed to his entrance into a religious order while making the journey to Paris in 1244. After a year he was liberated by John Teutonicus, the general of the order, but it is not certain whether he came immediately to Paris, remaining there for three years (1245-48) as St. Albert's pupil, or whether he went directly to Cologne and did not meet St. Albert until 1248, when the latter had returned from Paris to open a house of general studies in Cologne for the German province of his order. In any event, the German Dominican by his lectures and writings strengthened and encouraged the Aristotelian trend of St. Thomas' thought. Even his contemporaries remarked his dependence on St. Albert. By the middle of the thirteenth century, St. Albert had written two monumental works, the *Summa de creaturis* and a commentary on the *Sentences.* The former work is important because it contains St. Albert's opinions and teachings about creation, time and eternity, the corporeal and spirit worlds, psychology, and theology, both moral and sacramental. St. Thomas had this summa close at hand when he wrote the *Summa theologica;* when he wrote his *Commentary on the Sentences,* he had at hand the commentaries of St. Albert and St. Bonaventure. To be sure, St. Thomas and his teacher were equally willing to accept fundamental principles from Aristotle, and from St. Albert the pupil derived much astronomical and biological information. The points of difference and agreement in detailed questions are a subject for closer inspection; the fundamental attitude is to be noted here.

In comparing St. Thomas' *Commentary on the Sentences* with those of St. Albert and St. Bonaventure, we note his originality in abandoning the model laid down by the Lombard. Because of the nature of the subject matter, we should expect that he would retain the same division, examples, arguments, and formulations as his teachers, but beside these retentions we find frequent departures. Even when there is complete agreement, St. Thomas excels St. Albert not only in the external scholastic form, but above all else in his thorough systematizing, in his clarity and precision, in his use of later authorities and more profound reasoning, and by a clearer contrast to opposing doctrines. Superfluous questions are omitted; new questions are agitated which were unknown to St. Albert and St. Bonaventure. Here we note already the qualities which distinguished St. Thomas' later writings.

CHAPTER II

ST. THOMAS' CONTRIBUTION
TO PHILOSOPHY

The foregoing observations were in no way intended as a dismemberment of the philosophical system of St. Thomas Aquinas. The current tendency among scholars to reduce a scientific personality into many dependent relationships is a futile procedure. Indeed, for a long time a strange analogy in method has existed between the natural and the intellectual sciences. In the natural sciences various organic substances are studied by dissolving them into their component parts, and almost invariably the whole is lost sight of. Similarly in the intellectual sciences when a personality or a system is studied by means of an analysis of its dependent relationships, the spiritual bond which makes the all-embracing unity of thought and system visible is neglected. A knowledge of sources is, of course, necessary for the student of the Middle Ages, but the effort must not cease with this investigation of literary origins; only by a synthetic, macroscopic view can we understand a great system of thought. In spite of its receptive character, this is also true of the scholastic system of philosophy, although it cannot be denied that occasionally some discrepancy in the system must be subjected to a historical and genetic analysis, or explained as the effect of some earlier influence. In the same way, the great sections of the system which have been adopted into it from traditional thought must be studied in their structure. When, however, we wish to present the Thomistic system of thought as a whole, we must always proceed in reference to the all-embracing and unifying concept. Unity in the natural order, unity in the supernatural order, and the coordination of both in the higher unity of the divine plan of creation and preservation, this was the guiding principle of St. Thomas, in accordance with the motto taken from Aristotle's metaphysics, *"Sapientis est ordinare."* [1]

St. Thomas was no mere compiler, as was Vincent of Beauvais who gathers from various sources without respect to any order. He was no eclectic in the ordinary sense of seeking only the external and mechanical connection between thought elements and producing a mosaic of thought. Whatever St. Thomas drew from other sources he made to serve his all-embracing system. Indeed, it was his own teaching that it is not for the philosopher to collect what other men have taught, but to teach the truth; [2] with Aristotle he believed that a kernel of truth was to be found in every viewpoint. [3]

1. **Tradition and originality.** No one makes an absolute beginning in his intellectual labors; everyone builds on the state of knowledge he finds in his time. This state of knowledge forms the background against which he thinks, speculates, and questions, and from which he sets out on new paths. It is not the task of any individual to comprehend by his own efforts the entire universe of knowledge, but he should find his place in the vital process of knowledge and understanding. There is always growth, a maturing through generations, both in art and in science. "St. Thomas knew the world from books," someone has said; just as every scientist makes use of the knowledge and conclusions available in his time. "Even the greatest genius," Goethe tells us, "would not proceed very far if he had to rely entirely on his own efforts. But there are many who do not realize this, and so in their dreams about originality they waste half a lifetime groping about in the dark." Of those sciences in which St. Thomas was not an expert, we will speak later in detail. But in philosophy and theology his teachings are not mere dialectical elaborations; they are founded on fact and reason.

In one respect we note a difference between St. Thomas and the more relativistic modern mind. St. Thomas was convinced that certain truths were valid for all times; that these truths had been discovered, and that they could be further developed. He was not alone in this conviction. Spinoza declared that it was not his intention to found a new philosophy, but merely to bring the concepts already adequate and available into one system. Leibnitz said that the truths discovered in the past may be compared to gold refined from ore

[1] *Contra Gent.*, I, 1.
[2] *In 1 de coel.*, 22.
[3] *De malo*, II, 2.

or to diamonds brought forth from the mines. No one had a deeper realization of the contribution of each era to the priceless possession of truth than Hegel. All these thinkers approved the idea of a *philosophia perennis*. If one of the representative figures in modern philosophy has tried to point out that modern thought is being led in all important problems to the old positions of scholastic philosophy, it is merely an acknowledgment of the principle of continuity in the development of human thought.

Disinclined to any skeptical attitude, and convinced that the human spirit is driven forward to truth by truth itself (*ab ipsa veritate coacti*), St. Thomas teaches the continual progress of knowledge. Viewing the sociological character of our knowledge, he requires of every student that he accept the achievements of the preceding age and go forward in the search for truth.[4] Thus far there is no visible difference between Aquinas and the modern optimistic believer in progress, and the difference which does arise, arises less from his tenacity in adhering to the objectivity of truth than from the historical situation. St. Thomas thought of the universe as a much more limited and simple thing than it is in reality and, therefore, with Aristotle he felt himself closer to a scientific comprehension of this world than the modern scientist, who has an insight into the depths and spaces of this cosmos.

Analytical studies show again and again how much Thomistic philosophy is indebted to the thought of preceding ages for its contents. Great structures of thought enter into its world picture, yet scarcely a single philosophical idea not taken from tradition is found there. St. Thomas does not employ these thought structures as an external array; he assimilates their contents and builds them into a whole that is well thought out. It is rightly said that he possessed an architectonic feeling of the first order and was the greatest systematizer of the Middle Ages. He was distinguished by his universality in philosophy and theology, and by his thorough systematizing. Deeply indebted to tradition, his originality is evident principally in his masterful analysis of the scientific treasures of the past, and in the synthesis erected on this analysis. He enters completely into the spirit of the realistic world-picture of Aristotle, just as he makes the Platonic and Augustinian speculations his own. Thus ideas come forth from his mind as though they were new; they receive a fur-

[4] *In I Phys.*, 10.

ther development and a wider extension in their application to new fields. Thus Thomistic psychology, ethics, political science, epistemology, and metaphysics are new not only in their systematic structure but also in their contents. St. Thomas does not equal St. Albert in the extent of spiritual interests and knowledge of nature acquired by experience, but he does excel his teacher in the logic of his sequences, and in the solidity and symmetry of his system, which reviews all the problems of philosophy.

It has been customary in evaluating the Thomistic system to begin by studying its relations with the past. Such a method is calculated to eliminate both uncritical overestimates and undeserved depreciation. Indeed, some will say, St. Thomas' greatness lies in his synthesis, yet it is not a synthesis of truths that he himself has ascertained, but of the truths offered to him by the past. Or again, that his philosophy is not an objective philosophy of real things but mere book learning: an authoritarian philosophy. St. Thomas, it will be said, read more in the books of Aristotle and other thinkers than in the book of nature and of life. And again, his philosophy is alien to reality and does not represent the labor that went into the works of Aristotle, since the true Aristotelian is one who goes reverently to nature and learns from her who is the greatest of all teachers. St. Thomas, others will say, was no dynamic and productive thinker such as St. Augustine, Descartes, and Kant, for whom the questions of philosophy were profound personal problems.

Let us beware of exaggerations. We must choose the proper norm and standard if we are to arrive at the proper evaluation. Every thinker is confronted by a definite historical period in the development of human thought. When he arrives on the scene the temper of thought is formed in this or that way; he is placed in the presence of problems and in the midst of an intellectual fray without any choice on his part. Thus the thinker is called upon to assume a position, and his peculiar contribution will depend upon two things: on the certainty with which he grasps the nature of the problems before him, and upon the magnitude of vision and the amount of intellectual energy which he can command for the accomplishment of his task.

St. Thomas was above all else a theologian and he should be evaluated first of all in regard to his solution of the great medieval problem of harmonizing faith and science in one great synthesis.

Confronted with this problem, St. Thomas by his extraordinary intellectual powers made certain the victory of Aristotelianism over its opponents. Kant also was faced with a historical situation, involving the conflict of empiricism and rationalism, and the direction of his thought was determined by his involvement in this conflict, as well as by his preoccupation with Newton's mathematical natural sciences. St. Thomas' first contribution was made to theology by incorporating moral with dogmatic theology to form a single integrated science. His efforts benefited philosophy inasmuch as he approached philosophical problems both in themselves and as auxiliary to the truths of faith. He was the founder of Christian Aristotelianism and in this was far in advance of his time. His productive powers were active in a mighty work although they revealed themselves in a different way from those of Descartes and Kant. Even his contemporaries were aware that he was an innovator, and his biographer, William of Tocco, made mention of his innovations both in contents and method. The new intellectual movement within Christendom was the result of the personal activity of two men, St. Albert and St. Thomas.

The Thomistic system arose from the separation of the new Aristotelian from the old Augustinian tendency. Even in the beginning, St. Thomas had placed himself firmly on Aristotelian ground, and the rough outlines of his work were drawn early. Evidence for this statement is to be found in his youthful composition *De ente et essentia* which contained a sketch of his cosmos of being, in the later development of which he manifested greatly augmented powers of reasoning. At first, however, he was not certain about the unity of form, although he soon found himself drawn in that direction. And again in defining *materia signata* as the principle of individuation, he succumbed to various influences; in the explanation of the *intellectus agens* of Aristotle, the Arabian influence is noticeable. At first he even paid tribute to the Platonic-Augustinian theory of illumination only to reverse himself completely later on when the full force of Aristotelian principles drove his logical mind in another direction. In his early works, as in the *Commentary on the Sentences,* St. Thomas was often cautious in his formulations, but later he became more certain and definite; his intellectual development included not only an extension of knowledge but an inner organic growth together with categorical formulations and firmly founded reasonings.

St. Thomas never lost his reverence for the great ones in the realm of the spirit, but his respect for authority was limited by reason. Indeed he adopts the thoughts of authorities along with their reasoning; to these he adds his own reasons based on fact and experience. The student of St. Thomas will be surprised at the wealth of experimental knowledge he displays in ethics and social philosophy and at his appreciation of the empirical difficulties of putting things into practice. In contrast to many formalistic thinkers of modern times, he cannot be accused of being blind to the fullness of life; indeed no modern ethical system can be compared to his in its understanding of the extent of the ethical cosmos. Like his contemporaries he had keen vision in the realms of logic and of ideal entities; with regard to the understanding of being, St. Thomas was much more concerned with the permanent relationships and the structures of being that are the basis of the universe than with the knowledge of individual things. With a mind ever alert to essentials, he critically observed reality to attain the kernel of being.

St. Thomas was neither a professional mathematician nor a naturalist. In the natural sciences, he must be reckoned among the *philosophi in libris;* he did not derive his knowledge from an immediate observation of things and from their analysis, but from the books of Aristotle. Even when he compares the opinions of interpreters like Proclus, Simplicius, Philoponus, Avicenna, and Averroes, he makes his decisions on the basis of Aristotelian principles. At times, it is true, he makes a pointed observation in natural science and also displays some knowledge in optics, astronomy, and biology; nevertheless his knowledge is limited by his sources. This cannot be construed as a reproach since his task had been assigned to him in the realms of philosophy and theology by the exigencies of the thirteenth century. He cannot be expected to know more than the knowledge offered by his time in the natural sciences.

In that period of the dawn of the natural sciences a complete philosophical system could be of great help in providing a methodology and a definition of the field of inquiry. St. Albert the Great and Roger Bacon are eloquent proofs that Aristotelian principles did not obscure the way to an extensive knowledge of nature. Posterity still

pays tribute to St. Albert's knowledge of plants and animals, just
as it marvels at the profound vision with which the English Franciscan foretold the important inventions and discoveries of modern
times. The true Aristotelian, of course, is he who stands reverently
in the presence of nature and is taught by her; reliance on authorities alone is decidedly un-Aristotelian. The student who is animated
by the true Aristotelian spirit is looking always toward the advancement of knowledge. St. Albert and Roger Bacon are the naturalists
of the Middle Ages; still their studies of nature did not disclose to
them any new concepts of being or the knowledge of any new law
of being. Philosophical knowledge of essences is not derived from
natural science, but from a study of the phenomena; philosophy
would be in a sorry plight if it had to depend entirely on the testimony of the natural sciences gained by induction. The comprehensive metaphysical structure of St. Thomas is independent of his
knowledge of the natural sciences; nevertheless natural scientists
today are pointing the way more and more to the Aristotelian-
Thomistic synthesis, and psychologists are agreeing that the Aristotelian-Thomistic unity of body and soul is quite in accord with
their scientific findings. In modern times it has been found that philosophical vision led the way, and the natural sciences by their own
methods are arriving at the same conclusions. St. Thomas, it is true,
incorporated the erroneous astronomical, astrological, biological, and
physical concepts of his time into his system, and this imperfect
knowledge of nature was an obstacle in the way of his attaining
additional important philosophical insights. A reorientation of sciences such as biology, physics, and astronomy exercises an influence
on philosophy, proposes new problems, and requires a revision of
former judgments, but there are basic philosophical questions that
are beyond all the natural sciences. Wherever philosophy has reference to the natural sciences it must seek to keep pace with them by
ceaseless correction and research. Thus it comes about that the advance made in certain sciences since the time of St. Thomas prevents us today from agreeing with all of his opinions and conclusions.

Since, however, certain truths are independent of every historical
period, St. Thomas was able to enunciate philosophical truths of
permanent value. Today logicians are amazed at the advances made
in the Middle Ages in their field. Indeed, all that modern science
has striven to achieve in criteriology, logic, metaphysics, psychology,

and in the establishment of a basis for a realistic epistemology, was undoubted and unquestioned truth for St. Thomas. The medieval concepts of the state and the community, and the relationship between the individual person and the community, have not lost their validity even today. The famous jurist, Rudolph von Jehring, confessed that if he had known of St. Thomas' work on the natural law, he would not have written his book on law. Nicolai Hartmann declared in the foreword of his book on ethics that without the help of the Stagirite he would not have been able to write his work. Thomistic ethics contains the wealth of Aristotelian ethics complemented by the Graeco-Roman tradition and the principles of Christianity.

St. Thomas did not discover any new realms of being, yet his field of inquiry is almost coextensive with that of modern philosophers. Possessing all the concepts of the ancient world and of the Christian and non-Christian Middle Ages, he proceeded to an explanation of the universe. Both his greatness and his limitations arise from the fact that there were certain aspects of being which were disclosed only in modern times and that his knowledge of the natural sciences was conditioned by his historical period.

The literary form adopted by a thinker is influenced by the style of his thought as has been amply illustrated by Heraclitus, Plato, and Nietzsche. The medieval summa is an expression of the spirit and exigencies of the time. A great system was to be evolved that was to be a reflection of the divinely created cosmos. Although the Thomistic *Summa* does not descend to the level of the encyclopedia like the *Speculum universale* of Vincent of Beauvais, its magnitude prevents St. Thomas from investigating the subtleties of every detailed problem and from securing his reasonings on every side. The succeeding generations attacked the *Summa* precisely on these points. This was easy to do, now that the structure was completed and could be subjected to unmerciful criticism. The hasty completion of the system without too much development was partly responsible for the great lack of advancement among later Thomists. However, this outward form of the system should not deceive us. The system's concern with detailed problems is often evident beneath the bookish style that tries to brush minor problems aside, and anyone who has studied the *Quaestiones disputatae* and the various commentaries will appreciate the depth of Thomistic thought.

St. Thomas was convinced of the continuous progress of scientific knowledge, which was not the concern of any individual, but of many minds, of whole generations, of all humanity. He understood the force of error and the fruitfulness of intellectual hairsplitting. Like St. Bonaventure he understood that an advance was made in knowledge whenever new objects of knowledge appeared, when new methods of knowledge were adopted, and when a gifted thinker entered more profoundly into the subject matter of science. Dante's reproach hurled at those who do not seek the advancement of knowledge but merely repeat what others have said does not apply to St. Thomas.

The manner of presentation in the Middle Ages, in use for more than a hundred years before St. Thomas, was dependent on the thought methods of the time. It developed from the many attempts to reconcile the real or apparent contradictions between the authorities, especially between the doctors of the Church. The canonists Ivo of Chartres, Berthold of Constance, and Alger of Luettich began the development of this method of concordance that had been used earlier in the *Decretum Gratiani,* the medieval book of canon law. By his work *Sic et non* Abelard furthered its development, as did also the logic and the metaphysics of Aristotle. All of these works influenced the form of the disputations held in the Parisian schools and the methods of the Parisian summists Simon of Tournai, Philip of Greve, and later, Alexander of Hales, St. Bonaventure, and St. Albert.

St. Thomas simplified these methods by transferring the greater emphasis from the accumulation of reasons and objections to the solution and to the *corpus* of the article, and by giving only those objections which had some connection with the solution of the question. Every article is so arranged that it opens with a statement of the question, beginning with *utrum;* then the objections that oppose or seem to oppose the forthcoming solution are introduced by *videtur quod.* The *sed contra* introduces an argument generally supported by some authority and stating the Thomistic view. The solution itself, or the *corpus,* holds the central place in the article and begins with *respondeo dicendum,* and the article concludes with the refutation of the objections, or with an interpretation favorable to the solution.

The inner force binding together the parts of the article is, of course, more important than the outer form of the presentation. St. Thomas, preferring the deductive method, proceeded from the universal to the particular, from the known to the unknown, and from general principles to their application to individual instances. Principles are most important to him, and he understood what his principles required and excluded. He, who praised the intellect as man's noblest faculty, also understood the value of the aids to the intellect, such as the precise formation of concepts, conclusion, and proof. The syllogism plays an important part, supported by Thomas' ability to divide and separate, and especially to distinguish. This famous procedure of the Scholastics not only is justified as long as the real basis is not lost sight of, but is almost indispensable.

Valid objections can, it is true, be made against this zealous effort to harmonize. Irreconcilable elements are often brought together, placing the unity of the system in jeopardy, and, by the introduction of so many thoughts, the original aim is forgotten and the critical attitude toward the question is made blunt. Some centuries later a Thomist said of Nicholas of Cusa that his reading had been too varied and too extensive; the same might sometimes be said of St. Thomas.

2. Aristotle and Christianity. Critics of the Thomistic system have centered their attacks on the union of Aristotelian philosophy with the Christian religion. "What," they ask, "can Aristotle have in common with Christianity?" Aristotle is the philosopher of this world, the teacher of immanence who knows nothing of providence, of personal immortality, or of retribution, who expects everything from knowledge; who, in a word, is in so many ways directly opposed to the genius of Christianity. These objections heard in recent times were also raised in the Middle Ages. St. Bonaventure [5] held that the Aristotelian philosophy erected on natural reason was essentially un-Christian, that it contained numerous errors, that it endangered the faith and undermined the basis for any Christian philosophy. Duns Scotus made similar objections. St. Thomas, however, did not share these apprehensions. In his opinion Aristotle was a safe guide for this world, which bore upon itself the mark of its divine Creator. In his writings Aristotle had indeed never acknowledged the *credo ut intelligam,* but St. Thomas acknowledges the *credo* and strives to harmonize the Aristotelian *intelligere* with his faith. Thus in an

[5] *In Hexaem. coll.,* VI, nos. 2–6.

earlier era the religious Platonic system had been complemented by Aristotle; so also in the Hellenistic world the union of these systems had been accomplished by Philo of Alexandria and Plutarch of Chaironea, and by the theistic party among the Neopythagoreans. Why should Aristotelianism and Christianity be mutually exclusive? St. Thomas read Aristotle with Christian eyes and immediately began to correct where he found anything at variance with his faith. He knew how to rid Aristotle of the dross of Arabian interpretation, but he was not always able to escape the Aristotelian order of values. Here we recall his preference of the universal to the individual, and his opinion of woman.[6] Aristotle's teaching on act and potency does not constitute him a Christian philosopher, nor can it be said that even worldly wisdom found in him its highest development. Nevertheless the meeting of Aristotle with Christian thought had happy results in more than one respect.

Neoplatonism, especially in the Augustinian version, was strongly inclined to despise and underrate the world and earthly things, and, because of a certain excessive spiritualism, it sought some immediate divine illumination and assistance in the natural sphere. St. Thomas, on the other hand, was firmly convinced that the natural order was sufficiently endowed with powers and dispositions to enable it to fulfill its natural and ordinary tasks. He naturally rejected the Augustinian theory of illumination and adopted a new concept of body and soul. Thus St. Thomas formulated the idea of a Christian philosophy which is autonomous and independent of theology but which at the same time can be applied to theological questions in a new way.

When the Fathers of the Church came into contact with Greek philosophy, nothing seemed more natural than that philosophy and the Christian religion would be held apart. Nevertheless all the patristic writers, including St. Augustine, failed to make a clear distinction between faith and knowledge. Since they considered philosophy the germ of the *logos,* and Christianity the complete *logos,* they naturally placed their confidence more readily in Christianity and sought to know man's last end under the guidance of the light of Christ's grace. St. Augustine is not concerned with the distinction between faith and reason but with the Christian way of life in which both faith and reason, mutually supporting each other, strive for a harmonious development of human personality. For him it was *in-*

[6] *De an.,* 18.

tellige ut credas, crede ut intelligas. He taught that philosophy was nothing but Christian wisdom which not only showed the way to the knowledge of man's last end but also provided the means and the powers by which this end could be realized, and that, of course, could be done only with the assistance of divine grace.

The Bishop of Hippo does not deny that human reason can attain a certain profane knowledge, but he does deny that man of himself can come to the knowledge of his last end. St. Augustine had been profoundly impressed by the Skeptics; he had seen how reason had swayed from side to side in the ancient systems of philosophy and therefore he was unable to place full confidence in reason as a reliable guide to the true good. Since he believed that all philosophy was contained in the Scriptures and that divine illumination was necessary even in the natural sphere, he possessed no way of distinguishing between philosophy and theology either in their subject matter or in the viewpoints from which they approach their objects. Since the Neoplatonic-Augustinian theory of illumination dominated the early Scholastics, no definite distinction was made between philosophy and theology; indeed, no distinction was wanted and it was considered an impossibility for the believing Christian. Man is one; philosophy must come from this unity of the Christian man; therefore there can be nothing but a Christian philosophy. We find this attitude most clearly expressed in the generation of thinkers from St. Anselm to St. Bonaventure. The Benedictine monk, having adopted the Augustinian motto, *"Fides quaerens intellectum,"* did not seek knowledge in order to arrive at faith, but he believed in order to know; indeed, he maintained that without faith he could never attain to any knowledge. For St. Anselm faith is so intricately intertwined with man's soul that it not only absorbs his will and emotions, but is identified with his reason in many respects. It is from this viewpoint that the ontological proof for the existence of God must be judged. Although St. Bonaventure admits the existence of some differentiation in subject matter, viewpoint, and principles between philosophy and theology, he is unwilling to recognize philosophy as an autonomous science. Natural reason, disturbed by sin, is unable to enter into the sanctuary of divine things without the help of grace. Before Christ men had the light of reason; after Christ they possessed the light of grace.

Roger Bacon, too, is a defender of the Augustinian tradition inasmuch as he requires divine illumination for the knowledge of earthly things and especially for the knowledge of God. Thus even the greatest figure in the natural sciences during the Middle Ages, one who had done so much to establish a system of profane sciences, recognizes divine authority as the only certain source of knowledge and makes philosophy depend for its validity on revelation. Nevertheless he wished to reform the methods used in theology in keeping with the improved methods of the profane sciences.

With the appearance of St. Albert and St. Thomas on the scene, a change is to be noted in this attitude. Philosophy is now recognized as an independent science in its principles, methods, and subject matter. At the same time its conclusions are reconcilable with faith and theology. But, should any of its conclusions contradict the teachings of faith, it is to be corrected according to the higher teaching of revelation. Faith and science cannot really contradict each other, since such contradiction would refer to God from whom both the doctrines of faith and the first principles of knowledge are derived. For St. Thomas there can be no separation of faith and science; no separation of philosophy from the teachings of revelation, such as was desired by certain Averroists in the faculty of arts. He could not conceive of truth as twofold, and, although this proposition had not yet been theoretically propounded, certain Averroists were contrasting philosophical and theological truths in such a way as to lead to the conclusion that truth is twofold. St. Thomas foresaw this consequence, and, together with St. Albert and St. Augustine, he denied any contradiction between natural and supernatural truth.

St. Albert and St. Thomas established philosophy as an autonomous science based on pure reason and marked out the clear distinction between philosophy and theology in their principles, methods, and subject matter. During the twelfth century knowledge was considered merely a "useful thing," but now it began to be appreciated as having a value of its own, as the perfection of human reason.[7] A greater appreciation of this world spurred men on to a greater desire for knowledge of natural things, and the Aristotelian concept of knowledge pointed the way to an autonomous science of philosophy. With Aristotle, St. Thomas taught that all our knowledge is derived through the senses and that our intellect is able to abstract the spiritual content from the data of the senses and thus rise from the sensible

[7] *In I de an.*, I, 1; *Contra Gent.*, III, 25.

to the suprasensible.[8] Profane science and philosophy are coextensive with the power of the *intellectus agens*. Man is naturally endowed with the faculty of knowing both this finite world and the existence of God. In the *Summa contra Gentes* St. Thomas distinguishes between philosophy and theology with reference to their subject matter, methods, and principles.

The philosopher treats of things inasmuch as they have this or that nature, and because of the various classes or species of things philosophy is therefore divided into different parts. Theology considers things only in their relationship to God, and for this reason the consideration of the natural properties and laws of things is outside the limits of theology. Here St. Thomas points out an analogous situation with regard to other sciences, as, for instance, between the natural sciences and mathematics.

Furthermore, philosophy and theology make use of different principles; the former proceeds *ex propriis rerum causis,* the latter *ex prima causa,* inasmuch as revelation makes it known to us. Each science proceeds by a different route; philosophy studies creatures and from them proceeds to the knowledge of God, while theology begins with God and relates all things to Him. St. Thomas considers the latter method more perfect because it resembles the knowledge of God who knows Himself first and all other things through Himself.

In contrast to his fellow Dominican, Robert Kilwardby, who admitted only theological standards and criteria, St. Thomas together with St. Albert protested against any merging of the philosophical and theological fields of investigation. He defended the rights of human reason and secured for philosophy its rightful place in the hierarchy of the profane sciences. This liberation of philosophy from its dependence on theology marks a new period in Christian thought. Thus St. Thomas is rightly considered one of the founders of the modern concept of philosophy, and since his day philosophy has remained an autonomous science in the intellectual world of Western Christianity. St. Thomas had rescued philosophy from the all-embracing claims of dogmatism and fideism, and in spite of his connection with Christianity he became as significant a personality in philosophy as Descartes, Kant, and Hegel became in different social and historical circumstances.

In his defense of philosophy as an autonomous science, St. Thomas

8 *In Boeth. de Trin.*, Prol., I, 1.

wrote numerous monographs on philosophical problems: logical *opuscula;* writings on natural philosophy, ontology, and metaphysics; important works of his youth, *De ente et essentia, De natura accidentis, De natura generis, De aeternitate mundi contra murmurantes* (1270), *De substantiis separatis;* his controversy with the Averroists, *De unitate intellectus contra Averroistas;* and the important political writing, *De regimine principum,* which is his work only in part.

3. **The Aristotelian basis of science.** St. Thomas reared his philosophical structure of the universe on an Aristotelian foundation, and as Aristotle reasoned from a most extensive experimental background, St. Thomas' system bears the clear mark of the natural world around him. Aristotle adopted the Platonic thought that science refers to the universal, the necessary, the constant, the essential, but he taught that this constant and universal was to be found as the principle of form in the things around us, and that it could be known by us. It is the philosopher's task to exhibit these forms of being in the universe. These forms of being are found in the cosmic structure either in matter or independent of matter. Now, everything is intellectually knowable so far as its essence can be abstracted from matter and from the individual covering deriving from that matter. Indeed this abstractability determines the relation of things to the intellect and provides the principle of division for the various sciences.

Certain objects of knowledge are bound up with matter both in their existence and in their knowability; they have their being only in matter, and exist in principles of form. Natural philosophy concerns itself with those forms of being that are entirely submerged in matter; hence, in a definition of natural philosophy, the idea of matter is indispensable. Secondly, some objects of knowledge exist in matter, but can be known outside of matter; these form the subject matter of mathematics. Thirdly, certain objects of knowledge can exist without matter, of which some have never been joined to matter, such as God and the pure spirits; others are partly found in matter and partly not, such as substance, quality, potency, act, unity, and plurality. These are the subject matter of metaphysics, which is sometimes called theology, when God is its chief subject matter, and at other times fundamental philosophy, inasmuch as all other sciences derive their principles from it. St. Thomas adopts this traditional Aristotelian division, just as he accepts Aristotle's division of moral philosophy into monastics (individual morality), economics, and politics.

The naturalness of the Aristotelian-Thomistic system is based on its realistic attitude toward knowledge. All our knowledge begins with experience, namely, all that the senses perceive as far as the outer world is concerned. At the same time, however, both Aristotle and St. Thomas are far removed from any empiricism. With his external and internal senses man is able to obtain a picture of the outer appearance of things, and with his intellect he can penetrate to the content of being by relying on the data provided by the senses and on the conformity of the outer appearance of things with their essences.

From experience we derive the first concepts of being and non-being, the differences of being, such as potency and act, as well as all the concepts of sensible things which complement these basic concepts. From experience all fundamental knowledge is gained: the first principles, such as the principle of contradiction in its logical and ontological aspects, and the principle of the excluded middle; mathematical axioms, such as, the whole is greater than a part; the principle of causality, and that vast system of general rules and principles which express the general relations of being. From external experience St. Thomas rises to the heights of metaphysics and to the fundamental cause of all being. From actual data he goes to moral and social philosophy, and by analysis of actual life he arrives at the essence of things.

Universal propositions are obtained by induction (*universalia non sunt nobis nota nisi per inductionem*).[9] Here, however, induction means a great many things. It is not a mere summary judgment in which some property learned from the individuals in a certain class is predicated of all. Induction requires a certain amount of intuition and understanding of the state of sensible things, certain acts of comparison and division, and an accumulation of sensible experiences leading to a valid universal judgment. Throughout the process the intellect remains in command, and here Thomism, like Aristotelianism, bears a clear imprint of intellectualism.

4. **Philosophy and theology.** For St. Thomas philosophy is especially important in the service of theology. The problem of the relation of faith to science, or of religion to philosophy, had divided

[9] *In Anal. P.*, 30; *In VI Eth. Nic.*, 3.

the Church from the beginning into two parties. For many, faith in Christ together with a blameless life constituted the essence of Christianity. Neither philosophy nor the philosophical schools had been required by Christ or His apostles. At the beginning of the second century, the opposition to science and philosophy was especially strong because of the supposed danger to the purity of the faith, and Christians were forced to forsake Greek philosophy even as taught by its most worthy representatives. This movement in opposition to secular science was prevented from becoming dominant through the efforts of the catechetical school at Alexandria. St. Clement and Origen entered the lists and advanced unassailable reasons for the necessity and usefulness of philosophy. Excelling his contemporaries in his extraordinary personality and learning, Origen pointed the way toward a scientific basis for Christian teaching in his great philosophical and theological work, and also by his work in the development of the schools at Alexandria and Caesarea. Not only his immediate successors but also men like St. Athanasius, St. Cyril of Alexandria, Didymus the Blind, and the three great Cappadocians (St. Basil, St. Gregory of Nyssa, and St. Gregory of Nazianzus) continued under his inspiration.

In different historical circumstances, the same problem appeared again in the conflict between the dialecticians and their opponents. The dialecticians Anselm the Peripatetic and Berengarius of Tours, influenced by John Scotus Eriugena, taught that worldly knowledge was independent, and that reason was the only criterion even in matters of faith. In opposition to them arose Peter Damian and Manegold of Lautenbach who condemned all profane learning as useless and dangerous, declaring that faith is the first light of the intellect. St. Bernard of Clairvaux pointed out how philosophy undermined faith, referring to the dangerous proceedings of the dialecticians and to the errors of Abelard and Gilbert de la Porrée. He admitted that learning might be an ornament of the soul, but he condemned the subtleties of Plato and the sophisms of Aristotle and opposed any introduction of philosophy into the Christian religion. "Peter and Andrew, the sons of Zebedee, and their disciples, did not attend a school of rhetoric or philosophy, yet it was precisely through them that Christ wrought the work of salvation on earth." [10] The fear and love of God are required that man may attain his last end, and this

---

[10] Cf. Gilson, *Die Mystik des hl. Bernhard von Clairvaux* (1936), pp. 104, 251 ff.

end is not attained in the schools of philosophy but in the school of the Christian, preferably in the cloister. The opposition to the dialecticians often made use of this argument about the dangers to the soul. Philosophy, they said, encouraged arrogance, pride, and vanity, and destroyed the essential Christian attitude, which is humility of spirit.

Even the pagan Epicurus had called knowledge for its own sake vanity. St. Bonaventure and St. Thomas supported that view for more compelling reasons. All knowledge is directed to God, and every science must serve the knowledge of the divine. St. Bernard recognizes a mystic theology, but he does not admit a philosophical theology. The telling decision in this conflict was given by Anselm of Canterbury (d. 1109). Filled with the Augustinian spirit, he proposed the program: *Credo ut intelligam, fides quaerens intellectum.* Against the rationalists he defended faith which rested on divine revelation as being beyond their competence. Pure reason has no place where divine things are considered, and faith alone can give the experience that opens up the vision for the divine.

Anselm is, however, far from being a defender of assent by faith alone. The teachings of faith have a *ratio,* and this *ratio* can be comprehended by man's subjective *ratio,* his intellect. In opposition to the fideists, he requires a rational study directed toward the attainment of an insight into the teachings of faith, but this study must remain always under the guidance of the authority of the Church, the Scriptures, and the Fathers, and it must be founded on practical faith and moral living, without which no true judgment can be made about God or divine things. Thus Anselm fights at the same time on two fronts, for and against reason: against it, inasmuch as it claims a role that does not belong to it and that undermines faith; for it, in that he grants the ethically unbiased man an insight into the teachings of faith.

Hugh and Richard of St. Victor are brilliant proof that mysticism need not be hostile to science. Hugh is opposed to the prating of superfluous knowledge. The universe is the great natural revelation of God, and its contents must be heeded. Therefore he describes philosophy as the love of that divine wisdom which is revealed in creation and which can be studied there. Hugh of St. Victor's importance can be attributed to his unification of the mystical, philosophical, and theological disciplines into one great synthesis. Furthermore, in his work *De sacramentis christianae fidei,* which was completed toward the middle of the twelfth century, he erected the first great doctrinal structure of Christianity.

With the appearance of St. Albert and St. Thomas the movement of the synthesists took an Aristotelian turn. Now more attention was given to the inclusion of natural questions. These thinkers opposed the old monastic ideal even in their own order, and urged the study of philosophy and the profane sciences.

If human reason is a gift from God, if natural reason is directed to a supernatural complement, if grace does not abrogate nature but completes it, then natural reason must have a function in the intellectual and moral life of the human race. The Scriptures condemn only the abuse of philosophy; as an expedient, philosophy may be of great value. Aside from the training it imparts to our weak minds in the understanding of truth, philosophy is entrusted with a three-fold task. First, it must present the *praeambula fidei,* the existence and unity of God, and the underlying natural reasons. Secondly, it can make the teachings of faith clearer by means of analogies taken from the created world. Thirdly, it serves in the defense of the faith by showing that the opposing arguments are false or not convincing. Since the patristic era these duties have been assigned to philosophy both in theory and in practice. The defense of the faith was the first and most important task given philosophy; the preparation also of the *praeambula fidei* had been demanded of philosophy even before the days of St. Thomas, but St. Thomas placed religious faith on a much broader rational foundation. St. Thomas thus became the chief exponent of that explanation of the relationship between faith and reason that today is called the system of "partial identity" of philosophy and religion, and he placed all the profane sciences in the substructure of his theology. For him, the substructure included not only natural theology, but also a complete psychology of knowledge, a metaphysical psychology with the proofs for the substantiality, spirituality, and immortality of the soul, a philosophical anthropology, and a psychology of the will and the affections which provided for a transition to natural ethics. Besides these he included natural law, incorporating into it some important parts of Aristotle's political science.

Philosophy was not only to supply the foundation; it should also penetrate the whole content of faith. St. Thomas undertook the difficult and delicate task of determining the manner in which reason and philosophy could find valid application to the teachings of faith, and the extent to which such a procedure would be applicable. To draw the line between faith and reason requires a thorough knowledge of epistemology, of the validity of reason, and of the nature of faith, as well as a clear vision of the many errors and pitfalls one is apt to encounter. If the study of the faith was to become a science, more than a mere mechanical application of logical forms and apparatus was required. Philosophy was to serve theology in two ways, formally and materially.

Inspired by the scientific ideal of the faculty of arts at Paris, St. Thomas transferred the formal structure of methodical knowledge to the contents of faith which since the time of the Fathers had become ever more extensive. He used reason not only in the defense of faith but also as an instrument of progress in theological knowledge, and he introduced the method of proceeding from the known to the unknown (*discurrere de principiis ad conclusiones*) which was being used in the profane sciences.

In a material way the teachings of faith were made clearer by means of analogies. The motto *credo ut intelligam* presupposes, of course, that faith contains nothing opposed to reason and is therefore at least in part comprehensible by reason. St. Anselm had already gone a long way toward the scientific penetration of the teachings of faith and had sought necessary reasons for the teachings of faith. His dialectic was not the same as rationalism, because he did not pretend to give a full comprehension of religious mysteries; rather he attempted to make them intelligible so far as humanly possible, using analogies from this earthly life.

St. Thomas undertook to make the doctrines of faith more intelligible by means of scientific concepts and investigated scientifically many matters of faith. He was convinced that the concepts we gain from objects about us have a transcendental validity, and that the content of supernatural revelation might become clearer by comparison with our concepts. He taught: *"De divinis loquimur secundum modum nostrum, quem intellectus noster accipit ex rebus inferioribus, ex quibus scientiam sumit."* [11] He realized both the extent and the limitations of this statement; he was aware of the implication that our concepts are applicable in all spheres of being.

We are not surprised, therefore, to learn that in his *Theological*

[11] *De pot.*, II, I.

Summa, as well as in his other writings, philosophy is more conspicuous and receives more extended consideration than theology.
The designation of philosophy as the handmaid of theology was
adopted by the Scholastics from Philo, but the great services rendered by philosophy indicate a kind of handmaid that carries the
torch for her mistress lest she grope about in the dark. St. Thomas
admits, of course, that philosophy is not absolutely necessary for
theology and that philosophical arguments compared to the authority
of Holy Writ are only *quasi extranea et probabilia.* But, we may ask,
what would remain of the Thomistic system if the philosophical
foundation and the scientific argumentation were to be eliminated?
The apostolic faith protected by the Church's authority and explained
by the sayings of the Fathers would remain, but here the philosophical function would be reduced to a minimum, that minimum which
religion would require for the mere explanation of its terminology
and basic concepts. That minimum is not the ideal for St. Thomas,
although he once said that an old woman had more knowledge of
the truths of salvation after the coming of Christ than the philosophers before Christ.[12]

The harmony of the natural and the supernatural requires the
cooperation of reason and revelation. Reason, rising from below,
passes from the knowledge of the creature to the knowledge of God,
and God, coming down from above, descends to man by revelation.[13]
Knowing the independent value of faith, St. Thomas would rather
have the assent of faith to the truths of revelation without any scientific support than proofs from reason that are not tenable. Insufficient proofs only serve to injure religion.[14]

Even though St. Thomas considered philosophy of primary importance, he was far from permitting it to absorb theology. Not only
did he acknowledge that theology and revelation are necessary for
the instruction of mankind concerning truths which exceed the powers of human reason, and that they transmit a reliable and universal
knowledge of God to all people, but he also taught that theology has
its own subject matter and methods, and its own certainty. Theology
invites philosophy to participate in its field of labor and presents it

---

[12] *Expos. Symb. Apost.*
[13] *Contra Gent.,* IV, 1.
[14] *Ibid.,* I, 13; *Summa theol.,* Ia, q. 46, a. 2.

with problems and fields of application that it would never have discovered.

Students of St. Thomas are well aware of the importance of the *Quaestiones disputatae,* that form of philosophical writing which originated in the public disputations held by a master several times a year on some important question in philosophy or theology. Unlike St. Albert, St. Thomas made frequent use of this literary form, as did the members of the Franciscan Order (St. Bonaventure, Matthaeus ab Aquasparta, and others). In the intellectual arena, into which other masters and their students sometimes injected themselves, a teacher tried to give of his best and to present a well-founded argument in his *determinatio magistralis.* These *quaestiones* show St. Thomas in the midst of the intellectual movements of his time, and, owing to the fact that many of them were written during the same period as the *Theological Summa,* they are a valuable commentary on this great systematic work since they give us an insight into the problems confronting St. Thomas.

Each *quaestio* is a philosophical-theological summa in miniature, inasmuch as all important aspects of the subject are discussed. The most important of these *Quaestiones disputatae* is the *De veritate,* composed toward the end of his first period of teaching in Paris (1256–59). It presents all human forms of knowledge, both natural and supernatural, and contains a philosophical and theological epistemology. God, creation, and the Trinity are treated in the *Quaestio de potentia* (1265–68); the *Quaestiones de anima* are important for metaphysical psychology; and the *Quaestiones de bono, de virtute in communi,* and *de virtutibus cardinalibus* contain his ethics and the metaphysics of morality.

Valuable material may also be found in the *Quaestiones quodlibetales,* which were the literary outcome of disputations on various subjects (*de quolibet*) held twice a year, before Christmas and before Easter. Besides the commentaries on Aristotle, other commentaries by St. Thomas are important for a study of his philosophy, as, for instance, the *Expositio supra librum Boetii de Trinitate,* composed during his first sojourn in Paris (1257–58), in which he develops his ideas on science. Also important is the commentary on a work by pseudo-Dionysius (*De divinis nominibus*) in which St. Thomas makes important contributions to theology and the doctrine of causality, and the commentary on the pseudo-Aristotelian work *On Causes,* which he wrote in his last years.

Special attention must be given to the *Summa contra Gentes,* composed at the request of St. Raymond of Pennafort as a textbook for the use of young Dominican missionaries studying in Spain. Naturally this summa has an apologetic and polemic character. The theme of the *Contra Gentes* is: "From God to God." It begins, therefore, with natural theology; in the second book it treats of creatures; the third book proposes God as the ultimate end of all creatures; and the fourth book concludes with the revealed teachings on the Trinity, the Incarnation, the sacraments, and the Last Judgment. Out of this natural theology, cosmology, anthropology, ethics, and supernatural revelation, a whole is formed with a decided inclination toward philosophy. That this work was intended as an attack on a very proximate enemy such as the neopagan party in the Parisian faculty of arts or some Averroistic naturalism, is difficult to prove. It is true, however, that in this work St. Thomas attacks some important positions held by the Averroists and naturalists of any period or age.

St. Thomas' fame rests for all time on his great systematic masterpiece, the *Summa theologica.* It was composed as a textbook for the students of his time, and for us today it is an indication of the pressing demands made on theology in the thirteenth century. A summa, originally the designation for an abbreviated presentation of any science, about 1200 came to mean a complete presentation of speculative theology. Such a presentation was formerly known as Sentences (*Libri sententiarum*). The *Theological Summa* of St. Thomas had many predecessors, most of them still in manuscript, but none of these can compare with his in its extent of profane and sacred learning. St. Thomas reaches out so far in his discussion of a question that in dogmatic and moral theology he also treats of the aspects presented by natural and canonical law as well as by Christian mysticism and ecclesiastical liturgy. All the implements and weapons of philosophy come into play, but always under the direction of the teachings of faith.

Of the three parts of the *Summa theologica* we might write in explanation: "From God, to God, through Christ and His redemption." Since it is man who aspires to go to God by the redemption, the second part of the *Summa,* uniting the other two parts, comprises an extensive anthropology; a treatment of being and morals, the onto-logical structure, and the end of man. The first part contains the theology and the discussion of creation; the third part concludes the work with the doctrine of the redemption by Christ.

The harmony of the natural and supernatural orders is the univer-sal theme of this synthesis. The familiar comparison of the *Summa* with a Gothic cathedral is fully justified. The astounding wealth of material and the variety of structural units are held together by one plan and by one basic law as in all great works of art, by unity in variety. *"Omnia autem pertractantur in sacra doctrina sub ratione Dei: vel quia sunt ipse Deus, vel quia habent ordinem ad Deum ut ad principium et finem."* [15]

As is his custom, St. Thomas speaks of the end and purpose of his work in the prologue, distinguishing it from the summas and sentences of earlier Scholastics. In introducing beginners to the study of theology, he emphasizes three things: first, the elimination of un-necessary questions, articles, and arguments; secondly, an orderly procedure in the arrangement of the various disciplines; and lastly, the avoidance of frequent repetitions. St. Thomas had a definite pur-pose in mind in writing his *Summa*. The *Sentences* of Peter Lombard was defective in the arrangement and division of its material, and the commentaries on this work suffered from the same fault. The *Summa* of Alexander of Hales paid for its great adherence to the Lombard by a loss of structural unity and coherence. St. Thomas achieved his purpose. The qualities of clarity and thoroughness which character-ized his earlier writings are especially prominent in the *Summa theologica*. The Thomistic *Summa* is the most original contribution of its time to theology and philosophy. St. Albert's summa imitated the summa of Alexander of Hales both in content and structure, while the summa of Ulrich of Strassburg is greatly inferior to St. Thomas' *Summa* in its plan as in its symmetry.

[15] *Summa theol.,* Ia, q. 1, a. 8.

CHAPTER III

ST. THOMAS THE MAN

In contrast to other important figures in Christian thought, the intellectual development of St. Thomas Aquinas is marked by a certain serenity and peace. St. Augustine, the native of Africa and the child of parents quite unlike each other, is in a real sense a man of the transition period, in whose soul the battle between a decadent paganism and the new Christianity was fought. His origins were not in Christianity, but he developed into a Christian after many moral aberrations, and after being influenced by academic skepticism, Epicurean hedonism, Neoplatonic philosophy, and Cicero's *Hortensius*. St. Thomas, in whom Roman and Germanic blood flowed together to make a happy mixture, received his first training in the rule of St. Benedict, and later chose the religious habit of St. Dominic.

From youth he was happy in the possession of Christian truth and the blessings of the gospel, and he chose the religious life in the cloister that he might realize the ideals of Christian perfection.

St. Paul influenced the lives of both St. Augustine and St. Thomas, but in different ways and with different results. From the epistles of St. Paul, St. Augustine received the inspiration for his conversion, which he considered a special work of divine grace. His philosophy arises from the restlessness of his spirit and resembles the strife and struggle of our modern times. Truth is also for St. Thomas the guiding principle and the highest goal of life, but the struggling and wrestling for truth, the temporary despair, the profound melancholy and longing for death, the successive defeats and victories in which the life of St. Augustine is told and for which he appeals to the man of today, are all unknown to St. Thomas. St. Thomas had never found himself entangled in the world and therefore never had to flee from the world. He had no experiences like those related in the *Confessiones* and was therefore unable to write such a book. Because he had surrendered himself entirely to God, his life attained a steady, uniform rhythm. The program announced at the beginning of his philosophical summa applied to his whole life: *"Propositum nostrae intentionis est veritatem, quam fides catholica profiteretur, pro nostro modulo manifestare errores eliminando contrarios. Ut enim verbis Hilarii utar, ego hoc vel praecipuum vitae meae officium debere me Deo conscius sum, ut eum omnis sermo meus et sensus loquatur."* [1] He spent himself in the service of the knowledge of the divine, in lectures and study, and in prayer and preaching. St. Thomas remained always the man of science and the simple monk, unlike many Scholastics who climbed to high ecclesiastical positions. His career differed especially from that of his teacher St. Albert, who was not only an outstanding student and teacher, but also provincial of his order, bishop, preacher of a crusade, and judge in certain litigations. St. Thomas expressed himself concerning the importance and the responsibilities of the office of teaching, especially of teaching philosophy and theology. His biographers tell us of the throngs of students that came to his lectures, and of the clear and lucid way he presented his lectures. In view of the times, St. Thomas was a liberal teacher. While John Peckham bound his hearers by the authority of St. Augustine, St. Thomas permitted his students to follow any leader except in matters of faith and morals. [2]

The medieval thinkers were religious men, and their writings were composed in the service of the highest religious ideals. St. Thomas was inspired by a twofold passion, by the love of truth and the love of prayer. It might be said of him that he was almost a disembodied intellect, that his whole life was nothing but intellectual activity, to such an extent that he often forgot the necessary requirements of physical existence. Forgetful of all personal considerations, his whole being was consumed by an unbounded love of truth and things divine. His religious superiors felt themselves obliged to appoint another monk, Reginald of Piperno, to care for his physical wants. Whereas the Bishop of Hippo in the midst of his turbulent experiences regarded the will as man's greatest faculty, St. Thomas accorded the primacy to the intellect. [3] At the same time, St. Thomas was not oblivious of the limitations of the human intellect.

---

[1] *Contra Gent.*, I, 2.
[2] *Quodlib.*, III, 10.
[3] *De verit.*, XXII, 11; *Contra Gent.*, I, 2; *Summa theol.*, Ia, q.82, a.3.

His intellectualism was enlivened by a loving surrender to God and found its highest expression in his praise of a mode of life which combined contemplation with activity. In him, the philosopher does not oppose the theologian, and the mystic is not at variance with the thinker. In him the philosopher is always submissive to the teachings of faith; faith is always mightier than science. That high ideal which Plato proposed for all men, but especially for the thinker, the harmony of the spirit, was never so perfectly realized as in St. Thomas, and the ancient Greek exhortation (*Orando solum vere intelligitur*) had never been the norm for a life of science as perfectly as in his. The harmony which we find in his philosophical picture of the universe was a reflection of the harmony that reigned in his soul. St. Thomas was both a thinker and a saint. The title *Doctor angelicus* beautifully expresses the fundamental characteristic of his personality.

Because St. Thomas was so little concerned with his personal needs, he was able to give himself wholly to the study of the universe and to the development of a scientific picture of the entire universe. Not without reason has his system been called the most impersonal of all medieval systems. His opponents bear witness to his mildness and modesty in the disputations, although he knew well how to wield the cudgels of battle when the circumstances required it. The Averroists in the faculty of arts, and St. Bonaventure himself, experienced the sharp sting of his criticism.

Even the most pious soul cannot live in peace if the spirit of his time is the spirit of war and conflict, or if his intellectual freedom of scientific existence is threatened. For this reason the public life of St. Thomas is a series of battles. We have already mentioned his stand beside St. Albert in defense of the rights of the profane sciences against the reactionary defenders of the old monastic ideal. Soon afterward the intellectual activity of his order was threatened at the University of Paris. The new mendicant orders, the Franciscan and the Dominican, had not only made great progress in the care of souls, but now they were also taking their places in the front rank of scientific endeavor and forging ahead of the professors of the secular clergy. Signs of discontent appeared first in the pastoral ministry. Soon afterward discord raised its head at the University when the secular clergy contested the right of the mendicants to occupy professorial chairs. The Franciscans and the Dominicans were to be deprived of one of the two chairs which they held. Although Pope Alexander IV decided in favor of the orders, the conflict did not come to an end because the chief antagonist, William of St. Amour, issued his tract *De periculis novissimorum temporum* (1255). This attack was directed against the fundamental idea of the orders and prompted St. Bonaventure to reply with his *Quaestio de paupertate,* while St. Thomas wrote the tract *Contra impugnantes Dei cultum et religionem* in which he used the plea made by his teacher St. Albert before the pope in justification of the religious orders. Because of these conflicts, it was not until the autumn of 1257 that St. Bonaventure and St. Thomas were formally accepted as masters in the theological faculty. The strife continued, and even during his second term at the University of Paris, St. Thomas had occasion to write his *De perfectione vitae spiritualis* against Gerard of Abbatisvilla, and the *Contra pestiferam doctrinam retrahentium homines de religionis ingressu* against Nicholas of Lisieux.

The University of Paris was the center of the intellectual life and the arena for the intellectual battles of the time. In the Dominican Order were found men imbued with the spirit of progress, against whom a strong opposition began to form itself. St. Thomas fought a battle on two fronts, one offensive, the other defensive. He was on the offensive against the Averroistic Aristotelianism of the faculty of arts of the University with its tendency to undermine the whole Christian philosophy; he was on the defensive against the spirit of Augustinianism that was dominant in Christian philosophy. Since the days of the early Scholastics, St. Augustine's teaching had been the sacrosanct tradition determining all fundamental questions; to attack that tradition or to criticize it was tantamount to destroying all philosophy. St. Thomas was considered an upstart and a heretic, who had, it was true, some admirers and followers in the faculty of arts, but only opposition in the theological faculty. Among his opponents in the theological department were the masters among the secular clergy, not only William of St. Amour but also the more important Henry of Ghent who had enlisted the support of Stephen Tempier, the bishop of Paris. Also among the opposition were the masters of the Franciscan Order. St. Bonaventure, the friend of St. Thomas, had been succeeded in the chair of philosophy by the contentious John Peckham, whom St. Thomas opposed in a public disputation.

St. Thomas also found opposition in his own order among the older members who followed the leadership of Robert of Kilwardby. The prohibition issued by the Dominicans against the study of pagan literature, of Aristotle and his philosophy, was a blow directed against the new movement. Public condemnation was not long in coming. Three years after St. Thomas' death, in 1277, Stephen Tempier solemnly condemned a series of Averroistic propositions and among these he placed nine which belonged to St. Thomas. In his old age, St. Albert hastened to Paris to defend the teaching of his great disciple. Robert Kilwardby and John Peckham, each of whom became archbishop of Canterbury, likewise found occasion to condemn as dangerous certain Thomistic teachings. Soon after these official reproofs, the Franciscan William de la Mare joined the attack on Thomism and severely criticized 118 Thomistic propositions in his *Correctorium fratris Thomae*. The Dominicans replied with a series of writings, and the battle that waged so long about St. Thomas and his doctrine ended in a victory for him, at least in his own order.

An indication of the high esteem in which St. Thomas was held at the University of Paris may be found in the letter of condolence addressed by the faculty of arts to the general chapter of the Dominicans on his death. Even Siger of Brabant spoke of St. Thomas and St. Albert as *"praecipui viri in philosophia."* In his own order his critics were gradually silenced, and after his canonization in 1323 the condemnation of the nine articles was revoked and his system became the special doctrine of the Dominican Order.

The magnitude of the Thomistic system may be judged not only from the positive structure of the system, but also negatively from the large number of opponents it aroused. The system was attacked on the score of its methods and also in its content. It is regrettable, however, that Thomism found no defender or continuator comparable in stature to the great founder of the system.

PART II

THE STRUCTURE OF REALITY

INTRODUCTORY

The universe must be conceived as a whole before it can be explained. This universe may appear larger or smaller, depending on the mental horizon of a particular age or a particular individual, but at all times the parts are contained within the whole and refer to it. Here, too, the whole is before the parts. The fundamental problem of both religion and philosophy is the ultimate cause and the ultimate meaning of all being.

St. Thomas believed that the universe could be studied in two books, the Bible and this creation of time and space. The former discloses the origin and the meaning of the universe, in particular the meaning of human history and of each human being. The cosmos of time and space is an open book disclosing its own structure, the structure of its parts, their coordination to each other, and their relationship to their Author. He who thinks cosmically and is able to discern the harmony existing in the universe, will interpret the universe as an integrated whole. In the chapter "The Order of the Universe" we will present such a proportioned interpretation of the world.

We might be tempted to begin our presentation of Thomistic philosophy with the concept of being, especially since St. Thomas taught that the concept of being was the first that we formed and the one that underlies all other concepts. Nevertheless it is true that the idea of abstract being and all its properties can be understood only if the concrete reality from which it arises is first analyzed.

SECTION I

THE STRUCTURE OF INDIVIDUAL THINGS

Keeping in mind the lineaments of the whole, we need not lose sight of the nature of individual things. The frank realism of St. Thomas and the scientific method of Aristotle agree that the all-embracing reality which surrounds us and which can be perceived by the senses is composed of individual things. These thinkers were convinced that the processes of nature on this earth are designed for the production of individual things, whether individual things are composed of other things or even belong to the most widely separated orders of being. Among the substances then universally recognized were earth, water, air, plants, animals, men, heavenly bodies, and others. Individual things are the material object of the natural sciences. As the objects most immediately obtainable by our method of knowledge, they are the subject of a scientific research which seeks to penetrate to the principles of being.[1] Only to the concrete thing does St. Thomas accord an autonomous being in nature, and thus to it alone a perfected and complete existence. Everything in nature is actual being, and in it the origin and the cessation of being take place.[2] Like those who went before him, St. Thomas is intent on revealing the structure of the individual thing.

[1] *Met.*, VII, 1 f.
[2] *In IV Sent.*, 12, 1 ad 3; *In lib. de caus.*, 22; *De pot.*, III, 8.

CHAPTER IV

MATTER AND FORM

1. **Derivation and definition.** The famous teaching that every sensible being is composed of matter and form can be properly understood and evaluated only when we grasp the problem for which it is a solution.

a) Aristotle, the great teacher of the genetic method of observation, gained a knowledge of these two components through a study of the process of becoming. Like his predecessors, he was intent on the solution of the problem of the genesis of being, and he was convinced that this genetic process would throw light on the nature of matter and form. Even the ancient philosophers had been impressed by the existence of opposites in the universe, and like them Aristotle believed that the genesis of being moved from opposite to opposite. That which became warm, had been cold before. It seemed equally clear to him, moreover, that the opposites did not influence each other directly but that a substratum was required upon which they could work and into which they could be received.

Other observations led to the same conclusion. It was observed that the opposites were at no time substances, but accidents expressed in the predicate. Not only does the logical subject underlie the predicative expression, but it is also that which is ontologically prior and that in which the accidents have their being. This underlying substance, considered either in the individual or as a universal, has no opposites; it has the capacity of receiving opposites. Thus one and the same subject is at one time white and then black, now warm and then cold. In every process of becoming, a substratum is required in which the process takes place, and also another element: that which the substratum becomes, or the form impressed upon the substratum. What we observe in reality is paralleled in the plane of logic. We

59

may say that an educated man is composed of man and education. This is, of course, an accidental process, but the observation is also true for substantial being.

Aristotle adds another thought to this argument: the analogy from art, a methodical procedure which had been used by Plato to show the permanence of matter as the substratum. Just as an object of art becomes such when the matter (material) is clothed by an artistic form, so in every natural process each individual thing arises from the union of two elements. Two principles, matter as substratum and the form, must be considered separately in the genesis of being, or more exactly, three principles, matter, form, and the denudation, since not only is matter the substratum but it is something deprived of all form.[3]

Matter and form are defined according to the various methods in which the concepts are derived. Aristotle was well aware that he had derived his ideas from the genesis of accidental being and he was determined to establish his theory as valid in every instance of the genesis of being.[4] According to him, matter is the first substratum from which, as from a co-principle, every being takes its origin; it is that which is indestructible, the permanent recipient of all opposites, the mother of all being.[5] Then, because of the parallelism between thought and being, the separate elements found in the logical proposition became real components of the individual thing. Since all the determination found in the predicate referred to the form, matter was deprived of the character of being. It can be spoken of "neither as substance, nor quantity, nor as any other kind of being" (*Met.,* VII, 3). In accordance with the analogy of the artistic object in which the material is passive and undetermined, prime matter is also described as passive and indefinite. Form, on the other hand, is that which makes a thing what it is and confers on a thing a particular kind of being with specific properties. This does not complete the description of matter and form. Hardly any pair of concepts is more important in the Aristotelian system than potency and act, and scarcely any comparison appears as often as the comparison of matter with potency and of form with act.

Aristotle also derived the concepts of potency and act from his observation of the genesis of being. Disagreeing with the solutions of his predecessors, Aristotle thought that the genesis of being was a transition from potency to act, as the realization of that which was only possible. Aristotle saw how the Eleatics threatened the existence of natural philosophy and how Empedocles, Anaxagoras, and the Atomists denied the genesis of all substantial being. The Eleatics, relying on the principle that nothing came from nothing, denied all genesis and cessation of being as well as any diversity of being; the latter group considered all genesis of being as a mere mechanical union of two masses. Aristotle criticizes their failure to make the necessary distinctions, inasmuch as being and non-being do not exhaust all the possibilities. Being does not originate from non-being, but from accidental non-being; the new thing arises from the denudation or deprivation of form. Another way of solving the difficulty was to make the distinction between potency and act. The genetic process of being is a transition of potency into act, a development of the germinal disposition to full being. Being does not come from non-being, but reality comes from the possible; neither does being come from being, but from a real potency. Undoubtedly Aristotle had in mind here the organic genesis of being and the production of objects of art. The seed or germ contains the living being in potency which is actualized by the genetic process; seed and the living being are to each other as potency and act. In the realm of art, Aristotle considered the matter as the potency or the required condition for the artistic object. A block of marble is in potency to a statue; stones and wood are in potency to a house. Aristotle made the most extensive use of this concept of potency and conceived of every genesis of being, from the simplest physical process to the spiritual process of knowledge, as the transition from potency to act.

It is important to understand that here the Stagirite identified matter with the possible, and form with the principle that confers reality. This identification seemed permissible since the seed or germ from which the organism developed was not only the disposition but also the substratum in the genesis of being, and the original material used in the sculpture was the possibility and the prerequisite for the statue. The potency of the seed and the potency of the material do not, of course, lie in the same plane, inasmuch as the power of development is immanent in the germ of a living being and constitutes an active potency, while the material used for the statue is a passive potency that needs the activity of the artist for its actualization.

The identification of form and act is understandable when we remember that the material becomes a statue by being clothed with a form, and that the germ is actualized by the development of a certain form. The two pairs of concepts are not mutually coextensive, since they are of different derivation. By matter and form the individual being is divided into its two component parts; by potency and act the same thing is considered in two phases of being. Aristotle frequently emphasizes that matter and form can never exist separated from each other but only as integral parts of a composite.

These concepts of matter and form and of potency and act have formed the basis of all study of being since the time of Aristotle; for the Stoics, the Pythagoreans, the Platonists, the Fathers (especially for St. Augustine), and for Arabian, Jewish, and Christian Scholasticism.

Indeed interesting are modern interpretations of Aristotle which admit of another matter (metaphysical matter) essentially different from prime matter, but these are irrelevant in the present instance since St. Thomas consistently maintained the traditional interpretation of Aristotle's concept of matter.

b) St. Thomas seeks to develop faithfully these fundamental ideas of the Philosopher. He adopts the various derivations and definitions of matter and form, the proof *per viam motus,* the proof *per viam praedicationis,* the analogy between nature and art, and the derivation of potency and act.

According to St. Thomas, matter is uniform (*una numero in omnibus*) and excludes all numerical differentiation. It is the substratum of all things in nature; that which is capable of receiving opposites. It is that in which the origin and cessation of being takes place, but that which is itself exempt from being originated and which never ceases to be.[6] It was created by God. As the recipient of the form it enters into the constitution of things, making matter and form the intrinsic principles of all things.[7] With Aristotle, St. Thomas distinguishes between matter and privation. Although matter and privation are indistinguishable in their subject since matter is never without privation because union with one form denotes dep-

---

[6] *De princ. nat.; De nat, mat.,* chap. 1.
[7] *Summa theol.,* Ia, q.3, a.2 ad 3.

rivation of all other forms, they are nevertheless conceptually different. They differ because matter is being *per se* while privation is being *per accidens;* matter is in potency to reality, and as one of the principles constituting a thing it is *prope rem,* while privation is really non-being.[8] Privation does not enter into the constitution of things and is not therefore one of the principles of being, although it might be considered a principle in the genesis of being. Plato and Avicenna did not distinguish between privation and matter and consequently they fell into the error of regarding matter as non-being.[9] To matter belong definability and passivity, not activity. Matter is therefore the passive principle in the things of nature, that which is absolutely indefinite receiving definition through the form. Furthermore, matter has no actual existence but only a potential existence and thus it is the medium (*quasi medium*) between pure non-being and actual being.[10]

St. Thomas frequently pointed out the potential nature of prime matter and, following Aristotle, he wished to make it clear that matter is never found in nature as a reality. If it were an actual being, then there would be no difference between matter and the individual substance. On the other hand, matter is not pure non-being, but only being *per accidens.* As incomplete being, or in the words of St. Thomas, *"incompletissimum inter omnia entia,"* [11] matter has no autonomous existence, but can really exist only in a composite where it forms the basis for the changes that take place in sensible things. The concept of potency includes the notion of definability and the capacity to receive opposites.[12] Prime matter is pure potency; indeed potency expresses the nature of prime matter, inasmuch as it is a *principium in genere substantiae* [13] together with the form, not however as it is related to the form, since the essence of prime matter does not consist in a relation. This relation, however, is so intrinsic in matter that St. Thomas finally admitted that "to be in potency is nothing else than being in order to act." Like non-being, matter has no distinguishable marks; it belongs to the principles that are known only in their relation to others. Because matter may be conceived as

[8] *Ibid.*, q. 66, a. 2.
[9] *In VII Met.*, 2.
[10] *In I Phys.*, 9.
[11] *De spir. creat.*, I.
[12] *In XII Met.*, 2.
[13] *In I Sent.*, 3, 4, 2 ad 4.

being in relation to an indefinite number of forms, it may be called infinite (*infinitum secundum quid*).[14] But since this infinity is not actual, St. Thomas is not troubled with any philosophical consequences. After all, the potency of prime matter extends itself only to natural forms, and any infinity it might be said to possess would be limited.[15]

In company with Aristotle and Averroes, St. Thomas defends the numerical unity of matter which was so vehemently attacked by Roger Bacon. He explains what is meant by numerical unity by distinguishing between two kinds of unity. Unity appears in a single individual such as Socrates, but matter is not one in this sense since it possesses no form. That is said to have numerical unity which is without the dispositions upon which numerical diversity is based. Only in this abstract sense is matter numerically one. Matter is, furthermore, indivisible because the idea of matter precludes every kind of quantity in contrast to the point, which is indivisible as a principle of quantity.[16]

The form places a limit to the potency of matter.[17] It provides matter with existence and actuality and is itself act; indeed, it is "first" act, in comparison with that activity which flows from the form and is called "second" act (*operatio*).[18] Matter participates in existence only through the form. Matter and form are the causes of the composite, and as such therefore they differ from that which was caused. Matter is a cause inasmuch as it offers a basis or substratum for the existence of the form; the form is a cause inasmuch as it elevates matter to actual being. Everything possesses existence by reason of its form; this existence is of a certain kind because of the form; and besides this, the form confers unity. The form in general is able to unite with many substratums. The form exists now with matter, not as numerically one, but specifically one, individualized by the matter. It exists in a multiplicity of individuals, but in the process of becoming and cessation of being it retains at all times its own intrinsic uniformity. Limited by matter, the form attains an individual existence in an individual thing. Just as it is the principle of existence, the form

---

[14] *In I Phys.*, 15.
[15] *Summa theol.*, Ia, q.7.
[16] *In II Sent.*, 30, 2, 1.
[17] *In I Sent.*, 45, 1, 3.
[18] *Contra Gent.*, I, 27; *Summa theol.*, Ia, q.6, a.3; q.76, a.7; q.77, a.6; Ia IIae, q.85, a.6.

is also the principle of activity in things which are able to act in so far as they are in act. In this concept of act the dynamic philosophy of St. Thomas has its roots. The form is, moreover, the principle of knowability. Act contains all the perfections of being as well as all the perfections of activity. Act, which constitutes things intrinsically, also informs the knowing mind or intellect.

The form has more existence than matter because act is prior to potency, prior in concept, in time, in nature, and in purpose. Because of the higher existence of form, it follows logically that in comparison with matter it is the better and more perfect in every aspect. Act is the completion of potency and its "good." The whole form is in the whole thing as well as in every part and represents the perfection of the whole and of the parts.[19] St. Thomas calls the form a divine thing since it places the thing in relationship with God, and through the form the thing participates in divine being.[20] Every form has its own specific perfection, and any increase or diminution of that perfection creates a new species, just as in the realm of numbers any addition or subtraction constitutes a new species. By reason of this difference of perfection, forms are placed in a hierarchy and they function as principles of order in the universe.

2. **The relation between matter and form; potency and act.** St. Thomas explains the relation between matter and form in the Aristotelian manner. They are really distinct from each other but they are never separated. To speak of the existence of matter without form would be like speaking of a being in act without act, *ens actu sine actu*. Matter and form do not, as Avicebron taught, exist before they are united in the composite. Matter cannot exist without form, and forms likewise have no existence without a material substratum.[21] It is part of the idea of form to be in that subject of which it is the form; only individual things possess autonomous existence. Existence, therefore, cannot be predicated indiscriminately of forms and individual things. The form exists because something exists through it, *quia ea aliquid est.*[22] Matter is because of the form, and the form is the end of the matter, and only on the basis of matter can the form attain actuality. Because of this relationship the form is united directly

[19] *Summa theol.,* Ia, q.3; a.1.
[20] *In Boeth. de Trin.,* IV, 2; *Contra Gent.,* II, 43; III, 97.
[21] *Summa theol.,* Ia, q.45, a.8; q.65, a.4; q.66, a.2; Ia IIae, q.4, a.5 ad2; *Contra Gent.,* I, 27; II, 56, 82.
[22] *De pot.,* III, 8.

and immediately with prime matter and not through any third member.[23]

Owing to its indifference, matter is in potency to all forms, but it receives them in a certain order. It is first in potency to the elementary forms, and through them it is in potency to the other forms.[24] The potency of prime matter is never weakened, and when clothed with a lower form it still remains in potency to a higher form. "Prime matter is first in potency to the form of an element. Under the form of an element it is in potency to a composite body and therefore the elements form the matter for composites. As a composite it is in potency to the vegetative soul which is the act of such a body. In like manner the vegetative soul is in potency to the sensitive soul, and the sensitive soul to the rational soul. . . . Thus matter strives to attain the highest form." [25] Because of this inner relation between matter and form, it follows that in composites and even in the elements not every form can be educed from any matter. As Aristotle said, we cannot make a saw out of wool. Fire will not arise from every non-fire but from a certain non-fire (*ex tali non igne*).

Forms require a special disposition in the matter. Besides common prime matter we must also have proper matter (*materia propria*) which in practice plays the principal role. The potential element is that which is possible, determinable, and imperfect, and this element receives reality, definiteness, perfection, and form through the form which is the actual element. The form (act) is the principle of unity and totality. It is one substantial form, for instance, that makes the lion a substance, a body, a living thing, an animal, and a lion, just as one act of existence gives the thing reality. The form is the principle of specific unity while matter is the principle of numerical unity or individuation.[26]

Act and potency are important in the theory of universals. They penetrate through substantial and accidental being and they are found in all the predicaments. Within one and the same species, of course, a thing cannot be at once in a state of potentiality and of actuality, but it may be so with respect to different species. Considered in the abstract, act is infinite and is limited only upon being

[23] *Contra Gent.*, III, 97.
[24] *In I Sent.*, 43, 1, 1; *Summa theol.*, Ia, q.85, a.7.
[25] *Contra Gent.*, III, 22.
[26] *In I Sent.*, 43, 1, 1; *Quodlib.*, VII, 1.

received in a substratum, when the general form receives a delimited individual existence. In his hierarchy of being, St. Thomas constantly emphasizes that act is the perfect and valuable element, while potency is the imperfect; that a thing is more perfect when less potentiality is found in it.[27]

3. **Evaluation of the theory of matter and form.** The value of this doctrine of matter and form has often been a subject for discussion, and even today the Scholastics are divided into two schools, defending and rejecting it. Some Scholastics are bent on saving this theory at all costs and consider it the bulwark of the Thomistic system. They are especially attached to the theory of potency and act. A fair critique of the theory must take into consideration the origin of these two principles, matter and form. Aristotle adopted them as a solution for the problem of the genesis of being, and both he and St. Thomas, by extending the problems of natural science into the metaphysical sphere, applied these principles to the ultimate problems of being.

For Aristotle and St. Thomas, hylomorphism was a physical as well as a metaphysical theory. St. Thomas admits that it was through the problem of the genesis of substantial being that prime matter became known.[28] Both philosophers, it is true, are careful to distinguish between the problems of physics and those of metaphysics. Physics investigates the corporeal elements and the various forms of the genesis of being, while metaphysics studies the same things from the viewpoint of being in general and also the various kinds of being. In reality, however, both scientific viewpoints are merged in the construction of a uniform picture of the universe. If hylomorphism had only the supports of natural science, gained through induction, it would fall with the natural sciences, but in addition to those of the physical sciences it rests on logical and metaphysical supports.

As Aristotle had done before him, St. Thomas formulated the theory of matter and form from data obtained from an impartial observation of what takes place in art and nature. Is it not true that everything represents the formation of some material (matter)? Is not wood made into the form of a chair, and bronze into the form of a statue? In nature, is not matter formed into a man, a bear, a tree, and a crystal? What takes place so patently in the organic sphere, can be shown to happen also in the non-organic sphere. If

[27] *In V Met.,* 9.
[28] *In VIII Met.,* 1.

in objection the modern scientist should refer to the amorphic and diffuse condition of the spiral nebulae or to the vague form of interstellar matter, the argument would not have much force. The lack of form in these instances is relative. We would not be able to speak of spiral nebulae if the parts were not held together to form a whole. The form is so necessary that without it nothing could be comprehended.

The principle of form was especially important for the analytic mind of Aristotle. The things in the universe do not represent a chaos or some unintelligible combination of particles of matter. Organic nature especially appears as a realm of definite types. Everywhere we see the embodiment of ideas. In all this there must be some system of formation, some plan of organization, some principle of order which directs that at one time matter be changed into the form of a crystal and at another into the form of a plant, or animal, or a human being. Under this aspect, the argument that the numerical multiplicity of material objects of the same species points to the distinction between the individual and the specific nature gains in strength. For the study of the thing and the type, the idea of form is indispensable. It is well known how the idea of form and entelechy has again come into favor among modern natural scientists.

The importance of form extends also into the midst of ontological problems. Everything is dominated by an idea or a structural principle. Being is not, as modern positivism teaches, a purely factual, worthless existence. On the other hand, in opposition to the atomistic and mechanical concept of positivism, beings are complete and organic. Things are unities and wholes that cannot be dissolved into mere relations or even into unrelated parts. The realistic Aristotelian concept of nature and the idealistic interpretation of the Christian theory of ideas unite in the Thomistic concept of form. Although a thing may belong to various planes of being, it is nevertheless a closed unity. The same form determines the individual to the ultimate species; it becomes substance, body, living body, lion. This unity not only provides undividedness and separation from every other individual, but also a certain structural quality. Totality is included in this unity, for every thing preserves its being only as long as it preserves its unity, and it preserves its unity only as long as it preserves its totality. This thought is a key to the meaning of transcendentals.

No one will deny that the concepts of potency and act have real validity in any discussion of being or the genesis of being. We will meet them often in our presentation of the Thomistic system.

Our judgment, however, will be different when we consider the value of the concept of form in the natural sciences. Though the concepts of matter and form seem to recommend themselves immediately for the study of the phenomena of nature, in the non-organic sciences they are entirely insufficient. A more penetrating examination of phenomena in their causes will show the application of these concepts to be unsound here.

During the Middle Ages the purpose of a thing was the preferred object of study for the natural sciences. The final cause was to throw light on all other causes. To know the purpose and end of a thing was to know its nature and being, its form and structure, its activity and manner of reaction; in a word, its whole reality. The accomplishment of this difficult goal seemed much easier to Aristotle and the students of the Middle Ages than it does to a more critical modern age. The greatest difficulty was to find a methodology for the attainment of this knowledge which would be beyond criticism. Aside from their continual references to God, mysticism, and astrology, the Peripatetics and Scholastics erred in basing conclusions of too great universality on their phenomenology. They also erred in accepting forms and qualities as true causes, and in proposing mere terms as causal factors. The true knowledge of nature and of natural causes is not advanced when St. Thomas predicates certain dispositions of a thing because of its nature. Thus, for example, from the fact that all the substantial forms of lower bodies exist by virtue of the heavenly bodies, he concludes that the qualities arising from the form or species of the elements, such as heat and cold, are also produced by these heavenly powers. In the same manner he maintains that the principles of the lower bodies are only four *"propter primas tangibiles qualitates"* and that the elements are active *"mediantibus qualitatibus activis"* and that they are passive *"mediantibus passivis."* [29]

In the words of Pierre Duhem, Scholastic natural philosophy reposed an arsenal of properties in the substantial form and increased the number whenever it found it necessary to explain another phenomenon. This sterility was the cause of defections among scholars. Thus Gassendi, Robert Boyle (the founder of chemistry), and the

[29] *In II de coel.,* 10; *In III de coel.,* 6.

great Newton went separate ways. We know now that the nominalists at the University of Paris (Jean Buridan, Nicolas Oresme, and others) laid the foundations for modern science and that they soon had such disciples as Leonardo da Vinci and Galileo. A new orientation took place; the goal was no longer the nature and essence of a thing, but an explanation of the causes of the phenomena.[30]

Matter is the correlative of form. Matter was required as the substratum for the process of becoming and as the substratum for the reception of the definiteness and content of form. But even though the analysis of becoming and being reveals this substratum, it need not be a pure potency.

Aristotle arrived at the idea of prime matter by a progressive process of abstracting all positive determination from the substratum, and he actualized the resulting idea because of his belief in the parallelism between thought and being. The concept, however, gives rise to metaphysical difficulties. Absolute lack of being and real existence are not reconcilable. A thing cannot be a prerequisite without being something positive. In the realm of reality the concept of matter is an impossible middle between being and non-being. The argument that matter does not exist without a form is not sufficient to save it. Matter and form are really the product of an illegitimate conclusion by analogy from art to nature; they are the result of an exaggerated belief in the parallelism between thought and being.

It is instructive to note that both Aristotle and St. Thomas were forced to abandon the original concept of matter when they came to explain the actual processes of being in nature. Instead of pure potency we find a concrete matter with certain properties and dispositions which plays an essential part in the actualization of a thing. Some have tried unsuccessfully to save the theory by arguing that the ultimate metaphysical principles do not appear on the surface in the process of becoming.

Other considerations seem to make the theory of matter and form untenable. If matter is filled with a striving for a form, if it acts as the cause of certain qualities and imperfections, and as the principle of individuation, it cannot be a pure potency and the middle between being and non-being. Furthermore, the substantial form does not have a pure potency as its substratum because at the death of organisms when the soul-form departs, a corpse remains instead of prime

[30] Cf. Duhem, *Etudes sur Léonardo da Vinci*, 1913.

matter. The much derided *forma cadaverica* which St. Thomas was forced to invent is a mere subterfuge. As a Christian thinker, St. Thomas was obliged to accord prime matter some kind of being since it was the product of divine creation and reflected the divine Being even though it was a weak being, *"debile esse."* [31] Plato had not provided an idea for matter, but St. Thomas could not avoid providing some kind of idea in God, since there must be a resemblance in God for each of His creatures. He did not, however, admit a complete idea for matter but only an idea for the composite made up of matter and form. But after all, even a *debile esse* is being and not reconcilable with pure potency.

Criticism of this concept of matter was quick to arise. According to Roger Bacon, the substratum in the genesis of being is matter clothed with an incomplete form (*forma corporeitatis*), which rises from its indetermined generality to a definite kind of being in the process of becoming. Scotus, also, seems to be more logical in this question than St. Thomas. According to Scotus, matter as a product of creation possesses the *actus entitativus* and thus a being independent of the form.[32] If, he argues, matter were not in some act (*aliqua res actu*), its being would not be different from the being of the form, and thus no real union of two principles would be possible. Further, only something actual can be the basis of passivity. Differing with St. Thomas, Scotus teaches that matter could exist without form by God's power but not by its natural disposition; that matter possesses an idea in God; and that in its essence it is knowable by the divine intellect. He taught that *materia secundo prima* could exist together with the subordinate form of corporeity, and that *materia secunda,* second matter, together with the form, exists in reality with a complete existence. Just as Scotus had a forerunner in Henry of Ghent, so he also had a disciple in Suarez. Henry of Ghent had been unable to accord to matter an autonomous being independent of form, and Suarez, although he admitted with St. Thomas that matter was pure potency, nevertheless taught that it had the act both of essence and of existence; an act of essence because matter is a reality independent of the form, and an act of existence because as a product of creation and the subject of being matter must possess reality.[33] By inventing

[31] *De verit.*, III, 5 ad 1.
[32] *In II Sent.*, d.3, q.1.
[33] *Met.*, disp. XIII, s.4, nos. 9, 13 f.

this incomplete existence Suarez pays his respects to tradition and at the same time manifests his repugnance to the idea that something can be a substratum without being at all.

Modern natural science and natural philosophy have arrived at other conclusions than Scholastic hylomorphism. Elements are united to make forms and are subjected to new laws. In this respect the hylomorphism of the Scholastics is still valid. But how do the conclusions of this theory appear today? Recall the electro-dynamic theory of matter. Now we have electrons with electric fields of influence, and these centers of power are the foundations of material being.

4. Matter as the principle of individuation. The problem of individuation is not concerned with the role which the individual plays in logical predication, or with the origin and existence of the individual, or with the outward marks that make the individual intelligible, the *notae individuantes,* but it deals with the inner metaphysical principle of individuality, and the metaphysical root of numerical unity and singularity. Socrates possesses humanity in common with many other beings, but being Socrates is proper to him alone. What shall we say is the cause of this individuality? The answer will be intelligible if we remember the ancient realism of the theory of universals.

From this world of phenomena, continually subject to change and variation, Plato fled to his world of ideas which for him represented true being and the true object of knowledge. For him this world of pure essences not only was prior to the world about us, but it was also far more valuable. The world of phenomena with its individuals continually coming into being and again losing being possesses reality only inasmuch as it partakes of the world of ideas or inasmuch as the ideas appear in the phenomena. The things of this world have only an imitative being which is imperfect and, because they are imbedded in matter, they are only circumscribed, limited, and individual existences. Neoplatonism continued this thought to the point where a thing is more real the more general it is. It taught that matter is the last thing in the stream of emanation, farthest removed from the source of being, and that it is the prerequisite for the multiplication of individual things. As a realist, Aristotle strove to save the honor of the individual thing when he called it the first substance and true reality, but the Platonist in him prevented this doctrine from reach-

MATTER AND FORM

ing its full development for he immediately weakened its force by
the statement that the most important and valuable part of the individual thing is the form, the expression of the universal. In one
sense he rejected Plato's theory of ideas, but under a different guise
he accepted it with all its epistemological and metaphysical implications. Matter and form were indeed the result of the analysis of the
genesis of being, but the form was really nothing more than the
Platonic idea stripped of its transcendence. If, therefore, the universal
type is derived from the form, whence is the multiplicity of individuals within the same type derived?

Aristotle expressed himself only occasionally on this question of
the principle of individuation, but his opinion is nevertheless quite
clear. Immaterial things possess a simplicity which is the basis for
their unity.[34] The problem is different, however, with those things
composed of matter and form. The cause of the multiplicity of individuals is to be found in matter, and more specifically, in defined
matter. When Aristotle ascribed the principle of individuation to the
same factor that is responsible for that which is unreal and imperfect
in the composite, he placed the individual in dangerous company and
initiated a degradation of the individual. According to Aristotle's way
of thinking, Socrates is the universal form fashioned in this flesh and
these bones.[35]

The complete devaluation of the concrete was forestalled only in
those parts of Greece where Plato, the Platonists, and the Pythagoreans concerned themselves with the spirituality of the soul and its
welfare in the next world.

Among Christian thinkers a complete change was brought about.
Now the individual man with his uniqueness and peculiarities again
occupies the center of the stage. In some respects the Christian philosophers remained under the influence of the ancient Greeks. Even St.
Augustine, who valued the salvation of the human soul above all else
and who was so deeply concerned in his philosophy of history with
deciphering the meaning of the race's history, remained a Platonist in
his study of being and valued being according to its universality. This
higher valuation of the substantial essence or universal remained in
vogue throughout the period of high Scholasticism, and logically it
influenced the question of the principle of individuation. In the hey-

[34] *Ibid.*, VIII, 6.
[35] *Ibid.*, V, 6; VII, 8, 10; XII, 8.

day of Scholasticism this problem became the veritable apple of discord. Except a few Arabians who tried to derive individuality from
existence, the thinkers, including Avicenna and Averroes, the leaders
in the faculty of arts (Siger of Brabant and Boethius of Dacia), and
the Dominicans (St. Albert and St. Thomas), held the Aristotelian
theory.

St. Thomas came under the Aristotelian and Arabian influences,
and his solution of this problem wavered. One thing was certain: the
form, the basis of the substantial essence or quiddity, could not be the
basis of individuality because the form in itself is universal and can
be received in one or more substratums. The individual is founded
on the prime matter, inasmuch as matter is not capable of being received.[36] Not everything in the individual substance can belong to
the universal essence, otherwise the multiplicity of individuals within
a species would be indistinguishable. If the principle of numerical
unity were the same as the principle of the species, then two horses
would be one horse.[37] The principle of individuation is therefore matter through which the form is contracted to become this individual
(*contrahitur ad hoc determinatum*).[38] We must add immediately,
however, that St. Thomas was not referring to undetermined prime
matter but *"materia signata"* according to Avicenna. By this "signed"
matter he understands matter that has definite relations of extension
and magnitude and is therefore also divisible.[39]

At the same time, St. Thomas is careful to distinguish between
the part played by matter in individuation and the contribution made
by quantitative dimension. It is interesting to observe how St. Thomas
is sometimes under one influence and again under another. For a
time he is indebted to Averroes for the view that some indefinite dimensions must be admitted in prime matter before its union with the
form because otherwise the divisibility of matter and the reception of
different forms in different parts of matter could not be understood.
In the fourth book on the *Sentences* he declares that matter is the
first principle, and the dimensions on which the divisibility of matter
rests are the second principle of individuation. He also mentions these
undetermined dimensions in his *Opusculum in Boethium de Trini-*

---

[36] *De spir. creat.*, V ad 8.
[37] *Ibid.; Summa theol.*, Ia, q.11, a.3.
[38] *Quodlib.*, VII, 3; *De spir. creat.*, 1.
[39] Cf. *In 1 Sent.*, 25, 1, 1 f.

tate.[40] The form is individuated when it is received in this particular matter (*in hac materia vel illa distincta et determinata ad hic et nunc*). St. Thomas adds a distinction: the threefold extension can be considered in two ways. First, it can be considered in its limitation by dimension or by figure, and in this sense it is not the principle of individuation because this limitation is changeable in one and the same individual and thus the numerical identity of the individual might be endangered. Secondly, these dimensions can be considered without any firm limitation even though they never exist thus in nature. The *materia signata* consists of such indefinite and imperfect dimensions and in this way it individualizes the form (*sic individuat formam et sic ex materia causatur diversitas secundum numerum in eadem specie*). Not in itself, but as the subject of these dimensions is matter the principle of individuation. Thus St. Thomas refers numerical diversity partly to matter and partly to the difference of these dimensions.

The view advanced by Porphyry and Boethius that individuation consisted in the accumulation of accidents (*collectio accidentium*), was rejected by St. Thomas because it eventually led to a denial of the substance. St. Thomas taught that these indefinite dimensions are present in prime matter before the reception of the form. Whence do these dimensions come? To this question St. Thomas and the Thomists offer no solution.

In later years, however, St. Thomas abandoned this theory of the undetermined dimensions and, if the dissertation *De natura materiae et dimensionibus interminatis* is genuine, his reasons may be found there. These arguments are most effective and completely in accord with the basic principles of Thomism. In reality, he argues, these dimensions are quantities even though they are not actual in prime matter. Either they are educed from prime matter or not. If they are so educed this can happen only through the substantial form; but all dimensions which owe their existence to the form are determined. If these dimensions are not educed from the potency of the matter, then we are forced to admit three principles of being instead of two, matter, form, and these undetermined dimensions. Again: these dimensions separate parts of matter or they do not. If they do, then matter already has a substantial form since every distinction or division

[40] *In Boeth. de Trin.*, IV, 2.

derives from some form; if they do not, then these dimensions are reducible to nothing. No possible way presents itself by which dimensions can exist in matter without a substantial form. In this same work St. Thomas expressly declares that the first subject is matter, not with any dimensions, but in itself. If we say that three-dimensional matter is the principle of individuation, this does not mean that the dimensions cause the individuation, just as an accident does not cause the subject. The definite relations of extension are a sign of individuation (*indicium individuationis*), merely a means by which the mind is able to distinguish between individuals.

After rejecting the Averroistic position, St. Thomas still continues to talk about matter and definite relations of extension, and this has occasioned a long-standing controversy as to whether he admitted matter as the only principle of individuation or matter and quantity. In the short work *De principio individuationis,* matter is made primarily responsible for individuation while quantity is made a contributing factor only inasmuch as it is an inseparable concomitant of the individual.

The Thomistic principle of individuation has evoked much criticism, not only because St. Thomas was uncertain about it or because it was improperly understood, but especially because of the inherent weakness of the Thomistic position. It is erroneous to say that St. Thomas had sought the principles of numerical individuation rather than those of qualitative individuation, but it is true that he had in mind only relative and not absolute individuation. Viewing the number of individuals within one species, he judged that the species was derived from the universal form, and that individuation therefore came from matter. Epistemological reasons and the Aristotelian theory of abstraction supported this conclusion. If the universal in the human mind is obtained by precluding the sensible and material, then it seems that the material is responsible for the individual. Throughout the discussion of this question it is evident that he considered the universal the more important element.

But a critical examination of terms will present some weighty objections to this solution. How can matter which is pure potency and completely undetermined effect the individuation? If matter endowed with quantity and three-dimensional extension is proposed as the principle, the question immediately arises, whence does this quantity and three-dimensional extension derive? As a pure potency matter receives all definiteness from the form, and thus quantity must be referred to the form of the substratum. The objections do not disappear when the undetermined dimensions are introduced; St. Thomas himself seemed to realize this. Furthermore, every effect produced by an efficient cause must be referred to the form of the individual. St. Thomas would not have proposed matter with certain dimensions if he had not been of the opinion that these quantitative relations play the deciding role. But as St. Bonaventure and Suarez pointed out, a mere accident cannot be an intrinsic constitutive principle, nor can an accident, according to Scotus, be the basis of anything but accidental differences. Quantity does, indeed, presuppose the unity and individuality of a thing. It is the basis for external division, the external mark of material things; but it is only the index, not the principle of individuation. The characteristics of the individual are its unity, totality, undividedness, and definiteness.

The specific unity of the thing is founded in the form, but, as Scotus pointed out, the individual unity is more important than the specific unity. For this unity some intrinsic and positive principle must be found. The Thomists answer that since matter is pure potency, it cannot produce the act of individuation which must come from the form, and that the act of individuation can be effected only when the form is received in matter and limited by it. Aside from the fact that St. Thomas never taught anything like this, matter according to this explanation is only an occasion, or, at most, a coefficient principle. Here we have the difficulty of matter effecting a limitation, and, besides this, the form cannot produce the act of individuation unless it contains within itself some tendency toward a certain disposition in matter. When the Thomists speak of a potential relation of the matter, this relationship must again be predicated of the form.

When St. Thomas placed the principle of individuation for immaterial things in the form, and for material things in matter, establishing a double explanation, he made known his inability to find a uniform basis for the solution. Scotus was disturbed by this deficiency, and, later on, it led the youthful Leibnitz to reject the Thomistic solution. It seemed unnecessary that God and spiritual beings, on the one hand, and material beings on the other, should have different principles of individuation. Furthermore, in applying the theory to human beings it was seen to have some dangerous consequences. The Franciscans William de la Mare and John Peckham, and especially Tempier, the bishop of Paris, rejected the Thomistic solution because they feared it would lead to Averroistic monopsychism. The rejection of matter as the principle of individuation leads neither to a denial of being and the multiplicity of things, nor to nominalism.

Because of these difficulties it is not surprising that most Thomists sought another solution for the problem of individuation. In this connection, the superiority of Franciscan thought to that of Thomism is to be noted. Alexander of Hales regarded individuality as something intrinsically proper to every substance, and in this way he began a train of thought that links the Middle Ages with our own day. St. Bonaventure takes a step forward when, in spite of the authority of Aristotle, he rejects matter as the principle of individuation; a universal indefinite substratum so close to non-being cannot be the principle of definiteness and exclusion. He also considered any recourse to quantity as unfortunate since the accident quantity cannot be the source of individuation, and the difference between individuals is substantial and not accidental. St. Bonaventure admits that without matter there can be no numerical multiplicity, and that matter, therefore, is to be regarded as the condition *sine qua non,* but never as the *tota causa.*[41] He teaches further that the principle of individuation does not consist in a special and really existing form added to the specific form, as Averroes had thought.

If individuation can be traced neither to matter alone nor to the form alone, it must be derived from the actual union of matter and form. The physical inception of things is found in the mutual union of matter with form, just as the impression of a seal in wax comes into being through the union of the wax with the seal. The seal is capable of multiplication, but it requires a substratum for a multiplicity of impressions in wax; the undetermined wax by the impressions receives a form and numerical division at the same time. Such was St. Bonaventure's solution of the problem. However, when he was asked in what the principle of individuation consists, he distinguished between numerical and qualitative individuality. A thing is this thing principally because of the matter, which gives it position in time and space; it is this kind of thing because of the form. St. Bonaventure was careful to make it clear that personality is not derived from matter.

A new approach to the problem was made by Roger Bacon. In his

41 Gilson, *The Philosophy of St. Bonaventura* (1938), p. 280.

earlier years, as a young master writing his *quaestiones* on Aristotelian metaphysics, he derived individuation principally from matter and admitted the form as an instrumental cause. Later in his *Communia naturalium* he proposes a new solution. The individual and the universal, according to Bacon, may be compared to two parallel lines. The individual is determined by the substance and its principles. If Bacon states that a thing is individuated by a particular matter and a particular form in the act of creation, he is not trying to avoid the actual problem. He is trying to solve the problem of absolute individuation, which, from the standpoint of theism, can be explained only by referring to the ideas of individuality contained in the divine plan of creation. In this solution the individual being comes into its own.

Scotus continues this line of thought, declaring that the universal becomes real only when it is individuated; that this individuation is a great moment in the life of the universal, making it a much more valuable thing. The individual represents the closest possible unity, a positive entity, and one of the ultimates. What, Scotus asks, is the fundamental reason for this singularity? He rejects five explanations of his day, among them the theory that matter and quantity are the principles of individuation. He teaches that only one being is absolutely individual, namely, God. The universals are not individual of themselves; they require something to make them individual since they are in themselves indifferent. Scotus establishes the principle of individuation as a special form, an ultimate, incommunicable, indivisible, positive entity, which is added to the essence as the final difference determining it as an individual. The "thisness" (*haecceitas*) is the name which Scotus himself and his disciples gave this new form. According to Scotus, the universal form and the individual are not two different beings, neither are they two constitutive parts of a being. The universal and the individual, according to Scotus, do not lie in parallel lines, but they are in one continuous progressive line beginning with the universal and proceeding to the individual. Paying homage to the theory of parallelism between thought and being, Scotus concluded that, since the individual concept exists in our minds, the individual form must exist in reality. Thus Scotus halted the trend of thought fostered by the teachings of Aristotle and St. Thomas which tended to degrade the individual in favor of the universal. He taught that the individual is the perfection of the species, the only true reality, and the crown of the plan of creation. Individuals are the principal end of creation, and individuality is the most perfect mode of existence possible to creatures. Here the foundations were being laid for a new ontology and epistemology; the beginning of a new theory of values. Scotus stopped the trend toward the devaluation of the individual and paved the way for an understanding and appreciation of the individual. He marks the beginning of the triumphant march of metaphysical and ethical individualism.

Nominalism, through its principal representatives, William of Occam and Jean Buridan, taught that every thing is individual in itself; that being and individual being are identical, since the universal has no objective reality. Even Suarez, surpassing Scotus, said that individuality is given with the physical entity (*unaquaeque entitas est per seipsam principium individuationis*). Later Nicholas of Cusa was unable to emphasize sufficiently that the individual was the most perfect and most important being in creation. The natural philosophy of the Italians and the Germans during the Renaissance period supported this viewpoint. The evaluation of the individual reached its highest point in the monad theory of Leibnitz. This philosopher placed the formal principle of individuality in neither part, whether matter or form, but held that every thing in its entity is individualized. Without going over to nominalism, Leibnitz declared that individuals are the only substances that by their own power lead a proper existence and made their contributions toward the harmony of the whole. In the realm of ethics, individualism appeared in the personalist theory of Shaftesbury, and especially in the humanism and romanticism of Jacobi and Fichte.

CHAPTER V

ESSENCE AND EXISTENCE— THE PROBLEM OF UNIVERSALS

The problem of individuation is closely related to the problem of universals. Material things are composed of matter and form, and like the created spirits they are composed of essence and existence. This statement opens the door to one of the most fundamental problems of ontology, the science of being as such. Of every thing, of every being, we may ask the questions, whether it is, and what it is, and we can determine in reply that a thing is, and what it is. A concrete thing is a being that possesses essence and existence.[1] Existence denotes that something is present in reality; that it is actual and not possible. Essence refers to the content of this being, that with which the being is filled. An existing thing may be a stone, a plant, an animal, a man, a color, or one of many things. Each one of these beings presents a twofold aspect, its existence and its essence. If existence were nothing more than the realization or actualization of a thing, it would belong to all real things in the same way; to the thing and to its properties, to the whole and to its parts, to the changeable as well as to the unchangeable, and to the subsistent as well as to the contingent. It cannot be denied, therefore, that there are different kinds of existence. We will be able to isolate existence only when we have determined the being of ideal forms as distinct from the being of real things.

1. **The essence of things.** St. Thomas' position with regard to reality and ontological questions was greatly influenced by the Aristotelian and the Platonic traditions. This is evident in his discussion of the essence and existence of things. The philosophies of Aristotle and Plato are built around the theory of essence. In his early dialogues,

[1] *In II Sent.*, 37, 1, 1.

the Platonic Socrates asks: "What is virtue in itself, or courage, or justice, or the state, or the citizen." Here we are concerned with the nature of these forms. Rising above the ethical and political spheres, Plato asked similar questions about the whole realm of being, and, in so doing, he defined philosophy as the elevation of man to the study of being itself, as the Eros of the eternal and unchangeable. An idea represents true being and the real essence of a thing; the real essence which, in spite of its transcendence, shines through the things of this world and is apprehended by the intelligence of man. Aristotle, more conscious of reality, was unable to think of essences as separate from those things of which they are the essences. For him, an essence is the essence of something, and is in something. The idea is replaced by the form immanent in the thing. As Plato had done before him, Aristotle answered the "why" of a being by examining its essence; he made the form responsible for the "why" of a being. Whenever Aristotle treats of the substance of a thing together with its definition, he remains under the Platonic influence and understands essence in the definition as including form but not matter. He seeks to explain this difficulty by citing examples from art, mathematics, and ethics. In the things of nature, however, he finds himself forced to admit matter as part of the essence. He therefore distinguishes two kinds of definitions; the definition that refers to the form alone, and the definition that refers to the essence including both matter and form.

St. Thomas adopts the Aristotelian point of view. From his analysis of reality, St. Thomas concludes that the most important phenomenon is the fact that every thing is conceived not only as existing, but as existing in a certain way. All judgments made by the mind are answers to the question: What is it?, and in the predicate certain determinations are affirmed of the subject. When these determinations are not of an accidental nature, when they are unchangeable, and are invariably connected with the thing, then they are rooted in the core of the thing; that is, these determinations are then rooted in that which the thing really is. Every being, even that which comes into being and may again cease to exist, possesses an unchangeable essence, a structure which remains always the same, by which it is what it is and because of which it has a number of necessary properties. These essences are the principles of order in the undeniable multiplicity of individual things; they are the types, the specific natures that represent the definitional content of things. Sometimes this essence is called *qualitas,* but more often *essentia, quidditas, quod quid est, quod quid erat esse, natura communis,* or *substantia;* at times essence is designated by a compound of two of these terms, such as *quidditas sive natura,* or *substantia sive quidditas.*

St. Thomas explains the origin and meaning of these terms.[2] With Averroes, he derives *essentia* from *ens* (being), inasmuch as it designates that actuality common to all genera of being. *Essentia* refers to that nature common to all kinds of being, signifying not only the nature of substances but also the nature of accidents. Aristotle had pointed out that the *essentia* was not limited to the first category. We speak of the *essentia* as that by which a thing has being.[3] The term *quidditas* was introduced for essence because that which constitutes a thing in its particular kind of being and expresses its definitional content is the "what" of a thing, the *quid* (*est res*).[4] Frequently St. Thomas calls this "what" the *"quod quid erat esse id est, hoc per quod aliquid habet esse quid."* Essence is also referred to as form because, according to the explanation of Avicenna, form expresses the perfection and completion of a thing.[5] It is called nature inasmuch as it denotes the inner principle of activity and inertia, and consists of matter and form which constitute the essence of a thing.

In the simple substances, the form, the essence, and the thing itself are virtually the same, but material things in nature are not identical with their essences. In his youthful work, St. Thomas follows the teaching of Boethius and Avicenna, that the essence of a thing must contain not only the form but also the matter. The form is only a part of the essence, which is epistemologically expressed in the definition. The definition of a natural substance (material) must include matter and form, otherwise it would not be distinguished from a mathematical definition. In the definition of a natural substance, moreover, the matter is not merely something added to the essence. The essence cannot be said to consist in the relation between matter and form, but the matter and form constitute the nature of natural things. From this positive contribution of matter to the composite of things, it is again evident that matter cannot be pure potency.[6]

2. The problem of universals. Plato taught that true knowledge re-

---

[2] *De ent. et ess.,* chap. 1.
[3] *Ibid.*
[4] *Summa theol.,* IIIa, q.2, a.1.
[5] *De ent. et ess.,* chap. 1.
[6] *Ibid.,* chap. 2.

quired as its object the unchangeable, the constant, and the universal, which alone was true being for him. He therefore accorded an autonomous, transcendent existence to the ideal essence. Aristotle opposed this hypostasis of the universal for several reasons. He argued that the essence of a thing cannot exist separately from the thing of which it is the essence. According to Aristotle, the essence of a thing is immanent in the thing. According to St. Thomas also, the essence can exist only as individualized in the individual thing. The essential nature of man exists only in a particular man, in particular flesh and blood. Universal man cannot be found existing in reality, neither is there such a thing as a universal animal or a universal plant. Every essential nature exists only as a particular individual and it has an immediate, individual existence.[7] Every nature appears in reality as an individual nature, every specific type is found only as individualized in first substance, in some real thing. Thus the essence of each individual thing is numerically different from every other thing. In the individual, says St. Thomas, we do not find two essences, the specific and the individual, but only the specific essence realized in this individual.

When he said that all individual differences arose from the matter, Aristotle limited the essence too much. Later on he realized that this teaching was not in accord with things as they are in reality. Individuals differ from one another not only in this flesh and blood but far more in spiritual and mental properties. For this reason, Plotinus accepted an individual essential form which was really more than the specific form in the individual. St. Thomas, however, was too strongly influenced by Aristotle to admit the concept of an individual essential form. One obstacle was his principle of individuation. Nevertheless this individual essence was required in the Thomistic system, particularly in explaining the difference between essence and existence.

Inasmuch as the essence possesses the character of a universal, it has only a conceptual existence in the human mind; it is the product of abstraction, which, by eliminating the individual marks, lifts out the specific content. With Aristotle, St. Thomas teaches that the intellect contemplates things from the viewpoint of the universal (*agit universalitatem in rebus*), and that this universal nature has a twofold existence, one in individuals and the other in the mind (*unum*

---

[7] *De nat. gen.*, chaps. 5, 7.

in singularibus et aliud in anima).[8] The statement that the universal as such exists only in the intellect, does not prevent this universal essence, conceived by the human mind, from having an objective correlative in individual things,[9] but the nature of this correlative remains a moot question. St. Thomas is neither a conceptualist nor a nominalist. He denies neither the universal concept in our minds nor the objective correlative in the outer world. He accepts the scholastic formula dating back to Proclus, which affirms that the universals are *ante rem, in re, et post rem:* that is to say, first, that universals exist prior to the things themselves as models and ideas in the mind of the Creator; secondly, that they are actualized in things; and, finally, that they may be stripped of all that is individual and comprehended by our minds by means of abstraction.

In what does the objective correlative of the universals consist? St. Thomas is not an extreme realist like William of Champeaux (1070–1121), who admitted but one essential nature in each species and in this way, as Abelard has pointed out, made all individuals mere accidents of this one universal. According to St. Thomas, the essential nature is realized in each individual and is numerically distinct in each one. Beneath this individual character, however, the specific character is clearly discernible. While he insists that in the individual everything is individuated, St. Thomas teaches that in itself the form is universal and essentially applicable to a great number of individuals. A number of factors impelled him to retain the universal form, among them, the parallelism between thought and reality, and his principle of individuation. Thus he formulates the axiom: *particulare semper se habet ex additione ad universale.*[10] If immaterial forms are in themselves only specifically distinct, and if individuals are distinguished by matter, then the form cannot have any distinction within itself. As Aristotle had said, the form is the "one in many." Scotus goes still farther and teaches that the universal nature is inseparably bound up with the individual form; that the individual form determines and perfects the universal form, and defines it as a distinct individual. Socrates comes into being inasmuch as humanity is determined by "Socratity." The two, humanity and Socrates, are not really

---

[8] *De ent. et ess.,* chap. 3; *Summa theol.,* Ia, q.85, a.1 ad1; a.2 ad2; a.3 ad1 and 4; q.119, a.1.

[9] *In I Sent.,* 19, 5, 1; *In II Sent.,* 17, 1, 1; *Summa theol.,* Ia, q.13, a.9.

[10] *In I Sent.,* 19, 4, 2.

distinct; the distinction is formal and belongs to the logical and meta-physical orders. Suarez was the first to deny any actual difference between the species and the individual. In itself each thing is in-dividualized; it is the human mind that makes the distinction and apprehends these parts separately.

3. **The kinds of essences and their properties.** The study of the essence in its various aspects is broadened in the time of St. Thomas and Avicenna inasmuch as they investigate essence under still a third aspect. We are able not only to consider essence as existing in a particular individual, or as existing in the mind, but also to consider essence absolutely, keeping in mind only that which belongs to the essence as such. This contemplation of absolute being or essence, says St. Thomas, abstracts from its existence in the thing or in the mind. Thus it is not a part of man's essence that it exist in a particular individual, otherwise it could have no being outside the individual. Being considered absolutely does not have the character of the universal, because the concept of the universal includes the ideas of community and unity, neither of which is proper to the essence man considered absolutely.[11]

When we speak of specific being we must clearly distinguish between concrete and abstract things. Thus man and humanity are not the same. While the abstract essence (humanity) gives the essential principles and excludes the accidents, the concrete essence (man) denotes the whole, including both the essential and the accidental marks; the essential principles being definitely expressed while the accidents are given only indefinitely.[12] *"Homo significat ut totum, humanitas ut pars."* The *humanitas* is the formal principle of being, not the whole being; the animality is the generic principle, not the genus itself; rationality is the principle of difference, not the difference itself. Only with the substance that is without accidents, God, is there no difference between the concrete and the abstract. Here God is Deity.[13]

Humanity is that by which man is man. Having stated this truth, St. Thomas touches on the distinction between being and the cause or ground of being. Aristotle had come face to face with this problem without finding a solution. That which a thing is, is not the same as that by which it is. Many instances can be pointed out where the form

---

[11] *De nat. gen.,* chap. 7.
[12] *De ent. et ess.,* chap. 2.
[13] *In VII Met.,* 5; *De pot., IX, 4.*

is called the cause or ground of being; the complement and perfection of the whole being. By the form the material substratum is constituted a material being with certain peculiarities. Because the form is so vital, some came to the conclusion that the form is the same as the essence, but others were still of the opinion that matter also made a contribution in constituting a being and should be included in the essence. If the latter were correct, then that by which a thing is what it is cannot be found entirely in the form. That which a thing is must correspond in some way with that by which a thing is. If the essence of the thing includes the matter, then the essential cause must also include the matter. St. Thomas is following Aristotle when he says that the form is the essential cause of being, and he avoids certain difficulties by distinguishing between abstract and concrete essences. The abstract essence expresses only the specific principles by which an individual belongs to a species; it is only a part of the individual which has other integral parts.

Essences possess certain properties. They are unchangeable. This does not deny that they begin and cease to be in reality, but it merely affirms the unchangeableness of the specific character of the individual substance. St. Thomas compares the specific form with numbers; they permit no addition or subtraction without being immediately changed to another number. In the same way, any addition or subtraction in the definition of a species constitutes a new species.[14] Essences are said to be eternal, not inasmuch as they are actual in the world, but inasmuch as they are ideal forms in the mind, valid at all times. This eternal validity is, of course, founded in the divine universe of ideas. Essences are said to be necessary because they cannot be otherwise, and because they possess a number of necessary relations.[15]

4. The existence of things. Every thing possesses not only an essence but also existence. What does St. Thomas understand by this term existence? The verb "to be" has several meanings, as Aristotle pointed out. It may signify the truth of a judgment, it may serve as the copula in a sentence, or it may refer to something existing only in the mind which is at the same time founded in something objectively valid in reality. It also refers to things in the actual universe, but not always in the same way. These distinctions were not always made sufficiently

[14] *Summa theol.*, Ia IIae, q. 52, a. 1.
[15] *Ibid.*, Ia, q. 84, a. 1; q. 79, a. 9 ad 3.

clear in the presentation of the Thomistic system. Existence refers to
a real thing (*ens aliquid in natura existens*) with all that it is, whether
it be substantial or accidental. St. Thomas tries to make the distinction yet clearer; he contrasts the thing with its own reality, and the
act of existence is stripped of all the essential characteristics of the
thing.

Existence is found in all categories. It is not only the thing that
exists; its color, its extension, and the relation also exist. True existence, however, belongs only to the individual substance. All things
that do not exist for themselves but for another and in another, such
as accidents or the substantial form, have no true existence (*sed at-
tribuitur eis esse*). Existence is an ultimate, and therefore it cannot
be defined, but only described. Existence is the realization and actualization of things.

Existence is the greatest perfection of a thing, and with respect to
all other qualifications, it is comparable to act, inasmuch as things
possess actuality only in so far as they exist. Existence, therefore, is
the actuality of all things, including the form; with respect to things,
it is that which is received rather than that which receives. Existence
is neither a substratum nor the bearer of qualities; it is related to the
essential nature as act is to potency. Existence is that by which a thing
is realized (*sicut cursus quo currens currit*).[16] A thing exists because
it receives existence, and, after receiving it, the thing possesses its own
existence. The act of existence is the realization of the essence and
thus becomes the perfection of the form.[17] St. Thomas is careful to
contrast the existence with the subject itself which exists; they are
not identical. The existence (*ipsum esse*) is not the same as the subject (*subjectum essendi*), just as the act of running is not the same
as the running. We cannot say that running runs, neither can we say
that existence exists. A subject is required for the running as well as
for the existing. When St. Thomas says that things participate in
existence, he follows the Platonic Augustinian tradition. Participation (*partem capere*) takes place when something receives a universal.
Thus man participates in animal nature, Socrates in humanity, the
subject participates in the accident, the matter in the form, and the
effect participates in the cause. But existence cannot participate in this

---

[16] *Ibid.*, q.50, a.2 ad3; q.75, a.5 ad4.
[17] *In I Sent.*, 33, 1, 1; *Contra Gent.*, I, 52; *Quodlib.*, XII, 5.

way. It cannot participate as matter does in the form or as the subject does in an accident because existence denotes something abstract. Existence cannot participate as the particular does in the universal because existence is itself the most general and universal. Therefore everything participates in existence, and existence itself participates in nothing. To exist by participation is to possess an acquired existence. All created things owe their existence to another; they possess existence and hold it in fief.

Because every essence comes into real being only through existence, St. Thomas calls existence (*actus essendi*) the first act and the most perfect of all. More than any other thing, existence is form, the act of acts, the most perfect of all perfections that can be communicated to all things and that lives intimately in all things.[18] In countless passages, St. Thomas declares that the inner cause of being is existence, while on other occasions he attributes this function to the form.[19] Under the influence of the Aristotelian tradition, the form is said to be the agent that dispenses existence, but under the Platonic Augustinian influence it is existence that confers reality, even to the forms themselves.[20] The Platonic influence seems to be the strongest; in the *Liber de causis,* existence is called the foremost of all created beings. It is placed above the senses, the soul, and the intellect, and after the First Cause it is the most embracing and most effective of all causes; it is the highest of all creatures because it is closest to pure Being, closest to Truth and Unity. St. Thomas does not place much emphasis on this causality of existence in the Platonic sense, but he does regard existence as the first participation in the divine Goodness; the first divine effect in things, on which all other effects are based. The structure of the various forms of being in the universe is made up of the additions to existence. Since existence is the basis of everything else, it is the most valuable and is prior to all being.[21] But we might even imagine that existence is the substratum which is determined by others if we did not know that it is the act and that in which others participate.

5. **The relation between essence and existence.** The problem of the

---

[18] *In II Sent.*, 1, 1, 1; *Summa theol.*, Ia, q.7, a.1.
[19] *In I Sent.*, 8, 5, 2; *Contra Gent.*, II, 52–54; *Summa theol.*, Ia, q.29, a.4 ad 1; q.50, a.2 ad 3.
[20] *Summa theol.*, Ia, q.4, a.1 ad 3.
[21] *In I Sent.*, 8, 1, 1; *In II Sent.*, 1, 1, 4.

relation between essence and existence, and in particular the question of the real distinction between the two, created sharp difference of opinion among the philosophical schools of the Middle Ages.

In the writings of Avicenna, St. Thomas found the distinction between essence and existence discussed at great length. In handling the problem himself, St. Thomas made use of the terms *quod est* and *quo est* (*esse*) which were originated by Gilbert de la Porrée. *Quod est* refers to the essence, while *quo est* and *esse* refer to the existence.

The twofold question, what is it, and, does it exist, seemed logically to point to a distinction, and a logical distinction seemed to indicate a distinction in the thing itself. Furthermore, the essence of a thing can be comprehended even though it is not known whether the thing itself exists or not. We can understand what is meant by humanity without knowing whether a man exists. The principal reason for the distinction, however, is metaphysical and runs parallel with the fundamental distinction between Creator and creature. In God, essence and existence are identical. This identity is postulated by the concept of first infinite Being, the absolutely simple and necessary Being, that Being which is not caused and is pure act entirely free of all potency. Since God is not caused, He has not received His existence; He is Being *per se* (*esse per se subsistens*).[22] All created substances, however, have only received their existence (*Nulla creatura est suum esse, sed est habens esse*).[23] Creatures are not like God; they are composed of essence and existence. While the divine existence is infinite, created existence is limited to the substratum and is restricted by a certain specific nature. St. Thomas proposes the formula: every thing that belongs to any species possesses an existence distinct from its essence.[24] Through its study of the relation of infinite to finite being, the Platonic school had come to much the same conclusion; this St. Thomas had learned through the writings of St. Augustine, Boethius, Pseudo-Dionysius, and St. Anselm. Since every created thing is in relation both to being and to non-being, it does not possess being of itself, but by participation. But whatever a thing has by participation does not constitute its essence. In created things we find the difference between *habiti et habentis, participati et participantis,* and this participated existence is adapted to the capabilities of the

---

[22] *In I Sent.*, 8, 5, 1; *In II Sent.*, 3, 1, 1.
[23] *In I Sent.*, 8, 5, 2; 43, 1, 1.
[24] *Ibid.*, 8, 4, 2; *In II Sent.*, 1, 1, 1; 3, 1, 1 ad 1.

receiving substratum. St. Thomas distinguishes between two kinds of participation. That in which a thing participates may belong to the substance of that which participates, and in this manner species participates in the genus. Existence, however, does not enter into the definition of a thing, either as genus or as difference. Thus, it is by a second form of participation that a thing participates in that which does not belong to its essence.

Since essence is not identical with existence, essence and existence are related as potency and act. Every created essence is in potency to its existence.[25] In St. Thomas' words: *"Omne participans componitur ex participante et participato, et participans est in potentia ad participatum."* In every created thing, essence and existence complement each other to form the individual thing. Such a complementing presupposes a mutual relation between the two parts, and the process is carried out by a particular act. In this respect, existence and act may indeed be considered identical. The concepts potency and act are not restricted in their application to matter and form alone; they can be applied to essence and existence with equal advantage. But, so as to avoid any confusion in these comparisons, St. Thomas makes the following distinctions: in the composite of matter and form, matter is not a substantial essence, but only a part of it; likewise, existence is not the proper act (*proprius actus*) of matter, but the proper act of the whole being. Furthermore, the form is not identical with existence, but is related to it in a peculiar manner.

The created immaterial substances are also composed of essence and existence, of potency and act, and *"ex forma et esse participato."*[26] While material things are composed of matter and form and also of essence and existence, immaterial or spiritual substances are composed only of essence and existence. Thus the second kind of composite, that of essence and existence, is more extensive than the first, which refers only to material creatures. The essences of spiritual substances are simple, but the essences of material creatures are not simple, since they are composed of matter and form. For this reason, in spiritual substances the simple form is *quod est,* and existence is *quo est* and the act of the being. In material things, the *quod est* is neither the matter nor the form but the whole substance.

Being in common is divided according to essence and existence.

[25] *De ent. et ess.,* chap. 5.
[26] *In Boeth. de Trin.,* V, 4 ad 4; *Summa theol.,* Ia, q. 50, a. 2 ad 3; q. 75, a. 5 ad 4.

Essence, however, is realized in different ways in different planes of being, and its relation to existence is also therefore different. In *De ente et essentia,* St. Thomas places God at the beginning of his classi-fication of being. God's essence is identical with His existence. From this it does not follow, as Avicenna thought, that God has no essence at all, but rather that God is in no species, since in a species everything is distinct from existence. Neither does the identification of the divine essence with the divine existence lead to a pantheistic confusion of the divine Being with all substantial being. Because of His pure be-ing, God has an existence distinct from all others, and His individua-tion, according to the *Liber de causis,* is founded in His goodness.

In created spiritual substances, the spiritual essence is distinct from existence. Therefore the existence of these substances is not absolute but acquired, and it is limited according to the capacity of the nature or essence which receives it. The essence of spiritual beings is not received in matter, and therefore St. Thomas says that spiritual beings are limited from above, inasmuch as they receive their existence from a higher being, but that they are unlimited from below, since they are not limited in their forms by any receiving matter. Among the spiritual substances, no plurality of individuals is found in any spe-cies, except the instance of the human soul which is united to a body. In the third category of being, St. Thomas placed those es-sences that are composed of matter and form, whose existence is limited and circumscribed by the limits of the *materia signata.* The plurality of individuals within a species is founded on the divisibility of the matter.

In speaking of the relation between essence and existence, we also touch on the relation of the individual to essence and to existence. In God, the specific essence, the individual essence, and the hypostasis coincide because the form is identical with the essence and the prin-ciple of individuation. Between the suppositum and the nature there is no real, but only a logical, distinction.[27] The same applies to cre-ated spiritual substances in which the essence and the suppositum are the same. As stated by Avicenna's axiom, the essence of a simple sub-stance is itself simple.[28] Later St. Thomas receded from this view, declaring that only in God are the suppositum and the nature com-

---

[27] *In I Sent.,* 19, 4 1 ad 4.
[28] *Contra Gent.,* II, 54; *Summa theol.,* Ia, q.3, a.3; q.47, a.2; q.50, a.5; q.56, a.1.

pletely identical.[29] In created beings, however, nature and the suppositum are not completely identical, since the nature contains only that which belongs to the species. At this point St. Thomas makes a curious distinction between the species and the suppositum, saying that the suppositum connotes not only the essence but also that which is added to the essence, namely, the existence. He seems to think that the addition of existence might endanger the equality of essential form, species, and suppositum. By the existence these forms are merely transferred into the plane of reality.

In essences composed of matter and form, the essence is, of course, distinct from the suppositum. Natural essences do not subsist. The universal essence of natural things is found individualized only in the individual thing, and the individual substance is a composite of the universal essential nature and the individualized matter. The essence itself contains only that which belongs to the specific definition and is related to the thing as the formal part (*pars formalis*). But the individual contains much beside this: *Suppositum habet se per additionem ad naturam.*[30]

How, therefore, does the form fit in with essence and existence? In material things, the essence includes not only the form but also the matter; the form, therefore, is part of the essence. St. Thomas thought it important to distinguish clearly between form and existence. He said that form and existence were not identical, although they are never separated. Because of some necessary inner order, they always belong together. The form is the principle of existence, giving to every thing its existence. Things possess existence as long as they possess the form; if they lose the form they lose their existence.[31] Participation in existence, both in substantial and accidental existence, is by means of the form.[32] Therefore existence is called the act of the form and the complement of every form. If the form is sometimes called the act, it is, no doubt, because existence follows immediately upon it. From this it follows that no real distinction exists between form and existence.

Here a question may suggest itself: if the form is always immedi-

[29] *Quodlib.*, II, 4.
[30] *De un. verb.*, a.1; *Summa theol.*, Ia, q.3, a.3.
[31] *In I Sent.*, 8, 5, 1.
[32] *De an.*, 6.

ately followed by existence, why does not every form possess existence without further ado? The answer is as follows: the form does not need matter to exist, but in composite things, the form needs matter because it can exist only as an individuated form, i.e., as a form united to matter.[33]

Is there a real distinction between essence and existence? The bitter disagreement within Scholasticism is well known. While some regarded the teaching of the real distinction between essence and existence as fundamental to Christian philosophy, others considered the controversy of no importance.

The question with which we are confronted is whether St. Thomas taught that a real distinction exists between essence and existence. Students of Thomism are by no means agreed on this point. The majority of Thomists defend the distinction as real and hold that St. Thomas also taught it; even Suarez, who denied the reality of the distinction, admitted that it was St. Thomas' teaching. Today, however, voices are heard not only denying the real distinction, but firmly maintaining that St. Thomas did not teach that the distinction between essence and existence is real.

What do we understand here by the essence? We do not mean the ideal essence which is the eternal unchangeable prototype in the divine mind; neither do we mean the absolute essence, or the universal essence that the human mind abstracts from things. Here we are referring to the actual essence as found in things. To ask whether the specific or individual essence is meant is pointless, since essences appear in this world only as realized, individual essences. The question is whether a real distinction exists between this kind of essence, and existence. Differing with other Scholastics and his preceptor St. Albert, St. Thomas unquestionably taught that the distinction is real.

To prove this we must be able to show that St. Thomas, who always expresses himself clearly, never referred to this union of essence and existence as logical. He taught expressly that every creature possesses existence by participation, in contrast to God whose essence and existence are identical. The creature is not the existence, but it has existence. Because the creature has participated existence, it is finite, whereas God is infinite.[34] In every created spiritual substance, says St. Thomas, we find two things, the substance itself and its existence

[33] Ibid.
[34] In I Sent., 8, 4, 2; In II Sent., 3, 1, 5.

which is not the substance (*quod non est substantia ejus*).[35] We
should note carefully that these two parts are found in the substance
and not in our own thoughts, and, therefore, that we do not have a
logical distinction, but two distinct factors in the thing itself. St.
Thomas continues to adhere closely to the parallel between thought
and reality. Again he says, "In every creature we find one thing that
is itself the creature, having existence, and another thing which is the
existence." [36] The substance that participates in the existence is something else than the participated existence.[37] St. Thomas' sharp delineation of the essence as the potency that receives existence from
God, and the emphasis he places on the statement that everything
which is not found in the essence is added on from without (*hoc est
adveniens extra et faciens compositionem cum essentia*), permits no
other interpretation than that, in his opinion, the distinction between
the essence and the existence is real. Repeatedly essence and existence
are related to potency and act, which are, of course, really distinct
from each other. St. Thomas makes it clear that when he speaks of
potency in this connection he means the passive potency and not the
active potency.[38] Reality is predicated of a thing in the same way as
warmth or whiteness, yet between the substance and these accidents
there is a real distinction. Consequently St. Thomas states the formula
that existence inheres in things and is the complement and perfection
of them. Finally St. Thomas declares that everything which belongs
to the classification of substances is a real composite of essence and
existence, except God, who belongs to no class or species.[39]

The ancient philosophers knew nothing of a real distinction. Later,
it is true, the Platonic doctrine of participation made room for such
a theory, but both Plato and Aristotle were ignorant of any real distinction. Aristotle's discussion of essence and existence was kept in
the logical realm of being, and the parallelism between thought and
being that characterizes his system was not permitted to be effective
in this instance. According to Aristotle, the cosmos with its hierarchy
of forms possesses existence of itself. The simple forms, God and the
spiritual substances, have essence and existence because of an inner
necessity. Even the matter and the form of composite beings are eter-

[35] *Contra Gent.*, II, 53.
[36] *Quodlib.*, II, 3.
[37] *Ibid.*, III, 20; *De ent. et ess.*, chap. 5.
[38] *In I Sent.*, 8, 3, 2.
[39] *De verit.*, XXVII, 1 ad 8.

nal. Forms do not receive their existence from another, but they have it by the law of their beings. In such a concept of being where the form includes its existence, no real distinction is conceivable.

The idea of a real distinction originated in the philosophy of the Arabians; later it was encouraged by an erroneous interpretation of Boethius and was united to the Platonic theory of participation. Like his predecessors, Avicenna wished to separate infinite uncreated being from created finite being. Such a distinction depends on the concepts of necessary and possible being. While necessary being is uncaused and identical with its existence, possible being is produced by another. Everything that exists outside of the first and necessary being must have within itself the possibility of being translated into the existential order. The essences of both material and immaterial substances must contain the potency for existence, which is granted them in creation and which is really distinct from these essences in individuals. Such reasoning had its effect on Moses Maimonides and Christian Scholasticism; on William of Auvergne, St. Bonaventure, St. Albert, and especially St. Thomas. This argument from necessary and possible being was formulated by Boethius, who indeed had no intention that it should be thus applied since he understood it in an entirely different sense. Later the Platonic idea of participated being, together with Boethius' concept of possible being, was made to serve as the metaphysical basis of finite being.

However, the foregoing line of reasoning from necessary being is unable to support the contention for a real distinction between essence and existence. We marvel that St. Thomas defended the theory, which is, after all, irreconcilable with the Aristotelian basis of the Thomistic system. The union of form and existence is so intimate and close that no real distinction can survive. With both St. Albert and St. Thomas the form is the same as the *actus existendi,* the act of existence. The factual difficulties are no less formidable. The theory of the real distinction maintains that the existing essence of a thing is really distinct from its existence, which is contradictory. Because of the strong reliance on the parallelism between the logical and the actual universe, the logical distinction was transformed into a real distinction. It was not surprising that this theory would be rejected; the distinction between infinite and finite being does not depend on it.

CHAPTER VI

SUBSTANCE AND ACCIDENT

1. The kinds of substance. The concept of substance appeared in the earliest period of philosophical speculation and grew in importance with the development of scientific systems of thought. Even before Socrates, the idea of substance had been important. Plato and Aristotle defined the concept of substance and distinguished between its various kinds; the Neoplatonists, Boethius, and the Arabians continued on this foundation. Later, Christological and Trinitarian speculation made liberal use of this concept of substance, prepared by Greek philosophy.

Speculation as to the nature of true being was answered in various ways by the ancient philosophers. The Pythagoreans thought that numbers were true being, Plato turned to his universe of ideas, the ancient natural philosophers offered a primal matter and a number of elements. Aristotle, however, oriented to an empiric reality, taught that the individual was true being and reality. But by this mere statement, Aristotle had not touched the core of the original problem. Plato's world of ideas had indeed been rejected, but the question propounded by the natural philosopher still called for an answer; the question of the ultimate in the universe. Aristotle's response is well known: every thing and every individual substance that is subject to change is composed of two parts, matter and form.

Aristotle sought to divide the responsibility that the two integrating parts have in the individual substance as correctly as possible. The matter is the substratum and recipient of the form. Since the matter has no existence of its own and since it has existence in the individual through the form and only affords the possibility of existence, it is given the smaller part and is called the substance of possibility.[1] The

---

[1] *Met.,* VII, 3; VIII, 1 f.; XIV, 1.

form, on the other hand, which makes the thing what it is; form, the dispenser of complete existence, the principle of being and its essence, is the substance in reality.[2] Aristotle's conclusion in metaphysics is well known: "I call matter substance in the sense that it is possible; I call the form substance in the sense that it is real, and the individual thing I call substance in the sense that it is composed of matter and form." This theory of substance was so deeply rooted in the Aristotelian concept of being that no true Aristotelian was able to abandon it.

Also in St. Thomas' writings we find the declaration that the individual thing is the true reality, and that the term substance belongs primarily to the individual. Thus the individual is called first substance, in contrast to second substances. Even Aristotle had characterized the individual as the first substance and had given it ontological priority. First substance possesses existence without qualification and of itself, while all others have existence in only some respect or because of a relation to the first substance.[3] The distinctive mark of first substance is subsistence; only that which subsists has being in the true sense (*nobilissimus modus essendi*).[4] The first substance is called suppositum, subsistence, and hypostasis. A substance endowed with reason is called a person.

Subsisting in itself, first substance is perfect being which has no need for another in which to subsist or inhere. Subsisting being, perfect being in itself, substantial being, and absolute being are, according to St. Thomas, synonymous terms. If we search out the source of these marks, we shall find, as Aristotle found, that they are rooted in the subsistence of the thing. The individual substance is being *per se,* and by this *perseitas* substance is distinguished from accidental being, which exists in another. While perseity denies first substance any inherence in another being, no affirmation is made that substance is uncaused or that it is *a se.* To obviate any pantheistic consequences that might arise from the concept *per se esse,* St. Thomas carefully explains the meaning of the *per.* The preposition *per* denotes only the intrinsic formal cause, not the extrinsic formal cause or the efficient cause; in the last analysis, every finite substance restricted to some definite essence does not exist through itself, but through the divine

[2] *Ibid.,* VIII, 1 and 3; VII, 4 and 17.
[3] *In VII Met.,* 1 and 2.
[4] *In I Sent.,* 23, 1, 1 and 3; *Summa theol.,* Ia, q.29, a.2; q.30, a.4.

Being.[5] The concept of substance existing *per se* does not disturb its position in the system of causality; the individual substance possesses no existence in another subject, but it does originate from another subject.[6]

The idea of substance developed from the scientific explanation of the ancient concept of the individual that Aristotle had used when he needed a subject for the predicative determinations of the logical-grammatical order and a substratum for the genetic process of being in his natural analyses. From this twofold viewpoint (logical and real), St. Thomas refuses to allow the individual to be dissolved into a group of accidents. Since every accident is predicated of a subject, and since this logical relation is founded in ontological fact, quality, quantity, change, and origin are referred to some one subject. In the same way, every movement presupposes something that is moved, since there can be no act without that of which the act is the act. Thus from the concepts of change and movement follows necessarily the idea of some substratum capable of change.[7] "Everything that becomes is through something and out of something"; "all that becomes is because of being or toward being"; these were the conclusions formulated by Aristotle and Plato (*Met.,* VII. c. 1).

If the phenomena of the universe were reduced to mere happenings, movements, and changing accidents, all being and truth would be destroyed.[8] Substance, therefore, appears as the subject, the ultimate bearer of accidents and all other determinations and qualifications. Since substance includes in its concept being as opposed to non-being, so it represents constancy as opposed to continual change. It is not, therefore, condemned to any sterility and rigidity; change, movement, and development are not denied it. Substance changes, but it does not cease to exist in the change; it preserves its identity throughout every change. Inasmuch as substance changes, it comes into contact with time.[9] Substance is not only subsistence *in se* and *per se,* but it is also an individual and singular subsistence. It is individual inasmuch as it possesses a being undivided in itself, and it is singular (*singulare*) inasmuch as it has being distinct from any other. Substance has complete, distinct being; it has a complete sub-

---

[5] *In I Sent.,* 8, 1, 2 ad 2; *De nat. met.,* chap. 8; *Contra Gent.,* I, 25.
[6] *In I Phys.,* 12; *Contra Gent.,* II, 15.
[7] *In VIII Phys.,* 2.
[8] Aristotle, *Met.,* IV, 4.
[9] *In Perich.,* 4.

sistence in a certain specific nature.[10] Because substance is the foundation for all other being, it is given the first place and accorded the
greatest ontological significance.

The individual thing is not the only substance. As we have mentioned before, matter also is potentially substance, and the form belongs to the genus of substance (*de genere substantiae*) in like manner. In relation to the individual substance, matter and form are not
kinds of substance, but rather the principles of substance.[11] Besides
first substance there is also second substance, namely, the genus and
species. The essence, the nature of a thing, is referred to as a substance. To clarify St. Thomas' teaching on substances, it is necessary
to refer to the Aristotelian sources from which it is derived. The
influence of Boethius and the Arabians who came after Aristotle is
of secondary importance. Throughout this discussion, the form will
be of primary importance, because in discussing the various kinds of
substance, we must cite the form as the fundamental reason for substantiality.

Aristotle refers to form as a substance and accords it priority over
matter. Occasionally he calls it first substance, and attributes to it
every quality usually granted to the individual thing. In the genetic
process of being, the form won a position of the utmost importance.
The whole process of the genesis of being is directed to the essential
form, which is the best and most valuable part of being. The form is
identical with the end and purpose of being, and, in a higher sense
than the matter, the form is the nature of the thing, its inner principle of movement and rest. We can easily understand the high value
that Aristotle places on the form when we remember the influence of
Platonism on his thought and the relation of the form to the universe
of ideas. According to Plato, the ideas were the only true being, and,
as such, the eternal, unchangeable, universal object of knowledge.
Substantial forms retained these characteristics in Aristotle's system,
since he was faithful to the epistemological theory of his preceptor
and to the parallelism of thought and reality. Unwilling to allow
divergence between truth and reality, Aristotle felt himself obliged
to accord the character of substance to the form inasmuch as it is the
object of knowledge. But these substances are not colorless, shapeless,
suprasensible essences any longer; as forms they are the specific types

---

[10] *In I Sent.*, 26, 1, 1; *Summa theol.*, Ia, q.75, a.2 ad 1.
[11] *In II Sent.*, 3, 1, 1 ad 1.

which persist throughout the natural processes and serve in the individual as the unchanging object of our knowledge. Although Aristotle includes the matter in the species and essence of material things, the form remains the deciding and definitive element. From this it follows naturally that, according to Aristotle, the species and the genus are substances.

St. Thomas adopts the same viewpoint. He rejects the theory of ideas promulgated by Plato and denies to ideas the character of substance, asserting that universals have no separate existence. St. Thomas says that three reasons impelled Aristotle to oppose Plato in this matter: (1) an essence cannot exist separately from that of which it is the essence; (2) the species separated from matter cannot be the cause of being; and (3) sensible matter in general belongs to the concept of the species. St. Thomas continually refers to the essence, the form, the nature, and the species of a thing as substance. Whenever the matter enters into the essence, he emphasizes the importance of the form.

These species and genera, says Aristotle, are called second substances, and in relation to the substance whose essence they express, they are something qualitative. St. Thomas agrees with Aristotle. These second substances do not denote something individual (*hoc aliquid*) but a certain quality (*quale*); however, not a quality which is an accident, but rather a substantial quality.[12] The distinction between first and second substances is not identical with the distinction between species and genera, since second substances have nothing that is not also found in first substances. Second substance denotes the nature of the species taken in itself, while first substance denotes the nature in its individual existence.[13]

With Aristotle, St. Thomas declares that unity (*unum*) and being are not substances, since a thing is said to be one and a being by reason of its substance. Both concepts are predicated of the substance as the subject. The substantiating principle is not the unity of a thing; it is the form which constitutes the basis of the thing's being, its subsistence, and its unity. In comparison with the principle and cause of a thing, the *ens et unum* are much closer to the nature of the substance since they belong to a thing by reason of its substance.

   2. **Substance and accidents.** In the theory of the categories, the in-

---

[12] *In VII Met.*, 13.
[13] *De pot.*, IX, 2 ad 1.

dividual substance again holds the most important place for St. Thomas. Aristotle had referred to the substance as the individual with its properties, but more often in contradistinction to the accidents. In this latter sense, substance is the first in the table of categories. Aristotle defined substance "in its first and noblest meaning as that which is not predicated of another and which is not the substratum of another, e.g., this man, this horse" (*De categoriis,* chap. 5). Because of the connection between thought and reality, the categories bear the imprint of the logical sphere; accordingly, in Aristotle's definition of substance, both the logical and the ontological self-sufficiency of substance is expressed. Substance has no inherence in another being; it is the basis of all being and therefore the ultimate subject about which all predication is made. Of substance are predicated the accidents and the universals of the order of substance (*universalia de genere substantiae*), i.e., species and genus. Substance is never the predicate except when it is predicated of itself.[14] As a subject, substance resembles matter inasmuch as it is a recipient, but it differs from matter in that it does not receive its being from the accidents as matter receives its being from the form.

The parts of substance, whether physical or metaphysical, can be placed in the category of substance only through a process of reduction. St. Thomas does not deny that matter and second substances also can be the bearers of accidents for predication, but they do this only as integral parts of first substance. Man is white inasmuch as this individual man is white. Thus first substances are prerequisite for the existence of all others; if they did not exist, other things would not exist either.[15] Substance is therefore the first object of knowledge, and it is first also among concepts. What the foundation is for a house, what the heart is in an organism, substance is that in the ordered whole of a thing. As an individual being, substance does not exist in any subject; it is itself the substratum for opposites. Nothing is opposed to substance; it has no degrees of greater or less, i.e., that which substance is cannot be predicated of it more or less, since it exists as a whole at once (*tota simul*) and not successively.[16]

St. Thomas taught not only that a thing is composed of matter and form, but also that it is composed of substance and accidents.

---

[14] *In VII Met.,* 2.
[15] *Met.,* VII, 3.
[16] *Ibid.,* VII, 12.

Those things composed of matter and form and even created spiritual substances have accidents together with a specific essence.[17] The human intellect, by a process of analytical abstraction, separates those things that are united in a concrete unity and, having conceived the parts separately, it unites them again by judgments on its own part. The thing itself and the things that belong to it must be separated logically and really. In this connection, when St. Thomas speaks of accidents, he does not mean the predicamental accidents, i.e., the nine categories beside substance. The accident he refers to is a being that has a threefold relation to substance, and this threefold relation will throw light on the being of the accident itself. (1) Substance functions as the bearer and supporter of this accidental being (*praebens sustentamentum*), since the accident does not exist *per se*. (2) The accident possesses a unique essence and a unique existence distinct from the essence and existence of the substance, so that out of the substance and the accident arises an entity *per accidens* and not *per se*. (3) All accidents are forms superadded to the substance, and their existence is added on to the existence of the substance, but in such a way that in the natural order no accident can exist separately from the substance. The nature of an accident is to "inhere and to depend on another."[18] The accident shares this characteristic with the substantial form, except that the latter exists in the composite as a part, while the accident is "a bud on the stem of the substance."[19] With definite modifications, accidents are called beings (*non quia sunt, habent esse, sed quia eis aliquid est*). This inherence in another does not truly express being, but only being in a certain respect (*esse secundum quid*), that is, a form of being accorded to the accident because of the substance. St. Thomas, therefore, refers to accidents as coexistent beings and attributes to them only a weak kind of existence (*debile esse*), declaring that being is not predicated of substance and accidents in the strict sense, but only analogically.[20] Accidents, finally, can be the subject for another accident only in so far as they inhere in the substance.[21]

In spite of all these modifications, the much used concept of potency and act is applicable also to the concepts of substance and acci-

---

[17] *Summa theol.*, Ia, q. 85, a. 5 ad 3; q. 13, a. 12; *Quodlib.*, II, 4 ad 1.
[18] *Summa theol.*, Ia, q. 90, a. 2.
[19] *In I Eth. Nic.*, 6.
[20] *Summa theol.*, Ia, q. 45, a. 4; q. 90, a. 2; q. 104, a. 4 ad 3; Ia IIae, q. 55, a. 1.
[21] *De virt. in com.*, 3.

dent. Since an accident is an act it is also a form. The substantial and the accidental form agree in that each is in act and that through them something becomes actual, but they also differ in two ways. The substantial form creates being and its subject is pure potency, while the accidental form does not create being itself but only a kind of being (*esse tale aut tantum*), and its subject is actual being.[22]

An especially important distinction between substance and accident arises from the fact that the substance represents a dynamic center of activity and is related to accidents as the cause to effects.[23] The principles of substance are the immediate cause of accidents; the first and supreme cause of both substance and accidents is, of course, God. Substance may be regarded as a cause in several respects. It is a material cause inasmuch as it is in potency to accidents and receives them; it is an efficient cause inasmuch as it is in act, and it is a final cause inasmuch as the accidents serve to complete the subject. This triple causality applies to proper accidents only; with regard to the external accidents, the subject is only receptive when the productive principle is some external agent.[24] The essence does not influence accidents directly, but indirectly through the potencies that exist in the one essence. In the case of proper accidents, the substance reveals itself and exhibits its essential nature. The procession of accidents from the substance does not indicate a change of the substance, but only a natural consequence of deep-seated inner relations and the radiation of the metaphysical essence. In spite of the real distinction between the two, accidents grow out of the principles of substance; and in direct proportion to their proximity to the substance itself, they manifest the fund of potency grounded in the essence (*agere sequitur esse—operatio rei demonstrat substantiam et esse ipsius*).

Because of these relations, accidents are both really and conceptually bound with the substance. Just as accidents possess existence only in their subject, so they receive unity or plurality only from the substance. On the same ground, an accident cannot be defined without the substance, and in comparison with the substance, it must be considered something incomplete. At the same time, accidents do not enter into the definition of the substance, since they do not belong to

---

[22] *Summa theol.*, Ia, q. 87, a. 6.
[23] *Contra Gent.*, I, 22; II, 80, 97.
[24] *Summa theol.*, Ia, q. 77, a. 6.

the essence of a thing.[25] An accident may cease to exist in two cases; first, when its opposite replaces it, and secondly, when its subject ceases to exist.

Accidents are caused by the substance, and they have a closer or more distant relation to the substance according as they are caused by the parts, namely, matter and form, or by the composite. A number of accidents are bound up with the substantial kernel of a being; they are necessary and are always found in the essence whenever it is actualized. These accidents flowing from the essence are called proper accidents (*accidentia propria*); they are distinct from the essence, but they are the effect of substantial forms and manifest the nature of these forms. They are found in all individuals of the same species. Beings are not only specific principles but also individuals in which a species is realized. The individuating principle is prime matter, in which the basis for change in individual material things is also to be found. Individuals as such are subject to change, and matter is the basis for both change and accidental properties.

In addition to accidental properties, St. Thomas speaks of properties that are derived from the principles of the subject. Those that have an unfailing source or cause in the subject are called inseparable accidents inasmuch as they are always found in the composite, e.g., masculine and feminine. Since other properties, such as sitting or walking, are separable, they are to be distinguished from such accidents. Inseparable accidents are accidents *per se,* and St. Thomas divides them into two kinds. First, there are those caused by the essential principles of a being through a complete act, e.g., warmth through a fire. Secondly, there are inseparable accidents rooted in the essential principles only because of an aptitude (*secundum aptitudinem*), and they are fully realized only when some external cause becomes active; e.g., the translucency of the air, a phenomenon that is realized only through the presence of another illuminated body. In such instances, this aptitude is indeed an inseparable accident, but the complementary external factor is separable, since it is derived from a principle that does not belong to the essential constitution of the thing.[26]

In the individual, therefore, we find three classes of accidents, which, since even the structure of the individual is dominated by the

[25] *De an.,* 12 ad 7; *De spir. creat.,* 11 ad 5 and 7.
[26] *De ent. et ess.,* 6.

concept of order, are related to both the partial principles and the composite thing. We find two kinds of accidents *per se;* the first characterizing the specific form, and the second, the composite of matter and form. The third class is composed of the accidents *per accidens,* which are occasional, changeable, and separable, and founded in matter. Science is concerned only with those accidents that dwell in some subject *per se,* since properties which are not inherent in a thing do not permit a necessary conclusion. All accidents that belong to a subject necessarily must have their origin in the subject, and, given the subject, the accidents are also posited. There can be no science of contingent things inasmuch as they are contingent, but only inasmuch as they contain something that is necessary and derived from the form. Accidental being *(ens per accidens)* is excluded from scientific knowledge.[27]

St. Thomas realized the universal importance of this concept of essence, and he saw that it expresses the ultimate structure of a thing and its spiritual content; that it is the fundamental cause of a being's varied activity and its many relations. It is the great unknown, or at least insufficiently known, into which we must ever penetrate more deeply. We can comprehend the marks of the substantial forms, but the forms themselves remain in the background as the constitutive and regulatory principles, i.e., constitutive of the beings themselves and regulatory for our intellect, for which these forms are often the ultimate in attainment and the limit of our intellectual ability.

3. **The categories.** The categories hold the same important place in the Thomistic system as that accorded them by Aristotle. Logically they are the chief modes of predication; the supreme, universal, generic concepts under which all other concepts can be subsumed. Ontologically they are the most universal modifications of being. By slow steps, modern subjectivism and idealism have discovered the fundamental principle that being is prior to thought, but this principle served as a starting point for Aristotle and St. Thomas. The categories are not mental forms which the knowing subject by some categorical formation develops as the structural form of an object, rather they are objective modifications that belong to being independently of our thought or willing. A thing is what it is, in the fullness of its existence, independently of our concepts, which are

27 *Summa theol.,* Ia, q.86, a.3.

really an adaptation to a particular kind of being. A thing receives nothing from our thought, nor is it deprived of anything thereby.

We must distinguish clearly between the predicaments and the predicabilia. The latter represent the division of the logical universal into genera, species, difference, property, and accident. While the categories are divisions of being, and the various divisions represent different existential relations, the predicabilia are of second intention, forms of the mind that have no being outside the mind. In these two, it should also be noted, the principle of distinction is different.

Kant and Hegel denied that the Aristotelian table of categories possessed a guiding principle, and Tredelenburg failed to see any unity in it. But they were in error, since a principle of division can be and actually was found by St. Thomas. Being is not the genus that is divided into different species by the differences. Under the influence of logic and grammar, being is divided into genera according to the different ways of predication. In the words of St. Thomas: "Being is divided into ten predicaments, not univocally as the genus is divided into species, but according to the different modes of being. These modes of being correspond to the modes of predication." [28] Every species is actually being, and therefore the concept of being is not a generic term; it is found in everything that is. Being, however, appears in different modes which may be said to correspond to different genera.

The most important division in the categories is that between substance and accident, just as it is the most important division in the realm of being. First substance is the subject about which all other predications are made. These predications are divided into three groups according to the relation of the predicated content to the individual substance. (1) Sometimes the predication is of an essential nature, as when something that belongs to the nature is predicated of the substance, e.g., Socrates is a man, man is a living being. (2) The predication may express something that does not belong to the essence of the thing, something that is only inherent. This relation by inherence may be of different kinds. The predication may belong to the subject absolutely, and if it is founded in the matter it is called quantity, if it is founded in the form it is called quality. Or again, a predication may belong to the subject not absolutely, but

[28] *In III Phys.,* 5.

only in relation to another. This is the case with relations. (3) The last of the three classes of predications comprises those modifications that are external to the thing. Some of these are entirely external, such as the modifications of time and space, while others are found partly in the thing, such as *actio* and *passio*. A mode of being peculiar to man is habit. While other living beings are endowed by nature for the battle of life, man possesses reason to assist him in equipping himself for the task. This equipment is something external, but at the same time it is something that modifies the being of man.

Among the categories there is a firmly established order, determined, as Aristotle concluded, by the greater or lesser proximity of the categories to the substance. Since the category of quality is related to the form, and since the form is more a substance than the matter is, some thought that quality was closest to the substance. St. Thomas, however, following the principle of the priority of that which is presupposed, realized, as also did Aristotle and Plato, that quantity is closest to substance. Just as the form presupposes matter, so quality presupposes quantity. Color, for instance, comes to the substance through the surface, and by the division of the quantity, the other accidents are also accidentally divided. All other accidents are founded in the extension of the substance, and therefore quantity is prior to the others. Qualities are the principles of action and passion, and a series of relations. Quantity is also the basis for some relations. St. Thomas did not complete his organization of the categories, but it would not be difficult to do so. Habit holds the last place because it is entirely outside the subject and has no relation either to the measure or the causality of the thing.

4. **Quantity.** Quantity is the category that presupposes matter, and it is the first of the accidents to be predicated of substance. By its nature, substance is prior to quantity and in itself it is free of all quantitative determinations, which signify something added to the simple nature of substance.[29] Quantity is defined as that by which that which contains it is divisible and of which every part is a definite entity. Aristotle divided quantity into continuous and discrete, i.e., into extension and number. It is called extension when it deals with something measurable; it is called number when it deals with that which can be numbered.

Extension coheres within itself and is undivided; it is a continuum.

---

[29] *Summa theol.*, IIIa, q.76, a.3 ad2.

Whether extension and continuous quantity are identical is a debatable question, but according to St. Thomas they are the same. Extension consists in the disposition of the parts by juxtaposition within the whole. By three-dimensional quantity, the substance receives definite limits, an external measure, corporeity, and a definite site. It is made up of points, lines, surfaces, and corporeal forms which are the limits of the material substance. On quantity are based measurability and divisibility, unity and plurality: the first properties of being.[30] St. Thomas recalls Aristotle's statement that if quantity is removed, an indivisible substance remains.[31] He was far from saying, as did Descartes, that the essence of a thing is in its extension, and he also rejects the teaching of the Pythagoreans and Platonists that the corporeal substance consists in quantitative relations. Suarez' theory that every corporeal substance possesses an entitative extension whose various parts become impenetrable through the accidental extension is likewise not Thomistic.

Divisibility is based upon a thing's extension. The thing itself is divided, but the corporeal form is divided only *per accidens*. The parts of a continuous extension before the division have only a potential being, and the form, which is entirely in the whole, is only potentially plural before the division. After the division, the form is multiplied.[32] St. Thomas points out an important distinction for modern times. A mathematical body is divisible to infinity, since it consists only of extension and the concept of continuous extension does not preclude continuous division. The corporeal body, however, is opposed to continuous division. St. Thomas would not have admitted the objection that actual division, or at least mental division, ought to go as far as there is extension. He points out that, in addition to extension, a material body also has a definite form and definite fullness of power, demanding a certain quantity and precluding continuous division. With Aristotle, St. Thomas teaches that if one were to divide meat or water indefinitely, ultimately the parts would no longer be meat or water, since the corporeal substance would have been reduced beyond the minimum and a change would take place *propter debilitatem virtutis*. The increase or the diminution of every material body has its limits.[33] The form exercises an influence on

---

[30] *In I Sent.*, 8, 5, 2.
[31] *In IV Sent.*, 12, 1, 1.
[32] *In II Sent.*, 18, 2, 1.
[33] *Ibid.*, 30, 2, 2; 14, 1 ad 4.

quantity, inasmuch as everything belongs to some species, and every species by reason of its form possesses a certain quantity which is variable within limits. The entire essence is contained in both the larger and the smaller quantity. Matter, however, is not in potency to every possible quantity; quantity, like other accidents, is given to the matter according to the needs of the form (*secundum exigentiam formae*).[34]

The second species of quantity is number. Number arises from the division of extension; it has real existence only in things and becomes a mathematical form only by abstraction. Like Aristotle, St. Thomas distinguishes between the numbers that are in the things themselves, "the numbered numbers," and the numbers separated from things, "the numbers by which we count." Essentially, number is "multitude measured by unity" (*multitudo mensurata per unum*). Since every number consists of many unities, unity is the measure and principle of number, and this unity, like a point, is indivisible both potentially and actually. Quantitative unity and plurality must not be confused with transcendental unity and plurality. Because real and abstract numbers are different, they possess different properties.

5. Quality. Even today, quality is a concept embracing many things, some of which differ greatly from one another. Aristotle was eager to clarify and organize the great number of things included in the concept of quality. But when he defined quality as that by reason of which a thing is thus or otherwise and grants it the mark of definiteness as opposed to the indefiniteness of the quantum, he did not contribute much toward clarification. A study of the different kinds of quality may throw more light on the nature of quality itself.

Quality is one of the basic determinants of being. It is rooted in the core of the substance, since the essence or the specific difference of every thing is a quality (*quale*). Distinct from this substantial quality, we find the accidental qualities, which Aristotle divides into four kinds. The first class includes properties and dispositions; properties are of longer duration than dispositions. Knowledge and virtue are examples of the more persisting properties, while sickness, health, coldness, and the like, are examples of dispositions, which are more variable than properties. The second class comprises physical capabilities and incapabilities, e.g., proficiency in running or boxing, illness. The third class includes the sensible qualities, such as sweet,

---

[34] *Ibid.*, 30, 2, 1.

bitter, cold, warm, white, and black. They are called passive qualities, not because the subject which they modify suffers anything, but
because they produce changes in the senses. In this third group, Aristotle also places emotional changes and affections in the subject. The
fourth class of qualities comprises figure and form, and also straight-
ness, crookedness, and related qualities.

St. Thomas incorporated this teaching of Aristotle into his own
system, and eventually he attained even finer distinctions than his
predecessor by diligently comparing the latter's teachings with those
of other thinkers and by carefully applying his own conclusions to
many fields of thought. Distinguishing it from quantity, St. Thomas
describes quality as a disposition of the substance, as a mode of the
substance; and in explaining this mode, he makes use of the concept
of measure in so far as the qualitative determination is governed by
the substantial nature. This description, however, does not set definite limits to the concept of quality, because the concept of measure
belongs to quantity, and some dispositions, such as *situs* (local position), are also quantitative. Aristotle had merely enumerated the
four kinds of quantity; his commentators tried to establish order
among them. Simplicius designated as natural qualities those qualities that are within things by reason of their nature; other qualities,
added on from without or produced by an external cause, he called
habits and dispositions. Among the natural qualities are some that
express a potency; these belong to the second class of qualities. Other
qualities express something actual, and they are either deeply rooted
in the thing, as those that belong to the third class, or they are superficial, as those that belong to the fourth class of qualities.

St. Thomas criticizes this division of qualities. He points out that
many forms and sensible qualities are not natural, but something
added from without. On the other hand many dispositions are not
from without, but natural, e.g., beauty and health. St. Thomas proposes a new principle of division. Accidental qualities can be (1) conceived in their relation to the nature of the subject; (2) brought into
relationship with the *actio* and *passio* of the natural principles (matter and form); and (3) they can be brought into relationship with
quantity.

The last, quantitative quality, consists of form and figure. St.
Thomas calls it the quality that is related to quantity, and, because
the perfection of a thing consists in its peculiar form and figure, he

says that the figure is the clearest expression of the species. In illustration, he points to the plants, flowers, and animals whose specific differences are most easily discerned through the differences of their forms. As quantity is closest to the substance, so the figure is closest to the form (substantial). This quality is found only in corporeal things and is therefore rightly referred to as the "static" quality.

The concept of quality does not include motion or the idea of good or bad, neither does it refer to a good or bad disposition. St. Thomas' second and third classes of qualities include those that refer to action and passion. The second class includes the natural potencies, those important powers and dispositions from which natural activities proceed. The qualities of the third class are the sensitive qualities. The qualities of the first class include habits, dispositions, and all modifications concerning the nature of things. The concept of disposition includes the concept of potency, and it presupposes the concepts of totality and order inasmuch as we find dispositions only where the parts of a whole are ordered and directed to something. Here St. Thomas, Aristotle, and Simplicius distinguish three subclasses: an ordering *secundum locum, secundum potentiam, secundum speciem*. The first is the corporeal disposition and is really *praedicamentum situs*. The second subclass is the incomplete potency which is the preliminary for the third class, habit.

Because of its importance for moral science and also in the nature of things, habit is treated more thoroughly by St. Thomas than some other qualities. The word is derived from the Latin *se habere* and refers to how a thing disposes itself. Habit denotes a good or bad disposition of a thing with reference to its own nature or to some end. The mark of goodness or badness is so much a part of the idea of habit that whenever other forms or sensible qualities are said to be good or bad, they too are considered as belonging to the first class of qualities. Habit connotes the idea of persistence and complete inherence. Habit further connotes a lasting aptitude and inclination to certain activities, and therefore St. Thomas calls habits *qualitates inclinantes*. They are the dynamic qualities.

Habit is related to potency and to act. By potency, St. Thomas understands a thing's capacity for a passive or an active attitude. Habit is related to potency because potency is its immediate subject. Habit completes potency, and therefore it is the more perfect of the two. It is, however, closer to act. St. Thomas calls habit an incomplete act, and also *actus primus,* to distinguish it from activity (*actus se-cundus*).

The first class of qualities is restricted to certain types of being. Since disposition and habit are found only where that which is disposed and that to which it is disposed are different, and where these two are related as potency and act, they are not found in God. More-over, since everything that is in potency manifests determinability in several directions, this first kind of quality is not to be found in those things that by their very nature are determined to one definite act. An instance of this is found in the heavenly bodies composed of matter and form. The matter of these bodies is not in potency to different forms and activities, but only to a determined movement. Furthermore, since habits are found only where a number of factors unite for the disposition of the subject's form and activity, the simple qualities of the elements that belong to the nature of the elements only in a certain way cannot be called dispositions and habits.

On the other hand, health, beauty, and the like, since they include the ideas of order and dependence on several factors, are among the habits and dispositions. The question arises whether habits belong to the body or the soul of living beings. Averroes and others thought that habits belonged to the soul alone, but St. Thomas thought other-wise. If habit is considered a disposition to activity, then no habit corresponds to those activities which are determined to one direction by the natural powers. Those activities, however, that are carried out through the instrumentality of the body but originate in the soul, have corresponding habits belonging primarily to the soul and sec-ondarily to the body. Plants, since their vegetative faculties are de-termined in one direction, have no habits. Sensitive faculties as they are found in animals have no habits; instead, animals have instinc-tive, determined activities. But the sensitive faculties that are under the rule of reason are said to have habits. All sensible perceptions that proceed necessarily to their objects have no habit, whereas habits are found in the memory, phantasy or imagination, in the sensible part of the thought process, in the *intellectus possibilis,* and especially in the will. The very concept of habit includes a relationship to the will. Pure spirits have no material faculties and therefore no cor-responding habits; but, as they are not pure act like God, they are equipped with potencies and habits.

Whether this theory of qualities is tenable in every detail is not of great moment; the important thing is that in this discussion we see revealed an energetic struggle against any surrender of any qualities as they are found in the real world. St. Thomas had no inclination to deny to essences their most valued possession by reducing all qualities to quantities. Even the form is something qualitative. Everything in reality bears the marks of some primordial quality. A quantitative philosophy may ignore the qualities, but it cannot deny them. A philosophy strongly influenced by natural science and epistemology may strip some qualities of their objectivity, but it will not be able to deny that some objective correlate corresponds to the subjective quality.

   6. **Relations.** For the speculations of metaphysics and theology, especially the questions of the creation and the Trinity, scarcely any other category is as important as the category of relation. St. Thomas speaks of adorable relations in the divine Being, and this was for him sufficient reason for a detailed study of the ontology of relations. Aristotle laid the foundations for the theory of relations upon which later commentators (Boethius, the Arabians, and the Christian Scholastics) built. In this respect St. Thomas excelled the other philosophers by eliminating many errors, developing the Aristotelian principles and applying them to new fields.

   The definition of relation was first given by Aristotle. Relation is a particular mode of being; otherwise it would not be a separate category. Furthermore, relation possesses the mark of every accident, inherence in another (*in esse*). Relation is not only an external appellation, but a modification of the substance to whose being it adds another kind of being. While the other genera accord a thing some definite modification, relation goes beyond the thing itself and considers it with reference to something outside itself. Thus the relation is not, like quantity and quality, an accident continuing in the subject, but it is a reference to something else. The formal and essential peculiarity of relation consists in this reference or ordering to another. *Ratio relationis est, ut referatur ad alterum.* Relation depends for its being, not only on the existence of its subject, but also on the existence of something besides this subject. All these characteristics belong to its definition.

   Relation expresses nothing absolute about its subject, but only with respect to another, *qui ei inest ad aliquid extrinsecum*. According to Aristotle and St. Thomas, of all the categories relation is the weakest kind of being. It is also said to be the last kind of being because it presupposes all other accidents, not only substance. St. Thomas refused to admit that relation has no inherence in the subject; still, considering Boethius' declaration that relations do not inhere but are affixed to the substance, St. Thomas was willing to grant that the statement contained some truth. Sometimes, he admitted, the real foundation for relation almost disappears; but he strenuously opposed the statement that relations are only fictions of the mind.

Relation is indeed not a sensible accident, but the cause of the accident may be perceptible by the senses. The subjective idealist viewpoint, that relations are created only by thinking, was entirely irreconcilable with St. Thomas' realistic view of the universe. Relation could not be one of the categories if it did not belong to being itself, and if it did not inhere in things. Mere mental being is in contradistinction to real being that is enumerated in the ten categories. The concept of the world as an *ordo,* an ordered whole, reveals the real basis for relation and indicates how extensive is its application. Things alone do not constitute a universe. The interweavings and interconnections of things are required, with their mutual influences. Only from such give-and-take between things does a universe arise. Created things exist with a certain order among themselves, i.e., with real relations to one another. St. Thomas did not deny the existence of relations, neither did he reduce all things to mere relations.

A relation requires a foundation, *relatio fundatur in aliquo sicut in causa.* A real relation presupposes the existence of two real *supposita* really distinct; a subject is required from which the relation proceeds, and another subject really distinct from the first to which the relation extends. The bond of the relation unites the first subject to the terminus and vice versa; *relatio, quae est in uno sicut in subjecto, est in altero sicut in termino et converso.*[35] Therefore St. Thomas said that the foundation of relation is something inhering in the two termini and that the relation itself hovers midway between the subjects.

A relation is never with reference to another relation. Thus sometimes a relation founded in two subjects may have two aspects, as, for instance, fatherhood and sonship, or the relation may be really the same in both subjects and also bear the same name, as, for instance, similarity. The unity of a thing is no bar to a plurality of

[35] *In I Sent.,* 27, 1, 1 ad 3.

relations. Indeed, sometimes the simpler a thing is the more relations it is able to originate; for the more unlimited a power is, the
greater will be the extent of causality. St. Thomas points out that
the two members of a relation need not belong to the same plane of
being; a real relation exists between God and creatures. Relations as
such do not have any movement, nor do they admit of any increase
or decrease; these things may be predicated of the subjects and thus
accidentally of the relation.

The remote foundation of the relation is the subject or the substance. The proximate foundation, according to Aristotle, is quantity,
action and passion, measure and that which is measured. The measure
and measured, however, do not refer to any external measure, but to
measure of being and truth, *secundum mensurationem esse et veritatis*. St. Thomas used this division of Aristotle, designating the first
two as the foundations for predicamental relation. Quality as such
cannot be the basis of a relation, but only by reason of an attached
quantity or inasmuch as it is an active or passive potency. As a rule
it is true that the other categories follow rather than cause the relations.

The most important division of relations is that into real and logical relations, and those between these two, mixed relations.

Logical relations are those that have no real foundation and are
created solely by the mind. Here St. Thomas distinguishes four kinds,
which may, however, be considered as subdivisions of a division.

Relations of the first kind arise from the application of those concepts of order that are created by our minds, e.g., genus and species,
to things, and from the use of these concepts in bringing order into
our thinking.

The second kind arises from the method of thought, the *modus
intelligendi,* and is divided into four subclasses that St. Thomas
adopted from Aristotle and Avicenna. The first of these is the relation of identity by which something is referred to itself. In the second the relation itself is referred to the subject. In the third one of
the members of the relation is dependent on the other but not vice
versa. The fourth relation contains a comparison of being with non-
being. Logical relations, since they are purely mental entities, do not
belong to the categories representing the various modifications of
real being.

Real relations consist in an ordering of one thing to another whereby the foundation of the relation is real and actual in both subjects. This is always true of quantitative relations; it is not always true of the *actio-passio* relations, but only when the cause and effect are univocal, that is, when the causes bring forth effects like to themselves. The effect is always related to the cause, but the converse is not always true.

This last division brings us to the mixed relations, those, namely, that are partly real and partly logical. In this class are all those relations in which the terms of the comparison are not in the same plane of being. As an illustration St. Thomas selects the example of the one who knows and that which is intelligible. The act of knowing is in relation to the thing that is known, but the extramental thing is outside the intellectual order and it is not affected in its nature or existence by the act of intelligence. A relation created in this manner is indeed real in the intellect but not in the thing. The same kind of relation exists between the senses and that which is perceivable by the senses, between man and a picture, between man and a pillar with respect to the relations of right and left, above and below, before and after. The same relation also exists between the Creator and the creature inasmuch as the relation of dependence is real in the creature but not in God. This relation is not a mutual relation.

Relations may also be divided into relations *secundum esse* and relations *secundum dici*. The first are described as those in which names are imposed to describe the relations themselves, as master and servant, father and son; the latter are those in which the name denotes a quality or something similar upon which the relations follow. St. Thomas remarks expressly that this division is not co-extensive with the division into logical and real relations. There are, for instance, relations *secundum esse,* such as the right and left of a pillar, that are not real, and there are relations *secundum dici* that are not logical but real, e.g., the act of knowing and the thing known. The relations *secundum dici,* however, are identical with the essential or transcendental relations that express absolute essentials or some proportion or adaptation rooted in the innermost nature of a thing. The relation between matter and form, potency and act, body and soul, are favorite examples. The relation *secundum esse* is coextensive with the accidental relation, that is, the predicamental relation, in which the relationship itself and only an accidental form of being are expressed. This distinction into essential and accidental relations enters deeply into the speculations of ontology.

St. Thomas resolves the question about the relation of time as did Aristotle before him. Those members of a relation are simultaneous that are demanded mutually by the same reason, e.g., father and son, master and slave, double and half. Those actions from which relations arise are prior in time to the relation, e.g., the act of bearing witness. In those relations, however, in which the members of the relation do not belong to the same order of being, one member will be prior to the other by nature. Thus the object of knowledge is prior to the act of knowing, and God is prior to the creature. Whatever simultaneity there is in such relations concerns the relations and not the members.

The field in which the category of relations finds application is most extensive. While logical relations can be multiplied indefinitely, real relations are limited by the reality of things, but they are found in all grades of being. Quantitative relations are found only in the corporeal world, not only in the lower spheres but also in the heavenly bodies. The relations of *actio-passio* are found in every part of the universe and they assume a dominant importance since the whole universe is an ordered whole; because it is ordered, it is a great relation. Here again the law referred to above finds application: the simpler a thing is, the less its activity is restricted, and the more relations it is able to found. Real relations, although they are not accidents, form the essence of the triune God. Because God has no quantity, no quantitative relations are found in Him; but it is not true, as Maimonides thought, that all other relations are also eliminated. God appears as a member of the causal relation, and all creatures are referred to God as their beginning and their final end. From the comparison of created substances with God arise the relations of dependence and creation. The statement that relations possess reality in the creature but not in God and that the relation in God exists only in our minds, is closely connected with the teaching on the different natures of divine and created being which is an important part of Scholastic theology.

7. Action and passion. Since change and movement are real, action and passion which they presuppose must also be real. Change might have been made an independent category, but St. Thomas considers it only as the thing in the process of development. Prior to the change the form is in potency, during the change it is midway between potency and act, and after the change it is completed act. Because the process of change represents a thing in various phases, change like potency and act is classified under the genus of things. In order to be subject to change, however, a thing must possess certain equipment: it must have the power of action and passion.

The action can be twofold: it may terminate with some effect in an external object, e.g., the action of warming or cutting, and this is transient action; or it may occur entirely within the active subject, e.g., thinking, perceiving, and this is immanent action. This distinction is also made in passion, whose peculiarity it is to change from potency into act.

These categories of action and passion are not numerically the same, although they belong together for each other's completion. Only because of their mutual relation can the process of change and the particular effect take place. Action and passion are the constitutive parts of one and the same movement. In the relation of action and passion are found only those things that are generically the same but specifically different or opposite.

The contrasting relation between the active and passive terms is founded in the contrasting relationship between matter and form; every passive potency and every *passio* is rooted in matter, and every active power and *actio* is rooted in the form. St. Thomas adopts the Aristotelian conclusion that some things are exclusively active, others exclusively passive, and others both active and passive. He also agrees with the conclusion that activity and passivity may form one thing, as in the process of hearing. All being appears as active, and therefore the category of action is universal in its application. St. Thomas opposed Plato, and the Arabians who held that corporeal things possessed no active powers and that God and immaterial beings were the only active principles in the universe. *Passio* is no longer applicable in that realm where there is no matter and no potency, i.e., with God.

8. **The category of place.** Because of reference to a measure, the two categories of "where" and "when" result; the first refers to place, the latter to time.

The category "where" expresses the existence of a corporeal thing in a place. Since things move from place to place, Aristotle was led to inquire whether place and position are real, or whether place is only logically distinct from space. Just as space is founded on the extended corporeal world, and is inconceivable without corporeal extension, so also place and position connote extension. Spatial things are not identical with place since now one thing occupies a place and then the same place is occupied by another thing. Aristotle defines place as the stationary boundary of one corporeal thing enclosing another. The place or position contains and surrounds a thing, and without some corporeal quantity, place does not exist, since there is no limit unless something is limited.

Both Aristotle and St. Thomas are far from considering place and position as something subjective; for them place is real. Place depends on the extension of corporeal things. Corporeal things are measured and circumscribed by place, and thus the shape of the thing is determined. What is it that circumscribes a corporeal thing? Another corporeal thing by means of its surface circumscribes it, and therefore St. Thomas said that place was the same as the surface of the localizing body *"superficies corporis locantis."* He compares place to a container from which it is in some respects different. A thing is contained in place as wine is contained in a vessel; the vessel, however, may be moved with its contents, while we must conceive the place as stationary. At this point he came face to face with a difficulty. For a ship the water on which it floats is the delimiting place, but the water is always in motion and continually changing, and the place should represent stationary limits. Because of this difficulty, Aristotle was led to extend his point of reference and say that the whole universe was the container and the primary place of corporeal things. The modern definition of place as the equilibrium of natural forces was unknown to the ancient and medieval philosophers.

9. **The category of time.** Space and time are not ontologically the same, but as the formal presuppositions for the constitution of things they belong together. Beside the category of *where,* we find the category of *when.* Time presupposes quantity and it forms that subdivision which has no place or position but only an ordering of its parts. In his *Confessions,* St. Augustine pointed out those almost insurmountable difficulties that lie hidden in the concept of time. Every system of philosophy has to some extent considered these difficulties. To understand the Aristotelian and Thomistic concept of time, we

must keep in mind the plane of being which forms the basis for the formation of that concept. Certain things are taken for granted by St. Thomas and the Scholastics in connection with this problem: time is not something that exists only in our minds (Plotinus), it is not of the second intention, that is, merely a mode of thought (Descartes and Spinoza), it is not a subjective form of observation (Kant), but it is something that exists outside the mind. It is not indeed an independent entity like a river bed in which all other things flow, but it is a mode of being that modifies changeable things. With Aristotle the concept of time presupposed the concept of space and the concept of movement. St. Thomas adduces the inner phenomena of our being as the basis for the concept of time, and he gives less attention to the physical aspect, although the Aristotelian physical influence is strong enough to prevent him from entering into the psychological problems discussed by St. Augustine. St. Thomas is convinced that time is a part of movement; it is, he says, "the number of the movement (*numerus motus*) with reference to earlier and later (*secundum prius et posterius*). Time is an accident of movement. He does not, however, go as far as Duns Scotus, who held that between time and movement there is only a logical distinction, although he maintained that time and movement are intimately related.

Some have professed to see in this definition of time a begging of the question, since the distinction between earlier and later contains the notion of time. St. Thomas himself answered this objection. The *prius* and *posterius* enter into the definition of time *secundum quod causantur in motu ex magnitudine, et non secundum quod mensurantur ex tempore,* that is, the earlier and later are found in the definition of time not because they are measured by time but because they are caused by space or quantitative extension. Aristotle had already pointed out that the earlier and later are originally found in spatial extension, and then in movement, and finally as an element of time. Neither would St. Thomas allow the objection that the mind could not conceive the moving phenomena of the universe as temporal unless it had known what time is from its own inner experiences. We conceive the notions of time and movement simultaneously. When we apprehend the idea of movement, we also conceive the idea of time and vice versa. It is immaterial whether we perceive some process of movement in the sensible universe outside of ourselves or whether some change that takes place in our bodies caused by some external agent, or whether it is some imaginative or rational process in our minds. Events in both the outer and the inner worlds may form the basis for time. The fact that time possesses apriority with respect to movement is of no consequence. Because things are changeable they contain the idea of earlier and later and thus lay the foundation for time. Time is an unceasing stream, a ceaseless change of the "now," and it takes place in a continuous line which has no disruption. Time is the measure not only of the actual change, but also of possible changes, and it is also the measure of rest in which movable bodies may find themselves.

Some have remarked that this study of change and movement loses sight of the essential question of the constitution of time. But St. Thomas did not think so. For him the view of the succession of events was at the same time the view of the flow of time. Support for this contention is found in Aristotle, who thought that the "now" is always actually the same. Just as time corresponds to movement, the present moment, the "now," corresponds to that which is moved. That which is moved is at all times the same, and the difference between its being here and there is only a logical distinction. In the same way St. Thomas thinks that time consists in the flux of the "now," the present moment, which is continually becoming something logically different. Thus the "now" is given a factual foundation. Another factor, however, is needed for ordering the "now" moments into the stream of time. Although St. Thomas followed Aristotle in rejecting every attempt to make time a subjective thing, he recognized the subjective moment in time. The material foundation of time consists in the earlier and later of movement, but time receives its form from the comparing, ordering, and enumerating activity of our intellects. In this respect time differs from place or position. Whereas place is identical with the surface area of the enclosing body, time is not identical with any accident rooted in the substance. Again, whereas place finds its completion in the thing itself, time requires for its perfection the activity of an enumerating intellect. Time, therefore, possesses the *ratio extrinseci,* a reason from without, in a higher sense than place.

St. Thomas was aware that we are conscious of a uniform time. He derives the uniformity and unity of time from the first and simplest movement, which is the movement of the heavens. St. Thomas refers time to this first movement which causes all other movements and measures them, as the accident is referred to its subject, and thus he establishes the unity of time by anchoring it in the rigid immovable structure of the universe.

From an investigation of the present moment, Aristotle came to the conclusion that time is always, sempiternal. Since the "now," the present moment, is essentially a medium and transition, it is as necessarily connected with the past as with the future. Because of the problem of creation, St. Thomas rejected this Aristotelian theory. Aristotle had found resemblances between the present moment and the mathematical point. St. Thomas insists more than his teacher on this resemblance to the point, and he regards the present moment as the simple beginning and the simple end, suppressing the transitory idea of Aristotle. This sempiternity in Scholastic philosophy is not precisely the same as eternity. Eternity is the opposite of time and the negation of all time, it is timelessness. St. Augustine first proclaimed and Boethius transmitted to the Middle Ages that time is founded in changeable things, and that eternity is founded in the immutability, aseity, and totality of the highest divine Being. God alone is eternal. The concept of eternity includes complete immutability, complete limitlessness and the complete possession of the present, excluding any succession of moments.

Thus time and eternity are fundamentally different. The principal difference does not consist in this, that time has a beginning and an end, whereas eternity has neither. Even if time were sempiternal, the essential distinction between it and eternity would still remain. The difference consists in this, that eternity is entirely at one time, *tota simul,* whereas time is successive; and again, eternity is the measure of immutable being, whereas time is the measure of movement. The consequence of this distinction is that divisions of time can be marked off in sempiternal time, with a beginning and an end, but not in eternity.

Influenced by the theological tradition, St. Thomas inserts the *aevum* between time and eternity. Under the *aevum* are all those beings that are midway between God and mutable creatures, the heavenly bodies and the pure spirits. These do not possess the immutability of God, neither are they subject to change as are the sublunary creatures. The *aevum* has no earlier and later as we find in time, but it may be joined to the earlier and later, which is entirely impossible with eternity.

10. Criticism. The first object of knowledge is being, for the concept of being is the first one to be formed. Again and again St. Thomas emphasizes this statement as the fundamental principle of his ontological epistemology. Sometimes it seems that he wished to make being a kind of fundamental category, but categories, according to St. Thomas, have their place only when being is to be resolved into its various modes. Being and all that is not really distinct from it are above the categories.

St. Thomas accepts the categories almost as if they were first principles. Aristotle did not always enumerate ten categories; sometimes he was content with eight, or five, and sometimes even with three. St. Thomas held fast to ten and considered ten categories as complete and conclusive.

We should not be surprised if this, the first attempt to divide all existing reality into its ultimate modes of being, or into the ultimate and supreme concepts, should be somewhat defective. From very early times the voice of criticism was heard and it has not yet been silenced. St. Thomas laid it down as a requisite that these categories should be mutually exclusive, that one predicament should not be contained in another, but this requirement is not met in the table of categories. Many categories that are enumerated belong to the category of relation. Action and passion include not only relation but also the temporal-spatial determinations of where and when. Site or position (*dispositio partium in ordinem et locum*) belongs to order and relation, while the characteristics of relation are contained in quantity and quality. Relation even penetrates into substance itself inasmuch as the parts of substance have an inner relationship to one another. St. Thomas himself came to the conclusion that the categories were thus mutually in each other because, he thought, things were thus related to one another in reality.

Furthermore, the categories do not represent the ultimate, but since they possess structure and composition they presuppose other more basic concepts. Thus the concept of measure underlies the concept of quality, which in turn is based on quantity. Scotus points out that point and number belong to quantity because they are classed under measurement, and he adds that time and place, since they are measurements, must also be subsumed under quantity. He points out further that the idea of quantity is in danger of being absorbed by the concept of measure. The concept of posture, again, is based on the ideas of totality and order, and includes the concept of potency. In the same way, the idea of relation cannot exist without the concept of order, nor can the temporal-spatial determinations with their implication of dimensionality, exist without order. The charge that St. Thomas failed to distinguish sufficiently between the formal and the material categories is unjustified. The Aristotelian categories are material; the formal division is to be found in the predicables.

The criticism advanced by Plotinus against Aristotle is more formidable. Plotinus criticized Aristotle's categories as being based on the reality of the natural world and therefore having no validity in the spiritual realm. This argument was revived during the Middle Ages by Henry of Ghent and Duns Scotus; as it was developed, it pointed out the method by which a table of categories should be established. The various sections of reality should be examined as to their existential and essential structures, and from this study the ultimate concepts should be brought into relief, these concepts that would be required for an understanding of these great fields into which reality is divided. The list of the fields of being must correspond to the eventual categories. From this study it should become evident whether any categories went through all fields of being, and which fields were basically different from one another. The relationship between the various departments of being would be reflected in the relationship between the categories; the more the various departments of being were removed from one another, the more the modes of predication would differ from one another. Finally, the divisions made in the different kinds of being would find their counterpart in similar divisions made in the categorical structure.

A final criticism refers to the starting point of this teaching on the categories. The Aristotelian-Thomistic theory of the categories is individualist since it starts out from the individual substance as the ultimate reality. But is not the world, according to Aristotle and especially according to St. Thomas, a universe, a totality, a great order? Should not, then, the categorical theory be impressed with a universalist and totalitarian character? To this argument St. Thomas might answer that it is true the world is an order (*ordo*) and a totality, but the pillars on which this order rests are the individual

substances which by their conjoined beings and their conjoined op-
erations bring about the ordered unity of the universe. Like any
social community, the community of the universe possesses reality
but not substantiality. The structure of the universe can be known
from the supporting substances and from the relations that they
originate.

CHAPTER VII

THE CONCEPT OF BEING AND
ITS ATTRIBUTES

In agreement with Aristotle and Avicenna, St. Thomas repeats that the concept of being is of all concepts the most universal, and that all other concepts refer back to it. Whatever we grasp mentally we grasp as *being,* and thus the form *being* belongs to everything that we deal with in our mental processes. Every concept that we use in order to arrive at knowledge of reality presupposes the concept of being. Just as the concept of being is the most universal, so also it is the poorest in content. As to content, the concept of being tells us only that a thing is and that the relation of essence and existence is here present. Being is also the most extensive of all concepts; it is found in everything; it is therefore above all genera and species, which represent certain particularizations of being, and since it is above genus and species, it is called transcendental.

The concept of being implies and predicates the supreme laws of being: the principle of contradiction, the principle of identity, and the principle of the excluded middle. The evidence on which these principles rest is more important than the various controversies of the Middle Ages and later Scholasticism, about the priority of the principle of contradiction or identity. It is immediately evident to us that a being is, and is what it is, and that it is impossible for a being to be and not be at the same time or to be thus and not thus at the same time, and that between being and non-being there is no middle.

A. THE ANALOGY OF BEING

Because of the enormous extent of the field to which the concept of being is applicable, it is not always applied in the same sense.

127

Therefore it is one of the fundamental principles of Aristotelian and Thomistic ontology that being is predicated in many different ways. To each category a distinct kind of being is something else, and the same is true of the conceptual contents that are added to the concept of being. Indeed one and the same category may imply different things according to the different orders of being in which it is used. Thus absolute and contingent being, high and low, internal and external, material and spiritual, created and divine being, even being and non-being are given the same name, and sometimes all these manifest relationships of similarity and dependence. Even before the days of philosophers it was understood that the meaning of certain concepts was not predicated of the members of a comparison in the same way. Afterward the philosophers were not able to ignore this fact that was equally important for the order of being and the order of knowledge. St. Thomas defended the characteristic Aristotelian doctrine that the concept of being and the categories had only an analogous validity. He was acquainted with the usefulness of the analogy of being from his study of Augustinian theology. This analogous validity of the concept of being implies that in the order of being the marks and characteristics of being are actualized in different ways.

1. **The concept of analogy.** The meaning of analogy is best clarified by the exclusion of equivocation and univocation. A pure equivocation exists when two things incidentally have the same name without possessing any similarity, e.g., the word "bear," which may refer to an animal and to a constellation. While thus in equivocation the two expressions have entirely different meanings, in univocation the terms are used in the same sense, e.g., the term animal is used in the same sense for horse and ox. In univocation there is not only identity of names, but identity of meaning.

Between equivocation and univocation is analogy. Whenever St. Thomas speaks of analogy he insists that it is a relation based on a comparison, a proportion, a relationship of two or more things to some one thing (*ordo sive respectus ad aliquid unum*). The concept of proportion, that is, the process of thinking in relationships, belongs properly to the realm of mathematics and had its first application in the contemplation of numbers and their mutual relations. This mathematical method was transferred to apply to all things inasmuch as they are beings and also to the various relations between things. Here we should note that analogous relations can obtain only when there is neither complete agreement nor complete disagreement between two things; there must be a union of agreement and difference. In an analogy the same name or concept is predicated of different things partly in the same sense and partly in a different sense; in the same sense because of the reference to the same relation, in a different sense because of the different modes of the relation. St. Thomas illustrates the matter by an example adopted from Aristotle: the word "healthy" is used in many senses, the living being itself, the blood, the medicine, and the food are called healthy. The word "healthy," however, refers to only one thing; it is the same health that is found in the living being, that is indicated by the blood test, that is promoted by the medicine, and that is preserved by the nourishment. But the relationship is different. In this analogy the concept *health* does not indicate the same thing about these various objects, for the health of the organism is not the same as the healthiness of the blood, or of the medicine, or of the food. The word "health" asserts something about all these things in reference to some other thing. Three things should be kept distinct in an analogy; the common name, its application to a number of members, and the application of this one term to these members because of the different relations to one thing, and this one thing is moreover numerically one. The similarity of the members is only a similarity of relation and reference, a similarity *secundum quid,* while the difference is founded deep in the essential constitution of the members of the comparison.

2. **The kinds of analogy.** The division of analogy into its various kinds will further clarify the concept of analogy. Light will especially be thrown on the sense in which being possesses the unity required by an analogy. The viewpoint from which these divisions are made changes, and the examples chosen as illustrations are not used uniformly in the same sense.

If we recall the origin of the concept in the field of mathematics, we shall at once understand the division of analogy into that of simple proportion and that of proportionality. The former consists in the relation of two numbers, e.g., the relation of six to three inasmuch as six is twice three. The latter consists in the relation of two proportions to each other. As six is to three so ten is to five. St. Thomas calls a simple proportion a community between two or more objects based on a mutual relation in which the particular relation is determined by the purpose or the efficient principle or the subject; he calls the latter an analogy based on the similarity of two proportions. Both of these analogies are transferred from the realm of mathematics to other fields of real being and illustrated by examples. As in Aristotle, St. Thomas uses the relation of subject to accident, and the "health" example to illustrate the simple proportion. He illustrates proportionality with comparisons between physical and spiritual sight, or with the proportion: the helmsman is to the ship as the ruler is to the state.

A second division, going back to Aristotle, distinguishes between two kinds of analogy which to some extent are identical with the kinds of the first division. In this division the first kind is that in which the analogy is predicated of two or more members with reference to a third object; the second kind is that in which the analogous relation is predicated of two members, not with reference to a third but rather with reference to each other. The "health" example illustrates the first kind here, too, and the relation of substance and accident belongs to the second kind. St. Thomas thought it important to point out the following characteristics. In the first kind the point of reference belongs to only one of the members of the analogy, that is, by reason of an indwelling form. The other members possess the point of reference only with reference to the first member. In the example it is only the living organism that is really healthy; blood, medicine, and food, are not said to be healthy by reason of an indwelling form. The term "healthy" is derived from the relation to the health of the living organism. St. Thomas calls this kind of analogy, the analogy *secundum intentionem tantum et non secundum esse,* or the analogy of external attribution, i.e., the analogy in which the concept is applied to several things in different senses.

The ontological peculiarity of this analogy is reflected in the order of knowledge. In these analogies no definition is available without the first member of the analogy; there is no knowledge of the other members possible because these have the point of comparison only derivatively. The predicated nature, e.g., health, is present in only one instance. If we refer to this kind of analogy as that of external attribution (*denominatio extrinseca*), we should be careful to remember that this attribution is not entirely external. We must not think of the predication in the other members as extrinsic, otherwise we would have only equivocation. In our example, the blood is in the organism and is therefore an integral part of it, the medicine works in the body, and when the blood and the medicine are said to be healthy it is because there is a real foundation for the statement. A real relation exists between these objects and the body, but the quality of health belongs to the minor members not absolutely but only with reference to the major member.

Distinct from the foregoing analogy is that called *secundum intentionem et secundum esse*. It is present whenever no similarity is found either in the intention or in being (as, for example, in the case of substance and accident), but where a common nature is found in each of the terms of the comparison, if not in the same way at least in different grades of perfection. This occurs in the analogous relation between two members that refer to each other and not to a third member. The basis of the analogy is in such instances the constitutive principle of the members of the analogy. First substance accordingly is one term for all other being, and the categories appear as different representations of being with respect to this first substance.

The analogy of proportionality comes under this division. We must, however, be careful to distinguish between figurative and actual proportionality. In the former the analogy is attributed formally of only one of the comparisons and figuratively of the other. If we speak of a smiling meadow, we speak figuratively, because smiling is proper only to man, and when we speak of God as a lion, it is a figure because the form of lion is not an essential principle of the deity. This metaphorical analogy serves to express similarity in action or in the manner of activity. In the analogy of actual proportionality, however, the basis of the analogy appears as an essential constitutive in both comparisons; it has a metaphysical significance, especially in the case of the transcendentals.

To conclude: we have analogies of simple proportion and analogies of proportionality. Not every simple proportion is an attribution, for among the simple proportions some are found in which the point of the analogy belongs to only one member. At the same time some simple proportions are found in which the basis of the analogy belongs intrinsically to both members. In this one respect such simple proportions are like the analogies of proportionality. Furthermore, if we compare the figurative proportionality with the analogy of at-

tribution inasmuch as in both instances the basis of the analogy belongs to only one member, we must not lose sight of the difference
between them. Apart from the fact that one is really a simple proportion and the other is a proportionality, in the case of an attribution a real relation based on causality binds the minor members to
the main term, while in the case of a metaphorical analogy we find
only a similarity of activity.

3. The meaning of analogy. What is the ultimate meaning of the
analogy of being? From what discussion or controversy does it arise?
What does it serve to explain? The answer to these questions can
easily be given. Two realms of being require the analogy of the concept of being: the relation between substance and accident, of autonomous and dependent being, and the relation between the infinite
and the finite, the divine and created being. The first group of problems was known to Aristotle and to all who came after him, the second group of problems came with Neoplatonism. Substance and
accident are said to be being, but not in the same way. The being of
the accidents is of a different kind than the being of the substance.
In the same way, the being that is attributed to the Infinite and Absolute cannot belong to created and finite being in the same way.
Deriving from Neoplatonism through the patristic writers (Origen
and St. Augustine) and through Dionysius the Areopagite, this
thought was impressed on the philosophical and theological speculation of the Middle Ages.

The nexus of problems from which this question of the analogy
of being arose also throws some light on the further question of what
we are to understand by being in this connection, and in what sense
St. Thomas understood the phrase *analogia entis*. Being means not
only not non-being, not only existence, or belonging to reality. The
idea that being meant existence led to the acceptance of the concept of
being as a univocal concept, and doubtless with some justification,
for both substance and accident, finite and infinite, belong to reality.
However, our problem is not concerned with existence but with the
mode of being, and the mode of being is something else. It is quite
true that *ens* is derived from *esse*, but this *esse*, this *actus essendi*, contains the essential content and nature of the thing. Being therefore
is realized, brought into reality, in analogous ways, because in the
various realms of being the nature or essence of the existing things
is always different.

The analogous use of the concept of being implies the analogous use of other concepts. The various differences of being, such as essence and existence, potency and act, and also the transcendentals are concretized or realized in analogous ways. The principle of contradiction has a different significance for finite being than for infinite being.

In each of the stages or grades of being the mode of being is different. Being and the content of being are realized in gradations and steps in the universe. This gradation of being requires the analogy of being. For the medieval philosopher and theologian the *analogia entis* was the only way he could place the world in its right relation to God. The univocation of being leads to pantheism, while the equivocation of being leads to a radical dualism. God possesses an entirely different kind of being from that of the creature, but His being is reflected in the being of the world. Therefore all our knowledge of God is only analogous. This analogy of being is founded in the fact that all finite being is an image of infinite being. Cajetan expressed this fundamental thought of the Thomistic system in these words: Without analogy metaphysics is impossible.

B. THE TRANSCENDENTALS

Long before Scholasticism the problem of the transcendentals had engaged the attention of Aristotle and St. Augustine. The importance of the problem can be seen from the fact that it left its imprint not only on such metaphysicians as Suarez, Leibnitz, and Wolff, but even on Kant.

Aristotle laid the foundations of the theory of the transcendentals when he said that it was the purpose of his *Metaphysics* to determine being and all that belonged to it as such. A transcendental is that which is above all species of being and yet goes through all kinds of being (*circuit omnia entia*),[1] extending as far as being itself. Being has viewpoints, aspects, marks, one might call them facets of being, and these are found everywhere that being is found. The fact that being is the primary concept, the first concept received into the mind as being the best known of all concepts, and the concept to which all other concepts refer, pertains primarily to the order of knowledge; but these characteristics are immediately valid in the

---

[1] *In X Met.,* 3; *Quodlib.,* VI, 1.

order of being inasmuch as being is the repository of all special determinations of being.

The statement that the concept of being is poor in its content needs some qualification. Being embraces all the categories; further, it tells of a higher order not bound down to this earthly sphere, but referring to both the finite and the infinite. Being not only contains the fact of existence but also the nature and essence of things and thus it embraces the essential and intrinsic content of things. None of the transcendentals adds anything to the concept of being, but each one views being from a special angle.

1. **The individual transcendentals.** With such Scholastics as Alexander of Hales and St. Albert, St. Thomas gives prominence to the transcendentals *unum, verum,* and *bonum;* but like his preceptor St. Albert, he also mentions the other two, *res,* and *aliquid.* Inasmuch as every actual being is nothing more than the substance of the thing, *ens* and *res* may be considered identical. *Res* refers to the nature of the being. While the categories are to determine being more definitely, *res* expresses the nature of a thing indeterminately.

The term *unum* (one) is obtained by way of negation. *Unum,* the oneness of being, negates division, and expresses the idea that being is undivided, without adding anything new to the concept of being. Here St. Thomas rejects both the interpretations of Plato and the Pythagoreans and that of Avicenna. The former were correct when they said that being is one and that every substance represents an undivided unity, but they erred when they identified this unity with the unity that is the principle of number. This theory led them eventually to the conclusion that numbers were the substance of things. Avicenna held that *unum,* the oneness of being, added something new to being, since unity as a number added something. If, as Avicenna thought, substance received its unity from something else, then this something would have to receive its unity from something else again, and so on with the consequence of a *regressum in infinitum.* Thus unity and its opposite, plurality, do not arise as transcendentals by means of quantitative division of a *continuum,* from which number does arise, but it arises from the formal separation of different essences. Aristotle had expressed the necessary connection between being and unity (*Met.,* IV, 2), and St. Augustine, Boethius, and the philosophers of the Middle Ages followed him. St. Albert thought that unity was an effect of the form, which by one act conferred being, and by another act, only virtually distinct from the first, formed the matter into something unified. This simple unity of being, denoting its intrinsic inclusiveness, exists through the substance of the thing; and the plurality of properties, a plurality *secundum quid,* is entirely reconcilable with this unity.

This designation of oneness brings immediately to mind another transcendental, *aliquid,* something. As being is one inasmuch as it is undivided, so it is something inasmuch as it is separated from other things.

The last two transcendentals, the true and the good, rest on a relation, or on an agreement with knowledge and willing.

Truth expresses a mental relation to being, the agreement of the intellect with the thing. Since the being of a thing not only precedes the truth of the thing, but also supports it, St. Thomas acknowledged ontological truth and accepted the definitions formulated by St. Augustine, Avicenna, and St. Anselm: "That is true, which is," "The truth of every thing consists in the peculiarity of its established being," "Truth is the rightness of a thing."

Truth adds nothing new to being, no special mode of being is expressed by truth; only the conformity of being with an intellect is expressed, a conformity that is not implied in the concept of being. The orders of being and truth correspond to each other without however being identical, in the sense that a thing's agreement with an intellect is according to its being. *Ratio veri sequitur esse.* This definition, adopted from the ancients, indicates the direction that St. Albert's interpretation took. Every being possesses existence and also essence through the form. Every being possesses being inasmuch as it has form. By truth St. Albert understood the agreement of being with the form that inheres in it, and thus he implies the interchangeability of truth with actual being. St. Thomas reasons on the basis of a similar ontology. According to him every being is true inasmuch as it possesses the essential form of its nature and is identical with the substance of its being. The connection of the concept of truth with an intellect is so close, according to St. Thomas, that he is unable to abandon the idea of an agreement with some intellect. Truth in the intellect, too, is convertible with being, as the thing manifested with the manifestation, *manifestativum cum manifestato.*

According to the Aristotelian notion the definition of good includes a relation to an end. That is good after which all men strive.

One being, however, may be able to perfect another being and keep it in existence, and therefore in this respect it possesses the character of an end for this thing. Inasmuch as being is able to confer perfection, it is good. Even truth may be considered among the things that confer perfection, since a being by its essential content may perfect the intellect. No thing is able to give perfection to another thing unless it possesses some perfection itself. Therefore the good belongs to every being by its very nature, and every being is called good by reason of its very nature and being, by reason of its inherent goodness. In his explanation of the transcendental good, St. Albert remains with the immanent goodness of being, and St. Thomas in general agrees with his preceptor although he amplifies the idea with the addition of the relation to the outside.

2. **The properties of the transcendentals.** The transcendentals signify the same thing under different aspects. As they are convertible with being, so they are convertible with one another. They enter into all genera of being. Thus far with respect to the peculiarities of the transcendentals St. Thomas agrees with St. Albert, but he differs from him in the bases he alleges in his explanation of the good and the true.

After being comes unity (one), then truth, and after truth the good. Being is the basis, and it is followed by unity. Unity precedes truth because the mental grasp of an object presupposes its unity and stability.

If we look at truth and goodness in themselves, we see that truth precedes goodness because it is closer to being inasmuch as it considers being in itself, because knowledge goes before willing, and because truth perfects the intellect only by the specific content of being, whereas the good confers perfection not only with respect to the specific content but even as to being. Hence the idea of good contains more within itself than does the idea of truth, it seems almost to add something to the being. Further, if we consider both the good and the true with respect to the thing that they perfect, we see that the good is more imporant than the true since it is able to perfect many more things than truth (which can perfect only the intellect), and also because the perfection conferred by the good on being precedes the perfection received from truth.

3. **The philosophical importance of the transcendentals.** The theory of the transcendentals is, as it were, the focus for the whole of

Thomistic philosophy. The heart of St. Thomas' philosophy is rooted in the concept of the form which, as if by some magic power, explains being, becoming, knowledge, and the value of things. The form is that which makes a thing what it is. It expresses the specific content of a thing, and represents the basis for the essence and substance of the thing. With the act of being, the form confers both nature and existence. It is at once the principle that gives things their essential content and their unity, it indicates the truth content for knowledge and also the value of the thing (*forma est sicut divinum et bonum et optimum*).

As the phrase, *ens et verum convertuntur,* provides the basis for an idealistic ontology, the phrase, *ens et bonum convertuntur,* provides a program for a theory of values based on being itself; so the phrase, *ens et unum convertuntur,* calls for a totalitarian interpretation of things. According to this interpretation, every thing in the universe is a composite unity, and these things preserve their being only as long as they preserve their unity, and they preserve their unity only as long as they remain a whole. In this principle of the substantial form is founded the whole theory of being, knowledge, and value. It remains for us to add but one thought: every being is a unity, and thus it is a whole; every being is good and true, but it is also inwardly ordered. We might add this axiom: *ens et ordo convertuntur.*

Unity, truth, and goodness belong to every being by reason of the form that dwells within it. This form is nothing but the image of the highest unity, the highest truth, and the highest goodness impressed upon this being. Thus finite being in its essential constitution points to the Cause of all being in whose prototypical ideas the transcendentals have their ultimate foundation. Aristotle's realistic view of the universe and this transcendental interpretation of the Christian theory of ideas meet in the Thomistic concept of the form.

SECTION II

THE HIERARCHY OF THE FORMS OF BEING AND
THEIR INTERRELATION

Pascal declared it was blasphemy for man to attempt to analyze the constitutive parts of the universe and to try to unveil the universal plan of the Supreme Spirit. St. Thomas committed this blasphemy. He was not, however, the first. To view the universe as a whole, to understand the relation of the parts to each other and to the whole, was the scientific aim of the Greeks whose contemplation of the whole universe served as a model for Christian thinkers.

The hierarchy of the forms of being that progresses continuously from the lowest to the highest, each grade being distinguished by the degree of perfection of being, is always implied or expressed as the background for all the determinations of being. This hierarchy of being is, moreover, the philosophical basis upon which the interpretation of the universe as a cosmos is built in the Platonic, Aristotelian, Stoic, and Neoplatonic systems, as well as in the systems of Christian and Arabian thinkers. The Platonic theory of ideas in gradations that is actualized in this visible cosmos, and the Aristotelian theory of the forms of being give expression to the difference in being and in perfection of the things in nature. We know that the degrees of perfection of beings have been used as a proof for the existence of God which St. Thomas adopted from St. Anselm's *Monologium* and incorporated into his system.

In evaluating this hierarchy of being, St. Thomas sometimes views it from above, sometimes from below. At the highest point in the hierarchy is God, who is purest act, and in the lowest grade we find prime matter, which is purest potency. Between these two points is the surging stream of life and being. The closer a form approaches the purest act, the more perfect it is and the less potentiality and materiality it has in its make-up. The closer a form is to prime matter the more imperfect it is. In this universe the greatest difference and contrast are found between the corporeal and spiritual worlds. A certain similarity does exist, however, in this, that in both spheres certain beings are found to be in the process of development toward their own perfection, and others are found to be in possession of their perfection. Body and spirit are not found to be without some point of contact. Corporeal things, souls, and spirits are found in the following gradation. In the lowest place are the forms of the elements out of which the composite bodies are formed. Above this lifeless grade is the realm of living things—plants, animals, and man—while the heavenly bodies rise above this sublunary world, and the pure spirits in turn are above the heavenly bodies. The highest point, the climax, as it were, is God.

St. Thomas likes to use the Aristotelian comparison of the specific forms with numbers. As in the realm of numbers each number increased by one is specifically different from its predecessor, so in the material and in the spiritual worlds some forms are more perfect than others by reason of their essential natures. The composite bodies excel the elements in perfection, plants rise higher than the composite bodies, animals are above the plants, and within each of these divisions because of grades of perfection there are also different species.

Thus among the elements, the earth is the highest and fire is the noblest. Similarly within the mineral kingdom, we find a gradation leading up to gold. In the vegetable kingdom the gradation rises to the more perfect trees, and among the animals it culminates in man. Certain animals are very close to the plants, namely, those that cannot move and possess only the sense of touch; certain plants are also very close to the inorganic beings. Therefore Aristotle compared the kinds of being to the kinds of numbers in which an increase or decrease by one changes the species. Immaterial beings are no less specifically distinguished according to their grade of perfection.

Wherever there is a difference of degree, it arises because of the relation of the various degrees to some principle. In this way material beings are measured according to their specific differences from prime matter. The lowest grades are the most imperfect, the higher grades are more perfect because they arise from additions to the lower grades. Thus composite bodies have what the elements have and more; plants, too, are thus higher than the minerals; and animals are higher than the plants.

The spiritual substances, however, are not measured according to prime matter but according to a comparison with the first and most perfect principle of being, God. The closer an immaterial substance approaches to God, and the more it resembles Him, the more perfection it contains in its being. The highest perfection of God consists in this, that in His simplicity He possesses the essence of all perfection.

As prime matter holds the lowest place among the species of sensible things, so the human soul takes the lowest place among spiritual beings, because it requires sensitive potencies for its intellectual activity, and these potencies in turn depend on corporeal organs. The principle that a thing acts according as it is in act, is understood in the sense that perfection in activity is measured according to perfection in being.

The realm of corporeal beings and of beings bound to corporiety is also the realm of becoming and destruction. Such beings can lose their natural goodness, and are subject to change, to the conflict between contradictories, and so also to passion and evil.

God created things in order to manifest His goodness externally. For this purpose one creature was not enough. Therefore He created a multiplicity of different forms of being that represent and manifest in a divided manner that goodness which is simple and undivided in God; but altogether in their harmony these creatures are the divine masterpiece.

Creatures are *repraesentationes* of the divine being; either they are *repraesentationes per modum vestigii,* as are all creatures, or they are *repraesentationes per modum imaginis,* as are those spiritual beings endowed with will and intellect.

The perfection of the universe does not allow many forms of being to be missing. Thus we find in the universe a twofold law of structure, one the general law of the analogy of being; the other the law of continuity, the absence of any gap in the series of being, in the sense that the end of one being is bound up with the beginning of another, that a lower order of being participates weakly in the next higher order, that the lower grade of being, although it does not contain the higher, is able to touch on it.

CHAPTER VIII

CORPOREAL THINGS

Following Aristotle, St. Thomas, in accordance with the state of natural science in his day, taught that the four elements (earth, water, air, and fire) were the ultimate integral parts of all corporeal beings in this sublunary world. These four elements are therefore basic in nature and arise directly from a union with prime matter. Aristotle and St. Thomas also taught that in a physical sense these elements are bodies that cannot be resolved into other bodies of different kinds, and that they are the bodies into which composite bodies are resolved.

Every physical body possesses besides quantity, a number of active and passive qualities because of which it is separated from other physical bodies and given its own place in the universal system of efficient causes. These active and passive qualities (warm, cold, wet, dry, etc.) are proper to these things, *propriae passiones,* and their disappearance is followed by the destruction of the element itself. The quality of a simple body is not to be identified with the substantial form, although it is active only by the power of the form and as its instrument.

The elements unite with each other and thus they form mixed bodies, such as the minerals, the bodies of plants, animals, and men. The forces of the elements produce different mixtures and different mixed bodies. These composite bodies are higher the farther they are removed from the opposition of the elements, and their nobility is also based on the perfection of the balance in the mixture and on their approach to the heavenly bodies which were thought to be without any opposition in their elemental structure. The best mixture of the elements is to be found in the human body, which therefore became the dwelling place for the noblest form, the human soul. Following Aristotle again, St. Thomas taught that water and earth predominate in the composite bodies because otherwise fire with its intensive energy would consume the other elements.

Through the centuries the question continued to be agitated, whether the elements from whose union the composite bodies were formed were destroyed; and if not, in what form they persevered in the union. The question was broadened to that of the oneness or plurality of substantial forms in a composite body possessing potencies and powers that are specifically different.

Aristotle laid the foundation for this discussion but he did not give a satisfactory solution. He clearly distinguishes a mixture from substantial becoming, and he does not call every union of bodies a mixture. A mixture or composition exists only when the elements are separate before the union and are again separable afterward. Aristotle concluded that in the composite the elements remained not actually but only potentially, thus making use again of that concept of potency to which he always turned in a difficulty. But potency and act can be taken to mean two things: act may denote either the substantial form or the activity of that form; and potency may denote the absence of actuality or only a cessation in activity. Aristotle did not indicate in which sense he intended his statement to be understood and thus gave rise to different solutions. He maintained that in the composite the entelechy of the elements remained, that in mixed beings opposition of the elements was suspended, but that the substantial forms remained, and, finally, that there may be change but no destruction of the elements. We will not be surprised, therefore, when such Aristotelians as Alexander of Aphrodisias, Simplicius, and especially Philoponus in their commentaries felt obliged to declare for the preservation of the elements in mixed bodies.

At the time when St. Thomas entered the controversy, the theory of the plurality of forms was unquestioned. It was admitted by Avicebron and the Arabians as well as by the masters of the Franciscan Order, by Alexander of Hales, St. Bonaventure, Roger Bacon, and St. Albert. Influenced by Avicenna, St. Albert taught that in the composite the substantial forms persevered and that this was the teaching of antiquity. The Averroists taught that the elements and the accidents, as they did not possess complete forms, thus allowed an increase or decrease in their forms. St. Albert did not decisively reject this theory nor did he admit it; he inclined rather to a theory that the elements had two forms, primary and secondary. It is the primary form that persists in the composite, for otherwise the elements could not reappear when the mixed body is dissolved nor could the properties of the elements perdure.

St. Thomas strikes out in another direction. He does not oppose his teacher, but he attacks the sources to which St. Albert was indebted. After some early hesitation in his commentary on the Sentences, in which he still teaches a *forma corporeitatis* independent of the other forms, he gradually developed his theory of the oneness of the substantial form. He now openly opposed Avicebron's theory of a series of forms according to the genus and species of the thing (*ordo formarum secundum ordinem generum et specierum*) and also the theories of Avicenna and Averroes. Avicenna thought that in a composite body the active and passive qualities of the elements were reduced to some middle third while the substantial forms remained, otherwise he thought there would not be a composition but a destruction of the elements. St. Thomas rejected that theory for various reasons. The different elementary forms could not be received by prime matter at once (*secundum idem*) for they would have to dwell in separate parts of the matter. The union of a part of matter with a substantial form produces a physical body, and thus there would be several physical bodies, supposedly occupying the same place at the same time. This theory would end in having many physical bodies, while a mixed body should have all of its parts homogeneous.

St. Albert thought it was only a difference of words between Avicenna and Averroes. St. Thomas, however, saw a real difference and concluded that the Averroistic theory contained the most errors. To avoid admitting only an apparent mixed body, Averroes did not allow the elements in the mixture to remain unchanged, but reduced them to a middle state. St. Thomas objected that the foundation for such a theory was the wholly un-Aristotelian theory that the elementary forms admitted an increase and a decrease, and that they were the most imperfect kind of forms, placed midway between the substantial and the accidental forms. But no middle can exist between substance and accident, any more than a middle between affirmation and denial. If the elementary forms admitted an increase and a decrease, it would lead to the impossible conclusion that the becoming and cessation of the elements was like a *motus continuus*.

St. Thomas defended a mixture of the elements in the composite which is truly a mixture but in which the elements are not wholly destroyed. The active and passive qualities of the elements are opposites which admit of increase and decrease. From such qualities as remain in the composite, even though they remain only in a weakened state (*remissae*), there arises a middle quality uniting the natures of both extremes in itself. This middle quality, different in different mixtures, forms the peculiar disposition necessary to receive the form of the composite body. The forms of the elements do not remain actually in the mixture, but only virtually, because each individual can have but one substantial form. Because of the soul, this individual is not only a man, but at the same time also an animal, living, a body, a substance and a being. Neither a substantial form nor an accidental form precedes this form in the individual, since prime matter is the immediate subject for the one substantial form. St. Thomas was trying to preserve the idea of the composite, but he was still more desirous of keeping his ontological principles intact. He held that a plurality of forms was altogether irreconcilable with the absolute simplicity and unity of the individual. If there were several forms, the individual would not be *unum simpliciter,* but only *unum secundum quid*. St. Bonaventure admitted a number of subordinate forms besides the principal form, and Roger Bacon thought that a plurality of forms could be reconciled with the unity of the thing in the same way that parts of a whole are included in the one body. St. Thomas maintained, however, that true unity cannot arise from several acts, but only from potency and act. The nature of substantial being is absolutely indivisible being, it is what it is or it is nothing at all. The first substantial form by its union with prime matter produces this something *in actu;* all subsequent forms are accidental forms and any change in them does not affect the substance of the thing. Finally, St. Thomas considered a plurality of forms as superfluous, because the higher and more perfect forms unite in themselves the powers of the lower forms.

By thus rejecting the idea of the perseverance of the elementary forms in the composite, he was following his preceptor Aristotle faithfully, but his interpretation of the Philosopher is not entirely correct. It is surprising that St. Thomas in rejecting the plurality of forms as a Platonic peculiarity was moved more by dialectical reasons than by the conclusions derived from experience. The great Scholastics, St. Albert and Roger Bacon, who were in touch with the

conclusions of the natural sciences, declared for the plurality of forms
because experience told them that the qualities of the elements were
active in the composite and that after a composite was dissolved the
elements reappeared. Modern natural science has corroborated their
view. In distinguishing between free and bound elements, St. Albert
expressed a modern thought. In trying to maintain the absolute unity
of a thing, and the absolute unity of the substantial form, with which
even Aristotle had had difficulties, St. Thomas overstressed the idea
of unity.

Not only the powers and activities of the elements are proper to the
form of composite bodies, but other nobler powers and activities
founded in the specific form. These nobler qualities appear in every
individual of the species, but in different degrees depending on the
disposition of the matter and on the different constellations thought
to be influential when the individual comes into existence.[1]

[1] *De occ. op. nat.*

CHAPTER IX

THE LIVING BEINGS ON EARTH

1. The soul. The soul transcends the entire order of corporeal things. A profound chasm separates the lifeless world from living beings. The ancient Greeks loved to interpret the whole world in analogies of life, they loved to see life in everything. That inclination comes to light in the hylozoism of the old Ionian school, and because of it Plato was moved to admit a world soul. Even the realistic Aristotle was induced to place life and movement very close together. St. Thomas was unable to think of the universe as a living thing. Movement may be somewhat like life, but it is not actually life; only a similarity exists here.

How is the lifeless distinguished from the living? What is the essential determination of life? Only by taking the measure of activity as the fundamental principle can the essential characteristic be determined (*operatio sequitur esse*). That characteristic by which life reveals itself primarily and fundamentally is self-movement, self-formation from within, and self-determination to its own peculiar activity.[1] This concept of life is so inclusive that it reaches out to all manifestations of life, from the lowest to the highest, even to the divine. The perfection of the various grades of life increases according to the perfection of the self-activity. In the lowest grade of life are the plants, whose activity is regulated in a determined direction by an inner natural form. Animals are higher since their principle of movement is not a natural form but a kind of knowledge transmitted through the senses. The more perfect the senses, the more perfect will be the self-movement.

Those animals that are endowed only with a sense of touch move themselves by contraction and expansion, like mussels, and their

[1] *Summa theol.*, IIIa, q. 35, a. 1 ad 1.

manifestation of life is little above the movement processes of the plants. Those animals that possess all the senses and are able to perceive even remote objects possess unrestricted movement. They obtain a cognitive form through the senses, and the purpose of their activity is predetermined according to their natures, while their activity itself is carried out under the direction of the sensible cognitive form. Higher than these animals is man, endowed as he is with reason. Because of his cognitive faculties he is able to predetermine and prearrange his own ends, he can distinguish between means and end and he is able to bring about the realization of those things whose value he has appreciated and for which he strives consciously.

From these observations we come to know the four grades of life: (1) vegetative life, (2) sensitive life without local motion, (3) sensitive life with local motion, (4) intellectual life. In distinguishing the different forms of life, St. Thomas often takes the lifeless bodies as a starting point, and later in the classification itself he sometimes changes the point of view of the distinction. That viewpoint may be the greater or less dependence on organs for vital activities, or the perfection of the actions of the soul-principle, or the different end terms of the vital activity. The last viewpoint distinguishes not only plants, animals, men, but also the human, angelic, and divine knowledge from one another.

Wherever there is life, we also find a soul, that is, a special principle of the vital activities. In company with Aristotle, St. Thomas rejects a great number of concepts about the nature of the soul, among them the materialist concept, Galen's concept of the soul as a *complexio,* and the Pythagorean definition that the soul is harmony. The last two theories will evoke only passing interest, but the opposition to the materialist concept is of fundamental significance.

For St. Thomas, death was a proof of life. When the parts of a body disintegrate in death, the fact points to the existence of some principle that formerly held them together. If the soul were really a body and extended throughout the whole body, then two bodies would be in one and the same place. The acceptance of a materialist principle makes it impossible to account for such things as movement and growth, perception, cognition, and volition. The soul, therefore, is an immaterial, non-quantitative principle, and, being immaterial, it is not composed of matter and form.

Aristotle found fault with the definitions of the soul as the principle of motion and the principle of knowledge, and he laid down the requirement that the definition of the soul must apply to all kinds of souls and must take into consideration the necessary relation to the body. St. Thomas reiterated these demands, and he extended the relation of matter and form to the body and the soul, accepting a definition of the soul as the essential form of the body, or more precisely, as the first act of a physical body endowed with the power to live, and therefore an organic body. He had learned from Aristotle that every part of this definition is important. In the composite of a living being, the body is the matter and the soul is the form. The soul gives a body a special kind of existence, namely, life; since the disappearance of the soul is the signal for the cessation of all vital activity and the dissolution of the body.

If the term form-substance is to be replaced by that of act, it is intended to signify the soul as the principle that confers completion and actuality and the resulting condition of actual being. The expression *primary entelechy* means that the body receives from the soul primary reality and completion together with a certain number of dispositions for activity, although these dispositions are not immediately exercised. The distinction between possibility and reality that dominates all nature returns here and signifies the difference between the dispositions of the soul and their actualization. Moreover, St. Thomas points out that the term *first act, primary act,* excludes not only all act that is activity, or second act, but also the elementary forms which are always active unless they are hindered. The term *physical* excludes all artificial products and also the mathematical bodies. The enlivened body is an organic body because the soul is related to the body as art is to the artistic object, or as art to its instrument. The heart is the first of the organs because by it all other parts are set in motion. He finds a hierarchy among organic beings since the number of organs increases as the soul is found to be more perfect.

Aristotle bequeathed to the Middle Ages a very broad concept of the soul. The soul is not identical with consciousness, it is not *substantia cogitans,* but it is the principle of life (ἀρχὴ τῶν ξῴων). The biological viewpoint seems to predominate over the psychological in Aristotle's mind. When St. Thomas transferred the relationship of matter and form to the body and soul, a fundamental change was made in the Platonic-Augustinian concept of body and soul. Now body and soul were not thought of as separate individual principles but as two partial principles of one and the same substance, or as two integral parts that constitute a substantial, harmonious composite by reason of their inner mutual relations.

2. **The unity of the soul.** The foregoing observations were of no small value in solving the problem of the unity of the soul. Plato himself had been disconcerted by the problem whether it is one and the same power by which we effect the many diverse activities of the soul or whether we possess three different powers analogous to the three kinds of activity of the soul. Ultimately Plato decided for the latter alternative and distinguished between the appetitive, the audacious, and the rational parts of the soul. Each of these parts of the soul expresses itself in some vital activity, and yet, although these parts are different, Plato concluded that the soul possesses some kind of unity. In his *Phaedrus,* he compared this unity to that of a span of horses and the driver, and in his *Republic* with the unity of a chimera in which the form of a man, a lion, and a many-headed monster are joined together. Although the various parts in man are quite autonomous and sometimes antagonistic, they are all subject to the rule of the individual person. The rational part, according to Plato, is the real human being, in which self-consciousness is reposed, and which knows the rules for the activity of itself and also of the other parts of the soul.

Plato, therefore, in spite of this subjection to the rule of the rational part, considers that the parts of the soul are really distinct. Aristotle, however, without denying the multiplicity of the soul's activities, concludes for the unity of the soul. If the soul were constituted by a multiplicity of things, what would be the principle uniting this multiplicity into unity? Manifestly it is the entire soul that holds together the whole body. If the soul consists of parts, we cannot escape the conclusion that certain parts of the body are held together by certain parts of the soul. How will reason hold a part of the body together, and which part would that be? The concept of the soul as something fundamentally one obviates all these difficulties and is supported by the fact that plants and certain animals (insects) continue to live after they are divided, and are able to perform the same actions (sense perception and local motion) as before. The different parts obviously have the same soul as the whole living being, a soul not the same numerically but specifically the same, and in every individual this soul is one and it is divisible inasmuch as the same soul is found to be present in the various parts of the whole. When the parts are no longer able to perform vital actions, the cause is to be found in the fact that they no longer have the necessary corporeal organs. As the various powers of a certain kind of soul are anchored in the unity of that soul principle, we obtain a hierarchy of plant, animal, and human souls in which the next higher grade unites in itself the powers of the lower orders of souls. Just as mathematical figures in the higher forms include in themselves the figures of lower forms, e.g., the quadrangle contains the triangle, so the higher forms in the hierarchy of souls are related to the lower. Every living being is informed by one soul in which the different vital powers are rooted as in a dynamic center. In these souls the higher power always possesses the dominant and decisive place and it lends its name to this grade of living beings.

St. Thomas adopted these arguments. Only when one principle is to the other as act is to potency will the form unite immediately with the matter, and here the soul unites with the body without any external bond of union and thus represents a true unity. Plato was unable to progress forward to the concept of the oneness of the soul. According to St. Thomas he was prevented from reaching this conclusion because of his concept of the soul's relationship to the body. Plato taught that the soul was not indeed the form of the body but the mover of the body and that it resided in the body as a pilot is in the ship. By attributing the different movements of the body to different movers and subordinating one to the other, the oneness of the ship was indeed not put in jeopardy. Furthermore, Plato was attached to his principle that the existence of things depended on their participation in corresponding ideas. Socrates, for example, is a living being because of his participation in the idea of living being, he is a man because he participates in the idea of man. This participation in various ideas makes man appear as something pieced together, and precludes a genuine unity. Accepting the concept of act and its relation to the substratum, St. Thomas rejected all plurality of souls and forms in the organism. The body receives all the various grades of perfection from one and the same form. The division of the soul into three autonomous parts and their localization in the head, heart, and liver were not acceptable to St. Thomas. Reason cannot exist in a bodily organ. Finally, the mutual balance and check between the activities of the soul point to a common root in one principle.

3. The soul and its powers. Because of the soul's simplicity, Avicenna identified it with its powers and potencies, and St. Bonaventure concurred in this opinion. St. Thomas and Aristotle, however, maintained a real distinction between the soul and its powers. This was demanded by their ontological principles. Act and potency are in the same genus; if the act is not identical with the essence, then the potency is not to be identified with the essence. Only in God are essence and activity identical. If the soul were the immediate principle of action, we should find it in the perpetual exercise of these activities. This is, of course, not true. As first act the soul is the essential form of a particular kind of life and it is ordered toward the second act, to the expression of life. The essence of the soul is not the immediate principle of activity; it has its effects through accidental principles. The substantial form is the first principle of action but not the immediate principle.

The potencies or powers of the soul do not belong to the essence of the soul, they are rather accidents of the soul. The natural properties that flow from the essence of the soul stand midway between the essence of the soul and its activities. Since the activities of the soul are different in kind, they cannot be directly attributed to one and the same principle, but they must be conceived as grounded in different potencies. These powers must be of various kinds in order that the soul and the organism may attain its final end. Every potency is a principle of action and passion (*principium quoddam agendi et patiendi*); every potency is related to the action, and receives its name from its own particular action. The potencies of the soul are differentiated according to their different activities, in conformity with the ontological principle: *unumquodque operatur inquantum est ens.* The actions again are differentiated by reason of the difference in the objects, that is, the formal objects. A change of objects does not in itself require a difference in the potencies, but only when there is a change in that particular thing to which the potency is directed *per se.*

Again, in agreement with Aristotle, St. Thomas distinguishes between three kinds of souls (*tres animae*), four modes of life (*quattuor modi vivendi*), and five potencies of the soul. The difference in the souls is based on the degree to which a particular soul rises above the powers of a corporeal body. The rational soul rises so far above the body that it does not even require a corporeal organ for its activities; the sensitive soul indeed requires a corporeal organ, but no corporeal quality, whereas the vegetative soul is active only by means of a corporeal organ and with the help of corporeal qualities.

The modes of life are based on the various grades of life (*secundum gradus viventium*). Plants have only vegetative life, certain animals, besides the vegetative life, possess also sensitive life without local motion, the more perfect animals possess also the faculty of local motion. Man, besides possessing all these faculties, is distinguished by his reason. According to St. Thomas, the appetitive faculties do not form the basis for a mode of life.

The five potencies of the soul are differentiated according to their objects. The vegetative potency of the soul has as its object only the body that is united to that soul. The next two potencies of the soul have objects that are beyond the body to which the soul is united, the sensitive potency that perceives all sensible bodies and the intellectual potency that extends to being in general. Inasmuch as the soul is directed to objects that are external, it has also the faculties of appetite and local motion. The subordinate potencies of the soul will be considered later in detail.

The potencies of the soul may be active or passive. They are differentiated by reason of their objects; if the object is passive and undergoes a change, the potency is active; if the object is active, then the potency is passive. The vegetative potencies are active because the food is changed into nourishment and reproduction; the sensitive potencies are passive since they are changed and actualized by their objects. The spiritual potencies are partly active and partly passive since the intellect is itself partly active and partly passive. With regard to the passive potencies of the soul, the objects are principles and efficient causes, and with regard to the act of a passive potency they are the end and purpose of the potency.

A threefold order may be discerned among the soul's faculties. *Secundum naturam* the perfect faculties are prior to those less perfect, thus the sensitive potencies are prior to the vegetative. According to time, however, the less perfect potencies are prior to the more perfect faculties, thus the vegetative are prior to the sensitive in time. Some potencies are in a certain order by reason of their objects, and so sight, hearing, and smell are ordered because the object is first seen, then heard, and finally smelt.

The essence of the soul is the principle from which flow all the soul's faculties, but the soul is not the subject in which all potencies reside. The soul is the subject only for the reason and the will; the vegetative and sensitive faculties have as their subject the composite of the body and the soul.

CHAPTER X

THE DIFFERENT GRADES OF LIFE THE PLANT, THE VEGETATIVE SOUL

The lowest form of life is the vegetative soul, which is found in plants as their principle of life, and also in animals and men as a part of their souls. This vegetative principle is found in all stages of the development of a living being; it is found in the embryo, and also in the seed and germ because they possess the faculties of growth and development. In this sublunary world this temporal life that will pass away is dependent on this vegetative power because the preservation of species and individuals is dependent on the process of reproduction. In explaining this vegetative principle of life, St. Thomas followed his master, Aristotle, faithfully in all the essentials. The chief faculties of this principle are the potencies of nourishment, growth, and (after maturity) reproduction. St. Thomas rejects the explanation of the vegetative process as simply the interaction of the elements without an actual vital principle. St. Thomas argued that elements that had such contrary tendencies as fire and water could not suffice to bring forth the harmonious structure of an organism. He admitted that fire had certain powers of nourishment and increase and that it might be a co-cause of the process of life, but he thought that it alone could not be the cause of life. The fundamental difference between the growth of an organism and the increase of fire was that every living being grew within a form strictly determined by nature, while fire increased as long as fuel was present, i.e., it increased indefinitely. Furthermore, the growth of the organism represented its own preservation in all its identical parts, while the fire continued because it consumed new pieces of wood one after another. To express this in the modern manner: inorganic processes certainly

participate in the vital processes, and the science of inorganic beings
will throw some light on the problem of life, but it cannot completely
explain the entire phenomenon of life. Only when we admit a special
principle of life do the phenomena of the inner reception and adaptation of food for the purpose of self-preservation become intelligible.

The actual principle of nourishment is the vegetative soul. This
particular body is nourished by this soul that informs it, and the
means of the nourishment is food. Nourishment prevents the dis-
integration of the body, it furthers growth and full maturity, it
contributes to the formation of the seed, and is the means of reproduction. Nourishment, therefore, is closely related to the organism. The
nourishment of plants consists of the four elements, especially water
and earth, which are absorbed from the soil through the roots of the
plant which are its mouth. With the help of the plant's warmth
the nourishment is digested and transmitted to the various parts of the
plant. That nourishment not actually required for the support of life
is used for the formation of the seed and the fruit, and these in turn
include within themselves the conditions necessary for the existence
of a new organism.

The nourishment process of animals is far more complicated. The
mouth with its teeth, the stomach with the entrails, and the heart,
assisted by a number of lesser organs such as the liver and the spleen,
divide among themselves the task of preparing food for its reception
by the body. The mouth and teeth serve to masticate the food, in the
stomach the food is digested and transformed into a fluid. Certain
vessels transmit this fluid nourishment to the heart where the process
of blood manufacture is terminated. The nourishment of animals consists of inorganic matter, and especially of plants and other animals,
all of which again are composed of the four elements. In their various
combinations, these four elements are called primary nourishment,
and when they have undergone the aforementioned qualitative
changes they are called final nourishment, namely, when they have
been changed into blood and have become assimilable by the body.
The blood streams out from the heart through the arteries into the
whole body, delivering to all parts of the body the matter necessary
for their nourishment and growth. Nourishment, in the real meaning of the word, consists of sweets and of fats which are closely related
to the sweets, since both of these qualities by reason of their lightness
are easily cooked by the body's warmth. Things that are heavy and

bitter, on the other hand, are cast aside by the body as useless. The second potency, growth, serves the body in its attainment of the required quantity.

The third vegetative potency is that of reproduction. Whenever three potencies are anchored in one principle, they do not stand side by side without concern for one another; they always have some relationship to one another, and in a way exist for one another. This teleological mutual relationship is a fundamental principle of Aristotelian and Thomistic natural science. Nourishment serves growth, and growth serves the faculty of reproduction. While nourishment and growth are completed within the body to which they belong, reproduction produces another, new being. St. Thomas defined the limit of the plant's activity as coterminous with the realm of the plant's sense perception. The vegetative principle has only the limited task of preserving the life stream that courses through the organism and of bringing it to its fullest development. One of its functions, however, takes it without the limits of its own organism. The faculty of reproduction approaches the dignity of the sensitive soul which reaches out to external things. This potency of reproduction is the most important and the most perfect of the vegetative potencies, since the final purpose of all living beings, as far as their vegetative life is concerned, is not nourishment and growth but the production of another being of the same species. Every being can best be classified according to its final end, and thus the soul in this stage can best be conceived as the faculty that is directed toward the production of another being specifically the same. The urge of reproduction stands above the preservation of the individual and serves the preservation of the species and thus, according to Plato and Aristotle, secures the participation of the species in the eternal and divine. This continual renewal and preservation of the species is an ultimate fact which need not be referred to any other. The urge to reproduction is anchored deeply in the meaning of all being and is closely bound up with the value of all being as contrasted with non-being and the negative. Being is obviously a value, and the concept of being is a teleological concept. "Being is manifestly better than non-being, life is better than non-life, and among beings the living are better than the lifeless, the soul is better than the body. Therefore we have reproduction and for this purpose the distinction between male and female in nature, and from this follows the continual renewal of being and life." [1] St. Thomas accepted this Aristotelian judgment of values and Aristotle's method of referring all natural phenomena to their most profound metaphysical meaning.

The vegetative principle is active by means of three potencies, but it is always the same principle that resides in the seed and the germ cell, provides growth and nourishment until full maturity, at the height of vitality sets aside what is not needed for nourishment for the purpose of reproduction, and when the body is fully developed and reproduction has attained its end it does not disappear immediately but continues to function as a nutritive factor in the period of its decline and corruption. The vegetative principle does not accomplish all this alone, but makes use of auxiliary causes. Thus the active and passive qualities possess an instrumental function. Chief among these qualities is warmth, which belongs to all parts of the body and participates in all the vegetative functions, in the processes of digestion, nourishment, growth, and reproduction.

These ancient scientific explanations have, for the greater part, been revised by modern science. They are of little importance. But the ontological interpretation of the vegetative stage of life is still significant. St. Thomas' axiom is well known: the manner of activity reveals the manner of being. An organism is not a machine, composed of added parts; it forms its own parts. The life of the organism is an activity that proceeds and emanates from within the organism (*emanatio*), i.e., the organism accepts certain materials, transforms them, assimilates them, and forms them into various different members of itself. The plant soul, however, represents the lowest form of this vital emanation. Whereas the spiritual soul completes its activities without a corporeal organism and stands thus high above the body, and whereas the animal soul requires corporeal organs for its activities but no disposition of the corporeal qualities, the activity of the plant is of such a low order that it depends not only on the corporeal organs but also on the assistance of corporeal qualities. Among the vital principles the vegetative principle more than any other is bound to matter and subjected to physico-chemical forces. In explaining the various kinds of self-movement, St. Thomas accords the plant the lowest degree, that of movement from within toward externals.

[1] *De gen. animal.*, II, 1.

Three factors are responsible for the order found in the process of movement: the end, the form, and the execution. Everything that acts has an end or purpose, acts by reason of its own form, and the execution of the movement sometimes introduces the use of an instrument. In contrast to the animal, and especially to man, the end and the form of the movement in the plant are predetermined by nature in the plant. Only the execution of the movement properly belongs to the plant.

St. Thomas also judges the result of an activity from the standpoint of its inwardness. The higher any being is, the more inward will be that which is produced by that being, *quanto aliqua natura est altior, tanto id, quod ex ea emanat, magis est intimum*.[2] "In the lowest place we find the lifeless bodies in which every development requires the influence of an external body. . . . Next we find the plants. Here the fruit indeed comes from within and, being placed in the earth, produces another plant. The plant's imperfection is immediately manifest. The fruit, produced indeed from within, leaves the plant and as a product is totally outside it. The sap of the tree ceases to be within the tree in order to become the flower and the fruit which have only a tenuous connection with the tree. At maturity the fruit leaves the tree, falls to the ground, and from its seed produces a new plant. Indeed to be exact in our observation, we may say that the beginning of the formation of the fruit lies outside the plant inasmuch as the plant derives its nourishment from without through its roots."[3] When the plant concludes its task with the formation of the flower and the seed and the production of a new member of the species, it has revealed its essential purpose, the preservation of the species. The importance of the individual is far surpassed by the importance of the species.

[2] *Summa theol.*, Ia, q.18, a.3.
[3] *Contra Gent.*, IV, 11.

CHAPTER XI

THE ANIMAL

The sensitive principle of life in animals is likewise the vegetative principle, fulfilling the vital vegetative functions on which the sensitive functions are founded. In the exercise of its functions and in its entire being, the sensitive soul is completely dependent on corporeal organs, it is entirely limited by the body, merged in the body with which it begins to exist and with which it also ceases to exist. The senses have their seat in the heart; they are affected by external objects and may even be destroyed by superior force. Relying on his Aristotelian principles, St. Thomas rejected Plato's concept of the subsistence of the animal soul. Since the animal soul does not subsist in itself, it is not directly created by God, but comes into being in the natural process of generation. Every activity of the sensitive soul is attributed to the composite, and the sensitive potencies have as their subject the composite although they are derived from the soul as their principle.[1]

Under the influence of his teleological viewpoint in the study of the animal's soul and organism, St. Thomas proposes at the outset the axiom that nature has equipped every organism with all that is necessary for it to attain the purpose of its existence. The sensitive being possesses every activity that belongs to the concept of a complete sensitive being. Besides the faculty of local motion, the sensitive being is completely endowed with the sense faculties. The faculty of local motion is of such importance in the mind of St. Thomas, that he makes it the reason for his division of animals into great classes, those they are able to move and those that are immovable. In what does this complete endowment of the sense faculties consist?

1. **The sense faculties.** Normally the sensitive soul possesses five external senses (animated organs) whose business it is to perceive,

[1] *Contra Gent.*, II, 82.

not the essences of things, but the external accidents. Each of the five senses is directed to an object entirely proper and peculiar to itself, which it alone can perceive. Thus the sense of sight is directed to color, and hearing to sound. Besides these proper sense objects (*sensibilia propria*), we find objects common to several of the senses (*sensibilia communia*), such as movement, rest, figure and size, number and unity. These are common to the senses in that number, movement, and rest are perceived by all five senses, and all five objects are perceivable by the senses of sight and touch.

The number of the senses is not derived from the various organs differentiated by the predominance in them of air or water, or from the various kinds of media which may be connected with the senses or be separated from them, and finally not from various natures of the sensitive qualities. The number of the senses, St. Thomas continues, could not come from the nature of the organs, since the faculties do not exist because of the organs, but the organs exist for the senses. The number of the senses does not come from the second reason because again the media derive their fitness from the senses and not vice versa, and not for the last cause because the sensitive qualities are conceived as belonging to the reason rather than to the senses.

The senses are passive potencies that suffer a change from external objects. The difference in the changes determines the differentiation of the senses. St. Thomas speaks of two kinds of changes in the senses, one that is natural, and the other that is immaterial. The first he finds wherever the form of that producing the change is received in its natural state by that which is changed, e.g., as warmth is received by that which is warmed. The second he finds whenever a form is received according to its immaterial being. Such immaterial change is proper to the activity of the senses, for if a natural change were sufficient, then every body that suffered change would perceive something. The different senses arise from the fact that some of them experience purely immaterial changes whereas in others the changes are somehow bound up with natural changes. In the sense of sight the change is purely immaterial; in hearing and smell, besides the immaterial change, a natural change takes place in the sense object since the object of hearing consists of a natural change in the movement of the air, and since in smell the object is perceived only when a body affected by warmth emits odors. The senses of taste and touch experience changes in their sense organs. The hand is warmed when it touches warmth, the tongue is moistened by the moisture from tasteful things. Since the sense of sight is not subject to any natural change, it is the most immaterial. It is the most perfect of the senses.

After the sense of sight, St. Thomas places the faculties of hearing and smell, and of these two, hearing is the more important because the local motion involved in hearing is superior to the qualitative change involved in the sense of smell. The senses of touch and taste are merged in matter more than the others.

In agreement with Aristotle, St. Thomas accepts the number of five senses as conclusive and he also accepts Aristotle's reasons for this conclusion. Sensation is of vital importance for the animal. Because the animal has a body composed of a mixture of the four elements, it must be able to maintain the proper relation between cold and warmth and between moisture and dryness in order to escape dissolution. The maintenance of this balance is the task of the sense of touch. For this reason both Aristotle and St. Thomas consider the sense of touch the most necessary of all the senses and the foundation for the others. Touch comes into immediate contact with the texture of the outside world and keeps the animal informed about it and thus is able to ward off any destructive influence. However, since food is not obtained by immediate contact, the animal requires some kind of perception or knowledge. The knowledge of food that is at hand is obtained through the sense of taste, of food that is at a distance it is obtained through the sense of smell. The senses of sight and hearing pertain to the whole of those things that are necessary for the support of the animal's life. Touch and taste must not be lacking in any animal; all five senses are the mark of the perfect animal.

Although plants are entirely lacking in any knowledge of the things that they require, the lowest form of animals, without the faculty of local motion, do possess knowledge of necessaries when these are immediately present. The higher animals endowed with sight, hearing, and smell have knowledge of things that are not present to them either in order to seek them or to escape them. St. Thomas and Aristotle agree in denying that plants have any knowledge, but they concede it to animals even in the lowest grades. The Thomistic principle is that knowledge is accorded only to immaterial beings, and the immateriality and the perfection of the knowledge is judged according to the universality of the knowledge. Animal knowledge possesses a certain amount of immateriality because it receives the form without the matter. It is the lowest form of knowledge, however, because the whole cognitive process takes place in a corporeal organ. It is far inferior to human knowledge because it is limited to objects of the external world and to individuals alone.

For St. Thomas, as for Aristotle before him, sense and sensation mean more than mere sense perception (*apprehensio*); the activity of the senses includes a judgment. Sense perception is not always simply passivity; when it is complete it includes some activity on the part of the senses themselves and may be called knowledge (*quoddam cognoscere*). St. Thomas identifies this sense activity as the judgment about the proper objects of a sense, and this judgment, he says, is always true except when some obstacle exists in the organ or in the medium of sensation. This ability to make a judgment extends yet farther, since the senses are able to decide about objects that fall under their competence, e.g., they can distinguish between sweet and sour, and between white and black, etc. Animals are able to recognize things as they are, but they do not possess the consciousness of the knowledge of truth, i.e., the agreement of the subjective concept with the object.

For the complete exercise of its vital activity, a sensible being requires knowledge that rises above mere sense perception, as well as the ability to recall the past into its cognitive field. The complete sense endowment of a being therefore includes not only the five external senses but also the four inner senses. The first of these is the common sense (*sensus communis*), to which the objects of all five senses are proper. Aristotle had taught that this *sensus communis* has two functions; the apprehension of the perceptions of the various external senses, their distinction and classification and reference to their proper object, and secondly, the consciousness of its own perceptions. By this sense the individual knows that it hears, sees and smells. In it the activities of the five senses unite as in their primary and common principle. The *sensus communis* is related to the five senses as the point is to the various lines that converge in it, and at the same time it forms the basis for the imagination and the memory inasmuch as these presuppose the activity of the *sensus communis*. The heart is the organ through which the common sense acts.

The phantasy or imagination is the faculty that preserves the sense contents and forms and renews them; it is the treasury containing the forms produced by the external senses. It transmits to the sense appetite the representation of that which is not present, and it makes dreaming possible.

Sensible beings not only perceive sense contents, they also apprehend non-sense relations (*intentiones*), a knowledge that goes deeper, to something beyond mere sense contents. By means of sight and hearing, animals know their young and they recognize certain conditions, such as the harmfulness or usefulness of a thing. Animals have a certain knowledge of things (*substantiales conceptiones*); thus the lamb knows the wolf to be its enemy and it flees; and the bird sees that straw is useful for building a nest. These unreflective judgments are arrived at differently from those in man; they do not arise from a conscious joining of ideas but from the animal's natural instinct.

The animal also is capable of making value judgments. This capacity is called instinct, and by it the animal receives certain knowledge and is driven on to certain attitudes. This faculty of judging values (*vis aestimativa*) is related to the sensible appetite as the practical reason is related to the will, except that this faculty is confined to the individual. In the analogous faculty in man, because of the union of sensitive life and reason, the individual is apprehended by means of the universal species; the animal, however, knows the individual only inasmuch as it is the principle or end of an action or passion. All objects that do not belong to the field of action and passion are removed from the sphere of the animal's instinct. The sheep does not individualize this lamb as this lamb but only in so far as it gives it suck; it knows this plant only in so far as it is nourishment. Other things are of import to the animal only inasmuch as they are desirable or repulsive.

The complete endowment of a sensitive being requires also the faculty of memory. St. Thomas accords this faculty only to those animals that have some perception of time, but not to the immovable animals that perceive only those things with which they come into immediate contact. Memory is the custodian of the non-sensitive impressions that are derived from sensible objects, i.e., *intentiones particulares*. Memory is closely connected with instinct as with its principle with which it forms a specific entity. In agreement with Avicenna, St. Thomas repudiates the thought that memory and the phantasy are passions of the *sensus communis*. He considers them separate potencies based on different principles of activity, since the reception and preservation of sensations are dependent on different organs of the body.

The faculty of memory extends in two directions: it remembers those things already experienced and also the fact that it had the sensation. Clearly two things are contained here, namely, that the sensitive being distinguishes between the present moment and the past moment by virtue of its memory and has therefore some consciousness of time; and secondly that it recognizes an object previously perceived in the remembered object. St. Thomas does not grant to the animal any self-consciousness, but accords it only to man. The faculty of imagination in the animal is governed by the laws of association. From multiplied memories comes experience upon which the training of the animal is based. Avicenna speaks of a fifth internal sense, that unites and separates the imaginative forms (*mediam inter aestimativam et imaginativam*); but St. Thomas discards it.

2. **The sensitive appetite.** The inner structure of sensitive beings comprises not only the cognitive faculty but also necessarily the sensitive appetite. The cognitive equipment of animals does not function for itself, it is not an end in itself, but it is in the service of the appetite. All nature is built up according to an analogy, and thus to every higher grade in the hierarchy of being, a higher kind of appetite has been given. God, the first cause of all finite being, gave the different species of being not only their specific natures, but also certain principles and powers of striving which He ordered to Himself as the final cause. In every being there is a natural tendency, *desiderium naturale,* implanted by the Creator, by which the being strives for that which makes for the good and perfection of this particular being. Thus in each of the lower forms of being we find a natural inclination to that which is proper for it; living beings endowed with knowledge possess higher appetitive faculties. While inorganic beings and plants follow the direction of a natural urge, the appetite of animals and human beings extends to those things presented by the senses and the intellect. By delimiting it from below and from above, St. Thomas sought to clarify the concept of the sensitive appetite.

The natural appetite of plants, like all natural striving, is directed to the good, but there is no knowledge of the goal or any consciousness of motives for striving for the goal. The human will, however, reaches out for the end and the relationship between the action and the end. Therefore it apprehends directly the reason why a thing is desirable and is directed primarily to the good and useful, in a word, to something universal that may be actualized in many things, and thus the human will is directed only secondarily to this or that particular thing inasmuch as it contains goodness or value.

The sensitive appetite stands midway between the plant appetite and the human will. Like the rational appetite it goes out to some apprehended goal, and in this action the perceived good functions as the motive or *movens appetitum,* but throughout this process the sensitive appetite is directed to this particular good and does not apprehend the reasons of the desirability. On the one hand the sensitive appetite is not so bereft of consciousness as is the plant striving, and on the other it is not as wide in extension as is the human will. The knowledge of a thing as good and useful precedes the operation of the sensitive appetite and releases the activity of the appetite. The sensitive appetite and the human will have this in common: that both presuppose the transmission of a concept of the object by the senses, the imagination, or the intellect. While the human will possesses freedom of choice, the animal has no power over its appetite and is obliged by an inner necessity to strive for what it perceives to be desirable. The animal, it is true, possesses the principle of obedience, but it has no reason that would be able to command. It lacks all self-determination. The animal possesses the impulse or urge (*impetus*), but no power over itself (*imperium*). Therefore the animal has no power of giving or refusing assent to its striving, or of applying its appetite to some action or, of the power of making conscious use of anything. It lacks these faculties because it has no intellect with which to comprehend the relationship between action and end. All of the animal's activities ensue by reason of its instinct. St. Thomas offers a reason for this limitation: The sensitive appetite is a passive potency of the composite, possessing a corporeal organ and therefore subject to the dispositions of matter and corporeity, whose peculiarity it is rather to be moved than to move. The condition of animals cannot be more succinctly characterized than in these words of St. Thomas: *"magis aguntur quam agunt."* The animal requires no norm or rule above itself, since it bears in its own vital organization an immutable rule. Therefore the animal knows no ethics. Wherever a rule or norm is erected over an animal, it is injected by man in order that the animal may be made to serve man's purposes.

Following Aristotle, who in turn had followed Plato, St. Thomas divided the sensitive appetite into the concupiscible and the irascible. Even in the lowest form, in the natural appetite of inorganic beings, we find a twofold activity, the striving toward what will preserve nature and a defense action against what may destroy nature. The first function is rather receptive, the other more active. Together with Avicenna, St. Thomas taught that receptivity and activity in the soul always belong to different potencies. The proper object of the concupiscible appetite is that which is desirable as presented to it by the senses; the irascible appetite has for its object that which is arduous, *aliquid arduum*. These two powers are not, however, entirely disconnected from each other: the irascible appetite is the fighting vanguard that clears the way for the unhampered activity of the concupiscible appetite. To elucidate the question, both Aristotle and St. Thomas make use of the illustration of the animal's fight for food and the subsequent sexual intercourse.

In the animal, perception and striving are intimately bound together, and the bond uniting them is the desirable and the undesirable, for it is only the sensible content of what is perceived by the perception or recalled to the imagination that excites the appetite. St. Thomas distinguishes between three stages in the animal's vital process: the perception of sensible objects as favorable or harmful, the consequent apprehension of these things as desirable or undesirable, and finally the striving after the desirable and the avoidance of the undesirable. Not every appetitive action, however, originates because of some sensible object presented to the senses; the perception of inner conditions such as hunger, thirst, sexual desires, which are made known to the animal through the common sense, also lead to appetitive actions. If the means for satisfaction of a desire are not immediately presented, the imaginative mechanism is set in motion, the memory furnishes some object that will satisfy, and then the search for it is begun.

The animal constitution is also composed of certain affections or passions, which play an important part in the psychic make-up of the animal. St. Thomas speaks of different meanings of the word *"passio."* In its broadest sense it means susceptibility, and thus it can be predicated of all creatures inasmuch as every creature has in it some potentiality. In a narrower sense, passion means a change in which the thing affected receives something and casts off something.

This kind of passion, which connotes motion and is found only where there are opposites, necessarily requires a body and is found only in such creatures as are composed of body and soul.

To determine the meaning of the concept of passion, St. Thomas views it from four different angles. In conformity with the idea of passion, the factor that releases its activity should be something opposite and detrimental, not something pleasant and favorable, because passion denotes the change from a normal condition to the opposite. The change effected in passion is caused by some external agent, not by something internal, and furthermore this change must be total, not partial, it must be intensive and actual, not merely imperceptible. The seat of the passions is not the soul alone, but the composite of body and soul. The soul possesses passions only accidentally, inasmuch as it is joined to the body. Sometimes passions are predicated of the soul because it is the form of the body and thus certain changes, as, for instance, injuries to the body, react on the soul; again, the soul is the mover of the body, using the body to execute its activities.

Because of this twofold relation of the soul to the body, St. Thomas distinguishes between spiritual and corporeal passions: corporeal passions are such as originate in the body and have their term in the soul, and spiritual passions which are certain reactions of the soul leading to corporeal changes. The reason for this distinction is the origin of the passion in either body or soul. Essentially the passions are something psychic in form, and materially they are corporeal changes. They do not belong to the cognitive faculty but to the appetitive powers. Corresponding to the division of the appetitive faculty into the concupiscible and irascible potencies, the passions of both potencies are specifically different. The object of the concupiscible appetite is the good and bad presented by sensible perception. Those passions, therefore, that deal with the desirable and the undesirable, belong to the concupiscible appetite: joy, sadness, love, hatred, etc. The object of the irascible appetite is the good and bad, but in so far as the obtaining of the good or the warding off of the evil connotes some difficulty, something arduous. The passions of the irascible appetite, therefore, are daring, fear, hope, etc.

In the concupiscible appetite we may also distinguish according to the proximity of the object, namely, love and desire, joy and hatred, fear and sadness. In the irascible appetite, in the fight for the good, the knowledge of insurmountable obstacles may produce the passion of despair, and the knowledge of the possibility of overcoming the obstacles produces the passion of hope. With regard to the evil that is not present, fear or bravery arise, according as the evil may or may not be overcome. When the present evil can be overcome, hatred arises, but when it cannot be overcome there is no affection of the irascible appetite but only the passion of sadness in the concupiscible appetite. All of these passions may appear in various grades of intensity.

In both divisions of passions, some are more fundamental than others. These are prior to the others and it is from them that the others develop. The fundamental passions in the concupiscible appetite are joy and sadness; in the irascible appetite, hope and fear. The passions of both appetitive faculties are not, however, entirely unrelated. The irascible power is implanted in a being to overcome those obstacles that stand in the way of the concupiscible faculty in its positive striving for the good.

3. **Instinct.** The highest manifestation of animal life is instinct. The higher we go in the grades of animal life, the more perfectly equipped do we find the various kinds of animal life. Because of their sense of values and their memory, and also because of the supporting faculties of sight and hearing, the more perfect animals seem to possess a faculty similar to reason (*similitudo rationis*), a kind of prudence that directs their actions (*prudentia, directiva in agendis*). These animals enjoy the use of certain principles of action, certain norms for individual actions, although they are not general principles. Their activities are carried out with the greatest purposefulness and are directed to some future object as if some wise foresight were at the helm. Their activities serve the preservation of the individual and of the species. Blindly, without reflection, without forethought, animals follow the natural law, but in their obedience to the law there is no hesitation, nor do they have the support and benefit of any foregoing experience. St. Thomas compares the manner of their activity with the natural necessity with which inorganic beings tend toward their ends. The wise and thoughtful guidance in the animal's life comes from the Creator of the universe, who implanted in the animal these purposeful fundamental urges and impulses.

Even in the beginning the question arose whether reason was to be ascribed to the higher animals because of the manner of their activity. St. Thomas admits that because animals have some sense of values they must be accorded some weak participation in the faculty of reason, and, since they are able to do or not to do a certain thing, they must be accorded some likeness to free choice (*quaedam similitudo liberi arbitrii inquantum possunt agere vel non agere unum et idem secundum suum judicium ut sic sit in eis quasi quaedam conditionata libertas*). But they do not possess reason in the true sense or any power of reflection or choice. The proof of this is that all animals of the same species act invariably at all times; the swallow builds its nest in the same way at all times.

The animal stands midway between beings without any knowledge at all and rational beings. The former act without any choice, being determined to one thing; the latter act out of free choice; the animal acts with some determination, but not free determination (*arbitrio sed non libero*). By nature the lamb must flee before the wolf. Hence the animal can do no evil; all the requirements for a moral evaluation of its actions are lacking. Every appetite tends toward what is desirable as it is presented in a sensible or spiritual form. Evil, however, is possible only when the knowledge and the actions based on it are governed by some higher norm or rule. When, therefore, such a norm is lacking, there can be no departure from the rule. Animals have no higher norm for their actions than the sensible forms which they have apprehended and which are the only and necessary motives for their activity. Consequently in animals we discover only a similarity with moral good inasmuch as their passions are directed and influenced by their sense of values somewhat after the way reason directs the activity of higher beings.

4. **Summary.** St. Thomas Aquinas adhered faithfully to Aristotle's principles to explain the phenomena of animal life. All his observations and conclusions about animal life seemed to be in conformity with these principles. The animal organism is a psychophysical vital entity to which not only certain vegetative functions but also certain psychic activities are proper. Further, the animal is a complete whole, composed of faculties that fit into one another and require one another for the attainment of the animal's end. One activity depends on another in order that the chief purpose of the animal, the preservation of the individual and the species, may be attained. This great purpose requires nourishment, the procurement of nourishment requires local motion, both of these depend on the

appetite, the appetite presupposes the imagination and the memory, and these in turn rely on the external senses which connect them with the outside world.

The interpretation of animal life underwent many changes in the course of the centuries. Descartes taught an automatic and mechanistic theory of animal life by which he denied to the animal any soul-principle, extending the mechanistic interpretation of the inorganic world to the plant and animal kingdoms. On the other hand, recent Darwinians have attempted to reduce the difference between man and animal as much as possible and eliminate the essential distinction between them by representing the animal as quite intelligent. Both these camps are in error since they lose sight of the principle that we should not attribute to animals more or less faculties and powers than are necessary to explain their vital manifestations. Here, too, St. Thomas takes the middle path. Animals have a certain kind of knowledge, they perceive the qualities of things, they may attain to a kind of sensible general concept of things, they refer the elements of one situation to another, they apprehend things as desirable and undesirable, harmful and useful, they remember things, and they learn and gather experience.

To refer here in explanation to the mechanism of association is inadequate since phantasms and imaginations can associate themselves without any act of cognition. The mechanism of association prepares the material for cognition, but it is itself in no way an act of cognition.

We are, of course, prevented from reaching an adequate explanation of the animal's life since we are unable to relive consciously the course of the animal's vital processes and also because the sensitive forms of our own life are united to spiritual acts and penetrated by them. The psychological terminology of the life of the human soul is also limited in this respect. All of this, however, does not prevent us from attaining some essential knowledge about the life of the animal. In explaining the animal's process of apprehension, St. Thomas did not hesitate to speak of a judgment (*judicare*). This act refers to knowledge of a special kind, however, which is always limited to single sensible objects and goes no farther than the here and now of material being. The animal's sense perceptions only touch the outside, they do not reach into the inside, into the substance of things. Animals have no perception of things as such. They are in-

terested only in what has significance as an urge or impulse; they do
not perceive the objective world as composed of autonomous beings,
with definite natures and well-defined structures. Animals are unable to consider the individual from a universal viewpoint; they cannot apprehend the universal, the specific, the necessary idea, or the
idea of obligation. They have no faculties with which to inquire about
the meaning of things, to form individual or general concepts, nor
can they arrive at conclusions. Briefly, animals have only individual
impulses and guides for action which they must necessarily follow
and they have no concept of values or any freedom of choice. Hence
animals are not capable of making any progress or of developing a
culture and therefore they also lack the means of expressing thoughts,
the faculty of speech.

Voice, which St. Thomas defines in the Aristotelian sense and
denies to bloodless animals and to fishes, is a part of the animal's
make-up. The animal's voice, however, is midway between the articulate speech of human beings and the sound that inorganic beings
are able to produce. It is used to make known inner biological processes and experiences and possesses only an indicative character.

St. Thomas established the essential differences between man and
animal in much the same way as they are generally recognized today.
Indeed, St. Thomas attributed more to the animal than many animal
psychologists are willing to do today, when they deny that animals
see, hear, and perceive. St. Thomas was willing to admit the existence of the animal's practical "intelligence," but his views are not
in full accord with those of some modern animal psychologists in
their interpretation of animal phenomena. The assertion on the part
of some modern scholars, that there is only a quantitative difference
between a man using a tool and an animal using some implement,
would have been condemned by St. Thomas.

An animal possesses consciousness. It notices things that exist outside of it, it recognizes the surrounding world, it possesses functions
of communication which refer to the world about it and its parts,
and it reacts from within to the things it comes into contact with.
Therefore animal life represents a higher stage of life than that of
plants because it possesses self-motion. Animals do not establish for
themselves the end of their actions and movements; that end is predetermined by nature. But they possess not only the power of movement; they act because of a sensible form which they themselves

have obtained. In this connection we should not forget that the activity released by reason of these sensible forms bears the characteristic of passive necessity.

The degree of the animal's self-motion surpasses that of plants since, although the vital activities begin in the outside world, they are completed within the animal. Animals receive the sensible form of knowledge, store it in their memory, and later with its help they become active in their appetitive and instinctive center. Animals possess no higher intelligence than this; they have no consciousness of objective reality, no consciousness of the world or of themselves. The knowledge of objectivity and self-knowledge or self-consciousness correspond to each other. An animal is incapable of saying "I," and therefore it has no power over itself and no self-determination. As we view the animal organism we see that it is not complete and conclusive in the scale of being, but that it points to higher forms of existence.

CHAPTER XII

MAN
THE UNITY OF BODY AND SOUL

The concept of man is the nucleus of every philosophical system. As he searches for the truth and strives for the good, man asks first of all for knowledge about himself; he is interested in determining his place in the universe. Clarification of his position is important for a clear understanding of man's relation to God, to the universe, and to his fellow man, and it influences man's religious attitude, his moral outlook, and his social and political viewpoint.

In the development of philosophical anthropology it has long been recognized that man cannot be studied in a state of isolation and unrelated to his environment, and that the determination of the concept of man must proceed from the whole philosophical picture. Even though the representatives of the exact sciences proclaim that they have discarded all philosophical orientation, the philosophical attitude unconsciously underlies all their conclusions. In our study of man it is also important to choose a viewpoint from which man will be seen in his complete make-up so that no part of him will be suppressed or neglected in favor of another. Overemphasis of one part will injure the whole concept. St. Thomas approached the study of man from the viewpoint of his Christian philosophy, he looked at man from above, from the standpoint of his relation to God and his highest function, but he did not at any time lose sight of the lower parts of his nature in which he is bound to nature and to matter. For his understanding of man's natural make-up, Aristotle had prepared the way. For the study of man's relationship to the supernatural, St. Thomas drew freely from the concepts of Christian revelation.

1. **The unity of the substantial form.** By use of the measuring-

stick of activity, St. Thomas ascertained the essential make-up of man. *Propria operatio hominis est intelligere.*[1] Reason is man's most outstanding characteristic, and therefore man is a rational being. Without surrender of its vegetative and sensitive activities, the human soul is primarily and in its leading functions a thinking soul, and as such it is the first, exclusive, and adequate principle of life in man. Although it is essentially simple, it possesses a plurality of powers by means of which it fulfills its many tasks. Thomistic anthropology is dominated by the Aristotelian concept of the substantial unity of the body and the soul. This substantial unity is founded on the theory that the body and the soul are related to each other as potency and act, and as matter and form. As the essential form of the body, the soul penetrates and lives in every part of the body, and since it is the form of the body it provides the basis for the oneness of the human being (*unum esse totius compositi*). Because the soul is the form and the act of the body, it cannot be composed of matter and form; its act of cognition by which it knows things in the universal and absolute form precludes such a composition. As something that is essentially form and act, the soul needs no third substance to mediate between it and the body; the union of soul and body is natural and immediate.

St. Thomas also applies his teaching about the unity of the substantial form to man. According to this teaching, the more perfect form includes in itself the lower forms and transmits to the matter the different grades of perfection. From the soul the body and all its parts derive a substantial and specific being. When the soul disappears, not only the human being, the sensitive being, and the living being cease to exist, but the hand, the eye, flesh and bones, are no longer what they were. As Aristotle had said before him, only a nominal similarity remains. Man also derives his corporeity from the soul. On this point, replying to the objection that no one can give what he does not possess, St. Thomas declared that the soul did not possess corporeity *in actu* but *in virtute,* as the sun possesses warmth. To say that there were several substantial forms would interfere with the unity of man, and the relation between the living being and the human being would be accidental, the two would be separable, whereas a necessary connection exists between the two. It is one and the same soul that carries out all the vital activities

[1] *Summa theol.,* Ia, q.76, a.1.

through the powers that are anchored either in the soul alone or in the composite (*anima est quo primum nutrimur et sentimus et movemur secundum locum et similiter quo primo intelligimus*).[2] Here St. Thomas directly opposed the commonly accepted view at the University of Paris about the plurality of forms, and he also contradicted the doctrine of the Franciscan school and of Avicebron that the soul was composed of matter and form. St. Bonaventure's theory that light was the unifying medium, was also discarded. Primarily and of itself the soul is the act of the whole body and of all parts of the body, and it exists in the whole body as well as in all the parts. The reasons for this are found in the body itself, since the body is not an artificial whole, or a mere aggregate of parts, but a natural whole; and also in the soul, which is the form of the whole body conferring being and species.

A thing may be considered as a whole in three ways, according to St. Thomas; namely, inasmuch as a thing may have parts in three different ways. The soul is not a quantitative whole nor a whole *per accidens;* but, on the other hand, the soul considered as an essence does exist in every part of the body. With regard to its system of powers and potencies, however, the soul is not wholly in every part of the body; in fact, not even its entire power system is wholly in the body. The soul cannot be said to be wholly in the body since reason and will are not acts of the body. As to the other powers of the soul, they are wholly in the body, but not wholly in every part, since the different parts of the body serve some particular activity of the soul. Certain potencies inform different organs of the body for the execution of their own proper acts.

This unity of body and soul is not designed for the body but for the soul. The spirit of man, bound to the body and the sense world, needs corporeity and the assistance of the senses for the fulfillment of its vital tasks. Therefore the soul is not man, as Plato, St. Augustine, and Hugh of St. Victor thought, no more than the body is man. Both parts in their union with each other give the result, man. Thus St. Thomas rejects not only materialism but an exaggerated spiritualism. The soul is only a part of the human species, and does not belong to any genus or species. Even the attribute of personality does not belong properly to the soul but to the composite. The soul, because of an inner and essential necessity, is related to the body, and

2 *Ibid.*

it cannot attain perfection, even in the next world, except by being united to the body. Separation from the body is against the nature of the soul, and the union with the body is essential, although it is not metaphysically essential. For this reason, the soul in its attachment to the body bears a greater resemblance to God than when it is separated from the body.[3]

2. The soul's dependence on the body. The dependence of the soul on the body is contained in the very idea of man, since vegetative life is a kind of corporeal life, and sensitive life is body-bound and completely dependent on a body. When the body ages, the soul does not age; if an old man had the eye of a youth, he would be able to see as well as the youth. Even man as a spiritual being requires the body, not as an organ, but as an object, since the intellect needs the phantasms produced by the imagination, the imagination in turn needs the senses, and the senses for their perception depend on the body.[4] This dependence of the soul is conceived in such a way that the soul attains its perfection in the body but not through the body, and that either God or the soul itself perfects the soul with the assistance of the body (*cum adminiculo corporis obsequentis*), and that the soul constitutes the body's reality for its own use and as its organ.[5] The doctrine of the substantial unity of the soul and body, when it was logically carried to its conclusions, required the admission of a mutual interplay of influences on the part of body and soul, and the force of evident phenomena tended to give the corporeal part a more important position.

Plato's origins were deep in the Orphic Pythagorean religion; and when he considered the soul, Plato retained his religious viewpoint. Aristotle, however, remained the natural scientist, and looked at the soul from that viewpoint. According to Plato, the soul belonged originally to the kingdom of ideas, and because of some guilt or some natural law it had been lowered into the prison of the body. Thus the union with the body is something abnormal. The body is a hindrance obstructing the original and natural activities of the soul, and it is man's duty to strike off as soon as possible the fetters of corporeity, and permit the return of the soul to the realm of ideas.

Aristotle's concept of the soul is a purely natural concept. We have

---

[3] *Contra Gent.*, II, 85.
[4] *De verit.*, XIX, 1.
[5] *Ibid.*, XXVI, 2 ad 2.

already pointed out the preponderance of the biological viewpoint in Aristotle, but this does not prevent him from giving reason the more prominent place in the idea of man. This *nous* or reason appears only in the highest stage of life. St. Thomas joined Aristotle the naturalist and rejected the religious views of Plato. When it had once been corrected by the teaching of Christianity, Aristotle's teaching would find a logical place in the Thomistic view of the universe. Body and soul are united because they have been together from the beginning, and because the concept of a spiritual being merged in corporeity and sense life represented a stage in the great chorus of being; in order that it might be perfect, no step in the hierarchy of being could be lacking. For this reason St. Thomas was obliged to reject the teaching of Origen, that originally all spirits were equal and that their subsequent fall was the cause of their differentiation.

The body and the soul are not related to each other as two substances, but because of their inner ordering to each other they form one uniform substance. The expression, body *and* soul, does not perfectly conform to the reality, which is a whole that may be considered either as an animated, spiritualized body, or as a soul merged in a body. The body is disposed for its union with the soul by the *spiritus,* a gaslike something, from which, according to the view of the times, the principle of life resulted. However, in the centuries that followed, no concept of the relationship between body and soul has been as much in conformity with the facts as this idea of the substantial union. It is interesting to note that in our own times psychiatrists have returned to the idea of the substantial union of body and soul.

3. **The subsistence of the human soul.** Although the human soul is a form bound to the body, unlike other inorganic and organic forms merged in matter, it is not completely in the power of matter, but as reason it is independent of the body. As Aristotle had done before him, St. Thomas attributes to the rational soul activities independent of the body and the bodily organs, and since a being's activity is also the measure of its being, he attributes to the soul an existence independent of the body. Although in its vegetative and sensitive life the soul is bound to the body, as a rational being it belongs to a sphere of being far removed from all corporeity and all dependence on matter. The manner of its cognition is the token of its subsistence. Its existence is independent of that for which it

serves as a form.[6] This independence of the soul from all corporeity has certain consequences for the origin and the cessation of the soul. As to its origin: the soul does not owe its inception and existence to the natural process of generation as do plants and animals, but is directly created by God. As to its cessation: the soul does not cease with the body, but is immortal in its entirety. Here again man is the middle being. The pure spirits receive their existence from God without any dependence on matter or connection with matter; the natural forms receive their existence in complete dependence on matter; the human soul, however, receives its existence in connection with matter but not in dependence on it. Whereas the sensitive soul in animals is mortal, it is not mortal in man since it is substantially one with the rational soul.[7]

In this matter St. Thomas differed with Aristotle, who thought that those parts of the soul that depended on the body for their activity and existence perished with the body, and that the higher rational soul, i.e., the theoretical *nous,* alone perdured. In this way Aristotle sacrificed the unity of the soul. This solution was unacceptable for a Christian theologian. St. Thomas taught the immortality of the whole human soul and thus at the same time preserved the teaching of the unity of the soul. Aristotle tore the parts of the soul asunder; St. Thomas only separated the vegetative and sensitive potencies of the soul from the body and attributed the lower powers of the soul to the spiritual and simple substance of the human soul. He did this to safeguard his belief in the future reunion of soul and body. These powers of vegetation and sensation have as their subject not only the soul but the composite of body and soul. Having attributed them to the soul, he could not, however, predicate them actually of the soul when it was once separated from the body, he could only say that they were in the soul in *virtute,* as in their radical principle.

St. Thomas taught a unity of the soul from which proceeded vegetative and sensitive powers that needed organs, as well as the powers of the mind that needed no organs to function. Now, the question arises, whether the purity of the intellect is not endangered by this union in which the soul becomes the essential form of the body. St. Thomas answers this question in the negative, in the same sense in which he denied that the vital vegetative functions have no influence

[6] *De nat. mat.,* chap. 3.
[7] *Contra Gent.,* II, 86–89.

on thought and will. He was obliged to admit, however, that the intellect might be impeded accidentally inasmuch as it uses phantasms which are derived from the bodily organs which are in turn nourished by the vegetative functions. This is evident from the occurrences that take place during sleep and after meals. On the other hand, the intellect may have an obstructing effect on the imagination and through it on the vegetative faculties.

Thus St. Thomas explained the mutual interplay and influence that are occasioned by this substantial unity. In somewhat greater detail he inquired into the dependence of the spiritual on the corporeal. Sleep and dreams have a physiological basis. The various predispositions of men to this or that passion or indulgence depend on their corporeal constitution, as do also mental diseases, epilepsy, temperaments, and the normal and psychopathic types of personality. The defects of sensation and of reason can all be traced back to corporeal origins. In the strict sense of the word, mental diseases do not exist. Man's reason cannot be directly touched by a corporeal disturbance, since reason does not require a corporeal organ for its activities; indirectly, however, by means of the senses or the memory on which it depends, reason can be affected sympathetically. In the same way, the will cannot be influenced directly, but only indirectly through the sensitive appetite, the passions, and a disturbance in the mind.

Both those passions that are quantitatively abnormal and those that are qualitatively abnormal derive from corporeal processes. Even the moral attitude or disposition of men is affected by the bodily disposition. As Aristotle, so also St. Thomas makes the efficiency of the mind dependent on the perfection of the body, he makes the reason depend on the perfection of the sense equipment, the higher faculty determined by the lower. The more perfect the dispositions of the body, the more perfect will be the soul which it obtains, according to the general principle that the form is received into the matter according to the capacity of the matter (*quanto melius corpus est dispositum, tanto meliorem sortitur animam*).[8]

These conclusions of St. Thomas and St. Albert, relating to the details of physiological processes and organic functions, are based on the medical knowledge of their times, the findings of Hippocrates, Galen, Constantinus Africanus, and have for us only a historical in-

---

[8] *Summa theol.*, Ia, q.85, a.7; Ia IIae, q.82, a.4 ad 1.

terest. The important point in this matter is that, in his theory of the substantial unity of the body and the soul, St. Thomas realized that the corporeal constitution of man and its various changes are to be predicated of the whole man, and that man's spirit must nevertheless be kept free from any direct influence deriving from the body.

4. The individuality of the human soul. Humanity as such does not exist. Man exists only as individualized, as the man here and now, with this body and these properties. According to the principles of Thomism, the specific character is derived from the form, while the individuation comes from the matter. The often repeated formula, the same in species and different in number, emphasizes matter as the principle of individuation because it is the basis of numerical differentiation, and thus it lays undue stress on quantitative difference as against qualitative difference. St. Thomas himself became aware of the difficulty and cast about for a more satisfactory definition. In his commentary on the *Sentences,*[9] he speaks of the body as the direct cause of differentiation. Later he ascribed individuation not to the body but to the relationship to the body, and thus the souls of the deceased are differentiated by their different aptitudes to their bodies (*secundum diversam commensurationem ad corpora*).[10] Replying to the objection that the soul would lose its individuality at the time of death if it were derived from the body, St. Thomas said that the soul is not individuated by the matter itself but by the relationship to the matter (*non per materiam ex qua sed secundum habitudinem ad materiam in qua est*).[11]

In this sense he agreed with Avicenna, saying that the individuation of the soul depended on the body, with respect to its beginning but not as to its last end. It is a question of the relationship of this soul to this body. God creates the individual soul in view of the body generated by the parents, which the soul is to inform. Now the dependence of the soul on the body becomes intelligible. Since the individual soul is created by God for a particular body, we can readily understand how the organic dependence of the soul is bound up in the substantial unity of man and how the higher spiritual life of man is conditioned on the body and the senses. At the same time, it becomes clear how parents, although they are not the creators of

9 II, 32, 2 ad 3.
10 *Contra Gent.*, II, 75, 81.
11 *De anima*, 6 ad 4.

their children's souls, nevertheless may have an influence on the souls since these souls are dependent on the bodies. Thus creationism is preserved, but another difficulty remains. The soul possesses an autonomous individuality even though it is related and directed to the body. If, therefore, the body is no longer the principle of individuation, how is the body itself individuated? Indeed, whence is the body, man's corporeity, derived, if not from the soul, the one substantial form of man? St. Thomas might have avoided these and similar difficulties, if like the later Scholastics he had proclaimed the principle that every being is of itself, from the beginning of its existence, individual.

The soul is indeed only a part of the human species, but as the form it founds the species. The soul is the form, and also a something of itself, *hoc aliquid,* since it subsists in itself and continues to live after its separation from the body. It cannot be said to be an individual "like a substance that possesses a complete species, but like a part of a thing that has the complete species." [12]

As a composite being, man is transitory and perishable because of his body. Transitoriness belongs to the essence of matter and corporeity. Even the Creator Himself could not have created any matter that did not bear the mark of perishability. Since man is thus subjected to transitoriness, he is also subjected to evil and suffering.

[12] *Ibid.,* 1 ad 3.

CHAPTER XIII

MAN'S EQUIPMENT

St. Thomas evolved an ontology of the human person that is admirable as a complete and harmonious philosophical treatise. His achievement may be somewhat diminished by his references to Aristotle and the content of tradition, but the greater amount of his work is original and creative. In his study of man, we note the absence of the vivid experiences and immediate contacts with life that are so prominent in the studies of St. Augustine, and certain phases of human life are even passed over to which the psychological genius of St. Augustine had opened the doors. But in spite of these defects, St. Thomas gives us a study of man which, for its view of the whole structure of man's inner cosmos and for its understanding of man's spiritual acts, has never been equaled by succeeding thinkers.

1. **Man's bodily equipment.** Teleology, according to St. Thomas, is the all-embracing principle of nature. The divine artificer has given to every being the best equipment, not indeed the best absolutely, but the best for its particular purpose. The proximate purpose of the human body is the rational soul and its activities.[1] The kind of soul that a being has determines the corporal equipment, since body and soul are fitted to each other. The more perfect the soul, the more perfect the body will be, and the more perfect the body the more parts it will have. The perfection of activity follows the perfection of being. In the lowest forms of being a variety of accidents is sufficient, but in living beings a variety of parts is needed, and the greatest variation in the parts is found in man.

The human body contains the most perfect mixture of the elements and their qualities, of heat and cold, of dryness and moisture,

---

[1] *Summa theol.,* Ia, q.91, a.3.

etc., and because of its soft and delicate composition it is the most suitable organ for the sense of touch which is not only the foundation of all the senses but also the prerequisite for a good mind. St. Thomas concluded that man was the most clever of all animals because he had the best sense of touch. Man has the largest brain because it is required as the cooling organ for the heat generated by the heart, and has to provide material for man's activities in the imagination and memory, which in turn provide the basis for the intellectual activities.[2] The human hand, that "tool of tools," corresponds to man's intellectual pre-eminence and to the vast extent of his activities.

Although man excels the animals in the inner senses, he is inferior to certain classes of animals in the external senses. Man has the poorest sense of smell because, as St. Thomas reasoned, man's large brain deprives the olfactory organ of its required amount of moisture. According to a kind of compensation in his bodily make-up, man is surpassed by many animals in keenness of sight and hearing and in speed of movement. He does not, however, need natural weapons because he can provide the necessaries of life through the strategy of his reason and the instrumentality of his hand. Man's upright position is made possible through the surplus heat generated in the heart. His upright position is necessary for several reasons: since his senses serve not only the quest for food but also his quest for knowledge, his vision must encompass all things, those on earth and those in the skies; when the brain is in the higher position it allows the inner senses to function more freely; and finally, the erect position is a requisite for speech.

"If man had a bent position, he would use his hands as forefeet, and he would take his food with his mouth. For this he would need a larger mouth, larger and harder lips, and a hard tongue, so as not to be injured by external objects. Such equipment would make speech, the correlate of the mind, entirely impossible. By his erect position, man is especially distinguished from the plant. In man, the upper part of his body, the head, points in the direction of the upper part of the universe, and his lower part is in the direction of the lower part of the universe. Thus the structure of man's body corresponds to the structure of the whole universe. In the plant, however, the root, which corresponds to the human head, tends in the direction of the lower part of the universe, while its lower part is

[2] *Contra Gent.*, II. 73.

above. Between man and the plant is the animal, holding a middle position, the upper part being that which receives nourishment; the lower, that which provides for its elimination." [3]

2. **Man's sensitive equipment.** Man's sensitive faculties, including those of sense knowledge and sense appetite, do not form an isolated department in his being, but they are built into the whole structure and come under the influence of the spiritual soul. Because of man's substantial unity, therefore, his senses are higher and nobler than in other living beings. The sensitive faculties partake of man's spiritual nature, not only because they serve his reason, but also because they are illuminated by his intellect and empowered to perform higher and nobler tasks. The sensitive soul in man and in animals belongs to the same genus but not to the same species. Neither Aristotle nor St. Thomas makes any difference between man and the animals with respect to the number of the senses of the sensible forms; but it is important to note that man excels even the most perfect animal in the things he achieves with his senses. This is partly owing to man's superior sense equipment, such as his more perfect sense and organ of touch. Men's talents and gifts can be measured by the perfection of their sense of touch and the softness of the flesh. Man's sense equipment is more efficient especially because of its close relation to his reason. Thus man's common sense is capable of producing superior results. The human imagination by associating together certain pictures may produce new objects in the phantasm, and thus becomes a kind of creative power entirely lacking in the animal. In man, moreover, the memory may rise to the power of purposeful reflection, and in man the animal instinct is elevated to a kind of prudence, able to make immediate judgments about the individual. St. Thomas called this faculty the *ratio particularis,* and *intellectus passivus,* although completely dependent on the body, having the pineal gland as its organ. [4]

Just as the cognitive faculties of the sensitive soul participate in the reason, so also the appetitive faculties participate in the rational power and even in the freedom of the will. To what extent will be determined later.

The sensitive faculties are distinct from the spiritual, but the interconnection is by no means lost sight of. The sensitive faculties are

---

[3] *Summa theol.,* Ia, q.91, a.3 ad 3.
[4] *Comment. on the Sentences.,* III, 33, 2 ad 4.

all directed to the spiritual soul of man by which he reaches his highest perfection.

3. **The spiritual equipment.** As a spiritual being, man possesses all those attributes and qualities that belong to other spiritual beings. In a certain sense immaterial beings might be said to be everything with respect to their being and their activities. According to their being they are either the prototype of all beings, as God is, or they possess an image of everything. From a practical viewpoint, all spiritual beings have a relation to all things and a tendency to all things.

In his presentation of the ontology of the person, St. Thomas gives the more important place to the ontology of the soul. Man excels the rest of creation by reason of his *nous,* by his spiritual power, with reason and will as its essential parts.

In contrast to the threefold division of the soul's powers—into knowledge, willing, and emotion—advocated by the thinkers of the eighteenth century (Sulzer and Kant), St. Thomas recognizes only two faculties of the soul, knowledge and will. These potencies are distinguished because of their formal objects. Man either unites himself with things by receiving into himself spiritual images of things, or he adopts a practical attitude toward things in his desire for them or his rejection of them, in an attraction for them or aversion for them, in pleasure or displeasure at them. Truth and goodness are the two aspects under which man enters into relation with things.[5] Thus man's spiritual structure imitates the divine model, since God's actions are knowledge and willing.[6] These two fundamental functions cover the whole extent of man's spiritual equipment.

According to St. Thomas, the will is an extensive faculty, including not only the desire for some good but also the quiet possession of the good, the love of the good acquired, and the inner joy following the possession of the good. Joy is, after all, nothing but the quiescence of the appetite in the good, *"quietatio appetitus in bono."* [7] The act of the appetite, from the development of the desire out of our sympathy for some object to the increasing joy in the attainment of that object, is essentially one act that cannot be divided by being assigned to two different faculties.

[5] *Summa theol.,* Ia, q. 16, a. 1.
[6] *Ibid.,* q. 27, a. 5.
[7] *Ibid.,* q. 19, a. 1 ad 2.

Again, according to St. Thomas the beautiful is not an autonomous thing, and therefore no separate faculty is required for its perception. The three objective characteristics which a thing must have in order to be beautiful—perfection, proportion, and a certain brilliance— also belong to the essence of the good.[8] Therefore St. Thomas, following the ancient Hellenic axiom, identified the good and the beautiful, holding that the difference consisted in the viewpoint. The good, he said, is that in which the appetite rests; the beautiful is that in whose contemplation the appetite rests. St. Thomas thus acknowledges his adherence to the idea, first expressed in the *Dialogue* of Hippias Major (298) and often repeated since then, that only that is beautiful which pleases both the sense of sight and the sense of hearing. Only the visible and audible beautiful exist; the things that are pleasurable to the other senses serve to satisfy animal needs. The preferential place is given to sight and hearing because they have a higher cognitive significance and are more suitable for the needs of the reason. From the cooperation between the cognitive and appetitive faculties, the esthetic pleasure arises, or in the words of Aquinas himself, *"Pulchrum addit super bonum quemdam ordinem ad vim cognoscitivam."* [9]

a) **The cognitive faculty.** In the order of perfection of being, the cognitive faculty has a high and important significance. The perfection of every individual being and of every individual species is always a limited perfection; something is always lacking that is the perfection of other individuals and species. The Creator has compensated for this deficiency in those beings endowed with cognition inasmuch as they are able to make the forms and perfections of other beings their own, and thus are able to enrich their own beings with the forms of other beings.[10] The field of this spiritual conquest and acquisition is of the greatest extent. Since man is able to comprehend mentally the universality of things, he is in a sense all being (*homo quoddamodo totum ens*).

The intellect is a potency of the soul in which passivity and activity exist together. The intellect is a passive potency inasmuch as it is in potency to the intelligible universal forms, essences, and principles. As a passive potency it resembles, in the beginning, a clean slate, and

---

[8] *Ibid.,* q.39, a.8.
[9] *Ibid.,* Ia IIae, q.27, a.1 ad 3.
[10] See also St. Augustine, *De civ. Dei,* XI, 27.

also, because of its ability to be formed and determined, it bears a resemblance to prime matter. It is called the possible intellect, *intellectus possibilis*.[11] At the same time all spiritual cognition is an active faculty in which subject and object cooperate according to the law that every potency is brought into act by something active. What is this active principle of knowledge whose duty it is to extract or lift out the spiritual content from the material presented by the senses? The phantasms offered by the imagination cannot, of course, be considered as efficient causes since they belong to the sensible sphere, although they may be looked upon as instrumental agents in the process.

Therefore St. Thomas follows Aristotle in looking for a spiritually effective force in the intellect itself, and he calls it the active intellect, *intellectus agens*. The active intellect illumines the sensible phantasms and, by abstracting from all individual and sensitive detail, it releases the intelligible universal species which in turn informs the possible intellect and brings it into act. Knowledge itself is not in the province of the active intellect, only the illumination and purification of the sensible phantasms are in its sphere. For this function of purification and illumination the active intellect is in perpetual readiness; this task of casting its light on the spiritual structure of sensible things is its supreme purpose. The possible and active intellects, found together in the intellect when it is in act, are two distinct potencies in the human soul, the only two potencies in the soul that St. Thomas admits are really different. Since potencies are different by reason of their acts, and since the acts are different because of their objects, the possible and the active intellects must be considered apart, not because their objects are distinct natures, but because they consider objects that are formally distinct. The Arabians, in their pantheistic Aristotelianism, taught that the possible and the active intellects were separate substances. But St. Thomas maintained that they were only different potencies of the individual soul because of the fundamental connection between mind and sensibility, between sensibility and the body, and because we ourselves are conscious of ourselves in the act of knowing and abstraction.

The active intellect, as also the possible intellect, possesses three characteristics: separability from the body, incapability of suffering, and the absence of mixture, in the sense that it is not composed of

[11] *Summa theol.*, Ia, q.14, a.2 ad3; *Contra Gent.*, II, 59.

material parts and also in the sense that it is not completely bound up with the body. The *intellectus agens,* however, excels the possible intellect because of a fourth characteristic, namely, that with respect to its substance it is always in act. This does not mean, of course, that its activity is its essence, but that its activity is a consequence of its essence.

For St. Thomas the intellect is knowledge in the broadest sense. The intellect is the spiritual faculty that rises above the sensible world, and in the spiritual realm it is distinct from the will. Because it is immaterial and because its actions are not immersed in matter, it is, as Aristotle said, in a sense unlimited, it is as extensive as the universe of being itself. Although all knowledge may begin with the senses, and man may possess no other knowledge than that which is sense-conditioned, the power of the intellect ranges far above the sensible sphere. Together with Aristotle, St. Thomas sees the greatest perfection of the intellect in its comprehension of the whole order of the universe and of all the causes in the universe (*ut in ea describatur totus ordo universi et causarum ejus*).[12] Man, therefore, comprehends a world of things. Our understanding with its natural equipment knows primarily all that is being and all that is connected with being, including the supreme principles of thought and being with their unchanging validity. Its adequate object is the nature or essence of things, the *what* (*quod quid est*), that is found in all classes of being. The intellect comprehends the essence and nature of things, the manner of their inner structure, their unity and variety, their inner order and their relation to other things, and it is able, because of its use of analogy, to rise to a knowledge of the spiritual world, and because of the principle of causality it comes to a knowledge of the ultimate causes of the universe. In man, the natural striving of all things toward God, appears as an act of conscious comprehension. Because the mind is not immersed in matter, it possesses a kind of unlimitedness, and therefore it extends farther than the senses. Yet, in spite of this great number of objects, the intellect maintains a greater unity in itself than do the senses which are concerned with a much smaller number of objects. This unlimitedness, simplicity, and inner unity characterize the intellect.[13]

Nevertheless the human intellect remains bound to its corporeal,

---

[12] *De verit.,* II, 2.
[13] *Ibid.,* XV, 1; *In XII Met.,* 11.

sensitive existence, and from this fact certain consequences flow. Thus the human soul apprehends material things rather than immaterial things; by its nature it tends to the form of material things. St. Thomas concluded that the really proper object of the intellect that is immersed in the body is the essence or quiddity that is found in matter.

By means of his knowledge of the external world, man arrives at the knowledge of himself. He arrives first at the stage of self-consciousness and then at a more extensive self-knowledge. To a certain degree the senses are able to revert to themselves, inasmuch as they apprehend their own perception while they perceive external objects. But the senses do not attain to any knowledge of their own natures. Man, however, in his thought activity becomes conscious of his spiritual existence, and by discursive reflection of the subtlest kind he arrives at a knowledge of the nature of the soul, of the forces and powers dormant in the soul, and of the soul's structure. This knowledge does not, however, reach perfection during this earthly existence.

With regard to the problem of self-consciousness, St. Thomas adopts an attitude entirely different from that of St. Augustine, who taught that we are immediately and directly conscious of ourselves and that we come to know our own natures also in a direct manner. St. Thomas, on the other hand, defends the theory that we know ourselves only indirectly. In this matter these two great thinkers differ in principle. From the intensity of his self-contemplation and self-consciousness, St. Augustine proceeded to his knowledge of human nature and God; St. Thomas goes outside himself into the external universe and builds his metaphysical structure on the foundation of external experience.

Our knowledge extends as far as the realm of being. According to the Aristotelian expression, our souls become all things because of the unlimited extent of our knowledge. For this reason, St. Thomas was enamored of the intellect and in the beginning of his philosophical summa he starts singing the praises of the intellect and of truth and declares that the energy of the intellect and the desire for knowledge grow stronger even as the intellect seeks knowledge.

Again in agreement with Aristotle, St. Thomas clearly distinguishes between two activities of the intellect. The first is that natural and intuitive turning of the mind toward the supreme theoretical and practical principles, toward the essences of things seen with unhesitating certainty which it expresses in simple concepts. It is called the *intellectus incomplexus*. The other activity is that which judges, that is, combines these simple concepts or separates them and it is called the *intellectus complexus*.[14] While the comprehension of the essences of things is merely the passive reflection of the object in the intellect, the judgment of the intellect, combining concepts, is truly an act with a purpose. In this act of judgment the intellect becomes a creative faculty, producing something new when it attributes a quality to some object, or denies some quality to another object.

But this does not exhaust the activities of the intellect. The intellect ascends to a still higher plane. In its act of judgment it not only corresponds and agrees with the things it knows, it also knows its own agreement with the thing known, since the ultimate perfection of the intellect is not only the truth but the truth as known.[15] This excellence of the intellect is founded on its peculiar ability to return entirely upon itself, and thus the judging intellect is far above the senses as well as the intellect as it merely apprehends essences and principles. When St. Thomas proclaims that the excellence of the intellect consists in its ability to unite and separate concepts and not in its comprehension of essences, he makes an evaluating judgment which is somewhat out of harmony with the Aristotelian system. Aristotle had taught that in its intuitive power the human intellect manifested a certain resemblance to God, and St. Thomas himself had pointed out that God did not combine and separate concepts but saw them *simpliciter*.[16] Man does not possess a perfect intellect such as is found in the angels; he is not able to see directly and know unerringly all the essential characteristics of a thing or all the consequences that lie hidden beneath first principles unless by way of combination and separation of concepts and a somewhat tortuous succession of conclusions.[17]

Human knowledge is divided into discursive and intuitive; in both instances the object is the same, but the mode of knowledge is different. It is not a question of two different potencies or faculties, since it is the same faculty that apprehends the essences of things and also makes judgments and arrives at conclusions. The intellect

---

[14] *In I Sent.*, 19, 5, 1.
[15] *Contra Gent.*, I, 59.
[16] *Ibid.*
[17] *De verit.*, VIII, 15.

sees truth directly in the essences of things (*interius in ipsa rei essentia veritatem quodammodo legit*); reason, according to St. Thomas and in conformity with tradition (St. Augustine, Boethius), is the faculty that progresses from knowledge to knowledge. Reason is related to the intellect as to its basis and its goal: as to its basis inasmuch as every conclusion is founded in the first principles; as to its goal inasmuch as every conclusion is tested and verified by a return to the first principles. Neither God nor the pure intelligences possess this faculty of reason; it is peculiar to man, that middle being between spirit and matter, that being bound to the material and immersed in the sensible world, that being that is unstable and restless because it is still engaged in the quest for truth. Angels and men may be distinguished as intellectual and rational beings. Following tradition in the persons of St. Augustine and Boethius, St. Thomas distinguishes between a higher and a lower reason; the first extends · to the eternal and higher beings, the latter is concerned with temporal beings.

From the viewpoint of the end, the intellect is divided into the theoretical and the practical intellects; the theoretical intellect is concerned simply with the acquisition of truth, whereas the practical intellect seeks to place the truth in the service of action. The object of the practical intellect is not the good, but rather the truth as related to some activity (*verum relatum ad opus*). Since the true is also the good, inasmuch as it is desirable, and since the good is also the true inasmuch as it is knowable, and the good and the true each include the other, and since the true and the good therefore are not different objects, it follows that the practical and the theoretical intellects are not different potencies.[18]

The practical reason, which produces things, has its field of activity in the sphere of arts and morals. In the arts the practical reason tends to a particular end, to something that has been thought out by the mind; in the sphere of morals the practical reason aims at the general purpose of all human life. Thus the particular end should be subordinate to the general end.

In the order of values the theoretical reason is superior to the practical reason for three reasons: first, it is the noblest of man's activities since it may turn to God as its object; secondly, the acts of the speculative reason are desirable in themselves, whereas the

---

[18] *Ibid.*, III, 3; *Summa theol.*, Ia, q. 79, a. 11.

acts of the practical reason are desired because of the act; thirdly, man shares theoretical reason with God and the angels, but the practical activity corresponds to the activities of the lower beings. Through his speculative reason man enters into a union with the higher spiritual beings, and his perfect happiness in the life to come will consist exclusively in contemplation; even his imperfect happiness here on earth consists primarily in contemplation and only secondarily in the activity of the practical reason directed to the ordering of human actions and affections.[19]

An important part of human reason, that unites past, present, and future, is the spiritual or intellectual memory. Together with Aristotle but in disagreement with Avicenna, St. Thomas defends the existence of this memory. Avicenna was willing to admit only the sense memory, because he thought that only in the corporeal organs could an impression perdure. He thought that the possible intellect was dependent upon the active intellect whenever it was in need of intelligible forms. St. Thomas, however, emphasized the existence of reminiscences of spiritual forms, and attributed this *vis conservatrix specierum,* this treasury of all universal forms and essences, to the possible intellect.[20] We are here reminded of St. Augustine's teaching on the memory. The great doctor of the Church also considered the memory as the basis for all remembering, as the storehouse in which were gathered all human experiences. But for him the memory was still more; it had a still deeper significance. Within the inner memory (*memoria interior*) understanding and will united to form a centralized spiritual life. According to St. Augustine, this inner memory was not only that spacious chamber in which all the forms of being are received, but it was at the same time the place in which the soul comes to know itself, where the soul meets God, and where, by some law of gravitation, the soul tends toward God. Thus the imprint of St. Augustine's profound psychological studies is clearly seen in his metaphysics of the human personality.

b) **The will.** Just as the animal appetite supplements the senses, so the spiritual appetite, the will, supplements the faculty of spiritual knowledge. The potencies of knowledge and appetite belong together necessarily in immaterial beings. St. Thomas speaks of the will as

---

[19] *Summa theol.,* Ia IIae, q.3, a.5.
[20] *Ibid.,* Ia, q.79, a.6 ad 2 f.; *Contra Gent.,* II, 74.

the intellectual appetite, *voluntas est appetitus intellectivus.*[21] Thus man is lifted above irrational creatures by another distinguishing mark, namely, by his power to dominate his own actions, a power that rests on the freedom of his will.[22] St. Thomas was greatly concerned to define the relation between the intellect and the will and clearly to distinguish the will from the sensible appetite and the strivings of natural things.

The will and the intellect are not only specifically different potencies, but, because of the entire difference between their proper objects, they are really in two different genera of potencies. The object of the intellect is truth, the object of the will is the good. As in every other appetitive faculty, the movement of the will is outward toward things, while the movement of the intellect, on the contrary, is from things to the soul. The term of the appetite is the good which is in the desired object.

If, however, we consider the will and the intellect in their relations to that in which they are rooted, namely, the essence of the soul, we see that the will and the intellect are indeed powers of the same part of the soul, and that they have much in common. Both are clearly different from the sensible appetite, and both are immaterial potencies without corporeal organs. Both are directed to the universal, and because of their immateriality they are in a sense unlimited. The intellect includes in its field all being, and so also the will can have as its object all things.

As the intellect is directed necessarily to the absolute truth of the first principles, so the will is directed to the absolute good, the *beatitudo.*[23] Because they are fundamentally rooted in the same part, St. Thomas says that the intellect and the will are as principles to each other and that the one includes the other. Whatever is in the will, is also to a certain extent in the intellect. The objects of the two potencies are also mutually inclusive. From this follows the mutual interdependence and the close cooperation of these two faculties. Every act of the will is dependent on an act of the intellect (*nil volitum nisi praecognitum*), since the will becomes active only when the cognitive faculty presents some object to it (*bonum intellectum*

---

[21] *Summa theol.,* Ia, q.19, a.1; q.87, a.4.
[22] *Ibid.,* Ia IIae, q.1, a.1–3.
[23] *Ibid.,* Ia, q.19, a.3; *De malo,* III, 3; *Contra Gent.,* II, 47.

movet voluntatem). It is the practical reason that presents the objects and envisages the end and thus moves the will, whereas the judging reason points out the values of things or their qualities. This presentation of the objects with their valuations is a necessary prerequisite for the actions and decisions of the will. Without the knowledge supplied by the intellect there is no willing, no surrender to the object desired or loved. The intellect or the reason is the eye that lends vision to the will. Knowledge by its guidance and direction and the will by its commands unite in human actions to effect a common result. On the other hand, all knowledge is dependent on the will inasmuch as the will must will the knowledge. The will is the motor power of all of the soul's activities (except the vegetative faculty) and thus the will is the mover of the reason and the intellect.

The will belongs to the genus of appetitive faculties; nevertheless it is a faculty distinct from the sensitive appetite. The sensitive appetite strives for good things, whereas the will desires the good and individual things from the general viewpoint of the good. The will desires the good for itself, the animal appetite strives after individual things inasmuch as they share in the good.

Like all other appetitive faculties in the natural order of things, the human will also is directed by an inner necessity to its ultimate end of happiness. With respect to this end man has no freedom; his freedom applies only to the means to be used in the attainment of this goal.[24] This does not mean that violence is done the will or that the will is enslaved with respect to the final end; it is merely a result of that harmony that flows from the order of the universe. In the order of knowledge we recognize the axiom that like is known through like; in the appetite it is also true that every striving is toward that which is favorable and advantageous to the whole being.[25] By striving for the natural good the resemblance to God is attained. As an Aristotelian, St. Thomas finds the happiness of this life to consist in the contemplation of God, and the perfect happiness of the next life in the vision of God. All subordinate ends are only partially good, inasmuch as they are related to the final end.

Several different acts proceed directly from the will. At present we will consider three. The first belongs obviously to the will, the

[24] *Summa theol.*, Ia, q. 60, a. 1.
[25] *Ibid.*, Ia IIae, q. 8, a. 1.

willing and loving of the end. The second and third acts are intention and choice; since both of these are concerned with the attainment of the end, they are related to each other, but they differ
in having different functions. The intention consists in the striving
for anything in so far as it leads to the end. The relation of a thing
to the end is presented by the reason. The act of choice is the decision
between the means that may lead to the attainment of the end. In the
act of choice the freedom of the will may best be seen.

The two faculties of cognition and appetite cooperate in the act
of choice. The cognitive faculty provides the evaluating judgment
and offers counsel as to which object is to be preferred, while the
appetitive faculty supplies the approval. The simple act of willing
the end is intimately connected with the act of choice because, when
the will strives for a certain end, it necessarily determines itself to
will the means also. Between this act of willing the end and the
willing of the means, a judgment of the reason is made. St. Thomas
inserts another act before the actual act of choice, namely, the act of
consent (*consensus*), which is the act of the appetitive faculty directed to something that must be done, differing from the act of
choice inasmuch as it includes a number of suitable means, whereas
the act of choice determines the one that is to be used. Choice is the
last act of the will that deals with the means. Thereupon reason
plays another part in issuing the command; it not only judges that
it is good to will, but it also commands the will itself. Following this
act comes the act of use, that is, the desire to possess the thing in
actuality.

The inner relationship between the intellect and the will may be
made clearer by analogy. As in the cognitive plane principles are
related to conclusions, so in the appetitive plane means are related
to the end; as the intellect is related to reason, so the will is related
to free choice; and as intellect and reason belong to the same faculty,
so also do the act of the will and the act of choice.[26]

Since it is the human reason that knows the end and its significance, the road to the attainment of the end and the relationship of
means to the end, and further, since the act of choice is based on the
judgment of the practical reason with its ability to contemplate, compare, and evaluate, St. Thomas concluded with Aristotle that the
root of freedom was in the reason (*totus libertatis radix est in ra-*

[26] *Ibid.*, Ia, q. 83, a. 4.

tione), and declared that freedom went hand in hand with reason.[27]
The attribute of freedom, however, also belongs to the will since the
freedom of choice is an endowment of the will as well as of the intellect. Freedom has a twofold root, in the will as in its subject, and
in the reason as in its cause. St. Thomas supports this view with this
observation: the will is able to turn freely to several different objects
because the reason reveals the good in these different objects.[28] The
prerequisite for the decision of the will is the intelligible presentation
of various objects as they are evaluated by the reason.

Freedom belongs to the will in three ways: (1) with respect to its
act inasmuch as it is able to will or not will; (2) with respect to the
object inasmuch as it is able to will this and that and their opposites;
(3) with respect to the relationship to the end inasmuch as it is able
to will the good or the evil.[29] In contrast to the sensible appetite, the
will determines itself, its act is self-determination. The quality of self-
reflection belongs to the will and the intellect; in the intellect it manifests itself as self-knowledge and self-control, and in the will as
self-control and self-determination.

When he compares the human will with the divine will and that
of the pure spirits, St. Thomas points out that in God and in the
angels the will has for its basis the clear and unclouded intellectual
vision of their intellects, whereas man must depend on the deficient
and faulty basis of knowledge that is distorted by error and doubt.
The human will, like that of every created spirit, in contrast to the
divine will, is by its nature capable of good and evil. Man is able to
rebel against the order of nature, and sin; he is a moral being and
also a sinful being. St. Thomas ventures the statement: evil is most
frequently found in man (*malum est in pluribus in specie humana*).
On the other hand man is able to acquire the habit of virtue, and to
will and actualize the good.

Because he is equipped with reason and will, man stands out as
the only sensible being on earth that is at the same time conscious
of its actions. Adhering to the tradition that went before him, St.
Thomas attributes to man a twofold activity, *facere* and *agere*, making and acting. The first he conceives to be all handiwork, all technical activity that tends to the external world, all the activity that is

[27] *De verit.*, XXIV, 1, 2.
[28] *Summa theol.*, Ia IIae, q.17, a.1 ad 2.
[29] *De verit.*, XXII, 6.

controlled by the *recta ratio factibilium* and has as its purpose the production of external cultural objects.

But there is an activity that is nobler than the shaping of the external world, more important than the beautifying and improving
of external life, higher than craftsmanship and the arts, namely, the
perfection of the subject of the activity himself, the complete development of one's own personality. The moral development and
culture of one's own inner life is a prerequisite and at the same time
the norm for all activity that tends to the outside.

All action and willing in man proceeds from his practical reason.
In his synteresis, that is, his habitual knowledge of the primary principles of moral action, man possesses that faculty of his reason which
enables him to know unerringly and directly the first moral principles; it is a consciousness of true values, an evaluating knowledge,
scientia approbationis, that points out the good and turns the will
toward the realization of the good. In his conscience man has a
faculty that is able to apply the general moral principles to individual
cases. The conscience, says St. Thomas, has three functions: first,
it merely ascertains whether a thing has been done or not; secondly,
it evaluates and judges whether a thing should be done or omitted,
from which arises the feeling of obligation; and thirdly, conscience
recalls the norms of conduct and compares an action with them,
from which arises accusation, approval, or condonation.[30] Thus man
possesses an inner light by which he is guided, an inner law of his
actions, the self-legislation of his practical reason which is indeed
independent of his subjective attitudes because the moral order is
based on the order of being, and the moral goodness of our acts is
judged by comparison with this objective order. From this St.
Thomas concluded that the natural law was inscribed on man's reason, and that, since the natural law was only an integral part of the
universal law of God, man was placed in relationship with the highest law. Here is man's peculiar position in the universe: he is oriented
to a cosmos of values for whose realization and actualization he is
able to labor entirely conscious of his activity. This cosmos of values,
however, is not a strange and alien world; it is rather the essential
concept of the ideal human nature as it is developed in time, place,
circumstances, and in different individualities. Animals have a sensitive life of pleasure, and the pure spirits have as their proper form

[30] *Contra Gent.,* III, 47; *Summa theol.,* Ia, q. 79, a. 12 f.

of life an activity consisting in the development of the speculative intellect; but man's life consists in an activity that embraces the various forms of the moral virtues.

Human volition is not an exclusively spiritual thing, circumscribed by reason; it is, in accord with human nature, under the influence of the sensitive passions, a mixture of compulsion and freedom. The passions of the sensitive appetite play an important part in the economy of each human life. Since they are integral parts of the emotional life of the soul, they are able to hinder or further man's willing and acting. The passions, according to St. Thomas, have a threefold relation to the will. First, they may be the objects of the will, namely, when they are willed. Secondly, they may be as principles to the will inasmuch as they urge the will on or direct it, and they may do this in one of two ways: when the will accepts the sensible and makes it its own, and also when the passions drive the will in a direction opposed to the inclination of the will. Thirdly, the passions may be effects of the will inasmuch as the passions participate in the striving of the will or when the will spontaneously and on reflection calls the passions into being. Thus the sensitive passions may sometimes precede the will, sometimes they may also follow the will.

If passions preceding the will's activity arise suddenly and reach great intensity, they diminish or even destroy the will's ability to distinguish, upon which every virtuous act depends; and thus they hamper the freedom of the will and also the goodness of the act. In a truly virtuous man the passions are ruled by reason; a strong will enlists the emotions and passions in its own service. Whenever one of the passions serves the will, it is an indication of the will's energy. St. Augustine and St. Thomas formulate the law that intensive willing always releases a passion in the lower appetite, and the will can accomplish the act it intends more easily and more perfectly when it has called in the supporting cooperation of one of the passions of the lower appetite.

Mental and spiritual concepts can influence the passions in two ways, through the will and through the imagination. In the latter instance the mental concept takes on a particular form in the imagination and thus influences the sensible appetite. Inversely, the sensible appetite and the passions are able to affect the reason by proposing to it some apparent good in place of a genuine good, thus affecting the will's evaluation of an object. In such an instance man necessarily follows the goal placed by the passions. The passions do not necessarily influence the will's choice, however, because the autonomous power of the spiritual personality is arrayed against it and this power of the personality is able to perfect the faculties of the mind and will.[31]

The passions are legitimate parts of the human person; in conjunction with the whole and under the domination of the reason and the will, they serve the good. In the original state of justice, complete harmony existed between the spirit and the sensible nature, but when man turned from God disorder arose in the lower powers. If the natural order is restored by reason and the sensible nature is given a proper goal, and if the passions are bridled and directed to the good, they also become good. Whenever they are beyond the control of reason, however, they lead to evil. The control of the passions is one of the marks of man's perfection which is attained when the whole man turns to the good and when inclination and duty are coordinated in the harmonious relationship of a soul ruled by intellect and will.

In attempting to place the intellect and the will in the order of their importance, St. Thomas shows clearly that he is under the twofold influence of Aristotle the intellectualist and St. Augustine the voluntarist. In Aristotle, Hellenic intellectualism had reached its highest point. God, so they said, was devoid of any will and found eternal happiness in self-contemplation; accordingly the highest and noblest faculty was the thinking *nous* which devoted itself to the highest purpose, the comprehension of first principles. This thinking *nous* alone was immortal.

Taught by the wealth of his own personal experiences as well as by the Christian faith, St. Augustine approached this question of the relative value of intellect and will, and ultimately decided for the primacy of the will. St. Thomas tried to adjust this difference between the two great thinkers; however, he remained an intellectualist at all times. In itself the intellect is higher than the will because the object of the intellect is simpler, more abstract, more absolute, and more valuable than the object of the will; for St. Thomas, the object is the criterion of judgment in such a comparison as this.

Secundum quid, however, that is, in relation to another factor, the will may be higher than the intellect. Thus the will excels when

---

[31] *Summa theol.,* Ia, 81, a.2; Ia IIae, q.9, a.2; IIa IIae, q.156, a.1.

the being in which the good is found is higher or nobler than the soul in which the intellectual content is found; the intellect is higher when that being in which the good is found is beneath the knowing intellect. The knowledge of material things is therefore nobler than the love for them, but the love of God is nobler than the knowledge of God. Even from this viewpoint St. Thomas was unable to make a bridge over to the purely Augustinian theory; the intellectualism of Aristotle remained a dominant factor in his mind, and he accumulated reasons to show that the ultimate goal of the whole man consisted in the knowledge of the first truth, i.e., God. Man's supreme happiness, he said, consisted in the full development of man's essential characteristic, his intellect and reason.[32]

c) **Man's social and religious aptitudes.** Human activity arises from knowledge and willing. Man's equipment corresponds to his tasks. By his knowledge man expands and extends himself to the whole universe of being and makes it his own; his practical activity, however, is directed to cultural tasks in the external world and to the still more important task of morally improving his own inner life and also cooperating to bring about the moral and cultural progress of the community.[33] We would have an inadequate concept of man if we did not point out particularly an important characteristic, namely, the solidarity of humanity. By his very nature man is a social being. Aristotle had emphasized that thought, and St. Thomas developed it further: man has an essential relation to the community. Only in the community can the development of the spiritual and moral personality take place, only in the community can the personality of man reach maturity, only in the communities of marriage, the family, the parish, and the state can man's cultural activity be carried on. In the community, by means of his natural powers and his natural virtues of mind and will, man attains his natural happiness.

Man is not only a citizen of this earth; by his reason and spirituality, the imprint of the divine Spirit, man is lifted up above the other material beings and made a citizen of a higher, divine kingdom, "whose king is God, whose subjects are the angels and saints, whether these last reign in glory in their fatherland or whether they

[32] *Contra Gent.*, III, 25 f.
[33] *Ibid.*, II, 24.

are still on their pilgrimage here on earth." [34] Man's cultural activities are not ends in themselves, they are preliminary steps to a higher end. The ultimate goal of all spiritual beings is the knowledge and the love of God. The end toward which man tends is God, and all beings lower than man tend toward God through man. By his very nature man is religious, every fiber of his being turns naturally toward God. This direct and immediate relationship to God is a special characteristic of man's nature.[35]

The supernatural goal of man's life to be attained in the next life is something that transcends his natural powers and can be attained only with the help of God's grace. Even in the state of pure nature in Paradise man would have needed divine grace if he wished to perform acts that lay beyond his nature; all the more, therefore, will man, weakened by sin, need grace to obtain forgiveness of sin, perseverance in good, and eternal happiness.

Reason and will are the faculties that require supernatural helps in the form of the divine virtues. Reason is strengthened by the light of faith; the will is helped by hope and love. The subject in which grace resides in man is something more fundamental than the powers of the soul; it is the soul itself as a rational being which partakes of the divine nature by a certain regeneration (*per quandam regenerationem sive recreationem*).[36]

The act of faith is an act of the intellect assenting to a divine truth. This act is commanded by the will under the influence of divine grace; both intellect and will, therefore, take part in the act of faith.[37] Hope resides in the spiritual appetite and has God Himself for its object, being directed to Him as to its ultimate goal. The relation between hope and love accounts for the fact that love which is directed to God as the object of happiness is attributed to the same faculty as hope.

Because of his rational faculty and his life joined to God in grace, man receives the seven gifts of the Holy Ghost, which make him susceptible to the workings of divine grace. Piety, fortitude, and the fear of the Lord belong to the appetitive faculty; the others—under-

---

[34] *De verit.*, I, 9.
[35] *Contra Gent.*, III, 25.
[36] *Summa theol.*, Ia IIae, q. 110, a. 4 ad 1, 3.
[37] *Ibid.*, IIa IIae, q. 2, a. 9.

standing, wisdom, knowledge, and counsel—refer to supernatural knowledge based on faith. The content of faith is to be apprehended and understood by man. By supernatural acts, such as the blessed in heaven exercise in a perfect manner, the speculative reason attains the knowledge of the articles of faith and of all that is connected with them. By the gift of understanding, man's higher reason is perfected so that it may be properly subordinated to divine principles and norms. Although some resemblance exists between this act of wisdom and the knowledge of first principles, it belongs to the supernatural order because of divine cooperation. To persevere in faith, man must be able to make a right judgment about the content of faith; when this judgment refers to divine things he is helped by the gift of wisdom, when it refers to created things he is helped by the gift of knowledge. The correct application of all these things to particular instances is based on the gift of counsel.[38]

Out of the intimate union of knowledge and the spiritual appetite arises the affective vision of God (*cognitio affectiva*), which is a supernatural knowledge based on faith. One of the ennobling marks of the religious man is prophecy, an extraordinary and supernatural illumination which only a few of the elect enjoy for a time. Intellect and phantasy take part in prophecy, the former in a twofold manner, as knowing (seeing) and judging the subject of the prophecy. In prophecy the intellect goes far beyond its natural boundaries, and sometimes the prophetic illumination entails a suspension of the senses. The highest point in the divine working of grace is reached in ecstasy by which man is lifted up to a direct and supernatural vision of God, like that of the saints in heaven, and is temporarily endowed with the light of glory. God alone is the cause of this act of grace which until now, according to St. Thomas, has been vouchsafed to only two men, Moses and St. Paul.

All that Philo adopted from the religion of the Greeks and from the works of Plato and Poseidonius about the preliminaries, the progress, and the end of ecstasy was assimilated into Christian thought, and St. Thomas found plentiful sources in Pseudo-Dionysius, St. Augustine, St. Gregory the Great, and Hugh and Richard of St. Victor. The possibility of ecstasy is based on man's relationship with God. Even though in ecstasy the ultimate and exclusive cause is the working of grace, and although man is lifted above the use

[38] *Ibid.*, Ia IIae, q.62, a.1; q.68, a.1 f.

of his senses, still ecstasy does not destroy his human nature. St. Thomas explained the phenomenon of ecstasy by his well-known principle that, when one of the faculties is exercised to its utmost, the others are suspended. The intellect does not need the senses for its activity, and in ecstasy, this highest of religious experiences, the soul attains a purely spiritual vision independent of the senses. The point is in entire harmony with St. Thomas' psychology.

CHAPTER XIV

_____

THE HUMAN PERSON

1. The unity of the human person. In each of us the body and soul form a twofold unity, the unity of a nature and the unity of the person. The unity of a nature arises inasmuch as the body is united to the soul which confers on the body such a completion that out of the two a nature ensues in the same way as a nature arises out of potency and act, and matter and form. The unity of the person arises inasmuch as an individual possesses a corporeal-spiritual subsistence. The metaphysical structure of man could scarcely be expressed more succinctly. This unique union of body and soul forms the basis for specific and individual unity, and this individual unity in man is also unique. Man is a substance, he possesses an autonomous being, he is an individual, i.e., he has an undivided, self-inclusive, distinct, incommunicable being, but in this he does not differ from the other sublunary beings. Every animal, plant, and element is a substance and an individual; but man is more, he is a person, i.e., a concrete individual, an individual substance endowed with reason. The well known definition of person, taken from Boethius, as *rationalis naturae individua substantia,* or more briefly still, *suppositum rationalis creaturae,* expresses the idea of spiritual autonomy.[1]

Not every individual substance can be a person, but only those that have a complete specific nature. This point is of some importance, and St. Thomas puts great stress on it. The human soul in itself is not a person because it is only a part of human nature.[2] Only the individual man, composed of body and soul, is a person, and that because of the substantial and essential unity of his being. The term

[1] *In I Sent.,* 23, 1; 29, 1, 1; *In II Sent.,* 3, 1, 2; *Summa theol.,* Ia, q.29, a.1 f.; *De pot.,* VIII, 4 ad5; *De un. verb. incarn.,* 1.
[2] *Summa theol.,* Ia, q.75, a.2; q.75, a.4.

"person" is applied to that individual substance which, because of
its characteristic of rationality and intelligence, stands far above the
rest of material beings and which expresses the most perfect thing
in nature. From this spiritual autonomy follows man's faculty of self-
determination in willing and acting, and on it is based especially the
important philosophical corollary that man is a value in himself and
an end in himself.

The human person stands at the beginning of a line of beings
which continues on and finds more perfect expression and higher
forms in the pure intelligences. The concept of person is a concept of
a natural thing, the concept of personality is a cultural concept; persons should develop and unfold into personalities with the help of
the powers and faculties that lie dormant in the person itself.

This corporeal-spiritual unity of the person is shown to exist by the
happenings of everyday life. As a consequence we see how the different powers of the person react mutually upon one another, in-
fluencing one another, and have their common root in the person.
In accord with the principle, *ejus est agere cujus est esse,* all activity
emanates from the central ego. It is not the soul that hears, sees, feels,
thinks, and acts; it is man that thinks, acts, hears, and sees. Every
perfection of any one of the faculties is really a perfection belonging
to the person.[3] This fact, that the powers and faculties are rooted in
the personal unity, is manifest from the fact that, when sustained
and intensified activity of one of the faculties occurs, the other faculties are often suspended in their activity, and also from the fact that
acts of one and the same faculty mutually exclude each other. St.
Thomas illustrates the matter by referring to the phenomenon of
ecstasy. Because of this fundamental unity in the person, the higher
potencies are able to flow out over the lower, and the lower faculties
likewise may exercise a counterinfluence on the higher powers of
the individual. A surplus of activity in the soul may even flow out
into the body and vice versa. Thus inordinate joy or sadness may
cause physical changes, even death, in the body, while physical
changes may affect the soul and bring on unconsciousness. This
unity of the person in man also explains man's manner of existence
in the next life; the soul in glory will effect the transfiguration of
the body.[4]

[3] *De verit.,* II, 7; *Summa theol.,* Ia, q.75, a.2 ad2.
[4] *De verit.,* XXVI, 10 ad2, 16.

2. The substantial differences among human persons. Like his master Aristotle, St. Thomas was primarily interested in the study of what was similar in all individual beings. But he was not unaware of the differences that exist in human personalities and in the courses that human lives follow. He teaches not only that men differ from one another in their bodies, but also that their souls are individually different. On this point he is in agreement with the other Scholastics. In attempting to assign a reason for this difference in human persons, St. Albert was able to offer only one: that thereby the wisdom and power of the Creator would be more manifest. St. Bonaventure also accepted this reason, although he adduced another reason: that man's physical organization required a differentiation in the person. Richard of Middletown and Peter of Tarantasia sought for the cause of the differences in human persons in what they called spiritual matter. Souls are different, depending on whether they have more or less of this matter.

Relying on his theory of the relation between matter and form, St. Thomas offered another solution of the problem. The relationship of form to matter, of the soul to a particular disposition of the body, which we find in the various species, is also found to exist in individuals, and therefore in man a special soul, destined for a particular body, corresponds to each human body.[5] God creates a soul to correspond to the body produced by the parents and thus *this* man originates from *this* body and *this* soul. The soul transforms the body into an organism, but it does not enter into the body until certain conditions are realized. These conditions again have a countereffect on the soul itself. Each man, therefore, is distinct and substantially different from other men, and from this it follows that each man's activity is different from that of other human beings. From the first day of his existence the uniqueness of each man is firmly established. Every man is equipped with a fund of attitudes and dispositions; his physical dispositions are derived directly from his parents by inheritance, while his spiritual and mental dispositions and equipment are indirectly determined by his physical part since his soul is made to suit a particular body at the time of procreation. Every individual possesses a definite physical character, and this physical character has a causal dependence on matter and is moreover predetermined with its congenital dispositions and capabilities for perfection to a certain course

---

[5] *In I Sent.*, 8, 5, 2; *Contra Gent.*, II, 73; *De anima*, III, 19; *De pot.*, III, 9 ad 7

of life. St. Thomas points to the individual differences among men in their mental powers and intellectual contributions, in their temperaments and moral inclinations, and in their aptitudes and interests as unmistakable proof of the radical difference between man and man.[6]

3. **The difference between man and woman.** Differential psychology attempts to isolate and define the various types of personality, character, temperament, intellectual and emotional endowment, etc., found in men. In the same way the study of differential anthropology seeks to show the various forms of human existence that are based on sex, race, and the different stages of development. Although the students of the Middle Ages made some valuable contributions to the science of characterology, they remained far removed from the ideal of a differential study of character and personality. St. Thomas speaks only of the difference between man and woman, and he proposes the subject in a manner scarcely intelligible for the modern reader.

Being convinced of the substantial difference between individuals, St. Thomas drew the conclusion that person is not above sex, and that the difference between man and woman reaches down into the substance of human beings. Sex, therefore, is the basis for different physical characters.

His observations about man and woman are based on the conviction that woman is inferior to man. He was greatly influenced in this respect by the Stagirite's lack of esteem for woman and also perhaps by the opinions of the age. In agreement with Aristotle, St. Thomas reiterates the opinion that man represents in himself perfection, while woman stands for the imperfect, and that nature at all times is bent on the production of the male and produces the female only when it is thwarted by inner or outer factors. The woman comes into existence only *per accidens,* because some process of nature has gone awry, and woman is therefore actually "the male gone awry," *mas occasionatus.* Christian thought, however, forestalled any cruder conclusions and obliged St. Thomas to make the following distinctions: with respect to human nature in general, woman is not a mere accidental result, she is rather something intended by nature and willed by the Creator because of the propagation of the race. With respect to her own particular nature, however, woman is something defective and accidental, *aliquid deficiens et occasionatum,* because the active

[6] *Summa theol.,* IIa IIae, q.51, a.1; q.63, a.1.

power of generation in man seeks to produce something perfect like to man himself. If a woman is produced, this is owing to weakness in the man's power of generation, to some indisposition in the matter, or to some external factor, such as dampness which is often caused by the south wind.[7]

For this evaluation of man and woman, St. Thomas relied on the contemporary conclusions of biology. The woman possessed an imperfect faculty of procreation, she merely contributed the material for the production of the living being, and in contrast to man she was the passive principle while man was the active and form-giving principle. The superiority of the form over the matter is sufficiently well known. Not only does woman contribute the less important part to the production of the offspring, but she has the weaker body, the smaller growth, and a weaker intellect and less will power. Woman is to man as the senses are to the reason, or as the lower reason is to the higher reason. In woman the concupiscible appetite predominates, while man is the expression of the more stable element. Because both have reason, man and woman are said to be in the likeness of God, but man is the image of God in a special manner, because he is the principle and the end of woman, as God is the principle and ultimate end of the universe.

In the same way St. Thomas depreciates the functions of the woman. Woman depends on man in the act of procreation and for guidance throughout life, whereas man needs woman only in the act of procreation. His erroneous notion about the act of generation impelled St. Thomas to look on man as the master, and the woman as a mere helper. Man is able to accomplish all other tasks in life better than woman, even the care of the home and the education and training of the children.

St. Thomas makes woman intimately dependent on man; she is *aliquid viri,* a part, as it were, of man's body. Therefore man is her head and superior; he must guide her and may correct and discipline her. Woman is like a minor. Her lowly position extends also into public life. Obviously, according to St. Thomas, she is unfitted to fill any position in the Church; she is not a full-fledged citizen because she cannot exercise any civil rights. Within the home woman finds her position more favorable; here she is an equal to her husband and here she possesses some rights to personal freedom. But even here the

---

[7] *Ibid.,* Ia, q.92, a.1; q.99, a.2 ad1; q.115, a.3 ad4.

rights of man and woman are only proportional. Their rights to marital intercourse are not equal, and the duties of married life are distributed in the man's favor since man and woman in marriage have the relationship of master to servant. St. Thomas tries to preserve the religious dignity of woman; woman has the same supernatural end and is capable of receiving the same graces. Only in the natural sphere does she hold an inferior position, only with respect to her natural rights is she at a disadvantage.[8]

Seldom has it occurred that a thinker who has had such a profound influence on the thought of centuries has erred so profoundly with regard to the nature of woman as the medieval, cloistered St. Thomas. He thought that man would be able to perform household duties better than woman because he saw only brothers performing these tasks in his monastery. His lack of appreciation of woman as mother and wife is more amazing, as are his astounding views about women's souls and minds. The problem is partly explained by the fact that St. Thomas entered the monastery when he was only five years old, and thus saw no women about nor did he need the ministrations of women. Besides the influence of his monastic life, he came under the influence of the thought of his times, which accorded scant consideration to woman's civil rights and her position in the state.

4. **The moving principle in the life of a personality.** The human person is equipped with various powers by which it carries out its tasks. These powers are rooted in the same principle and are related to one another. Where is the moving principle that sets the lower and higher vital powers in motion? This principle is synonymous with the natural system of urges, with the basic natural urges (*ad quae natura primo inclinat*), and with the natural inclinations, all of which are concerned with the preservation of the individual and the species, the formation of the community, and also the development of the spiritual, mental, moral, and religious qualities of the personality. Often, of course, the various forms of knowledge are only instruments and aids serving to satisfy man's needs, but in the higher plane the urge to know takes its place in the process of attaining the truth and of reaching the last end, God. These fundamental urges are intensified when they are joined to the affections and emotions, they receive a moral quality when they come under the rule of the practical intellect.

[8] *In III Sent.*, 3, 2.

Thus we see the psychological and anthropological aspects of human personality; the intensity and direction of the basic urges, the course of the affections and emotions, the various goals, and the durability and permanence of the principles of its acting and willing. Modern psychology and anthropology make a far more systematic study of these subjects than did the Middle Ages, but occasional references remind us that St. Albert and St. Thomas were not entirely ignorant of their implications.

CHAPTER XV

MAN'S METAPHYSICAL AND RELIGIOUS POSITION THE MEANING OF HIS EXISTENCE

From the earliest times the theories about the origin, make-up, and essence of man diverged in opposite directions. Even today opposite opinions are embattled against each other; of these, two were unknown to St. Thomas. He did not at any time think of man as a mere natural being, as a product of biological development, that is closely bound spiritually and corporeally to its starting point, the animal. Nor did he think of man as that problematical being whose true nature is only gradually revealed by the development of history. Man is not the summation of all that the various sciences have been able to conclude about him. The Thomist concept of man is composed of two integral parts, one philosophical, the other religious. The philosophical part is derived principally from Aristotle, the religious part comes from the teachings of the Christian faith.

Hellenism bequeathed to the Middle Ages a concept of man that was based on the opposites of theism and pantheism, of mortality and immortality, and the concept was ably defended by Plato, Aristotle, and the Stoics. According to this notion, man is a rational being; he is not a god, not even a miniature god. But he is endowed with a logos and he is able to know the universe and himself and accomplish certain tasks alone. He is not derived from subhuman nature, although he comprises within his nature both the vegetative and the animal form of being, uniting them into one psychological unity in such a way that these lower forms of being contribute to his being under the direction of his spirit. St. Thomas did not consider this concept a great discovery; it was rather something that could be discerned on the face of the facts of nature, knowledge that could easily be obtained by an analysis of man's essence. This concept is the supporting idea on which is built the structure of the Christian teaching about creation, man's state in Paradise, the Fall, and the redemption.

Here on earth man is the pinnacle since he is the most perfect of all natural beings; in the universe he is the middle being since in him the most perfect body is joined to the lowest of the spirits to form the unity of body-spirit-person. He is therefore a microcosm in which all the principles of being in the universe are gathered together.[1] "In a certain sense all things are found contained in man. He shares his intellect with the angels, his senses with the animals, his vegetative faculties with the plants, and his body with inanimate creatures." [2] According to the principle of continuity, all beings have their end in man. Prime matter is in potency to the forms of the elements, under the forms of the elements matter is in potency to the forms of the mixed bodies, under the forms of the mixed bodies it is in potency to the vegetative soul, the vegetative soul is in potency to the sensitive soul, the sensitive soul to the intellectual soul.

Matter seems to aim at the ultimate form, the form of man.[3] As all subhuman forms of being are united in man, so his intellect is a connecting link with the purely spiritual intelligences. Man is at the same time a summation and a bridge. His intellectual soul is *"quasi quidam horizon et confinium corporeorum, in quantum est substantia incorporea, corporis tamen forma.*[4] Man dominates all subhuman creation, which looks to him as the imperfect tends to the perfect.[5] Man, however, since he is a person, is an end in himself.[6] Although his body and spirit are separable, he is the beginning of those creatures that are not the trace of God but the image of God. As the image of God, he has an autonomous value and he is therefore not directed to the universe but to God as to his last end[7] In the incarnation of the Son of God human nature was united with God directly, and because man is by his nature directed to God, all other forms of being return to God in him and with him.[8]

---

[1] *Summa theol.,* Ia, q.91, a.1; Ia IIae, q.2, a.4.
[2] *Ibid.,* Ia, q.96, a.2.
[3] *Contra Gent.,* III, 23.
[4] *Ibid.,* II, 68.
[5] *Summa theol.,* IIa IIae, q.66, a.1.
[6] *Contra Gent.,* III, 112.
[7] *Ibid.,* III, 25; *Summa theol.,* Ia IIae, q.2 a.8 ad2.
[8] *Prol. in III Sent.*

Like every other creature, man possesses a finite, limited form of being, determined and defined within genus and species, a form of being that is imperfect because it is mixed with potentiality. The only perfect being is pure act which is also eternal. All created being is subject to change, and thus the attribute of time, temporality, is a quality of its form of existence. Finite beings not merely exist, they also come into being, they originate, they grow, develop, unfold powers and dispositions, and they strive toward certain ends set for them by the order of the world. The twin concepts of being and time have a place in the Christian philosophies of St. Augustine and St. Bonaventure, and for St. Thomas they are of special importance. The physical concept of time as the measure of movement, which St. Thomas adopted from the physics of Aristotle, was inadequate to explain the march of spiritual and historical progress, and therefore it had to be discarded for a more profound metaphysical concept.

Time is something created, it originated with the world, it is closely connected with the transition from non-being to being, and it is the existential form of all created being. Time belongs to the essence of the human being; it is in time that man unfolds his existence. In the history of Christianity time has a religious significance. No thinker has expressed himself more eloquently on this subject than St. Augustine. Since man is destined for another world, he finds no rest in this world, and since he bears within himself the divine spark, he is destined for eternity. St. Thomas readily accepted the thought developed by the Neoplatonists, that man stands on the border line between time and eternity (*quasi in horizonte existens aeternitatis et temporis*).[9]

St. Thomas is also a realist in his philosophizing. This fact may not appear immediately on the surface, as it does with St. Augustine, whose entire life was almost exclusively spent in a bitter strife about himself and his relation to God. In his inner life St. Thomas had no experience of the anguish, fear, terror, distraction, or despair that St. Augustine knew; from the beginning he was in the undisturbed possession of the content of Christian teaching and of the Christian way of life. In St. Augustine's life the whole meaning and purpose of human life was the point about which the strife raged, and the intense contemplation of his own soul and being was the way that led to truth and to God. During his wrestling, St. Augustine expressed the profound thought that man will discover what he is only in himself.

[9] *Contra Gent.*, II, 81; III, 61.

St. Thomas does not contradict the conclusions of the great doctor, but he seeks to support this knowledge of man's nature by making it a metaphysical and integral part of the knowledge of the whole universe. He placed anthropology firmly in the midst of a comprehensive study of all being and all values, and from this all-embracing science conclusions and consequences would, of their own accord, follow about man and his existence. The meaning of man's concrete existence, however, will not be clear without some knowledge of the essence of man.

No justification exists for the fear that St. Thomas may have been blind to the problems of an existential philosophy because he followed a master who was so intent on isolating the abstract essential structures of things. Ancient philosophers as well as the thinkers of the Middle Ages gave their attention to realistic problems, but they were careful not to sink into the exaggerated preoccupation with externals that characterizes modern secularized thinking. I call it secularized thinking because it originates in Protestant theology, especially that of Kierkegaard and to some extent that of Luther himself. It also finds expression in various Protestant works of prayer and piety. Ancient thought also had its pessimistic phases, but in general the great figures in ancient philosophy did not succumb. They admired the cosmos and tried to coordinate all things in this everflowing, eternal, cosmic life. Ancient man felt that he was a part of this great cosmos and he also felt that it was good to be in this cosmos. Even Plato, who looked with such great longing to a higher and spiritual world, was able to evaluate this world below as the image of a higher world. The Eros that lived in ancient man was at once the son of wealth and poverty, placed midway between the gods and the utter idiots, conscious of its own ignorance and destitution, but filled on the other hand with a burning desire for the highest knowledge and carried away far above this world to the highest good that alone would make life worth while.[10]

Aristotle, the philosopher of this actual world, saw the reason and meaning of things in themselves. From all eternity this cosmos included all the forms of being in itself, all those forms that manifest their characters and fulfill their teleological purposes. Aristotle has no doubt that "being is better than non-being, that life is better than

---

[10] Plato, *Symp.*, 211 f

non-life, that pure spirit is better than the soul." [11] The kingdom of being ascends hierarchically, and man excels all other mundane beings because of his characteristic mark of reason, and by his reason and his will he contributes his part to complete the meaning of the whole universe. The *Nicomachean Ethics* sang the praises of the rights and dignity of the human personality in the great cosmos.

Ancient philosophy was as devoid of nihilism and despair as it was of self-degradation. We need only consider the Stoics, their wonderment at the universe, their praise of the divine first cause, their assent to the course of the universe, and their submission to divine providence. Since he was an integral part of the cosmos, man had a duty to perform and he was obliged to complete his particular stage of being by developing his reason. He is able to attain this end even in spite of the vagaries of fate and the evil in the world. Besides this, he has no other concern in the world. We recall the noble figure of the imperial philosopher, Marcus Aurelius, who governed his life and prepared for death so calmly. "Do your duty," he said; "do it as if every action were your last, and when life's end comes, depart cheerfully, saying a grateful farewell to the tree on which you ripened as an olive and to the bough that bore you." The Hellenist stood solidly in this world, whether he thought that he was a member of a pantheistic cosmos, or whether he was in a Neoplatonic Pythagorean world that would serve as a springboard for his ascent to a mystical union with divinity.

If the position of the ancient was so solidly established in philosophy, the thinkers of the Middle Ages were even more secure in their philosophical outlook. Christian philosophy was able to give a less hesitant answer to the basic problem of all philosophy, the question why things are. Viewed metaphysically, the world is a cosmos created by God by a free act of His will, a manifestation of His power and wisdom. Within this cosmos man has a definite metaphysical position. No thing is without a purpose, and thus *ens et bonum convertuntur*. This axiom became the bulwark standing against any devaluation of being, and in the same way the concept of the universe as an order prevented any denial of the intrinsic value of being.

All things are signs, vestiges of the Creator, and man is more, he is the image of God. Man, indeed, like all other material and earthly

[11] *De gen. animal.,* II, 1.

creatures bears the marks of temporality, nothingness, limitation, and a certain inclination toward death, especially since he lost the primeval direction of order by original sin. But since he is the image and reflection of God, he still has a relation to God, a kinship with God, and because of the fact of the divine redemption man may be elevated to the sonship of God by grace. The apparent contradictions to his being that are offered by his sufferings, his guilt, and death itself are erased, and these things take on a meaning. He may be torn hither and thither between closeness to God and separation from Him, he may be tossed about in a kind of metaphysical storm,—St. Augustine is the great example—but this unrest is only another proof that the universe has no meaning without God. A profound, living faith during the Middle Ages prevented men from sinking into the abyss of nihilism.

Man's ultimate end is in the world beyond, it consists in a perduring union with God. From God man receives the law of his being and of his actions, impressed on his reason, and toward God man is directed as to his beginning and his end. This relationship to God, this ordering to God, is an essential attribute of man's nature. Only from the divine viewpoint can any light be thrown on man's existence, and only from that viewpoint can man's nature and his value be estimated. Like that of St. Augustine, the anthropology of St. Thomas Aquinas is theocentric.

Religion seeks to offer an explanation for the individual's destiny and for the history of the race. In both instances free will is found to be a magnificent as well as dangerous gift. Man actually abused it and sinned. Then the order in nature established by God was overturned. Christian revelation tells of the mystery of original sin and relates how sin became universal and touched all with its mark. Each individual has sufficient experience in himself of the corruption of human nature, of the power of evil, and of the force of wickedness in his own attitudes and condition. The original ordering to God was lost, although the consciousness of sin included in itself a consciousness of God. Within man's nature, however, the possibility for a healing of his condition remained; the re-establishment of his relation with God by means of grace, merited by the divine act of redemption, could still be hoped for.

As a historical being, man is the center of the world, his history is the history of salvation, the great process of human recovery which, in this life, does not indeed lead to his original state in Paradise but which will restore to man a relationship to God, and also a right relationship both to himself and to his neighbor. By the position accorded him in the mystical body of Christ, man's natural relation to God, by reason of his creation, is given the highest consecration. Thus the philosophy of St. Thomas is not a heroic nihilism, or a heroic acknowledgment of futility, but rather a heroic confession of the infinite and divine basis of our being in which all finite things are contained and in which the value and purpose of the human person are firmly established.

How shall we evaluate the anthropology of St. Thomas? Its religious elements, of course, are a matter of religious assent and do not concern us as philosophers. Nowadays philosophical anthropology is always disturbed by the problem of the proper approach to man. Both ancient and medieval thinkers were right when they fixed man's position in the cosmos after an impartial consideration of the facts of nature and a comparison of man with other beings beneath him as well as above him. But, we may ask, is man really that middle being? If we are to determine the middle, we must have a comprehensive knowledge of the terms and of the intermediary beings. Certainly we do not know all the grades of being that actually exist or that are possible in the universe. May there not well be, in the vast extent of the universe, kinds of being which we have no inkling of? The medieval thinker had a comparatively narrow concept of the universe and, about determining the middle point in the grades of being, he had no hesitation such as we have today.

The problem might be solved as Pascal tried to solve it. He thought that the middle point among creatures was a matter of subjective feeling. Man can feel that he is midway between the infinitely great to which he looks up with awe and wonderment, and the infinitely small which seems to recede ever farther from him. Such a concept of the middle being was not acceptable to the Middle Ages, nor would the modern subjective viewpoint be acceptable.

Throughout all his speculations St. Thomas never lost sight of man's place in nature, but he might have given more thought to the study of the history of man's development. Again, St. Thomas might have given more attention to what is instinctive in man, to the various urges, the animal part of his nature, and even that which is bestial. He took into consideration the technical achievements of man, although he did not give them nearly as much attention as does the modern world. In principle, St. Thomas was undoubtedly right in giving the greater prominence to the metaphysical and religious man, because the technical man is, after all, guided in his actions by the dictates of his higher being. In a sense, it seems that St. Thomas might have envisaged the future when the technical man would go beyond his proper limits and upset the balance of his personality because he evaded the control and direction suggested by his ultimate goal.

CHAPTER XVI

THE HEAVENLY BODIES

Man is the middle being between the physical and the purely spiritual worlds. Another sphere of being, however, shares this position with him, since the heavenly bodies also are midway between the sublunary corporeal world and the separated substances, partaking of the nature of both these spheres. They are corporeal but in such a way that they seem to be related to spiritual objects in at least one respect. St. Thomas rejects the theory that the material cosmos is of a uniform construction, and with Aristotle he teaches that the heavenly bodies are not composed of the four elements, but of ether. He concludes that ether exists because the movement of the heavenly bodies is different from the movement of the four elements. The four elements move opposite to one another, and this movement accounts for the generation and corruption of beings; but the heavenly bodies move in orbits. All generation and corruption is excluded from their natures. In contrast to earthly things, the sun, moon, and stars are perfect beings with respect to substance, power, size, and figure from the beginning and without any process of becoming. Here on earth matter is in potency to the most varied forms, and, in the course of the process of becoming, matter actually takes on many forms, but the forms of the heavenly bodies perfect their matter in such a way that no potency to being remains but only the potency to place (*potentia ad ubi*). Perfection is far greater in the upper part of the universe than here below. In the upper regions each individual is so perfect that it completely fills the nature of the species. In spite of this great perfection, however, St. Thomas continues to consider the earth as the center of the universe; the planets, the sun and moon, surround the earth in concentric spheres.

The heavenly bodies are subject to two kinds of motion. The first is common to all stars; it is the uniform rotation from east to west about the earth's poles. The other movement is from west to east, around a line drawn perpendicular to the ecliptic; this motion differs in different planets. Together with the radiation emitted by the heavenly bodies, this movement exercises an influence on the processes of generation and corruption on earth, especially on the generation of living beings, including man. Therefore the saying, "Man is produced by man and the sun." The ninth heaven, the heaven of the pure spirits, is free from this movement, but in the other heavens, the closer they are to the earth the faster is the movement.[1] Since the heavenly bodies have no independent movement, they must receive their impulses from without. The important function of setting the heavenly bodies in motion is exercised by the pure spirits.

[1] *De nat. mat.*, chap. 3; *De verit.*, XII, 1; *Summa theol.*, Ia, q. 55, a. 2; q. 66, a. 2; q. 68, a. 13.

CHAPTER XVII

THE CREATED PURE SPIRITS

1. The existence of the spirit world. The existence and nature of the pure spirits had been discussed amply before St. Thomas in the writings of Greek, Jewish, and Arabian philosophers, and by the Fathers of the Church and the Scholastics. "But Dionysius has written more ably about the angels than any other." [1] The Areopagite is indeed the foremost writer on the subject of the pure spirits.

The existence of pure spirits was firmly established for St. Thomas because it was demonstrated by Christian revelation, but besides this he also adduced natural reasons. In presenting his reasons for the existence of a world of pure spirits, St. Thomas proceeded differently from Anaxagoras, who thought a spiritual substance was required to explain the process of decomposition; he differed from Plato, who considered a multitude of spiritual substances (ideas) as the source of earthly species and genera; he differed also from Aristotle, who supposed a plurality of spiritual substances to explain the eternal, uniform movement of the heavenly bodies.

Like other scholastic teachers (St. Bonaventure, St. Albert, and Hugh of St. Victor), St. Thomas drew his principal argument from his idea of the structure of the universe. The concept of the perfect universe guarantees the actualization of the possible essences in the whole order of the universe. According to his concept, a subsisting spiritual being is able to exist without animality, and from this possibility the actuality follows.

St. Thomas arrives at the same conclusion by means of his study of the structural laws of the universe. According to these laws the highest individuals of a lower order touch on the lowest individuals of the next higher order, and thus pure spirits must come after the

---

[1] *De subst. sep.*, chap. 16.

human soul that is body-bound. Again, because of the fundamental principle of the natural priority of perfect beings, perfect and incorporeal forms must supersede the corporeal imperfect forms of material beings. Furthermore, the order in the universe requires that the transition from one extreme to another take place by intermediaries, e.g., the transition from God to the material world. St. Thomas was able to make use of this argument because, in opposition to St. Bonaventure, he held from the beginning that the difference between men and angels was essential and not merely accidental. Finally, the good of creation, i.e., similarity to God, is best attained when the creative Cause is reflected in pure spirits.[2]

2. **The nature of the pure spirits.** The pure spirits also participate in being; their being is finite and limited, created by God from nothing. Unlike the divine being, it does not contain all things in itself, but is specifically determined. St. Thomas did not accept the teaching of the Greek Fathers, that the angels had been created before the corporeal world, since the spirit world is only a part of the universe with a relation to the whole from which it receives its perfection. A previous creation of the angels would not be in accord with the perfection of the universe.[3] Because the pure spirits are created, their substance is limited, and because they are next to God almost all composition is excluded from their being. Only God, however, is absolutely simple. Like other created things, the pure spirits are composed of essence and existence, i.e., potency and act.

Pure spirits, considered in themselves, had the possibility of existence from another, but this existence is their actuality. From this fact St. Thomas drew the conclusion, as had St. Augustine before him, that pure spirits are composed of subject and accidental forms. Thus they differ from corporeal substances that are composed of matter and form. Plato held that his ideas (pure spirits) were composed of a material and formal factor, and the Neoplatonists, especially Plotinus, went over to the extremely realistic theory that all finite beings are composed of matter and form.

This view came into scholastic philosophy by two routes: first, through St. Augustine whose leadership was espoused by Hugh of St. Victor, Peter Lombard, and others; secondly, this view came also through Avencebrol, the Jewish philosopher, whose book *The*

---

[2] *In I Sent.*, 8, 5, 2; *Contra Gent.*, II, 50–54; *De spir. creat.*, 1; *Quodlib.*, IX, 6.
[3] *De ent. et ess.*, chap. 6; *Summa theol.*, Ia, q.61, a.1; *De subst. sep.*, chap. 16.

Fountain of Life was highly regarded by the Scholastics. Under Avencebrol's influence the Franciscan school, from St. Bonaventure and Alexander of Hales to Duns Scotus, taught the composition of pure spirits out of matter and form. Like St. Albert before him, St. Thomas defended Aristotelianism against the new methods of Neoplatonism. The reproach that he followed pagan philosophers rather than theological tradition, he turns against the Franciscans themselves, from whom the reproach had originally come. He tried valiantly to exonerate St. Augustine, Hugh of St. Victor, and other authorities from the blame of having adhered to this doctrine. In his controversy with Avencebrol, he attacked his principles and method, especially his underlying concept of matter.

Among the Franciscans the views of Aristotle were quite acceptable. St. Bonaventure thought of matter as completely unlimited possibility, present also, therefore, in spiritual beings. "Viewed in itself, matter is neither spiritual nor material, and that essential quality of matter by which it receives a form is indifferent to the form imposed, whether it be material or spiritual." [4] This metaphysical view of matter is still more evident in Duns Scotus, who thought that matter was the inner principle of all created actuality by which the whole creation is unified. God made all things out of this *materia primo prima* by adding corresponding forms. But Duns Scotus did not mean to assert that the angels and men's souls are made of the same matter as are corporeal things; he merely wished to emphasize that angels and human souls are subject to passivity, changeableness, and the possibility of receiving new perfections. If they were to be viewed as pure forms without matter, they would be approaching too close to God, for God alone is pure act.

St. Thomas differs from Scotus. If matter is conceived in the Aristotelian sense, as that which receives forms and privations, it cannot be attributed to spiritual substances. Those forms that are arrayed next to God in the universe cannot be composed of the lowest of all being, prime matter; they should rather be elevated above all matter. St. Thomas thought of prime matter as having an intimate relation with corporeality. He built his strongest refutation of Duns Scotus' theory on the principle that the activity of a being is in conformity to its nature, and in this instance the activity of the soul is entirely immaterial. If the intellect were not immaterial it would not be able to perceive the species of things in a purely spiritual manner, purified and divested of a material shell.

The immateriality of pure spirits is the basis of their incorruptibility. Since they have no matter which would separate a universal nature into individuals, this immateriality also furnishes the reason for the subsistence of the essence, the identification of the subject and the essence, and it is the reason, finally, why every angel is a species in itself. Since similarity of species denotes similarity of form, and numerical differences denote the differentiation by matter, St. Thomas denies the existence of individuals in the species of angels because the angels are not composed of matter and form. This concept was in entire agreement with the theory St. Thomas had accepted from the ancients that the universal is higher than the individual. If the heavenly bodies had each but one individual to every species, it was much more congruent that the pure spirits should exclude all individuation within the species.[5]

Because the angels are bodiless creatures they have no place; they are not like corporeal creatures bound down to some place. They can have only a relation with some place when some localized body is supported by their power. Since an angel by its limited powers can completely dominate only one body, we may say that an angel can be in only one place at a time, and that more than one angel cannot be in the same place. According to Aristotle's physical and temporal concept, the angels are above time, yet they are bound to time since their spiritual being implies the transition from non-being to being, and their spiritual activity is exercised in successive acts.[6]

This contradiction in Aristotle's views shows how much his theory was in need of reform. The relation of pure spirits to the heavenly bodies is twofold. Some spiritual substances are movers of the heavenly bodies, not their forms, and they are related to the heavenly bodies as the mover is to that which is moved. Other heavenly bodies are the reasons for which the heavenly bodies are set in motion and they have a separate existence.

Since they are purely spiritual, the separate substances are beings that know and will. Their knowledge is not identical with their sub-

---

[5] *Ibid.*, 8, 5; *Contra Gent.*, II, 54, 55, 93; *Summa theol.*, Ia, q.50, a.2–4; *Quodlib.*, IX, 6.

[6] *In I Sent.*, 37, 3; *Summa theol.*, Ia, q.52, a.1; *De pot.*, VI, 6; *De spir. creat.*, 6; *Quodlib.*, I, 4.

stance or with their being, since that is true only of God. Nor is their faculty of knowledge the same as their essence, since in no creature is the faculty or potency identical with the nature or essence of the being. Each angel possesses a nature, and from this nature his vital activities proceed.

3. **The activities of pure spirits.** The act of knowledge is the primary activity of the angels. The angels differ from God and man with respect to the organ, the extent, origin, and method of their knowledge.

As pure spirits, the angels have no physical organs, and thus they do not have those faculties of perception that are dependent on physical organs. Both St. Augustine [7] and St. Thomas accord the angels a spiritual memory. They know nothing of the distinction of intellect into possible and active, since pure spirits are not like man, at one time in potency to knowledge and at another time actually knowing. The angels are at all times in act as to knowledge. The objects of angelic knowledge are immaterial, and do not require the illumination of the *intellectus agens* as with man.

The source of angelic knowledge is different from that of God and man. God knows because He is truly infinite and contains all things within Himself, for all things are in His essence. The angel, however, does not include all things within itself, and therefore does not know all things in its nature. Since the angel is a spiritual, subsisting, and actually intelligible form, it knows itself through its form; its nature is an object of knowledge for its intellect. Further, the angel knows God, but its knowledge does not approach the perfection of divine knowledge, since God knows Himself in His essence in such a way that the divine essence is in Him who knows.

The knowledge of the angels is, however, lifted above the imperfections of human knowledge. The latter is like knowledge obtained through a mirror, since the intelligible form is not derived immediately from the object itself, but from some other thing that reflects the object. Man knows God through creatures by way of causal conclusions, and the form of this knowledge is more negative than positive. The nature of God transcends both the powers and the form of our human knowledge. Angelic knowledge holds a middle place between divine and human knowledge. It is based on an intelligible form that is derived directly from the object. God impressed His

---

[7] *De Trin.*, X, 11.

image on the angelic nature, and thus the angel is able to know God through his own substance; but it does not fully comprehend the divine nature because no created image is able to express fully the essence of God. At all times that chasm between God and creatures remains infinite.

In his *Theological Summa,* St. Thomas declares that the knowledge of the angels is more closely related to the "mirrored" knowledge of man, since angels only reflect the divine nature. In the beatific vision, however, both men and angels will see the nature of God directly. Then the means of knowledge will be no reflection or picture, but the divine essence itself. In this knowledge the divine essence does not become the form of the intellect, it merely acts in place of a form. In that beatific knowledge the light of glory is the supernatural faculty used by the intellect.

In knowing other things, the intellectual faculty is perfected by the intelligible species; angels do not know other things and the other pure spirits in their essences. Following St. Augustine and Dionysius, St. Thomas teaches that the angels do not receive the intelligible species of created things, as men do, by abstraction; God imprinted on the angels' spiritual nature at the time of their creation all the intelligible species of things, both material and spiritual. Thus the species of all things are a natural endowment of the angels, providing them with the knowledge of those things to which they are directed by their natures. Unlike the human intellect, the angelic intellect cannot be compared to a blank tablet; it is rather comparable to an inscribed tablet on which are written the ideas of things. The angelic intellect excels the human intellect as a formed thing excels an unformed object. While God, who is purest act and actuality, sees everything in the simplest and most centralized manner, created intellects see the things of the universe in a multiplicity of ideas. Relying on the principle that the effectiveness of a thing depends on its actuality, and that the more effective a power the more centralized it is, St. Thomas attributed to the angels fewer and more universal ideas and a greater intellectual power according to their position in the angelic hierarchy. Besides this knowledge by means of intelligible species, St. Thomas attributed to the angels a knowledge of vision with respect to the divine Logos, without, however, conceding to them a perfect knowledge of first causes.

Because of the comprehensiveness of their knowledge and its perfection, the angels excel man. An angel knows itself by means of its own substance and it knows itself actually at all times; man does not always know himself actually. The angel's knowledge of God is much more perfect than man's; the angel knows all other pure spirits and all corporeal things in their universal nature as well as in their individual exemplification. Since the angels must function as forces in the physical world, especially as the movers of the heavenly bodies, they must have some knowledge of individuals. The present, past, and future also come within the sphere of their knowledge. With respect to the angel's knowledge of the future, St. Thomas makes a distinction. The future as such cannot be known by any creature, but only by God who is above all the distinctions of time. Creatures can know the future only from its causes. Inasmuch as the future proceeds necessarily from natural causes, it can be known much more perfectly by the angels than by man. Again, that which happens frequently will be known by the angel with some probability, but also with greater accuracy than by man. About free acts and contingent events, angels like men can only surmise. These things are known only to God. Those angels to whom is granted a more perfect insight into the dispositions of divine providence know future contingencies better than others.

Concerning conditions existing within man, St. Thomas again makes a distinction. In so far as these inner conditions are revealed in physical conditions, they can be known by the pure spirits as well as by man. With respect to the knowledge of our thoughts, St. Thomas teaches that the angels can know the species that exist in our minds; but he denies that the angels have any knowledge of how our free wills will apply these ideas and species. In the same way the angels have knowledge of our meritorious thoughts that are connected with our moral refinement and purification. The angels, however, must be especially initiated into the mysteries of grace that take place in men's souls. From the beginning the angels had some general knowledge about the Incarnation, the basic fact of the work of the redemption, although even the higher angels remained ignorant of the details of the Incarnation. Thus we find in the angels a certain amount of intellectual potency, not indeed with respect to natural objects, but with respect to the contents of divine revelation. Again, an angel is in potency inasmuch as it does not always apply its knowledge of natural objects. In one respect the angels are always in act:

in their vision of the Logos which is their supreme happiness; here they are never in potency.

In method, too, angelic knowledge differs from human knowledge; here we find no discursive thinking, no syllogistic conclusions, and no uniting or separating in judgments. No mental process is required to perfect the knowledge of the angels, since their knowledge is perfect and actual from the beginning. St. Thomas compares the knowledge of the angels to the condition of the heavenly bodies. Just as the stars and planets are in a state of perfection from the beginning and are not gradually perfected by growth and movement, so the pure spirits in the upper regions always enjoy the peace of the secure possession of knowledge. The pure spirit beholds everything at once, its intellect is intuitive; it sees the principle together with all of the conclusions and consequences, it sees the effect in the cause, and the cause in the effect. As the angelic intellect beholds the essence of a thing, it understands immediately all that belongs to this essence and all that opposes it. Because man lacks this perfect spiritual illumination, he is obliged to unite and separate in his judgments. Our intellects assemble the universal form from many particulars, but the angels have a total comprehension of things inasmuch as they comprehend the universal directly. In comparison with the divine intellect, the angelic intellect is, of course, particular in its comprehension of truth, for God comprehends all being and all truth at one time, whereas the angel cannot comprehend all things in one act of knowledge or in one idea.

Since pure spirits do not make judgments, they are free from all error. St. Thomas accepted from Aristotle the theory that the intellect is no more able to err in comprehending the essence of a thing than the senses are able to err in apprehending any quality adequate to them. If that is true of the human intellect, it is all the more true of the angelic intellect. Error arises accidentally in the human intellect when man in laying down a definition makes a false union or separation of ideas, or when he makes an unwarranted extension of a definition. Such a cause of error does not exist in the angels because, when an angel comprehends the essence of a thing, the complete structure of the thing is contained in its idea. This secure possession of the knowledge of the essence of things and this freedom from error are such an essential part of the angelic nature, that it is retained by the angels with respect to natural things even after their fall. The good spirits possess the further distinction that they are able to understand rightly the supernatural, divine plan in created things, while the fallen angels, misled by their evil disposition, often fall into error. The angels are also able to understand many things at once. In accord with the principle that a thing is actually intelligible only when its image is in the intellect, several things can be understood at one time only if they are seen as one spiritual unit. When the angels behold the divine Logos, they behold all things in one spiritual species (*quae est essentia divina*), and all things at one time; [8] when they know things by means of acquired forms, they know all that is contained in that intelligible form. Thus they know all individuals of one species in one intelligible form.

The will is an essential part of a being's intellectual equipment, and thus the angels, too, possess a will. Since they do not have a psychophysical nature, they do not have a sensible appetite or emotions. Love, joy, as acts of the will without any sense accompaniment, are found in God and in the angels. The natural striving for good found in every being is also found in the angels, and with them it takes the form of a natural, rational love. St. Thomas builds up his concept of the angelic will from what he knows of man. The angels have freedom of will in a much higher sense than man. Their will does not suffer division into a spiritual will and a sense urge; it has for its object all good in general and it apprehends all particularizations of the good as partial ends. Man by his nature tends toward his ultimate goal, happiness, and he freely chooses the means to this end. The same thing occurs in the angel, with this difference: the angel possesses a more acute appreciation of moral values and thus without hesitation or reflection sees immediately all the connections between secondary ends and means and the ultimate end. In its natural love the angel tends toward itself and seeks its own perfection, just as man does in a rightly ordered self-love. This natural love extends also to the other angels inasmuch as an angel shares the same angelic nature, and it is especially directed to God, the greatest good of the universe.

From Dionysius, St. Thomas learned that the angels possessed no evil nature nor any natural inclination to evil. An evil inclination is possible only when a conflict arises in some being composed of two natures in which the lower nature tending to some particular good successfully opposes the inclination of the higher nature to good. But

[8] St. Augustine, *De Trin.*, XV, 16.

the angels are not composite beings, and even in those instances in which St. Thomas teaches that the pure spirits are united with a body, as in the demons, the higher nature is not subjected to the lower in the same way as in man. Therefore evil can arise in pure spirits only through the will. Sacred Scripture teaches the fact of sin; St. Thomas tries to explain the possibility of sin by his delineation of pure spirits.

If the angels had a body and a sensitive soul, as the Platonists taught, the explanation would be easy; but St. Thomas does not accept the Platonic theory entirely. The pure spirits sinned because they did not order their own proper good and their own perfection to the highest end, but rather set themselves up as the ultimate end and drew the norm of their actions not from the divine will but from themselves. The first sin, the first attack on the order of being and values, was the sin of pride, from which necessarily flowed other sins: hatred of God and the envy of man. The pure spirits are like human beings in that their sin is a lack of the proper order toward God, but they do not share another characteristic, that of the lack of the proper subordination of the lower to the higher nature. Such subordination has no place in the angels because they are, of course, not composite beings.

Sin cannot be committed by a being that possesses pure actuality; only such beings as have potentiality can sin. The angels, it is true, possess actual perfection and the actual happiness consonant with their natures, but they remain in potency to supernatural happiness. The angels could not have sinned with respect to any natural order, but only with respect to the supernatural order. The angelic sin was not the striving for absolute equality with God (the angels saw clearly that that was unattainable); rather it consisted in their reliance on their own nature and its powers in the attainment of their supernatural good instead of relying on God and His grace. Together with all the masters who were teaching at the University of Paris, St. Thomas rejected the theory that the angels were evil from the first moment of their creation because of their wills.

In the same way St. Thomas condemned Origen's teaching about the universal apocatastasis (the final blessedness of all sinful creatures). In opposing this doctrine of Origen, he was less concerned with the unchristian view of the eternal return of all things, a view that had deeply impressed the Alexandrian teacher, than he was with Origen's belief in the possibility of the moral conversion of the pure spirits. St. Thomas attributes Origen's error to a false idea of the freedom of the will. An essential part of the freedom of the will is the ability to turn to a diversity of things. This diversity refers, first to those things that play a part in the choice of God, the pure spirits, and man, of means to an end; it refers, secondly, to the choice of good and evil; and thirdly, it refers to the changeableness of the will's decision, by which the will abandons some end for which it had been striving. This last quality is not essential but only accidental to the will's freedom, since it arises from the changeableness of human nature. This variability in the human will may come from an inner or an external cause; internal when in the course of time the knowledge of the individual undergoes some change or when the appetite is differently disposed; the cause is external when God is able to turn the will from evil to good by His grace. Neither cause is found in pure spirits since the angels are unchangeable in their knowledge and in their wills with respect to the things that concern their own natures, being in act with respect to these things at all times. They are in potency only with respect to the supernatural and only here can there be question of attachment and aversion. In the same way no change is possible through an external cause, because for the angels the time of probation is passed and any conversion through grace is not in accord with divine wisdom. In the bad angels the effects of their first act continue on and so all their following acts are bad; after their first act of free choice, the decision is made forever. St. Thomas accepted this theory as an article of faith long recognized in tradition; St. John Damascene said: "For the angels the commission of sin was as conclusive as death is for man." Further, St. Thomas held that the proposition was demonstrable in psychology.

The will is naturally in accord with the cognitive faculty. The angelic intellect comprehends all things unalterably, even as we perceive first principles. The human intellect and will are subject to change, but the angelic will remains unalterably attached to the object of its first choice. The human will is subject to change both before and after the act of choice, but the angelic will is subject to change only before the act of choice. Therefore the bad angels remain hardened in evil and therefore also they abuse the good for evil purposes. In the same way the good angels cannot sin any more; their minds and wills are permanently attached to God, and their complete happiness consists in the vision of God.

From Aristotle's principle that those things that are opposed to nature do not occur as frequently as those things that are in harmony with the universe, St. Thomas tried to prove that the number of good angels was greater than the number of those that fell. The sin of the angels was such a violation of the natural tendency of nature. Above the angel's natural happiness there is also a supernatural happiness which can be obtained only as a gift from God.

In discussing the number of the pure spirits, St. Thomas makes it clear that he is not in agreement with Plato, Aristotle, and Moses Maimonides. Following Dionysius, he concludes that the number of the pure spirits is very great because of the principle that the measure or number of things increases with their perfection. This measure or number consists of size in corporeal things and simply in number in the realm of the spirits.[9] In his *Compendium theologiae ad Fratrem Reginaldum,* St. Thomas explains how the angels are divided into three hierarchies because of their three stages of knowledge, how each hierarchy is again divided into three choirs, and how these three choirs and hierarchies act as the *universales executores divinae providentiae* (chap. 126). None of the angels is able to create or influence directly the natural order of things; these are powers that belong solely to God. Any influence that the angels may have on the physical world is limited to the channels of natural powers. The human intellect is akin to the spiritual activities of the angels, and therefore the angels are able to strengthen the intellect of man and to illuminate phantasms for the purpose of forming unusual concepts.

---

[9] *De subst. sep.,* chap. 2, § 8; *Summa theol.,* Ia, q. 110, a. 2 f.; *De malo,* XVI, 9–12.

CHAPTER XVIII

GOD

God is the first cause and the last end of the universe. He is the underlying presupposition of everything that is, and He is supreme over all being. He is, however, in no sense a part of the universe, for God and the universe are separated by an infinite abyss.[1]

1. **The formation of the concept of God.** If we are to understand the Thomist concept of God, we must remember the influence that tradition exerted on St. Thomas. Several schools of thought are united in his teaching. The idea that we are able to know the existence of God but not His essence had been given prominence by Philo and Plotinus and, having been accepted by the Neoplatonists of the patristic era, it was transmitted to St. Augustine and the Areopagite, and thus reached St. Thomas. Again, St. Thomas adopted the thought, derived from Aristotle, that with respect to the highest immaterial substances our intellects are like the vision of nocturnal birds in the bright light of day.[2] These schools of thought strengthened the tendency of St. Thomas' mind to erect insurmountable barriers in the way of our knowledge of God and to term our knowledge of God ignorance. This attitude seems more pronounced in his earlier writings, but he never abandons it. We find it in both summas, and at all times he is careful to restrict our actual knowledge of God.

St. Thomas went to great lengths to substantiate his theory about the possibility of knowing the essence of God. Since human knowledge is primarily directed to sensible phantasms, any other source of knowledge is lacking. The intelligible forms obtained by abstraction from sensible data are entirely insufficient to transmit any knowledge of God because of the infinite distance that separates God from the

[1] *Summa theol.,* Ia, q. 61, a. 3 ad 2.
[2] *In Boeth. de Trin.,* I, 2; *Summa theol.,* Ia, q. 12, a. 12.

created world. The concepts drawn from sensible objects may be able
to throw some light on non-sensible relations, but they cannot reach
the divine nature, since sensible things and God are not in the same
genus. St. Thomas makes use of Maimonides' term when he says
that anything we say about God is *"fere aequivoce."* He also uses
Dionysius' expression that the likeness of sensible things to God is
really a "dissimilar similarity," and he goes so far as to say that neither
our natural knowledge nor the knowledge we have about God from
revelation approach close to the divine essence. As Dionysius said,
the ray of light from divine revelation comes to us in conformity with
our natures.[3] All knowledge is adapted to the condition of him who
knows: a restriction that the speculative theologian might well
ponder.

Because our minds are bound down to the sense world, the nature
of God represents the unattainable for our speculative efforts. The
most perfect knowledge of God is that the nature of God lies completely beyond anything we can conceive in this life and that God
remains for us unknown.[4]

St. Thomas restricts man's knowledge of God from another angle.
Even when creatures reveal God in themselves, the mind of man is
still unable to fully comprehend the content of divine knowledge
contained in creatures.[5] The boundaries of man's knowledge of God
are most narrow and man is dependent on revelation for his knowledge of God.[6] The usual method of obtaining knowledge of a substance through its remote or proximate genus determined by its
properties is not applicable here because God belongs to no genus. In
place of the genus in the knowledge of God, St. Thomas speaks of the
knowledge *per negationem;* instead of the properties he refers to the
divine relations to sensible things, that is, the relation of cause and
pre-eminence. Thus St. Thomas, referring to Dionysius and Boethius, replaces the knowledge of the essence of God with a knowledge
by way of negation, causality, and pre-eminence (*per negationem, per
causalitatem, per excessum*).[7]

How important St. Thomas considered the method by way of

---

[3] *In Boeth. de Trin.,* VI, 3.
[4] *Ibid.,* I, 2.
[5] *De verit.,* II, 1.
[6] *Ibid.,* V, 2 ad 11.
[7] *In Boeth. de Trin.,* I, 2; VI, 3.

negation is well known.[8] The incomprehensibility of the divine nature forces us to fall back on the negative way of knowledge, and St. Thomas points out the value of this method even in other instances. We know a thing much better when we understand how it differs from other things. Everything has its own peculiar nature by which it is clearly distinguished from other beings, and this is the foundation (*fundamentum in re*) for negative knowledge.[9] If this negative method is used in the Aristotelian sense to make clear distinctions and direct the intellect away from the finite and if it prevents the mind from reaching unjustifiable conclusions about God, then it becomes of positive value and is not to be confused with the kind of negative knowledge that leads only to the greatest vagueness about God. When we try to approach God by way of negation, we first remove all that is corporeal, then also the spiritual, inasmuch as we find it in creatures, and then nothing remains in our minds except that God is, nothing more. Last of all, we remove even this being as far as it is like created being and now remains the divine being in a certain darkness; and that is the form in which we know God in this life.[10] Conclusions such as these led some theologians to quote St. Thomas in support of a negative theology.

Plotinus, in his *Enneads* (III, 8, 9; V, 2, 1), expressed the opinion that God is beyond all those things we can reach and that He cannot be comprehended with the help of any concepts derived from finite being. God, according to Plotinus, possesses neither corporeity nor sensation, neither consciousness nor spirituality nor being. The only thing that is knowable about God is His existence. Similarly Dionysius indulges in unmeasured phrases when he describes God as being beyond all determination and human expression, beyond all concepts and ideas, but the cause of all being.[11] Only the nameless name, "I am who am," approximates the divine being.

The fundamental reason for this attitude toward our knowledge of God lies in the difference between the relation of essence and existence in God and in man. While in creatures essence and existence are separate, and existence must be added to the essence or intelligible content of a thing, in God essence and existence are identical. St.

[8] *Contra Gent.*, I, 14; *Summa theol.*, Ia, q.3.
[9] *Contra Gent.*, I, 14.
[10] *In I Sent.*, 8, 1; *De pot.*, VII, 5.
[11] *De div. nom.*, I, 1, 5, 6; *De coel. hier.*, II, 3.

Thomas does not intend to deny that God has essence when he says that it is identical with His existence. We can readily understand the contrast that exists between the limited contents of created beings and simple being; in God, however, the infinite content of His nature and simple, absolute being are readily reconcilable. When St. Thomas says that God is simple being, he does not intend to explain away the divine nature or empty it of all perfection. Divine being is incapable of further perfection or growth; it contains all the perfections of all other kinds of being, but in a more perfect way, that is, simply and absolutely.[12] Being is predicated of God not as being emptied of all content, but as being containing infinite being.

From tradition St. Thomas gathers reasons why the term *"qui est"* ("who is") is the most proper: (1) it expresses the perfection of the divine being (St. Jerome); (2) it corresponds to our negative knowledge of God because it is an indefinite expression of the unlimited being of God (St. John Damascene); (3) being is the first and the fundamental imitation of the divine goodness (Dionysius); (4) in creatures whose essence and existence are not identical, the designation is derived from the essence, but God is best known from His being since in Him essence and existence are the same (Avicenna). The expression *"qui est"* is, therefore, the most adequate term for God since it expresses both a maximum and a minimum in God. It expresses the maximum because it predicates the fullness of all being and all perfection; and since essence and existence are the same, it signifies the actualization of pure act. It expresses a minimum when, because of its generality, it refrains from any determination that would restrict and distort the divine being. This maximum and minimum give rise to no difficulties for, as St. John Damascene says, God is an infinite and indetermined ocean of substance (*quoddam pelagus substantiae infinitum et indeterminatum*).[13] Thus the negative and positive are united in our knowledge of God.

2. **The positive idea of God.** The theology contained in the two great summas of St. Thomas present much more positive material than the aforesaid limitations would lead us to expect. Even here, it is true, he introduces his dissertation with the statement that we can never comprehend the nature of God and that we approach closer to God the more we deny and exclude from Him. Where are we to

---

[12] *De ent. et ess.,* chap. 6.
[13] *In I Sent.,* I, 1.

find the standard that will govern our exclusions? This criterion consists in the conclusions resulting from the various proofs for the existence of God and from certain ontological principles. The proofs for God's existence not only show that He exists, they also reveal Him as the unmoved Mover, as the first efficient Cause, as necessary being, as being *a se,* as possessing intelligence, as supreme in being and perfection. Thus the knowledge of God's existence contains within it some knowledge of His nature. We can have no negative knowledge, no negative theology, without some positive presuppositions.

In discussing the natural knowledge of God, St. Thomas rejects both logical and psychological apriorism; he opposes St. Anselm's ontological proof of God's existence as well as the theory of our congenital knowledge of God proposed by the Augustinian-Franciscan school. In explaining the statement that the knowledge of God is implanted within us, he concedes only that the faculty of knowing God is implanted in our natures. God is not for us the first known, as some theologians taught, relying on an unwarranted interpretation of St. Augustine. As an Aristotelian, St. Thomas admitted the sensible world as the only source of our knowledge, and the proof from causality as the only legitimate method. In St. Albert's writings the proofs from causality began to predominate, but in St. Thomas they are the only kind of proof admitted for establishing the supreme cause of the universe.[14] The five well known proofs for God's existence found in the *Summa theologica* proceed from the world as it is perceived by the senses and, with the insertion of quidditive abstractions and essential analyses and by means of the principle of causality, conclude with a validity that is transcendental.

The first proof, developed by Aristotle and adopted from the Arabians and St. Albert, concludes from the fact of movement to the first moving cause that is itself unmoved. The second proof concludes from the order within efficient causes that there must be a first cause since causes do not cause themselves and since a retrogression into the infinite is impossible. This second proof was developed by Avicenna and introduced into Latin Scholasticism by Alan de Lille. The third proof, the proof from contingent being, was partly developed by Maimonides; it concludes from the existence of those beings that may or may not be to the existence of a being that must exist necessarily and of itself. The fourth proof from the stages of perfection is derived

[14] *Ibid.,* III, 1 f.; *Summa theol.,* Ia, q. 12, a. 12.

from St. Anselm's *Monologium* (chap. 4) and makes use of trains of thought that are of Augustinian and Platonic origin. The fifth proof relies on the teleological argument and concludes from the fact that certain things that have no intelligence act for a purpose and therefore they must be directed by some other being endowed with intelligence and will. The underlying principle in this proof is that wherever there is a purpose there must also be an intellect.

Even within the fold of Scholasticism these proofs for the existence of God were assailed by critics, especially by Duns Scotus and the Scotists. As a matter of fact, they contend, these proofs contain a weakness that cannot be denied. They say that, granted a first mover exists, as well as a supreme efficient cause, something that exists necessarily, and some supreme intelligence, no proof has been advanced that this principle is the personal God of Christianity substantially different from the universe. Scotus had pointed out that the proof from motion merely proved the existence of a mover who is locally unmoved, and like many other Scholastics after him he struck the proof from motion from the catalogue of proofs for God's existence. Other voices were raised to proclaim that the acceptance of God's existence on faith was more reasonable than on the basis of such arguments.[15] Could not this first mover and the first efficient cause be some non-personal substance, some blind irrational cause, or some necessarily acting will? Could not the apparent design of the universe be traced to some rational principle immanent in the universe? Must this necessary *ens* be a personal God? So they asked.

To judge the matter fairly we must recall that St. Thomas presented these proofs in sketchy outline and later in the two summas he adduced the detailed proofs and explanations. If we adopt a critical attitude toward these proofs, we must keep in mind that our present-day philosophy is too much under the influence of subjectivism and positivism and too much given to logical analyses.

Before entering on a study of the theology of the two summas, we have a few words to say about the manner of our knowledge of God.

3. **The analogical knowledge of God.** The positive idea of God was in accord with the views of the eminent philosophers and theologians, and at no time was speculative theology content with a merely negative idea of God. Even Plotinus added an idea of God that he

---

[15] Scotus, *Oxon.*, I, dist. 8, q. 5.

derived from things: that the One and First was the Creator of all things, the giver of life, the principle of being and the good, the end of the universe. All these concepts are repeated by Dionysius and acknowledged by St. Thomas. In the twelfth book of Aristotle's *Metaphysics,* St. Thomas found a positive presentation of theology, and in the writings of St. Augustine he also found a positive doctrine. This positive presentation in St. Augustine was given in spite of the Neoplatonic influences which maintained that any categories obtained from finite beings were inapplicable to God and that we had better maintain a respectful silence about God since we could say only what God was not and nothing about what He was.[16] In the mind of St. Augustine, God was an eternal, infinite, absolutely simple, spiritual being, in whom substance and properties were identical. God, according to St. Augustine, is the essence of all being, the supreme cause existing of Himself, the highest wisdom which has brought all other things into existence according to the images subsisting within itself, the essence of truth, and the highest value.

St. Thomas developed the positive idea of God and defended it especially against Maimonides, who taught that our positive and affirmative ideas about God were really only negative in character.[17] The essence of God, of course, remains excluded from our knowledge, but it is certain that He possesses some attributes as the supreme cause of the universe and that certain facets of His being can be known.[18]

Since every efficient cause produces something like itself, whatever God makes must in some way be like Himself and permit some ray of His perfection to fall on His creatures.[19] Every perfection and every positive quality found in the effect will be found in the cause in the same way when the cause and effect have the same form; they will be found in the cause in a more perfect manner when the cause excels the effect as to form. God is related to the universe as in the latter instance. Because the created things represent God's perfections in an imperfect manner and because the distance between God and His creation is infinite, the forms of our knowledge also are only imperfect representations of God's essence. A perfect representation

---

[16] *De Trin.,* V, 2.

[17] *Summa theol.,* Ia, q. 13, a. 2; *De pot.,* VII, 5.

[18] *In I Sent.,* 19, 5, 2; *Contra Gent.,* III, 55; *Summa theol.,* Ia, q. 12, a. 12; *De pot.,* VII, 5.

[19] *Contra Gent.,* I, 29; *Summa theol.,* Ia, q. 4, a. 2; *De pot.,* VII, 5.

would have to correspond to the unity and simplicity of the divine Being and thus be in one intelligible form. Our imperfect knowledge requires a multiplicity of forms which give only an imperfect picture of the divine essence, but which are nevertheless all valid.[20] As a loyal Aristotelian, St. Thomas taught that this limited knowledge of God was far more valuable than the more perfect knowledge we have of created things.[21]

The following distinctions are of some importance. Our concepts and ideas are based on the make-up and perfection of created things, and in them the thing itself and the manner in which it is actualized must be kept distinct. Some concepts express some perfection that is only imperfectly realized in things, other concepts express qualities whose imperfection is inseparable from created things, and these can therefore be applied only to finite being. Among the latter are such ideas as man, stone; all these contain some matter and can be predicated of God only figuratively. Other concepts express some perfection even though this quality is only imperfectly actualized in things. These concepts are the so called transcendental ideas; among the first and most fundamental is the idea of being. Other transcendental concepts are those of the supreme principle of being, of unity, truth, the good, and also the ideas of cause, effect, causality, life, intelligence, will, wisdom, etc.[22] Their validity goes beyond the universe from which they are derived by us; they penetrate the whole cosmos of being, and they belong to God primarily and in the most perfect degree, since no creature is able to receive these qualities in that degree in which they are found in God. Here St. Thomas makes extended use of the terminology of the Areopagite and of Neoplatonism to express God's pre-eminence.[23] With Dionysius, St. Thomas agrees that the negations about God are absolutely true, but the affirmations are true only *secundum quid*.[24] None of our concepts have any univocal validity with respect to God, since univocal ideas are applicable only to a multiplicity of things which have the same form of existence. This condition is not fulfilled with respect to God and creatures. From the divine viewpoint, in God essence and existence are identical, and the divine essence is actualized but once in God's

---

[20] *De verit.*, II, 1.
[21] *Contra Gent.*, III, 25.
[22] *In I Sent.*, 8, 1; *De verit.*, I, 1.
[23] Dionysius, *De div. nom.*, II, 3; *Myst. theol.*, I, 1, 2.
[24] *In I Sent.*, 22, 2; *Contra Gent.*, I, 30.

being; from the human viewpoint, a univocal predication can be made only when cause and effect are adequate to each other.

No effect is able to receive the image of the first cause except in a distorted manner, and whatever we find in the effect is there *divisim et multipliciter et particulariter,* while the same thing is in the Cause *simpliciter et unite et universaliter.*[25] Not only must the cause and effect belong to each other, they must also have the same existential mode. Thus, the material house and the house in the mind of the builder are not conceptually different, yet a univocal predication would not be permissible because the house itself has a material existence and the house in the mind has an immaterial existence. Oftentimes the difference in the mode of existence is based on the conceptual difference, as is the difference between independent and dependent being, essential being and being by participation. No univocal predication can be made about God and creatures because any such predication would be classified under one of the five *predicabilia,* none of which is applicable to God.

Thus our knowledge of God is only analogous.[26] In reviewing the different kinds of analogy, St. Thomas permits only one to be applied to the relation between the universe and God. He excludes that analogy in which something is said about two or more members with respect to some third member, because in such an analogy the third member is prior to the others. This would not be true in the analogy of God and the universe, where God is prior to all members. The other analogy is that in which the predication is made only *secundum intentionem,* and this also must be eliminated. The only applicable analogy is that in which something is predicated of all the members with respect to one of the members. In this instance one of the members is prior to the rest but all the members have something in common, even though the grade of perfection may vary.

St. Thomas rejects the analogy of proportion in favor of the analogy of proportionality (cf. pp. 129 ff.) because the analogy of proportion presupposes a necessary and permanent relation between its members. Creatures, however, are not in any relation to God that determines the divine perfection. On the other hand, a difficulty was raised by some who said that no relation could exist between God and the universe because of the infinite distance between them. St. Thomas

[25] *In IV Met.,* 1; *Summa theol.,* Ia, q. 13, a. 3.
[26] *De pot.,* VII, 7; *In I Sent.,* 19, 5.

replied that it was for this reason he had adopted the analogy of proportionality which was so broad that in it even the finite and the infinite could be brought into relationship.[27]

Some controversy has arisen about the point whether St. Thomas fell into error about the applicability of analogy to God. If we look at the matter from a broad and sympathetic viewpoint, we will see that St. Thomas predicated of God only such attributes as have a transcendental character and an inner, essential similarity to God, except where he predicates certain specific and generic concepts in a figurative way. All those things that we might predicate of God are based on the causal relation, on that relation of creatures to God as their first cause in which all the perfections of things exist in an infinite degree. This causal relation is not a mere external relation, in the sense that God is the producer and the universe is that which is produced, without any inner relation between them. Between God and the universe this relation implies that what is caused is like the cause and that the essential form of the effect exists in some way in the cause. The essential content of creatures does not exist alongside God's essence without any relation to it. Is not everything good because of its inner resemblance to the divine goodness (*similitudine divinae bonitatis sibi inhaerenti*)? [28] The essential form of the effect, however, is actualized in the cause in a different manner. Here St. Thomas speaks of similarity and dissimilarity: similarity because the universe imitates God, dissimilarity because the effect is far below the cause. Since the analogical relation is founded on the causal relation, it cannot be reversed any more than the latter. Creation imitates God and is like Him, but the converse is not true.

4. **The theology of the two summas.** In the *Summa contra Gentes* St. Thomas begins with the conclusion of one of the proofs for God's existence, from the attributes of unchangeableness and immutability. From this he concludes to God's eternity. The concept of the first uncaused cause, of the first necessary being, leads to the same conclusion of God's eternity. Because God is eternal, because He is the first cause, and because all possibility of not-being is excluded from Him, He is without any potency and He is pure act (*actus purus*). Because God is without potency, He is also without matter; and because in

27 *De verit.*, II, 11 ad 4; XXIII, 7 ad 9.
28 *Summa theol.*, Ia, q. 13, a. 6.

Him there is no difference of potency and act, He is not a composition.

The same conclusion is derived from the concept of first cause, the highest good, and from the fact that a composition is later than its parts and that every composition requires one who makes the composition. Since God is not composed of parts, since He is without any potency, devoid of all movement and all limits, since He is the highest and first being, He is not a corporeal being. Again, since He is not composed of parts, He is identical with His essence. This truth is shown also from the fact that in God there are no accidents, that the divine essence is not individuated through matter but by itself. The essence of a thing is either the thing itself or the cause of the thing. But God has no cause, and therefore His essence is Himself.

The notions that God is the first and necessary being, the supreme cause, pure act without potency, a simple being without composition, are also proofs that in God essence and existence are the same. Since the divine substance is identical with its existence, everything in the divine substance belongs to that substance. Therefore, again, accidents cannot be found in God, nor any of the determinations of genus or species.

Since God is identical with His being, and since He possesses being in all its fullness, He must be absolutely perfect. This perfection connotes the highest good, and from this concept of the highest good follows the idea of God's unity. God's infinity is deduced from His absolute fullness of being, from the idea of the identification of God with His being, from God the pure act, and from His eternity.

That God is an intelligent being is deduced from His immateriality and absolute perfection and from the teleology of the universe, which requires an intelligent principle. That God has intelligence follows also from the fact that He is a subsisting form which must have knowledge.

The will always accompanies the intellect. God has a will which loves first of all Himself, and then all other things that are like Him. He loves Himself necessarily, all other things freely. A perfect and intelligent being is a living being, and in God essence and life too are identical. If this were not true, God would have His life by participation and then He would be composed of parts. Hence God's life is eternal.

The greatest perfection of a being consists in its most perfect activity. The perfection of activity depends on four factors: first on the magnitude of the object and then on three conditions. The three conditions are, that the activity remain within him who acts, that it be an activity of the highest power, and that the activity be carried on easily, perfectly, quickly, and with pleasure. These four factors are found in God's activity.

Since happiness is an activity of the intellect, and since God is essentially the same as His intellect, His essence consists of His happiness. Hence God's happiness transcends the happiness of all other things. Having come to this conclusion, natural theology has reached the highest point it can attain.

St. Thomas developed his picture of the divine being as Aristotle had done in the twelfth book of his *Metaphysics*. Aristotle beginning with the idea of the unmoved first mover, proceeded to the idea of a spiritual person who led a complete and happy existence in the knowledge of himself.

In the *Theological Summa*, St. Thomas begins with the idea of God's utter simplicity, excluding any kind of composition, and also any kind of corporeity. This notion is bound up with the idea of the unmoved mover, pure act, and first being. God is not composed of matter and form, because the concept of pure act excludes all potentiality and also all materiality. In a composite of matter and form, the being receives its perfection from the form, its perfection is participated, but God is essentially perfect. Since God is not composed of matter and form, there is in Him no distinction of essence and *suppositum;* the form in God is a *suppositum subsistens,* and God is His own deity (*Deus est sua deitas*). God is not only identical with His own essence, He is also identical with His existence. If God's existence and essence were not the same, God would have been caused, a conclusion that is irreconcilable with the first cause. In God essence and existence must be identical because essence and existence are to each other as potency and act, but in God no potency can be found. Finally essence and existence in God must be the same, since in those beings in which essence and existence are distinct the being is participated being, which is repugnant to the idea of first being.

Since in God no real distinction exists between essence and ex-

istence, and between potency and act, God is not in any genus or
species, and the composition of genus and difference is not found in
Him. Similarly, God possesses no accidents, because the subject and
its accidents are related to each other as potency and act, and also
because in God there is nothing caused or added. As non-corporeal,
uncaused, and without any potency, as pure form and first being,
God possesses absolute simplicity. He is not composed of parts, nor
does He enter into any composition. He is neither the soul of the
universe nor the formal principle of all things nor the primal matter of all things. These three notions are repugnant to the idea of
God as the first efficient cause and first being.

God's perfection is deduced from the concept of first efficient cause.
As the first cause, God is at the same time the highest actuality, and
since a thing possesses perfection inasmuch as it is in act, God possesses the greatest perfection. According to the principle that the perfection of an effect is found in some way in the cause, the perfections
of all things are found in God because He is the first cause and first
being. Further, since every cause produces effects that resemble itself
in some way, some resemblance to God is found in all things. This
similarity, of course, is only an analogous one.

Goodness is closely related to a being's perfection. Being and good
are convertible, and a thing is good inasmuch as it is desirable, it is
desirable inasmuch as it is perfect, and it is perfect inasmuch as it
is in act. As the supreme efficient cause of all perfection, God is the
highest good, excelling infinitely the good of created things. Because
of the identity of His essence and being, God's goodness is essential
to Him.

God's infinity follows from the fact that His being needs no receiving substratum, that it is without any limitations, and that it
subsists in itself. God's immutability is deduced from the idea of
pure act, which precludes all possibility and thus all change; His
immutability may also be seen from the absence of any composition
in God, and finally from the fullness of the divine being which admits of no addition or growth. The concept of immutability includes
the notion of eternity, because every kind of movement and all time
are alien to God. God's unity follows from His simplicity, from the
idea of absolutely perfect being, and from the unified order in the
universe, which presupposes a supreme unifier. Thus God possesses

the greatest indivisibility and the greatest unity. From the ideas of first efficient cause and ultimate end, we see God as the director and governor and preserver of the universe.

The structure of the theology in the two summas and in the *Compendium of Theology* is the same. We find in each instance the development of a series of ideas and concepts from which, by an analytical and deductive process, negative and positive ideas are obtained about God. The more fundamental concepts are analyzed and then by logical processes an advance is made in knowledge. The principles of metaphysics are often called in to support an argument, and, according to the Thomistic view, since these principles and the concepts that are used possess real validity, the result is not a mere conceptual fabrication or fiction, but a series of conclusions that have actual validity. This logical process begins with the results of the proofs of God's existence, which in turn rest firmly on the objective validity of the causal nexus and the fundamental principles of ontology.

As a result of these positive and negative notions about God, we come upon the unbridgeable abyss that lies between God and all that is created. By negation a series of finite imperfections is excluded from God: change and all beginning and cessation, all potentiality and materiality, all composition and multiplicity, all time and space, and all distinction between substance and accidents. By the positive way, God is determined as the absolute fullness of being and the highest perfection, pure act, as always in total possession of His being, as essential unity, supreme cause, as the ultimate end and governor of the universe, as that being above all space and time, eternal, living, and spiritual. By the same positive way, God is known to be the highest wisdom and the greatest good, as the being that subsists in Himself, supremely happy and sufficient to Himself. God is infinite because He comprises all things in Himself; He is negatively, not privatively, infinite because He knows no limits. He has infinite power, He alone is active by reason of His substance, He is the first and last end and purpose of all His thinking and willing and He is in continuous possession of that end and purpose.

In any treatise of theology it is of great importance to draw a clear line of demarcation between pantheism and the substantial distinction between God and creatures. St. Thomas had occasion to reject the pantheism which taught that God is the formal being (*esse formale*) of all things. He condemned this theory as a confusion of the universal concept of being with God's absolute being and the mingling of the real and logical orders. He solved the problem of how other beings could exist beside God, the absolute fullness of being, by referring to the analogy of being. God is indeed the fullness of being, He *is* being itself, in Him essence and existence coincide. Finite creatures have being, but it is being of an entirely different kind; they only participate in being, their being is only a faint imitation of the divine being. The relation of the universe is expressed in the words: "*Deo assimilari.*" If creatures have being only by sharing in another's being, they possess goodness only by participation.[29]

God is also the first truth. The supreme principles of thought and being are based on His being inasmuch as they are only images of uncreated truth. The eternal validity and absolute unchangeableness of these principles is guaranteed by God Himself.[30] God is the reason why thought and being correspond. God called all things in the universe into being after the model of the ideas essential to His own nature, and everything in the universe has its being and truth by reason of its form, and this form is an imitation of the divine idea. The human intelligence possesses the faculty of thinking those divine thoughts that are actualized in the objective universe. The form of every created thing points the way to knowledge for the human intellect. God is the measure of the being of every thing, and the form of the thing is the measure of our knowledge of it. To conceive of truth as the agreement of thought and being is to think of truth as founded on a theistic concept of God. The supreme validity is found in God, He is the supreme good from whom the goodness of all other things is derived. In Him the natural moral law in its immutability is founded, and finally God is the goal, i.e., the happiness of all created beings.[31]

Even though God transcends all other beings, He is intimately present in every being; He is immanent in everything in the universe by His presence, His essence, and His power.[32] We will understand the meaning of this statement better when we come to consider the divine plan of the universe, divine providence, and the activity of creatures carried out through the power of God.

[29] *Contra Gent.*, I, 26; *Summa theol.*, Ia, q.54, a.2.
[30] *Contra Gent.*, III, 47; *Summa theol.*, IIa IIae, q.8, a.1; *Quodlib.*, X, 7.
[31] *In I Sent.*, 8, 1, 3; *Contra Gent.*, III, 17, 25.
[32] *In I Sent.*, 37, 1, 2.

Some have objected that this Thomistic concept of God as the first mover, the supreme cause, and as pure being *a se* has little in common with the religious concept of God. They say this is not what the religious man understands by the term "God." But the fullness of being and power in God, from whom all other beings receive their existence, is contained in the religious concept of God. When man surrenders himself and submits himself to the infinite and divine persons, he performs an act that has a profound metaphysical significance. St. Thomas knew, of course, that the religious concept of God was enriched by many other elements and attributes.

SECTION III

THE ORIGIN AND CORRUPTION OF THINGS

CHAPTER XIX

BECOMING AND CHANGE, ORIGIN AND CORRUPTION OF THINGS

Becoming and change, the origin and cessation of things, the increasing and decreasing movement, development, and decay of things, are among the fundamental facts of our experience and among the basic data of life and the universe. Anyone who would try to deny the multifarious change among things would find himself not only in conflict with everything about him but also in conflict with himself. Everyone is subject to change in his spiritual and mental life as well as in his physical being and everyone finds himself borne along in the continual flux of things. Thus, when the Eleatics denied the existence of becoming and change, their contention met with little approval, because from the beginning philosophy was concerned with the problem of change. The origin and passing of the universe presents a problem which, with all its detailed questions, clamors for explanation and solution. From an ontological as well as from the psychological viewpoint we can see how the first inquiry should be directed to that primal matter from which all things are made and to which they again revert. One of the world's most original thinkers, Heraclitus, was keenly aware that the whole universe was in a ceaseless flux and in an unceasing process of change.

In approaching a problem and offering a solution, the viewpoint from which a thinker sees the problem is by no means a matter of indifference. St. Thomas characteristically considered the problem of the natural becoming of the universe from the viewpoint of Aristotelian principles, and the existence of the world from the standpoint of Christian philosophy. Aristotle observes nature as it simply and unassumingly makes itself manifest to man, and he interprets nature with the help of those principles that nature itself seems to offer him. St. Thomas follows in the footsteps of his master and accepts the conclusions of Aristotle's study of the phenomena of nature.

All change and becoming is excluded from God because He has no potency and no matter, because He is pure act. The axiom: *"Per se fieri non possunt,"* applies to all immaterial beings. Thus the metaphysical presupposition for the becoming of any being is its composition of matter and form.[1] Act denotes actuality and, if things are exclusively act, any further becoming is impossible. Since, however, every creature possesses potency and privation, and since there is a real distinction between substance and accidents, the necessary conditions are given for change and becoming something else. We have becoming of a thing whenever something new is predicated of a thing, whether this new thing is the thing itself or some property, whether it is a condition or a relation of the thing.

In corporeal things we clearly distinguish between the conditions of rest and movement. Corporeal things are capable of movement, but in themselves they are unmoved. In the Aristotelian tradition the idea of movement (*mutatio, motus*) not only denotes the process of becoming in nature, but it is a fundamental ontological concept and an essential characteristic of every natural form. This thought is implied in the definition of the natural sciences, since they are those that have as their object material things and those that are subject to motion.[2]

The movement of natural things is not an end in itself: it exists to serve being. All movement is directed to an end that should be realized. It is a metaphysical axiom that, in comparison to rest, movement is the less perfect, and this concept of rest as it is applied to the various planes of being is used in an analogous sense. St. Thomas goes beyond the philosophy of Aristotle when he declares that the movement of the heavenly bodies has for its purpose the attainment of the full number of the elect. When the number of the elect reaches the predetermined number, the heavenly bodies will come to rest and then the movement of earthly things will also cease, and all corporeal bodies will come to rest.

In his *Sophist,* Plato taught that movement was one of the genera of being. According to the Aristotelian and Thomistic concept, move-

---

[1] *In I Sent.,* 8, 1; *In IV Sent.,* 10, 1, 2; *In VIII Met.,* 4.
[2] *In Boet. de Trin.,* V, 2; *Contra Gent.,* III, 74.

ment is not a category but one of the post-predicaments, classified in the relation of *actio-passio,* and found more definitely within the categories of quantity, quality, and place. Corresponding to these four categories, both Aristotle and St. Thomas distinguish between four kinds of movement.[3] The potency-act relation permeates every realm of being, and, since potency and act are among the primary differences of being, they are prior to movement and can therefore be used in a definition of movement.

To be in movement is a process or transition from an incipient stage, the potency, to a final stage, the act. That thing is said to be in motion which is midway between potency and act, which is partly in potency and partly in act, and that which has left the state of potency and is steadily approaching the state of act. This condition is expressed in the definition of movement: the act of potential being inasmuch as such being is tending toward act, or the progressive actualization of possible being (*actus entis in potentia quatenus in potentia,* or *actus mobilis inquantum hujusmodi*). In this definition, the term *act* expresses the relation to the earlier potency, while the term *potency* expresses the relation to the perfected act. To call movement act is justifiable since we may call act anything by which a potential being is actualized, and potential beings are actualized by movement. St. Thomas distinguishes potencies to two different acts: the potency to the completed act, and the potency to the imperfect act which is the movement itself. The movement is not a special nature or essence, but is the form in the process of becoming, in the state of imperfect act; "it is not complete being, but the way to being, the intermediary between potency and act."[4]

As he observed the phenomena of change, transition, origin, and corruption of being, St. Thomas discerned the properties of movement. Movement, which, properly speaking, is found only in corporeal things, requires, first of all, something that moves, whether an internal or external principle, which gives the impulse to movement. Every movement process implies a causal relationship; every movement process occurs between two terms, *a quo* and *ad quem.* These two terms are opposites, and therefore we have the saying: "*Omnis mutatio est inter opposita.*" What was cold becomes warm, what was small becomes large, what was here is now there, what was

[3] *In V Phys.,* 3.
[4] *In III Phys.,* 2; *In IV Sent.,* 1, 4.

water becomes air. A movement derives its species and value from its goal. A change is considered great according to the distance between the terms. Each of the four categories of movement includes a spanning relation, and a relation between two opposites. This relation "from something"—"to something" is an ontological part of the structure of movement.

Movement is not made up of other movements, but of indivisible moments each of which is related to the movement as is the indivisible point to the mathematical line. Properties of movement are continuity and succession: by continuity, movement is measured in space; by succession, it is measured in time. These succeeding moments in movement are only in temporal succession, not in a causal succession. One does not produce another, but they are produced by the efficient cause as moments in the transition from potency to act.

The term members of movement come under the same order of being. In the case of spatial, quantitative, and qualitative change, they are in the same genus; in the case of substantial origin and corruption, they are united in the same potency of matter.

The nature of the opposition of the term members differs in the various kinds of movement. In the first three kinds they oppose each other by contrariety; simple origin and corruption oppose each other by contradiction. Since affirmation and negation do not allow a middle term, and since they border directly on each other (e.g., fire and non-fire), the movement between them does not take place through a temporal transition but suddenly (*in instanti*). Examples of such sudden mutation are *illuminatio, generatio, corruptio*. If St. Thomas had had a closer acquaintance with the inner processes of becoming, if he had studied substantial becoming in the example of the development of a living being, he would have seen that all movement is successive being which, as imperfect act, tends to completion, and that the final form is always acquired gradually, and that becoming always precedes existence.[5]

Movement requires something movable, a subject, which is the passive recipient of the mutation or movement. Both terms coincide in one subject, otherwise we could not speak of a transition from one to another. This common subject in local, quantitative, and qualitative movement is some real being; in substantial mutation it is

[5] *In VI Phys.*, 2; *Contra Gent.*, II, 17, 19; *Summa theol.*, Ia, q. 45, a. 1 ad 2; q. 73, a. 2; IIIa, q. 75, a. 7 ad 2; *De pot.*, III, 2 ad 3; *Quodlib.*, 11, 4, 4.

potential being, prime matter. After the movement or change the subject is different from what it was before, but it does not surrender its being, it perdures in the process of change and becoming. Movement meant no more and no less to St. Thomas than it did for Aristotle; for both it was the *actus* of the *potentia* itself, a process taking place in time in some movable object.

Since movement takes place within different categories, St. Thomas distinguishes different kinds of movement. The first is local change, and this, in a sense, is a condition for the other kinds of change. Things not only occupy different places, but this local movement is required for their action upon one another. According to the principle that whatever is first in a certain genus is the cause of all that follows in the same genus, this local change gives rise to other changes, especially qualitative changes.

The second kind of movement is quantitative change, the decrease and increase in things. Decrease comes about by the loss of matter, and the movement from a perfect state to a less perfect state ensues; increase comes about by the incorporation of more matter, and the movement from a less perfect state to a more perfect state ensues.

The third kind of movement is qualitative change (*alteratio*), which proceeds from the active qualities of things and produces similar qualities in other things. Thus warmth produces warmth. St. Thomas grouped these three kinds of movement together as movements in the real sense of the word because one and the same actually existing sensible subject is common to the two opposed terms.

The change that takes place in the generation or corruption of a thing is, however, much more radical. Substantial forms have their own peculiar activities to a greater degree than the accidental forms, and they are able to effect their formal content in new things. The changes they effect are not only accidental, but an entire substance is either produced or ceases to exist. Here we have the absolute production of a thing in contrast to a mere production *secundum quid*. When an element changes over into another, when the seed is transformed into blood, when from the seed or germ new living beings are produced, and when living beings are destroyed, we are confronted with substantial changes, in which almost always the production of one being signifies the destruction of another. Generation is the acquisition of a substantial form, corruption is the loss of the substantial form. In order that there may be corruption, things must be composed of parts.[6] In all these changes we find no such thing as *actio in distans:* each change is brought about by contact which is either immediate or mediate. Origin or production in the absolute sense, namely, creation, by which temporal things with all their possibilities for change are posited, is not movement at all.

The statement that whatever moves is moved by some other being, is a fundamental law of the Thomistic system. In this declaration St. Thomas extends the concept of movement so that it includes the activities of the intellect and the will. Like the concept of being, the concept of movement is an analogous concept, taking on a different meaning according as it is used.

[6] *In V Phys.,* 2; *In II Sent.,* I, 1, 2; *De verit.,* 28, 1; *Lib. de caus.,* 26, 27; *De princ. nat.*

CHAPTER XX

BECOMING AND CAUSALITY

All becoming takes place within the framework of causality. Every process of becoming is caused, and the causes may be of different kinds. Looking at the history of the theory, we see that St. Thomas harmonized the theories of causality proposed by Aristotle and by the Neoplatonists which, it is true, had to a great extent been discussed by the Arabians. This theory of causality is based on the analogy of art and such principles as are offered by the phenomena of things in the process of becoming and change. Thus the theory in its essential features was supported directly by reality.

As becoming and change, so causality is intimately related to the existence of things. Becoming is indeed a movement directed toward the form, and thus toward existence. Causality embraces all those factors out of which substances build themselves up in the great complexity of movement in the universe; causality is the expression of the rules according to which substances are constructed, properties are changed, and changes are made in conditions. Causality is the explanation of all activity and, for St. Thomas as well as for Aristotle, it was an important part of ontology. The concept of cause is subordinate to the concept of principle, which is more general.

In company with Aristotle and Averroes, St. Thomas attempted to define clearly the line between principle and cause. According to the Aristotelian concept, principle is something primary, whether in the order of being, of origin, or of knowledge; it is that from which something proceeds in some way (*a quo aliquid procedit quocumque modo*). The concept of principle also contains the idea that it does not depend on anything else and that everything else in that particular genus depends on it. Every cause is a principle, but not every principle is a cause. The concept of principle is the broader of the two, as cause is more universal than element. Cause always implies the essential distinction between itself and that which it causes, but the principle may be consubstantial with that of which it is the principle. Thus a point is the principle of a line, but it is not the cause of the line.[1]

In the order of origin or generation and being, cause is a principle, since the cause is that from which a thing derives its being. An essential part of the concept of cause is that the substantial or accidental being of a thing depends on the being of another thing, and that one being and its powers intervene in the sphere of another. This other thing, that is, the effect, depends for its existence on the cause. The cause is the inner power, and often it is also the supporter and preserver of the new thing. For all kinds of cause, it is true that the cause is really distinct from the effect. In causality, therefore, we do not have a mere temporal succession of beings, but between cause and effect there is a connection of being.

As Maimonides and Averroes, so St. Thomas was quick to reject Algazel's view that the theory of causality has no reality or objectivity, being merely a succession of certain phenomena to which we have become accustomed.[2] Indeed he points out immediately that this succession of things is not essential to the causal relation, as, for instance, in the creative causality of God. This succession is proper to movement, but not to casuality, and creation is not a movement, nor is it the term of a movement as is generation. The important thing is the proceeding of one thing from another.

With the early Scholastics and St. Albert, St. Thomas asserts that if a sufficient cause is present the effect follows necessarily. Because of this necessary connection we see that the effect is completely dependent on the cause: *"manente causa manet effectus; cessante causa cessat effectus; remota causa removetur effectus."* [3] We must not, however, misunderstand this necessity of the causal relation; the cause is not unalterably determined to some particular effect. St. Thomas here distinguishes between natural causality and the free causality of the will which includes in itself the creative causality in which this note of necessity is lacking. Further, when he asserts this necessary connection of cause and effect he adds the limitation

---

[1] *De princ. nat.; In V Met.*, 1; *In I Phys.*, 10; *In I Sent.*, 12, 1, 2; *Summa theol.*, Ia, q.33, a.1; *De pot.*, X, 1 ad9.

[2] *Contra Gent.*, II, 19; *Summa theol.*, Ia, q.33, a.1 ad 1; *In I Phys.*, 1; *In II Phys.*, 10.

[3] *Contra Gent.*, III, 94; *Summa theol.*, Ia, q.2, a.3.

that by a sufficient cause we are to understand an unhindered cause even in the case of natural causes.

In contrast to the old natural philosophers, who denied the existence of all chance and taught absolute necessity of all causality, St. Thomas pointed to certain causes in nature which did not attain their effects necessarily but only frequently. Sometimes, he said, there is failure among the causes; although a thing may appear as a sufficient cause, its effect may be impeded by the activity of some other cause that intervenes. He refuted the objection that this intervention and impeding also occur necessarily, by saying that only beings *per se,* and not being *per accidens,* which is not really being, had a cause.

In formulating the causal principle, he gives it a Platonic and Aristotelian dress. From Plato's *Timaeus* came the sentence: "Everything that happens has a cause; an uncaused occurrence does not exist." [4] More frequently, St. Thomas uses the Aristotelian formula: whatever is moved, changed, formed, or made, is moved, changed, formed, or made by another (*omne quod movetur, ab alio movetur*).[5] The question has been raised whether this statement is to be understood physically or metaphysically; both Aristotle and St. Thomas affirm that it is to be understood both physically and metaphysically. At first St. Thomas applies this formula to the corporeal world, and then with some modifications he uses the concept of movement in the sense of change, and transfers the validity of the principle of movement to all changes, establishing the metaphysical validity of this principle on the difference between potency and act. Thus the statement on movement is changed over to the causal principle; every change has a cause, and an uncaused occurrence does not exist.[6]

St. Thomas begins inductively with the observation that all things that are seen to move are moved by other things. But this does not yet afford a universal validity for the principle. Again, when he proceeds deductively and derives his principle of movement, presupposing a concept of the physical world and of movement that is untenable in view of our present-day knowledge of the natural sciences, his theory of causality seems to be seriously threatened. But the validity of the causal principle is bound up with the correctness

[4] *Summa theol.,* Ia, q. 46, a. 1 ad 6.
[5] *Contra Gent.,* I, 13; *Summa theol.,* Ia, q. 2, a. 3.
[6] *Summa theol.,* Ia IIae, q. 75, a. 1.

or falsity of the concept of movement. We must not forget that a true metaphysical idea may be hidden beneath an erroneous concept of physical motion.

St. Thomas was aware of the close relation existing between first principles. Just as the concepts of being and non-being are our first concepts and are also the presupposition for an understanding of the concepts of the whole and its parts, so the principle of contradiction, which declares that being and non-being are mutually exclusive, is presupposed in the statement that the whole is greater than any part. When we consider the principle of causality, we see that it likewise deserves the rank of first principle because it is obtained by an analysis of the process of becoming and by an explanation of the factors contained in the process of becoming and in the concept of becoming.

In another respect, however, it does not appear to be a first principle, because St. Thomas is obliged to adduce proofs for it. But the principle of causality does possess that analytical character required for first principles although it is only mediately analytical. According to St. Thomas, a statement is analytical when its predicate is contained in the subject or when the predicate has a necessary relation to the subject. This necessary connection with the subject need not be originally thought of when we think of the subject; it may be the product of long and tedious cogitation. Thus potency and act are to each other as non-being to being. If potency is to become act, i.e., if non-being is to become being, this must happen either of itself or through another. It cannot occur of itself because non-being and being exclude each other, because a thing cannot be in potency and act in the same respect at the same time, and because no sufficient reason exists for non-being to become being.[7]

St. Thomas accepted from Aristotle the division of causes into four kinds: *Omnis causa vel est materia vel forma, vel agens vel finis.* The existence of causality in nature presupposes that things have active and passive potencies and powers (*virtutes*), for only then can they be active or passive, only then is a mutual influence possible between them.[8] A thing is active only in so far as it is in act, it produces effects only by reason of its actually existing nature. From its essential form proceeds its principle of activity. The essential form

[7] *Contra Gent.,* I, 13; *Summa theol.,* Ia, q.2, a.3.
[8] *Summa theol.,* Ia, q.25, a.1.

of a thing and the activities that proceed from its potencies (*operatio*) are related to each other as "first" and "second" act. The activities of a thing are themselves divided into those that tend to the outside (*actio transiens*) and produce changes in things, and those that are completed within the subject itself (*actio immanens*) and perfect that subject (e.g., knowledge).[9]

In this Aristotelian division of causes, some have pointed out the lack of a principle of division derived from the nature of cause. This apparent failing is in reality an advantage. In this instance Aristotle refrained from a deductive derivation of the kinds of causes and drew his distinctions from the very process of becoming, from the formation and actualization of a potency.

A substratum is required in every process of becoming or generation of being; something that is itself unformed but is capable of being formed, some matter from which the new being comes, in which the process of becoming takes place and which is in passive potency to being. When there is a genesis of substantial being, this substratum is prime matter, which possesses no definite being but is in potency to substantial being (*materia ex qua*); if there is a genesis of accidental being, a real subject exists in which the accidental formation takes place (*materia in qua*). The form is the cause of being, it gives prime matter a determined being; in substantial becoming it gives being itself, in the genesis of accidental being it gives a definite accidental being. With respect to being, matter and form have a mutual causal relationship; the form is the cause of the matter inasmuch as it gives the matter actual being, and the matter is the cause of the form because it is the depositary of the form. Since matter and form are the inner constituents of a thing, St. Thomas calls them [10] the intrinsic causes in distinction to the efficient and final causes, which are extrinsic causes. Only the intrinsic causes can be called principles.

As is well known, St. Thomas speaks of privation besides these two principles of the genesis of being, matter and form. Privation is not a cause, but only a principle and, unlike matter and form which are principles *per se*, it is a principle only *per accidens;* it is a principle of becoming but not of being. Privation is necessary for the genesis of being since any matter clothed with a form is at the same

---

[9] *De verit.*, VIII, 6.
[10] *Met.*, XII, 4.

time in privation with respect to some other form and also since the process of becoming begins with a state of privation.

Since the genesis and production of a form can take place only in matter, St. Thomas calls matter a cause of the form. In the genesis of being, matter and form react on each other and this mutual reaction produces the individual thing (*Phys.*, I, 7). Another thought that is fundamental in the Aristotelian-Thomistic theory of the genesis of being is that what is produced is not matter and form, but the composite; what is produced is the individual thing constituted by matter and form. Matter is in potency to the composite because it is in potency to the form, and the form comes into existence because the composite is produced through it. If matter and form would result from the process, then there would have to be a matter for the matter and a form for the form, and so *ad infinitum*.[11]

Movement means the educing of something from potency to act. What is in potency cannot actualize itself. This condition exists in art as well as in nature. The form is present only in the actual thing. A principle, therefore, is necessary to lead the potency to the fullness of existence: the efficient cause (*causa efficiens vel movens vel agens vel unde est principium motus*).[12] As an extrinsic cause, the efficient cause produces something distinct from itself, and it is obviously distinct from the matter and form. To establish a sufficient cause, one thing is not always enough; frequently several factors must work together to produce the one effect. In agreement with Avicenna, St. Thomas distinguishes four kinds of efficient cause: *causa perficiens, disponens, adjuvans,* and *consilians*. The first is the cause which produces the final perfection of a thing, namely, the form. A disposing cause is one that prepares the matter for the form; and this cause may be either remote or proximate with relation to the induction of the form. An efficient cause is called assisting (*adjuvans*) when it serves the principal effect, but is distinct from the chief cause; and an efficient cause is called counseling when it intellectually determines the end. Three kinds of efficient cause must be mentioned here because of their importance in the Thomistic system: the equivocal cause, which coincides neither nominally nor conceptually with the effect; the univocal cause, which coincides both nominally and con-

---

[11] *De princ. nat.; In II Sent.,* 18, 1; *Summa theol.,* Ia, q.9, a.2; q.25, a.1; q.77, a.6; Ia IIae, q.55, a.2; *De pot.,* III, 1; *In I de coel.,* 6; *In I Phys.,* 13.

[12] *Contra Gent.,* I, 17, 20; *Summa theol.,* Ia, q.2, a.3; q.6, a.1.

ceptually with the effect, as when a man produces a man, warmth produces warmth; and analogous cause, which is not in the same genus of being with its effect but retains some resemblance to the effect, as is true of God the cause of the universe.

Every active thing is active in the pursuit of some intention, i.e., it acts for some purpose, whether that thing is some natural thing or some will. Thus we have the purpose or end as a cause. The end is that toward which the appetite of the active thing is directed and because of which some other thing happens. The end, purpose, and purposeful action had their origin in the field of conscious human activity of the will, and here it was that Aristotle began to analyze these basic concepts and later brought them into contact with the concept of the good. Man acts for a purpose, in his mind he determines something in the future and strives to actualize by his will some good that he knows and values. Aristotle, the greatest teleologist of antiquity, thought that finality and purpose could be clearly seen in nature; indeed, he thought that more purpose could be discerned in nature than in the works of art. Here again St. Thomas is in entire conformity with Aristotle. He explains final causality inductively when he relies on reasons offered by the psychology of the human will; he offers an explanation by way of deduction from the genesis of real being as follows. Since no potency can proceed to act by itself, an efficient cause is required. The activity of this efficient cause needs some direction to an end, otherwise we could not explain why this thing and not another was done. This direction to something determined is what is meant by end and purpose. Everything that acts, acts for a purpose. If we remove this first in the series of causes, we remove the rest, for the first among causes is the final cause. Matter does not attain to the form if it is not moved by some active thing, and this active thing moves only in view of some purpose.

In rational beings this direction to an end is accomplished through the will; in other natural beings, through the natural appetite. The purpose becomes the wherefore and in the mind it begins to act. What is in the future appears causal to some extent, and, while assuming this causal nature, it still remains a principle. The end or purpose is the dominating power over the genetic process of being, and thus the whole exists before the parts, not in reality, but as an idea. The final form of the being stands at the beginning of the process of its genesis, and throughout it determines the means and methods to be used for its actualization. The activity of the human will differs from the purposeful activity of things in nature in this, that the will is intent on a known end which it is able to consider, whereas irrational beings are intent necessarily on one goal and by this unconscious striving for an end they give testimony of the divine intelligence working in nature.[13]

The purpose or end is the most important of all causes; it is the *causa causarum*. It gives the impulse to the other causes; it is the cause that all other causes are causes. The efficient cause is active because of the end, and because of this activity the form completes the matter and the form determines the matter. By its very nature the final cause deserves priority.[14]

Besides these four causes St. Thomas also mentions the exemplary cause. This cause had its origin in Platonic Christian circles, and played an important role in Plato's *Timaeus* as well as in St. Augustine's doctrine of creation. The exemplary cause is the model existing in the divine mind, according to which things are made in the universe.[15]

These various kinds of causes appear also in various forms, enumerated by Aristotle and the Arabians. Thus *causa per prius* is distinct from *causa per posterius,* the proximate cause is distinct from the remote cause. According as a thing acts or has the capability to act, it is an actual or potential cause. St. Thomas makes a clear distinction between *causa per se* and *causa per accidens;* the former produces the effect as such, the accidental cause does not. The cause *per accidens* is given several senses: at one time St. Thomas speaks of a house built by a man who is also a rhetorician, and again of a cause *per se* when it produces unintended effects besides its principal effect. Frequently St. Thomas speaks of the cause *per accidens* as that cause which overcomes obstacles in the way of the cause *per se.*

St. Thomas lays particular stress on the difference between the principal cause and the instrumental cause. The principal cause is that which determines the activity by its own form; but often an instrumental cause must be inserted in the causal process. In speaking of the instrumental cause we must distinguish between its twofold activity and effect; that which is effected by its own form and power,

---

[13] *Contra Gent.,* III, 2; *Summa theol.,* Ia, q.5, a.2 ad 1; Ia IIae, q.1, a.2.
[14] *Summa theol.,* Ia, q.15, a.2; q.5, a.4.
[15] *De verit.,* III, 1.

and then that effect attained by the movement of the principal cause which goes beyond the powers of the instrumental cause. The saw and the ax cut the wood, but they cannot of themselves make the table; this can be done only by the craftsman using the tools. The effect produced by the peculiar form of the instrumental cause is prior to the effect produced by the activity of the principal cause, but the activity of the instrumental cause coalesces with that of the principal cause.

This distinction between the principal and instrumental cause is important in the Thomistic system because the divine artisan conserves His masterpiece, the universe, by means of intermediary causes as His instruments.[16]

In St. Thomas' philosophical view of the universe, the distinction between general and particular causes is also of great importance. Among the former are the heavenly bodies, the pure spirits, and especially God; among the latter are the powers of sublunary beings that produce individuals.[17]

1. **Fundamental principles of causality.** An examination and interpretation of the principle of causality leads to important conclusions which might be called axioms or fundamental principles of causality. These propositions can be traced back to Aristotle and the Neoplatonists. Like Nicholas of Amiens before him, St. Albert had collated these propositions, and St. Thomas increased their number and thus cast still greater light on the original principle of causality.

Foremost is the Thomistic anchoring of all that is dynamic, all that is active, in being itself: act follows upon being, the manner of a thing's acting follows its mode of being (*agere sequitur esse, modus agendi sequitur modum essendi*).[18] Being unfolds itself in its action. If everything that is potential attains actuality only through something that is itself actual, it follows, according to St. Thomas, that things are active only so far as they are in act or actual; or again, things are active by reason of their forms, since it is through the form that things obtain actuality.[19] The principles of being and actuality and activity coincide.

Another conclusion follows: every efficient cause produces some-

[16] *Ibid.*, XXVII, 4; *Contra Gent.*, II, 24; *Summa theol.*, Ia, q. 45, a. 5.

[17] *Summa theol.*, Ia IIae, q. 85, a. 6.

[18] *Contra Gent.*, III, 69; *De pot.*, IX, 1 ad 3; *Summa theol.*, Ia, q. 89, a. 1.

[19] *Contra Gent.*, I, 73; *Summa theol.*, Ia, q. 3, a. 2; q. 45, a. 5; IIIa, q. 8, a. 5; *De pot.*, III, 11.

thing like itself (*omne agens agit sibi simile*). The artist impresses on his material the ideal form that exists in his mind and thus produces a work of art. Fire generates fire, man generates a man, and the grain of wheat produces more wheat. When a horse produces a mule, the process still holds true, at least within the next higher genus. This principle applies only to genus and species and not to the individual (*hoc aliquid*). All natural activity takes place within the boundaries of the species (*nihil agit ultra suam speciem*), and the law of synonymity declares that generation is the transmission of the species. The individual difference between the producer and that which is produced is not affected. Because of this relation the effect must be contained *in virtute* in the cause, a certain resemblance to the effect must exist beforehand in the cause, and finally a certain resemblance to the cause must be found in the effect. This resemblance, however, refers only to the proximate cause, not to the more remote causes. Thus a man resembles the man who produces him but not the sun which is an auxiliary cause in his generation. The perfection of the effect is found in the cause; if it is a univocal cause, the perfection will be of the same order; if it is an equivocal cause, the perfection in the cause will be of a higher order. A man produces another man, but the sun possesses more than that which was produced by its power, and God possesses all perfections in an infinitely higher degree than created things.

This theory of causality has the most far-reaching influence in the Thomistic ontology. Since the act and the form of a thing represent the perfection and goodness of a thing and since the process of becoming is a process of similarity, the process of becoming aims at producing act and form and thus also the perfect and the good. Evil is entirely beyond the scheme of generation (*praeter intentionem et generationem*). We arrive at the same conclusion from a consideration of the final cause. Since everything acts for a purpose, it is always intent on the good. Since the cause is good and the effect receives the good, every effect turns by nature back to its cause. The teleological structure of the principle of causality is the reason why that which is first in the cause is the last in the effect.[20]

Causality does not denote a mere succession of phenomena according to some order; causality is rather a process in which things

---

[20] *Contra Gent.*, I, 49; II, 21; III, 21; *Summa theol.*, Ia, q.4, a.2; q.5, a.4; q.19, a.2; q.63, a.4; IIa IIae, q.106, a.3; *De div. nom.*, IV, 2.

form or are formed, it denotes a production of something similar, the transmission of being, the forming of substances. A comparison of the Aristotelian and Thomistic concept of causality with that of the present-day shows how intimately the concept of cause was connected with the concept of being. In the mind of Aristotle and St. Thomas being was not a mere factual, valueless existence as it is for the modern positivist philosopher; for them, being was permeated with the elements of order. Every being was dominated by an idea, by an inner structural principle, by a form with a purpose; every being was a totality to which all individuals had a determined relationship. In the process of becoming, the being hands on its own structure and its peculiarity and its mode of activity, it reproduces its properties in other beings, not as if the cause entered into the essence of the effect but in such a way that a peculiar effect proceeds from a peculiar cause.[21] The process of becoming takes place in time and concludes with the visible effect. Thus the process of becoming is a process of actualization, the process that Aristotle called entelechy, which is nothing else than the form intent on producing a definite type. St. Thomas incorporated this thought in his natural philosophy and utilized it in his theory of form originating from the potency of matter.

This theory had a long history. St. Thomas attributed it to Aristotle and Averroes; St. Albert and St. Bonaventure had used it. The basic thought which goes back to Aristotle is the following. If matter is to be actualized, the act or form must be present potentially in the matter. Aristotle had derived the concepts of matter and form from artistic objects, as he had derived the concepts of potency and act from the generative process of organic being. He then identified matter and potency on the one hand, and form and act on the other, and finally he transferred the relation between the potential and the actual to matter and form. Consequently all movement was conceived as a disposition for actualization, and the genesis of all being was conceived after the analogy of organic being as the development of actuality performed in the germ or seed.

St. Thomas thought that this theory safeguarded the doctrine that substantial forms were developed by natural agencies as against the Neoplatonists who held that natural agencies only disposed the matter for the reception of the form, which was induced by a separate

[21] De pot., III, 5 ad 1.

principle. According to St. Thomas, the substantial forms were educed by natural agencies from the potency of the matter. In this process, of course, the potential basis in the matter must correspond with the dynamic equipment of the active principle.

One difference must be noted here. St. Albert and St. Bonaventure held that this potency in matter, from which the form is educed, is an active potency; St. Thomas calls it a passive potency. Relying on Porphyry, St. Albert thought that the potency of matter was something positive as the inchoation of forms; St. Bonaventure, under the influence of St. Augustine, thought that matter had a *ratio seminalis* in it for the production of future forms and being. Both therefore permitted the idea of some germinative foundation for the future being. The educing principle is not therefore superfluous, since in both views the disposing element requires something to release it. But St. Thomas, accepting the Aristotelian concept of matter without modification and bereft of all determination, taught that matter was only a passive potency from which the form was not really educed; the acting principle actually confers the new form and therefore it would be more correct to say that the form was induced instead of educed.

In every process in which being is originated some substratum is required; but this rule has one exception, the creative activity of God. The acting principle applies itself to this substratum, and the being is originated *per informationem,* by informing the matter. No acting principle can be thought of without some passive principle, no actual being exists without some corresponding potential being. We have already remarked the metaphysical priority of the act over potency, but in the genesis of being, when act and potency are dependent on each other, they must be simultaneous.

Like potency and act, cause and effect are also closely related. The cause is always conceptually prior to the effect, but it need not be prior in time. The idea of a thing being its own cause is a contradiction; "nothing can be its own cause, for then it would be prior to itself, which is impossible." [22]

St. Thomas is not content with a general expression of the relation between cause and effect. He examines the relation of the four kinds of causes to the effect and arrives at the following conclusions. Matter and form precede the effect; the purpose is not prior to the effect

[22] *In III Sent.,* 18, 1, 3; *Contra Gent.,* I, 18; II, 47; *Summa theol.,* Ia, q. 1, a. 2 f.

in being, but it is so in intention; the form as such has no priority. Since a thing receives its being through the form, the existence of the form is simultaneous with the existence of the effect. Inasmuch as the form is the purpose, it may precede in the intention of the cause. A cause that acts by means of movement necessarily precedes its effect in time, since the effect stands at the end of the activity while the cause is the principle of the activity. In the order of existence the matter and the cause have priority, but in the order of perfection the form and purpose have priority.

Cause and effect are proportioned to each other. One cause corresponds to one effect, the same effect will correspond to the same cause. This does not deny, however, that different causes will produce the same effect. The necessity of the effect depends on the necessity of the cause. Whatever acts by reason of its natural form will carry out its activity with greater intensity and perfection than that which acts only through participation with some higher cause. Thus fire heats more intensively than a heated object. General effects correspond to general causes, particular causes correspond to particular effects. A strong effect comes from a proximate cause, a weak effect from a remote cause. The proposition that the cause is higher than the effect and that the cause contains more than the effect was introduced into Scholasticism from St. Augustine. Aristotle, when opposing the Pythagoreans and Speusippus, denied that the perfect could be developed from the imperfect. St. Thomas agrees with him. Act is always by nature prior to potency, and therefore the imperfect can be derived only from the perfect.

2. **God and secondary causes.** St. Thomas seems never to be content with extolling the eminent significance of the first cause and God's causality. It is God who moves all things, who directs and guides all things, who Himself is moved, directed, and guided by no one. Not only did He grant things their being, but in His ineffable goodness He also granted them the dignity of causality. Created things function as secondary causes in the universe by reason of the essential forms which God impressed upon them. When He gave them their forms, God endowed things with natural inclinations to definite ends; He granted them inner principles from which their actions and movements proceed. God uses nature as the instruments for the completion of His plans. These principles are handed on in the process of generation and genesis of being.

Just as finite things do not exist of themselves, so they are not able to act of themselves. All that second causes produce they produce by virtue of the first cause. The effects of secondary causes are attributable to the first cause. This does not militate against the proper activity of things, it merely expresses the idea that the divine power cooperates everywhere. God is the cause of every activity inasmuch as, by His creative and preserving actions, He secures the existence of things and with their existence grants them the power to act and continues to support that power. Without this higher divine causality, the lower causes could not have any activity. Every secondary cause has its causing ability from the first cause.[23]

In answering the question, how God acts in secondary causes, a sharp division arose among the interpreters of St. Thomas. On one side the thesis was defended that according to St. Thomas the essential forms were sufficient with the principles of action that God had placed in them and that St. Thomas taught that there was only indirect cooperation by God. Opponents on the other side maintained that St. Thomas taught that God imparted to secondary causes a special impulse for every action and that St. Thomas had taught a direct cooperation with secondary causes. Although the defenders of the first view have assiduously accumulated many texts from the writings of the Angelic Doctor, they cannot surmount the fact that St. Thomas actually mentions a fourfold cooperation on the part of God and that he clearly differentiates between them.[24]

St. Thomas not only teaches that God grants things powers and preserves them in the use of those powers, but that besides this He applies their movements and is directly active in the instrumental effects of secondary causes. This view corresponds with the Thomistic idea that God acts most intimately in things. It appears that the Thomists are right when they believe their master upholds the *praemotio physica*. It is especially true that God cooperates directly when we speak of the life of grace.

The first cause and secondary causes cooperate, in the sense that the first cause confers being as such whereas the secondary cause produces this particular kind of being. Being as such is a specific effect

---

[23] *De verit.*, V, 9 ad 10; *Contra Gent.*, III, 67, 70, 88, 89; *Summa theol.*, Ia, q. 105, a. 5; *Lib. de caus.*, 1.

[24] *De pot.*, III, 7; *Summa theol.*, Ia, q. 105, a. 5; q. 22, a. 3; Ia IIae, q. 9, a. 4; *Contra Gent.*, III, 70.

of God. In their activities, secondary causes stand in continual need of the creating, preserving, and applying activity of God, on which they rely as their support and foundation. Only in union with God's creative power can any creature produce a complete thing. Here it is not a question of two separate effects, one produced by God and the other by natural causes; the effect proceeds wholly from both causes but in different respects. The effect comes from God as the Creator of the matter and the giver of the powers by which the secondary cause acts; it comes from the secondary cause inasmuch as the effect is the term of its limited activity. Important principles are bound up with the relation of secondary causes to the first cause. The simpler a cause is the more closely it approaches to the first cause, and the more it is able to share in the proper activity of the first cause. The less matter a cause has in its being and the more form, the more active it will be; the higher and nobler a cause is the more its effects will extend, the deeper it will penetrate, and it will be able to actualize remoter potencies. The weakening of the effect of a cause goes apace with the removal of that cause from the first cause.

Even though the influence of the first cause may exceed that of the secondary cause in intensity and duration, the effect will resemble the secondary cause more since it is the secondary cause that determines the act of the first cause to this particular effect. Therefore the effect is denominated according to the secondary cause and not according to the first cause. The influence of the first cause reaches the effect only through the intermediary instruments; nevertheless the influence of the first cause is greater on the effect than that of secondary causes.

CHAPTER XXI

THE IDEA OF CREATION

1. The origin of the universe according to the Greeks. The idea of creation is not derived originally from philosophical speculation but from biblical revelation. For those who believe in revelation, creation is something that is to be accepted and not demonstrated, something that is not to be doubted since it is a fact made known to men by God even though it is not demonstrable or comprehensible by the finite mind of the essentially finite man. For the Jews, Arabians, and Christians, creation was firmly founded on faith. St. Thomas, however, thought so highly of the human intellect that he dared to incorporate the concept of creation as a homogeneous member into his metaphysics. Human insight finds one field open to it, that of the human will, which at least provides an analogy of the fundamental causality of creation, for by the action of the human will something conceived and valued in the mind receives extra-mental reality.

From its earliest beginnings when it had a distinct hylozoistic outlook, Greek philosophy accepted a special efficient cause to explain the origin of the universe. This cause, according to Empedocles, was the mystical power of love and hate; later Anaxagoras elevated the concept to that of the *nous*. Thus a supreme spiritual principle for the origin of the universe was established, but the idea of creation remained alien to Greek philosophy. The *nous* of Anaxagoras returned in Aristotle in the form of the first unmoved mover, but even now the universe is neither formed nor created by God. Creation out of nothing was excluded from the universe as well as from God according to Aristotle. Indeed that famous principle, nothing comes from nothing—to safeguard which he had sought the distinction between potency and act—prevented any such concept as creation. In its existence the universe rested on itself, and that was true of the cosmos of the forms of beings as well as of the substratum, prime matter, which existed necessarily. Individual beings, indeed, are contingent, but not the universe as a whole.

Everything in the world is explained, according to Aristotle, by the world itself, except the beginning of movement. This universe existing of necessity from all eternity in the fullness of being has one relation with God, who directs the process of movement that extends from the highest sphere of the fixed stars through the whole universe and incessantly renews all the forms of being. The idea of creation is also excluded on the part of God. Instead of attributing to God the fundamental activity underlying all others, Aristotle declares that any action or production must be removed from the idea of God as an imperfection. The divine essence consists in contemplation, in the highest activity of the intellect. God has no will, said Aristotle; when asked how God directed the movement of the universe, he replied that God moved the world as that which is loved moves the lover. The material world moves itself in desire toward the highest form.[1]

We might concede that Aristotle had formulated fundamental principles that would have required the acceptance of creation as their consequence, especially when he said that what is most true and most actual is the cause of the being of all other things. But St. Thomas was little justified in enumerating Plato and Aristotle among the adherents of the doctrine of creation.[2] His sharp judgment, that the error of those who accepted an uncreated matter was "unbearable," strikes the two great Greek philosophers as well.

Plato seems to have come somewhat closer to the concept of creation. Led by the analogy of the fundamental causality that he found in human activity, Plato advanced to the idea of God as the former of the universe and the architect of the world. In his *Timaeus* he went into detail in explaining the analogy between the origin of the universe and the formation of a work of art. As the artist produces the work of art from material already present according to the plan conceived in his mind, so the divine demi-urge forms the world from the matter present from all eternity according to the eternal ideas. The Platonic idea of God is, therefore, closer to the

[1] *Met.*, VII, 7; *De coel.*, II, 12.
[2] *Summa theol.*, Ia, q. 44, a. 1; *De pot.*, III, 5.

Christian concept than is the Aristotelian, since Plato endows his God with love and speaks of the origin of the world as the product of unselfish goodness. In its development of the idea of God's relation to the universe, Neoplatonism made no advance toward the Christian idea.

Plotinus, who abandoned the Platonic picture and the intention that animated it, compared God to the source from which a river rises, to the root from which a tree grows, to the sun that radiates light and dispels darkness, to the number one from which the whole system of numbers proceeds; but he did not conceive the world as originating in the thinking and willing of God. According to him matter was not independent, it was the least important factor in his process of emanation. He rejected any equality of the world with God and defended God's substantial independence from the world. But when he thought of the origin of the world as a process of emanation in which the world proceeds from the divine being by an inner necessity, he was far from the Christian idea of creation although occasionally some resemblance to creationism may be found in his theory. Most of the religious and theistic thinkers continued to adhere to Plato's *Timaeus*.

From Philo, the Alexandrian Jew, we might expect to hear an expression of the idea of creation. He does indeed call God ποιητής and also κτίστης, but the Platonic notion that the universe was made of some pre-existing material had such a powerful influence on him that he used it in his interpretation of the Pentateuch. In the beginning some of the Fathers of the Church tried to free themselves from this Platonic concept. The Christian concept of God requires the pure, unmodified concept of creation. Again and again it was necessary to defend it, even as late as the time of St. Augustine against the Manichaeans. The idea of a world formed from matter is opposed to the absolute perfection of God; no other reality can exist beside Him. Within this created world, causes needed a substratum for their activity. The human artist is able only to form his material, the divine artist produces the form and the material from something that was not before, from nothing. Metaphysically the thought might be expressed: God is simple and absolute being, and every other being is through Him.[3]

Among Christian thinkers creation out of nothing was interpreted

[3] *De div. nat.*, III, chap. 5.

in yet another sense entirely unacceptable to St. Thomas. John Scotus Eriugena (d. 877), under the influence of Neoplatonism, concluded that because God was perfectly undetermined He was the nothing from which the world was made. He explained the nothing, however, as a "full, superabundant nothing, as something more than being, as the pre-eminence of the divine superbeing," and from this nothing all things proceeded by a necessary process. Creation is "God made visible," theophany, God's self-development or unfolding.[4] But according to the Christian view, creation is a work of God and not the realization of divine possibilities.

2. **The concept of creation.** To create means something more than to cause to exist, more than to form a being. The idea of creation denotes that things are produced in the fullness of their being by the first cause (*emanatio totius entis a causa universali*). Among the various modes of the origin of being, it is supreme, because its final term is the whole substance of a thing. The concept of creation therefore includes the notion that it proceeds from non-being, from nothing (*ex nihilo*). This nothing is not a substance, it is no reality at all. The preposition *ex* in the definition expresses a negation, it denies the explanation of the world's origin out of some pre-existing material. The world came into existence by an absolute positing of being *nullo praeexsupposito* (*productio entis in quantum entis*). God is the cause of being as such. Nothing is found in the thing that is not new and that was formerly present. In contrast to the other kinds of origin of being, creation's causality extends to all parts of the being. Creation is not movement nor is it change, because both of these require a substratum; creation is a simple emanation.

The objection that being needed some receiving substratum did not deter St. Thomas. If God posits being, He also posits what receives that being. Essence and existence, it is true, are different, but when God gives existence to the essence He creates not only the existence but also the essence. The preposition *ex* also expresses an order of things, it tells us that the thing is "after the nothing." [5]

The concept of creation is intimately bound up with the idea of God. Creation presupposes a personal God as the only sufficient explanation for the fact of creation. He alone can produce things out

---

[4] *Ibid.*, chaps. 5, 19.
[5] *In II Sent.*, I, 1; *Contra Gent.*, II, 21; *De pot.*, III, 1 ad 17; 5 ad 2; *Summa theol.*, Ia, q. 41, a. 3; q. 45, a. 5.

of nothing. For St. Thomas creation was not a truth of faith as it was for Maimonides and St. Albert; it was not a miracle that defied proof. Following Avicenna, St. Thomas attempted to make creation evident by demonstrations that rested on the fundamental principles of his metaphysics and his theory of the genesis of being. The supreme principle of action is that a thing acts only in as far as it is actual. The mode of a things's activity depends on the mode of its actuality. Every individual thing may be said to be in act with respect to two things. It is in act with reference to itself, and here it is in act not as far as its whole substance is concerned but only by reason of its form; further, it is in act with reference to other actual things. No thing possesses the fullness of act and the perfection of all actual things; a thing has only a certain specific perfection.

According to the principle that everything produces something like itself, a specific thing does not produce simple being but being of a specific kind. This natural activity proceeds after the manner of movement and requires the substratum of matter. God, however, is pure act; with reference to Himself and with respect to other beings He possesses all perfections of things (*est virtualiter omnia*) and He is also their origin and cause. God alone, therefore, is able to produce a thing without any pre-existing material in the fullness of its subsisting being. At the same time this conclusion is in accord with the other principle, that that being which possesses the perfections in a certain genus to the highest degree is the cause of those perfections in all other members of that genus. God is the supreme being and therefore He is the cause of all being outside Himself. The proportion between cause and effect requires that a particular effect have a particular cause, and that what is common to all effects have a common and universal cause. Thus being, which is common to all effects, requires God as its cause. St. Thomas appropriates the statement found in the Neoplatonic *Liber de causis,* that being has its origin by creation, while life and the other perfections of things are added *per informationem.* All this reasoning is based on the fact that finite beings have existence only by participation, having received it from a being in whom essence and existence are identical. This difference between beings that have being *per essentiam* and those that have being *per participationem* establishes this unbridgeable abyss between the Creator and creatures and prevents any monistic confusion of the two.

Among the different kinds of genesis of being, creation is the first because it presupposes no other, and its effect, simple being, is the first effect which also presupposes no other. The first and most universal cause, God, produces simple being; all other activities determine this being and produce specific and individual being (*hoc ens vel tale ens*).

In essence creation is a relation. Since the universe depends on God, but not vice versa; this relation from God's viewpoint is not real.

Having established the doctrine of creation, St. Thomas did not rest; it was still necessary for him to defend the doctrine from attack and from efforts to distort it. In objection to the doctrine of creation, some have said that it was impossible because between being and non-being an infinite distance intervenes that cannot be bridged over. St. Thomas answered with a distinction: if the distance were infinite considered from both sides, then indeed it would be unbridgeable, and such would be the case between non-being and the infinite being of God; if, however, the distance is from non-being to the finite being of creatures, it can be bridged over. Especially the ancient axiom, "nothing comes from nothing," was advanced against creation. Even Aristotle had accepted this proposition of the Pre-Socratics as an axiom. St. Thomas acknowledged its validity in all particular effects and for all natural mutations in the universe, but he denied its validity with respect to the first cause of all being. The ancients erred, he said, because they had not advanced to the idea of a universal cause, and therefore they could not rise to the grand concept of creation.[6]

Working as the supreme cause, the divine artisan by the free causality of His will brought into existence the universe modeled after the eternal ideas in His intellect. This is the great contribution of Platonism which found its way into Scholasticism through St. Augustine and the Pseudo-Areopagite. These ideas express the nature of God in its relation to the multiplicity of things. Even though they are multiple they do not destroy the unity of the divine nature, and they refer not only to genus and species, as Plato and Averroes taught, but also to the individual, as Plotinus and St. Augustine held. Whenever ideas are active, all origin by accident or necessity is eliminated, for here intellect and will are at work. These ideas corroborate the concept of creation and they are the unifying members between God

---

[6] *Contra Gent.*, II, 16; *De pot.*, III, 1 ad 3.

and the universe. The idea exists in the divine mind as *essentia crea-trix,* and when it is applied to the world it is the *forma factiva.* St. Thomas rejects the creation by means of intermediary beings, as well as the cognate theory that God intends the creation in general and the division into individuals is carried out by subordinate beings.

Another difficulty presented itself: How can the supreme spiritual being produce corporeal beings? Should not this first principle also be corporeal in order that corporeal beings might issue forth from it? Or should not this supreme principle be beyond both corporeity and spirituality in order to explain the various planes of being? Or must we trace matter back to intelligible qualities as its source? St. Thomas solved the difficulty by referring to the analogy of the divine artisan. The artisan need not be everything that he produces. In His mind God forms these divine essences which, when ushered into existence, manifest a likeness to Himself in as far as they are.[7]

The purity of the concept of creation requires that the creatures be produced directly by God. The Arabians, Algazel, and Avicenna, and Siger of Brabant of the faculty of arts, proposed a theory accord-ing to which God created some primary being which produced a second being, and so on to the corporeal world. They were led to this theory because they thought that God as a simple being could produce only one being. St. Thomas rejected this theory as erroneous, and was reminded at the same time of another error: the concept of God's activity as a natural occurrence. In nature, it is true, only one thing proceeds from a simple thing, but God acts with His free will and posits the external world in existence according to the world of ideas contained in His essence.

St. Thomas excludes from creatures all creative activity. Creatures themselves are not able to create because they have not the power themselves nor have they received it from the first cause. They can-not create by their own power because only the first cause can be the principle of being; they cannot create by virtue of the first cause because every effect of an instrumental cause depends on its powers. But the powers of a second cause are finite, while creation requires an infinite power because of the infinite distance to be bridged over between being and non-being. Again, everything acts inasmuch as it is in act. Only pure act can produce a thing in its whole substance.

St. Thomas opposed any attempt to teach that the first causal prin-

---

[7] *De verit.,* III, 1, 2, 8; *Summa theol.,* Ia, q. 15, a. 1.

ciples were more than one, especially the Manichaean theory of a dual principle, one good and the other bad. Things are active inasmuch as they are in act, i.e., by reason of their form; but inasmuch as a thing is in act it is good and perfect. Nothing therefore is active inasmuch as it is bad.

3. Creation and time. From Plato's *Timaeus,* by way of Philo of Alexandria and the patristic tradition, the idea that time originated with the universe came into Scholasticism. Before the beginning of the world there was no movement and therefore no time. According to St. Thomas also, the beginning of the universe and the beginning of time are simultaneous. Time is not a presupposition for creation; it is not an autonomous stream within which something is created, it is merely implied in creation. For this reason St. Augustine is careful to emphasize that the universe was not created in time but with time. That moment in which the world began is not time or a part of time, but a point marking the boundary or limit of time. Creation took place in an indivisible act. Both St. Augustine and St. Thomas protest against understanding the "before" of the nothing in a time sense. This nothing has neither measure nor duration.[8] We cannot speak of the last moment of nothing and the first moment of being, since before created being time did not exist, even though the human imagination seems to be able to extend time beyond the beginning of the universe. The nothing from which the universe was created precedes being not in duration but in nature, i.e., ontologically.

We must keep in mind these observations of St. Augustine if we wish to comprehend the Thomistic viewpoint with respect to the question of whether the world had a beginning.

On this point, among the Arabians two tendencies manifested themselves: Arabian philosophy, like Aristotle, taught the eternity of the world; Mohammedan theology, on the other hand, sought scientific proof for the fact of creation. Against these opinions Maimonides, the leader of Jewish thought in the twelfth century, proposed the theory that we can know about creation only through revelation, even though some philosophical proofs seem to incline toward the eternity of creation. He had a decisive influence on St. Albert, who taught that creation, as the absolute positing of being and as a free act of God's will, was entirely outside the realm of philosophical proof. We know about the miracle of creation only

[8] *Contra Gent.,* II, 35.

through our faith. Afterward, indeed, when we know about creation, we also know that this created world must have begun, for, according to St. Albert, to be created and to be without beginning is a contradiction since a temporal being that does not possess its being and its life in one indivisible act necessarily must have a beginning.

St. Thomas differs from his master on two points. First, it is his opinion that the creation of the world can be established by proof; but the world's creation in time cannot be proved by reason. Creation out of nothing, in the sense of excluding all pre-existing matter, can be proved, but not creation out of nothing in the sense of creation after the nothing, for to be created and to be without beginning do not imply a contradiction. A cause must precede the effect, the nothingness must precede being only by nature or ontologically, not necessarily in time. The cause that produces its effect instantaneously need not precede its effect in time.

In every creature we find the mark telling us that it was created, but it does not go so far as to tell us how it was created or in what moment of time. We cannot ascertain whether the world had a beginning in time from the nature of things, since these essences are elevated above all temporal and local determinations (*universalia sunt ubique et semper*), nor can we discover it from God, since the existence of the world depends on God's free will, which is also above time. The universe and time began when God willed them. The changeableness of the world does indeed preclude eternity, but it does not preclude an unlimited duration. St. Thomas rejects the attempt to attribute to the world an eternity like that of God, as do St. Augustine and Boethius, because the idea is repugnant to reason and faith.[9]

Time originated with the universe; before the beginning of the universe there was no time. What is to be said about the question, whether God could have created the world before that moment in which He actually created it. No temporal "before" really exists. St. Thomas expressly denies that God has any temporal priority and attributes to Him the priority of eternity. The "before" of the nothing in creation is to be understood ontologically and not temporally. If we start out with the Augustinian view that the world and time began with a free act of God's will, we must abandon the idea that the world is a theophany or an essential expression of God's nature, and

---

[9] *In II Sent.*, I, 1; *Quodlib.*, III, 14, 31; *Contra Gent.*, II, 31-38; *Summa theol.*, Ia q. 46. a. 1-3; *De pot.*, III, 14 ad 6, 17.

then, too, the question about a temporal priority appears futile. Two possibilities remain: The universe is either equally eternal with God and then it would be a theophany, or it is created by God along with time. The course of time viewed from the beginning of the world might have been greater or less than it actually is, but such considerations do not go outside the realm of time and do not concern any duration outside the universe.

St. Thomas, influenced by Aristotle, tried to push back the beginning of the universe to something like a disappearance of the beginning. In St. Bonaventure, Henry of Ghent, and later in Suarez, the Augustinian influence made itself felt. These thinkers held that succession and eternal duration were irreconcilable and that a finite being implied a temporal beginning without further proof. *"In principio,"* according to St. Augustine, means the beginning of creatures; but time is itself a creature and therefore it, too, had a beginning.[10]

[10] *De gen. ad lit.,* III, 8.

CHAPTER XXII

THE ORIGIN AND PASSING OF THE UNIVERSE AND ITS PARTS

An essential quality of the universe is that it is a creature of God. As the natural revelation of God, as the herald of His power and wisdom, it is more than the object of natural philosophy; it also claims the right to be viewed in its whole structure with the eyes of religion. It was in this spirit that Origen, St. Basil, St. Gregory of Nyssa, St. John Chrysostom, St. Ambrose, and St. Augustine interpreted the account of creation. This did not, however, prevent them from adducing the findings of natural science and natural philosophy for a better understanding and a deeper appreciation of what the biblical narrative had presented. Conforming to tradition, St. Thomas for the greater part studied the origin of the universe within the framework of the biblical story with the help of the principles of science and philosophy. He emphasizes the fact that the biblical author was obliged to adapt himself to the comprehension of his readers. He refuses to admit that the Scriptures can be used to support any particular theory of natural science, and he vindicates an unrestricted freedom with regard to those things that lie outside the teachings of faith.[1]

We must not expect to find a new cosmogony in the Thomistic system; like his predecessors he adhered to the theories of the past, striving to adapt the picture offered by natural science and the metaphysical principles of Aristotle with Christian thought. The greater part of his observations have lost interest for us; only his attitude toward the basic problems will be presented here.

1. **Simultaneous or successive creation.** In cosmogony two theories

---

[1] *In II Sent.*, d. 12–15; *Summa theol.*, Ia, q.65–74.

stood arrayed against each other. The first originated with Philo and was handed down to the Alexandrian school; it was later defended by St. Augustine among the Latin Fathers. It taught the simultaneous creation of the whole universe. The second theory maintained the successive creation, and was adopted by the school of Antioch, and later by St. John Damascene and Peter Lombard. St. Augustine said that the idea of simultaneous creation offered a more worthy picture of the Deity. He explained the six days of creation in a twofold sense: either as different moments in the understanding of the angels, or as an expression of the order in which all that was potentially and simultaneously created made its appearance in its temporal development. While St. Bonaventure [2] rejected simultaneous creation, St. Albert accepted it in the sense of a simultaneous and actual creation (cf. his commentary on the Sentences, his *Summa de creaturis,* and his *Theological Summa*). In his commentary on the Sentences, St. Thomas inclines to the Augustinian view as the more reasonable and more advantageous for defending the hexaemeron. He expresses a similar opinion in his *De potentia,* but in the *Theological Summa* he refuses to express a preference for either view, being intent on minimizing the importance of the difference between the two views.[3]

In the beginning God created matter with a definite form but with the potency to all other forms. Since matter cannot exist without a form and since it receives its mode of being from the form, unformed matter did not exist in time before it received a form. Matter posited without form would be a being in act without act, which is an obvious contradiction. For this reason St. Augustine taught the simultaneous creation of matter with its particular form. St. Basil and St. Gregory of Nyssa proposed the temporal priority of unformed matter in the sense that matter had an imperfect form until it was elevated to its natural and complete form. Here again St. Thomas held that both theories were reconcilable with the concept of creation, although the principle that God created all things in the beginning with their perfect forms should have inclined him to the Augustinian theory. He excludes only the theory that matter received a common form. If that were true, all changes and mutations would take place on this one matter alone, and would therefore be merely accidental. Becoming and cessation of being in the real sense would therefore

² *Brevilog.,* II, 5.
³ *In II Sent.,* 12, 1, 2; *De pot.,* IV, 2; *Summa theol.,* Ia, q. 74, a. 2.

no longer exist. Such a theory he held to be un-Aristotelian and not in agreement with the facts.

St. Thomas divides the origin of the world into three stages: the creation, the separation, and the ornamentation. By the first he understands the creation of the unformed matter of heaven and earth along with time, by the second he understands the equipping and perfecting of heaven and earth with the integrating substantial forms. This formlessness, however, did not precede the formation in time but only in nature. This formation separated the essential parts of the world, the heavens, water, and finally the land and the sea. But the work of ornamentation is both really and temporally distinct from the work of formation and separation. On the three days of the ornamentation the stars and the planets were produced in the skies, the fishes and birds in the water and the air, and the land animals on the land. St. Thomas placed the plants, since they grow out of the earth and thus belong to it, under the work of formation and separation.

While explaining his theory of simultaneous creation, St. Augustine interpreted the narrative of the creation in the sense that God did not bring living beings complete into existence; He produced plants and animals only *causaliter* by placing their seeds in the elements of the universe. Thus the earth received the power to produce living beings. God implanted the specific germs as seeds (*rationales causales, rationales primordiales*) in the bosom of nature, where they lay hidden and invisible, but from them came plants and animals, depending of course on certain conditions and natural laws. Although St. Thomas always records the doctrines of St. Augustine with the greatest reverence, here he clearly differs and teaches that God actually created the pure spirits, the heavenly bodies, the elements of the world, and the first pair of each species of animals that are generated through semination.[4] He is especially clear concerning man's direct creation, about whose origin he goes into great detail.

Since the origin of a thing is the road to its being, the manner of its origin will resemble its being. The rational soul has a subsisting being, and therefore it has an independent origin. It originates neither from a corporeal matter, because then it would itself be corporeal, nor from a spiritual matter, because then all spiritual substances would be indistinguishable. The soul, therefore, is created.

[4] *De pot.*, IV, 2, ad 28; *Summa theol.*, Ia, q. 66, a. 1, 4; q. 70–72.

The human soul is not produced before the body. On this point Origen [5] is in error, as is also St. Augustine. The former is in error when he teaches that all spirits were created together and that they are united to higher or lower bodies according to their merits; the latter's teaching is unacceptable since it is a part of the seminal theory, declaring that the human body was placed in the world as the beginning *causaliter* while the soul was created with the spirit world and later seeks out a body for itself. Such a theory, remarks St. Thomas, could be accepted only by a Platonist, that is, one who considers the soul a complete nature and an independent essence that lives in the soul as its pilot. But those who regard the soul as the form of the body and an integral part of the human essence, cannot admit that these two parts are severed in their very origin. In the original creation of things God made them in their perfect nature, and thus He made the whole man at once. The creation of the body, like that of the soul, takes place directly through God.

The pure spirits cannot create; they can only change what has already been created. Moreover, the creation of the body by a finite spirit would be repugnant to the principle of similar production.

Woman was formed from the rib of the man to signify the close union of man and woman and to foreshadow the institution of the sacraments. [6] The world of the pure spirits, since it is a part of the universe, was not created before but simultaneously with the other parts. [7]

2. **The process of preservation.** In the original founding of the universe were placed all the causes by reason of which all things are preserved and by which also they multiply themselves. At one time the essences of things were made, and the rule was established according to which they would act. The far-reaching realm of the second causes was defined in the beginning. The universe was perfect with respect to causes and the species of things, even though it was not perfect with respect to the effects of the causes and individual things.

St. Thomas is greatly concerned to defend the reality of natural causes. Things are active by reason of their forms, and they are passive by reason of their matter. Their activity does not consist in the

---

[5] *De princ.*, II, 1 ad 9; III, 5.
[6] *Summa theol.*, Ia, q. 90, a. 2, 4; q. 91, a. 1 f.; q. 92, a. 1–4.
[7] *Ibid.*, q. 61, a. 3.

production of things as to their whole substance, but in giving form to matter (*in imprimendo formas in materia*). Because they are bound down to matter, natural causes are restricted and particular. The origin of forms proceeds through the activity of natural powers. The forms are only potentially hidden in the matter, and the matter is not merely disposed to the reception of the forms, which are produced by God or by some intelligence. The forms are rather educed from the potency of the matter in intermediary stages according to well-defined rules.

By means of their active qualities, things act upon one another. The active qualities produce both accidental and substantial forms; they produce the former by virtue of their own power, the latter by virtue of the power of the substantial form whose instrument they are. Since the active qualities are active by virtue of the power of the substantial forms, the effects produced show a resemblance not only as to quality but also as to species.[8] In agreement with Aristotle and the Arabians, St. Thomas teaches that these active principles are not sufficient in themselves but must be supported by the heavenly bodies. To the uniform movement of the heavenly bodies the multifarious changes in the sublunary world must be referred as to their cause.[9] By a preliminary change the matter is disposed by the efficient cause and thus directed toward the new thing that it is to enter into. When this disposition of the matter is completed, then the new form immediately and necessarily enters into a union with the matter.[10]

The processes of becoming and cessation of being are possible because matter is able to receive actuality from only one form and thus is in a state of privation with respect to the other forms. The four elements are the ultimate corporeal constituents, which may change over into one another, and from them the rest of the corporeal world is composed. St. Thomas took over the results of Aristotle's natural science. Aristotle had classified the elements according to the differences perceived by the sense of touch. These differences of cold and warm, dry and moist, are sometimes called the causes of the basic elements and at other times qualities of these elements. Aristotle arranged the pairings of these qualities in such a way that fire repre-

[8] *Ibid.*, q. 45, a. 8 ad 2; q. 48, a. 4; q. 59, a. 2.
[9] *In II Sent.*, 1, 1; *Contra Gent.*, II, 20; *Summa theol.*, Ia, q. 45, a. 8.
[10] *In II Sent.*, 5, 2; *Summa theol.*, q. 113, a. 7; q. 85, a. 6.

sents the warm and dry, air the warm and moist, water the cold and moist, and the earth as the cold and dry. The relationship between the elements is such that each one is related to two others by one member of its pair and is entirely opposed to the third. All the elements may be changed over into one another. All change and becoming, as is well known, takes place between opposites, and the elements have in them two opposite qualities, or at least one. The change of the elements into one another takes place more readily in those instances where there is a point of agreement, i.e., where two qualities are alike. Thus the change from air to water takes place more readily because the quality of moistness remains and only the warmth must be overcome by the cold. If total opposites are to be changed over into each other, a middle member is necessary; thus water does not change directly into fire, but only by changing first into air. In these processes of change, the warmth and coldness represent the active functions, while the moist and dry qualities are the passive functions.[11]

Mixed bodies are composed of the four elements; sometimes of similar elements and sometimes of dissimilar elements. In the bodies composed of similar elements the smallest part is the same as the whole body, as the inorganic forms, stone, iron, gold, silver, etc., and the integrating parts in certain organisms, such as flesh, bone, blood, hair. In the mixed bodies the elements surrender their substantial being; they are no longer actual beings (as Avicenna, Averroes, and St. Albert taught), but they exist only virtually in the mixture. This mixture is something entirely different from a mere aggregation. The distinctive properties of the elements remain in the mixture, although they may be somewhat weakened, and thus the elementary forms show that they are still active and that they have not been dissolved to prime matter or that a complete corruption of being has not destroyed them.[12] The dissimilar bodies are formed from the similar bodies, as the face, hand, and foot, which, separated into parts, are not like the whole.

Living beings originate by the process of natural generation. Natural generation is the cause of a living being that arises from another living being; the new being is of the same species as the principle. In

---

[11] *In II de gen. et corr.*, 2–4.

[12] *Contra Gent.*, II, 56; *De mist. elem.*, *In I de gen. et corr.*, 21; *Summa theol.*, Ia, q. 76, a. 4 ad 4; *De coel. et mund.*, III, 2, 1.

sexual generation the male principle is the forming principle, while the female element merely contributes the matter.[13] Like Aristotle and the Arabians, St. Thomas calls in the heavenly bodies as principles that are active in the generation of man and the more perfect animals. St. Thomas rejected Avicenna's opinion that animals may originate from the mixture of the elements without any seed, and thus, by denying any spontaneous generation, he promulgates an important principle of natural philosophy. Nature produces its effects at all times strictly according to rule (*natura determinatis mediis procedit ad suos effectos*). When a being is produced by semination it cannot at the same time be produced without seed, for this would be a setting aside of the law of nature.

St. Thomas shares with antiquity and the Middle Ages the opinion that imperfect animals are produced without seed by the heavenly bodies from slime and corruption.[14] All that he teaches about semination, nourishment, the processes of nutrition and growth, the change of food into blood, and the process of assimilation in the body, is essentially the teaching of Aristotle. In the same way, the basic laws of development laid down by Aristotle recur again in St. Thomas. The central organ, the heart, is the first to come into being and the last to dissolve; the more general form arises before the more special form. First man receives being (*esse*), then he receives life (*vivere*), and finally he becomes man. Since the specific type unfolds itself in each individual, the constancy of the species is secured.

The various kinds of soul principles originate according to their metaphysical structures.[15] The becoming of things is like their being. Thus those principles that do not exist of themselves and that are bound to the body in their existence and in their functioning come into being with the body in the same manner as the body. St. Thomas is opposed to the idea that the animal soul is created by God. Neither the plant soul nor the animal soul is a *substantia perfecta per se subsistens*. Plants and animals have no independent being and no independent activity, and they do not require a special intervention by God for their origin; bound to matter, they come into being as all other corporeal forms.

Inorganic forms produce beings like themselves without the help

---

[13] *Summa theol.*, Ia, q. 27, a. 2.
[14] *Ibid.*, q. 21; *De pot.*, III, 8 ad 15.
[15] *Ibid.*, q. 118, a. 1: *Contra Gent.*, II, 57, 68, 86, 89; *De spir. creat.*, II ad 8.

of an intermediary, thus fire produces fire. Living beings also produce similar beings without an intermediary, as when in nourishment flesh produces flesh. Generation, however, takes place with the help of intermediaries. An active force radiates from the soul of that which generates, and this force is neither the soul nor a part of the soul, but a movement of the generating soul. The soul has no special organ; it is borne by the spirit of life, which is itself enclosed in the seed and is supported by a threefold warmth, the elementary warmth, the warmth of the heavenly bodies, and the warmth of the soul. In those beings that originate from sexual generation this active force resides in the male principle, while the material contribution is made by the female. The woman possesses the vegetative soul-principle from the beginning. By the power of the male's seed the female matter is changed, and the vegetative principle is elevated to the act of the sensitive soul. Once the sensitive soul becomes active, the seed is dissolved and loses its power, becoming now merely what St. Thomas calls *"corporis regitiva,"* perhaps some kind of dormant governor.

A question often discussed was that of the origin of the spiritual human soul.[16] From ancient times, patristic thought was influenced by a twofold tradition: on the one hand, the Platonic theory that the soul descends from a higher spiritual realm. This theory persisted in Aristotle, not in its original form, but inasmuch as the *nous* of the soul came from the outside. On the other hand, the Stoics offered the theory of generationism or traducianism, according to which the entire human soul was produced by parental generation. This latter theory was accepted by Tertullian and St. Gregory of Nyssa. The former theory, derived from Plato and Aristotle, gradually led by way of Neoplatonism to the creationism of the Fathers of the Church.

St. Thomas opposed generationism and defended the theory of the direct creation of the rational soul. His reasons were based on the principles derived from his teaching on the origin of beings. A thing's activity is always in conformity with its being. The spiritual soul has a subsisting being, is able to act without a corporeal organ, is essentially separable from the body, and, since its nature is far higher than that of the body, it originates in a manner different from that of the body. Everything that comes into being arises either from matter or from nothing. The soul does not originate from matter since it contains no matter; therefore it is created out of nothing. Furthermore,

---

16 *De pot.,* III, 9.

St. Thomas refers to a law according to which those things that origi-nate by way of generation must be educed from the potency of mat-ter. The soul, however, cannot arise from a corporeal matter since it does not require a corporeal organ for its activity.

St. Thomas opposed the traducianism of St. Gregory of Nyssa. The theory that the soul like the body is contained virtually in the seed and that it develops only gradually, was opposed by St. Thomas be-cause it led to one of two alternatives, both of which were unaccept-able. Either the soul is contained in the seed from the beginning in the fullness of its species but is prevented from exercising its acts because it has as yet no corporeal organs, or the soul is in the seed in the beginning as a force or form that has not yet reached the specific nature of the soul. The first alternative is unacceptable because no complete spiritual soul is able to exist in the seed that is contributed by the generating parent; the latter theory must be rejected because substantial forms do not come into being gradually and do not permit of a greater or less.

St. Thomas did not assent to all forms of creationism. He opposed Aristotle's theory that the vegetative and sensitive souls originate through natural generation and that finally the rational soul is cre-ated, because this theory destroyed the unity of the substantial form. For the same reason he rejected the concept that the vegetative soul is in potency to the sensitive soul, and that the sensitive soul repre-sents the act of the vegetative soul, and that the rational soul, finally, is similarly the act and perfection of the sensitive soul. In this theory, in which the vegetative and sensitive souls are as matter to the form of the rational soul, the immortality of the soul is put in jeopardy. A third theory failed to win the Angelic Doctor's approval: that the embryo had no soul of its own prior to the reception of the rational soul, and that its activities were to be referred to the mother. The actual vital movements of the embryo cannot be referred to an exter-nal principle.

In the same way, St. Thomas rejected the teaching that all souls were created at one time outside their bodies. The perfect always precedes the imperfect by its very nature (Aristotle, Boethius), and therefore God called all things into existence in their natural per-fection from the beginning. Outside the body the human soul does not possess a perfect existence, and therefore it requires to be united to the body in the beginning of its existence. Besides, the numerical differentiation of the body could not be established without such a union (Avicenna). Thirdly, the human soul forms one uniform substance together with the vegetative and sensitive principles; since these latter need the body in their activities, the human soul also needs the body. If the human soul were created alone before the body, no valid reason for uniting it to the body could be assigned. In fact, the human soul depends on the body inasmuch as the body is united to it in the beginning, *quantum ad sui principium;* not with respect to its final end. Thus it is that after the destruction of the body the soul preserves its existence, even though that existence is not complete, *non in completione suae naturae.* The human soul has perfect existence only in union with the body.[17]

This, then, is the teaching of St. Thomas himself. The seed is not informed by a soul, but only by the kind of power that we find also in irrational organisms. This power disposes the matter to receive the soul. Differing from the origin of the elements in which, for example, the form of water immediately replaces the form of air, the origin of living beings proceeds through a series of becomings and destructions of being. First the formative power originates in the seed; then, when the seminal power disappears, the vegetative soul comes into being. After the disappearance of the vegetative soul, comes the sensitive soul, including the vegetative powers. After the sensitive soul disappears, the rational human soul comes into existence by creation, endowed with vegetative as well as sensitive powers. By this theory St. Thomas hoped to accomplish two things: the safeguarding of the unity of the human soul and the defeat of generationism.[18]

This theory of the origin of the soul, however, was hard to defend. Loud opposition was heard in many quarters. Indeed some objection was raised immediately based on St. Thomas' principles of the origin and becoming of things. If every cause produces something similar to itself and acts through its form, then man in his entirety must be the cause of the new man. In reply, St. Thomas made a distinction that extended the principle to the breaking point. Man is said to produce an effect similar to himself through his form inasmuch as the generative power in the seed disposes the matter and makes it a perfect organ for the human soul.

He resorts to a similar distinction in answering the objection based

---

[17] *Ibid.,* III, 10.
[18] *Contra Gent.,* II, 89; *De pot.,* III, 9.

on the principle that an efficient cause always produces an effect of the same species. This is true, says St. Thomas, when the forms are not subsistent, for then they function as causes of the new forms. But things are different in the case of subsisting forms. Here the genitor is only the cause of the union of the rational form with the properly disposed matter; it is not the cause of the form itself. The final disposition of the matter is *necessitans ad formam*. The whole man may be said to originate from the seed inasmuch as the power of the seed is active in bringing about the union of the body and the soul. Because of this union man is man, and not because every part of the man originates from the power of the seed.

Other objections were based on the fact of inherited characteristics. Long ago the Stoics pointed to the fact that spiritual and other characteristics were inherited from ancestors, and therefore they taught the origin of the whole man by way of parental generation. St. Thomas was aware of these phenomena and readily acknowledged their existence, but he judged that they could be explained on a corporeal basis, since the spiritual and mental characteristics and properties were determined and influenced by the physical. Forms differed according to differences in matter and in physical structure. God creates souls in view of the soul's essential relation to the body; He creates a soul for each particular body.[19]

From the standpoint of religion some pointed out that original sin could not be explained except by generationism. In reply St. Thomas referred to the difference between original sin and sins committed later. Original sin, since it was committed by the head of the race, is a sin of the whole human race, a community sin; the sins committed after original sin are attributed to the particular person committing the sin. Original sin is in the soul because the soul belongs to human nature. Human nature is transmitted by the parents to the children by way of the procreation of the body upon which the soul is afterward poured out. Since the soul together with the body enters into one nature, it too is affected by evil. If it were not for this union there would be no staining of the human soul.

Thus the noblest being on earth, man, the middle being between two universes, arises from the cooperation of natural powers and the divine act of creation. Just as man excels other beings in nature in his being, so he also excels them in the manner of his origin.

[19] Cf. *Expositio in S. Pauli apostoli epistolas, in Rom.*

Creation is the work of a moment. Whatever comes after the act of creation is the work of the preservation of the world. God certainly possesses the power to recall the world into nothingness after He has produced it by a free act of His will. Because of His ineffable goodness, however, He preserves the universe in existence; nothing is ever annihilated. Immaterial beings possess no potency to non-being; in material beings this potency is permanent. The movement of the heavens, which serves in the multiplication of human souls and of the elect, will cease sometime, and with it all becoming and corruption of being will come to an end. After the end of the world there will be no mixed bodies, no plants, and no animals. These creatures are indeed necessary for the perfection of the universe while it is in motion, but they are not necessary absolutely for the perfection of the universe. The four elements, as the material principles of the universe, and the heavenly bodies as the active principles of the universe, will continue to exist. The human body, too, will be preserved in its composition because the perfection of human happiness requires the perfection of natural equipment.[20]

[20] *Summa theol.*, Ia, q. 104, a. 3 f.; *De pot.*, V, 5, 9, 10.

SECTION IV

ORDER IN THE UNIVERSE

An axiom of the Thomistic system of philosophy states that "every-thing in the world is ordered." This concept of order was the basic idea of St. Augustine's thought and philosophy, and St. Thomas may in truth be called the philosopher of order. We find few pages in the Thomistic writings where something is not said about order, the relationships of order, and the connections of order. The foundations of any theistic teleological philosophy, and especially any system that views the universe with the eyes of Christianity and is dominated by the Pauline spirit (*quae autem sunt, a Deo ordinatae sunt,* Rom. 13:1), demand the serious consideration of order and its relations in the universe. The viewpoint of faith was corroborated by natural reason. Those philosophical developments to which St. Thomas owed most, built up the idea of order more and more and thus furnished a commentary on St. Paul's words.

CHAPTER XXIII

THE CONCEPT OF ORDER BE-FORE THE TIME OF ST. THOMAS

As the positive is primary to the negative and is its presupposition, so the cosmos is primary to chaos and is a presupposition that we may even speak of chaos. An absolute chaos, complete disorder, does not and cannot exist; the most we can have is a relative chaos, chaos with a background of order. For anything to have a stable existence it needs an ordered relation to being and an inner structure. The fact that the Platonic and Aristotelian systems saw the essence of a thing in its order is a matter of great metaphysical import. It is not necessary to refer the order of every being to its adequacy with the divine idea in order to realize that every being has a kernel of being from which properties flow, without which it would not be what it is, and the loss of which would mean the destruction of the being. It is significant that mechanical atomism was obliged to conclude that the ultimate elements of things were equipped with determined qualitative and quantitative properties and tendencies.

Whoever thinks of the universe as a unit and as a whole must think of it as an ordered structure. The parts in their diversity are able to form a unit and a whole only if they have a definite relation and an established order among themselves. As soon as the Hellenic mind had conceived the universe as a harmonic whole with an adequate cause, it proceeded to inquire about the principles of order in the whole. Thales, the most ancient of Greek philosophers, was the first monistic thinker to conclude that this multifarious universe came forth as a unit from water. In the only extant fragment of the writings of Anaximander we read about the order of time in which things mete out to one another punishment and penalties for their guilt. For the Greek, who everywhere sought for measure and harmony and proportion, the cosmos, this ordered universe, is the visible reality.

The Pythagoreans thought that numbers were the principles of order and that the universe was a corporealized mathematics. At times Heraclitus used to compare the universe to a haphazard dust heap because he was so conscious of the opposites in the world; yet in spite of his pessimistic evaluation of the world, he was the first to introduce the logos as the principle of being, of becoming, and of knowledge, and he derived all proportion and harmonious agreement in the world from the influence of this logos. To explain order and harmony in the universe, Anaxagoras established a spiritual principle of action, the *nous,* because he was aware that order was maintained only where thought was dominant. An ordered universe cannot be explained without an intellectual principle, and this idea retained a leading position in philosophical idealism. In opposing Democritus' mechanical materialistic concept of the world, Plato became the advocate of teleology, that spiritual form of natural philosophy.

Associated with the explanation of the world as an image of an eternal world of ideas, and as a divine masterpiece, is the concept of the world as an animated and rational being. In this being has been planted a world soul that participates in the mind and harmony of the eternal world of ideas and, as a spiritual power, brings about the realization of the grand idea of the universe. Thus the visible world is a living cosmos. All that is represented in it must be explained from the viewpoint of another spiritual world of ideas, which alone is really existing. Through this other world an ordered cosmos was made out of the chaos of matter, and this cosmos is the greatest, best, most beautiful, and most perfect of worlds, so that the world of ideas might have a reflected existence and this nether world might participate to the fullest in the goodness and perfection of the ideal world.

These ideas are not only true beings; they are the real values and, because of their dynamic and teleological significance, they confer value on other beings. Reaching their culmination in the idea of good and of God the highest value and the supreme end, these ideas have an inner order among themselves. Through the highest divine efficient cause this order has been imaged in the visible universe. With respect to the realm of moral ideas, man is to adopt this knowable supra-empirical order into his life and make it the order of his actions.

This theory of the ideal cosmos which is prior to the physical world and forms the presupposition for all that is and for all that will be, is the core of the Platonic system which was later incorporated into Christian thought and even today remains as an important part. The work of carrying out the idea of order and applying the theory to nature was undertaken by Plato's greatest disciple, Aristotle. Plato complained that Anaxagoras had neglected to continue this labor [1] of referring all things to the intellect and its directions. Aristotle's principles of form are really principles of order of the highest rank. The form, essence, end, or natural logos of a thing is the more important and more valuable part of a thing; it is the actual good, the immaterial principle which determines the origin and the complete structure, it creates balance and order, fits and adjusts parts and members proportionately to one another, prevents excess and dearth in the thing; in fine, it makes every natural product a work of art. Aristotle personifies the nature of a thing and compares nature to a wise husbandman and the thinking man who does nothing without a reason or vainly, who never acts by whim, but does all things with a purpose.

Thus nature is not a succession of tragic failures but a well-ordered whole. Aristotle ventured the statement that more purpose could be seen in the works of nature than in the works of art. Led by this conviction he set himself to investigate in a special work, "why in living beings every part is so and not otherwise." Each individual thing is built up in its being in an orderly manner, its becoming is subject to regulations of order, and its dispositions, attitudes, and activities are all directed in an orderly way to an end. But more than this: the individual forms are also ordered to one another. The world is an ordered hierarchy of forms, and the universe as a whole with its multiplicity of forms is itself related to the highest form, to God. This order also includes man with his diversity of activities, and in the individual it results in the knowledge and formation of moral living and in the formation of the civil community.

In the teleological view offered by monistic Stoicism, Aristotle approaches closely to Heraclitus. The deity, that artistic fire, the *logos spermatikos,* is an intellectual being that proceeds according to plan in the formation of the world; as it develops the individual *logoi,* it produces an ordered universe that is complete in the smallest detail.

Among the Fathers of the Church, St. Augustine with his unusual

[1] *Phaed.,* 97 f.

insight delves deep into the order of things, accepting it as a natural revelation of God, and makes an attempt at interpreting the drama presented by the universe. Almost everything that St. Thomas has to say about the concept of order and its relation to other ideas, about God and order, about the natural order, about order in the individual and in the parts of a thing, about the order in the universe and about chance, about order in the family and in the state, etc., was foreshadowed by St. Augustine. In the following words the great Bishop of Hippo gave expression to his idea of order in his *City of God:* "In the physical realm peace consists in the ordered agreement of the parts, the peace of irrational souls consists in the ordered quiescence of their urges, the peace of rational souls is in the ordered harmony between knowledge and activity, the peace between body and soul is in a well-ordered life and in the well being of the living being, peace between mortal man and God consists in an ordered obedience to the eternal law activated by faith, peace among men is in an ordered harmony and concord, the peace of the family is in the concord of the members in commanding and obeying, the peace of the heavenly kingdom is in the perfectly ordered and harmonious enjoyment of God, and lastly the peace of all things consists in the quietude of order."

St. Thomas also found the idea of order prominently featured in the philosophy of Boethius and Dionysius the Pseudo-Areopagite. The early Scholastics also, under the Platonic-Augustinian tradition, and the Franciscan school made extensive use of the concept of order, as did afterward the Jewish, Arabian, and Christian forms of Aristotelianism.

CHAPTER XXIV

ORDER

All that the speculation of Greek and Christian schools of thought had attained with respect to the order of the universe received a new meaning and new force in St. Thomas' system. The concept of order goes through all parts of his philosophy, his ontology, cosmology, theology, psychology, epistemology, ethics, and political science. The concept of order has a relationship with all the fundamental concepts of the Thomistic system; it has a reference to the idea of God, of reason, of nature, to the idea of causality, of form and purpose, of the good, perfection, substance, measure, proportion and relation, etc. And the idea of order is thus related because it is essentially bound up with the concept of being, which forms the basis of all these other concepts.

St. Thomas always limited himself to clear-cut ideas in his study of the universe, and therefore he began his dissertation on order by clearly defining the concept of order according to the tradition of the Aristotelian and Augustinian schools. First, the concept of order includes in itself the relation of earlier and later (*rationem prioris et posterioris*). We cannot speak of earlier and later, however, without referring to some principle, i.e., something that is first in its genus. That is said to be earlier which is closer to the principle (*principium*). The presence of some principle is so necessary for the structure of every relation of order that the axiom arose, "wherever there is some principle, there is also some order."

Every order implies a kind of proportion or a relation and presupposes a distinction between things since an order can exist only between objects, forms, and elements that are distinct from one another. The various kinds of order relations are determined by the principle of the order. Since a thing may be a principle or the first absolutely,

or by its nature, or relatively with respect to some subject, a thing
may also be earlier or later according to place, time, movement,
origin, perfection, or knowledge. Thus there are orders of time, orders
of value, orders of origin, orders of causality, orders of knowledge,
etc.

But these differences are not enough; the difference must be accompanied by an agreement. Unless the possibility for agreement and
similarity is found in things that are different, no connection of order
can be found among them. If such a connection exists between a plurality of things, then a disposition is said to be present.

In accord with St. Augustine and Boethius, St. Thomas holds that
the concept of order is contained in the concept of disposition, and
that the order of the parts in a whole and the direction of the whole
to its purpose are expressed in the concept of disposition. He further
requires that for every relation of order there be a community of
action, some cooperation. Besides these characteristics of order, Aristotle and St. Augustine taught that the attribute of unity necessarily
belonged to order. Whenever beings, integral parts, elements, etc., are
in a relation of order they are bound together into a certain unity.

The unity thus attained may, however, be of several kinds. Since
principles are found in every sphere and plane of being—principles
of being, principles of origin, of knowledge, of action—and since every being, every species, and the whole universe, is each a unit, evidently the concept of order permeates the whole universe. *Ad hoc
autem quod aliqua habeant ordinem, oportet quod utrumque sit ens
et utrumque distinctum et utrumque ordinabile ad aliud.*[1]

The concept of order is not a bare concept of being; it is also a concept expressing value. Continuing the Aristotelian as well as the
Platonic traditions, St. Thomas considered the concept of order a
perfection and attribute of being, something good, *ordo autem ad
rationem boni pertinet sicut et modus et species.* St. Thomas quotes
St. Augustine's dictum that *modus, species,* and *ordo* are the three
universal goods that God gave to all things.[2] At the same time, in
accord with the Platonic tradition, everything that is ordered has the
mark of beauty in it.

To grasp the universe as an order, the idea of unity of order is of
special importance. St. Thomas, still following Aristotle, distinguishes

---

[1] *De pot.,* VII, 11; *Summa theol.,* Ia, q. 22, a. 1–4.
[2] *De nat. boni,* chap. 3.

between substantial wholes which are absolute unities, *unum sim-pliciter,* for example, those that are composed of matter and form, and unities and wholes *secundum quid,* in which a real plurality forms a unit by juxtaposition or interrelation and in which the parts do not completely lose their autonomy. This unity of order, therefore, is judged to be the least of the unities.

St. Thomas applies the concept in the most diverse connections. A heap of stones, a house consisting of many parts, an army composed of many soldiers, a body consisting of many organs, the powers of the soul, the family and other social forms, the state, the Church, the angelic world, all these are examples of the unity of order. From this varied collection of instances we may conclude that the idea of unity of order is nothing more than the opposite of simple unity, *unum simpliciter.* We find here the haphazard connection of being merely thrown together, the mere juxtaposition of things as well as permanent relations of order and unity that enter into the constitution of the things themselves.[3]

1. God the Author of order. Whence are those principles upon which the universe is founded as a unity? The idealist interprets the universe from above, and therefore he holds that an appreciation of the order in the universe can be had only from the cause of all being and value, from God alone. St. Thomas proclaims the axiom: *sapientis est ordinare, ordinatio est rationis ordinantis,* the work of a wise being is ordered, and the order in the universe is referred back to God. God is the all-wise artisan who brought the universe into existence according to a predetermined plan and directs it to a determined end. The form according to which the world was made exists in the mind of God, and this theory of the ideas that exist in the mind of God is a warrant not only for the doctrine of creation but also for the concept of order. These ideas themselves represent an order, for in the mind of God is contained the idea of the whole universe, the whole order of the universe, and the ideas of those different things that constitute the order of the universe. The divine artisan begins His work in thoughts, He determines and chooses the parts according to the end He desires and orders these parts to the end. The order existing in things has been precogitated in the mind of God.[4]

We cannot have a concept of the whole without knowing the par-

---

[3] *Contra Gent.,* II, 58; IV, 35, 6; *Summa theol.,* Ia IIae, q. 17, a. 4.
[4] *Contra Gent.,* III, 99; *Summa theol.,* IIa IIae, q. 91, a. 1 ad 1.

ticular structure of the things that compose the whole. Hence, when we have an idea of the universe, we must also know the number of its essential parts, the nature and essence of each thing, and the way it participates in the perfection of being. The order existing in the model is a guaranty for the order of the image.[5] The universe is a unity, indeed a unity of order, and it is a unity because the unity of the world cause is reflected in it. Even though the inner Trinitarian life of God is ordered, and the divine nature and the creative power belong to the three Persons according to an order, no obstacle arises for true unity because the three divine Persons possess one essential nature. According to this inner divine order creation is attributed primarily to the Father, wisdom to the Son, and to the Holy Spirit goodness and government (*deducens res in debitos fines*) and the power of giving life.[6]

St. Thomas distinguishes a twofold order in things. A creature has an order to other creatures, as, for example, the part to the whole, accidents to the substance, the thing to its purpose; secondly, a creature has an order to its end.[7] On another occasion he distinguishes between *ipsa species et ordo ejus ad finem*.[8] The forms of both these orders pre-exist in God; the exemplary forms are ideas in God's mind, and the forms of the ordination of creatures to their end make up providence.

With his decided preference for clear distinctions, St. Thomas holds apart this twofold order in things: the order of things in their origin from a first principle and their ordination to their ultimate end. The divine knowledge becomes practical when things are actualized, and the divine knowledge becomes a disposing power when it arranges parts with respect to the whole. Inasmuch as this order proceeds from the first principle, St. Thomas calls it the order of generation; it is divine providence when it refers to direction to an end.

2. **Order in the universe.** The divine idea of order reaches realization in the universe. The ideal concept is eternal, but the arrangement and execution of order is within the temporal sphere, and also requires the assistance of second causes. Although all being and all becoming is subordinated to the all-embracing divine order, many

[5] *Contra Gent.*, II, 42.
[6] *Summa theol.*, Ia, 47, a.3.
[7] *Contra Gent.*, III, 77.
[8] *Summa theol.*, Ia. q. 13, a. 5.

partial orders also exist. Each of these depends on a created cause and includes everything that is subordinate to this second cause.[9] God alone, the cause of all order, is not subject to order. Following St. Augustine, St. Thomas teaches that God guides all things in free sovereignty according to order.[10]

a) **Order and the individual.** "All things love to exist in peace and unity with themselves; they abhor any jarring note or any disturbance or dislocation of their properties. This perfect peace, assured by their unmixed and individual species, preserves all things in a solid relationship to themselves and firmly establishes the inner peace of things." [11] These words of the Pseudo-Areopagite may be taken as the mystic expression of that fundamental idea in the Platonic, Aristotelian, and Thomistic systems, that the inner nature and essence of each thing is firmly and solidly established. Each individual thing is an ordered connection in its being and in its structure. More than this, everything refers back to certain principles by its essential order.

Even the ultimate elements out of which the individual being arises, matter and form, essence and existence, have an inner relation to each other. By its nature, matter tends to specific completion, and the essence of a thing is ordered to participated being. Matter and form belong together inwardly; only when they are joined do they have perfect being. The same is true of potency and act: *esse in potentia nihil aliud est quam ordinari ad actum,* and *actus proprie habet ordinem ad potentiam.*[12] Matter exists because of the form, and the body exists for the soul. Though not in origin, yet in the order of perfection the form possesses priority. Aristotle and St. Thomas evaluate things as good, and the good is measured according to the plane of being of the form. The form is the principle of actualization and denotes perfection and value. Between matter and form there is a definite order of goodness. The form is good in itself, the composite substance is good inasmuch as it has form, and matter is good inasmuch as it is in potency to the form.

Actual being is derived from the form, as are also the degree of resemblance with God and the grade of perfection. Because there are different forms, different relations are found in matter. Certain forms

[9] *Contra Gent.,* III, 98.
[10] *De civ. Dei,* IV, 33.
[11] *De div. nom.,* XI, 3.
[12] *Summa theol.,* Ia, q. 5, a. 1 ad 1.

require a simple matter in which to be realized, others require a complex matter. The form is the regulating principle in created things. St. Thomas defines this form or nature as a mark that God has impressed upon things, according to which they guide themselves to a certain end. This nature is also an order, or more precisely, it is a cause of order.[13]

Without this inner arrangement, things would act without order. But the fact is that in all its actions nature follows an order. Every created thing is directed to some good as to its end, whether it apprehends this end or not. In a composite being the form establishes an order among the parts. Every part exists for a particular purpose and is related to the other parts. The lower parts are there for the higher, the matter for the form, the body for the soul, the lower powers of the soul for the intellect, all external parts are for the inner parts, and all the parts are present for the perfection of the whole, and finally, the whole thing exists for some purpose outside itself.[14]

We also express the idea of order when we say that substance is the first of all beings and that the accidents depend on the principles of the substance as the imperfect depends on the perfect. As there are different principles, there will also be different kinds of accidents. Everything that the accidents are, they are with reference to the substance, and they are rather species, modes, and orders of the substances than of themselves. They exist for the perfection of the substances, and by a well-established order they grow out of the substances.

All substances possess essence, power, and activity, and between these three there is a definite order. The power is rooted in the essence, and the activity proceeds from the power.[15] Among the powers of the soul the spiritual powers have precedence over the sensitive powers and dominate them. In the same way the sensitive powers are prior to the vegetative, but in the process of generation the vegetative powers are the preparation and presupposition for the higher powers.

As he followed Aristotle, St. Thomas knew he was in accord with St. Augustine and St. Bonaventure, and he may have thought of himself as the commentator on the words of the Book of Wisdom: *Omnia in mensura et numero et pondere disposuisti*. Nothing can be found

[13] *In VIII Phys.*, 3.
[14] *Contra Gent.*, III, 129, 141.
[15] *In II Sent.*, 36, 1, 5.

in the world that does not possess measure, form, and order as its imperishable and inalienable endowment from God.

b) Order in the hierarchy of forms. It has been rightly said that the problem of universals is the problem of order in being, and that nominalism is the destruction of the ancient and medieval idea of order. From the time of Plato, the essences, species, and generic types of things represented the structural framework of the cosmos. The forms of things, those divine elements, are since Aristotle not only the principles of order in the individual, but also the structural principles of reality and the principles of order in the cosmos. The order of things results from the diversity of forms. God wished to communicate His perfection as much as possible to other beings, and thus created things that imitate the divine goodness. They are images, or at least resemblances and reflections, of the first cause, and among themselves they are ordered under the highest good according to the different grades of goodness.

The forms of things are a hierarchy of perfection inasmuch as the higher forms always add a perfection to the lower grade. St. Thomas rejected Empedocles' theory of accident in nature as well as Origen's theory that the different corporeal beings arise from different degrees of guilt in an earlier world. Accordingly corporeal beings would exist not because of their own goodness but for the punishment of the sins of other beings.

The gradation of beings arises originally from divine ordinance.[16] Like Aristotle, St. Thomas compares things to numbers, which have different ranks according to their position in the series. A multiplicity of things was required because the divine goodness could not be represented in one species.

When St. Thomas speaks of a graduated order, the order may refer to a particular plane in the order or to the relation that exists between the various grades in the order. Even among the elements an order of rank is found because of their position.[17] Ascending step by step, the composite inorganic things are more perfect than the elements, plants are more perfect than the minerals, animals are more perfect than plants, men are more perfect than the animals, and within each sphere one species is more perfect than another. The relationship between the spheres is such that the potencies and perfections of the

[16] *Contra Gent.*, II, 45.
[17] *In I Sent.*, 8, 5, 2.

lower grades are present in an eminent degree in the higher sphere, so that the higher are built on the lower.[18] This hierarchy is continued into the sphere of the heavenly bodies, where the forms, in contrast to those of this lower world, are actualized in only one individual. The ascent goes still farther, to the pure spirits, about whose order, place, and significance in the universe St. Thomas has much to say in detail. The crown and conclusion of this hierarchy is God.[19]

c) **Order in becoming and in the activity of things.** Logically the theory of being turns into a theory of becoming. The forms of being not merely tower above one another, but in their being they are dependent upon one another. The order in things does not consist simply in a superordination and a subordination of forms, but it extends to movements and activities of things since every thing, by reason of its form, has its proper activity. Thus a static order becomes dynamic. Just as being, so also the becoming and activity of things are under the domination of the concept of order. This order is revealed in a special way in the interconnection of activities; for, as they act upon one another, things are bound together in the unity of order. All activity takes place for some purpose; becoming is directed to being, potency is ordered to act, and the corruption of being is again ordered to the origin of being. The system of order embraces that which a thing is as well as that out of which the thing comes; creation itself is not beyond the embrace of order. In the origin and corruption of being, we find a certain order and succession of rank. The higher a form, the higher will be its activity; the more general a form is, the later will be its origin, and in the corruption of being the reverse is true.[20]

Causality expresses a relation of order, and the idea of cause includes in itself the idea of order because it has the character of a principle. The Stoics, especially Poseidonius, had studied the order that prevailed in the causality of nature, and later St. Thomas was able to read in the writings of St. Augustine about the order of causes. St. Thomas made these investigations his own, and he established an order of effects to correspond to the order of causes. Thus particular causes have particular effects, universal causes have universal effects. Between universal causes and particular causes there is likewise a

---

[18] *Summa theol.*, Ia, q. 47, a. 2.
[19] *Contra Gent.*, II, 95; III, 109.
[20] *Summa theol.*, Ia, q. 77, a. 6 ad 1; *De malo*, XVI, 9; *In II Phys.*, 14.

close relation. As the cause is above the effect, so the order of causes is above the order of effects. United to the order of causes is an order of instruments and an order of ends.[21]

The universe is held together by higher and lower secondary causes, but the gradation in the rank of these causes is not permitted to ascend to the infinite; the solution of the problem is God as the highest efficient and final cause.[22] A total order includes all the parts of the whole, inasmuch as one thing acts on another or one thing is the end or type of another. If a thing should escape from the framework of a lower cause, as, for instance, a miscarriage, the thing remains within the scope of the order of a higher cause and within the realm of divine Providence. No being and no occurrence is able to escape the order of Providence.[23]

All things are bound together to form a closely united order because of the interaction of efficient causes and because things are often ends for one another. A hierarchy of efficient causes exists, corresponding to the hierarchy of being; it descends from God to the pure spirits, to the heavenly bodies, till it reaches the elementary forms, and every cause uses the lower forms of being as its instruments. Composite bodies are made up of the elements and their qualities, the plants feed on the mixed bodies, animals feed on plants, and man uses all these things for nourishment and clothing, using them as tools and placing them in the service of knowledge. Thinking that the heavenly bodies had a part in the production of living beings, especially man, and considering that all things beneath man were for his use, St. Thomas was able to adopt the medieval anthropocentric view of the universe; according to this view, man is the central point in which all parts of the universe converge.[24]

In the order of the universe some things not only are good in themselves but also assist the good of others. Thus rational beings differ from corporeal creatures in that they are called on by God to care for other beings. The great imperishable substances, according to St. Thomas, namely, the heavenly bodies, never depart from their purpose, being constantly turned toward their first principle and never failing in their movements. But he was disturbed by the fact that

21 *Lib. de caus.*, 1; *Contra Gent.*, I, 15; *Summa theol.*, Ia, q. 22, a. 2 ad 1; q. 18, a. 3; q. 105, a. 6.
22 *De verit.*, V, 5; XXV, 4; *Contra Gent.*, I, 16; III, 17.
23 *Summa theol.*, Ia, q. 48, a. 1 ad 5; IIa IIae, q. 51, a. 4; *De pot.*, III, 18 ad 22.
24 *Contra Gent.*, III, 22, 77–82.

perishable natures often defect from the right purpose and the true order. He derived consolation, however, from the Aristotelian view that in the order of the universe the imperishable substances are like the children of the house, while the perishable beings are like the slaves and domestic animals that sometimes act contrary to the behests of their master. But none of these occurrences falls beyond the framework of the total order.[25]

d) **Order and the universe.** A fourfold purpose is realized in the universe. First, every creature exists for its own act and its own perfection. Secondly, the lower creature exists for the sake of the higher. Thirdly, individual creatures exist for the perfection of the whole. Fourthly, the whole universe with all its parts is directed to God as to its ultimate end.[26] Frequently St. Thomas repeats Aristotle's thought that the good of the army is not only in the order of the army but also in the general.[27] The order of the purposes mentioned in the second and third instances requires further explanation.

The perfection that arises out of the relations and gradations of different and dissimilar creatures is the "good of order," the *bonum ordinis,* the inner good of the universe, that common good which is above all individual orders and is, as it were, the ultimate form of the whole. Aristotle and St. Augustine had arrived at this conclusion, and St. Thomas accepted it with a theistic foundation. This order did not arise by accident; it was planned beforehand by God, it was willed by Him and created by Him. This order is the purpose and end of the universe, toward which all the parts are ordered and directed.[28]

In comparing this inner good of the universe with the good of the parts, St. Thomas attributes greater value to the former because it participates more perfectly in the divine goodness. Individual things in themselves are, of course, good, but they are especially good because of the order of the universe. The preference of the whole to the part (with a restriction to be mentioned later) is a fundamental law of the world. The whole benefits each part because the part exists for the whole; only from the viewpoint of the whole can we estimate the value of the parts. No created form of being, even the highest, is a

---

[25] *De verit.*, V, 4, 8.

[26] *Ibid.*, I, 65, 2.

[27] Aristotle, *Met.*, XII, 10.

[28] *Contra Gent.*, I, 78, 85, 86; II, 39, 42, 45; *Summa theol.*, Ia, q. 15, a. 2; q. 42, a. 3; q. 103, a. 2 ad 3, a. 3 ad 2; *De malo*, XVI, 9; *De subst. sep.*, 10; *Lib. de caus.*, 9.

universe in itself, but it is a part of the universe. No part is perfect separated from the whole. Every corporeal and immaterial substance has a definite relationship to other substances, whether that relation or order is necessary or voluntary. The Thomistic concept of the world conforms to the Platonic-Aristotelian and Augustinian tradition in that it interprets the universe as an organic whole, as a planned work of art.[29]

Not all the parts have the same relationship to the good of the order; the most prominent place is held by the spiritual substances. They express a greater resemblance with God because of their spiritual knowledge by which they are able to grasp the universe. Furthermore, this order of the universe exists in the upper regions of the universe in its ideal form, in contrast to the lower regions. The difference between the two regions lies in this, that in the upper region every individual is at the same time a species, while in the sublunary world every species is dispersed into many individuals; the same essential nature is not completely exhausted by the individuals, but must be integrated into the system of order by individual principles and accidents.[30]

According to the Aristotelian view, nature is always intent on the eternal and the unchangeable, namely, the species; nature always strives for the eternal. In this matter, St. Thomas was completely under the dominance of that school which taught the higher value of the universal. Nature's principal intention is the good of the species, and perfection consists in the preservation of the species. The good of the species always outweighs the good of the individual, and this preference for the species might have had important consequences in the case of man. St. Thomas, however, avoids the difficulty by making man an exception. Man is intended *per se* by the Creator for the sake of his soul. Providence takes into consideration, therefore, all the integral parts of the universe *per se,* such as the spiritual substances and the heavenly bodies; and the other parts only *propter alia.*

St. Thomas proposes the problem, whether the universe or spiritual beings participate in a greater degree in a resemblance to God. He concludes that the universe possesses the greater perfection *diffusive*

---

[29] *De verit.,* XXIII, 1; *Contra Gent.,* III, 64, 69, 101, 112; *Summa theol.,* Ia, q.21, a.1 ad3; q.23, a.7 ad2.

[30] *De spir. creat.,* 8.

et extensive, but *collective et intensive* the greater resemblance to God
is found in the spiritual substances because of their ability to participate more in the highest good. He remarks with justice, that we
cannot rightly contrast the whole with a part, but rather part with
part, since the whole always includes the part, and the resemblance to
God that belongs to the spiritual substances belongs also to the universe.[31]

The mutual order of the parts exists only because of the order of
the leader, *ordo ad ducem.* Above the order that holds the universe
together in all its parts, is the order by which all things are referred to
their last end. Here the wisdom of the Old Testament and the doctrine of the New Testament join with Platonic and Aristotelian
principles to corroborate his teaching. All things that act, act for a purpose, and in the order of purposes we find an ultimate purpose or
end. The ultimate purpose of the universe is God, to whom all the
parts of the universe look and are referred, the intellectual substances
directly, the others indirectly.[32]

Since the natural order is a created product of God's free will, it
does not exist by a natural necessity. It regulates and dominates after
it has been established by God, and nothing can oppose it. God might
have established another order, and St. Thomas explains the presuppositions for another order in some detail.[33]

Presupposing things as they actually are, the universe could not
be better, for everything has received all that is proper to it in the
total order. The individual is a part of this order and is adjusted to
the harmony of the whole. If a thing or a species were better, the
proportion of the order would be disturbed, just as the melody on a
harp would be disturbed if one string were tightened too much.[34]

Order and providence are most intimately united since they both
depend on the intellect and will of God. Order is defined as the proper
effect of providence. St. Thomas was not unmindful that, when we
speak of the providence of God, we transfer human relations to God,
and that his picture of the divine artisan had the unmistakable features of anthropomorphism. In explaining God's relation to the order

---

[31] *Summa theol.,* Ia, q. 93, a. 2 ad 3.
[32] *In I Sent.,* 1, 2; 39, 2; *De verit.,* V, 1 ad 9; *Contra Gent.,* I, 78; II, 24; III, 17,
18, 98, 99, 112; IV, 54; *Summa theol.,* Ia, q. 21, a. 1 ad 3; q. 22, a. 2; q. 47, a. 3; q. 65,
a. 2; Ia IIae, q. 2, a. 8 ad 2.
[33] *Contra Gent.,* II, 28; *Summa theol.,* Ia, q. 25, a. 6 ad 3.
[34] *Contra Gent.,* III, 98 f.; St. Augustine, *De civ. Dei,* XII, 4.

of the universe, St. Thomas found it necessary to introduce the idea of providence. This concept of providence includes the idea of the divine disposition of things. He points out that the idea of disposing refers to the arrangement of things toward their last end as well as to the order in the whole. The execution of this order belongs also to providence, and the governing principle of providence is the eternal law.[35]

The question of the extent of divine providence had received different answers. St. Thomas found himself obliged to repudiate Democritus' theory of accidental occurrences, since it denied all providence, as well as other views that were irreconcilable to his philosophical principles and to Christian doctrine. He opposed Averroes who, because of an erroneous interpretation of Aristotle, declared that providence referred only to the species and to necessary beings among individuals, i.e., the heavenly bodies. In the same way he opposed Maimonides, who went a little farther than Averroes by including human beings among those included under divine providence. According to St. Thomas, providence extends to all things in the universe.[36]

The Christian doctrine of providence is derived in its essentials from the teaching of the Stoics, with certain modifications, and from the Neoplatonic system that developed under the influence of the Stoa. Even the Stoics had proclaimed a providence extending to the whole universe because of their pantheistic views, and Neoplatonism definitely stood for a universal providence, with the exception that it allowed the providence to sink to the level of a natural necessity. By uniting the doctrine of providence with the concept of a personal, supramundane God, St. Augustine and St. Thomas lifted the theory of providence from the plane of natural laws to an act of a free spiritual being.

Like the divine power, the divine wisdom extends even to the lowest creatures. In the execution of the world-order, God makes use of intermediary causes, because in His ineffable goodness He wished to endow creatures with the dignity of causality. Secondary causes are the executors of divine providence; without these secondary causes we would have no order of causes but only an order of effects.[37]

---

[35] *De verit.*, V, 1; *Contra Gent.*, III, 77–80, 98.
[36] *Summa theol.*, Ia, q. 23, a. 1.
[37] *Contra Gent.*, III, 75–77; *Summa theol.*, Ia, q. 22, a. 2.

Within the framework of his theory of providence, St. Thomas shows not only the possibility but also the necessity of physical evil in the universe, based on reasons handed down by tradition.[38] The perfection of the universe, which is the most desirable good after God, requires the actualization of all stages of being. The beauty of the world requires the synthesis of all differences. In this realm of graduated beings we find some that have the ability of defection from the right order, and thus arises what is disordered, what is evil, since it lacks goodness and order (*defectus boni, privatio boni, privatio ordinis*). Since the good consists in perfection and act, and since the act may be first act, i.e., the form and integrity of a thing, or second act, i.e., operation or activity, we may have a lack of goodness in first act, such as blindness, or lack of a member, or a lack of goodness in second act, such as sin in rational man.

Appealing to the authority of St. Augustine and Dionysius, St. Thomas repeats the dictum of the Neoplatonists that the whole is more perfect when it possesses parts that can lose their goodness and their being because of their changeable nature, and that the beauty of the universe consists only in the ordered mingling of good and evil. How much goodness would be lost if no evil were admitted! The existence of the lion posits the annihilation of other animals. Without the dreadfulness of tyrants we would have no martyrs. Thus evil contributes to the perfection of the whole, not indeed of itself but accidentally (*ratione boni adjuncti*). Evil in the absolute sense is not found in the universe, it is always founded in some good. Therefore no evil goes beyond divine providence. Defects in the things of nature are offenses against a particular nature but not against nature in general. Accidents escape a particular order of causes but they do not fall from the universal order of causes.

In the order of divine providence, prayer also has its place. Prayer cannot change the eternal plan and order, but within a particular order it is able to influence a cause that is subordinate to providence. The whole natural order depends on God's free will, and God is able to produce effects beside this order, or He may produce things that are above the powers of secondary causes. Against the background of Christian thought, St. Thomas develops these ideas.[39]

---

[38] *Contra Gent.*, I, 85; II, 42, 44; III, 64, 71–75; *Summa theol.*, Ia, q. 22, a. 2 ad 1, 2.

[39] *Contra Gent.*, III, 96, 100–2; *Summa theol.*, Ia, q. 105, a 6; *De pot.*, III, 2; VI, 1 ad 2 f.

Thus the order of the cosmos and its parts arches itself up to God, and sometimes St. Thomas attributes to it such beauty that we wish it would actually be so. The greatest violation of this order, the greatest disturbance of this order, came about through sin, through the misuse of free will by intellectual creatures. Physical evil is independent of this evil, sin, and St. Thomas justifies its existence by reason of the make-up of the order of the universe. Physical evil must exist if the structure of the universe is to be such as it is. The process of becoming, that signifies the origin of one being and the corruption of another, implies negation and imperfection; the lower created, material, and matter-bound things descend the ladder of being, the more they have within them the factor of the possible, the potency of failure and of defection from the goal set for them by nature. Since the time of Aristotle, matter as opposed to form, the principle of order, has been regarded as the principle of the imperfect, of the contrary, of what is opposed to the goal or purpose, and St. Thomas allowed this disturber of order in the universe to have a place in his picture of the universe.

CHAPTER XXV

SENSE PERCEPTION

We have already spoken of man's prominent position in the universe, and of his task in the whole as a part of the universe. His high purpose corresponds to his essential make-up. Just as his body and soul have an ordered relationship to each other, so there is a well established order among the powers of his soul. By a natural order the powers of the soul rise out of the essence of the soul, and the individual powers are regulated by an order of origin, an order of perfection, and an order of mutual cooperation.[1] No doubt can exist, therefore, that in the fulfillment of his life's task man is subject to the law of order in knowledge, in practical activities, and, in short, in all his cultural acts.

1. **The order of knowledge.** Aristotle said that the human soul is, in a certain sense, everything, a microcosm, and that the soul receives within itself the forms of all things, and thus becomes the depositary of the concepts of the universe. This saying is important because it gave direction to the epistemology of St. Thomas. Knowledge has certain properties precisely to attain this goal of a universal ideal depositary. Knowing is an immanent activity, it remains within the subject, and is the perfecting of an active subject. At the same time knowing requires an essential relationship with its object.[2] What is known enters into the knower, the knowing subject takes the objects of knowledge into itself, it makes them part of its inner being in conformity to its own inner nature. In this intimate relationship, what is known can come to the knower only after the manner of the knower (*secundum modum cognoscentis*), according to the na-

[1] *De anima*, 13; *Summa theol.*, Ia, q.77, a.7.
[2] *Summa theol.*, Ia, q.18, a.3 ad 1.

ture of man's consciousness (*modus cognitionis sequitur modum naturae rei cognoscentis*).[3]

In all respects the Aristotelian-Thomistic epistemology is decidedly realistic; according to St. Thomas, *verum habet fundamentum in re,* and *ratio veri fundatur super ens,* and *omne intelligere est aliquid intelligere.*[4] Things are the previous objects of knowledge, i.e., they are presupposed as existing beforehand for knowledge. St. Thomas rejects every kind of phenomenalism. Our cognitive powers not only apprehend our own subjective states; they are not limited to the contents of what is immanent in our own consciousness. The first and direct object of knowledge is not the cognitive picture or form or the species, but rather the thing itself, the object itself. This is true, says St. Thomas, of the senses as well as of the intellect. Phenomenalism is opposed to the natural consciousness of knowledge, because it denies the attainment of any knowledge beyond inner consciousness; since it maintains that every judgment is about contents that are immanent to the subject, it leads to the abandonment of all objective knowledge, and ultimately to the conclusion that contradictory things are true at the same time.[5] St. Thomas attacked such skepticism at the very root. Logical consciousness about the objectivity of our knowledge rode out every storm of skeptical attack since the time of Plato and Aristotle, and in St. Thomas it received the following classical formulation: It is evident that there is truth, for a denial of truth is equivalent to saying that there can be no truth. If there is no truth, then it is still true that there is no truth. But if anyone says that anything is true, the fact of truth has been demonstrated.[6]

Knowledge is a causal connection between the thing and the knowing subject, and it comprises all those factors that are essential for such a connection. Therefore St. Thomas rejected that exaggerated activism which taught that the soul produced knowledge in itself, and also the theory that ideas were congenital or that the soul formed the cognitive pictures whenever it came into the presence of sensual objects. Knowledge comes into existence when a proportion or an ordering of the knowing subject to an object of knowl-

---

[3] *Ibid.,* q. 12, a. 11.
[4] *De verit.,* I, 1 ad 1; 4; 5 ad 19.
[5] *Summa theol.,* Ia, q. 85, a. 2.
[6] *Ibid.,* q. 2, a. 1 ad 3.

edge takes place. The cognitive image is the intermediary between the thing and the knowing consciousness.

St. Thomas was unaware of many of the criticisms of epistemology of the modern mind, but he was far in advance of modern thought when he sought to explain the meaning and the task of our cognitive powers by finding the place of the intellect in the great order of being in the universe. He sought to understand the part from the meaning of the whole. To know is a teleological process, knowledge is a teleological connection.

To be the conceptual depositary of the universe, man is equipped with different cognitive faculties, and within his cognitive functions we discover a varied order. The functions of knowledge are ordered with respect to one another. Knowledge begins with the senses and rises from the sensible to the intelligible. Nothing is found in the human mind that is not based on sensible data. Even the most sublime metaphysical thought arises from the sensible. The human spirit is able to lift out higher spiritual contents from the sensible and, relying on the knowledge of the ideal contents imbedded in the sensible, it forges ahead to the knowledge of the divine.[7] The order of the objects of knowledge corresponds to the order of the faculties of knowledge, *secundum ordinem intelectuum est ordo intelligibilium.* We find a definite order and succession in the comprehension of the objects of knowledge. Therefore the order of knowledge is like the order of being, and thus there is an order of potency and act to correspond to the order of objects. Even the objects of one potency or power have a definite relationship of order. "The first object of our intellect in this life is not any being or any truth, but it is the being and truth in material things from which the human mind goes forward to the knowledge of other things." [8] St. Thomas remained faithful to this Aristotelian program.

2. **The objects of the senses.** The senses are intermediaries between the knowing consciousness and the external world. When our bodies are equipped with the senses they are given receiving stations for the impressions of the things of the outside world. Here St. Thomas accorded the sense of touch a special importance.[9]

Every sense appears in conjunction with a corporeal organ. It is

---

[7] *Ibid.,* q. 1, a. 9.
[8] *Contra Gent.,* II, 96.
[9] *Summa theol.,* Ia, q. 76, a. 5; Aristotle, *De anima,* II, 9.

a passive potency that suffers a change in itself caused by some external sensible object, and thereby the sense is transformed to a state of actual perception. The differences of the sense organs are in accord with the differences of sense powers, and the different senses are in accord with the different objects of the senses. Not all the accidents of physical beings are objects of the senses, only those that are qualities of the third kind.

Each of the senses first of all perceives its own proper object; the sense of sight perceives color, hearing perceives sound. Sense knowledge is a process of change, and in this process St. Thomas distinguishes between a natural and a spiritual or immaterial change. The first is present when the form of that which causes the change is received in the one changed according to its natural being, e.g., warmth is received by that which is warmed. The latter is present when the form of that which causes the change is received in that which is changed only in its immaterial being, e.g., the form of the color in the pupil of the eye, which is itself not colored. St. Thomas points out that if natural change were sufficient for sense perception, then all natural bodies would perceive whenever they were changed.

Besides the objects proper to the senses, others are common to all the senses, e.g., size, number, rest, motion, figure. All these may be referred to quantity, which is the immediate subject of qualitative change. The common objects of the senses do not act directly on the senses and of themselves but through the sensible qualities, e.g., the surface acts on the senses through the color.

St. Thomas mentions a third object of the senses, the accidental object, *sensibile per accidens,* by which he understands what is not perceived by the senses at all but is immediately perceived by another cognitive faculty as soon as the data of the senses is perceived, e.g., when through a movement the life of that which moves is apprehended.[10]

In adopting this threefold division, St. Thomas took over the teaching of Aristotle as he had developed it in his own psychology:[11] "We may speak of the object of the senses in a threefold sense. Two classes of objects are such that they are perceived by the senses of themselves; the third class of objects is perceived acidentally. Of the

[10] *In II de anima,* 13.
[11] *De anima,* II, 6.

two first classes of objects, one is the proper object of a sense, and the other is an object common to all the senses. The proper object of a sense is that which is not perceivable by any other sense and in which no error is possible, e.g., color for the sight, sound for the hearing, taste for the sense of taste, while the sense of touch perceives several qualities. Each of these sense perceptions judges about its adequate object and never errs in knowing that its object is color or sound, etc., but it may err about the what and where of the colored or sounding object. Objects of this kind are called proper objects.

"The common objects are motion, rest, number, figure, and extension, because they are not ordered to one particular kind of sense perception but to all kinds in common. A movement may be perceived by the sight as well as by touch. We have before us an accidental object of sense perception when we know that this white object is the son of Diares. We speak of an accidental perception because the object that we actually perceive, the whiteness, is given an added determination. In the nature of things, the sense suffers no change from the object that is only accidentally perceived. Among those objects that are perceived of themselves, the proper objects are primary, because they determine the nature of each kind of sense perception." This text is important because in it we learn that the term "perception" has several meanings: it may be taken in a narrow or a broad sense. St. Thomas uses the word with these many meanings. Later we shall see that perception is not a simple act, but a complex act signifying much more than the mere having of sense contents.

3. The nature of sense perception. In enumerating the various objects of the senses we have not touched on the fundamental problems of sense perception, nor have we even named them. At this time we will examine more closely the perception of the proper objects of the senses, their natural purpose and their contribution to the whole, since, after all, this act of perception provides the basis for the other acts. In the order of knowledge the proper object is indeed primary and is that which is perceived of itself. The knowledge of all other things follows the proper object and is obtained through another and accidentally. St. Thomas does not always regard the precedence of the proper object as a priority of time; frequently it is a priority of order. At the same time St. Thomas states that the knowledge of the proper object is perfect, but the knowledge that follows it is burdened with many imperfections.[12] Many problems come to the fore.

The things of the external world do not enter into the subject in their material mode of being. What is in him who knows is not the thing itself but a cognitive image; in this instance the sense species (*species, similitudo, intentio, forma*) enters him who knows. Even here at the beginning of a discussion of the Thomistic epistemology we must give warning that the expression "cognitive image" should not lead to any idea of a theory of images. The expression is unfortunate as a choice to designate what is intended; a more detailed analysis of Thomistic epistemology will clarify the matter. One of the first difficulties is the question whether the cognitive image within us or the objective thing is the object of knowledge. That problem was important during the Middle Ages and is important today; it is the centuries-old problem of the opposition between idealism and realism. No one has ever attempted to classify St. Thomas as an idealist in this matter. On the other hand, some disagreement exists as to whether he held that the external thing itself or the species was the actual object of knowledge. No doubt, however, seems to exist about what the natural realism of the Thomistic system requires. The direct object of knowledge is not the species, but the thing that is represented by the species. "*Species intellectiva secundario est id quod intelligitur, sed id quod intelligitur primo est res, cujus species est similitudo.*" [13] This sentence refers to spiritual knowledge, but the same thing is analogously true of sense knowledge. The eye perceives the stone, not inasmuch as the stone is in the eye, but through the species it perceives the stone in its objective being.[14] Therefore it is the property and quality of the external object that is perceived. How is this possible when only the sensible image exists in us? A study of the process of knowledge will solve the problem.

In sense knowledge the external objects and the sense faculties cooperate in such a way that the external object changes the sense faculty by its activity and produces in the sense an image of the thing or one of its qualities, which is called the *species impressa*. St. Thomas

---

[12] *Summa theol.*, Ia, q. 18, a.3; q.37, a.1 ad 2; q.78, a.3; q.88, a.1.
[13] *Ibid.*, q.78, a.2.
[14] *Ibid.*, q.14, a.6 ad 1.

points out the receptive character of this impression, and that in this species the objective nature of the thing, or the sensible form of the thing, is expressed. When this species is imprinted upon the sense, the sense perception is not completed; only the foundation has been laid. St. Thomas expressly distinguishes between the change in the sense organ and the completion of the knowledge by the act of sense perception.[15] In the case of the sense of sight St. Thomas visualizes the matter as if the color produces the cognitive image in its medium (the atmosphere), and in the eye only with the assistance of light. This cognitive image that is imprinted on the organ is a physical determination through which the actual psychic cognitive image is produced. This *species impressa* is the principle by which the process of knowing proceeds. The material change in the organ and the immaterial formation by the perceptive faculty correspond to each other. "In the mind we find forms of knowledge produced by the effect of things on the mind. All this activity takes place through the form, and therefore the forms in our mind are primarily and principally related to the forms of extramental things." [16] This is all analogously true of sense knowledge. The peculiar relation of the species to the sensible quality of the thing is a guaranty that it is the objective thing that is known in sense knowledge. St. Thomas goes still farther; he speaks of the union of what is perceived with the perceiving sense, and of the identification of the sensation with what is perceived.[17] "The sense is simply a passive potency which is disposed by nature to be changed by an external sensible object. This external something that produces the change is what is apprehended by the sense." [18]

It is surprising that the commentators of St. Thomas could not agree on whether St. Thomas had accepted a *species expressa* in sense knowledge, because when he actually discusses the question of sense knowledge he states explicitly that sense knowledge is directed immediately, without the intervention of a *species expressa*, to things and their qualities in their physical objectivity.[19]

Do we then, according to St. Thomas, know things in their actual sensible being? Does St. Thomas defer to an immediate realism? If

[15] *De pot.*, VII, 10.
[16] *De verit.*, X, 4.
[17] *Summa theol.*, Ia, q. 12, a. 2; *Contra Gent.*, I, 51.
[18] *Summa theol.*, Ia, q. 78, a. 3.
[19] *Quodlib.*, V, 9 ad 2.

so, how are we to explain this immediate perception of reality? The problem itself is difficult, and a certain lack of agreement in some of St. Thomas' utterances may have been the reason why his interpreters are unable to agree even on what is meant by immediate realism.

To correctly explain the Thomistic position, we must keep in mind the fundamental principle that in knowledge we consciously come into an immediate relation with that which is sensibly perceivable and its qualities. On the other hand, St. Thomas is equally certain that in our consciousness is found only the cognitive image produced in the senses, which is identical in content with the objective sensible quality. Is not the species, therefore, the actual object of our knowledge? Do we not find passage upon passage in the Thomistic writings, from the *Commentary on the Sentences* down to the *Theological Summa,* in which St. Thomas teaches that the act of perception can be directed to an external object only in as far as a species of that object exists? Is this not true because nothing is seen besides the species?

The answer can only be in the negative. It is not true that we perceive the species and accept it as the intermediary because of its resemblance with the object. It is not true that the external object reflects itself in the mirror of our senses and that we read the properties of the original from this reflection. The service that knowledge renders man in life would prevent such an interpretation. In life we not only perceive things, we act on them, change them, deal with them, and not with cognitive images. We might be able to obtain some kind of knowledge of things from the image since the object stands behind it, but this theory is decidedly un-Thomistic. The objective thing and the species unite into one in the act of knowledge. He who knows is in possession of the object of knowledge without any intermediation.

This conclusion is corroborated by the fact that, by the simultaneous perception of various objects of the senses, we attain to a concept of a being in which these objects are united. This would be impossible if we perceived only the color and not something colored, only bitterness and not something bitter.[20] This union and identification of the object and the species is something real and ontological.

A difficulty arises at once. The senses sometimes err. The sense per-

[20] *In V Met.,* 11.

ceives something bitter while the objective thing is sweet. In this instance the species and the thing do not coincide. With Aristotle, St. Thomas explains that in healthy sense organs, that is, normally, the representative in the senses coincides with the thing itself, but when the organ is indisposed the species and the object are in disagreement. Like Aristotle, St. Thomas makes the distinction that the sense in perceiving itself is always true, *circa ipsum sentire,* but that with respect to the thing itself it may occasionally err.

Later St. Thomas was obliged to admit the subjective side of the species, its property of being a quality of the one who perceives, more than he was willing to do in stressing the objective point in his theory. Nevertheless he maintains that the cognitive form and the thing itself coincide, *idem est ferri in similitudinem rei et in rem, quae per similitudinem talem cognoscitur (De verit.,* II, 3 ad 3). This union and identification of the species and the object is a natural procedure of order, presupposing a healthy organism.

But the object perceived by the senses is not always the same as the existing thing, that which is perceived by the senses is not always the same as the actual thing. Here St. Thomas introduces an important distinction: we must keep separate in the thing its objective existence and its peculiar nature. It is only with respect to the latter that the species and the thing itself sometimes disagree, but the species always shows unerringly the existence of some object.

For perception two things are required, the one that manifests itself is not enough. If something manifests its peculiar being, that is not enough; the one who knows must have the faculty of comprehending. Man has this faculty if he possesses healthy sense organs.

What is to be said about the certainty of the reality of the external world? In spite of all skeptical and idealistic attacks, mankind has held firmly to its conviction that the world is real. St. Thomas knew of no attacks on the world's reality, and therefore he had no occasion to defend it or prove it by special argument. He valued the reliability of the sense and rational knowledge endowment highly enough to conclude that the reality of the universe was established. He often said, *"Videmus, sensu constat,"* and that silenced all doubts. The external world is impressed on our consciousness in such a way that its objective reality is assured. St. Thomas had at hand facts and reasons to verify this universal human conviction. In his knowing, man comes into contact with another causality. Knowledge is a causality, or a relation, in which things act through their forms and impress themselves upon a consciousness through these forms. In this fundamental connection a thought expressed previously now becomes valuable as an argument. St. Thomas had mentioned that the sense of touch is the basic sense. He accords this sense special significance since it obtains knowledge of the existence of the external world by pressure and collision from without and is able to convince us of the material reality of the world. St. Thomas makes use of an argument, at least implicitly, that is used in modern times to demonstrate the reality of the external world, namely, the experience of opposition. In discussing the reality of the world, Maine de Biran, William Dilthey, and Max Scheler have placed this argument in the forefront of the defense of the reality of the universe. St. Thomas, however, is probably more correct when he understands the experience of opposition as merely an experience of perception.

In this matter, St. Thomas also makes use of an argument that does not go beyond the closed circle of the conscious world and yet is able to throw light on our knowledge of the external world. In a much discussed passage of his work *De veritate*,[21] St. Thomas considers the possibility of arriving at truth with certainty. He declares that the intellect reaches out to the objective nature of things in its judgments and thus knows the truth. Certainty about this knowledge of truth can be obtained when the relation of the intellectual act to reality is understood. Such knowledge is possible because the intellect is able to reflect on its own act and analyze the nature of its own act. Furthermore, it is necessary that we have an understanding of the nature of the active principle involved, namely, the intellect itself, whose nature it is to be made conformable to things in the universe. Truth is known and assured by the act of self-reflection. What St. Thomas says about the intellect has analogous value for the knowledge of the senses. The intellect analyzes the nature of the sense as such, which is conformed to the quality or property of some

---

[21] "Veritas est in intellectu et in sensu, sed non eodem modo. In intellectu enim est sicut consequens actum intellectus et sicut cognita per intellectum; consequitur namque intellectus operationem, secundum quod judicium intellectus est de re, secundum quod est; cognoscitur autem ab intellectu, secundum quod intellectus reflectitur super actum suum, non solum secundum quod cognoscit actum suum, sed secundum quod cognoscit proportionem ejus ad rem: quae quidem cognosci non potest nisi cognita natura ipsius actus; quae cognosci non potest, nisi natura principii activi cognoscatur, quod est ipse intellectus, in cujus natura est ut rebus conformetur. Unde secundum hoc cognoscit veritatem intellectus, quod supra seipsum reflectitur" (I, 9).

external thing, and the intellect comprehends the teleological relation of the cognitive faculty to its proper object. This principle of
relation between the cognitive faculty and its proper object is, according to St. Thomas, a universally valid principle throughout the
universe, and it dominates and governs every cognitive relationship
and guarantees that we comprehend both the existence and the nature of things in their spiritual and sensible beings.

The importance of this question of the certainty of truth and the
way St. Thomas attempts a solution have caused this passage in *De
veritate* to be loaded down with commentaries and extensive discussions. Here we must immediately point out that this text does not
say that the knowledge of the nature of our intellect will vouch for
the certainty of all knowledge of truth; only the certainty of the
objective reality is attributed to an understanding of the nature of
our intellects.

But is this teleological conception of the cognitive faculty and of
the cognitive act able to support this guaranty of the certainty of
truth? Must we not establish this teleological nature of our intellects
first? Or have we arrived at the ultimate that can no longer be rationally proved?

The following may be important for a solution. Undoubtedly this
inner contemplation of the intellect and the senses resulted in a kind
of intuitive certainty in the mind of St. Thomas, and it was, moreover, a coordinated part of his philosophical system, which has, as a
fundamental principle, that every faculty and potency is directed by
nature to its proper object. If no obstacles are interposed, every natural urge and every natural striving is, according to St. Thomas, attainable and none is futile or in vain.[22] These relational tendencies
may be shown by induction; experience proves them to exist and
establishes the principle that every thing is good in its act (*omne ens
est bonum*). If *per accidens* an obstacle arises and prevents the attainment of the purpose, this does not invalidate the principle or
destroy the whole order, because such an obstruction itself has a
significance in the total order. The ultimate basis for this relation
(of a faculty to its proper object) is founded in God as is every other
creature. St. Thomas would not share the hesitation of modern epis-

[22] *De verit.*, I, 11 f.; III, 1; XXIV, 2 ad 8; *Contra Gent.*, II, 33; III, 44, 107; *Summa
theol.*, Ia, q.60, a.1 ad 3; q.80, a.1 ad 3; *De pot.*, III, 6; VIII, 1; *In III de anima*, I,
11; *In XII Met.*, 12.

temologists in basing this principle of relation on the existence of
God. He was convinced that he possessed real proof and he also
believed that all parts of his system supported one another and derived strength and meaning from the whole. It is not a weakness but
rather an advantage of the Aristotelian-Thomistic system that it permits no knowledge separate and divorced from the whole.

4. **The structure of the acts of perception.** St. Thomas and Aristotle
distinguished between three different kinds of objects in sense perception and thus permitted no doubt about the fact that in sensation
a variety of distinct, interlocking, and overlapping acts unite to
assure our knowledge of the outside world. St. Thomas' statement
that the senses are purely passive potencies is amplified and continued to include certain acts of judgment by the senses. The mere
possession of sense content must be supplemented by sense judgments. The mere sense impression is not a matter of sense consciousness; in their complete form the senses include a judgment about
their proper objects.[23] Pure sensation merely provides the material
for the higher formation of knowledge.

The first activity begins when the sense apprehends the proper
quality and objectivizes its content. The sense distinguishes among
its proper objects, e.g., vision distinguishes black from white. The
common sense continues the line of determination. This common
sense first of all perceives the acts of perception, it functions as the
immediate consciousness of perception; but besides this it records
the number of impressions in the senses, it grasps the quantitative
dimensions and orders them in their spatial connections.

The acts by which the accidental objects are perceived are especially far-reaching. The simultaneous contents of various senses are
referred to one and the same thing, and thus the thing is logically
perceived.

Now follows the closer determination of the thing. At a distance
this clarification takes place according to a certain order: first the
more universal and then the less universal is apprehended. First we
know that something is a body, then a living being, then a man,
and lastly that it is Socrates or the son of Diares. These examples
are instructive. We perceive not only corporeal things, but a living
being, personality and personal relationships. A great number of
complementary and supporting acts that compare, interpret, and

---

[23] *De verit.,* I, 11; *Summa theol.,* Ia, q. 85, a. 6; *De anima,* 13; *Quodlib.,* VIII, 3.

distinguish cooperate in order to build up a varied and ordered world of events and objects in our perception. Each act of perception makes use of the material of our memories and the whole deposit of our experiences.

This opens up the great complexity of question about the epistemological basis of our perception of things, of living and animated being, of spirit and persons. We cannot expect to hear the final word in these difficult problems from Aristotle and St. Thomas, but they did point the way for more penetrating analyses. An important contribution was their realization that the act of perception was a complicated spiritual structure of acts; although there is an essential difference between the knowledge of the intellect and the knowledge of the senses, no separate activity of sense and intellect is possible.

CHAPTER XXVI

INTELLECTUAL KNOWLEDGE

St. Thomas' tour of knowledge leads from below to above, from the senses to the intellect, from the external to the internal.[1] "We can enter into the innermost parts of a thing only through those things that stand about, as through a door. This is the method of human knowledge that progresses from effects and properties to the knowledge of the essence of a thing." [2] Relying on the knowledge of the senses, the human intellect is active in several ways. The intellectual activity begins with the abstractive comprehension of the essential contents of a thing, by judgment the intellect analyzes these contents, and by proof and reason these contents are carried on farther.

1. **The object of intellectual knowledge.** Plato stood for the dominance of the universal over the particular, of the essential over the contingent, and he declared that the universal essences were the true realities. Because of the parallelism between thought and being, the true object of knowledge is the discovery of the universal and essential. That opinion of the pre-eminence of the universal prevailed from Plato's time to the days of Hegel and the phenomenologists. According to Aristotle and St. Thomas, the forms and essential contents are the end and goal of all study and research and the object of the various sciences. Science as a whole seeks out essences, wherever and whenever they may be found. *"Intellectus humani proprium objectum est quidditas rei materialis."* [3] The Middle Ages rejoiced in the belief that the human intellect by its very nature tended to truth and to the *what*, to the essences of things. The striving for truth

---

[1] *Contra Gent.*, IV, 11: *intellectus ingreditur ad interiora rei.*
[2] *In III Sent.*, 35, 2, 2.
[3] *Summa theol.*, Ia, q.57, a.1; q.85, a.5 ad 3.

indicates the general direction of the intellect and includes that presupposition without which knowledge would be meaningless; the second striving to attain the quiddity of a thing expresses the intellect's direction to a specific goal. It is not mere chance or preference, but an aprioristic tendency imbedded in the human mind that directs it to knowledge.

The individual as an individual cannot be known scientifically. The perception of a thing is by no means the knowledge of the thing. The reason on account of which the individual is unknowable is the individual matter. Every science has a genus or class of beings as its object. In what respect is this genus of being considered? Following Aristotle and Plato, St. Thomas says that the intellect strives after the universal, whereas the sense perception is busy with the individual. That is universal which belongs to a plurality of individuals, that which belongs to every individual in a genus or species, and that which belongs to a thing inasmuch as it is what it is. We deal with the universal when we treat of the essential type or the natural law. Besides the universal in the form of the essential type and the natural law, we find the universal in the first principles of being and thought and in the universal obligation of morality. What is valid universally is valid not only here and now, but everywhere and at all times. Thus the universal is also necessary; the two belong together.

As the object of science must be universal, so it must also be necessary. What is known may not take on a different guise at different times. What is subject to change can be perceived only as long as the appearance remains. The object of knowledge is universal, necessary, and also unchangeable, and this is at the same time the essential form of things or is at least founded on the essential form.

Thus St. Thomas, like Aristotle and Plato, accumulates reasons why the universal is the object of science. In another place he points to the universal as the more powerful; he who knows the universal also knows the individual, because the individual is contained in the universal, but not vice versa. Again, he who knows the universal knows the earlier and thus also the later, at least in potency. Furthermore, the individual represents the perishable element because of the matter which is the principle of individuation; the imperishable element, however, is the form which is preserved unchanged through the course of generations. Matter, as the principle of individuation, is like the unlimited. The universal as the form, however, is simple and definite, and confers limits and boundaries on the unformed matter.

The knowledge of the universal is also the knowledge of the causes and the why of a being, since the universal is the first subject to which an essential property is given. Whoever knows the universal, knows the thing best in its own nature, inasmuch as it is what it is.[4] The concept of the universal is not a mere subjective thing, it is not an instrument of knowledge invented for the practical purpose of overcoming the multiplicity of individual phenomena; it is real in the sense that it has an objective correlative in things. St. Thomas emphasizes the point that it is true that we find only individuals in reality, but these individuals have an inner essential kernel, they manifest a specific character, which is not numerically the same in a multiplicity of individuals, but which exists unchanged and unchangeable as to its content in individuals and continues throughout a whole series of generations of individuals.

Every science studies those properties that properly belong to some genus of being, the essential marks of beings composed of matter and form. Science is concerned only with those accidents which belong to an object *per se,* because those accidents that do not belong to an object *per se* do not permit a necessary conclusion. All accidents that belong necessarily and at all times to some subject, must have that subject as their cause, and when that subject is posited the accidents are posited as well. About contingent being there can be no science inasmuch as they are contingent, but only inasmuch as something necessary is found in them derived from the form. Accidental being is excluded from scientific knowledge.

St. Thomas mentions three kinds of essential contents and three stages of abstraction. In the first place the intellect abstracts the species of natural things from the sensible individual matter; not from sensible matter in general. It abstracts the species of man from this flesh and these bones, not from flesh and bones in general. Secondly, the intellect comprehends mathematical essences by abstracting from all sensible matter, both individual and in general. It also abstracts from intelligible matter, but only from the individual, not from intelligible matter in general. In this instance, intelligible matter is substance inasmuch as it underlies quantity. The concept of quantity is bound up with the universal notion of some bearer of quantity.

---

[4] Aristotle, *An. post.,* I, 24.

But the intellect is able to lift the absolute nature of quantity from sensible matter, and comprehend it as a universal concept in its essential elements and essential laws of being. The highest form of abstraction is metaphysical abstraction, in which the intellect leaves behind even intelligible matter in general and forms concepts like being, unity, potency, act, etc., which attain actualization without any matter in the region of immaterial substances.[5]

2. **The intellect's knowledge of essences.** The essential core or kernel and the universal essential relations of things are the object of intellectual knowledge. The subject of the knowledge is also a factor in determining the nature of the cognitive process. Man knows differently from a pure spirit or God. The abstraction of the conceptual content of the sensible world is a process that corresponds to the body-spirit nature of man; and the fact that all knowledge is obtained indirectly, through cognitive forms, is also a consequence of man's natural equipment. In the process of knowledge St. Thomas distinguishes four things: the thing that is known, the intelligible species by which the intellect is actuated, the intellectual act, and finally the conceptual image in the intellect.

St. Thomas expressed himself clearly about what is known in the thing. The intellect knows the essence of the sensible individual thing, separate from all individual determinations. St. Thomas at no time understood this essential nature to mean the content of the intellectual concept obtained by abstraction; this essential nature is always the essence of the thing purified of all that is individual or accidental.

How is this knowledge transmitted? The process begins when an intelligible form is formed in the intellect. Whence comes this intelligible form or species? What powers enable the intellect to form this species? Before any actual knowledge is present in the intellect, the intellect is in potency to all that is intellectually knowable. This potency, called the possible intellect, requires an active principle to lead it over into act. Now the sensible images of sense perception, such as the phantasms, belong to the sensible sphere and, since the physical cannot act on the spiritual, and since the lower cannot form the higher, these phantasms cannot be considered principal causes, but only instrumental causes. Intellectual knowledge is far above the mere perception of the individual. This higher ac-

[5] *Summa theol.,* Ia, q.85, a.1 ad 2.

complishment requires a higher power. We know how St. Thomas, relying on Aristotle, solved the problem. He attributes a power to the intellect itself, called the active intellect (*intellectus agens*). Its task is to illumine the phantasms and release the intelligible species from all its sensible and individual accompaniment. Then this intelligible species informs the possible intellect and leads it into act. The possible intellect has a natural tendency to the universal and essential that is illumined by the active intellect. Both intellects work together in the process of actual knowledge; the active intellect is active to the same extent that the possible intellect is receptive. The active intellect imprints on the possible intellect the species that have been released from the phantasms as representatives of corporeal things.

What do the phantasms contribute to this abstractive process? St. Thomas emphasizes their great importance for the process, for only in relation to them, only in them, does the intellect comprehend the spiritual content of things. They are not the total cause of intellectual knowledge, but they are the material causes. The phantasms are resemblances of sensible things formed, not by the activity of the external senses, but by the inner senses. They are not distortions, but they are directed by the reason to the end that things may be known from them. Different intelligible species in the intellect correspond to the different structures found in phantasms.[6] The phantasms represent sensible things and their essences.

Phantasms supply the objects for the activity of the active intellect. How much has already been written about this intellect! We do not intend here to parade before the reader the many views and interpretations. The following, however, seems to be important. The active intellect is the light that illumines the phantasms. Continuing the reasoning of Aristotle, St. Thomas repeatedly emphasized that "whatever is known is known only inasmuch as it is illumined by the active intellect and received by the possible intellect." He explained again and again that the active intellect illumined what is

---

[6] "In imaginatione autem non solum sunt formae rerum sensibilium, secundum quod accipiuntur a sensu, sed transmutantur diversimode, vel propter aliquam transmutationem corporalem (sicut accidit in dormientibus et furiosis) vel etiam secundum imperium rationis disponuntur phantasmata in ordine ad id quod est intelligendum; sicut enim ex diversa ordinatione earundem litterarum accipiuntur diversi intellectus; ita etiam secundum diversam dispositionem phantasmatum resultant in intellectu diversae species intelligibiles" (*Summa theol.*, IIa IIae, q. 173, a. 2).

potentially intelligible when by abstraction it made it actually intelligible. All this can mean only that the active intellect by its power of illumination lights up the essential core of a thing, the intellectual content of a thing, lifts it from its individual accessories and presents it thus purified to be received by the possible intellect.[7]

All this is in accord with the concept of knowledge as a teleological relation. The active intellect makes a contribution by producing a purified species (*species depurata*) in the possible intellect. This spiritual intelligible form has the same relationship to the possible intellect as the form of a stone has to the eye. Thus the imprinting of this cognitive form is a *passio* and expresses the receptive character of knowledge.

But knowing is an activity. When the cognitive form has been impressed on the intellect, the process of knowing is not yet concluded, indeed the process by which the concept is formed is not yet completed. The cognitive form is the principle that sets in motion the activity of the intellect which forms and develops the imprinted form into an intellectual concept. This intellectual concept has an inner relation with the thing that is known. The intellect forms this concept precisely for the purpose of knowing the thing.[8] The intelligible species must develop into the intentional species, i.e., the imprinted resemblance of the essence of the thing must become an inner concept of the intellect, and the intellect must consciously refer it to the thing itself. The *species expressa* so formed, sometimes called *verbum mentis, verbum interius,* comprehends the thing in its essential content because of its inner relation to the thing. Just as in the sensible plane of knowledge the species is not the object of knowledge, it is merely the means of knowledge.

Receptivity and activity combine to form this subjective-objective cognitive form and achieve the goal of comprehending essences. In the intellectual cognitive faculty, however, the mark of activity and spontaneity is more strongly stressed than in sense knowledge. The activity and spontaneity of the intellect is already present when the phantasms are to be illumined and when the essential content is to be purified, and later it rises to the production of the spiritual intentional concept. Thus the objectivity of the process is carefully

---

[7] *In I Sent.*, 3, 4, 5; *In II Sent.*, 20, 2; *In III Sent.*, 23, 1; *Contra Gent.*, I, 56; II, 77; *Summa theol.*, Ia, q. 54, a. 2 ad 2; q. 79, a. 3, 5; q. 85, a. 1 ad 4; *De anima*, 4, 5.
[8] *De pot.*, VIII, 1; *Contra Gent.*, IV, 11.

preserved; the illumining, purifying, and abstracting all take place with respect to some actual thing or its representative. When this goal has been attained, the intellect is united to the essential content of the thing by contact, by intuitive comprehension, and by a kind of vision. According to St. Thomas, the process of knowing is a productive process in which receptivity and activity unite to produce something new. The terms "concept," "conception," "to conceive" (*concipere, conceptus*) point to this analogy. Aristotle designated this spontaneous and active power as that which is divine in us, and St. Thomas develops the idea with alacrity. To have this intuitive vision of essences would be impossible for man if he did not share in the divine light.

St. Thomas incorporates the Augustinian doctrine of knowledge in the eternal ideas into his system. He agrees with St. Augustine that the ideas of all created things are already in the divine mind. In conformity with these ideas all things are formed, and by them also the human mind knows all things. But St. Thomas does not mean that we see these ideas in God and that we see the created essences of things in these ideas. Knowledge in God and through God in the Augustinian sense, especially as it was taught during the Middle Ages, was not accepted by St. Thomas. We do not look at a mirror and see the reflection of things in it. Just as everything that we see is seen inasmuch as the light of the sun makes it visible, so we comprehend essences and ideas because the light of our intellect has an inner relationship with the divine light and participates in the uncreated light of God's intelligence.[9] But in all other respects the process of human knowledge is carried out with the data supplied by the senses and by the intellectual powers of human nature.

The Platonic mind thought that it beheld the guiding idea hovering over each individual thing, and the *nous* of Aristotle thought that it had the faculty of reading the essences of things in individuals and beholding the entire supporting scaffold of forms on which the sensible world is constructed. Aristotle had been maneuvered into this position of defending an *intellectus agens* partly because he wished to supplant Plato's theory of the knowledge of eternal ideas.

The frequently repeated statement that by its very nature our intellect goes out to essences was subject to objections from various quarters. In some explanations it seemed that the active intellect

[9] *De verit.*, X, 6.

made contact with the essential kernel of a thing. Modifications and limitations were quickly added to this statement. St. Thomas realized that essence was a word of tremendous significance; he knew that it expressed the ultimate structure of a thing and the spiritual content of a thing, and that it is the ultimate basis of a thing's activity and its manifold relations. To require the full knowledge of a thing's essence was an idealistic plan that was impossible of fulfillment. St. Thomas, because of the stand he took in his ontology and the realistic orientation of his epistemology, would have been unwilling to admit that we know only the relations of a thing. He was obliged to admit, however, that our knowledge of essences is only partial, restricted, and sketchy. Complete knowledge, he said, is not necessary in human cognition. From the accidents, and that is all that the phantasm supplies, the intellect penetrates to the essential principles by means of the metaphysical connection between substance and accidents. It proceeds to knowledge not by intuition but by reasonings, by laborious, cautious reasonings.

"In the things that we perceive with our senses the essential differences are unknown. We determine them by the accidental differences that are rooted in the essences, just as the cause may be determined from the effect." [10] With respect to the abstraction of metaphysical and mathematical essences, the theory stands on somewhat surer ground. We would expect more, however, since we possess the illumination of the divine intellect in us. Our hopes are dashed when St. Thomas proceeds to further limitations and declares that frequently the external accidents take the place of the essence in things. Finally, St. Thomas emphasizes the limitations of the human intellect by saying that up to his time no philosopher had known the essence of a fly.[11]

Other questions and objections are heard. Who will tell us what is essential and what is non-essential? In what does the criterion for knowing the essence consist? According to the original Aristotelian-Thomistic theory the answer is quite simple. In its active as well as passive potency the intellect is a priori propelled to the essence and it knows the essence intuitively and distinguishes it of itself. St. Thomas was obliged to retreat from this stand to stating that this vision of the essence is replaced by a laborious analysis of the es-

[10] *De ent. et ess.*, chap. 6.
[11] *Exp. in Symb. Ap.*, a.2.

sence. That aprioristic tendency to the essential remains in general.

All knowledge reaches its completion by the comparison of the knower with the thing. The basis of this comparison is the comprehension of the essence, and the comparison is expressed in the judgment. But how do we obtain certainty from this comparison made in the judgment? The criterion of certainty is the same as that mentioned in the discussion of sense knowledge. That frequently quoted passage from *De veritate* (I, 9) refers primarily to spiritual knowledge, which is attained when the intellect reflects on its own act and on its nature as the principle of this act. Truth is attained by the reflection of our thoughts upon themselves and by the knowledge that our intellectual faculty has an essential direction to the external thing as its object. St. Thomas displayed his unusual understanding of the problem of knowledge and certainty, when he tried to establish the certainty of our attainment of truth from the purpose of the structure of the act of intelligence and not from the thing itself the knowledge of which is in question. If in the act of intelligence there is no indication that we can certainly attain to truth, then the evidence of things is impossible.

3. **The essential contents of things and the knowledge derived from them.** By the three grades of abstraction described earlier, we obtain three kinds of ideas of the essences of things.

In the order of knowledge metaphysical abstraction holds the first place. The concept of being is the first concept that we form and it is at the same time the most basic of all concepts, containing within itself all other concepts, while all other concepts are referred back to it. Our knowledge is constantly directed to being, it is totally immersed in being. Before any other determination is attached to an object, we first determine that it is being. All other ideal contents are parts, aspects, facets, and marks of being, which are examined and separated in our knowledge. All other concepts arise by some addition to being.[12] In the practical sphere the concept of good is analogously the first concept since upon it are built the special moral concepts.

The simple comprehension of ideas and essential contents is by no means complete knowledge. For that the joining of concepts in judgment, is required. The comprehension of concepts is preliminary to judgment, but it is judgment that tells us that a thing is some-

[12] *De verit.*, I, 1.

thing or is not, that a thing exists and examines what is contained in the first concepts.[13] With the knowledge of the first concepts we possess immediately the knowledge of the first principles. No statement can be composed of only one concept; two concepts are always necessary. These statements, such as the first principles, arise from the knowledge of the terms and from the comparison of these terms. Among the first principles of knowledge is the principle of contradiction in its ontological and logical aspects together with all its particular applications: the principle of the excluded middle, and the mathematical axioms, such as, the whole is greater than a part; if equals are taken from equals, the results are equal; if two quantities are equal to a third they are equal to each other. The principle of identity is not mentioned among these principles, obviously because it is contained in the principle of contradiction.

These first principles are not unrelated to one another; rather they are connected by an inner order. In Aristotle and St. Thomas the principle of contradiction is the supreme principle in which all others are anchored. It occupies the most prominent place as the *"dignitas omnium dignitatum"* and the *"ultima opinio omnibus communis."* We must first understand this principle before we can understand the rest, as, for instance, the statement that the whole is greater than a part. As the concepts of being and non-being are first concepts and are basic for an understanding of the concepts of whole and part, so the principle of contradiction, which implies that being and non-being exclude each other, is the basis for the statement that the whole is greater than a part.[14] The principle of causality is closely related to these first principles, and after it comes the larger number of general statements and universal rules which are the vital nerve in the Thomistic deductions. These universal statements are usually introduced by *"videmus, apparet, manifestum est."* Since they are not merely conclusions derived from first principles but arise from an experimental foundation, their validity and force depend on this experimental basis.

A problem that has often been agitated is, whether St. Thomas taught that the apprehension of first principles is the function of the active or possible intellect. St. Thomas is himself responsible for this division of opinion. Some commentators thought that the active intel-

---

[13] *Ibid.,* I, 3; *In Boeth. de Trin.,* VI, 2.
[14] *In IV Met.,* 5, 6; *Summa theol.,* Ia IIae, q.94, a.2.

lect apprehended first principles, while others attributed the light
that illuminated the first principles to the possible intellect, explaining that this light is derived from the active intellect. In reality, both
powers cooperate in the knowledge of first principles. To the possible intellect belongs the habit of the first principles, but it is unable
to obtain any knowledge of first principles without the abstracting
function of the active intellect. The possible intellect is signalized by
a natural habit that tends toward the first principles. The function
of this habit is dependent on the activity of the active intellect, which
lifts out the intelligible species. Afterward this species is received by
the possible intellect, and as soon as the first concepts are known the
knowledge of the first principles has been attained.

The validity of these fundamental principles is guaranteed by the
order of knowledge. These principles are built on the basic concepts,
these concepts in turn are derived from external sense perception.
The sense perceptions provide within us a phantasm which is the
basis for the formation of concepts. The perception of the senses is
based on the perception of external objects and provides material
for the intellect. The validity of experience and the experimental
origin are a pledge for the validity of the first principles.[15]

These first principles occupy an important position. No error is
possible about them. They are the most certain and secure elements
of our knowledge, and on them rests the whole certainty of our scientific knowledge. Scientific certainty can be ascertained at any time
by referring back to them. All science is contained in them potentially; they are the germ cells of all knowledge, small in extent but
great in their power. They are universally known and immediately
evident. Once the meaning of the subject and predicate is known
and compared, their certainty is assured.[16]

The process of knowledge of first principles is an immediate act
of intuition (*simplex et absoluta acceptio principii per se noti*).[17] St.
Thomas describes the apprehension of first principles as a sudden, immediate, effortless act of the mind, a mental process well within the
framework of the Aristotelian system, even though the influence
of Cicero's and Boethius' Stoic theory of the concepts developed by
all men is clearly evident.

[15] *Summa theol.*, Ia, q.89, a.1; Ia IIae, q.51, a.1.
[16] *De verit.*, XV, 1; XVI, 1; *Contra Gent.*, I, 61; *Summa theol.*, Ia, q.2, a.1; q.62,
a.8 ad2; Ia IIae, q.3, a.6.
[17] *De verit.*, VIII, 15; *Summa theol.*, IIa IIae, q.180, a.6 ad2.

Among the Stoics these concepts are not indeed actual, but they are congenital and potential. Cicero and Seneca thought that seeds of truth and virtue were implanted in us by nature. As an Aristotelian, St. Thomas rejected the Platonic theory of inborn ideas. The human intellect is not by its very nature in possession of the intelligible forms, and learning is not merely a matter of remembering, because of the manifest connection between experience and the formation of concepts. Our minds are like blank tablets, and possess merely the power of forming concepts. Nevertheless St. Thomas found a grain of truth in the Platonic theory. He restricted the theory of inborn ideas to mean that a certain beginning of the knowledge of first principles is given us by nature. This inchoate knowledge is the Aristotelian habit of first principles.

No finished knowledge is given us by nature, but only the habit, the disposition, the faculty to form these first principles. As in Aristotle, this habit is twofold: in the cognitive sphere it is the *nous,* in the practical field it is called *synteresis.* This habit is not one that is obtained by repeated actions, but is a primitive original power innate in our minds (*innatus menti nostrae ex ipso lumine intellectus agentis*). Just as in all natural phenomena certain embryonic powers exist beforehand in readiness for the actuality, so in mankind we find two habits that are ready for immediate action, i.e., for the knowledge of theoretical and practical first principles.

By accepting this piece of nativism, St. Thomas paid tribute to the Stoic theory that he found in the writings of Seneca, Cicero, and the Fathers of the Church. He developed a potency into a full-fledged faculty. The theoretical as well as the practical habit of first principles tends by nature to these first principles. The concept of being and the principle of contradiction possessed priority not only in the ontological and logical orders, but also in the psychological order.[18]

St. Thomas did not accept St. Augustine's theory of illumination. Yet the knowledge of first principles is anchored in the spirit of God inasmuch as the light of the intellect was given to man by God and also inasmuch as the first principles of the theoretical and the practical intellects are images of uncreated truth. Besides the normal cooperation, St. Thomas did not require any special divine illumi-

[18] *In III Sent.,* 23, 2; *De verit.,* XI, 1; XVI, 1; *Summa theol.,* Ia, q.84, a1; *In de an.,* 5.

nation; the powers that the Creator gives the human intellect are sufficient to obtain the knowledge of basic principles.[19]

In the second stage of abstraction the intellect forms mathematical ideas and forms. The path by which the human mind arrives at mathematical forms is that of abstraction from sensible data. Things have several properties, among them quantity. The human intellect isolates this quantity from sensible matter and all other properties and contemplates only what it apprehends as quantity. This abstraction is possible because accidents are found in substances in a certain order, and quantity comes first, followed by the qualities based on quantity, and thus the knowledge of quantity can be obtained without the knowledge of the sensible qualities.

Matter also plays a part in mathematics, not the sensible matter but intelligible matter. The mathematician abstracts from all sensible matter, both individual and universal matter, but he does not abstract from intelligible matter. In mathematical knowledge the sensible matter is eliminated, and in its place comes intelligible matter, first mentioned by Aristotle, and adopted by the Neoplatonists, the Arabians, and St. Albert. By this intelligible matter St. Thomas understood substance inasmuch as it is the basis of quantity. As every science abstracts from the individual, so mathematics abstracts from individual intelligible matter but not from intelligible matter in general.[20]

Thus the mathematician has for his subject matter neither really existing objects nor purely subjective forms, but rather abstracted forms lifted out of sensible matter. Quantity, with a meaning different from that which it has in real nature, is the realm of the mathematician. The mathematical forms have their real foundation in the quantitative aspect of things. St. Thomas says that the structure of natural things is primarily mathematical and that the mere addition of sensible matter is sufficient to constitute them. Even though lines, points, and areas are not able to produce a thing of themselves, these mathematical relations are contained in the thing and they penetrate it thoroughly. A violation of mathematics is, according to St. Thomas, a violation of nature.[21]

[19] *Contra Gent.*, III, 47.
[20] *Summa theol.*, Ia, q. 85, a. 1 ad 2; *In Boeth. de Trin.*, V, 3.
[21] *In I de coel*, 3; *In III de coelo*, 3; *In I de gen et corr.*, 3.

Here we must mention the question of the relation of mathematical forms and principles to experience. As Aristotle before him, and the other Scholastics, St. Thomas did not mention or discuss all the problems that are implied in this question. Until his time mathematics was thought to deal with quantitative forms that abstracted only from sensible matter and for the rest found their fulfillment in the quantitative relations of things. On the other hand, these thinkers did not lose sight of the fact that mathematical propositions, especially those that are geometrical, did not refer to actual relations in things but to the non-sensible forms in our minds.

According to Plato, mathematical forms were not derived from reality since no true triangles, circles, etc., exist in reality. Reality is only the occasion which makes us conscious of these fundamental concepts.[22] Later, Proclus objected to the Aristotelian theory of abstraction on the ground that geometric concepts could not be taken from sensible objects since the physical triangle and circle do not possess the absolute precision of the geometric forms.[23] This Platonic apriorism is, of course, not reconcilable with the Thomistic theory of knowledge.

In order to form mathematical concepts, the intellect needs previous experience. These concepts are not merely revived in the mind by sensible matter; they are developed out of the matter presented by experience. They are contained potentially in the quantitative relations of things, and they become actual by the activity of the *intellectus agens*. Thus, here again, the actualization of the potential finds a new application in the Thomistic system, and the theory of mathematical knowledge is integrated in the whole cognitive system. To sum up the Thomistic position: the intellect is able to isolate the absolute nature of quantity in all its purity, undistorted by sensible matter, and deal with it as a universal concept with all its universal rules and essential elements.[24]

Thus the Aristotelian and Thomistic epistemologies occupy the middle position between apriorism and sensualism. Mathematical relations are not presented through the senses and they have no real existence as in the Platonic world of ideas; they are not mere beings

[22] *Phaed.*, 74, A.
[23] *In Euclid., elem.*, 12.
[24] Aristotle, *Met.*, IX, 9; XIII, 3; *De anima*, III, 8; *Summa theol.*, Ia, q. 1, a. 2; q. 85, a. 2 ad 2; *Quodlib.*, VIII, 1.

in the mind since they exist previous to our thoughts. We are able to isolate them in their purity from experience simply because they inhere in some way in things.

This abstraction is not an arbitrary and subjectively conditioned process. By its very nature the human intellect proceeds to the apprehension of the essential nature of a thing. This subjective disposition and the objective data correspond to each other. At first the mathematician abstracts the idea of quantity, but this is not enough; he proceeds now to compare and combine, and to form syntheses and theories of linear transformations, and finally the nature of space and the essence of number are revealed to him, as the object matter of his science. As he builds his scientific structure, the fact that no contradiction arises is the proximate criterion of certainty.

Since concepts of quantity, purified of all sensible matter, lie at the very basis of mathematics, Aristotle was forced to concede to Protagoras that sensible phenomena are not the actual object of mathematics. The visible relations of things and the mathematical propositions are not identical. The tangent does not touch the circle at only one point, as is stated in the Euclidian proposition about the circle. The sensible matter is responsible for the distortion. We see the mathematical relations with the eyes of the intellect because we are dealing with definitions and conclusions derived from them. The concepts of the rectilinear and of area make known to us that the sum of the angles in the Euclidian triangle is equal to two right angles.

As a Platonist, St. Augustine rejected the theory of abstraction and maintained the suprasensible origin of mathematical ideas, and thus for him mathematics became the model of aprioristic and absolutely evident knowledge. For St. Thomas too, mathematics was the science of essential laws although it was based on abstraction. Even though concepts cannot be gained without the matter provided by experience, they may lead to knowledge which requires no substantiation by experience. St. Thomas expresses the distinguishing mark of mathematics as against the natural sciences in the fact that mathematics deals only with the essences of things. In mathematics proofs are not given about one thing by means of another thing, but simply by the proper definition of the thing itself (*non de una re per aliam rem, sed per propriam definitionem illius rei*). St. Thomas explains further: Although certain demonstrations are deduced from the circle about the triangle and conversely, this happens only because the triangle is potentially in the circle and con-versely.[25] In contrast to the critical Kant, St. Thomas was cognizant of the analytical character of mathematics. At the same time St. Thomas did not have in mind that narrow concept of analytical judgment that we find in Kant's *Critique of Pure Reason*. This nar-row concept of analysis includes only such knowledge as can be gained by a dismemberment of the subject with the aid of the prin-ciple of identity. No progress comes of such analysis. St. Thomas realized clearly that both ontologically and logically a closed and necessary connection existed in mathematical knowledge but that intermediary middle terms are required for our knowledge, so that mathematics is a science in which our knowledge makes definite progress.

Kant distinguished between mathematics and dogmatic philo-sophical knowledge inasmuch as the former evinced some progress in its aprioristic conclusions while the latter was nothing more than the dismemberment of concepts or their application to empirical data.

St. Thomas, however, conceived mathematics to be a strictly de-ductive and aprioristic science because its conclusions are obtained by an analysis of the ideal contents of its axioms. Mathematical con-clusions are always true, and in mathematics we find an aprioristic necessity, but conclusions about things in nature are true only for the greater part, by a necessity *a posteriori*.

The fact that mathematics is based in reality and that the results of mathematical speculation can be applied to external things is a feature of the Thomistic system and an expression of St. Thomas' natural realism.

The third kind of ideas abstracted by the intellect includes essen-tial contents of natural things. We have already touched on the method by which they are obtained. We may add the following remarks. Everything in nature possesses, by reason of its essence, cer-tain necessary relations and properties, and places certain definite ac-tions, and this in spite of its individuality and contingence. The natural scientist studies these necessary relations in all things that are material. The basis for these necessary relations, however, and for all the laws that govern things, is the essential content of the thing.

These three classes of abstracted ideas are not independent of one

[25] *In Boeth. de Trin.*, VI, 1; *In I Phys.*, 1.

another. The ideas and principles of metaphysics are valid for mathematics and for the natural sciences, and the conclusions of mathematics are valid in the natural sciences.

4. The knowledge of the individual. Being and knowledge correspond to each other. Since St. Thomas held that matter is the principle of individuation and that the individual is lowered by matter, and since he emphasized that individuals are distinguished from each other only by a quantitative difference, he could not logically admit that we have any knowledge of the individual. His view of the great realm of being followed both the Platonic and the Aristotelian tradition in their exaltation of the universal and in permitting no place for the individual. The senses, of course, transmit some knowledge of the individual which is necessary for our practical lives, but for the rest St. Thomas taught that "the intellect knows sensible individual things only indirectly and by a kind of reflection." [26] What are we to understand by this knowledge?

St. Thomas speaks of the matter on two occasions, in the *De veritate* and in the *Theological Summa*. In the first instance he describes the process as follows: When the intellect knows its object, the universal essence, it turns to obtain some knowledge of its own act, then it goes farther to know the species that is the principle of its act, and then finally it looks at the phantasm from which it has abstracted the species and thus it obtains knowledge of the individual.[27] The same viewpoint is assumed in the *Theological Summa*, with the difference that the reflection on its own act by the intellect is omitted. Since the knowledge of the universal is obtained only by reference to the phantasm, this mediate knowledge of the individual is concomitant with the immediate knowledge of the universal. For a solution of the problem it is not necessary that the intellect should reflect on its act; the deciding thing is the peculiar relation of the universal to the phantasm.

Thus, in some way, the declaration that the individual cannot be known is watered down, although the Thomistic system does not thereby rid itself of all that is objectionable in this indirect knowledge of the individual. Had St. Thomas not been content merely to state that the knowledge of the individual is mediate and reflective, and if he had indicated what is known about the individual in this way, many different objections would have been heard. As it was, St. Thomas aroused much opposition by his teaching about the knowledge of the individual. Among the members of the Augustinian tradition, William de la Mare, Matthaeus of Aquasparta, Scotus, and the Scotists, all raised serious objections. Later the nominalists (Durandus, William of Occam, Aureolus, and Gregory of Rimini) taught the immediate knowledge of the individual because of their stand in epistemology.

These thinkers declared that the immediate knowledge of the individual is a fact; some, like Matthaeus of Aquasparta, declared that an individual species existed for the knowledge of the individual. Scotus' criticism was the most incisive. The universal, he said, could not be abstracted from the individual without a knowledge of the individual, since he who abstracts must know from what he is to abstract. Every act of intellectual abstraction takes place with reference to an individual, and in this the knowledge of the individual is included. The denomination of something presupposes the knowledge of that thing, and it is a law of logic that the knowledge of the difference between two members of a relation presupposes a knowledge of the members. From these facts it is clear that the individual is not known by reflection.

Furthermore, reflective knowledge would take place by means of a spiritual or a sensible cognitive image. It cannot be by means of the former because the spiritual image represents the essence; and it cannot be the latter because the sensible image cannot have a determining effect on the intellect, although it can influence the process of the imagination. Scotus had adopted an original stand with respect to the principle of individuation and therefore he was necessitated to take a different stand on the question of the knowledge of the individual. A principle of his ontology was, the more being the more knowability; therefore he required the direct knowledge of the individual. According to Scotus, the individual has a being that is more definite and richer in content than the universal. He reminds us that God Himself and the pure spirits are individuals, and that they know themselves and the other individual beings. In this connection it is interesting to note that St. Thomas himself was unable to avoid making concessions.

This theory of the unknowability of the individual does not pervade the whole Thomistic system. St. Thomas says that it is not the individuality but the materiality of a sensibly perceivable thing that is the reason for its unknowability.[28] In those substances that are individual and at the same time immaterial nothing stands in the way of their knowability. Such substances are God and the pure spirits. As an immaterial being, each of these substances is a species and also an individual.[29] Here the principle of individuation consists in the form itself, that is, in the greater or less perfection of the form. *Omnes angeli differunt specie secundum diversos gradus naturae intellectivae.*[30] Every form that cannot be received in matter and has an independent existence, is also an individual, because it cannot be received in matter. This is true of God, and it is also true of pure spirits since each of these forms is individual, *quod non est nata in aliquo esse.* But every form, according to St. Thomas, inasmuch as it is a form can be participated in by many, but in the case of a pure spirit an obstacle exists preventing this participation because this form is not intended to be received in a subject which would make it an individual.[31]

In this case, St. Thomas, like Aristotle and the Arabians whom he quotes, transfers the principle of individuation to the form, and, as far as the sphere of the spiritual is concerned, he surrenders his theory that all knowledge is of the universal. He would have been obliged to make this concession because of that principle which states that a thing is the more knowable according as it possesses more of being. Thus that thing is most knowable which is most free from matter.[32] Since God and the pure spirits have a singular existence, the individual can be the object of knowledge in the highest sense of the word.

Even for a part of the material world St. Thomas was obliged to make restrictions about the knowability of the individual. Matter was supposed to be the principle of disorder, of the indefinite, the changeable, and of the partial. All this was true of the sublunary world, but it did not hold in the more perfect world of the heavenly bodies. St. Thomas pointed out that the pure spirits and the heavenly bodies had a common characteristic: that in both worlds one in-

---

[28] *De anima,* 3 ad 17.
[29] *De ent. et ess.,* chaps. 5 f.; *Contra Gent.,* II, 93.
[30] *Summa theol.,* Ia, q. 50, a. 4.
[31] *Ibid.,* q. 13, a. 9.
[32] *De verit.,* II, 2; XXXIII, 1, *secundum gradum immaterialitatis est gradus cognitionis.*

dividual is found in each species. This happens in the heavenly
bodies because all the matter directed to one species is embraced by
one individual. Thus we have one sun, one moon, out of all the matter of that species.[33] It remains true, of course, that the form is of
its nature communicable. The reason for this unity of the individual
is not, therefore, to be found in the form, but in the matter. In
the realm of the heavenly bodies the matter is not the principle of
division and multiplicity, it does not cause change. The heavenly
bodies are distinguished by their unchangeableness; and thus the
matter of the heavenly bodies is not an obstacle to knowledge.[34]

Even in the case of the sensible things of this world it is not un-
conditionally true that individuality and concreteness are unknowable; in fact, St. Thomas attributes to God and the pure spirits a
knowledge of the individual. God is the cause of a thing, both its
matter and its form. The idea in the divine mind is an image of the
thing with respect to its formal and material aspects, and the knowledge of the thing embraces the whole thing. Since the cognitive
forms in the angelic mind are entirely similar to the ideas in the
divine mind, the angel knows the universal and the individual
through them.[35] Now the materiality of the thing is no longer a
reason for its unknowability. The all-embracing spirit of God and
the divinely illuminated angelic mind master the individuality of
the thing founded in materiality. But our inability to comprehend
them persists.

This conclusion arises from the imperfection of the human cognitive faculty, which is not adjusted to the individual. The knowing
subject, instead of the object to be known, is the deciding factor.
Matter and the individual weighed down by matter are the barriers
to our knowledge; in the presence of God and the angels these barriers fall.

5. **Self-knowledge.** According to a law that applies both to the
individual and to the race, man because of his attachment to the
external world seeks to make it his own in order to promote his
own welfare and to satisfy his quest for knowledge. First he looks
about him and sees the physical world and then he tries to take it
to himself by his senses and his intellect. From this real phenomenon

---

[33] *Contra Gent.*, II, 92; *Summa theol.*, Ia, q. 13, a. 9.
[34] *In VIII Phys.*, 21; *Summa theol.*, Ia, q. 9, a. 2.
[35] *Contra Gent.*, II, 100; *Summa theol.*, Ia, q. 57, a. 2.

he reverts to another reality, much closer to himself. This reality is his own inner being, his own ego. And even though skepticism may threaten the existence or the nature of the external world, for most thinkers the consciousness of self and the certainty of one's own thinking is the impregnable rock against which the waves of skepticism break in vain. Self-knowledge increases in value and importance when, through the inner nature of man, the way is found to God, and through self-knowledge the meaning of human life is discovered.

St. Augustine is the author of the metaphysics of inner experience, he is the artist who excels in the analysis of the inner life, he is the eulogist of the immediate certainty of consciousness, the great advocate of self-knowledge and the defender of the direct vision of the substance of the soul.[36] The Augustinian tradition accumulated reason upon reason to support this direct vision of the soul. We err if we think that St. Thomas opposed St. Augustine in the beginning in this matter of self-knowledge. For a long time St. Thomas agreed with St. Augustine as a good Aristotelian, but finally the time came when he was forced to disagree by his principles and by facts, and he was obliged to deny that the soul knew itself through its essence.[37] The attempted adjustment of his position to Augustinian expressions, especially in *De veritate,* should not mislead us.

In answering the question whether the human soul knows itself through its own essence, we must keep in mind the Aristotelian principle that a thing is knowable inasmuch as it is in act and not inasmuch as it is in potency. By its very nature the human soul knows only potentially and its knowledge becomes actual through the intervention of the cognoscible object and the subsequent activity of the active intellect. Our soul knows itself therefore not by means of its essence but by means of its acts, and this occurs in two or three directions.

The soul's first knowledge of itself is the knowledge of existence. A man knows that he has a soul. When he becomes aware that he perceives, performs vital acts, he knows that he has a soul. Since there is no knowledge that is not knowledge of something, a man must first know something before he realizes that he knows. For this knowledge of the existence of his soul the mere presence of

---

[36] *De civ. Dei,* XI, 26; *De Trin.,* X, 10; *Solil.,* II, 1.
[37] *De verit.,* X, 8; *Summa theol.,* Ia, q. 87, a. 1-4.

his soul is sufficient since it is the principle of the act in which the man engages in self-knowledge. This self-knowledge is infallible; no one can fall into error in this knowledge.

With this knowledge of the existence of the soul is joined the knowledge of the peculiar nature of the individual soul, the knowledge of the soul's particular structure in this individual. St. Thomas does not further explain this knowledge, but from the reasonings in his anthropology we can conclude that this knowledge is obtained through the acts of the soul.

The third step is the knowledge of the soul and its nature in general. For this knowledge the mere presence of the soul is not sufficient; a penetrating and careful research is needed. This form of knowledge of the soul is subject to frequent errors. Because they lack intellectual power and mental training, many men are not able to obtain a profound knowledge of the nature of the soul. St. Thomas compares the human mind, the lowest in the series of intellects, with prime matter, the lowest grade of physical being. As prime matter can be known only through the forms that are received in it, so the human soul and the human mind can be known only through the knowledge of external objects and through the cognitive forms that act on the soul. St. Thomas briefly describes the path followed by those who investigate the nature of the human soul: the human soul knows the universal nature of things through immaterial species; from the immaterial nature of the intellectual forms of knowledge they concluded to the soul's independence of matter, and from this attribute of immateriality other properties of the soul were deduced.

A comparison with the higher intellects throws some light on the self-knowledge of the human mind. God knows Himself in His essence since His essence is identical with His knowledge. An angelic intellect is not identical with its essence, but the first object of an angel's knowledge is its essence. Although an angel's knowledge of its knowledge and of its essence must be kept logically separate, an angel knows both in one and the same act. The human intellect is not identical with its knowledge, nor is it directed to the human essence as its first object. The first objects of the human mind are external objects, then, in second place, man knows the act by which he knows the object, and by way of this act he comes to the knowledge of the intellect itself whose perfection consists in knowledge.

An objection arises immediately. Does the human soul manifest its activities only in knowing? Are not its striving and willing also important? St. Thomas was aware of this problem and he tried to incorporate the knowledge of the will into his theory of self-knowledge. He recalls the analysis of the act of the will, which is nothing more than an inner movement guided by a cognitive form. According to the principle that the inclination in a thing conforms to the mode of the thing's being, this inclination of the human will is understood in the intellect as in its first principle and its proper subject.[38] Hence the will is known by the intellect. Man knows that he wills and then he comes to know the nature of this act.

Such, in rough outline, is the Thomistic teaching on self-knowledge. Some points stand in need of clarification and further explanation. Does not the order of knowledge of the object, knowledge of the act, and knowledge of the nature of the faculty conflict with that important text in *De veritate* (I, 9) in which the certainty of truth is made to depend on the reflective act and the necessary relation of the act to its external object, while the knowledge of the nature of the act is here made to depend on the knowledge of the nature of the faculty? Again, with regard to the knowledge of the nature of the intellect, what is to be said of its dependence on the knowledge of the act? Here we have an apparent conflict with psychological priority.

Without doubt, the foregoing reasonings indicate that St. Thomas intended to say that the knowledge of the nature of the intellect is the result of careful study and that it logically depends on the knowledge and interpretation of the intellectual act. Later when St. Thomas, in determining the criterion of certitude for our knowledge of the external world, refers primarily to the nature of the intellect, we are confronted by a contradictory statement in the Thomistic system.

In evaluating the Thomistic position on the question of self-knowledge, we need to distinguish clearly between the question whether the intellect can know itself without the stimulus of the content of external knowledge, and the question whether the soul, incited to activity by immediate experience or by rational thought, can know its own act, powers, and essence. The first question deals with the genesis of our self-knowledge; the second refers to the logical method employed in self-knowledge. St. Thomas answers the first

---

[38] *Summa theol.*, Ia, q.87, a.4: *inclinatio intelligibilis, quae est actus voluntatis, est intelligibiliter in intelligente sicut in principio primo et in proprio subjecto.*

question by saying that our knowledge of our inner world is obtained by way of our knowledge of the external world. Once the soul has been stirred to activity it knows its acts, powers, and nature. With regard to this knowledge of the soul's acts and powers, it is important to point out that these things are the immediate data of consciousness. St. Thomas says that this knowledge about the soul is the most certain of human knowledge inasmuch as each one experiences in himself that he has a soul and places certain spiritual acts.[39] In this connection St. Thomas calls on the authority of Aristotle and St. Augustine; the latter's analysis of consciousness is far more penetrating and subtle. Here no difference exists between the Augustinian and the Thomistic lines of thought. Like St. Augustine, St. Thomas does not consider the knowledge of self as knowledge of the second order, and he is so completely in accord with the great doctor of the Church that he adopts his language unreservedly.[40]

St. Augustine, however, went much farther than St. Thomas, when he taught an intuitive, direct knowledge of the soul by its own essence. His medieval disciples, St. Bonaventure, John of Rupella, and John Peckham, followed him on this point. Another disciple, Matthew of Aquasparta, taught that the soul was aroused to activity by the external world but, "once it has entered on intellectual activity, it is recalled to itself by this activity, although previously it seemed to have been lost entirely in the consideration of external things. Now it is able by an immediate vision to see itself, its own acts, and its own nature. It knows itself, therefore, not by means of conclusions and reasonings, but by direct vision as if it directed its sight on its own content. This viewpoint is substantiated by four facts which together supply ample proof. Four things are required for this spiritual vision as four things are also required for the perception of the sense of sight: the presence of some visible object as such, a proper visual faculty directed to this object, a mutual relation between the faculty and the object, and the reflection of the light from the object, for everything that is seen is seen in some light." [41]

St. Thomas opposes this theory strenuously because his attitude was much more realistic and factual. If the soul knew itself by its own

[39] De verit., X, 8 ad 8.
[40] Contra Gent., III, 46.
[41] Cf. Spettmann, Die Erkenntnislehre der mittelalterl. Franziskanerschule von Bonaventura bis Skotus, 1925.

essence, then every man would know what the soul is, and then no error would exist about the soul. This is patently not true. Again, in the order of knowledge, those things that are known of themselves are prior to those things that are known through others. If the soul knew itself through itself, the science of psychology would begin with this basic knowledge of the soul. But instead, it is the nature of the soul that is being sought after. We really start with the accidents and try to forge ahead to the substance, and from partial activities we try to understand the whole of the soul. Only by reasoning, by reflection, and by intensive turning upon ourselves can we know the nature of the soul. "At first the activity of the intellect turns to that which is comprehended from the phantasms, then it returns to a knowledge of its act, then to the intelligible species, the habit and powers of the soul, and finally to the essence of the intellect and the soul itself." [42]

[42] *De verit.*, X, 9.

CHAPTER XXVII

THE KNOWLEDGE OF TRUTH

All knowledge aims at truth. In our practical lives we lay our comprehensions of truth beneath our decisions and actions as their foundation. In our theoretical life, we are bent on the acquisition of truth, and every science is nothing more than a system of knowledge that lays claim to being a part of truth in general. From the time of Plato and Aristotle many problems had arisen about the concept of truth which called for some solution from St. Thomas.

1. **The depositary of truth.** All knowledge signifies the conformity of him who knows with the object that is known, the agreement of the thinker with things. This conformity or adequation of the intellect and the object expresses the full content of the idea of truth.[1]

Truth comes into being through the participation of both the object and the intellect, and thus the question arises whether truth resides in the intellect or in things. We can speak of the truth of a thing only with reference to the conformity of that thing to the intellect. Thus St. Thomas, together with Aristotle,[2] concludes that truth exists primarily in the intellect and figuratively in things. The things of nature, which have received the measure of their being from the divine intellect, are themselves the measure of man's speculative reason. (*Sic ergo intellectus divinus est mensurans, non mensuratus: res naturalis autem mensurans et mensurata, sed intellectus noster est mensuratus, non mensurans quidem res naturales, sed artificiales tantum.*) The thing in nature, therefore, is set between two intellects, in reference to which it can be said to be true.

A thing may be said to be true with reference to the divine intellect inasmuch as it fulfills that for which it was intended by the divine

[1] *De verit.*, I, 1 ad 2; *Summa theol.*, Ia, q. 16, a. 1.
[2] *Met.*, VI, 4.

intellect. A thing is true with respect to a human intellect if it can allow a true concept of itself to be formed; it is false in so far as it presents an existence or a nature which it does not possess. The truth of things with respect to the divine mind possesses temporal as well as ontological priority. A thing that is known is ordered by its very nature to the divine mind; with reference to the divine mind that contains its form and the idea of its proper nature, it is said to be absolutely true. This truth is inseparable from things, for without the divine intellect which gave them being they could not exist. When things are known they have only an accidental relation to the human intellect, for without the human mind things would continue to exist.

Truth which exists in its proper sense in the intellect and only secondarily in things, necessarily includes in itself this relation to some intellect. If no human created intellect existed, things would still be true with reference to the divine intellect. If every intellect should be obliterated, the idea of truth would also be destroyed, but that is, of course, impossible.[3]

The knowledge of truth implies a causal relationship. From the viewpoint of things, the divine mind is the cause inasmuch as it produces the essence and the content of truth. Truth in the human mind is the effect inasmuch as the human intellect receives its knowledge from things which are the cause of its knowledge. In spite of this causality of things, truth belongs properly in the intellect, since it is the being of things, and not their truth, that is the cause of truth in the intellect.[4] St. Thomas distinguishes clearly between the logical forms to which truth is attached and the real external things, and also between these forms and the mental processes. A logical entity is the product of the intellect, outside of which it has no existence, except in some language symbol, and even here it is distinct from the intellect's act of production. Just as in the external actions the act and the result, e.g., the act of building and the building, must be kept separate, so in the activity of the intellect the act of the intellect must be distinguished from what is produced by such acts, namely, judgment, syllogisms, proofs, etc.

St. Thomas refrained from turning the logical entity into something psychological, so he refrains from making logical structures ontologi-

---

[3] *De verit.*, I, 2; *Summa theol.*, Ia, q. 16, a. 1.
[4] *In I Sent.*, 19, 5; *Summa theol.*, Ia, q. 16, a. 1 ad 3; a. 5 ad 2.

cal in the sense of Platonic metaphysics or of modern logicism. The concept of truth cannot be separated from the thinking and knowing subject as its depositary. Every thought process consists of a productive mental act and is rooted therefore in the thinking subject and in the logical product by which it refers to some object. Thus the logical entity stands midway between the psychic realm and the real being of the external objective world; it is indebted to both, to the psychic realm for its existence, and to the external world for its validity. For St. Thomas there are neither truths nor statements that exist in themselves; only objective things exist in themselves, whether or not they are thought by some empirical subject. Logical truth consists in the conformity of the intellect with the objective thing; it is therefore truth that is known and thought.

2. **The depositary of logical truth.** Repeatedly St. Thomas says that truth exists primarily in the intellect, in the uniting and separating intellect, i.e., the judging intellect. For the sake of clarity we must keep in mind that Aristotle and St. Thomas speak of two distinct activities of the intellect; the first is the activity that forms simple concepts and comprehends the essences of things, the *intellectus incomplexus;* the second is the activity which judges, that is, unites or divides these simple concepts, the *intellectus complexus.* Like Aristotle, and like Leibnitz and Kant later, he declared that it is only the *intellectus complexus* that is true or false. Truth and error rest therefore on this uniting and separating. Furthermore, sentences, the external signs of the thoughts formed by the intellect, are also true or false. The uniting and separating by the intellect corresponds to the affirmation and negation in the sentence.[5]

Truth is pre-eminently a property of judgment. Therefore it is imperative that we obtain a clear idea about judgment. The simple comprehension of an essence precedes the judgment and is intended to serve in the uniting or separating of the essences in the judgment. As a union and separation, judgment is a synthesis, but it is a synthesis preceded by an analysis. The individual thing that is comprehended is not a simple thing, but is composed of a subject and accidents. All that has been united into an entity in the thing must now be dissolved by analytical abstraction, and then again predicated of the thing.

St. Thomas speaks of a twofold difference between the uniting and

[5] *In I Sent.,* 19, 5, 1; *De verit.,* I, 3; *Summa theol.,* Ia, q. 16, a. 2.

dividing judgment and the conceptual image. While the concept comprehends the essence, the judgment comprehends the being of things and gives it expression. Again, the judgment is not a passive occurrence, but it is an act, a purposeful activity. In making a judgment, the intellect is to a certain extent engaged in a creative activity since it produces its own proper mental image, something that does not belong to the objective thing. The intellect, when it forms mere concepts, does not have a proper mental image but only an image of the thing that lies beyond the conscious sphere. In this phase the intellect is like the senses, which likewise receive the sensible species by passive reflection and not by any creative activity.

A true judgment consists in the agreement of the mental judgment with the objective state of things. In every judgment a certain form, called the predicate, is affirmed or denied of some object called the subject. In itself this activity of the intellect is a union, but with reference to the objective thing there is a union when the intellect knows the actual union of the object and certain dispositions and at the same time sees the agreement of the objective world with its own mental world.

Truth is found in the intellect inasmuch as a resemblance to the known thing is found in the intellect. The intellect is able to understand this conformity of the content of its consciousness with external things and thus it knows the truth. *"Conformitatem istam cognoscere est cognoscere veritatem."* [6] As it has this advantage, the judging intellect excels all other cognitive functions. The highest perfection of the intellect is this power to unite and separate. This conclusion sounds somewhat strange against the background of Aristotelian Scholastic thought. The Platonic theory that the intellect possesses an intuitive power as its highest perfection would have been more reasonable since it would have displayed more similarity with God, who does not unite and separate in mental judgments.

The proposition that truth and error are found only in the uniting and separating of judgments needs some modification. St. Thomas found himself obliged to make the concept of truth applicable to the comprehensive power of the intellect and the perceptive power of the senses. The mental judgment depends on sense and the mental images that it uses in its acts, and the truth of the judgment will depend to a certain extent on how faithfully these images reflect the external

---

[6] *Summa theol.,* Ia, q. 16, a. 2.

world. St. Thomas subjects the simple act of the comprehension of essences to the test of truth. The product of that act is, of course, not false in itself as is the case with the joining and separating of judgments. By its nature the intellect tends to the essences of things and comprehends them as its proper object. This comprehension is always true, since the intellectual faculty cannot fail with regard to that object which it must resemble in order to be informed by it. The intellect receives its form by being made like the essence of the thing, and therefore the intellect cannot be in error with regard to that thing.

This simple, incomplex thing, the definition, does not include in itself either the idea of agreement or non-agreement, and therefore it cannot be said to be false or true. But St. Thomas found it necessary to modify this statement later with regard to the intellect's act of comprehending essences inasmuch as an act of comparison is connected with the act of comprehending an essence. When the intellect comprehends an essence it is always true, but error may enter *per accidens,* that is, when the judging intellect enters and falsely applies a definition true in itself, or unites irreconcilable parts to form a definition. Such error can arise only in the case of composite things; with regard to the essences of simple things the intellect does not err. It either comprehends the truth or it does not comprehend at all.[7]

The senses, too, as in Aristotle, are subjected to the test of truth. Like the intellect comprehending essences, the senses by their nature tend to their proper objects and they are true inasmuch as they image or perceive these objects as they are. This sense knowledge, to which St. Thomas conceded a kind of judgment, includes in itself a resemblance to the perceived object, and truth exists in the senses as a consequence of their acts. The healthy condition of the senses is, however, presupposed. The senses are never able to comprehend this conformity to the object; only the intellect is able to do this. The sense conforms to the object, but it does not know that it conforms; the consciousness of the possession of truth is lacking to the senses because they are entirely incapable of reflection. Even though the peak of sense knowledge is a kind of self-consciousness, the senses never know their own nature or the nature of their acts, and therefore they do not know their own conformity to external objects.

[7] *In I Sent.,* 9, 5; *De verit.,* I, 2; *Contra Gent.,* I, 59; III, 108; *Summa theol.,* Ia, q. 17, a. 3; q. 58, a. 5; q. 85, a. 6.

The reason for this is that the senses are not able to turn back on themselves. Although the senses, besides knowing the sensible object, also know that they are perceiving, and thus have a slight resemblance to reflective action, they are unable to make the complete reflection on themselves. Ultimately this is because the senses are bound down by corporeal organs.[8]

St. Thomas proposes the question whether the senses are subject to error, and he replies with a distinction. In themselves the senses are entirely free from error, for they merely manifest their disposition to the intellect, and with respect to this disposition they are always true. But if the senses are considered as reporters about something, they may portray the matter to the intellect differently from what it is. Inasmuch as the senses are able to furnish the judging intellect with false sense data for the judgment of things, they may be said to be false. The senses always give a true report about their own status, but they may report falsely about the condition of things.

With respect to the relations of the senses to things, St. Thomas together with Aristotle distinguishes three kinds of sense objects, as was noted in the section on sense perception. With regard to the proper object of the senses, no error arises, because the senses receive their form through the resemblance with the object. *Per accidens,* however, even here an error may arise when the senses are indisposed or distorted. But even in healthy senses errors may arise with respect to the common objects of the senses because the senses are affected, not directly, but only through the sensible qualities. Again, these common objects of the senses, and especially the accidental objects, are perceived only after the proper object and through a comparison and composition of the senses. As the senses are unable to know their own knowledge of truth, so they cannot tell when they are in error. Such a decision belongs to the competence of the judging intellect. In the senses the affection and the perception are identical, and sometimes the senses are affected in a way which the object does not warrant, and thus the report of the senses departs from the truth.[9]

3. Ontological truth and its connection with the concept of God. Things are the cause and the standard of human knowledge. Truth in the human intellect corresponds to a foundation in things. Along

---

[8] *In I Sent.,* 19, 5; *De verit.,* I, 9; *Summa theol.,* Ia, q. 16, a. 2; *In de III an.,* 11.

[9] *Summa theol.,* Ia, q. 17, a. 2 ad 1; q. 17, a. 3; q. 78, a. 3; *De verit.,* I, 11; St. Augustine, *De vera relig.,* chap. 33.

with the Platonic Augustinian tradition, St. Thomas recognizes an ontological, transcendental truth, a truth in things. Thus a thing is true inasmuch as it possesses a proper essence; *propria forma, secundum quam imitatur artem divinam.*[10] Each thing's form is the guidepost for the knowing human intellect. Things are knowable because they possess an essential content that is mentally comprehensible, and the human intellect is by its nature disposed to comprehend these essential contents of things. The inner constitutive elements of things inform the knowing mind; as the Pythagoreans said of number, the form dispenses knowledge.

The perfection and truth of things and also of the intellect come from God, whose being is the cause of all being and whose knowledge is the cause of all other knowledge. The divine radiance penetrates everything with its power and casts its light into every intellect and supports the correct knowledge of things. The Thomistic theory of spiritual and intellectual knowledge can best be characterized by the term "ideal realism." It is realistic inasmuch as the *res,* the thing, is the beginning and the standard of knowledge; it is idealistic inasmuch as the ideal content of things is the proportioned object of the human mind, and also inasmuch as God, i.e., the divine idea, provides the reason for the thing's being and knowledge.

The Pythagorean principle that knowledge is possible only when the knowing intellect has a certain relation with the nature of things, lies at the bottom of every system of ideal realism, as it is the basis of the Thomistic system. This principle has an unbroken succession from St. Augustine to St. Anselm, Avicenna, and Franciscan Scholasticism, and then through St. Albert the Great to St. Thomas. Ontological truth is founded in the essential content of things, and since things, because of their perfection, represent a hierarchy, St. Thomas was able to assert: The greater the being, the truer it is.

Positive assertions of truth correspond to some idea that has been actualized in things. What is to be said about the expression of privations and negations? These have no positive form as their objective correlate, they are not an imitation of the divine prototype, and they do not express an ontological truth. The truth of a negative or privative statement is different from that of a statement founded on a positive quality in things. We cannot speak in the same way about a true stone and true blindness. The truth of the stone includes the essence of the

[10] *De interpret.,* I, 1; *In I Sent.,* 19, 5; *Summa theol.,* Ia, q. 16, a. 1.

stone, and the truth of the assertion rests on this real foundation. The truth of the privation rests on a comparison made by the mind without a positive foundation in being. Non-being is a creature of the intellect and becomes knowable through the mind in contrast to being. To express the matter logically: the truth of negative assertions is founded in the truth of the positive assertions. We comprehend a negation after the manner of being; we first refer to being, we think of something positive, and then we deny it.[11]

4. **The eternity and unchangeableness of truth.** St. Thomas considered the much discussed question about the eternity and unchangeableness of truth. He does not admit the existence of a separate sphere composed of metaphysical essences that exist of themselves. Since truth is in the intellect, eternal truths are found only in the eternal mind, i.e., the divine mind, and never in the created mind. God is the presupposition before we can speak of eternal truth. Every truth has its foundation in being, and the concept of truth implies the comprehending activity of the intellect. The idea of truth comprising these two elements, foundation in being and comprehension by an intellect, can be said to be eternal only with respect to God. Only the divine being is eternal and unchangeable, whereas the being of contingent things is subject to change. Only the divine intellect is by its nature eternal and unchangeable. From this divine, eternal truth are derived the truth of all things and the truth of the human intellect. There is but one divine truth through which everything is true, yet there is a multiplicity of truths in things and in the human intellect. The human mind is not eternal; therefore the truths that it thinks are not eternal. Likewise things are not eternal; they go from being to non-being, from this form to another, and the truth in an intellect must be guided by these changes.[12]

St. Thomas found the eternity and unchangeableness of truth expressed nowhere more clearly than in St. Augustine. The often repeated theme of the Augustinian writings is that mathematical laws and logical principles, the laws of beauty and the norms of morality, are things independent of experience, and that they are eternally valid, rising above all individuals and binding all equally. These truths are eternally valid and necessary because they come from eternity. There

[11] *In I Sent.*, 19, 5; *De verit.*, I, 5 ad 2; *Summa theol.*, Ia, q. 16, a. 3 ad 2; a. 5 ad 3.
[12] *De verit.*, I, 4, 5; *Contra Gent.*, I, 35; II, 84; *Summa theol.*, Ia, q. 16, a. 6–8; *De pot.*, III, 17 ad 27.

is an unchangeable Truth containing all unchangeable truth, and that is God.[13]

Ancient philosophy had a tendency to give all a concrete existence, as may be seen from Plato's universe of ideas and Plotinus' *nous*. St. Augustine halted this excessively realistic tendency when he placed this world of truth in God and expressed the system of truth as the world of ideas in the divine mind. St. Anselm and the Franciscan school were under the Augustinian influence when they said that God was the highest truth, subsisting in Himself, and the ultimate cause and norm of all other truth.

Some scholars think they see a difference here between St. Augustine and St. Thomas. The latter is supposed to have discarded every Augustinian-Platonic view of the objectivization of all truth. But the difference is of little importance; although ideas and truths are expressed somewhat as autonomous forms, the ultimate metaphysical basis for both thinkers is the same; first principles are resemblances of that first truth and from it they derive eternity and unchangeableness. We are not able to see the first truth in its essence in this life; we can know truth only in its reflections.

[13] *De lib. arb.*, II, 8–12; *De ver. relig.*, chaps. 29 f.; *De immort. an.*, chap. 4; *De Trin.*, XII, 2; XIV, 15; *Solil.*, II, 8; *Retract.*, I, 4; *Conf.*, XII, 25.

CHAPTER XXVIII

THE ORDER AMONG SCIENCES

1. The division of sciences. No statement can be made about absolute non-being. The matter of scientific knowledge must in some way possess being. Here St. Thomas distinguishes three kinds of being: real being that has reached full existence, potential being implanted in its causes, and being in the consciousness of an intelligent being.[1] Different sciences are concerned with these various kinds of beings and they are distinguished from one another according to the kind of being they deal with.

In accord with tradition, St. Thomas defines the subject of a science as what is presupposed in that science, or that which is to be studied in its properties; the object of a science comprises these properties which are seen to come from the essence of the subject. The subject and the properties together form the matter of the science. The objects of the sciences differentiate the sciences, and here the distinction between material object and formal object is important. The object is not alone the deciding thing for the differentiation of a science; the viewpoint from which a science considers its object provides the ultimate reason for the differentiation. All the things and material that come within the field covered by a science constitute the material object of that science; the aspect of these things that is to be examined constitutes the formal object. Aristotle laid down this distinction, the medieval Aristotelians adopted it, and St. Thomas incorporated it into his system.

The matter of a particular science represents something that is joined together into an order which the human intellect strives to comprehend. All knowledge tends to the connections of order, and the intellect manifests the actual ability of comprehending the order that dominates things. From the viewpoint of the intellect, this order

[1] *In I Sent.*, 38, 4; *Summa theol.*, Ia, q. 16, a. 3 ad 2.

is fourfold: (1) the order which the intellect does not create but which it observes, i.e., the order in nature; (2) the order which the intellect produces through certain mental acts when it disposes the concepts of things; (3) the order to which the intellect gives rise through the acts of the will; (4) the order which the intellect produces by its activity in the external world.

The activity of the intellect is perfected in its habits and thus, since there are four activities, four habits or sciences correspond to these activities. The first order is the matter of natural philosophy, of which metaphysics is a part. The second order is the concern of rational philosophy with its subdivisions of rhetoric and logic. Rhetoric considers the parts of speech; logic deals with the mutual order among first principles and their relation to the conclusion of a syllogism. Moral philosophy deals with the third order. The fourth order is the field of the mechanical arts.

This division does not comprise all the disciplines mentioned by St. Thomas. Mathematics is not mentioned; metaphysics is merged with natural philosophy although they are separated by an important distinction. The relation of logic to the other sciences is not expressed, and sacred science, *sacra doctrina,* is omitted.

Since the idea of science depends on the concept of being, the thinkers of the Middle Ages, under the influence of the Platonic and Aristotelian traditions, were intent on the study of essences, which they tried to comprehend by their theory of abstraction. The sciences of the Middle Ages, founded as they were on certain logical and metaphysical presuppositions, presented a hierarchical structure that was closely interconnected, culminating not in worldly science but in the Christian science of divine things. The system of instruction, beginning with logic, continued through mathematics, the natural sciences, ethics, metaphysics, to theology.

a. **Logic.** Even before the time of St. Thomas the question of the place of logic in the scientific structure was often raised. St. Thomas followed the lead of Aristotle's *Organon,* of Boethius, the Arabians, and the Christian Scholastics. Aristotle had written two works of logic: the *Topica* and the two *Analytica.* The *Topica,* a textbook for the art of dialectical disputation, contains instructions for debate and argumentation. The *Topica* plays the part of the auxiliary and instrument for thought and supplies, for right thinking, a wealth of rules and admonitions which are themselves rooted in other theoretical reasons. The actual science of logic is to be found in the twofold *Analytica* (*Priora* and *Posteriora*) and consists of a treatise on conclusions, proofs, and the definition and its parts. For Aristotle, logic was primarily a theory of methods which also embraced the theory of the concept and judgment. The practical directions for giving a correct definition are lost sight of in this treatise. Aristotle is really the founder of logic as a theoretical science, as the science of the scientific structure of our knowledge, which attains a certain dignity inasmuch as it serves as the instrument for the other sciences. The Platonists and Stoics placed logic alongside physics and ethics as a part of philosophy, but the Peripatetics considered it only as an auxiliary science. Later, Proclus' disciple, Ammonius, took the middle viewpoint, that logic was both an auxiliary science and a part of philosophy, and this viewpoint found acceptance with Boethius and the other Scholastics who felt the Arabian influence.

The object of logic is the thing in the mind, *ens rationis,* all those mental forms that are produced for the purpose of knowing reality, such as judgments, conclusions, proofs and their elements, concepts of order, such as genus and species. Logic is the science of those mental forms that constitute a science, it is the science of science, the science of the scientific means of knowledge. As a methodology, logic furnishes the means for scientific work. St. Thomas separates logic from metaphysics. Metaphysics considers things in their existence as independent of our thoughts; the logician studies the intellectual forms of order as they are related to things. Since our thoughts are oriented to matter and objects, logic is an objective science, and our concepts of order have validity in the things of nature. But since logic looks at things only from the viewpoint of formal principles, it is closely related to mathematics.

St. Thomas considered logic, in its ultimate sense, as a theoretical science, although he often referred to it as the instrument of science. St. Thomas also valued logic as a science of methods and the science of the art of thinking. Since it is a theoretical science and the teacher of the art of thinking, logic is the science that should be studied before all other sciences.

b. **The theoretical material sciences.** The traditional Aristotelian division of theoretical philosophy into natural philosophy, mathematics, and theology, was adopted by St. Thomas. The principle of division in this instance is the principle of abstraction, applied in so many cases, which rested on the basis that a thing is intelligible only so far as it is separable from matter.

We find as objects of our knowledge certain things that are bound to matter both in their being and in their knowability, things that exist only in matter and that have definitions in which sensible matter is an indispensable part. With these things natural philosophy is concerned. Other things are bound in their existence to matter, but not in their knowability, for their definitions do not include sensible matter. This second class of beings is the object of mathematics. Thirdly, we have objects of our knowledge that can be without matter in their existence, either because they have never been joined to matter, as God and pure spirits, or because they sometimes appear in matter and sometimes without it, such as substance, quality, potency, act, unity, plurality. These things are the subject matter of metaphysics and its divisions.

In the first place among the material sciences, St. Thomas places natural science, since it is the knowledge of sensible perceivable effects, a knowledge progressing from the knowledge of these effects to the highest causes. Natural science ranks ahead of mathematics because natural things are better known to us. The subject matter of the natural sciences is all those things that are in matter and in motion. A thing is completely embraced with its properties, activities, and changes, when it is analyzed from the standpoint of the fourfold causality. As it was for Aristotle, causal knowledge is for St. Thomas the highest kind of knowledge, in a deeper sense than in modern thought. He took it for granted that the first thing to be studied was the forms of things, the principles of being which determine the species of things and the extent of their effects.

Psychology is a division of the natural sciences. St. Thomas classes it among the natural sciences because it is the form of a physical organic body. It is a part of the physical world not only because it is the principle of motion but also because the effects of the vegetative and sensitive soul are possible only in conjunction with the body. Most of the dispositions belong to the composite and are therefore not separable from the body and thus come within the range of the natural sciences. As St. Thomas used the principle of separability from matter as the principle for division among the sciences, so he distinguishes the parts of the various sciences, especially the natural sciences, by the same principle, *secundum diversum modum separationis et concre-*

tionis. Hence the human *nous,* including the *intellectus possibilis* and the *intellectus agens,* since it is not the act of a corporeal organ and is not merged in matter, was considered in the realm of metaphysics with the pure spirits.

The fundamental attitude of Thomistic psychology had been determined by Aristotle; its problems were those outlined by Aristotle and St. Augustine. Thomistic psychology was concerned with more than the metaphysical problems of the substantiality, spirituality, and immortality of the soul, the relationship of the soul to the body, and the activity and freedom of the will. It considered the whole constitution of man, and the whole field of the spiritual and mental organism was the goal of its inquiry. It disclosed the various potencies and powers of man and studied the functions and acts that proceeded from these powers. This knowledge was obtained reductively, going from the object to the act, and from the act to the habit from which the act flowed. The study concluded with a precise analysis of the structure of this act. This Thomistic psychology explained the participation of different potencies in the same act and the mutual dependence between various psychic powers that were rooted in the unity of the soul. From the object the soul came to know its act, and by this path it attained to a knowledge of its own nature.

Comparisons were made with superior beings, the pure spirits, and with inferior beings, the animals, in order to throw light on the life of man's soul. The lack of experimental psychology is richly compensated for by a profound understanding of the peculiar structure of the soul's acts and by an insight into the essential interconnections of man's inner microcosm in which the different powers are rooted.

Mathematics deals with the essential laws of quantity. Its objects are number and dimension. In determining the division of mathematics and in assigning it a place among the other sciences, St. Thomas consistently followed tradition. Mathematical objects are superior to those of the natural sciences because they are abstracted from matter, they yield to the objects of metaphysics because they are sensible and perceivable by the phantasm. Mathematics, according to St. Thomas, is among the most sublime and certain sciences.

Metaphysics is the science of being as being, and thus it is concerned with the supreme concepts of being, first principles, fundamental laws of being, and also with the highest cause of being, God. Its first department is ontology with which epistemology is closely allied because of its foundation in being, as well as the theory of values, because value also is based on being. The most important part of metaphysics is theology; because of the sublimity of its object and the certitude of its principles, it takes the most prominent place among the profane sciences and also represents the transition to the *sacra doctrina,* the science of faith.

c. The practical sciences. Actually the practical sciences in the framework of the Thomistic system hold a much more important place than we are led to expect from the scantiness of the original outline. When the system unfolds we are surprised to learn how much matter and method St. Thomas brought to bear that he might secure and establish the supreme practical principles and the conclusions that flow from them. With regard to the science of human relations, this matter will receive detailed treatment when we come to speak of the moral order, the social order, and the order of law and justice.

The distinguishing mark of practical philosophy noted by St. Thomas and Aristotle is that it aims at some production, whereas the speculative sciences are directed to the knowledge of truth. An important part of practical philosophy is the science of morals, which is concerned with relationship of human nature as a rational person in private life and in the life of the community. Moral science was given a threefold division: monastics (see *supra,* p. 41, economics, and politics, and this division, established by Aristotle, was developed by the Peripatetics and adopted by the commentators, the Arabians, and the Christian Scholastics. St. Thomas, however, considered it only a classroom division, which he promptly discarded.

Among the practical sciences, St. Thomas enumerated the mechanical arts, such as medicine, shipbuilding, strategy. The vagueness in the division of the practical sciences was overcome later when St. Thomas adopted Aristotle's division into the liberal and productive sciences (*activa et factiva*). The former is concerned with those acts that reach completion as acts; the latter refers to acts that end in some external thing. Both parts of the division agree in this, that they have individual and contingent things as subject matter and therefore furnish less certainty in their conclusions than do the speculative sciences.

d. History. St. Thomas knew nothing of a philosophy of culture in the modern and proper sense, and consequently he also did not recognize any epistemology of the cultural sciences. Nor is history a science. Aristotle (*Poetica,* chap. 9) had denied the scientific character of history because it dealt with the individual and not the universal, and all the thinkers of the Middle Ages aligned themselves on his side. The Augustinian school relegated historical occurrences to the realm of faith, and the Aristotelians simply repeated their master's dictum. In company with St. Albert the Great and Ulrich of Strassburg, St. Thomas taught that we can have no scientific knowledge of human events because they are individual and contingent.

On one point we discover an essential difference between Aristotle and St. Thomas on this question of history. In the sphere of nature and of culture, Aristotle taught the eternal return of all things. Not only the things in nature but the various cultural entities have a form, or entelechy, to work out; when this has been fulfilled, the final goal has been attained. Aristotle recognized no pause in the cultural process because, according to his view, the world is visited again and again by great catastrophes and the men who survive such occurrences bear within themselves the same or a similar culture. On the basis of this primitive historical morphology, Aristotle could have developed the science of history to fit into his concept of science. St. Thomas, however, did not admit the concept of an eternal world or the eternal return of all things. Much earlier, St. Augustine in opposing Origen had pointed out that this teaching was irreconcilable with Christianity. The concept of the world's history as a movement that occurs once, having a beginning, a climax, and a final goal, is part of the Christian view of the world. St. Augustine, in his writings, displayed the material for building a true philosophy of history, but the theory of science failed to reach that point in its development when history would be given its rightful place in the scientific system.[2]

2. Methods. The scientific method is of telling importance in every science. With Aristotle, St. Thomas distinguishes between two great classes of methods, the analytic method and the synthetic method. The former, called also *via resolutoria, modus processus resolutionis,* proceeds from what is composite to what is simple, from the last to the first, from the whole to the parts, from the effect to the cause, and from the particular to the universal. The synthetic method, called *via compositiva, modus processus compositionis,* proceeds from the simple to the composite, from the first to the last, from the parts to the whole. from cause to effect, and from the universal to the particular. In this process the starting point is first in knowledge as well as in being,

[2] *Summa theol.,* Ia, q. 1, a. 1 ad 3; *In Boeth. de Trin.,* III, 1.

whereas in the analytic method the starting point is, of course, first in the order of knowledge, but later in the order of being. An instance of synthesis is deduction; instances of analysis are induction, abstraction, and division. Definitions may be reached by the synthetic as well as by the analytic method.

An order is to be observed in the use of all methods in general, in the formation of concepts, in the process of proof, and in the formation of definitions, because in each instance the order of being is the determining factor. Thus definition supposes the concept of the universe with many forms of being in various grades; the universe is regarded as a kind of family tree which has being as its root and which, by means of the different genera and species, is differentiated down to the individual. By indication of the genus and the specific difference, everything is assigned its proper ontological and logical place. In a philosophy for which the world is a closed system of genera, species, and subordinate species, no insight into the whole may be obtained except by the dismemberment of these genera and species.

Every science has principles, general principles and special principles. If each science deals with one genus of being whose essential properties are to be studied, then this particular mental work must have a starting point, a principle within this genus of being. Thus each science has not only its own subject matter but also its own principles, which cannot be used as the basis for another science unless the subject of this second science is included in the concept of the subject of the first science. No science proves its own subject matter, and no science proves its own principles, but a science does prove things from this matter and these principles. As each science is assigned its subject matter by metaphyics, which divides being into its genera, so the special scientific principles are supported by the principles common to all sciences. Here the supreme principles of theoretical and practical science come into prominence again, attesting their importance in the Thomistic system.

No special proof is needed to show that the whole theory of science and method was in accord with the learned classes of the time. In the course of time other goals were set for scientific endeavor in conformity with changing scientific outlooks, and then the tasks of the various sciences also changed to fit the new goals. To enumerate the progress in science step by step would require the writing of a history of science from the Middle Ages down to the present time.

CHAPTER XXIX

MORALITY AND ITS RELATION TO BEING, KNOWLEDGE, AND WILL

If unity and the complete absence of a multiplicity of theories is the supreme requirement for an ethical system, it seems that the Thomistic system of ethics is gravely deficient. In this system we find different thought motives coming together, some of which arise from different traditions and some from a varied manner of approach to the problems of a moral system. We are not, however, referring to the charge made by some, that St. Thomas violently combined the natural ethical system of the "battle for existence" with the Christian ethics of love. That reproach is, of course, quite unjustified. In the Thomistic system such things as nature and grace, man's original state, sin, redemption, and sanctification, are merely different phases of the story of man's redemption, phases, however, which are inwardly united with one another.

The multiplicity of theories is found mostly in the natural sphere. The idea of life in accord with nature, the idea of the perfection of being and of virtue, the idea of end and purpose, the viewpoint of happiness, the idea of regulating the will through the order of reason which in turn rests on the order of being, and the theonomic system of morality, are all in themselves guiding viewpoints, each one of which alone might be a sufficient ethical principle. With his great powers of harmonizing and his far-sightedness, St. Thomas made excellent use of all these thought groups. Because these various viewpoints were found to be inwardly reconcilable, a certain unity was given the system. Someone might inquire which of these many viewpoints is given the leading role in the system; but the question would be superfluous. We soon discover that for St. Thomas, as for St. Au-

gustine before him, morality is synonymous with order, and that sin
is synonymous with disorder. We will readily see, in an exposition of
Thomistic ethics, that all other viewpoints come into their own in
their orientation to the concept of order. Although St. Thomas continued to think within the framework of the traditional categories,
he was able, principally on the basis of this concept of order, to master
the ethical reality and present his treatises on virtue and moral values
as the finest contribution to medieval ethics.

As soon as we begin to determine the subject matter of ethics, the
concept of order appears as a constitutive element. St. Thomas assigns
to moral philosophy as its object human actions that are ordered to
one another and to some end. All those activities that are not subject
to the intellect and the will, namely, those natural and unconscious
vegetative and sensitive functions, have no place in an ethical consideration. The subject matter of ethics is "human activity directed to
an end, or man when he acts because of the free choice of an end," [1]
i.e., man as a person. Freedom of the will is a necessary presupposition and the basis for all human activity. Morality begins when the
free will is active.[2] Morality is not synonymous with the universe of
values and purposes; it is the actualization of a certain value in man,
and depends on the decision that man makes, the decision to carry
out the order which he has come to know. As a personal being, man
represents that particular point in the universe where imperative values are transferred to reality. Morality is the transformation of a known
order of values, and the transformation is based on an inner attitude
and a decision of a free will; or again, morality is the freely actualized
order of reason.

Thomistic ethics is generally described as an ethics of purpose and
end. And, as a matter of fact, St. Thomas begins with the idea of purpose and end, referring to the fact that all human acts are placed for
some end. Since the series of ends cannot be allowed to extend to infinity, he requires a last and highest end which is desired because of
itself alone; all other things are desired, consciously or unconsciously,
because of this last end. Therefore the correct way seems to begin with
a consideration of the order of purposes, and from it to the planned
regulation of human activity, bringing the order of reason into relation
with the order of purposes.

[1] *In I Eth. Nic.*, 1.
[2] *Summa theol.*, Ia IIae, q. 1, a. 1.

But if we look more closely at the matter we shall find that the Thomistic ethics is not quite so. St. Thomas states expressly that a thing can become the end of the will only because it is a value or because it is considered to be of value by him who acts. Sometimes it was said that St. Thomas is in opposition to the other Scholastics, including St. Albert, because his teaching was regarded as being that the concept of end is the beginning of morality, whereas the Scholastics taught that the concept of good is this beginning. In reality, however, no difference exists between St. Thomas and the other Scholastics. St. Thomas also begins with the idea of good, or rather the idea of value. In the first article of the ethical considerations of the *Theological Summa* he says: *"objectum voluntatis est finis et bonum."* Again and again he says that a thing takes on the aspect of an end because it is good. The end is the form which a thing assumes when it enters into relation with an appetite. The reason why an object becomes the object of an appetite lies in its goodness and value. St. Thomas frequently repeats this idea: *"omnis appetitus non est nisi boni,* and *amoris proprium objectum est bonum."* [3]

What is desired by the will is the apprehended good, and whatever is desirable has the aspect of good, and therefore the evil is desired only under the aspect of good (*sub ratione boni*). In the philosophical summa, St. Thomas arrays reason on reason in support of his view that the statement *"omne agens agit propter finem,"* means the same as *"omne agens agit propter bonum."*

Every appetite tends toward something that is in conformity with the nature of him who strives; all striving is directed toward the perfection of the subject. Inasmuch as a thing is agreeable to the subject it is good, inasmuch as it is repugnant it is evil.[4] This concept of the perfection of the subject is a concept of value; since value is based on being, we must first consider absolute being and absolute value.

1. **Absolute being and absolute value.** Good and bad are not primarily moral terms; they are determinations of being itself. We shall best understand the Thomistic view if we begin with the ideas of good and bad in being. The ontological principle that being and good are convertible reaches its development in ethics. If we wish to understand Thomistic ethics, we must separate the various lines of reasoning that overlap and actually form a whole in the system.

---

[3] *Ibid.*, q.8, a.1; q.27, a.1.
[4] *Ibid.*, q.29, a.1; q.27, a.1.

Referring to Aristotle, St. Thomas says that the concept of good, like that of truth, merely adds a relation to the concept of being; that a thing is good inasmuch as it is the end of some striving. The goodness of a thing, therefore, consists in the desirability of a thing and in its capacity of being an end.[5] The concept of value is a primary concept in the order of our practical concepts, it is the first concept we form in this order, it is an original concept that is not referred to some other concept, and it can be explained only by means of later concepts. With this, St. Thomas means that the concept of value is ultimate in its genus.[6] Hence the concept of value in being implies a relation to a subject; a thing is valuable to some subject. At the same time the concept of value is in no way made subjective, in Aristotle, St. Thomas, St. Bonaventure, or Duns Scotus.

The good is desired by the appetite, but the good or value has a real foundation in the thing. A thing's mere capability of taking on the aspect of an end is not enough to describe its goodness. A thing is good and desirable and can therefore give perfection only because it itself possesses perfection. A thing is good and valuable inasmuch as it is perfect.

A thing is good inasmuch as it is perfect, but it is perfect inasmuch as it is in act. In speaking of being, we must keep separate the essential content of the thing and its existence, by which the thing is placed in the state of reality. Aristotle understood that being is always better than non-being, and that being and life denote a good. According to St. Thomas, being has the character of good, and every being is good because it possesses being. Because of a natural urge or tendency within it, every subject that does not have being strives for it, and everything that has being loves it and seeks to preserve it with all its energy. Existence is a further perfection, completing the subject and the essence.

The value of things is based on their perfection, and the perfection is founded on the actuality of the things, *esse actu boni rationem constituit*. This movement in things to become something valuable, this basic urge belongs to the innermost structure of things. Inasmuch as things have existence, they may be called good. The axiom, *omne ens est bonum*, expresses not so much the teleological direction of the thing as the realized perfection in actuality.

Existence, therefore, and actuality are good. Does this exhaust the

---

[5] *In I Eth. Nic.*, 1; *De verit.*, XXI, 1; *Summa theol.*, Ia, q. 5, a. 5.
[6] *In I Eth. Nic.*, 1.

meaning of the statement *"omne ens est bonum"*? No. Does bare existence hold such a high place? It is the being of a thing that expresses the actuality and form of a thing. Existence may exhibit the content of a thing's form, and that is good and desirable, but the true good is the essential good.

Everything is created valuable; it does not, as some moderns wish to think, become valuable through the valuing subject without which it would be valueless. The thing is valuable because God gives it value as He gives it being. A thing is good because it has fullness of being; it is bad when it lacks this fullness. St. Thomas makes one more important distinction: between absolute goodness and goodness *secundum quid*. For the absolute goodness of a thing, St. Thomas required that it have subsistence in its essential principles, and that it be perfected by the addition of the accidents that belong to the essence, for the union of a thing with other things is established by activities that proceed from the essence in the form of powers and properties.[7]

St. Thomas thus places the value of a thing primarily in its perfection and in its act. The distinction between first and second act is of some importance here. First act is the form and substance, and second act is the activity of the thing. By its nature every thing is valuable by reason of its form, and from this arises the goodness of its dispositions and activity.

2. **Moral values.** We have followed the ancient line of Aristotelian reasoning and we have seen that the goodness of a thing consists in the full development of its peculiar nature and the attainment of its own peculiar perfection. This brings us to a consideration of the development of human nature and moral goodness. By this time we are aware that value is founded in being, and also that ethics is really the science of being, a continuation of ontological principles into a higher anthropological plane. But, we must remark immediately, human beings are different from other beings.

As a spiritual person, man ranks high above the realm of unconscious, blind, urge-propelled natural beings and forms a new plane of being. While the development of all other natural beings is necessary and therefore right, it is not so in the case of man. His stage of being is a spiritual plane, and that denotes the stage of freedom. As a personal being, man makes acts of the will. Inasmuch as man desires

---

[7] *De verit.*, XXI, 5; *Summa theol.*, Ia, q. 5, a. 1.

his natural being, life, and happiness, St. Thomas ascribes natural goodness to man's will and to its acts (*De malo,* II, 3 ad2).

All nature below man reaches its objects through the natural law, but in man there appears, illuminated by his spiritual being, an imperative which he recognizes consciously and which he is to actualize by his acts. This moral activity is also a part of the great universal activity.

Apart from the divine cooperation, moral activity presupposes on the part of the subject rational reflection and the free decision of the will. As a whole, the moral act, and thus also moral being, arises from the union of two factors: the rational reflective and free act of the subject and the objective goods and values that result from this activity. The moral act, therefore, looks to two sides: to the subject that makes the act and to the object that is intended.

Objectively the moral act is made up of several elements which St. Thomas enumerates in accord with the other Scholastics; the object, the end, and the circumstances. He also makes use of the Aristotelian concepts of matter and form and the concept of genus from the predicables together with the idea of the specific difference in trying to throw light on the moral act. The incorporation of these various factors into his theory occasionally led him into difficulties, and his explanations do not always concur.

Everywhere, except in the *Commentary on the Sentences,* St. Thomas regards the generic good as objective, or ontological, good.[8] Generically, therefore, every act is good, that is, inasmuch as it is an act and possesses being and essence. In this respect the human act is an object of ontology determined by the ontological determinations. It is only when the specific difference is added that the act of the will takes on moral value. The specific goodness or badness of an act is determined by the object. The moral goodness depends on the proper object (*materia circa quam*), on the object which is governed by the order of reason and represents the proximate end of the act. Matter it is that gives to every action its form and its specific imprint.[9] Thus

---

[8] St. Thomas (*In II Sent.,* 41, 1) is here not considering ontological good. Here the generic good is the conformity of the moral act to a corresponding good, and it includes agreement with the circumstances and direction to an end *per habitum gratiae et caritatis.*

[9] *Summa theol.,* Ia IIae, q.18, a.2–5; *Quodlib.,* III, 27.

such acts as taking nourishment, toiling, assisting our neighbor, are materially and formally distinct.

Some matter is bad in itself and it stamps the act as bad, e.g., theft, murder.

In the second place the moral quality of an act depends on the circumstances which are added to an act like accidents to an object. The good or evil that results from the circumstances is an individual determination of the act excluding any moral indifference. A circumstance is something that is outside the substance of the act, it "stands about the thing." From the causes of the act we derive the circumstances why and how; from the measure of the act come the circumstances where and when; and the act itself varies according to matter and effect. All the circumstances are included in the following enumeration: *quis, quid, ubi, quibus auxiliis, cur, quomodo, quando.*

The circumstances not only decrease or increase the goodness or badness of an act, they may also determine the species of the act, when, for instance, the circumstance makes an essential change in the object. A new species of sin may arise when some act is materially or formally more narrowly determined by a circumstance. Thus, to use something that belongs to the neighbor becomes adultery when that object is his wife, and theft becomes a sacrilege when the stolen article is taken from a sacred place. Sometimes a circumstance creates an entirely new species, e.g., when stolen goods are used for a simoniacal purpose.

The third factor in the moral structure of the act is the relation of the object to the right end. In accord with the other Scholastics, St. Thomas teaches that for the absolute goodness of an act all the factors for moral goodness must be present; the absence of one factor makes the action bad.[10]

The end of the act also acts as a specific difference. St. Thomas was obliged to determine the proper relationship between object and end. He therefore distinguished between the internal and external act of the will; the proper object of the internal act of the will is the end; the matter (object) is the proper object of the external act. He places the internal act in relation to the external act as the form to the matter, and then he formally derives the species of the moral act from the end, while the matter is supplied by the object. But the question could not rest there. He went on to show how in many important instances the object of the external act had an inner relationship to the end, and that

[10] *Summa theol.*, Ia IIae, q 18, a. 4 ad 3; q. 20, a. 3.

the more general specific difference came from the end, whereas the more proximate differentiation came from the object as it was directed to the end.[11] These two distinctions are not easily reconcilable. If the end is the form, then it is the determining element with respect to the undetermined matter of the object. But in the second instance St. Thomas establishes two determining specific differences; the difference of their object with respect to the more general nature of the end becomes the really deciding determination.

When we compare this course of reasoning with the thought of the other Scholastics, we realize how these thinkers wrestled in order to master the multiplicity of factors in the problem. St. Bonaventure distinguished between three kinds of goodness: the goodness of nature, the goodness of morals, and the goodness of convenience or profit, but he referred the moral goodness arising from a free decision of the will to the same factors as did St. Thomas. The generic goodness that is derived from the proper object is specified and determined by the circumstances. Final perfection in the act is obtained through the direction to the right end, and this is indispensable for the goodness of an action.[12]

Duns Scotus derived the generic goodness from the proper object, and the specific goodness from the end. Both must coincide for the moral goodness of the human act. The proper object, as restoration of property or almsgiving, does not suffice when the intention for a right end is not present; and the intention is not sufficient when the object is not adequate. Sometimes Duns Scotus accepts the circumstances as determinations of the object, but more frequently he subsumes the end among the circumstances, making the end the most decisive of the circumstances in determining the species of the act. It is quite clear that Duns Scotus strove to merge the end with the object or with the circumstances.

When St. Thomas establishes the end as the formal element, he is probably closest to the actual state of things and also most in accord with his system. The goodness of the will's act does not depend solely on the proper object, but also on the intention, the attitude and direction of the will. The end is the basis and reason for the will, *ex fine sumitur quasi formalis ratio volendi*. The highest end in human life is God. St. Thomas required that all particular goods and ends be

[11] *Ibid.*, q. 18, a. 6; *In III Sent.*, 33, 1; *Contra Gent.*, III, 9.
[12] *In II Sent.*, d. 36; d. 41 ad q. 1.

directed and related to God and that the human will be conformed to the divine will.[13] In the *Commentary on the Sentences*,[14] Aquinas discusses the question whether infidels can do good acts, and he replies in the affirmative with a qualification. An infidel cannot do acts that are meritorious for the supernatural end; but, since he has natural reason, he can do acts of natural virtue which can be directed to the last end even though they are not actually related to that end. In perfect virtue in which both nature and supernature play a part this direction to the last end must not be lacking. That direction is always present when man acts and wills *ex caritate*. In this respect, St. Thomas aligns himself with tradition, with St. Albert and St. Bonaventure especially, as he also does when he teaches that the love of God includes all other motives, even the motive of fear, which is so much discussed in Christian ethics.

The following distinction is important. Duns Scotus was aware that the objects are concrete states of things (e.g., generation, and the good to be obtained, the child, posterity), and that the ends (e.g., love of the common good, fidelity, justice, love of God) are ideal values belonging to an entirely different sphere of values. This distinction is of great importance in the metaphysics of value. No other Scholastic before him had so clearly differentiated between these spheres, and many after him lost sight of the distinction. Not every human act is a moral act, but only that which is referred to some ideal value.

Although St. Thomas thought of every object of the will as an end and thus considered the order of objects as the order of ends, the end or purpose really becomes something to which something else is related without any consideration for the sphere of values. This distinction of the sphere of values does not, therefore, appear in the Thomistic system as clearly as with Duns Scotus. As a matter of fact, the relation to an ideal value, to the order of reason, and to God, has a constituting importance for morality in Thomism. St. Thomas is aware of the difference between the matter and the motive of the will, but he is more interested in their cooperation. The end and the means for attaining that end are indeed different objects of the will, but inasmuch as the end supplies the reason why the means are willed, they merge into each other to form one object. The goodness of the intention is shared by the object. To express it in another way, we may

---

[13] *De verit.*, XXIII, 7, 8; *Summa theol.*, Ia IIae, q. 1, a. 6; q. 19, a. 7.
[14] *In II Sent.*, 41, 1, 2.

say that the goodness of the internal act of the will is poured out on the external act of the will, just as the goodness of the external act, derived mostly from the intellect, is transmitted to the internal act.[15]

In this way St. Thomas answers the question proposed by the modern theory of values: How can moral values be realized if human acts are directed to the actualization of real relations and the attainment of concrete goods? That is possible because the moral phenomenon is composed of two parts that belong together by an inner relation. Whether we go from the ideal value to the concrete thing or from the thing to the ideal value, both are the foundation for the goodness of the moral act. The ideal values express the norms for the development of man's nature; they are genuinely human values established by God to correspond to the idea of man. These values can be attained only when human activity establishes certain real relations in things and makes certain concrete goods. This is what is meant by conforming to the will of God.[16]

Thus moral value possesses an inner structure; the individual parts are not merely added to one another, they are members of a whole. We find this in Scotus and also in St. Thomas as well; "the degree of goodness and evil in moral acts is threefold: first this goodness comes from the object, then from the circumstances, and thirdly from the right virtuous intention." [17] Since the virtuous intention has the right end in view, the end is really the forming principle in the whole structure.

The order of values and ends is proposed to the will by the intellect. Now the statement, the good depends on the object and on the right end, is developed to mean that moral goodness of the will depends on the conformity to the order of reason.[18] Aquinas goes farther in the development of this idea when he says that in a higher degree morality depends on conformity with the eternal law, and ultimately with God. By his very nature man carries within himself the seal of the divine intelligence in the form of the general principles of action according to which the ends and purposes of his strivings are measured.[19] The proximate rule for the acts of the will is the human reason; the supreme rule is the eternal law and the will of God

[15] *Ibid.*, 38, 1; *Summa theol.*, Ia IIae, q. 12, a. 1 ad 4; a. 2, 4, 9.
[16] *De malo*, II, 4 ad 11.
[17] *Ibid.*
[18] *In I Sent.*, 39, 2, 2; *De verit.*, V, 7; *Summa theol.*, Ia IIae, q. 18, a. 5; q. 19, a. 2 f.
[19] *Summa theol.*, Ia IIae, q. 91, a. 2.

that it gives expression to. The moral act derives its quality from its agreement or non-agreement with some norm. This norm and rule is derived ultimately from God and is expressed in the *lex aeterna*. Human reason is able to comprehend this norm; indeed much of the order of value and worth is revealed in natural happenings which are governed by divine law. The moral phenomenon is only part of the universal world phenomenon.

According to the theistic, teleological, and Christian view, the universe is the realization of the good and value contained in a pre-world idea. This good or value of things existed in the divine mind before it was realized in the world. God had already thought the ideas of all things, He had apportioned to each a measure of being and to each stage in being He gave a certain value, He endowed each grade with His love and made it lovable. Thus the order of the universe was established by God. According to the degree with which things approach to God, they possess greater or less value, they are *magis et minus bonum et verum et nobile,* they manifest greater or less perfection according to how they reflect the divine being.

The goodness of things is founded in the forms of being, and these represent a hierarchy with their various powers, faculties, and relations. The development of the essential forms in things through their innate tendencies to movement is the realization of the world plan, that is, what is to be done according to the divine ordinance. Man is a part of this great actualization of being. Led by his natural inclinations, man knows many tasks commanded by the natural law, he knows many genuine human values, such as self-preservation, marriage, the procreation of children, community life, right and justice on which community life rests, the knowledge of truth and of God.[20]

3. The order of the reason and the order of the will. Goethe's criticism of Kant's ethics, that it never reached objects, cannot be applied to the Thomistic ethics. St. Thomas' ethics never loses sight of actuality. The value of things is not derived from our subjective evaluation of things, but exists of itself. The essential forms with their dispositions and teleological tendencies are the standards for measuring the value of things. Nevertheless St. Thomas had ample reason for stressing the importance of the order of reason. The will, it is true, is always by its nature intent on the good, but this good is always the good that is known. The order of reality must be known, it must become the

[20] *Ibid.,* q. 94. a. 2.

basis for a system of ordered truths intended for practical living if it
is to move the will. St. Thomas frequently repeated the statement
that a thing must first be known before it can move the will as something desirable, *nil volitum, nisi praecognitum.*

One of the primary notions for St. Thomas was this guidance of
the will by the reason as the *"propinqua et homogenea regula voluntatis."* [21] The good is comprehended by the intellect as the true, and the
true and the good include each other. Being is comprehended as good
and true by one and the same complex act, and the practical intellect
directs that which is known as good and true to some work.[22] The
comprehended order of reality can become the norm of action only
when it enters into relation with the will. The intellect lights the way
for the will. Thus a subjective order corresponds to the objective order, and this subjective order is twofold: the order of reason and on
it as its basis the order of the will, which is an order of our intentions,
of attraction and repugnance, of hate and love, of preference and rejection. Ultimately it is the reason that orders and the will that is
ordered.[23]

St. Augustine, whose symbol might well be a flaming heart, placed
love as the basic affection of the will, and in the will he discerned
that weight which determined the whole direction of human nature
(*pondus meum amor meus*). St. Thomas followed him in this view;
perhaps not with the same glowing fervor of personal experience but
still with the same understanding. Love belongs to the appetitive faculty. Since there are three stages in the appetite, he distinguished a
natural, sensitive, and spiritual love. The natural love is found in all
the powers of the soul since the good and beautiful is lovable for all
beings. Everything has a natural inner connection with all that conforms to its own nature.

This natural urge or love is perfected when it is elevated to the
sphere of the order of reason. Here love becomes the mainspring of
human activity. All activity takes place because of some purpose, but
the purpose is always loved, and that which is loved is always something valuable or at least apparently valuable. In agreement with St.
Augustine and Dionysius, St. Thomas declared that man always acts
because of some kind of love, *ex aliquo amore.* This becomes clearer

---

[21] *Contra Gent.*, III, 9, 107.
[22] *Summa theol.*, Ia, q.79, a.11 ad2.
[23] *Ibid.*, IIa IIae, q.26, a.1 ad2 f.

when we reflect that all the other passions, such as sadness, joy, and desire, arise from love.[24]

St. Augustine spoke of virtue as the order of love inasmuch as man joyfully assents to the hierarchical structure of ends and purposes and accepts this order as the principle of his activity.[25] St. Thomas adopted this formula, and stated that by virtue our love is ordered and that an ordered affection belonged to every cardinal virtue. Out of right love come a right will and good deeds; perverted love and distorted preferences are an offense against the universal moral order. The natural order has a close connection with the moral order, and from the observance of the natural order arises the morality of the will. Thus we have the proposition: *lex aeterna est ratio divina vel voluntas Dei ordinem naturalem conservari jubens et pertubari vetans.*[26]

Since the times of Origen, St. Augustine, and Peter Lombard, the order of love has been a favorite subject in Christian ethics. St. Thomas did not escape this tradition. Man looks on all the objects in the world with his inner faculty of participation. All things are good, but they are not equally good. The higher must be preferred to the lower, and on the pinnacle of the order of love is God, the highest good and the common good of all. Since God is the principle of all good, man must love Him more than himself and all other beings with a beneficent and appreciative love. Man loves himself inasmuch as he shares in the divine goodness, and in himself man must prefer the spiritual goods to the corporeal goods. In themselves the corporeal goods are higher than the external goods.

With respect to the order of love that affects persons, man must love himself more than his neighbor. This is simply the order of nature: that a thing first perfects itself and then shares its own perfection with others. The order of love is built on the order of nature which it perfects. Self-love comes before the love of neighbor for another reason: if self-love is based on self's participation in the divine goodness, then the neighbor is also to be loved because he is joined to this divine goodness. The neighbor is to be loved according to his proximity to God, i.e., according to his perfection. Divine justice demands that we wish for everyone happiness according to his

[24] *Ibid.*, Ia IIae, q. 26, a. 1 ad 3.
[25] *De civ. Dei*, XV; *De doctr. christ.*, I, 27; *De mor. eccl.*, 15.
[26] St. Augustine, *Cont. Faustum Man.*, XXII, 27.

degree of perfection. The neighbor is to be loved more intimately the more closely he is related to us, and persons are closer to us the more they have an essential and not only an accidental relation to us. Therefore blood relatives are to be loved more affectionately and are to be supported more than strangers, friends are to be loved more than enemies, the common good of many more than the private good of one individual, provided this good is in the same sphere.

In another place St. Thomas divides the order of love into the blood community, home community, state community, war comradeship, Christian church community; and he adds that, depending on the viewpoint, each of these may receive the preference. Thus we support blood relatives in the preservation of life, we assist our fellow citizens in matters of the civil community, we support our fellow soldiers in those things that pertain to war. Our friendship for our blood relatives is the more natural, original, and firmer affection, even though our attachment to others may seem stronger in other respects.

In self-love as well as in the love of neighbor, the inner spiritual man must be loved more than the external, corporeal man; and certainly the spiritual man is to be loved more than mere material things. Our neighbor's spiritual welfare is higher than the welfare of our own body. With respect to the constitution of our nature, our bodies are closer to our souls, but with respect to the participation in salvation we are closer to the soul of our neighbor than to our own bodies.

St. Thomas also sought to establish an order in the love of blood relatives. Origen had arranged the order in a descending scale: God, parents, children, servants; St. Ambrose and St. Albert required the greater love for the parents; but St. Thomas made a distinction. With respect to the object of the love, the father is to be loved more than the children because of his greater resemblance to God, since he is the procreating principle; but with regard to the closer union, the children are to be loved more than the parents.

Because of the Aristotelian theory of procreation, St. Thomas was misled to require a greater love for the father than for the mother. As the effective and forming principle in procreation, the father is superior to the mother, who is only the passive principle providing the formless matter. Viewed objectively, the parents as principles are to be loved more than the spouse. Ultimately, however, St. Thomas made some compensation by saying that the greater love belonged to the spouse, and the greater reverence to the parents. The attributes of the soul require us to love the better stranger more than the worse relative.

Since God is the greatest good and since all other things are loved because of Him, and since things are to be loved according to their relation to God, the goods of grace are to be loved more than all temporal goods. One act of grace excels all the natural goods of the universe. The order of love continues into the next world and there, too, God is loved above all else, and others are to be loved according to their proximity to God, *totus ordo dilectionis beatorum observabitur per comparationem ad Deum.* The fact of blood relationship and other reasons for preference recede into the background. If they remain at all they are changed into love determined by closeness to God.[27]

St. Thomas speaks of a threefold order in the human will. The first of these arises from reason and consists in the regulation of our actions and affections; the second order is derived from the divine law which is the norm for all human relations; the third order is that which governs man's relations with his fellow man. Aquinas was aware of the fact that these three orders do not exclude one another, and that the third is readily seen to be a part of the first. An offense against the order of reason or against the divine law constitutes for St. Thomas the essence of sin. He made use of this threefold division of orders because they afforded him a convenient basis for the groups of sin. Each offense against these orders is based on a perverted love and is a sin (*peccatum est actus inordinatus*).[28]

From this inordinate love arise sins against God, against self, and against the neighbor; the right love, however, finds expression in the three theological virtues, in the virtues of self-control and fortitude and justice. At St. Augustine before him, St. Thomas taught that evil has no autonomous reality, thus opposing the error of the Manichaeans. A natural evil in itself does not exist and cannot exist in God's creation. Evil is indeed non-being, but it is not negation; it is rather a lack of the good (*privatio boni*). A thing is evil when it lacks that perfection that it should have by reason of its nature. And an act is evil when the object of the act is in conflict with the nature of

27 *In III Sent.*, 29, 1; *Summa theol.*, Ia IIae, q. 113, a. 2; IIa IIae, q. 25, a. 7; q. 26, a. 1–13.
28 *De malo*, I, 3; II, 2.

him who does the act. Evil or sin is a defection from the order of
reason, which is the same as the divine order of the universe; it is
an act of the free will which robs man of his dignity and degrades
him to an animal servitude.[29] Every sin arises from the rejection of
some higher good and the preferring of some lesser good, and ultimately inordinate self-love is the cause of every sin.[30] The evil of
punishment is opposed to only a part of the order of the universe,
but the evil of guilt is contrary to the order of the whole universe.[31]
With Aristotle, St. Thomas declared that disorder (*peccatum*) enters
into all natural, artificial, and voluntary acts only because something
has not attained the end to which it was directed, because the
act lacks the proper order, form, and measure. When there is a defection from order in the natural law, it occurs from necessity, but
in acts of the will the defection is voluntary. Thus the defect of the
will takes on the aspect not only of sin but also of guilt.[32]

About this question of evil, St. Thomas was able to find much in
the writings of St. Augustine. He learned there, for instance, that
every disturbance of the order of nature must be punished, that
the punishment of sin is itself a part of the order of the universe, that
different orders of punishment must correspond to the different orders of good, and that evil does not disturb the order of the world in
every respect but makes a certain contribution to the harmony of
the universe.[33] St. Augustine, and St. Thomas too, ventured to justify
the existence of evil in the universe because of certain ontological, religious, historical, and metaphysical viewpoints. Having optimisti-
cally affirmed the goodness of all being in the axiom, *ens et bonum
convertuntur,* they went further in coordinating evil in the realm of
being and allowing it to play a part in the significance of history.
St. Thomas' theodicy is not only possible on the ground of his theory
of order, it is really required by it.

4. The order of good and the order of purposes. Since ancient
ethics was concerned with the order of goods and values, it tried to

---

[29] *Contra Gent.,* III, 140; *Summa theol.,* Ia, q.48, a.1 ad 2.
[30] *Contra Gent.,* III, 109 f.; *Summa theol.,* Ia IIae, q.77, a.4; q.84, a.1 f.
[31] *De pot.,* VI, 1 ad 8.
[32] *In I Sent.,* 48, 1; *De malo,* II, 2. In the work *De malo,* St. Thomas clarifies this
use of the word "sin" (*peccatum*). Evil exists when a subject or act lacks order or
form; sin exists when some act of nature, art, or morals lacks form or order; and
finally guilt is present when the sin is voluntary.
[33] *De civ. Dei,* XIX, 13; *Ench.,* 11.

establish a table of values. Some commentators thought that the Thomistic system of ethics, so strongly influenced by the teleology of Aristotle, had departed from the ethics of good and value. As a matter of fact, it cannot be denied that in St. Thomas the idea of purpose and end is decisive, and that the principle, *agere propter finem,* is the fundamental law of all happenings, and also of all human activity. The determination of an ultimate end, in whose service all other ends are subordinated as means, and the establishment of an order of intention and an order of execution, are important parts of the Thomistic ethics. Nevertheless the difference between an ethics of good and the ethics of St. Thomas is non-existent when we recall that St. Thomas identifies good and end and purpose. The object of the will is the end and the good, but the end has the character of good, and the highest good is synonymous with the ultimate end.

A thing can be the object of willing because it has value; it can be an end because some good, real or apparent, is seen beneath the end. This emphasis of the teleological relation of good does not endanger the objectivity of good.

In setting up its list of goods, ancient ethics studied human goods and put them in a certain order. Plato and Aristotle made use of an old division, based on the chief components of human nature, and distinguished between the goods of the soul and those of the body, and with the latter they associated external goods. St. Thomas adopted this table of goods. In the first place are the goods of the soul, which ornament the inner man. Among these are the virtues and also all those things that foster virtue. Above all else the happiness that comes from the practice of virtue is listed here. A certain order is also found among the virtues themselves. After the spiritual goods come the goods of the body (strength, health, and beauty), since the body exists for the soul in the natural order. All goods, purposes, and the whole universe form a hierarchy, and this hierarchy finds expression in the division of goods into those that are desirable for their own sake, those that are desired for the sake of gain, those that are desired for the satisfaction of the subject (*honestum, utile, delectabile*).[34]

Even in ancient ethics external goods played no insignificant part, since it is impossible, or at least difficult, to attain the morally beautiful without the assistance of certain means. Although Plato and the

---

[34] *Summa theol.,* Ia, q.5, a.6.

Socratics did not value external things as highly as Aristotle, the importance of possessions for moral living was not lost sight of in the Attic period. Aside from the advantage for establishing personal independence, for which the liberty-loving Greek had a keen sense, personality could be more easily developed and the right attitude maintained toward fatherland and friends if the individual had possessions. The ancient Greek clearly understood the moral dangers that followed on the lack of possessions. The social problem was seen to be a moral problem. In his *Politics,* Aristotle said succinctly: "Poverty engenders civil war and crime."

The ancients were also aware of the dangers of wealth, and consequently the maxim was soon formed that only the right use of goods and a certain measure of riches would serve man's purpose. St. Thomas is no despiser of external goods; he knew how important they were for the support of life, for the development of personality, and for maintaining a state in life, and how helpful they were in practicing the duties of friendship and charity. The value of external goods is not, of course, a moral value, but they have a significance for morality. They are good when they further virtue; they are evil when they lead away from virtue. Virtue is sufficient in itself, but external goods contribute to the easier practice of virtue. In this connection, St. Thomas had wealth in mind; with respect to honor, and especially friendship, he was obliged to admit that these are not external but that they are a part of man's inner spiritual habit.[35]

External things have a profit and use value independent of their relation to morality. We can admit that moral acts have a material foundation in external goods because the moral relation is a relation to persons with respect to some valuable thing or relation. These material things take on a moral character only when they enter into a moral relationship.

St. Thomas also discusses the value of physical perfection, and he subordinates everything that is biological in the human make-up to man's spiritual welfare. If we are to determine the value of the goods of the body we must first determine the value of life. According to the way an era, a people, and a thinker value life, they reveal their own spirit. We need only observe the Greeks. Although St. Thomas does not discuss the matter expressly, he indicates clearly that life, health, and physical perfection are goods that mean much

[35] *In Joh.,* 4; *Contra Gent.,* III, 127, 129, 131, 133, 141.

for the person as well as for spiritual and moral perfection.[36] But they are certainly not the highest good.

The highest earthly good is virtue. The reproach has been directed against ancient ethics that it listed the virtues after the external goods. The reproach, if it has a foundation, strikes the medieval ethics, especially Thomistic ethics, as well, since St. Thomas adopted the ancient division. But the reproach is without foundation. Virtue is a good not only inasmuch as it represents a good for another man; virtue is rather a good for him who possesses the virtue, since it represents the essential perfection of his person. If virtue is what makes a man good, then it is a good for man.[37]

Among spiritual goods, eudaemonia takes the first place because it really consists in virtuous living. Virtuous living in this world is only a means to an end, a means to attaining happiness here on earth and especially in heaven. Objectively God is the highest good, who by His infinite value is alone able to fulfill perfectly the activity of a human person. Subjectively the highest human good is that happiness which consists, not in the love and fruition of God, as St. Augustine, St. Bonaventure, and even St. Albert the Great said, but in the intellectual vision of God (*visio divinae essentiae*). It consists, therefore, in the activity of what is most perfect and highest in us, our intellect. Hence the subject of happiness is not the will but the intellect; but concomitantly the love of God is effected immediately and directly by the knowledge of God.

St. Augustine distinguished between goods of enjoyment and goods for use. God as the highest and unchangeable good is the object of enjoyment, and by enjoyment St. Augustine meant the loving attachment to an object for its own sake. As a true Aristotelian, St. Thomas could not share St. Augustine's viewpoint. Because of its intrinsic worth the intellect is above the will, and psychologically the intellect is the mover of all the soul's activities, even of the will, because it presents to the will its object. Thus the end of the intellect is also the end of all other human activity; the last end of all human living is the knowledge of God.

Man is prepared for his union with God by a process of adaptation in this life, and this process includes in itself the realization of many

---

[36] *De reg.*, I, 15; *In VII Eth. Nic.*, 13 f.; *Contra Gent.*, III, 26–37.
[37] *Summa theol.*, IIa IIae, q. 68, a. 1 ad 1.

values. Man can attain his highest subjective good only through a union with the highest objective good.

With respect to happiness, morality possesses the primacy, even though happiness has an intimate connection with morality. The relationship between morality and happiness, with which Kant had wrestled vainly, is ontologically and psychologically explained by St. Thomas, since the fundamental urge to perfect happiness can be satisfied only by making human life morally good. Only moral good has happiness in its train.

This eudaemonist turn of Thomistic ethics and religion is something entirely secondary. Like the other Scholastics, St. Thomas knew that joy and happiness are concomitant values. The good man is concomitantly a happy man and not vice versa. The essence of happiness arises from the union with the absolutely good, final end.[38] Reward and punishment, sometimes excessively stressed in Christianity, are incorporated into this relation by St. Thomas; they are phenomena that follow according to the laws of nature (*poena consequitur peccatum*). "Since sin is an inordinate act, every one that sins offends against some order. It is only a consequence if he himself is seized by this order; and this seizure is the punishment. The order that can be violated is threefold, and therefore the punishment is also threefold. Man is subject to the order of his own reason, the order of the community and the state, and the divine order of the universe. A threefold punishment corresponds to a violation of this threefold order; the reproach of conscience, punishment by human authority, and punishment by God." [39]

[38] *Ibid.*, Ia IIae, q. 2, a. 1–8; q. 3, a. 1–4; *Contra Gent.*, III, 25, 34.
[39] *Summa theol.*, Ia IIae, q. 87, a. 1.

CHAPTER XXX

VIRTUE AND ORDER

The goods and values listed in the various tables by philosophers do not have the same relationship to the moral man. Some of them refer to the value of the human person and signify man's moral habits. These are the virtues, *bona secundum naturam interiorem hominis,* which according to the well known Aristotelian axiom make both the person and his activities good. For the good of a human being as a human being consists in the perfect development of his rational faculty, and this consists partly in the proper relation to God, partly in the knowledge of truth, and partly in the ordering of the lower appetite by the reason and in the right use of external things. The whole treatise on virtues, which is the kernel of the Thomistic system of ethics, is permeated by the thought of order: virtue is ordered love, and virtue is an ordination to the good; sin, on the other hand is an offense against the order of reason.[1]

1. **The definition of virtue.** Virtue is a habit that makes the person and his works good; it perfects the faculties of knowledge and willing.[2] This Platonic-Aristotelian description of virtue, which is often repeated by St. Thomas, forbids the identification of virtue with the natural disposition to virtue, or the Socratic identification with knowledge. St. Thomas does not undervalue the germs of virtue which are innate in every man by nature, and with respect to these germs of virtue he distinguishes between the general dispositions to virtue that are given to every man as a rational being, and the individual dispositions that are given along with the structure of the individual

---

[1] *In III Sent.,* 33, 2; *Contra Gent.,* III, 25–40; *De virt.,* I, 7–13; *Summa theol.,* Ia IIae, q. 55, a. 1–3; IIa IIae, q. 44, a. 8.
[2] *Ibid.,* Ia IIae, q. 55, a. 1.

person. These general dispositions consist in rational principles of
the intellectual and moral virtues and in a natural direction of the
will toward the good. The individual dispositions consist in the better or worse disposition to certain virtues, depending on physical
qualities or on the influence of the heavenly bodies.[3]

The dispositions to virtue must be cultivated, and the habit of
virtue is acquired only by corresponding activity; thus man becomes
just only by just actions. The quality of the habit depends on the
quality of the action. This delimitation of the concept of virtue was
adopted by St. Thomas from Aristotle and has been a part of the
Scholastic system since the time of Abelard and Peter of Poitiers.

According to the Thomistic system of ontology the concept of virtue implies the concept of order. A habit has a relationship to the nature of a being and also to the activities of this being; potency and
habit are ordered to the act as to their final completion and perfection. Virtue stands for the final perfection of a potency, a finish and
perfection for valuable action; it signifies all that man can come
to be, continual progress in value and in the end the highest achievements of human nature. The perfection of a potency consists in the
determination to act; and this determination is not present in the
beginning as in the natural potencies. Animals, for instance, have no
moral habits. This determination to act, this habit, is acquired by
activity. Such a habit, since it is a kind of inner tendency, has a
twofold relationship to the act; through it man receives the faculty
to do a good act and at the same time the proper use of this faculty.[4]

The habit of virtue directs the potencies of the soul to the good,
and it also is a habit of operation; thus it not only is a good habit
but is also productive of good. It is part of the essence of virtue that
through it man performs a moral act, consciously and infallibly, immediately and resolutely, without hesitation or difficulty. Thus man's
whole being is directed to the good, his consciousness, his will, his
intention, and his affection. This direction to the good is so essential
that there can be no question of the abuse of a virtue. Consequently
a virtue creates order since it produces an ordered action each time.
St. Thomas accepts the definition of St. Augustine: that virtue is a
quality of the soul which causes correct living, excludes every abuse,
and is effected in us by God without us. Later he was obliged to

[3] *Ibid.*, q.63, a.1; *De virt. in com.*, I, 8.
[4] *Contra Gent.*, III, 22; *De virt.*, 1–5.

add that the phrase "produced in us by God without our cooperation" referred only to the supernatural infused virtues.[5]

2. Division of virtues. St. Thomas did not establish his table of
virtues on the basis of an original study of the ethical reality. He
was influenced by a threefold tradition which was for the greater part
in alignment with the reality of life. This tradition included the
Pythagorean-Platonic doctrine of the four cardinal virtues, the far
more extensive Aristotelian system of virtues, and the Christian doctrine of supernatural virtues.

The division into the four cardinal virtues by Plato was made
from the viewpoint of the subject and is based on the different parts
of the soul inasmuch as wisdom is the virtue of the rational part
of the soul, courage the virtue of the irascible part, temperance the
virtue of the appetitive faculty, and justice is referred to the perfection of the entire soul. This does not imply, however, that the
difference in the direction to objects plays no part at all.

As is well known, Aristotle distinguished between two classes of
virtues, the intellectual virtues and the moral virtues. The intellectual
virtues consist in the activity of the intellect exclusively; the moral
virtues are based on the right relation of the irrational appetite to the
rational part of the soul and are activities of the composite of soul
and body. Aristotelian ethics was deeply impressed by the Platonic
division of the soul into rational and irrational parts, and this psychology is often quite evident.

Aristotle divides the intellect into the theoretical and practical intellects, depending on whether the intellect is concerned purely with
the knowledge of truth or with truth that is in harmony with right
appetite. Of the five intellectual virtues, three belong to the theoretical intellect, namely, science, understanding, and wisdom; art and
practical prudence belong to the practical intellect. Among the theoretical virtues Aristotle gives the highest praise to wisdom because
it is the union of science and understanding and because its character is purely theoretical. Wisdom also brings with it the highest
degree of happiness. The important virtue of the practical reason is
prudence, which plays a decisive part in the formation of the moral
virtues.

After the intellectual virtues Aristotle presents a great array of
moral virtues. If we were to compare the Platonic division with the

[5] *Summa theol.*, Ia IIae, q. 55, a. 4.

Aristotelian scheme of virtues, we would place wisdom among the intellectual virtues, while courage, temperance, and justice belong to the moral virtues. Aristotle manifestly extended the Platonic list of virtues and, because of his keener insight into the fullness and extent of moral living, he revealed many new phases of moral relationships. Besides the virtues of courage and self-control, he mentions liberality, magnanimity, love of honor, meekness, love of truth, friendliness, and politeness. All these virtues express a human relationship, and, since Aristotle was apparently led by the question about what the relationship touched, he based his classification on an objective rule, the difference of moral matter.

St. Thomas accepted this division into intellectual and moral virtues. He based the division on the fact that a virtue is the perfection of human activity, and since the intellectual and appetitive faculties are the principles of all human activity, every virtue belongs either to the intellectual or to the moral sphere. For St. Thomas, however, the moral virtues are virtues in the proper sense (*virtutes simpliciter*), because the act of the will is not only good *materialiter* but also *formaliter;* its object is the good from the viewpoint of the good.[6]

Among the theoretical virtues of the intellect, wisdom holds the first place. For Plato, who was not yet acquainted with the division into theoretical and practical reason, wisdom included theoretical and practical knowledge and was the best guide to true morality. Among the Stoics wisdom was the ideal of the scholar and the complete expression of all virtue.

Aristotle withdrew wisdom from the practical sphere and described it as the virtue of the wise man who is removed from the world and immersed in contemplation. St. Thomas adopted the Aristotelian view of wisdom. The theoretical virtue of understanding deals with basic principles, the virtue of science deals with the knowledge of particular spheres of being, and the virtue of wisdom deals with ultimate causes and reasons and is therefore the virtue of the highest metaphysical knowledge.[7]

If we consider the Latin word *sapientia,* or the root *sapere* ("to taste"), we might surmise that wisdom, *sapientia,* the virtue of tasting, would have the greatest proximity to reality. In reality, however, the virtue closer to actuality is the virtue of the practical reason,

---

[6] *In III Sent.*, 23, 1, 4.
[7] *Summa theol.*, Ia IIae, q. 57, a. 2.

prudence, which is important in the formation of the moral man. The Middle Ages declared that man to be wise for whom all things in the world tasted (appeared) as they really are, and medieval thought required a profound knowledge of reality and a realistic approach to the external world as the basis for morality. The virtue that accounted for the union of the imperative with this reality was prudence.

St. Thomas had a clear idea of the position of prudence in the system of virtues. Prudence is not a fortunate choice of name for this virtue, for it does not refer to a kind of cleverness or craftiness, but rather to a realistic attitude of the mind in practical living. The measure and standard that is received through knowledge from external things becomes the norm of action. Inasmuch as prudence determines what is morally good, it becomes the progenitor of moral virtues and the inner form of the virtues. By nature prudence is an intellectual virtue, but it deals with the same matter as do the moral virtues; and therefore St. Thomas assigned to prudence a middle place between the intellectual and moral virtues.

The moral virtues are distinguished as habits by their objects. Some moral virtues regulate actions as their object; others regulate affections and passions. Even Aristotle had distinguished the moral virtues according to whether the external or the internal life of man was being made subject to the order of reason. And also according to St. Thomas, two spheres of human activity are ordered: the external actions and the inner world of affections. Thus the order of reason is actualized in external circumstances and relations and in the assignment of what belongs to the neighbor, and it is also actualized in inner circumstances.

The doctrine of the four cardinal virtues handed down by a sacred tradition was something so firmly established and so replete with truth for St. Thomas that he considered a critical investigation of its origin or a justification of its existence equally superfluous. This doctrine was an important part of patristic ethics and by this route came into medieval ethics. The division of the virtues was made among the parts of the soul in such a way that prudence was attributed to reason, courage to the irascible appetite, self-control to the concupiscible appetite. Not all the Scholastics followed Plato in attributing justice to the whole soul; some, among them Philip the Chancellor and St. Albert, divided prudence into a reflective and a deciding virtue, assigning the first to reason and the latter to the will; others, including St. Thomas, simply assigned justice to the will.

St. Thomas labored to show that the four cardinal virtues arise from their formal principles and also from the subject of virtues. The formal principle of virtue is the good of reason. If we view this good in the intellect itself we have the virtue of prudence, if we view the order of reason as it is actualized we have the virtue of justice when activities are regulated, and self-control and courage when the passions are ruled. If we begin with the subject of virtues, we again have four cardinal virtues: prudence belongs to the reason, justice, temperance, and courage to the will, the appetite, and the irascible part. They are called cardinal virtues because they possess the characteristic of virtues in a pre-eminent degree.

Justice, in the narrower sense, deals with equality and proportion and it regulates the relationship to others; in its essence it consists in giving to every man his due. Justice signifies the perfection of the human community. This objective aspect of justice stands out more prominently in St. Thomas than the act of the person. With Aristotle, St. Thomas distinguishes several forms of justice: a general justice (legal justice) and a particular justice; and the latter has two divisions, commutative and distributive justice. This division is not a mere academic exercise; it corresponds to the essential structure of the community which manifests a threefold relationship: the relation of the members among themselves, the relation of the whole to the members, and the relation of the members to the whole. The first relationship is governed by commutative justice, which proceeds on the principle of arithmetical proportion. The second relation is governed by distributive justice, which proceeds according to geometric proportion and distributes according to worth and merit. The third relation is ordered by legal justice.

In its broader sense justice embraces all the legal relations of a community and thus all the virtues that refer to the commonweal. Aristotle incorporated that concept of justice into his ethics, and St. Thomas realized the importance of morality in public life and relations. Like Aristotle he highly valued legal justice. Although St. Thomas was firm in determining the obligations of the individual person toward the community, he did not lose sight of the perfection of the individual, which is indeed the presupposition for the perfection of the commonwealth. Inasmuch as justice may refer to obligations due to God, parents, the country, and benefactors, we have special forms of that virtue: religion, piety toward parents, patriotism, gratitude to benefactors, reverence, and homage.

The good does not come to man without effort; it is not without reason called the arduous good, *bonum arduum*. It is the task of the moral virtues to impose measure and limits and to restrain the onslaught of the passions and protect the good of reason. This thought recurs again and again in St. Thomas' writings, especially when he speaks of temperance and courage, both of which serve to regulate the affections. St. Thomas recognized how important fear is in human life and how it is able to keep the will from being subject to the intellect. Courage has as its object fear of difficulties, especially the fear of death. Courage may come into play either in the act of attack or in submission and endurance. Resoluteness and perseverance, as well as the readiness to make an attack, belong to the essence of the virtue of courage. The virtue of self-control is the virtue that puts a bridle on the passions of the sensitive appetite, on the natural desires and urges to self-preservation and to the preservation of the species, the accompanying pleasures, and the satisfactions of the sense of touch.[8]

As a realist St. Thomas knew the importance of the passions in the development of the whole man and in the formation of the moral man. As movements of the irrational appetite, the passions are morally indifferent; they become good or bad according to their subordination to the reason and the will. The affections and passions are the centrifugal power of the soul, they are the root of emotional life and the basis of the development of the personality. They are material that must be formed. Therefore St. Thomas opposed the Stoics, who taught that the passions and affections were evil and that they must be killed off.[9] St. Thomas required that the life of the affections and their development be brought under the regimen of the reason and that an inner order be established; he also required that man hold dominion over himself and that inner harmony be established, or rather be re-established, such as man possessed before the Fall. Because of his Christian viewpoint, St. Thomas did not teach that human nature was evil in its roots and in its emotional life; he taught that man lost his original justice and that then disorder arose among

[8] *Ibid.*, IIa IIae, q. 141, a. 1–3.
[9] *Ibid.*, Ia IIae, q. 24, a. 1–3.

the powers of the soul because of original sin, that the will and especially the lower appetite were damaged. These powers must now be regulated and controlled by reason and the Christian law.[10] In the *Theological Summa*,[11] St. Thomas declared that man's good actions are carried out in conjunction with the passions, *"bona autem operatio hominis est cum passione."*

Thus St. Thomas incorporated the emotions and passions into the moral structure. The view of the Stoics in this matter appeared to him to be an apathy that was worse than criminal, and here he was in agreement with St. Augustine.[12] St. Thomas went farther in overcoming the traditional rigorism of some of his predecessors, such as Origen and St. Ambrose, by recognizing the value of natural things even in the ascetical life. Sometimes St. Augustine, too, who generally tried to be just in his evaluation of this world, condemned earthly things in a way that St. Thomas could not approve. Thus St. Augustine, and St. Jerome too, joined the sexual and corporeal with the sinful in a way that seemed to St. Thomas unjustified. He understood that it was praiseworthy if a man practiced self-denial for reasons of health or religion, but he thought that for the sake of his own welfare and that of the race man must sometimes be permitted certain necessary pleasures. The flight from all pleasures, he said, was the vice of insensibility.[13]

The virtues have manifold relations with each other, some are presuppositions for others, some again include other virtues within themselves. Some virtues coincide in their purposes and in their effects but differ in their motives; some are occasions for others, some are the roots of others, while some are causes of other virtues. Some virtues and vices are renowned for their progeny; we need only read St. Thomas' articles about the progeny of anger, avarice, gluttony, and luxury. Those are called progeny of a virtue or a vice which serve the same purpose as the principal vice or virtue.[14] The principal virtues and vices are, as it were, the generals, while the virtues and vices that spring from them are the army (St. Gregory the Great).

When St. Thomas reduced the great diversity of moral virtues to the three cardinal moral virtues, he made a step that was not in every

---

[10] *Ibid.*, q. 82 f.
[11] *Ibid.*, q. 59, a. 5 ad 3.
[12] *De civ. Dei*, IX, 5; XIV, 9.
[13] *Summa theol.*, IIa IIae, q. 142, a. 1 ad 2.
[14] *Ibid.*, q. 118, a. 8; q. 128, a. 6 f.; q. 132, a. 4 f.; q. 148, a. 3 ad 2, 5, 6.

respect fortunate. This effort toward simplification contained in it the danger of obliterating the differentiation of the good that Aristotle had revealed. St. Thomas distinguishes between three kinds or parts of virtues: integral parts, as it were, elements of which the virtues are composed; subjective parts, the parts of virtues which are determined by the objects; and the potential parts, those which coincide with the principal virtue and must be attributed to it formally. These attaching virtues are classed with the principal virtue inasmuch as they apply the characteristic of the principal virtue to a secondary matter. The essence of justice consists in the creation of an equality; the essence of courage in the strengthening of the soul, and the essence of temperance in the bridling of the most vehement urges of the sense of touch.[15]

When St. Thomas brought the integral parts of virtues into relief, he was acting on the correct knowledge that virtues are complex things, that they have a fundamental relation to one another, and that some virtues are included in others. Courage and temperance, if we view their whole phenomenon, are seen to have included in them other virtues than those we might suppose from their definitions. Courage that tends to attack and aggression, is permeated with the virtues of self-confidence and great daring; while courage that persists has the virtues of patience and endurance woven into it. St. Thomas even finds that anger is a part of courage. Temperance is accompanied by the moral horror of anything shameful, and a sense of decency and a love of the beautiful.[16]

In revealing the integral parts of virtues, St. Thomas did much for a proper understanding of the structure of virtues, and when he distinguished the potential parts of virtues he stood on sure ground. In some of his divisions he may have gone too far in detail, as, for instance, when he derived theft, robbery, and murder from violations of the virtue of justice which included the worship of God, reverence, homage, gratitude, and obedience. He distinguished these virtues by the degree or difference of what was due another, and no doubt some justification exists for that reason; but other values and considerations are included in these virtues, as reverence, homage, worship of God, and gratitude. He rightly designates fidelity as a part of

---

[15] *Ibid.*, q. 157, a. 3; q. 161, a. 4 ad 2 f.
[16] *Ibid.*, q. 128, a. 1; q. 143, a. 1.

justice., since it signifies the carrying out of a contract or promise.[17]
He admits that truthfulness is a part of justice only by association.
In truthfulness there is a kind of equality in the agreement of what
is said with what is in the mind, and, as St. Thomas thought together with Cicero, not in the agreement of what is said with the actual
state of things. When a man is in error he does not offend against
truthfulness, even though what he says does not agree with the concrete thing. To say that truthfulness protects the mutual confidence
of men and thus supports well-ordered life in a community is true
but it is not the decisive matter in this instance; all the moral virtues
have the same relation to the common good. St. Thomas even subsumes the Ten Commandments under the virtue of justice.

When St. Thomas declared that one man owes another truthfulness in his speech *ex honestate,* we might say that under truthfulness
many other personal considerations are to be found, such as a certain
inner decency, self-respect; and finally truthfulness has a relation
with courage and bravery. In speaking of liberality as an appendix
of justice, St. Thomas himself admitted that it is not a species of
justice and that only a minimum of the characteristic of justice can
be found in it. The two marks which St. Thomas regarded as distinguishing justice—external things as the matter and a relationship
to others—do not enter into liberality at all. Liberality gives when no
obligation exists, *ex quadam decentia.*[18]

St. Thomas included the virtue of magnanimity in the divisions
of courage inasmuch as it represents the strengthening of the mind
in the attainment of what is difficult. But this is hardly a correct
description of that virtue which includes ideas of the right appreciation of moral values and a flight from what is ignoble. Aristotle had
pointed out that this virtue of magnanimity includes in itself a whole
system of virtues. St. Thomas is equally unconvincing when he
speaks of grandiosity as a part of courage by a piece of ingenious reasoning.[19]

No one will deny that humility is connected with modesty and
temperance. But it includes many other things, as may be seen in
the twelve degrees of humility enumerated by St. Benedict, which

[17] *Ibid.,* q. 58.
[18] *Ibid.,* q. 109, a. 1, 3.
[19] *Ibid.,* q. 134, a. 4.

St. Thomas himself quotes.[20] It is equally difficult to agree that the desire of knowledge is a part of temperance.[21] Every grouping of virtues and moral values in any system of ethics has its defects; even St. Thomas, the great coordinator, was unable to master this matter completely.

Above the natural virtues are the supernatural virtues (faith, hope, and charity) infused by God, which are required that man may attain his supernatural end. They are directed principally to the last end and therefore they are virtues in the perfect sense. They merge into one another within a sacred circle; love strengthens hope and these two again strengthen faith, and at the same time they form the foundation for the Christian virtues and bring about their elevation to the sphere of grace.

By faith we have certain knowledge of the first truth and all other truths founded in it, and this knowledge surpasses all natural knowledge. In hope our will, relying on divine assistance, is directed to the highest good and eternal happiness. Love reaches out to God Himself and in Him it finds its rest. By love the will is united to its end and it is spiritually changed into the end. Love directs all actions to God as the last end and lays the foundation for a true friendship with God. Since the form of an action is derived from the end and purpose, love is the essential form of all virtues. Further, since infused prudence cannot exist without love, and since all the moral virtues are derived from prudence, love is shown to be the root of all virtuous living. In the order of perfection love holds the first place and faith the last place. The development of the supernatural life begins with the acts of faith and culminates in the acts of love; while the destruction of the supernatural life begins with the loss of love and is completed with the loss of faith: *Quod est primum in constructione, est ultimum in resolutione.*[22]

In thus emphasizing the prominent place of love in his teaching on the supernatural virtues, St. Thomas remains faithful to ancient tradition. In his presentation, however, some minor changes may be noted. As an Aristotelian he did not share the rigorism of St. Augustine, who connected all true morality with supernatural love and in one of his extreme moments exclaimed that the virtues of the

---

[20] *Ibid.*, q. 161, a. 6.
[21] *Ibid.*, q. 166, a. 1 f.
[22] *Ibid.*, q. 1–26; q. 23, a. 3–8; q. 34, a. 5; Ia IIae, q. 62, a. 3 f.; q. 65, a. 2.

pagans were no more than brilliant vices. At the same time love, according to St. Thomas, is somewhat changed, not with respect to
its object, but with respect to its content and nature. St. Augustine's
love of God was a love of fruition, so also it was for St. Albert. But
for St. Thomas this most sublime gift of grace that may be developed
into infinity was a love that was mutual and benevolent, an absolute
and unreserved surrender of the creature to God, a love purely because of the divine goodness and perfection. Although he sometimes
speaks of the fruition of God, he really teaches a purer form of the
love of God that makes him more akin to St. Bernard of Clairvaux
than to St. Augustine. The happiness of the next life is a minor end,
a *finis sub fine,* and the desire for this happiness is an act of hope
and not of love. The subject of love is the will, and love develops
in three stages: freedom from sin, progress in good, and union with
God.[23]

3. **Virtue and the practical reason.** In man we find the chaotic and
that which is ordered. Matter is the chaotic element, while the order
comes from man's creative principle, his practical reason; and from
this principle too, comes virtue.

This conviction is a part of all the ancient philosophical schools,
sometimes in the sense of a strict intellectualism as in Socrates and
the Stoics, sometimes blended with voluntarist elements as in Plato,
Aristotle, and the Neoplatonists. This conviction of the function of
the practical reason in man is found throughout the Thomistic system. As in Aristotle, here too, there is a blending of the intellectual
and the voluntarist view. According to the former view the intellect
is the sole foundation for virtue; reason is the cause and the root of
all virtue, in it are all the germs of all the virtues. Moral action is
really action in conformity with reason. The first principle of all
human action is the intellect, and whatever other principles of action may be found in man they must all obey reason in some way.
St. Thomas goes so far as to say that the virtue of the appetitive
faculty is no more than a form imprinted by the reason on the sensitive appetite. The true human good is the good of the intellect, and
by this standard all other goods and virtues are judged.[24] The high
valuation of the intellect in the structure of human personality cor-

---

[23] *In II Sent.,* 38, 1, 2; *Summa theol.,* IIa IIae, q. 17, a. 8; q. 24, a. 6; q. 26, a. 3 ad 3.
[24] *De virt.,* 4 ad 3; *Contra Gent.,* III, 9; *Summa theol.,* Ia, q. 18, a. 5; q. 19, a. 1 ad 3;
Ia IIae, q. 61, a. 2; q. 66, a. 1; IIa IIae, q. 47, a. 6.

responds to its high position in the structure of the moral person. If we wish to understand the importance of the intellect for virtue and morality, we must understand the various functions of the intellect.

4. **Synteresis.** This habitual knowledge and the virtue of the practical reason (prudence) play important and decisive roles in the actualization of the order of the universe. Of these two, synteresis is the more important. By its very nature the will tends to the good, says St. Thomas. In each person there is natural disposition to virtue, and this disposition needs perfecting. The perfecting of this virtue takes place under the tempering of reason. Reason chooses the right means, and thus it appears that prudence is active in the very beginning and perfects virtue with its ordinating activity.[25] Sometimes St. Thomas seems to have in mind an original knowledge of the good rather than an original tendency of the will to the good. In reality, however, the direction of the will to the good is bound up with the original knowledge of the good. St. Thomas acknowledges an original tendency to the good in the intellect as well as in the will. In the will there is a natural inclination to a good end or purpose, and in the practical reason are present certain innate and connatural ends, *innati fines connaturales homini.*[26] Just as the theoretical reason forms the concept of being as its first concept, and as in the intellect certain principles lie ready for use, so the practical reason comprehends the concept of the good in an original act. From this arises a special habit of the mind, called synteresis, the knowledge of the first moral principles. These principles are known unmistakably, immediately, as if they were innate.[27]

As its first and universal principle, the practical reason is illuminated by the principle: The valuable, the good is to be done; the evil is to be avoided.[28] This statement, this expression of a primary value judgment, is, according to St. Thomas, an analytical sentence. Its content is not against reason; the concept of the human good (*bonum humanum*) includes the notion that it be actualized without further reasoning. But St. Thomas does not stop with these generalities. Keeping in mind the idea of the human good, he determines good and evil in the sense that the good in any life is obedience to God.

---

[25] *De virt.,* 8 ad 1.
[26] *In III Sent.,* 33, 2, 4.
[27] *In II Sent.,* 24, 3, 2.
[28] *De verit.,* XVI, 1; XVII, 1; *Summa theol.,* Ia, q. 79, a. 12.

Reason judges all the inclinations of man to be good in themselves:
self-preservation, marriage, the rearing of children, community living, and the prerequisites for communal life, namely, respect for
right, justice, and the personality of the neighbor.

Moral knowledge starts with these natural inclinations, since they
are the object of the conscious activity of synteresis. At first the inclination rises from a natural source, but it is immediately subjected
to the light of reason which after a penetrating analysis approves
these movements as being connected with the development of man's
nature. Synteresis goes farther than mere generalities: all that is
prescribed or forbidden by the natural law is within its province.
Besides the fundamental and primary act of the practical reason in
which the concepts of good and bad are born, synteresis stands for
the moral consciousness, it signifies the first and original contact
with morality and with the unchanging standard by which all values
are measured. This primary and a priori apprehension of value in the
reason's fundamental act is continued by synteresis and applied to
the concrete objects presented in real life. If man did not by nature
possess the faculty of distinguishing between good and evil, the
basis for a judgment value and for making a choice would be lacking.

Here we are immediately faced by the question: Does the natural
reason always function correctly? St. Thomas points out that man
must reach a certain age before he understands the supreme moral
truths. He attributes the knowledge of the supreme moral principles
to all men who have attained the use of reason. A disordered reason, depraved inclinations, bad habits and evil dispositions, however,
will prevent man from drawing the proper conclusions from these
first moral principles.[29]

By this teaching of synteresis, St. Thomas made his own a nativist,
or rather a priori, teaching of tradition which is in entire accord with
the saying of the Apostle, that by nature the law is inscribed on the
heart of man.[30] Plato, Aristotle, the Stoics, and the Fathers of the
Church acknowledged a similar apriorism, though occasionally in
somewhat different form. St. Thomas was able to read about the
natural moral law in the heart of man in the writings of Tertullian,
St. Ambrose, St. Jerome, in the Augustine of the earlier period, as

[29] *Summa theol.*, Ia IIae, q.93, a.6; q.94, a.4.
[30] *In III Sent.*, 37, 1; *In IV Sent.*, 33, 1; *De verit.*, X, 6 ad 6.

well as in William of Auvergne, St. Bonaventure, and St. Albert. When he considers this moral habit together with the instinct of animals, from which he is careful to distinguish it, he wishes to point out its infallibility and the sureness with which it tends to its end.

When St. Thomas designates this moral knowledge as natural, he intends to express the manner of its origin in our intellects and also the relation of this knowledge to the orders of being and nature which are independent of us. He met with the idea of the innateness, at least of the germs of our knowledge of moral principles, wherever he turned, but the concept of synteresis did not enter medieval ethics until the twelfth century. Alexander of Hales and St. Bonaventure made use of the idea, but they made it a habit of the will, a natural inclination that strives for the good and rejects the evil, while the knowledge of the first universal moral principles and their application to individual instances are a habit of the intellect called conscience. St. Albert thought that the practical reason is the subject of synteresis, which as such is a faculty distinct from the will and the reason, and which knows the first moral principles and is an unerring judge of good and evil and of one's individual actions. Like St. Albert and St. Thomas, Duns Scotus defined synteresis as a function of the intellect. The inclination to good and the rejection of evil were attributed to the habit of synteresis, which was thus made to conform with the original inclination of the will.

To prudence St. Thomas assigned the twofold task of discovering the means to the ultimate ends and the application of the universal principles to the individual cases of life.[31] Synteresis and prudence often appear in the closest connection. But before we define prudence more exactly, we must first consider the close connection between synteresis and conscience. With St. Albert, St. Thomas taught that the application of universal principles to individual cases is the business of conscience. He does not mean that this always occurs in the form of a syllogism. Synteresis and conscience are related as habit and act, as the principle and its application. In its universal principles and as the first rule of conduct, synteresis is infallible and unfailing; conscience, however, which is a regulated rule, in its application to individual cases is subject to error. Conscience consists in the application of what we know to what we do. When the conscience considers an act before it is placed, it gives testimony, it obligates

[31] *Summa theol.*, IIa IIae, q. 47, a. 6 f.

us, and it urges us on; when it considers the act completed, it praises, it reproaches, it accuses, and causes pangs of regret.[32] Synteresis and conscience, therefore, are completely in the service of the order of the moral man.

If we follow this course of reasoning carefully, the fact that the functions of conscience and those of synteresis are partly quite similar, if not identical, cannot escape us. We must concede that the two different lines of thought, running parallel here in the Thomistic system, have not been harmonized. The doctrine of synteresis and conscience is derived from the medieval Christian tradition, whereas the doctrine of prudence and right reason comes from the Aristotelian theory. In adopting the Aristotelian doctrine of prudence, St. Thomas also adopted certain qualifications of the concept of conscience, and in his ethical system two principles run parallel, sometimes competing with each other, and always identical in their functions.

More important, however, than this dissonance that arises from different historical influences, is the following problem. The supreme and first comprehension of value by synteresis is: *Bonum est faciendum*, good must be done. Does St. Thomas here propose a rigorist doctrine in the sense that the good is always a binding command, and the greater good a still greater obligation? Do the series of values and the series of obligations run parallel? Does the good obligate of itself? Is there nothing ethically counselled? The Thomistic viewpoint is clear; "All evil, every sin, is to be avoided. Everything must positively be done that falls under the prescriptions of the natural law, namely, what the practical reason naturally recognizes to be a human good." [33] Among these obligations are the fundamental relations of man to himself, to his fellow man, to his community, and to God. In the same way, for a Christian the supernatural life of virtue in order that he may attain his last end, is an unconditioned obligation. Certain goods and values ought to be actualized in the human race, but these are not within the power of the individual or each individual, and certain goods are surpassed in obligation by other goods. With regard to these, no man can be obligated to what is beyond his ability. Even within the sphere of what he is able to do, man is not obligated to do the greater good;

---

[32] *Der verit.*, XVI, 2 f.; XVII, 1, 2 ad 7; *Summa theol.*, Ia, q. 79, a. 13.
[33] *Summa theol.*, Ia IIae, q. 94, a. 2.

he is not obligated to "heroic" action. St. Thomas' explanation of almsgiving also excludes any rigorism. He merely requires that what is moral may be done and that all that is evil is forbidden. The Scotist formulation of the supreme moral principle, "Each one must approve what is morally good, and disapprove what is morally wrong," excludes rigorism more radically, but is not actually different from the Thomist statement.[34]

The autonomy of conscience is not a discovery of modern times; it was an integral part of the ethics of Socrates, Plato, and Aristotle; during the Middle Ages it also occupied an important place. St. Thomas takes it for granted that conscience is the supreme instance and final court of human conduct. In order that man may submit to human authority he requires the approval of the judgment of conscience.[35] The command of a superior cannot be obeyed if conscience judges it to be evil.[36] Opposing Peter Lombard and agreeing with St. Bonaventure, St. Thomas decided that a man must rather submit to the sentence of excommunication than obey an ecclesiastical command against the dictate of his conscience.[37] According to St. Thomas, the autonomy of conscience is different from the autonomy taught by Kant. St. Thomas did not have in mind a conscience independent of everything else; the dictates of conscience give expression to the requirements of the natural law and the divine law, and the requirements of the objective order of the world.

According to St. Thomas, an erring conscience also obligates. The objective order and the subjective order are not always identical, and the erroneous conscience has a place in the moral order inasmuch as it issues its commands under the appearance of good, *sub aliqua ratione boni*. Only the guiltlessly erroneous conscience leads to good actions; if the error is the result of an act of the will only sinful actions result. Error is a sin when it is avoidable and when it refers to something that everyone should know.[38] The classical example of the obligation of an erroneous conscience is found in the *Summa theologica:*[39] Faith in Chirst is a good thing and necessary for salvation; but if a man, because of his erroneous conscience, should

[34] Scotus, *Oxon.*, IV, 14, 2, 11.
[35] *Summa theol.*, IIa IIae, q. 104, a. 1 ad 1.
[36] *De verit.*, XVII, 5 ad 4.
[37] St. Bonaventure, *In IV Sent.*, dub. 38; St. Thomas, *In IV Sent.*, 38.
[38] *De malo*, III, 6–8.
[39] Ia IIae, q. 19, a. 5.

think this faith in Christ to be an evil thing, he would be obliged
to shun it. St. Thomas has more to say about other restrictions within
the religious sphere when he treats the natural claims to freedom
of conscience.

To show the immense importance of the virtue of prudence in
the great ordered structure of morality, it will be best to have in mind
the Thomistic statement that two things are required for the goodness of human actions: a right purpose and the means to this end
or purpose. Man is directed to the right end partly by synteresis,
and partly by a well-ordered appetite. The task of judging the right
means to the end belongs to prudence. Just as the knowledge of first
principles by the intellect is the beginning of science, so synteresis
starts prudence in motion. Just as the knowledge of an art is the norm
of artistic activity, the *recta ratio factibilium,* so prudence is the norm
for moral actions, the *recta ratio agibilium,* and therefore prudence
is a constitutive element of moral virtue. When prudence begins to
function, the natural inclination toward virtue is elevated to conscious and perfect virtue.

The great general purposes are easily known; with respect to
these, error is not likely, but the fundamental moral values in life
are always actualized in particular persons and in particular circumstances. Here the illumination of the intellect is required for
the here and now instant and the discovery of the present good. It
is a habit of the practical reason that is alert to actualize the moral
good in particular instances.[40] Earlier St. Thomas had assigned to
synteresis the task of determining the supreme purposes and ends,
while prudence determined the means to these ends. Prudence, however, also determines ends, not the ultimate ends, but proximate ends
of particular actions. Prudence recognizes what is moral in an individual instance. Prudence keeps in view the general principles
furnished by synteresis, and then it weighs and reasons about the
end of this particular act and, considering the whole situation, it
decides which means are best to attain this end in these circumstances.
Thus the proximate purpose and the means to attain it are determined by prudence as it takes counsel, judges, and prescribes.[41]

Such is the function of prudence. If we recall that ethics is, after

[40] *De virt.,* 6.
[41] *In III Sent.,* 33, 2, 3; *Summa theol.,* Ia IIae, q. 58, a. 4; q. 66, a. 3 ad 3; IIa IIae.
q. 47, a. 6 ad 3; *De virt. card.,* 1 f.

all, the ethics of practical living in which means play such an important role, and that these means can be known only after a penetrating study of reality, we shall realize the importance of prudence in the establishment of the moral order. Evil is always a contradiction of the truth of reality; it opposes the knowledge of the truth of reality, and this knowledge is the function of prudence.

The chief function of prudence is the discerning of the golden middle of moral order wherein consists the essence of moral virtue. (*"Sine prudentia nulla virtus moralis esse potest, . . . inter alias virtutes est maxima, quia est moderatrix aliarum."*) [42] Relying on his wide experience in human affairs and conforming with a view deeply rooted in the Greek mentality, Aristotle judged that the essence of moral virtue consisted in the observance and maintenance of the right middle. The matters to be regulated are the affections and passions; excess must be controlled and suppressed, and deficiencies must be heightened and increased. Besides this, it is important to have these passions at the right time, with regard to certain persons, for certain reasons, etc. Besides the affections and passions, man's actions also must be regulated since they, too, may exceed proper bounds or fail to reach them.

Thus virtue is an attitude which is, of course, not always in the exact mathematical middle, but it is somewhere between the two extremes, sometimes nearer to one than the other. Aristotle did not extend this principle to the intellectual virtues, and he was obliged to abandon it with respect to the virtue of friendship, and later he was forced to acknowledge the restriction that certain affections and actions are intrinsically bad and therefore can have no right middle, such as adultery, murder, envy, and malicious pleasure at the misfortune of others. On closer examination we see that the term "right middle" is mostly figurative; the immediate circumstances of life, the when and wherefore, have no differences of quantity or intensity and cannot therefore be subjected to the principle of the right middle. At the same time Aristotle held that the value of virtue is something absolute, and not a medium value; with respect to its worth, virtue is an extreme. In his *Eth. Nic.* (II, 6), he expresses this distinction: "From the viewpoint of metaphysics and being, virtue is a middle; but viewed as a good, it is an extreme." Two things must be ob-

[42] *De virt. card.*, 3.

served, therefore, in virtue: the essential content and the moral value. The middle which we speak of is not a middle as to the moral value but with respect to the essential content.

St. Thomas introduces the Aristotelian definition of virtue in the following words: "Moral virtue signifies the fulfillment of an appetitive faculty by some determined matter. Reason is the norm and standard for the appetitive faculty. The goodness of that which is regulated consists in its conformity to the norm, just as the perfection of a work of art consists in its agreement with the rules of art. Evil consists in a departure from the norm, and this departure arises from the too-much or the too-little. Virtue consists in conformity to the norm of reason, and this conformity consists in the avoidance of the too-much and the too-little, in the right middle therefore." [43] St. Thomas accorded great importance to the proposition that goodness consisted in the right middle and conformity to a norm and he even subjected the intellectual virtues to this rule. Even in regard to the theological virtues he tried to salvage the principle, although he was obliged to admit, as was St. Albert, that with respect to the object of the theological virtues there can be no excess. He answered the question why one particular attitude is virtuous among many possible attitudes, by saying that this one alone conforms to the norm of reason. With regard to conformity to the norm of reason, virtue constitutes the golden middle, while the extremes are made up of the two vices. With regard to the matter, virtue possesses the character of the middle since it avoids the excess and deficiency.[44] Prudence discovers the right middle, moral virtue realizes it; what is prescribed by prudence is accepted by the moral intention.[45]

Prudence is not only a cognitive function; it is also a commanding virtue. It was described as such by Aristotle and the Stoics, by Cicero and William of Auxerre. According to St. Thomas, its functions are not exhausted in its counseling and judging of particular cases; its commands extend to the ultimate end of man. Because the moral value cannot come into existence without the command of prudence, St. Thomas concluded that the commanding function of prudence was characteristic, although Aristotle had taught that the counseling

---

[43] *Summa theol.*, Ia IIae, q.64, a.1; *De virt.*, 13.
[44] *Summa theol.*, loc. cit., ad 1.
[45] *In III Sent.*, 23, 1: *De virt.*, 13.

function was more important. Thus prudence is given a structure analogous to synteresis, which also consists of knowledge in the form of a command.

To establish harmony between the objective reality of things and the willing and acting of man, is the important task of prudence. In order to fulfill this duty, prudence possesses a distinctive inner structure, consisting of eight integral parts: memory, understanding, docility, aptitude, reasoning, providence, circumspection, and caution. Memory provides the basis for making the proper decisions in practical life, by preserving the experiences of the past. Understanding furnishes the supreme moral principles that are necessary for arriving at moral conclusions and also the knowledge of the proper immediate ends which serve as minor premises in the practical syllogism. Since the experience of each individual is limited, he tries to profit by the experience of other men, especially by the wise counsel of his elders. The readiness to be taught and to accept advice is called docility. This does not mean that the individual's judgment is superfluous. Independent investigation together with the faculty of making rapid decision constitutes mental agility. Reasoning refers to the moment of reflection, when the mind concludes from the known to the unknown. Circumspection takes care that the individual actions have the right relation to the end with respect to the immediate circumstances, and caution prevents an apparent good from becoming an end.

Whenever a thing is composed of a plurality of parts, one part always has the primary position, and the other parts are subordinate to this part, and the whole receives its unity from this primary part. Among the parts of prudence, this preferential position belongs to providence. The task of prudence is to order the particular actions of a man, and these actions are always in the future. Providence assumes the office of directing the ways and means which are determined by the other parts of prudence to the proper end. The concept of providence includes the idea of a proper ordering toward the purpose, and this in turn includes the ideas of wise counsel, correct judgment, and unerring command.[46]

As is his custom in the treatise on virtues, St. Thomas distinguishes between potential and subjective parts besides these integral parts. The subjective parts designate the various fields in which prudence

[46] *In III Sent.*, 33, 3; *Summa theol.*, IIa IIae, q. 49, a. 1–8.

is active. More important are the potential parts which St. Thomas introduces as adjunct virtues. These have subordinate acts to perform and remain subordinate to the principal virtue. The three subordinate virtues under prudence are eubulia, synesis, and gnome. The first signifies ample reflection; as one must collect his thoughts before writing so eubulia precedes prudence. A certain choice is made after the reflection, and then follows a judgment; this judgment is made by synesis and gnome. The difference between synesis and gnome consists in this, that synesis makes its judgment under ordinary and normal circumstances, while gnome judges in extraordinary conditions and by applying special rules.[47]

As moral virtue is impossible without prudence, so prudence is impossible without moral virtue. Prudence is concerned with the particular good about which man may be in error in contrast to the general principles offered by synteresis, which are unerring. The proper application of the general principles may be impeded by the passions, and an apparent good may take the place of the true good. The chief task of prudence, to counsel wisely, judge correctly, and prescribe correctly, cannot be performed unless the obstacles placed by the passions are removed. As a man has a natural habit or aptitude for comprehending the general principles, so he must obtain the proper attitude toward a particular end by means of moral virtue. The will, it is true, inclines by nature to the good, but it needs the moral virtue of justice in order to choose the proper means for the end. The irascible appetite must be perfected by the virtues of courage, perseverance, endurance, and heroism; the concupiscible appetite, by the virtues of temperance, purity, meekness, and humility, so that the way may be cleared for prudence.[48]

In summary, St. Thomas was able to speak of a threefold order brought about in the passions and affections by the intellect: first, the intellect governs the passions and the affections that they may observe the right middle, and thus a certain control is exercised over internal and external activity; secondly, reason governs man with respect to his passions so that he will maintain some stability in his virtuous attitude; and thirdly, reason brings about an adjustment of human actions to conform to something external, such as an end or the fellow man, and thus it causes man's actions to be correct. The

[47] *In III Sent.*, 33, 3; *Summa theol.*, IIa IIae, q. 49, a. 1; q. 51, a. 1–4.
[48] *In III Sent.*, 33, 3; *Summa theol.*, Ia IIae, q. 57, a. 5 ad 3.

three characteristics of all moral virtues (measure, stability, and correctness) are the result of the ordering functions of prudence.[49]

The prudence that we have thus far been speaking of manifests an imperfection inasmuch as it is always directed to a special end. True and perfect prudence is that which is concerned with the end of the whole life, with the ultimate end. This it can do only together with charity. Infused prudence cannot exist without the supernatural virtue of love.[50] Only when nature and supernature are united, only when natural virtue is penetrated by supernatural virtue, will there be a perfect exaltation of virtue.

5. The subject of the virtues. The concept of order plays a part also in the problem of the subject of virtues, especially in determining the subject of the moral virtues. Even more emphatically than their master Aristotle, the Peripatetics ascribed all virtues to the will, and in this they opposed the Stoics, who held that the subject of the virtues is the intellect. St. Augustine, too, held that the virtues were the concern of the will. St. Thomas taught that, although reason was an important factor, moral goodness depended on the will, and that the habits of the intellect without reference to the will could be called virtues only *secundum quid*. Only the will or a faculty moved by it can be considered the subject of virtue.[51]

Each habit in a faculty represents a perfection of that faculty. Such habits preparing and disposing a potency for act are superfluous whenever the potency by its nature is inclined to its proper object. The object of the will, however, is the good of reason proportioned to the will. To this object the will is inclined by nature; here no perfecting habit is needed, and the natural potency is sufficient. St. Thomas defines this object of the will as *bonum passionis moderatae,* as a good referring to the individual's person. Only when a certain good is beyond the powers of man does the faculty need the habit of virtue, as in the case of that good which refers to God.

Without reference to the will, the intellect is the subject of virtue only *secundum quid,* and the intellect becomes a subject of virtues ultimately only by reason of its relation to the will. Thus the speculative reason is the subject of the virtue of faith in which the intellect is moved by the will to give its assent; and the practical reason is the

[49] *In III Sent.*, 33, 1.
[50] *Summa theol.*, Ia IIae, q.65, a.2.
[51] *Ibid.*, q.56, a.3.

subject of the virtue of prudence with respect to the right will.[52] In
the proper sense, the will is the subject of morality, for in the last
analysis it is the will that is regulated by morality.

6. **The rank of the virtues.** In his treatise on the virtues, St. Thomas
assembled all that was offered by the ancient Hellenic schools of
thought and whatever was known about the nature of value in the
Christian tradition. He believed that he had achieved a complete
table of values and that he had embraced the whole extent of moral
good. Therefore he felt able to approach the problem of ranking
of virtues among themselves, and to determine the various classes of
virtues. Aristotle conceived his table of virtues to be a graduated list
of values; the differences between the virtues were expressed in value
predicates. St. Thomas offered a list of virtues, and he also attempted
to discover the reason underlying the differences in the value of
virtues.

The value of a virtue is actualized in the virtuous act. The subjective contribution toward the value of the virtuous act consists in
the right intention, the right attitude, the strength of the will, and
the greater or less freedom. These elements, already mentioned by
Plato and Aristotle, became the traditional possession of Christian
ethics.[53] Since the positive is more valuable than the negative, the
doing of the good is of more value than the omission of the evil.[54]

For the rest, many objective standards are found by which the perfection of virtues may be measured. Most of these standards have an
inner relation to one another and have a kind of ranking order among
themselves. When this is not the case, the evaluation of a virtue may
be different according to the different standards used. The value of
a virtue and of a virtuous act in which the virtue is actualized is
measured in the first place by the object with which the virtue is concerned. The noblest object is God. Therefore a virtue is greater the
more directly it has God as its object, the more intimately it unites
someone with God, the more it serves the last end; and a sin is
greater the more it turns away from God. Among human goods,
the soul is higher than the body, the body is higher than external
goods, and the common good is higher than the private good.

The intellect has an essential part in virtue; the order of virtue is

[52] *Ibid.*
[53] *De virt.*, 74, 2 ad 1; 107, 3; 110, 4; 113, 2.
[54] *Ibid.*, 44, 2 ad 3; 79, 4.

also the order of reason. Therefore the rank of virtues is measured secondly by the relation of the virtue to reason, or to the good of reason.[55] This good includes the objective order although it does not completely exhaust it. Thirdly, the value of virtue is measured by the part of the soul that is its subject.[56] Fourthly, other things being equal, virtue is measured by the extent to which its good is spread, the greatness of the benefit it causes. It is measured further by the length of the virtuous activity; and lastly by the immediate circumstances.

The theological virtues are higher than all other virtues because their object is God. Infidelity, despair, and hatred of God are among the greatest sins. In the order of existence, faith comes before hope, and hope before love; but in the order of value, love has the first place. This value judgment is derived from St. Paul and St. Augustine and is based on the constitutive importance of love for all virtuous living. Love is the mother and root and the form of all virtues, and thus also the form of faith and hope. The same order of rank is the result of the standard of closeness to its object. God is the object, and whereas love touches God Himself and rests in Him, faith and hope touch God only in so far as the knowledge and attainment of good are derived from Him. While faith is concerned with what is unseen, and hope with what is not possessed; but love is in possession of the beloved object.[57] When he thus emphasizes the importance of love, St. Thomas weakens somewhat the primacy of the intellect which he had accepted from Aristotle, and he likewise weakens his earlier intellectualism by thus giving love its proper place in the perfect state of eudaemonia.

The intellectual virtues are more excellent than the moral virtues because of their subject, which is the intellect itself. They also excel because of their object, since the object of the intellect is the universal while the object of the will is some particular thing. As with Aristotle, the virtue of wisdom holds the first place among the virtues of the mind because of its object, since it is directed to God the highest cause. According to the principle that an effect is judged from its cause, and the lower causes are judged by the higher causes, wisdom

[55] *Ibid.*, 123, 12; 154, 12; 161, 5.
[56] *Ibid.*, 123, 3.
[57] *Summa theol.*, Ia IIae, q.62, a.4; q.65, a.5 ad2; IIa IIae, q.4, a.7; q.10, a.3; q.13, a.3 ad1; q.104, a.3; q.105, a.2.

is the natural orderer of the other virtues of the theoretical intellect. In defining the intellectual virtues, St. Thomas attributed to them qualities that are not entirely without some ethical connotation. This is especially true of prudence as the presupposition of the moral virtues. Between prudence and the moral virtues we find that peculiar fundamental relation on which the high position of prudence rests. Prudence ranks next to the theological virtues, which are directed to the highest good, because the order of reason with respect to ways and means to attain an end is derived from prudence.

The gradation of the moral virtues was simplified for St. Thomas when he grouped them under the cardinal virtues of justice, courage, and self-control. On the basis of the threefold criterion of relation to object, relation to reason, and the subject in which the virtue is found, we obtain the following gradation: justice, courage, and self-control or temperance.[58] Justice is given the first place. Legal justice excels the other moral virtues just as the common good excels the private good. Particular justice precedes the other moral virtues because of the subject in which it is, namely, the will, and also because of its object, since it goes beyond the individual and orders the relation to the neighbor.[59] Even Plato, because of his social and ethical attitude, placed the common good above the individual good, and thus gave to justice the first place. Aristotle and St. Thomas followed this line of thought.

The good of man consists in the good of reason. Prudence possesses this good essentially, justice produces this good, and courage and temperance preserve this good. Courage comes before temperance for several reasons. Courage exists for the service of justice and therefore deserves every commendation that is due to justice. Temperance is principally concerned with the individual. Courage controls the most powerful movements of the sensible appetite, those which deal with life and death, whereas temperance tames the desires of the sexual and nutritive life. By overcoming the fear of the danger of death, courage does more to preserve the good of reason, just as it is closer to reason because it is situated in the irascible appetite, while temperance is found in the concupiscible part.

St. Thomas was not content with this general classification of the

---

[58] *In IV Sent.*, 33, 3; *Summa theol.*, Ia IIae, q.66, a.4; IIa IIae, q.123, a.12 ad 2; q.136, a.2; q.141, a.8; q.161, a.5.
[59] *Summa theol.*, IIa IIae, q.30, a.4.

virtues. Making use of the above-mentioned standards, he sought to delineate the finer differences between the individual virtues in the various groups. Under justice, the first place belongs to religion because it is directly ordered to the honor of God.[60] Therefore pride is the most grievous sin because it is essentially a turning away from God, while all other moral failings have this turning away from God only as a consequence.

The standard of the relation to the object is thus formulated by St. Thomas: among the moral virtues, one virtue is said to be higher than another according to the magnitude of the good that is set aside for the sake of God. Since obedience implies the setting aside of one's will, which is in a sense the greatest spiritual good, this virtue deserves "more praise" than the other moral virtues. Obedience grows out of reverence for God and is contained in all the virtues that manifest honor and service to God or human authority. Inasmuch as obedience arises from the reverence of God, it falls under the virtue of religion, and is a part of its principal act, the surrender to God. Inasmuch as the moral virtues are commanded by it, obedience has a causal relation to them.

A virtue is considered to be higher according to the manner in which it actualizes the good of reason; hence St. Thomas places humility immediately after justice and after the theological and intellectual virtues, but before all other moral virtues, since it establishes in man an aptitude for the order of reason. Viewed from the standpoint of the order of reason, temperance is more perfect than abstemiousness since in the temperate man the sensible appetite is subject to reason, whereas in the man who must practice abstemiousness some opposition still exists against reason.

The order of reason is the same as the order of nature, and the order of nature is identical with the divinely established order of the universe. Therefore the value or lack of value in a virtue or a vice is greater or less according to the greater or less degree in which such virtue conforms to the order of nature or violates it, especially in the group of virtues that refer to the sex life.[61] This natural viewpoint did not, however, prevent St. Thomas from according to virginity the first place among the group of virtues that refer to chastity. The dominion over the sexual appetites, which especially disturb reason,

[60] *Ibid.*, q.81, a.6.
[61] *Ibid.*, q.154, a.12; q.152, a.1-3.

and the complete abandonment of sexual pleasures in order to contemplate divine truth, is entirely in conformity with the order of nature and in agreement with man's spiritual character. The command to reproduce and multiply was directed to humanity as a whole, not to the individual.

As long as we accept the guidance of the ideal of the good of reason we will value those virtues higher which refer to this good than those which merely abstain from evil. Thus St. Thomas ranks mildness and meekness after the theological and intellectual virtues and also after justice, but higher than the other virtues that repress evil inclinations.[62] Liberality is the ordered use of external goods; hence it comes after temperance, which has as its object the regulation of the sensible appetite, and especially after justice and courage. Patience is placed after the theological and intellectual virtues, since a virtue is higher when it prevents a greater loss or evil.[63]

St. Thomas not only evaluated the virtues, he also judged the various states of life according to the same standards. The contemplative life is higher than the active life because it is in possession of the highest object, because it is more in conformity with man's reason, because it has a greater resemblance to God, and finally because it endures longer. This does not preclude the possibility that in certain circumstances the active life is better.[64] Virginity is higher than marriage because the divine good is higher than human good, because the welfare of the soul is more important than the welfare of the body, and because the contemplative life is higher than the active life.[65] A life of enjoyment and indulgence is condemned as unworthy of a man; the desire for "wretched comfort and ease" is alien to the spirit of St. Thomas; he demands the strenuous activity of all the powers of man's personality.

An inner order exists in the life of virtue. St. Thomas distinguishes three grades of virtue: (1) the imperfect virtues, or dispositions to virtue, which are different in each individual and which lack the guidance of the moral intention; (2) the virtues that are regulated by the moral intention as their immediate rule; and (3) the highest plane of virtue which recognizes God as the supreme norm of morality

---

[62] *Ibid.*, q. 157, a. 4.
[63] *Ibid.*, q. 117, a. 6; q. 136, a. 2.
[64] *Ibid.*, q. 181, a. 1 f.
[65] *Ibid.*, q. 152, a. 4 f.

and is always united with love. Only the infused virtues are absolutely perfect virtues, because they direct man to his last end.

When love is infused, all the moral virtues are infused. Love is the principle of all good works directed to the last end. Love is the supreme Christian value and also the basic and underlying value. Whoever possesses love has all the other virtues; whoever possesses prudence has all the moral virtues. The theory of the unity of virtue defended by the Stoics appeared afterward in many forms and also left traces in the Thomistic system. One virtue is indeed not the same as another, but the virtues do overlap. Prudence appears in all the moral virtues, and all the moral virtues have a mutual relation because of their matter. All the affections and passions proceed from love or hate and they culminate in joy or sadness. In the same way actions are related to one another and to the affections. The man who has conquered the lust of the senses will be able to accomplish the easier thing of controlling his foolhardiness in the face of danger. How evils grow out of one another is mentioned frequently by St. Thomas and especially in *De malo* (VIII, 1); and consequently it was necessary to show how virtues are rooted in one another, how they are related to one another, and how they reach out into one another's sphere.

CHAPTER XXXI

MAN'S SOCIAL NATURE AND THE NATURE OF SOCIETY

Ethics deals with the practical man. But the practical man is never alone. The isolated man, man separated from all others, is a fiction. The moral world not only includes the moral attitude of the subject of morality, but it contains in itself as its members all the forms of society. Chief among these is the state, because man is able to fulfill his life's task only in the framework of the community. Since the days of Homer and Hesiod, the thought has been repeated again and again that only from the soil of an ordered community existence can morality and culture arise and only there can they make progress. Philosophy accepted this thought and emphasized the importance of the community for the development of virtuous living.

Even in Plato we find the social tendency of ethics coming clearly to the fore. The importance of the state for the mental and spiritual development of the individual is underscored. At the same time two things are noted: the morality of a community is determined by the degree of morality found in the hearts of its citizens, and the morality of the individual depends on the morality of the whole. Plato could assert this mutual relationship between the individual and the community because he realized that the attitudes and dispositions of the state are derived from the individuals who make up the state, while the individual is subject to a decisive influence from the state with which he is so closely bound up. Because of these opinions, we might well expect to find Plato laying greater stress on the total character of the state.

That tendency toward the total state, however, was deflected by Aristotle. In opposing the dissolving tendencies of the radical Sophists, Aristotle originated the formula that man was by nature a social being, to which Democritus, Protagoras, and Plato assented. Aristotle developed the idea of the organic state and to him also belongs the credit of showing that man's nature is social. The absence of the state was for Aristotle the mark of a subhuman being, i.e., an animal, or of a superhuman being. Far more than the bees and the animals that live in herds, man is a social being; he alone possesses a moral sense of good and evil, of right and wrong, and he alone has in language a means for giving expression to this sense. A community of such moral ideas and moral feelings is the foundation for the family and the state.

Plato, in the *Republic,* designated the manifold exigencies of the individual which he cannot satisfy himself as the cause of the formation of the state. Aristotle adopted this viewpoint and in the eighth book of his *Ethics* said that communities arise because of the benefits they bring to men. He does not retract this statement in his *Politics,* although he extends it by saying that man has a natural desire to live in a community even though he would derive no benefit from it. But it is the idea of benefits that brings men together; men associate in order to preserve the good which is their life.[1] These factors in the formation of the state, pointed out by Aristotle, are not entirely unrelated to each other. Man's natural requirements and his power of speech are indications pointing to community life, his sense of morality and right are presuppositions for an ordered community within which he is able to perform his life's tasks.

This teaching of man's social nature and of the idea of the organic state became a deposit in the writings of the Stoics and was bequeathed to Cicero, who in turn transmitted these ideas of the philosophy of the state to Christianity.[2] This thought of the social characteristic of man's nature was found to be in complete harmony with the New Testament idea of an organic corporate community. In the writings of St. Paul we read that all are one body in Christ, that all have a mutual relationship, and are active in various states and vocations in the community.[3] Because of these texts the Fathers of the Church were not slow to adopt as a whole the basic ideas of the Hellenic philosophy of the state. St. Augustine made extensive use of

---

[1] *Pol.,* I, 2; III, 9; *Eth. Nic.,* I, 6, 13.
[2] *De offic.,* I, 44; II, 21 f.; *De fin.,* III, 20, 65; V, 23; *De rep.,* I, 25; *De leg.,* 1, 10.
[3] Cf. I Cor. 12: 12; Rom. 12: 4–6; Eph. 4: 15 f.

these ideas and drew liberally from Cicero.[4] Aristotle, the New Testament, and especially St. Augustine were the great authorities and guides for St. Thomas. Of these Aristotle was the most important for it was his clear insight into reality that lived again in St. Thomas and made him conscious of the social and economic conditions of his time.

1. **Man's social nature.** In all his writings St. Thomas proclaimed that the human community was essentially rooted in man's nature.[5] More than any other living being, man is intended for sociability, for community living, for political life. Man is a civil, social, and political animal. Being a man is synonymous with being a co-man. For man the community is a natural necessity, because man is not an independent, self-sufficient being. For the preservation of life, for the satisfaction of their material needs, and for the development of their spiritual faculties, men depend on their mutual support. No one can lose sight of these manifest facts that show how man is thrown on his fellow man for assistance, for complementing his being, and how he is closely bound up with other men.

Like Aristotle, St. Thomas began his study of human society by considering man's biological background. He did not overlook the essentials or reach out into a vacuum in so doing, because he began with the study of that without which even man's personal nature could not exist, life itself. In itself life is a good, and this good cannot be preserved without mutual defense and help. The propagation of life requires the union of the sexes, and man's material needs require mutual cooperation. What one man cannot do, is done by another, and thus the labor of many produces what the individual needs. Similar support is needed for the development of man's higher faculties. Without the community man could not attain his own particular goal, the perfection of his spiritual and moral nature. Intellectual growth is furthered by contact with other minds, and moral development is hastened on the path of virtue by life in common with good men. Perhaps no words express this inner mutual relationship of men to one another as well as the axiom: *homo homini amicus*.[6] Later Thomas Hobbes formulated the counterpart of this saying in his

---

[4] *De civ. Dei*, XII, 27; XIX, 12; IV, 3; *Enn. in ps.*, IX, 8.

[5] *De reg. princ.*, I, 1; *In I Eth. Nic.*, 1; *In VIII Eth. Nic.*, 12; *In I Pol.*, 1, 5; *Contra Gent.*, III, 85, 117, 125, 128–30, 134, 136; *Summa theol.*, Ia IIae, q.72, a.4; q.95, a.1; q.96, a.2; IIa IIae, q.129, a.6 ad 1.

[6] *Contra Gent.*, III, 117, 125; IV, 54.

homo homini lupus, which expressed briefly the atomic mechanistic concept of society.

Like the birds that have no social instinct and are therefore birds of prey, so men who shun and hate society have an evil and corrupt nature. Men like St. John the Baptist and St. Anthony the Hermit, who preferred the solitary life from religious motives, are exceptions and phenomena above the average; but even these were connected with society.

An unmistakable sign of man's social nature is his language, which by its nature is the means of expression intended for another. Language is the transmitter which bespeaks the spiritual and intellectual bond between men, and at the same time it is the strongest factor in the formation of the community. Above all things, language must announce the truth, express the difference between good and evil, between justice and injustice, and thus lay the foundation for every community. Hence St. Thomas declared that, when men forget the natural relation of speech to truth and abuse language to express falsehoods, they undermine the community and the social order.[7]

The various forms of community life are necessary for the preservation of life, the propagation of the race, the attainment and secure ownership of material goods, for material welfare, for physical and intellectual growth, for religious and moral instruction, for the maintenance of tradition, and for the defense of right and justice. And since the division of labor is the basis for economic and intellectual life and progress, St. Thomas declared that the various vocations and professions within the community of the state are also necessary.[8]

This relation of the state to man's nature and the purpose of his being is so essential, that the state, like marriage, would have come into being in Paradise, apart from the benefits which it produces.[9] The state is as little the product of sin as is marriage. Even in the paradisiacal state men would also have been unequal with regard to sex, age, and the faculties of soul and body. The possibility of mutual support and complement and the establishment of an order depend on this inequality. Man's social nature is not a blemish or a defect. St. Thomas viewed it in an optimistic light. In the beginning God had endowed men differently that the "beauty of order might shine

[7] *Summa theol.,* IIa IIae, q. 109, a. 3 ad 1.
[8] *Contra Gent.,* III, 134; *Quodlib.,* 7, 17.
[9] *Summa theol.,* Ia, q. 96, a. 4.

forth in the human race." [10] The relation of subordination and super-ordination is essential for this beauty of order. Therefore Plato, Aristotle, Cicero, and St. Augustine had recognized the unwritten law of nature that the more intelligent and nobler members of the race are called to rule those who are less able. From an adequate understanding of the nature of society we can proceed to the knowledge of the true community and the true state.

Social life is founded on the innermost principles of man's being, and it flows from man's very nature. Human nature is related to the principles of time and space and it exists with individual differences and with physical and spiritual limitations. On the other hand, man's substantial form, the soul, makes all these individuals men and forms them into a community. Because all men participate in one species they are, as it were, one man. Their social nature is based on the peculiar limitations of the individual and specific factors of the human composite. [11]

The human community is the whole, the individual is a part, a member of this whole. Referring to the relation between the community and its members, Aristotle in his *Politics* (I, 2) said: "In this instance the whole is prior to the part." St. Thomas accepted this idea of organism and applied the comparison of the human body and its members extensively to the problem of society. The individual men are related to the community of the state as the individual parts of man's body are related to his entire physical organism. Just as the hand or the foot cannot live without the relationship to the human organism, so the individual man in isolation is not sufficient for himself. Accordingly the whole possesses a conceptual and natural priority with respect to the parts, and these parts receive their specific nature as parts from the whole and they do not remain what they are when their connection with the whole is destroyed. This conceptual priority does not completely describe the matter; the whole is also prior to the parts as to perfection since the whole has greater wealth of being and a larger participation in divine being. [12]

Objections have often been made against the application of the organism idea to the community and the state because the individual

---

[10] *Ibid.*, a.3.

[11] *Ibid.*, Ia IIae, q.81, a.1.

[12] *In I Pol.*, 1; *Summa theol.*, IIa IIae, q.31, a.3 ad2; *In Rom.*, 12, 2; *In I Cor.*, 12, 1–3.

person is thereby degraded to the status of a mere member and deprived of his autonomous rights and his autonomous significance. The organism idea is, however, fully justified, but we must always remain aware, as was St. Thomas, of the limitations of this Aristotelian concept. We must not interpret the organism in a physical sense, as John of Salisbury did, but in a moral sense. Aristotle did not carry out this comparison with the physical organism absolutely; he realized its restrictions. St. Thomas, however, because of his Christian viewpoint, had more opportunity to proclaim the right of the individual person.

In attempting to solve those important problems with which we shall be presently engaged, it will be well for us to keep in mind the intent of Aristotle's statement about the physical organism. That statement applies not only to the essential parts but also to the integral parts. Man's being is not exhausted in his corporeal existence; he possesses deeper veins of being from which is derived his aptitude as a social being. Even this natural priority of the whole as against the parts is not true in all instances, as we shall have occasion to point out later.

A natural disposition or aptitude to society is not the same as the natural origin of society. Like those thinkers who preceded him, St. Thomas was not oblivious of the important part played by the human mind in the structure and development of the various forms of the community. Man possesses a natural disposition to social life just as he has a natural disposition to virtue, and both these dispositions press forward to actualization. The proximate formation of the community takes place through the activity of human beings themselves, and this activity in turn is directed by human reason. Like Aristotle, St. Thomas calls the state the noblest product of reason, and he considers it a masterpiece and a creation of the human spirit which approaches perfection the more it resembles nature. He knew the importance of detailed regulation and the division of duties in the community, and thus the role that the individual plays.

Later, during the Renaissance, the state was considered a work of art, the conscious individualist creation of the human spirit. St. Thomas' attitude is not in accord with this view or with the political theories of the later Middle Ages. He remained faithful to the expression of the real state of things; man's natural social disposition, revealed by his natural attachment to society, is developed by the human reason and the will and thus attains concrete form. The organic form of the state or community is only the conscious continuation of a process inaugurated by nature, and this beginning knows nothing of a contract made between several individuals. If a contract appears somewhere in the process, this does not affect the natural origin and foundation of society. No contradiction between these two factors exists. We do not find it contradictory that the human intellect is an essential part of man and that he is able, by his power of reflection, to know his natural endowments and labor for their fuller development. Marriage is rightly adduced as a living example to show how a harmonious social structure arises from a natural disposition and a voluntary agreement or contract. Aegidius Romanus, one of Aquinas' disciples, expressly states that the part which human reason plays in the founding of the state does not preclude its natural origin.[13]

2. **Grades of the community and the state.** The impulse toward the community is itself divided into a number of partial urges or impulses from which arise different communities that serve various ends and purposes. Every community comes into being for the sake of some good or value, and since a value takes on the aspect of a purpose in the human will, the community comes into being for some purpose. The aspect of value is the primary one; the teleological aspect is secondary. Corresponding to the graded order of goods and values is a graded order of communities. Since the differences of value and purpose differentiate the various community forms from one another, the family and the state and the community differ not only quantitatively (by reason of the number of their members), but also qualitatively and specifically. The essential content of the higher forms of the community is something more than the sum of the lower forms; the higher forms excel because of their own peculiar nature and essential content.[14]

Aristotle did not say that the natural priority of the state to its parts was without qualification. Not only in the order of origin, but also in another sense the individual precedes the family, as the family, individuals, and communities are prior to the state. Aristotle declared that the family possesses a natural priority to the state, because he considered the family more necessary and earlier than the state,

---

[13] *De reg. princ.*, III, 1, 1.
[14] *In I Pol.*, 1; *Summa theol.*, IIa IIae, q.58, a.7 ad 2.

because the propagation of all sensitive beings was more important than any other function, and finally because the germinal powers of love, the community, and justice are first active in the family.[15]

According to the natural law that dominates all living things, progress is always made from the imperfect to the perfect, and from the simple to the composite. Thus arises the first social union that is found in marriage or domestic society. St. Thomas said that this domestic society is more closely related to human nature than the state itself (*homo naturalius est animal conjugale quam politicum*), because marriage with its acts of procreation and nourishment on which all life is conditioned is more necessary and therefore prior to the state.[16] The principal purposes of domestic society are the procreation and nourishment of children, the training and education of the young, the mutual assistance obtained by a division of labor, and the mutual spiritual and moral demands made on each other by husband and wife on the basis of their mutual love. Thus marriage arises from man's nature but develops into the moral sphere. Domestic society embraces the relations of order between husband and wife, parents and children, of lord and servant, and of master and slave. Domestic society, itself but a modest structure, possesses its own specific nature, and it is not only a preparatory step for higher forms, but it is the perduring basis, the germ cell of the state and the model of all other forms of subordination and superordination.[17] If we discern the patriarchal idea in Thomistic social thought, it is derived from the family and applied to the other forms of society, just as the authority of the king arose from the rule of the head of the family or of the clan.[18]

St. Thomas understood that in Christianity marriage served higher ends than those envisaged by the pagan Aristotle. St. Thomas complemented Aristotle with the teaching of St. Augustine. According to the latter, marriage seeks a threefold good: *fides, proles, sacramentum,* faith, offspring, and the sacrament. St. Thomas adopted this threefold good, but he rearranged it according to the threefold character of husband and wife. Inasmuch as these have an animal nature and are generically the same as other living beings, the purpose of marrige is the offspring; inasmuch as the parents are human

---

[15] *Eth. Nic.,* VIII, 14; *Eth. Eud.,* VII, 10.
[16] *In VIII Eth. Nic.,* 12.
[17] *De reg. princ.,* I, 1.
[18] *In I Pol.,* 1.

beings, the good of marriage is mutual fidelity; and inasmuch as they are Christians, the good of marriage consists in the sacrament and its blessings.[19]

The good of the education and training of the children requires the monogamic form of marriage and its lifelong duration. Marriage includes more than a biological distinction, however constitutive this difference may be. It is the state of life of two persons who assist each other in mutually complementing each other in order to attain their supernatural end. As a model of the close union of spiritual love, marriage was therefore incorporated into the Christian scheme of grace.

When several families unite under one authority, they form a community which excels in the extent of its production, its mutual assistance, and therefore also in its autonomy.

From a plurality of communities the state arises as the frame for the perfect economic, spiritual, and moral life of a people. As the depositary of earthly happiness the state is the goal and end of all the preceding communities. Differing from Aristotle, St. Thomas [20] did not consider the state the highest, most perfect, and most self-sufficing community, but only as the most perfect community for the things that are necessary for life. For St. Thomas the *civitas* was not the supreme form of society as the *polis* was for Aristotle. He did not deny that the state was the condition for the actualization of all natural human values and for attaining natural happiness. St. Thomas praised the first founder of a state as the greatest material benefactor of mankind and he accorded to the state the most honorable place among all social forms, because the good of the state is the noblest of all human goods, *"quod bonum rei publicae est praecipuum inter bona humana."* [21] To forestall any misconceptions, we should point out here that when St. Thomas, like Aristotle, speaks of the state as the perfect community he does so without any reference to theology or religion.

Thus the various forms of community rise in hierarchical order, growing organically out of one another, continually increasing in extent; yet the lowest form remains in its totality and integrity al-

---

[19] St. Augustine, *De bono conjug.*, I, 1; *De civ. Dei,* IV, 14, 21–23; *De gen. ad lit.,* 9, 7; St. Thomas, *In IV Sent.*, 26, 1.

[20] *De reg. princ.*, I, 1.

[21] *In I Pol.*, 1; *De reg. princ.*, I, 1.

though it enters into the higher forms as an integral part with functions in the higher form. Only through intermediate groups is the individual incorporated into the state, and he remains at all times united to the other members by his natural relation to them and by the common bond of thought and love. Corresponding to the various forms of community are different degrees of union: the love of blood relatives, the friendship of those who live in the same place, and the community of thought of fellow citizens.[22]

When St. Thomas was writing about the *civitas* he had in mind the medieval city which had come into being to supply its own needs and which formed a self-sufficient economic sphere. The medieval city had also attained certain autonomous political rights and thus resembled the ancient *polis*. St. Thomas in no wise departed from the original Aristotelian thought when he applied it to the contemporaneous forms of community life. No essential change was made when St. Thomas replaced the picture of the ancient state with that of the medieval city.[23] For St. Thomas the city with its divinely willed division into occupational groups and its competent defense of private possession signified a form of life far better than any other, excelling by far life on the land, a form of life best suited for the actualization of the common good. After the various occupations, St. Thomas enumerated the states of life, the *ordines,* farmers, craftsmen, judges, soldiers, merchants, priests, and the rulers, all having their legal position and legal rights. When St. Thomas reduced the occupations to three in imitation of the threefold division of the angelic world, viz., the patrician, the citizen, and the common man, he forgot his original scheme since the standard is now birth and possessions instead of occupation and actual contribution to the community.[24] His economic thought is oriented to the medieval industrial city, just as his social ethics is concerned with the same data.

Unlike the Aristotelian *polis*, the *civitas* is not the highest and ultimate form of the community. Above it is the province with a greater measure of self-sufficiency, and above the province rise the kingdom and the Empire.[25] St. Thomas is, however, little concerned about the differences existing in his data. A great diversity of forms met his

[22] *In III Sent.*, 29, 1, 6.
[23] *In I Pol.*, 1.
[24] *Summa theol.*, Ia IIae, q.91, a.6; q.95, a.4.
[25] *De malo*, I, 1.

eye: the absolute monarchy of Naples and Sicily with its Oriental cast of absolutism, the Lombard cities, the papal state, the French monarchy, the German *regnum,* built on its hereditary dukedoms, and finally the all-embracing bond of the Empire. The historical reality as St. Thomas viewed it should have shown him the people as distinct from the state and taught him certain values created by the people, such as the popular rights claimed by the German people. But St. Thomas did not venture so far from his literary data.

Every community requires a central authoritative direction which keeps in view the common good and tries to make it real. If man were only an individual being he would have but one end and that would be attainable by his reason. He would be solely under the rule of God and in all other respects he would be his own master. This would be an instance of absolute individualism. But besides the end of the individual, mankind has the end of the community to strive for, and everywhere in the world where several individuals are striving for one end we find some dominating principle. It is a universal law active throughout the universe, and what takes place in the universe as a whole is reflected in the parts. No total order exists without a supreme authority. God rules the whole universe, the heavenly bodies govern the earthly bodies, rational beings rule corporeal things, the soul governs the body, reason rules the irrational powers, heart and head govern the members of the body. Neither the demons, the angels, nor man in the paradisiacal state are exempted from this universal authoritarian order. Wherever we find plurality and difference, order can come into being only through subordination and superordination according to the divine precept that the higher being always governs the lower.

All particular orders are contained in the universal order, they are special instances of the general order. Comparing the power of authority to the soul, St. Thomas said it was the essential form of the organism. Authority, therefore, is the vital, life-giving force in a community, directed to the attainment of the end of the community. He distinguishes between two kinds of organisms: the physical organism in which the individual member lacks independent existence and independent activity, and the moral organism in which the members have an independent existence and activity. That disorder may be avoided in both kinds of organisms, a dominating principle is necessary. The community is a moral organism, and the dominion exercised in it is over free beings. In the political community the ruler directs the conflicting interests of the individuals to the common goal. If all the individuals were absorbed in their own particular interests, the common good would be jeopardized. That element in the community which divides the individuals must be corrected by the central power which looks only to the common good. Thus St. Thomas could say that the common good was really the good of the ruler, *bonum principis*. This double order, the relation to the ruler and the mutual relation of the members is found in all forms of the human community.[26]

St. Thomas' discussion of the significance and nature of authority shows how he will solve the problem of the original depositary of civil authority. Some have tried to align St. Thomas with modern thought by professing to see in him a representative of the moderate theory of popular sovereignty. At this point it will be of some value to retrace the stages of the development of this theory from St. Thomas to the present day.

Rousseau and Hobbes are the best known representatives of the theory of absolute popular sovereignty, which is always preceded by the absolute sovereignty of the ego in each individual. By uniting their wills in the social contract the individuals create the popular will, and this popular will is to be regarded as the sole and ultimate foundation of all civil authority. Moreover, since the will of the majority is always the right will, the popular will is always right. The ruler is merely the deputy or delegate of the popular will. St. Thomas, by reason of his social principles, is far removed from such a theory of popular sovereignty, which is nothing but a doctrine of extreme individualist liberalism founded on the fallacy that the people are no more than an aggregate of individual wills. The people are not a mass without a head and members; the people are always an organic whole.

Suarez, who is often called the representative of moderate popular sovereignty, knew well that the people were not an inorganic mass. According to his theory, civil authority is derived ultimately from God; it lies dormant in the people within the natural community, and it is conferred on the ruler by the express or tacit consent of the

---

[26] *In IV Sent.*, 24, 3, 2; *De reg. princ.*, I, 1; *Contra Gent.*, III, 81, 85, 98; IV, 76; *Summa theol.*, Ia, q.96, a.4; IIa IIae, q.182, a.2 ad3; *In I Pol.*, 3; Aristotle, *Pol.*, I, 5; III, 5; Cicero, *De rep.*, III, 25; St. Augustine, *De civ. Dei*, 19, 13.

people. Having adopted this viewpoint, Suarez logically concluded that democracy was the original and the most natural form of the state. His political theory must be interpreted in the light of the times in which he lived. Suarez opposed the legitimist political doctrine of King James I of England, which maintained the divine right of kings on the principle that God had originally conferred on rulers the power to govern. Suarez admitted only one instance of such direct transmission of power to a definite person, the power to rule the Church conferred directly on St. Peter the first Pope. Thus the people as a whole remain the subject and depositary of civil authority. When clans and tribes unite they form a people and a state in the form of an immediate democracy. The exercise of authority may be delegated by the whole people to an individual or to a group of men, and thus, mediately or indirectly, the secondary forms of the state are established, monarchy and aristocracy (Suarez, *Defensio Catholicae fidei* and *De legibus*). It cannot be denied that Suarez' theory of popular sovereignty enjoys a much more logical development than the later theory of Marsilius of Padua, published near the close of the Middle Ages.

The idea that the ruler received his power and authority from the people was widely accepted during the Middle Ages. This theory descended from the Roman institutions to the glossarists and canonists (Rufinus, Stephen of Tournai, Hugucio, Lawrence of Spain, and others), and it was probably known to St. Thomas. At first sight we might be inclined to find an echo of this theory of the transmission of authority from the people to the ruler in the works of St. Thomas. Many thought they had found substantiation for this view of popular sovereignty in the *Summa theologica*.[27]

The first reference seems to be the more decisive in support of that view: The law aims at the common good by its nature. To be concerned about the common good is the task of the whole populace (*totius multitudinis*) or of that person who represents the whole people (*vel alicujus gerentis vicem totius multitudinis*). Thus the making and issuance of laws is the business of the whole people or of that public person who stands in the place of the people. In support of this argument St. Thomas added: *ordinare in finem est ejus, cujus est proprius finis.*

In these instances, however, St. Thomas is not discussing the ques-

---

[27] Ia IIae, q.90, a.3; q.97, a.3 ad 3.

tion of the original subject of civil authority. He merely says that the power to make laws rests either with the people or with that person who represents the people. His conclusions and reasonings about the attitude to be maintained under a tyrranical ruler and his open preference for monarchy in the *De regimine principis* cannot be made to conform with the theory of popular sovereignty. St. Thomas' position with regard to the bearer of civil authority follows logically from his fundamental principles. In every community the existence of the power of authority is necessarily implied because no community can come into being or continue to exist without it. The power of authority rests on the basis of the natural law, and it is posited without further ado with the idea of an organism. Therefore it is added neither directly nor externally by the will of the majority. The people is a whole in which the power of authority is immediately and directly present, just as the soul is present in an organism as an expression of the order divinely willed in all things.[28]

Historical conditions and circumstances determine the way a community comes into being. The form of the authority may be varied, but St. Thomas preferred the monarchical form as the original and the best although not the only form. St. Thomas seems to prefer to consider the community as a following with a leader. The common good is the goal of the whole people, which is to be attained by the particular leadership of the people. Therefore St. Thomas called the common good not only the good of the whole (*bonum totius*) but also the good of the ruler (*bonum principis*).

Following Aristotle, St. Thomas distinguished three good forms and three evil forms of the state. The good forms are monarchy, aristocracy, and democracy; the evil forms are tyranny, oligarchy, and ochlocracy. In evaluating these forms of the state, St. Thomas also follows Aristotle in all essentials. The first three forms are good if they keep in view the highest goal of the common good. Every form, however, possesses its weaknesses and bears within itself the danger of being corrupted into an evil rule. If we are to decide which is relatively the best form of government, the teleological viewpoint will require that we make the decision on the basis of the principal end of the state. The rule of a single individual is the best because thereby the unity and peace of the state are best assured. Nature, which always

[28] *Ad Rom.*, chap. 13, 1; *In II Sent.*, 44, 1, 2; 2, 2, et ad 4 f.

follows the best method, knows but one principle, and a work of art is greater the more it resembles nature.[29]

Aristotle had based the excellence of monarchy on the pre-eminence of the monarch in knowledge and virtue.[30] St. Thomas makes use of the same argument, invoking the authority of the Scriptures and St. Augustine.[31] St. Thomas seems to have a greater preference for monarchy than Aristotle did, although he does not consider it the only form of government as he does in the case of the Church. St. Thomas does not approve the absolute form of monarchy, but rather a combination of monarchy, aristocracy, and democracy. In such a combination the deterioration of monarchy into an oppressive tyranny would be prevented while an interest in the government would be instilled in the citizens by their participation in the government. In general, however, St. Thomas remains close to the traditional theory that the monarchical principle is preferable in any mixed form of government.

The state is the creation of human reason and in particular it is the product of the mind of the ruler. The things that reason creates, works of art, are imitations of what is found in nature. St. Thomas is guided by the analogy of nature and he distinguishes two phases: the establishment of the state and the government of the state. The first task is seldom necessary; but if a government is to be established, the ruler must lay a secure foundation of the state by selecting a place noted for its fertility of soil, pleasant climate, and natural defenses. The principal and continual duties of the ruler are the preservation of the state and the attainment of the last end. The highest goal of the citizens of the state is their union with God in a virtuous life. Thus the ruler must provide for the virtuous living of his subjects by introducing, preserving, and perfecting a good order of life. This good order of life requires three things: peace and harmony among the citizens, the encouragement of good deeds, and the necessary economic background for a good life.

The preservation of the good order in the state depends on three kinds of activity by the ruler: he must secure the continuance of good government by replacing the deceased officials of the state through

---

[29] *De reg. princ.*, I, 2; *Contra Gent.*, IV, 76.
[30] *Pol.*, III, 12 f.
[31] *Summa theol.*, Ia IIae, q.97, a.3 ad3.

wise appointments, he must foster virtue and suppress evil by laws, punishments, and rewards, and finally the ruler must defend his subjects against external enemies. The art of ruling extends to a wide field of activity.[32]

If we have in mind the ultimate goal of the state, the following duties seem to follow. Of special importance are the defense of the state against external enemies, the establishment of inner peace and harmony, which depend on the observance of justice. Thus the creation of justice and right in the state by wise laws and just courts of law are the prerequisite for the great good of peace.[33]

Peace and harmony are warrants for the material and spiritual well-being of the citizens, and this state of well-being is established by agriculture, the crafts, and trade, and itself is the basis for the establishment of higher cultural activities, which consist in the fostering of education and learning, and the promotion of virtue in the citizenry.

The promotion of public morality by positive legislation is a primary duty of the state, but this does not mean that the state should not foster private virtue and repel any attack on the practice of virtue by private individuals.[34] Since the worship of God is required by the natural law, St. Thomas rejects the concept of a state without religion.[35] Like St. Augustine he assigns religious rights and duties to the state. He permits the state's intrusion into the religious sphere in order to support moral standards and he requires the state to defend and support the Church.[36]

From the purpose of the state it follows that the state itself and civil authority are founded on the natural law and that all those things that are necessary to carry out the duties of the state, such as the making of laws, judicial sentences, and punishment of law violations, are a part of the natural law of the state. Since the natural order and the natural law come from God, we may say that civil authority has a theocratic derivation. The state has no immediate concern with the

---

[32] *De reg. princ.*, I, 14 f.

[33] St. Augustine, *De civ. Dei*, 2, 21; 15, 8; 19, 13; *De reg. princ.*, I, 15; *Summa theol.*, IIa IIae, q.62, a.7; q.66, a.8.

[34] *Summa theol.*, Ia IIae, q.92, a.1.

[35] *Contra Gent.*, III, 120; *Summa theol.*, IIa IIae, q.81, a.2 ad3.

[36] *De reg. princ.*, I, 14; *Contra Gent.*, III, 120; *Summa theol.*, Ia IIae, q.7, a.1 ad1; q.99, a.3; q.96, a.4; IIa IIae, q.85, a.1; q.99, a.4.

supernatural order.[37] The subordination of individuals under authority in the civil community is required by the natural law, and the supernatural order merely supports this arrangement.

3. **The nature of the civil community.** What is the nature of the civil community or of the social entity? Social philosophy has the duty of providing an ontology of the community, and St. Thomas addressed himself to this task. In the first place the community is a unit. Since unity has degrees, St. Thomas modified this statement by saying that the community is not an absolute unity, but a unity *secundum quid,* namely, a unity of order.[38] The terms "matter" and "form" are used to explain the point. The mass of humanity is the matter that is formed into a unit by the order. The civil community does not perdure in its matter, since the individual human beings disappear and make way for others; the unity of the community is preserved and continued by reason of its form, which is the unity of order in its different offices.[39] One form existing in different *supposita* can only be a form of order. The model for the Aristotelian-Thomistic concept of the community is the universe, and St. Thomas also compared the community to the biological organism in which the matter is continually changing while the form is preserved.

The limitations of this comparison are immediately evident. The individual members of the state are more than the matter; they are also the active agents who by their wills form the civil community.

The state is an autonomous entity, comprising not only the citizens of one time but many generations; thus the state extends horizontally and vertically. The individual citizens die, the state lives on, like the olive and laurel trees that remain green although some leaves fall while others grow.[40] The order that holds together the multiplicity of subjects in the state is not an arbitrary order assumed at will, otherwise any organization of men for a determined work would be a state. The order in the state is perduring, it exists under a common authority, it is born of the natural desire for social activity, and it is determined by its last end and goal.[41] According to St. Thomas, the state or nation is not an inorganic thing that attains some

[37] *Summa theol.,* IIa IIae, q. 12, a. 2; q. 104, a. 1, 2, 6.
[38] *Contra Gent.,* IV, 35; *Summa theol.,* Ia IIae, q. 17, a. 4.
[39] *Quodlib.,* VIII, 5; *Summa theol.,* Ia, q. 39, a. 3.
[40] *Summa theol.,* Ia IIae, q. 96, a. 1.
[41] *De reg. princ.,* I, 15.

unity when an order is imposed on many individuals from without. The civil community is a social structure in which we find a people with an organic growth developing political, social, and juridical organizations.

A community is, therefore, not an arbitrary union of men with common interests; it is a structure with a natural growth perfected by conscious organization. Today the true inner community is often rightly contrasted with a mere external association of men for some external purpose.

In what does the uniform order of the community consist? Every community comes into existence because of some good or some value, by the concerted direction to this end and good.[42] The common good, the common end and purpose, call this order of the community into existence and keep it alive. Therefore every community is an order of relation which manifests itself in an agreement on values, thinking, and feeling, and in a common activity.[43] The whole of the community has an activity that does not belong to the part or member. The attack made by the whole army, the progress made by a ship when many men are at the oars, are examples used by St. Thomas to illustrate simply this community activity. Thus we see that the community is an order of thought, love, and action,[44] an ordered whole of human activity, or an association of men who, led by a common goal and end, strive for some common object. Out of the individual powers of many men one power of the whole is formed, and this one force produces the common effect, which can be attained only if the many are formed into a unit. The community is not a unit of being but a working unit, not a whole being but something acting as a whole.[45]

Every community is a whole whose members were not absolutely autonomous and self-sufficient from the beginning, but they are united with one another and for one another. Because of blood relationship and membership in the same clan, the individuals are members of a whole. This whole has its being in the members and through the members, but as a whole it is above the members and is a form that is supraindividual ranging above the individuals. As the state does

[42] *In VIII Pol.*
[43] *In I Eth.*
[44] *De car.*, 2, 4 ad 2.
[45] *Contra Gent.*, IV, 7; III, 66.

not come into being by the mere aggregation of the individuals, so the common good is not the sum of the individual goods. As the state is a whole, so the common good is a whole, a good that is higher than the individual good and possesses its own autonomy as against the individual good.

This thought was expressed in the words: "The common good of the state and the particular good of one person differ not only in degree but by a formal difference. The nature of the common good and the individual good are different just as the nature of the whole is different than the nature of the part." [46] Hence the common good can be the cause or basis of something qualitatively new. By this common good the civil authority is able to justify its existence, laws come into being to serve the common good, and, because of the kinds of common good, various kinds of community arise. This is not the Platonic preference of the universal to the particular, but the Platonic-Aristotelian preference of the whole to the part.

The community is, of course, much more extensive than the individual, but it is always something concrete and real. The Middle Ages regarded the community as a whole and understood the value of the higher orders of being, while modern Positivism and individualist liberalism lost all appreciation of such higher orders.

Remaining always the philosopher of the middle, St. Thomas is equally removed from the extreme of the unreality of social entities and the extreme of regarding society as a substantial and objective entity. He asserted that the community had a specific being but he did not attribute to it a substantial being, independent of the being of the individual persons who are the members of the community. Here we must distinguish: the community possesses reality but it does not have a substantial being. Reality and substantiality, according to St. Thomas, are not the same; only the individual persons, in this connection, are substances. We might be inclined to regard this question, whether St. Thomas thought the community had substantial or accidental being, as of no significance; but this determination was actually of importance in the mind of St. Thomas. He attributed to the community an accidental existence, since, for him, order is a relation, and every relation, no matter how important it may be, is placed in the category of accident.

The community is an accidental relation based on a transcendental

<hr />

[46] *Summa theol.*, IIa IIae, q.58, a.7 ad2.

or essential relation. Since human nature must of itself depend on the community for its full development, the relation to the community is natural and essential. The community is, therefore, never a substance, but it is a substantial and essential requirement of human nature, founded on the relation of *actio-passio*. However, the concrete form of the community is an accidental or predicamental relation because by its nature humanity is not bound to any particular kind of community. In this way St. Thomas' teaching about the community and the social entity is integrated with the fundamental principles of his metaphysics.

The community exercises its own independent activity, but it does so only through the *supposita* of the individual persons who are brought together by the actualization of their social dispositions and their common relationship to some value. Thus here too the principle, *agere sequitur esse,* is acknowledged. A man acts as an individual person and as a member of the community, and St. Thomas keeps the two aspects separate. He was familiar with the corporate idea: all men are, as it were, one corporate body, and this corporate body is like one man (*De malo,* IV, 1). The different men with their different functions are members of one organism. The value judgment or the command that motivates their actions originates either from the ruler or from the majority of the members of the community. Such actions of the community are subject to moral principles, and St. Thomas assigns them to ethics as part of its subject matter. Since the community has an activity it may also commit a crime, and therefore it also possesses a conscience.

St. Thomas did not discuss the question of the social conscience in all of its aspects, but this much is clear, that the social conscience is not the sum of the consciences of the individuals, yet the individuals are the subjects in which the social conscience resides. The social conscience is the knowledge of the common good in the mind of the head of the state and the individual functioning leaders of the state and the obligations that flow from the knowledge of the common good. These obligations descend upon all the members of the community to whom the common good is in any way entrusted.[47] St. Thomas enunciated an important principle in this regard: the community becomes concrete only in the persons of the individual members.

Opinion is divided about whether St. Thomas went on and de-

47 *De malo,* IV, 1.

veloped the idea of the organic state to the concept of the state as a juridical person and as an independent subject of right and duty. If we read the pertinent texts carefully, we will not doubt that St. Thomas closely approached the concept of the moral and juridical personality of the state although the detailed determination was left for later times.[48]

[48] *Summa theol.*, Ia IIae, q.97, a.3 ad 3.

CHAPTER XXXII

THE INDIVIDUAL AND THE
COMMUNITY

The question of the mental and moral relationship of the individual to the state was unknown in the time of the ancient *polis*. The free citizen was bound by his whole being to the state; all his activity belonged to the state or to that group to which he belonged. His service of the community was at the same time his service of God. Points of strain may have arisen between the individual and his community, but never opposition.

That situation changed in two ways, practical and theoretical. Groups and individuals placed their own interests above the common good, they made use of political power for economic exploitation, and they distorted the political convictions of the individual to such a degree that the problem of the individual's relation to the community arose of its own accord. The radical wing of the Sophists proclaimed the individual right of the stronger and taught that the state had come into being by a kind of social contract, or that the state was even hostile to human nature. Plato said that the Sophists merely coined the theoretical formula to fit the practical conditions of the time. In the highest stage of Attic culture the philosophers made energetic war on the disturbing individualism of the Sophist enlightenment. Although Plato had a congenital preference for the politician's profession, he was unable to enter the lists actively because of the uncertain state of things. To reawaken the consciousness of the people for the community and to fend off the decline of the ancient *polis,* Plato wrote about the state. But he never saw his theories and efforts rewarded with success. Later times, however, have found his work a treasure house of important political truths.

The duty of the individual is determined entirely by his subordination under the purposes of the whole community. Each individual, according to his talents and dispositions, is incorporated in some particular group, and each group and every individual in each group have a determined task to fulfill. The state is a social organism whose well-being depends on the harmonious cooperation of all its parts, and each of these parts is assigned a task to perform in view of the ultimate end of the whole organism. Plato was convinced that the good of the whole was identical with the good of the individual, but for him the state was an end in itself in which the individual was a partial end. Even though the three estates include a gradation of personality, the state is always the dominant social organism in whose service the various groups and estates must act.

Because of these concepts, Plato imposed drastic limitations on the individual in favor of the state. On the other hand, he required that the state make important contributions to the good of the individual. The state's most important duty is to secure for the individual his last end, happiness both here and in the other world. Whenever Plato's metaphysical and religious reasoning comes to the fore and this earthly life is considered the anteroom of the next life, the state is treated as a preliminary means for man's transcendental end.

Aristotle felt obliged to recede from the more extreme socialistic views enunciated by Plato, particularly in his *Laws,* where, for instance, he says that the children belong to the state more than to the parents, and that the state has the right to determine the education of both children and adults. Aristotle admits that both the individual and the family must be oriented to the state, and he requires a common civil education and training because no citizen belongs to himself, but to the state. The solicitude for the whole includes the solicitude for the part, and thus the training of the individual is the business of the state.[1] Aristotle also limited the individual in favor of the state, but he is far removed from any attempt to eliminate the personality of the individual. He defended the particular existence of the family against any encroachment of the state, and he distinguished between the good man and the good citizen. The whole *Nicomachean Ethics* is a canticle in praise of the rights and excellence of personality. When personality is fully developed it accrues to the benefit of the state, just as the state will perform important tasks for the benefit of the individual. When the destruction of the independ-

[1] *Pol.* VIII, 1, 2, 13.

ence of the city states of Greece had finally been accomplished, the Stoics began to labor for the ideal of a common community of the people, but Epicureanism depreciated the community and enthroned the individual.

An analogous process took place in the Middle Ages. Here, too, the individual was so completely imbedded in the group that no question arose about the antagonistic attitude of the individual with respect to the community. The medieval man had been formed by the community spirit of the Church, and through her religious, moral, and social doctrines the individual had been firmly established in a determined relationship to his neighbor, to civil laws, and to the head of the state. The static form of the vocational groups completed the framework of his social life. But even in the Middle Ages points of tension developed between the individual and the state. This tension was first felt in the communities themselves, in the vocational groups, guilds, and sections of guilds, until finally the individual himself found that he was set against the whole community.

Thus individualism came into being, reaching its maturity in the Renaissance and the liberalist Enlightenment. With regard to the social problems, St. Thomas was obliged to assume a position by his historical forebears, Aristotle and St. Augustine, and by the necessity of offering a solution to the real and practical problems presented by social and political life about him.[2]

1. **The person of the individual as an organic member of the community.** At the present time the social whole is considered the only proper starting point in determining the relationship of the individual to the community because the opposite view is considered too dangerous as leading to individualism. As a matter of fact, we may begin with the community or the individual and arrive at the same conclusion if our reasoning is realistic and unprejudiced. St. Thomas makes use of both methods, choosing the one that best suits his purpose. If, for instance, he is analyzing the individual in the community, he begins with man's social nature.

In this connection we must keep in mind the well-known propo-

---

[2] Cf. De Wulf, "L'individu et le groupe dans le scolastique du XIIIe siècle" in *Revue Neoscolastique,* 1920; Roland-Gosselin, *La doctrine politique de saint Thomas d'Aquin,* 1928; Mandonnet, "Saint Thomas d'Aquin et les sciences sociales" in *Revue Thomiste,* 1912, Vol. XX.

sition that man is by his nature a member of the community, and that he is related to the community as a part is to the whole, and as the imperfect to the perfect. As a part belongs to the whole, so man belongs to the community. As the whole, the community possesses a higher being; and as the perfect entity, it possesses a higher value. This particular specific value of the community is the common good, which is better and more divine than the good of the individual. St. Thomas frequently brings into relief the Aristotelian thought that the organic community excels the individual member and the particular good.

The position of the common good is clearly delimited on all sides. As the community of the state does not arise from the mechanical sum of individuals, so the common good is not made up of the sum of individual goods and benefits. The common good is something qualitatively new, an independent good of special significance, namely, the perfection of the essential form of the state community. Along with Aristotle, St. Thomas designated this common good as the highest among earthly human goods, and he placed all private goods far below divine and community values.

A basic law of being and value makes the good of the whole the end and purpose of the part, and besides this, the magnitude of a good corresponds to the extent of its worth. Moreover, the community and the common good display greater fullness of being and a higher significance, they express more perfectly the idea of divine goodness and divine being and therefore they possess a greater resemblance to God. This thought is of the utmost importance since it contains the metaphysical justification for the subordination of an autonomous personality under a non-personal entity. The preferential position of the community and the common good is based ultimately on the fact that the infinite nature of God is reflected more fully and with greater purity in the community.

The pre-eminent position of the common good is illustrated by the following considerations. The wise ruler is far more intent on the common welfare than on the welfare of any individual. Again, the principal virtue of legal justice strives for the common good as its proper object and it orders all other virtues toward the common good. Prudence, too, which assists at the birth of all virtues, through the form of social prudence directs all men to the common good. Finally, all laws are in the service of the common good, they work for the realization and securing of the common good, and they derive their worth from the fact that they foster the common good.

In this way the obligation of the individual toward the social whole is clearly expressed. Since man is a member of the community, everything that he is and has belongs to the state. This proposition is taken from Aristotle, and may sound rather strange coming from Aquinas; later, St. Thomas modifies it. First, however, he draws every possible conclusion from the fact of man's membership in the community to establish his duties toward the community. These conclusions culminate in the statement that the good of the part is measured by its relation to the whole. Therefore the individual man can never be good if he is not in the proper relationship to the community and toward the other members of the community.

Here a natural law is at work. By nature the part loves the whole, and reason imitates nature. Therefore the individual is obliged to dedicate his whole self and all his faculties to the whole. Viewed from the standpoint of the common good, self-mutilation and suicide are forbidden; on the other hand the state is justified in imposing great burdens on the individual for the benefit of the community. The state, as a product of reason, has an analogy to nature, and in nature the part may be pruned for the good of the whole. Human nature in itself deserves the greatest respect, but the common good is so far above the individual good that anyone who endangers it or destroys it, may be punished, imprisoned, mutilated, or condemned to death by the proper authority.[3]

The membership of the individual in the community is so essential and the relationship between the members in the social organism is so intimate that the actions of men have an immediate effect on the community and on the members. Everything whether good or evil, whatever injury is inflicted or whatever benefit is conferred, has an immediate effect on the whole. All St. Thomas' thinking is organic. He who injures the hand, injures the whole man. Since the whole and the parts are in a mutual relationship, whatever befalls the whole is felt by the parts. He who is concerned about the common

---

[3] *In I Pol.*, 1; *In V Pol.*, 2; *In I Eth. Nic.*, 1; *De reg. princ.*, I, 14; *In IV Sent.*, 19, 2, 3; *De verit.*, V, 3; *Contra Gent.*, III, 17; *Summa theol.*, Ia, q.60, a.5; Ia IIae, q.90, a.3; q.92, a.1 ad3; IIa IIae, q.26, a.3 ad2; q.31, a.3 ad2; q.39, a.2 ad2; q.47, a.10; q.58, a.5 f.; a.7 ad2, 9 ad3; q.60, a.5 ad1; q.61, a.1 ad5; a.2; q.64, a.2, 5; q.68, a.1 ad3; q.141, a.8; q.134, a.1 ad3; *Comp. theol.*, I, 124.

good, is at the same time concerned about his own welfare, since the private good cannot improve without the good of the family, of the community, and of the state. The individual is a member of the family and the state, and the well-being of the member depends on the well-being of the whole.[4]

Only in the order of the community can the individual welfare be secure. The benefits of the whole redound to the welfare of the individual. The good condition of families, communities, and states furthers the good of individuals. Members of the community have certain positions of rank, different functions and tasks, and also certain rights and duties in the social organism. Therefore they do not share in the good of the community according to some mechanical and arithmetical measure, but rather according to an organic and geometrical progression. According to his position and social standing, the individual is fructified in the development of his personality by the common good.

As the community is not something that floats in the air above the members, so the common good is not something that is independent and above the members, but it finds expression in the private welfare of the members. Here we are confronted with the quantitative aspect of the common good, which has a significance not to be lost sight of. Aristotle and St. Thomas often refer to this quantitative aspect. The social community possesses a quantitative structure in the multiplicity of its members, which has some significance in the relation of the common good to the private good. Material welfare and comfort, the justice of law, the order of right, public morality, and the like, must be actualized in all the members of the community; and the more the common good is realized in the members, the better will be the condition of the community.

The superiority of the common good and the community is firmly established. But all values and kinds of values are not in the same plane. The universe of values is multidimensional. Hence St. Thomas laid down the following limitation: the common good is better than the good of an individual when both are in the same genus.[5] Therefore the common good is above the individual good only in the same sphere, but not where goods of different genera are in competition,

---

[4] *Summa theol.*, Ia IIae, q. 21, a. 3; q. 61, a. 5 ad 4; IIIa, q. 7, a. 13 ad 3; IIa IIae, q. 47, a. 10 ad 2; *De car.*, IV ad 2.

[5] *Ibid.*, Ia IIae, q. 113, a. 9 ad 2.

e.g., earthly and spiritual goods.[6] The salvation of the individual soul, which is in the supernatural order, is superior to the earthly common good. In the purely earthly sphere of this life, the common good, the laws that protect it, the state authority and its machinery, are above the welfare of the individual. But even here in the natural sphere the ascendancy of the community over the individual is not absolute, as we shall see later.

Man can attain his ultimate supernatural goal only as a member of a supernatural order. Alongside the state, the highest earthly community is the Church, the administrator of the divine order of salvation, whose origin, center, and life-giving principle is Christ. The organic concept of the Church expressed in the figure of the mystical body of Christ is enunciated in the New Testament, particularly in the Gospel of St. John and more formally in the Pauline Epistles. Afterward the thought was received into patristic literature and was cherished as an important teaching by Scholasticism. St. Thomas was thoroughly imbued by this doctrine.[7]

Through the union with this mystical organism, especially with the head, vitality is transmitted to the individual members that they may attain their ultimate end. The religious community also has its common good which, in contrast to the non-personal goods of other communities, is a person, namely God. Only as a member of the ecclesiastical community can an individual work out his salvation, only with the help of his fellow men and the Church can man reach this union with God. This community, of which Christ is the head, continues to exist in the next world.

The objection that it is the individual and not the community, nor the Church, that is to share in eternal happiness, has little force. In the *De regimine principis* (I, 14) St. Thomas assigns to the religious community the same religious last end as to the individual. With all clarity he says that not only the individual but the community will attain the enjoyment of the vision of God. Thus a new light is thrown on the Thomist concept of the community as a true organism, and at the same time the thought is expressed that the total order of the community will stand before the throne of God, and the individual will be there as a member of the family, as a citizen, and as a member

---

[6] *Ibid.*, IIa IIae, q. 152, a. 4 ad 3.

[7] *Ibid.*, IIIa, q. 8; *In III Sent.*, 13; *De verit.*, XXIX, 4 f.; *In I Cor.*, chap. 12, 3; *Eph.*, chap. 1, 4.

of his particular group. Therefore God is the last end of the individual and of the community; He is the *bonum privatum* as well as the *bonum commune*.

Even man's eternal happiness is in accord with his social nature. Indeed, the community goes beyond man's social nature and we behold a community of all the spirits. The kingdom of God itself appears as a community. "The last end of all rational creatures consists in the attainment of happiness in the kingdom of God. This kingdom is nothing more than the ordered community of those who are enjoying eternal bliss in the vision of God." [8] The coexistence of individuals and the community in the next life displays a new order. The vision and love of God, of course, remain the acts of the individual persons, but this does not prevent the establishment of an intensive and intimate community life among all those who are united in this great community whose end is again God.[9]

Finally St. Thomas enunciates an important truth: all the empirical, earthly communities are related to the supreme community whose head is the infinite and supreme divine being. From this head all communities are derived as from their source, and after this supreme community all other communities are modeled and placed somewhere in the great plan of the universe.

Man and community have a transcendental relation to each other. Outside the community man cannot come into existence, he cannot develop physically or mentally, he cannot become a good citizen or a perfect Christian. Only within the community can he develop and unfold into a personality. Man never ceases to be a member of the community; in no phase of this life or of the next life is the individual person dismissed from the community. The lower forms of the community, retaining their independence and their measure of glory, have a position of service beneath the higher forms, and thus each social entity does its part for the fulfillment of the ultimate end.

2. **The position of the individual in the community.** St. Thomas is painstaking in his consideration of the individual as a member of the community and of his many duties toward the various forms of the community. But in spite of this, the individual man is not permitted to be dissolved in the community. We need only refer to St. Thomas' writings on the ontology of the human person. In this pres-

---

[8] *Contra Gent.,* IV, 15.
[9] *Summa theol.,* Ia IIae, q. 111, a. 5.

ent connection it may be well to emphasize the important points of
that teaching.

If it is true that every creature in the universe exists for the sake of
its own act and its own perfection, that is especially true of man. Because of their resemblance to God, the rational creatures are the
noblest, and because of their nobility they are placed directly in the
providence of God. The fact that man is a member of the community does not prevent him from being a preferential part (*pars prin-
cipalis*) of the universe which exists for him and of which he is a
secondary end. The particular character of the members does not
conflict with their coordination in the whole.[10]

Man is indeed a spiritual person, a being endowed with reason
and free will, capable of self-reflection and self-determination; he has
a special value and dignity and a particular perfection, and he has a
destiny beyond this life, a supernatural union with God. Even though
the community is the condition for his physical origin and for his
mental and bodily development, metaphysically every man, according
to St. Thomas, is the image of a particular divine idea. Metaphysically
man is independent of the community with respect to his origin. The
community itself is only the actualization of a preformed reality that
exists germinally in every individual person. The structure of the individual is the metaphysical presupposition of the community.

The individual persons are the pillars on which the community
rests. St. Thomas found it necessary to say that the community is not
a metaphysical entity as is a physical organism; it is only a working
entity. This union to attain an end and produce an effect is not total
and absolute in the sense that it affects the entire activity and the
complete attitude of man. Many activities remain that are carried out
only by the individuals and that refer to the individual alone.

From these ontological conclusions follow many important directions for the practical order of life. St. Thomas sharply distinguishes
between the end of the community and the particular goods of the
individual.[11] Private goods may indeed be directed to the common
good, but in themselves they are separate. Since the whole universe
and all its parts are directed to God, man because of his important
position in the universe has a personal share in this relationship.

[10] *Contra Gent.*, III, 110–13; *Summa theol.*, IIa IIae, q.64, a.2 ad3; Ia, q.65, a.2;
In XI de div. nom., 2.

[11] *De reg. princ.*, I, 1, 15; *De car.*, IV, ad2; *Summa theol.*, Ia IIae, q.96, a.3;
IIa IIae, q.58, a.5 ad3.

St. Thomas rejected the attempt to abandon man to the rise and fall of his social fortune. "Man, with all he is and all he has, is not entirely subordinated to the political community." His relation to the political community does not decide the merit and demerit of his actions. With all he is and has man is subordinated rather to God.[12] Rightly understood, this does not attack the idea of organism. The individual person remains an individual and he can really be incorporated into the community by means of his individuality. The rights of the community over the individual are by no means limitless and absolute; the natural and divine laws have established barriers in defense of the individual. The concept of the common good actually precludes any suppression of the individual person, and the person possesses rights that may never be touched by the community, and others that may be abridged only when the community is in actual peril.[13]

Such is the picture which St. Thomas sketches of the individual in the community. The individual person and the community are not opposites; they have a mutual relation to each other which implies a certain mutual dependence. Just as the individual cannot exist or develop his essential nature without the community, so the community cannot actualize its end, the common good, unless the individual men live together and work together in the concrete. The well-being of each is inseparably bound up with that of the other. The welfare of the members is rooted in the welfare of whole, and the perfect whole can be constructed only out of solid, healthy members. St. Thomas recalls his basic principles. The ultimate basis for the mutuality of this relation must be found in the structure of human nature. Specific nature and individual existence belong to man from his origin; but the quality of membership in a whole, his tendency to live and work with another for a common good, are just as fundamental as his particularizing attributes. These qualities do not militate against each other, for the individual and the community are by nature directed to the good. The direction of the will of the virtuous man and the direction of the prescriptions of the laws that aim at the common good are identical.[14]

How are the individual and the community adjusted in this mutual relation? The fact that both have the same goal in view forbids that

<hr/>

[12] De reg. princ., I, 14; Summa theol., Ia IIae, q.21, a.4 ad3.

[13] Contra Gent., III, 155; Summa theol., Ia IIae, q.95, a.2; q.96, a.4; q.97, a.4 ad3; IIa IIae, q.66, a.8.

[14] Summa theol., Ia IIae, q.96, a.5.

either one be made the means to serve the other's purpose. The individual person is not a mere means toward the realization of the good of the community; the individual possesses his own value and he has his own destiny and end. The independent position and value of the individual is not annihilated by his proper incorporation into the community, but through the fullness of the perfection of the whole the individual is able to attain his own elevation and perfection.

The community is not merely a means to an end. St. Thomas was aware that the family, the community, and the state, exist for the individual person, and that the higher forms of society exist for the lower forms, but this does not prevent the various forms of the community from having their own immanent ends and their own values. St. Thomas remains true to reality when he places the individual and the community, the higher and lower social forms, in the relationship of mutual service and cooperation.

The individual persons are the dynamic fonts that actualize the common good by their individual wills and their individual status; on the other hand the community with its common good supplies those sources of power by which the individual is assisted in the attainment of a fuller physical and mental existence. This is true of the existence here below as well as of that existence beyond the grave. Frequently the statement is made that man's last end is the happiness of each individual in the next world. To this every form of the community is directed as a means and, when that end is attained, the community loses its significance since it is to serve only the good of the individual. Such was not, however, the concept of St. Thomas. According to his basic metaphysical principles the whole universe, all the various grades and orders of being, are directed to God, and all actualize the great idea of creation, and all reflect the fullness of the divine being, although in an imperfect manner. In this great cosmos the community also has a place of its own as one of God's creations.

By this organic interpretation of the community and human society St. Thomas was able to avoid the false concepts of the community as well as the socialistic suppression of the individual, and at the same time he made use of this theory of organism in the community only to the extent that his data, the structure of free, spiritual persons, permitted.

3. Church and state. Medieval man was an adherent of that Christian Church which made his eternal salvation secure, which formed his conscience, which transmitted all culture, and which prescribed his attitude to the state. The Church made totalitarian claims on her faithful and obtained for herself in the mind and affection of the individual a far more important position than the state, because she introduced the individual to the highest values, to goods which the state knew nothing of. In a letter written in 829, the Frankish bishops speak of Christendom as one great Christian body, divided into two principal parts: the priesthood and the royal power (*unum corpus christianum principaliter divisum in sacerdotio et regno*). The opposites here are not, however, the Church and state. The letter envisages the all-embracing, universal kingdom, the mixed body of Christendom, that holy empire foreordained by divine providence in which the spiritual and secular powers are separated, and in which later the secular and spiritual forces were to wage a bitter conflict for the supremacy.

According to the Augustinian-Gelasian theory, these two powers were to be independent and coordinated to each other. The papal decretals accepted this view with the added emphasis of the indirect power of the Church. More important than these theories, however, was the fact that in the actual strife the Church obtained the supremacy in this holy empire. St. Peter, it was said, had received the secular supremacy together with the spiritual primacy. The secular ruler received his power from the Church just as the moon received its light from the sun. Two supreme authorities, two powers, cannot exist together.

St. Thomas made no great departure from this traditional medieval concept of the relation between Church and state, but he introduced a far-reaching element into the discussion. In essentials he agrees with the Augustinian-Gelasian view, although he does not become a partisan of that school or of any of the embittered camps on this question. He followed the path traced for him by his Aristotelian principles. From Aristotle he had learned the concept of an autonomous state, not beholden to the favor of the Church, but erected on a foundation of the natural law, a perfect society. Even before St. Thomas had been able to look into Aristotle's *Politics,* he had defended the independence of secular and spiritual authorities in their own spheres. Aristotle had heightened his appreciation

for the autonomy of the things of nature; and since these two communities actualized different purposes, he distinguished between the
communities themselves.

Thus St. Thomas was led to differentiate sharply between the
profane sphere, including the profane intellectual sphere, and the
strictly spiritual sphere. Nature and supernature serve different ends
and therefore must be kept strictly apart, in order to determine their
mutual penetration, their cooperation and coordination, as well as
their historical opposition. Unfortunately St. Thomas did not write
a separate *quaestio disputata* on the relation between Church and
state, but his occasional utterances on this question permit a clear
understanding of his position in the matter.

In the *Commentary on the Sentences,* St. Thomas offered the following explanation: "The spiritual and the secular power come from
God. The secular power is subordinate to the spiritual power to the
degree that God placed it beneath the spiritual power, i.e., in the
things that concern the salvation of the soul. In these things we must
obey the spiritual authority more than the secular. In matters of civil
welfare we must obey the secular power rather than the spiritual,
according to the saying of our Lord (Matt. 22:21), 'Render therefore to Caesar the things that are Caesar's.'" In all matters of civil
welfare the secular power is here designated as the power of the
highest instance, while to the Church is assigned the care of the
spiritual welfare.

The thought that the civil welfare was included in the care of the
spiritual welfare is expressed occasionally in the Middle Ages, but
it is alien to St. Thomas and irreconcilable with his explanation of
the duties of the secular ruler. The supreme authority of the state
is rooted in the natural law; it is not derived from the Church, and
in itself it is not attached to the true faith. It may exist therefore
unhampered in a state of infidelity. Because of this distinction, St.
Thomas attributes to the secular authority the right of interpreting
the natural law, while the spiritual authority has the right to determine the proximate application of the law in spiritual matters.[15]
In the sphere of such things as the payment of interest and the restoration of property, the civil regulations may be different from the
ecclesiastical law because the state may take other things into con-

---

[15] *Ibid.,* IIa IIae, q. 147, a. 3.

sideration, but the divine law does not abrogate the human law.[16]

What, then, is the relation, practical as well as theoretical, between the state and ecclesiastical authority? In no instance does St. Thomas say that the highest secular power is united to the primacy of the Pope by its very nature. The frequently quoted statement taken from the *Commentary on the Sentences,* "The secular power is united to the spiritual, as with the Pope who has both powers in his hand according to the disposition of Him who is priest and king for all eternity," refers merely to the actual fact that under divine providence the two powers were united in the Pope.[17]

When St. Thomas discusses the question of the relation of faithful subjects to an unbelieving ruler, he distinguishes expressly between an established authority and one to be newly erected. When the civil authority already exists, the ruler's power of dominion is entirely removed from the control of the Church because ecclesiastical authority extends only to those who are members of the ecclesiastical community. But when a form of government is newly established, the Church cannot permit that an infidel become the ruler, because of the possible danger to the faith of the believing subjects. Such a ruler might easily, especially in despotic forms of government, issue commands that would conflict with the faith and that might be obeyed by the faithful subjects because of the weakness of their characters.

St. Thomas further concedes to the Church the right of proceeding against an apostate ruler and deposing him by judicial sentence. Both these powers are derived from the Church's supreme authority and right to care for the salvation of her subjects and to establish penalties for those who disobey her laws. Unlike the proponents of the hierocratic system, St. Thomas did not argue for the Church's direct power in temporal things and for the absolute dependence of the secular sphere on ecclesiastical authority, but he defended the Church's influence in religious concerns and her indirect power in secular things. (Since the time of Cardinal Bellarmine the term "indirect power" came into general use.) St. Thomas realized that the application of such penalties should be tempered by the conditions of the times. The Church could not proceed against Julian the Apostate because of her weak position, and therefore she permitted the

---

[16] *Ibid.*, q. 10, a. 10; q. 78, a. 1 ad 3; *Quodlib.*, XII, 28.
[17] *In II Sent.*, 44, a. 3 ad 4.

faithful to obey him in all things that were not against the faith.

In those things that concern the salvation of souls, the Church must be accorded the supreme power; her rulers and subjects as faithful believers are subject to the authority of the Church. Undoubtedly St. Thomas viewed Church and state as two separate realms with separate tasks. The Church serves the supernatural, those things that are spiritual and distinct from earthly things, *a terrenis spiritualia distincta*. On the other hand, St. Thomas knew well that these two powers existing in the actuality of human society must find a point of balance and adjustment even in the smallest decisions of the individual person. This adjustment is required first of all by the fact that the supreme and ultimate end is one and all-embracing; only one last end exists and to it all other ends and purposes are directed. St. Thomas makes use of the Aristotelian thought of the hierarchy of ends in order to clarify this relationship of secular and spiritual powers.

In reading St. Thomas, we must keep in mind the great difference between the times before Christ and those after Christ. Aristotle was confronted in his day by an entirely different situation. In the Aristotelian *polis* religion was integrated and incorporated in the community of the state; religion was a part of political life, and since it was primarily intent on earthly ends it was naturally subject to state authority. St. Thomas himself pointed out that among the pagans the priesthood and religious worship, since they served temporal ends, were subordinate to the rulers of the state upon whom devolved the duty of furthering the common good. Even the Old Testament countenanced such subordination of religion.[18] St. Thomas also recognized instances in which religion is subject to the authority of the state: in those cases in which the external and internal worship of God comes under the natural law. In these instances religion is a common human concern which is subject to the ruler of the state as a part of the common good.[19]

The ultimate end of man, of man as an individual as well as a community, is union with God. If man were able to attain this end by the power of his nature alone, the secular authority would be obliged to assist him in attaining that end. But man is able to attain

[18] *De reg. princ.*, I, 14.
[19] *Contra Gent.*, III, 120; *Summa theol.*, Ia IIae, q.99, a.3; q.101, a.2; IIa IIae, q.81, a.2 ad3; q.85, a.1.

this end only with the help of divine and supernatural forces, and thus this duty of assisting him to his last end belongs to some divine supernatural authority. That authority belongs to that King who is not only man but God also, our Lord Jesus Christ, who makes men children of God and leads them into the glory of heaven. Christ gave this authority on earth, not to earthly princes, but to the Supreme Pontiff, the lawful successor of St. Peter. To him all the kings of Christian kingdoms are subject. St. Thomas was clearly speaking of subordination in matters of religion and faith, as is evident from the statement: "The administration of this kingdom was entrusted, not to earthly kings, but to the priests, that spiritual things might be kept distinct from earthly things." [20] Material things, however, are subject to the kings. But since the princes of Christendom give allegiance to the Church because of the conviction of their faith, they may be called vassals of the Church, *vasalli ecclesiae,* in contrast to infidel kings, who sometimes persecute Christians and put them to death.[21]

The pre-eminence of the Church is often expressed by the figure of the body and the soul: the earthly power is subject to the spiritual as the body is subject to the soul. If, however, the Church is thus said to be superior to the state, this does not mean that the Church in itself has a right to earthly things. St. Thomas was careful to point out in detail when the ecclesiastical authority can command in temporal affairs. An instance would be when the earthly authority leaves certain temporal affairs to the jurisdiction of the Church.[22]

From Aristotle, St. Thomas accepted the idea of the *polis* as a perfect community or society. The concept was applied to the pre-Christian state. Was it still applicable to the Christian state? St. Thomas answered unhesitatingly in the affirmative. The Christian state in which the civil authority serves the interests of the Church, in which the Church promotes the supernatural life with all its varied moral and religious activities, in which Church and state cooperate in attaining man's last end, is an autonomous and perfect society. The historical reality, it is true, often departs from this high ideal and from this ideal harmony. St. Thomas was well aware of this, and therefore he often turned his gaze from the imperfections

---

[20] *De reg. princ.,* I, 14.
[21] *Quodlib.,* XII, 13, 19 ad 2.
[22] *Summa theol.,* IIa IIae, q. 60, a. 6 ad 3.

of this world to that community and perfect society, the triumphant Church, which is governed in the best possible manner, to that society which was called the *civitas Dei* in the world to come.[23] For him this was the perfect community, and Aristotle's concept of the perfect state is given a religious turn.

The high ideal of the perfect state evolved by St. Thomas deteriorated in later times. Aristotle's idea of the autonomous state was used by political theorists in support of the national state and for the disruption of the medieval idea of the perfect state.[24]

[23] *De verit.*, VII, 1.

[24] Cf. W. H. V. Reade, *The Cambridge Medieval History*, Vol. VI (1929). This work treats of political ideas before 1300. Cf. also. Joseph Lecler, "L'argument des deux glaives" in *Recherches de science religieuse*, XXI (1931), 298–339; R. Rolland Gosselin, *La doctrine politique de S. Thomas d'Aquin*, 1928.

CHAPTER XXXIII

THE ETERNAL LAW

Wherever we find law we find order, at least a tendency to order, since laws are made for the sake of order, which in turn is the prerequisite for the attainment of the common good. Law and right precisely define the status and function of every individual in a community and of the community itself. Law and right make possible the harmonious cooperation of individuals in a community and of lesser communities with higher communities, and thus make a substantial contribution to the attainment of the chief purpose of the community.

The treatise on the philosophy of law and right in the *Secunda Secundae* of the *Theological Summa* has merited the unqualified praise of all who have given it their attention. Such recognition need not, however, descend into a kind of apotheosis. Even if we point out certain discrepancies and defects, enough remains of solid worth and excellence. An important quality of the Thomistic treatise on law and right is that it does not expend itself in any particular direction or in support of some special thesis; it sets itself to view the whole phenomenon of law and justice and impartially makes use of whatever the past has to offer toward a solution of the problem. Furthermore, it always keeps in mind the metaphysical core of the concepts of law and right, yet it is not deficient in its consideration of the nature of positive law, its meaning, its significance, and its various manifestations.

St. Thomas represents a high point in the development of the scholastic theory of law and right. Not until the thirteenth century did Scholasticism concern itself at any length with quesions of jurisprudence. Early Scholasticism either ignored problems of law or gave them scant attention, and even those theological summas written about 1200 fail to offer a special tract on natural law and natural right. These problems were first treated in the *Summa aurea* of William of Auxerre. Since that time they were given an important place in the works of Franciscan Augustinianism, such as the writings of Alexander of Hales, St. Bonaventure, and Matthew of Aquasparta, and in Aristotelian literature, as, for instance, in the works of St. Albert the Great.

In his treatment of law, St. Thomas was able to draw from the Roman law as well as from canonical law. He knew the works of Isidore of Seville, from whose *Etymology* most of the legal definitions of scholastic literature were taken; he knew also Gratian's *Decretum,* a work that stood midway between theology and the study of civil law. The primer of scholastic theology at that time was Peter Lombard's *Sentences,* which owed much to Gratian's *Decretum.* The *Corpus juris civilis* and the collected pronouncements of the Popes published in the decretals of Gregory IX were also used by St. Thomas. He occupied an advantageous position in the development of jurisprudence because he was able to exploit the contributions of Aristotle and St. Augustine to the fullest extent, and make a critical comparison of the legal theories of his scholastic predecessors and contemporaries.

In the following pages we will try to show how St. Thomas remained true to the highly developed medieval sense for right and equity, how he completed and corrected the thought of his predecessors, how by his creative thinking he formed everything into an organic whole, and infused new life and meaning into the traditional concepts.

1. **The concept of law.** For St. Thomas "law" meant a norm of action, a norm that is obligatory. Therefore, like St. Bonaventure and Duns Scotus, he derived the term *lex* from *ligare (dicitur lex a ligando, quia obligat ad agendum)*, and not as Isidore, St. Augustine, and Cicero, from *legere,* even though he made use of the latter derivation when it suited his purpose on occasion.[1] All action takes place for some value or some purpose. This ordering toward a purpose is the function of the practical reason. Hence it seemed evident that law was a concern of reason. The general prescriptions of the practical reason made to govern actions have the character of law. We are not surprised to learn that St. Thomas puts the basis of law in the practical reason and not in the will. Even Aristotle had declared that

[1] *Summa theol.,* Ia IIae, q.90, a.1, 4 ad3.

the establishment of standards, regulation of actions, direction and guidance, were matters of the reason. In the same way the Stoics and Neoplatonists, influenced by Roman jurisprudence, and also the Fathers of the Church had looked at the matter from the intellectual viewpoint.

But, no less than Aristotle, Cicero, and St. Augustine before him, St. Thomas did not lose sight of the relation of law to the will. He knew that the prescription of the law proceeded from a will and applies to another will. Therefore he said that law was a matter both of the intellect and of the will. Later Scotus isolated the element of obligation more definitely and attributed it formally to the will. In the fundamental relation of the expression of the will and the intellect, the latter holds the higher place, because the expression of the will has the force of law only when it is founded on reason. If this manifestation of the will is opposed to reason, it is evil, a perversion of law.[2] The reasoning behind this conclusion may be sketched as follows: if a norm or standard rests on reason, it is in accord with reality and it is true since reason has truth for its object. This truth is the conformity (*adaequatio*) of the intellect and reality. The ordinance of reason, as an element of law, contains truth and conforms to actuality.

This fundamental reasoning is important. When St. Thomas thus based law and right on reason oriented to actuality and real things, he built a bulwark against legal Positivism and legal voluntarism which denied a universally valid objective order in the world. At the close of the Middle Ages this voluntarism was represented by William of Occam. Many years before, Cicero had rightly concluded that, "if justice and injustice were merely popular opinion or a princely edict or a judicial sentence, that is, if law depended solely on the human will, we would have a law approving robbery, adultery, and the falsification of last testaments."[3] If the will alone were the determining factor in the law, then law would be an arbitrary thing depending on human wills or on the divine will. As a matter of fact, some of the voluntarist disciples of William of Occam said that theft, murder, and adultery might be considered as possible divine ordinances.[4]

[2] *Ibid.*, q.92, a.1.

[3] *De leg.*, I, 16.

[4] Cf. William of Occam, *II Sent.*, q.190; *IV Sent.*, q.14; Nicholas of Autrecourt, *Chart. Univ. Paris*, II, §1124; Peter d'Ailly, *Quaest. in I Sent.*, q.9, 12.

All the characteristics of law are expressed in the famous definition: *lex est quaedam rationis ordinatio ad bonum commune ab eo qui curam communitatis habet, promulgata,*[5] law is a regulation in accordance with reason promulgated by the head of the community for the sake of the common welfare.

St. Thomas explains the parts of this definition. Law, as a rule and standard, is either in him who regulates and measures or in that which is regulated or measured. Only in the former sense is law a matter of reason. Inasmuch as law may be found in things as a certain inclination, it is law only in a participative sense. Law requires an intelligence from which it issues, an intelligence that is either divine or human. The first principle governing human actions that is established by the practical reason is man's supreme end, i.e., his happiness. Law serves the perfect community, it aims at the good of the community, but it includes in this concern for the common purpose the ends of the individual and knits the activities of individuals together. Only he can direct to the ultimate end who has the care and responsibility for a particular community. Thus God is the lawgiver for the universe, and in the human community the lawgiver is the civil authority. The publication or promulgation of the law may never be omitted. This promulgation is different in the case of the natural law from what it is in the case of positive laws; either the law is written by God on the tablet of man's heart, or it is expressly revealed, or it is made known by human authority in such a way that everyone knows it or can know it. When the law is put in writing, it possesses a continuous promulgation.

St. Thomas follows St. Isidore (*Etym.,* V, 19) in enumerating the various acts of the law as: commanding, forbidding, permitting, and punishing. Each of these acts, however, is not equally essential to the law. Every law, inasmuch as it is essentially a norm, rule, and prescription, possesses a directive force, just as the lawgiver himself possesses such directive power. In cases where the legal prescription is not fulfilled, the coactive force, or the sanction of punishment, is united to the law. This coactive power can be applied only to those who are subject to the lawgiver, and not to the lawgiver himself since no one can force himself. While the directive force of law is an essential part of the law, the coactive and punishing powers are only accidental, in the sense, however, that they are intimately con-

---

[5] *Summa theol.,* Ia IIae, q. 90, a. 1–4; *Contra Gent.,* III, 14; *Etym.,* V, 19.

nected with the meaning and purpose of the law. Because of the
malice that exists at times in human wills, a law without coactive
force would be illusory and without effect.[6]

St. Thomas distinguishes between four kinds of laws: divine laws,
which direct to a supernatural end and are made known to man by
revelation; human laws, i.e., the positive human legislation; above
the human law is the natural law, which is itself a derivation of the
higher eternal law of the universe. Empiricism and positivism recognize no natural laws and thus they are forced into the position of
legal positivism.

2. The eternal law. In attempting a more exact delineation of law
and right, we might begin with a consideration of positive legislation, and this method would eventually lead us to our goal, although
it would entail an excursion into the field of positive law and positive right. Let us inquire, for a moment, about the origin of the idea
of law incorporated in the first positive law. St. John Chrysostom [7]
proposed this question and answered it by saying that present-day
lawgivers may perhaps act under the influence of tradition when they
legislate about marriage, wills, murder, etc., but that the ultimate
basis of all laws is man's God-given conscience. The law of conscience brought the courts of law into existence and gives force to
penal laws.

This law of conscience is not a collection of legal principles in a
formal sense, but it is a collection of prescriptions that have a material content. We may sometimes refer to these prescriptions of
conscience as self-evident, reasonable laws, but the ultimate basis
for the law of conscience is laid in the nature of man and of things;
it is therefore some law incorporated in the very nature of things.
This universal or eternal law has an intimate connection with the
natural law, but it is not identical with it, even though we find the
earlier Stoics confusing these two laws because of the pantheistic
trend of their thinking. If we have in mind the nature of things in
the universe, we are considering the natural law, but we do not yet
proceed to the more fundamental eternal law. To come to the
eternal law we must proceed to an interpretation of the universe
and of all essences in the universe from the standpoint of the ultimate
divine principle.

[6] *Summa theol.,* Ia IIae, q.92, a.2; q.90, a.3 ad2; IIa IIae, q.67, a.1.
[7] *Ad pop. Antioch. hom.,* 12, 3 f.

In his theory of eternal law, St. Thomas represents the highest point in a long tradition, its more important stages marked by the figures of Cicero and St. Augustine. Cicero himself, however, was under the influence of Greek philosophy and thus he incorporated many Stoic ideas into his theistic philosophy. Thinkers with religious convictions long recognized the existence of laws and prescriptions having a validity based on the cosmic order established by the Deity; and they admitted the force of these laws although in many instances they were ignored in public life. Ancient poets and writers gave expression to these sentiments, as, for instance, Sophocles in his *Antigone* (V, 456 f.). So also Empedocles in his *Canticle of Atonement* proclaimed that the universal law extended through the length and breadth of the all-embracing ether and the immeasurable brilliance of the heavens, while the Pythagoreans chanted the praises of the cosmos permeated by one great law.

This thought received a fruitful turn when Heraclitus identified the primal divine pneuma, the cosmic intelligence, and the cosmic law, and said that all norms of human action are derived from this divine eternal law.[8] With regard to the promulgation of the natural law and natural right, special attention must be accorded the Sophists (Antiphon and Alcidamas) who were able to cause great disturbances by their teachings. As representatives of the radical wing of the Sophist school, they distorted the idea of the natural law by establishing the individual as the norm of all action and proclaiming the natural law of the stronger individual. In immediate reaction to this teaching, Plato, the defender of the higher spiritual man and the spokesman of the higher spiritual world, arose and declared that the moral order is bound to eternal and unchanging norms and laws. Before we speak of positive law and positive right, a certain right and justice was firmly established, a law that is eternal and valid in a higher world, an eternal imperative for this empirical world, an eternal prototype that every ruler must observe and imitate without fail.[9] Although Plato's ideas possessed autonomy, they did not represent something ultimate and uncaused; they were referred back to God as their cause, and therefore law, right, and morality are rooted in the ultimate reason of the universe.[10] Especially in his

[8] *Frag.*, I, 2, 41, 112, 114.
[9] *Rep.*, VI, 500.
[10] *Ibid.*, X, 596–98.

Laws, Plato derives the natural order as well as the legal order from God the supreme cause.

Within the framework of his teleological philosophy, Aristotle made extensive use of the concept of a natural law based on metaphysics. He defends the idea of natural law as against positive law, but he knew no eternal law. The reason for this is that he did not understand the close connection between the order of the universe and the concept of God. For him God is only the first mover. The world derives its existence from itself, all power in the world is attributed to its nature or φύσις.

An interesting development took place in the natural pantheism of the Stoics. The primal pneuma, from which all things in the universe proceed, contains in itself also the forces that course through matter, the world soul, the world intelligence and the universal or cosmic law to which everything must yield.[11] This theory of a universally valid cosmic law was given a theistic metaphysical basis by Philo and Cicero and afterward by the Fathers of the Church.

Cicero holds an important place in the history of thought as the transmitter of the ideas of Hellenic philosophy to the thinkers of the patristic period. With the building material of Greek philosophy he erected a structure of thought that was accepted by Christianity and developed to completion in the Middle Ages. Some of the Roman jurists took over Greek terminology without being able to penetrate to the original meaning and the ethical content of Greek thought, but this was not true of most Roman thinkers and especially not of Cicero. He is not indeed an original thinker, but he gave such enthusiastic expression to the concepts of natural and eternal law that Christian thinkers gladly followed his leadership. The world is a cosmos and a work of God. Everything has been produced by the intelligence and will of the Supreme Being and is ruled by Him. For this planned universe, in which every being, including man, is enclosed in a certain order, a supreme law of being and action has been established. In this law is included the law of man's life, and in this law, which is the same as the intelligence of the Supreme Being, all law is founded.

From Cicero the line of the history of thought goes to the Fathers of the Church and especially to St. Augustine. St. Augustine taught that the eternal law is the ultimate fount of law and right, and he

[11] *Frag.,* III, 308–26.

describes it as the divine wisdom, and divine intelligence. It is the divine wisdom or the divine will commanding that the natural order must be preserved and forbidding that it be disturbed.[12] Just as the supreme wisdom is the unchanging truth, so it is also the unchanging eternal law from whose realm nothing is exempt.[13] This doctrine of the eternal law was in organic agreement with the theistic teleological philosophy of St. Augustine. He presupposed a divine idea before the appearance of the phenomenon of the universe, he taught that a divine plan underlay the course of the universe. The divine wisdom contains the idea of the universe (*ratio condendae creaturae*), and the invisible, unchanging, eternal forms and reasons of all things that come to exist in the empirical world.[14] The plan of the universe comes to completion in a hierarchy of grades of being each more perfect than its predecessor. Each grade of being has received its own form of being, a definite form, a definite principle of activity, and a determined rule of life from the wisdom of the almighty Creator of the universe. While all beings, from the inorganic state to the animals, actualize the eternal law of the divine plan unknowingly by reason of an inner necessity, man, because of his intelligence, is able to understand the order that applies to him. The eternal law abandons the imperative of the natural law when it comes to man and appeals to him as an obligation that should be fulfilled. Thus the natural law arising from the eternal law becomes the moral law for man, it becomes the expression of the divine order as willed by God. Essentially the eternal law is always intent on the preservation of a perfect order.

When, in the thirteenth century, jurisprudence was incorporated into the philosophical and theological system, the Augustinian theory of the eternal law was accepted as its metaphysical foundation. St. Thomas was completely loyal to the Augustinian tradition when he taught that the principles of order for all existing beings were established beforehand by the Ruler of the universe. As the Creator of the universe, the divine wisdom contains the ideal prototype within itself, as the mover of all things toward their end divine wisdom acts as the law of the universe. Therefore St. Thomas defined the eternal law as the "plan of government in the supreme Ruler," and as "the

12 *Cont. Faust. Man.*, XXII, 27.
13 *De ver. relig.*, 31; *De civ. Dei*, XIX, 12; *De ord.*, II, 7, 23.
14 *De gen. ad lit.*, IV, 24; *De civ. Dei*, V, 11.

divine wisdom inasmuch as it directs all movements and actions."
The eternal law of the universe is the most profound and most fundamental law underlying the whole order of the universe, and, like
St. Augustine, St. Thomas declared that because of this law everything is in the best order (*omnia sunt ordinatissima*).[15] In this eternal law are contained both the natural law and the moral law, the
natural order and the moral order. Order consists in this, that God imprinted on every form of being in nature certain principles for proper
acts. Together with these principles, every being receives an objective
direction to its end.[16]

Everything is subject to the eternal law, nothing can withdraw from
it; whoever attempts to recede from it violates it. The eternal law
bears the promise of supreme bliss as well as punishment and damna-
tion.[17] St. Bonaventure and Duns Scotus do not differ in principle
from St. Thomas on this question. If the act of creation proceeded in
accord with the eternal intelligence and the eternal prototype in the
divine spirit, if the divine will is based on the divine wisdom and acts
in accord with the highest concept of order, this order of the universe
must be manifested in a universe completely subject to law. No
theistic and teleological system of philosophy that acknowledges an intelligent supreme Being can omit the concept of a supreme and eternal law.

[15] *Summa theol.*, Ia IIae, q.93, a.1; St. Augustine, *De lib. arb.*, I, 6.
[16] *Summa theol., loc. cit.*, a.5.
[17] *Ibid.*, a.6 ad 3.

CHAPTER XXXIV

NATURAL LAW

1. The concept of natural law. The eternal law of the universe is not revealed in its entirety to the mind of man; it is known, however, by the blessed, who enjoy the beatific vision of God's essence. To some extent the eternal law is manifest to us in created things by means of the natural law. All creatures participate to some extent in the eternal law, at least so far as "they possess a tendency to their own peculiar acts imprinted on their natures by the eternal law."[1] To bring the plan of the universe to realization, the Creator called into existence beings with a circumscribed nature and assigned to them certain tasks for certain ends, and the eternal law serves the accomplishment of this divine plan for the universe. Every particular nature in the universe possesses certain activities, and these activities correspond to the particular nature, according to the metaphysical principle that the peculiar activity of a being corresponds to its nature.[2]

The course of the development of each being is charted by the fact that every being by its nature is directed to its own proper activity and that it possesses tendencies and natural inclinations to actions and purposes conformable to its own nature. Therefore it appears that the natural law is the complexus of tendencies toward ends and inclinations to actions which are based on the constant essences of things. By these inclinations each thing fulfills its own purposes and establishes the order in the things of nature. This idea of the natural law is in agreement with the definition of Ulpian, with that of Justinian in the *Corpus civile,* and that of Isidore: *jus naturale est quod natura docuit omnia animalia.* Thus the natural law includes such things as the union of male and female, propagation of the species, and the nourishment of offspring.

[1] *Summa theol.,* Ia IIae, q.91, a.2.
[2] *Contra Gent.,* III, 129.

Rufinus, Gratian's third commentator, narrowed down the concept of the natural law so that it applied only to man. Later William of Auxerre distinguished natural law in the strict sense from the vague Roman concept of natural law and defined it as all that reason commands us without special reflection. For St. Albert, too, the natural law was a law of reason comprising the obligations of rational human nature. St. Thomas adhered to this line of thought, and he conceived the natural law to be essentially a law of reason so that he spoke of law only with reference to rational beings and not to irrational beings. In its proper sense law can be said to be active only when rational beings participate in the eternal law through their own reason. Man alone is a creature susceptible of law. This modification requires also that the law be found essentially in him who prescribes the measure and standard that are the law. In irrational beings we speak only of a certain similarity to law. Therefore we have the definition: the natural law is in no way different from the eternal law, it is merely the participation in the eternal law by a rational creature.[3]

Man possesses a distinctive nature and therefore determined laws of activity. Rational beings differ from the lower creatures because man by his reason guides and directs his actions.[4] These natural inclinations are really tendencies to an end. But these ends are objects of the appetite and will, they have the character of good and the valuable, and they have an attraction for the appetite. In this juncture the reason, *ordinativa omnium quae ad homines spectant,* becomes active and takes cognizance of this material of the appetitive faculty which it directs and governs. Thus the ends that arise before the natural tendencies are lifted up into the sphere of the intellect, and here they are evaluated, affirmed, approved, corrected, and ordered in a proper relationship.

In man's original state this rational course of action was always infallible. But when the harmony of the soul was disturbed by sin, reason lost some of its pre-eminence.[5] In general, however, whereas the animals follow a natural instinct in their vital actions, reason is dominant in man; the eternal and universal law appears in animals in the form of blind tendencies, but man participates in the eternal law by his knowing and striving. This law appears in man in the

---

[3] *Summa theol.,* Ia IIae, q.91, a.2 ad 1; q.93, a.5; *Contra Gent.,* III, 114.

[4] *Summa theol.,* Ia IIae, q.94, a.3; *In IV Sent.,* 33, 1.

[5] *Summa theol., loc. cit.,* a.2 ad 2; a.4 ad 3; q.91, a.6.

form of an imperative which aims at the actualization of the idea of human nature. St. Thomas says: "Man participates in the eternal law inasmuch as he knows and inasmuch as the inner moving principle of his activity is derived from the eternal law; irrational creatures participate only inasmuch as the principle of action is derived from the eternal law."[6] "The natural law is primarily in the eternal law and secondarily in the natural judgment of the human reason."[7] In the human spirit the eternal law becomes a prescription of reason and assumes an obligating force.[8]

The natural law is therefore the complexus of all those prescriptions which flow from human nature, which are directed to the fulfillment of man's ultimate end, which are known by the light of reason, and which appear in the consciousness of man armed with a claim to absolute obedience. Everything that is not in accord with man's proper end is opposed to the natural law. Thus Gratian's definition of the natural law—all that is contained in the Decalogue and in the Gospels—is replaced by a more realistic statement, and at the same time the natural law is distinguished from the divine law.[9]

In this teaching on the natural law, St. Thomas united some well-known conclusions offered by tradition. No doubt can exist that the moral teaching of the New Testament and also that of the Fathers of the Church rest on the basis of a theory of the natural law, on the theory that all the basic moral principles are written on the heart of man and are therefore unknown to no one. These were said to be prescriptions that made themselves known to reason of their own accord. If sometimes among the Fathers the formula bears a touch of the Stoics, the thought itself is thoroughly Christian. In entire accord with the theory of the natural law, is the concept of the nature of things as the principle of action, being, and order, and the interpretation of natural tendencies as an expression of a natural order of things. We find references to this thought in Plato, Aristotle, and the Stoics, and a development of it by Cicero, St. Augustine, and the Scholastics.[10]

---

[6] *Ibid.*, q.93, a.6.
[7] *Ibid.*, q.71, a.6 ad 4.
[8] *Ibid.*, q.19, a.4; q.94, a.2; a.4 ad 3.
[9] *In IV Sent.*, 33, 1; *Summa theol.*, Ia IIae, q.94, a.4, ad 1.
[10] Cf. Marcus Aurelius, IV, 4; VI, 44; VII, 9; Seneca, *Epist.*, 4, 90, 95; *De ira*, II, 31; *De benef.*, IV, 12, 17; *Natur. quaest.*, III; Cicero, *De leg.*, I, 8, 15–17; *De rep.*, V, 4; *De nat. deorum*, I, 15; *De fin.*, V, 15, 21.

From the beginning St. Thomas pointed out the connection between the natural law and reason, calling it the law of reason. We find this thought expressed in some way also by the Fathers of the Church, in Neoplatonism, by the Stoics, Aristotle, the Cynics, and Heraclitus, all of whom looked on the natural law in man as the law of reason, as the spiritual appeal to man's will directed by his reason, far excelling the passive direction and submission of irrational creatures.

Certain discrepancies which some fancied they found in this course of Thomistic thought really do not exist, since this law of reason is in no sense said to be without relation to the order of being and nature. At the most we might be inclined to see a lack of such factual relationship when St. Thomas says that the natural moral law is derived from an illumination by some higher world. He makes that statement in a discussion of the Neoplatonic Augustinian theory of illumination. This theory, however, never became dominant in his mind. Already in the *Commentary on the Sentences,* and later in the *Theological Summa,* he taught that by nature certain principles reside in every thing by means of which a thing places its proper actions which are conducive to attaining its own end. These principles are the forms of things: in rational beings they are the rational forms, especially the faculties of knowing and willing. In the faculty of knowing we find a *naturalis conceptio* and in the will a *naturalis inclinatio.* Both potencies, therefore, have a natural disposition or aptitude.

The Thomistic concept of truth as the *adaequatio rei et intellectus* requires that a real connection exist between the object and the knowing faculty. In fact, man knows the ends and purposes comprised in his human nature and the relation of his actions to these ends and purposes, and by knowing his own nature man comes to the knowledge of the norms of his actions so that they will conform to his ends.

To say that St. Thomas alone discovered the ontological natural law is to go too far. The basic thought is derived from Greek realism, but St. Thomas incorporated it more aptly into Christian thought than did his predecessors. We need no illumination from above when things themselves point the way and when they show the measure of perfection in their own natures. With this argument nominalism was rejected. Our concepts of the natural law are not mere subjective forms created out of the relationships of individuals about us, they are actually forms that express real objective relations. Thus the objective and universal validity of the prescriptions of the natural law is safeguarded. In its fundamental principles the natural law is the same in all individuals both as to its knowability and as to its certainty.[11] Thus St. Thomas, by giving the natural law an ontological foundation, established a natural and evident basis for morality and law, and he avoided a mystical exaggeration as well as the disturbing theories of skepticism and relativism.

2. The content of the natural law. To obey the natural law means nothing more than to give free rein to the natural human striving for good.[12] The natural law is the expression of natural morality; therefore St. Thomas enumerated all virtuous acts under the natural law. In the theoretical order of knowledge we saw that the concept of being is the first concept and that the principle of contradiction is the supreme principle. Likewise in the moral order the concept of good is the first concept, and the supreme principle was enunciated by St. Albert and St. Thomas as follows: Good is to be done and evil is to be avoided. This principle is the root that underlies all the prescriptions of the natural law.[13] Man necessarily tends to the good, that is, toward his happiness. The will cannot do otherwise than will the good; in this respect man possesses no freedom. Whenever man strives for something, he seeks it under the aspect of the good. He may fall into error in the choice of the means, but he always has his gaze fixed on the good, real or apparent.

Like the denial of the first theoretical principle, the denial of this first moral principle leads to self-contradiction. If a man would try to oppose the good and his own happiness, he would be seeking his happiness and his good in this supposed freedom and thus he would merely be giving an added proof that he is still under the attraction of the good. The multiplicity of prescriptions that apply to man are merely particularizations of the good or evil.

The great object of the Thomistic system is to make all parts of the system harmonize with the supreme epistemological and metaphysical principles, and to show that every conclusion rests firmly on

---

[11] *Summa theol.*, Ia IIae, q.94, a.4.
[12] *In IV Sent.*, 33, 1.
[13] *Summa theol.*, Ia IIae, q.94, a.2.

the basic principles. This characteristic of the system is especially evident in the teaching on the natural law. The search for truth in the theoretical field has its counterpart in the practical sphere. Here the search is for the good, which is really identical with being and truth, and this search strives for the perfection of being, the perfection of one's own personality or of other beings. This is the positive part of the principle: good must be done. The negative part is expressed in the words: we may never inflict evil on another.

In explaining the contents of the natural law, St. Thomas follows the direction of nature. "Since the good always has the character of an end and since evil is opposed to the end, reason evaluates all natural inclinations and tendencies as good and worthy of realization, and therefore it commands that the good be done and the evil be avoided."[14] In morality and in the natural law only the original inclinations, the fundamental tendencies, those that correspond to the development of the human person and thus supply the psychological foundation for the natural law, are important. St. Thomas oriented his theory of the natural law and human right to the ontology of the human person. Man possesses several different spheres of being, but all of these belong to the whole person by means of an organic subordination to each other; and all are subject to the rule of reason which directs them to the fulfillment of the end of human life.

The hierarchy of the prescriptions of the natural law corresponds to the principal gradations in the relations to the good and to the various strivings that issue from human nature. The order of the precepts of the natural law corresponds to the order of the natural inclinations.[15]

The most fundamental inclination or urge which supports all others is the urge to self-preservation, and in this respect man resembles all other beings. The natural law includes all precepts aiming at self-preservation as well as all those that forbid suicide, self-mutilation, and the murder or injuring of others.

The second group of precepts in the natural law is based on man's animal nature which he has in common with all sensible beings, on the urge to the production and rearing of offspring. Since in the case of man it is a question of the sexual union of rational beings and the

14 *Ibid*.
15 *Ibid*.

procreation of persons, monogamy appears as the only permissible form of marriage. Marriage, like the state, is a natural thing, but not a thing necessary by the natural law. Because of his inner urge to continue the race, man has a natural inclination to marriage, and this inclination is actualized by his intellect and an act of his will.

The purpose of marriage, as Aristotle had already said, is twofold. The primary purpose is the offspring and its welfare, its generation, nourishment, and education. The secondary purpose consists in the mutual assistance of the spouses and in their mutual fidelity. In agreement with St. Augustine and Christian tradition, St. Thomas added a third purpose or good of matrimony. He distinguished a threefold good, therefore, in accord with the threefold character of married persons. Inasmuch as married persons are in the same genus with other living beings, the purpose of marriage consists in the offspring; inasmuch as they are human beings, the purpose of marriage consists in their fidelity; and inasmuch as they are Christians, the good of marriage consists in the sacrament.[16]

All that is contrary to nature is opposed to the natural law. To place an obstacle in the way of the primary purpose is to violate the primary precepts of the natural law. That which impedes the attainment of subordinate ends or disturbs the prosecution of the primary end is a violation of secondary precepts derived from the primary precepts of the natural law. Polygamy is not opposed to the primary precepts of the natural law because it does not prevent the generation and rearing of offspring. But it is against the sacramental character of marriage and against the second purpose or good of marriage. A love and friendship that perdures for life belongs to the essence of marriage. The woman would not be the free and equal companion of the man if he were permitted to have many wives. To a certain extent polygamy imperils the primary purpose of marriage also, inasmuch as the husband could not adequately care for the education and training of the children of many wives. Even in the animal kingdom one male unites with one female when the offspring require care for some length of time.

Since polygamy does not prevent the generation of offspring and is not therefore opposed to the primary purpose of marriage, God

[16] *In IV Sent.*, 26, 1; *Summa theol.*, IIIa, q. 41, a. 1; q. 49, a. 2; Aristotle, *Eth. Nic.*, VIII, 14; St. Augustine, *De bono conj.*, I, 1; *De civ. Dei.*, XIV, 21–23; *De gen. ad lit.*, IX, 7.

may permit it for some higher good, in order, for instance, that members of the true faith may be increased.[17]

The security of the offspring and the continuing care for the physical and mental development of the children and the mutual happiness of the father and mother require that marriage be indissoluble.[18] Polyandry is opposed to the first principles of the natural law since it makes the generation of the offspring, if not impossible, at least difficult, and especially since it jeopardizes the education of the children because of the uncertainty of the children's paternity. Since the first principles of the natural law are decisive in the formation of positive law and for custom and tradition, polyandry cannot be sanctioned by positive law or custom.

Concubinage is a violation of the primary precept of the natural law because such a union is sought for itself and not for the purpose of producing offspring. Such a union is entered into to satisfy sensual desires and, if children are born, their education and training will be in danger. Thus a manifest injustice is inflicted on the offspring since their welfare is not sufficiently secure.

Only when the dictates of the natural law had become clouded and obscure in the minds of men did the pagans consider sexual intercourse permissible outside of marriage. Because houses of prostitution are against the natural law, primitive Christianity condemned them in pagan civilization. The assumption that slavery included the right to extra-marital intercourse was likewise a violation of the natural law. The slave is indeed obligated to serve the master, but she is not obliged to sexual intercourse.[19]

The natural law forbids moreover marriage between blood relatives, between father and daughter, mother and son. In such marriages the principle object of marriage could be obtained but not in the proper way. If we learn that sexual unions between parents and children occurred among certain savage peoples, this can be attributed only to the darkening of their intellects. Referring to St. Augustine[20] and the Old Testament, St. Thomas declared that such unions were an offense against that respect which children naturally owe to parents. With regard to marriages between sisters and brothers, he said

---

17 *In IV Sent.*, 33, 1 ad 1.
18 *Ibid.*, 33, 2; *Contra Gent.*, III, 122 f.; *Summa theol.*, IIIa, q.67, a.1.
19 *In IV Sent.*, 33, 1, 3; *Summa theol.*, IIIa, q.65, a.3, 5.
20 *De civ. Dei*, XV, 16.

they were not forbidden in themselves; in fact, in the beginning of the race they were necessary. Such marriages, however, are opposed to the concept of marriage as the union of different persons, because sisters and brothers have as it were the same origin.[21]

Divorce, too, is against the natural law because it jeopardizes the welfare of the offspring and at the same time it is a violation of marital fidelity. Manifestly those sins called "sins against nature" are against the natural law because they oppose the purpose of the sexual act. Among these are self-pollution, bestiality, sodomy, and any unnatural intercourse between man and woman. In these actions man oversteps the barriers which nature herself has erected around the use of the sexual organs and thus he sins seriously against God, the Author of nature.[22]

Therefore lifelong monogamy is the form prescribed by the ultimate ends of the universe for man's sexual life. From the whole concept of marriage it follows that the parents' care, physical as well as spiritual, for the children, is commanded by the natural law, as is also the respect and love of the children toward their parents.

A third relationship to good and thus a third group of demands made on man by the natural law flows from the rational nature of man. Among these duties St. Thomas counts man's mental development, the search for the truth, with respect to his last end and to his vocational perfection, and finally man's moral development. Since the finite and limited being is directed to the infinite and absolute Being, and since the subject is directed and oriented to the Master, evidently religious development and activity belong to prescriptions made by the natural law.[23] Further, since man not only is an individual person but possesses in his innermost being social attitudes, St. Thomas insists that the social forms, such as the family, state and the community, are deeply rooted in the natural law.

At this point we can see that the entire Decalogue belongs to the natural law. We must not, however, conclude that the Decalogue is a derivation from some general and vague principles called the natural law. This purposeful interpretation of the various aspects of human nature will lead to definite and practical directions for attaining the end of the law, the natural development of human nature.

---

21 *Summa theol.*, IIa IIae, q. 154, a. 9 ad 3; *Contra Gent.*, III, 125.
22 *Summa theol.*, IIa IIae, q. 154, a. 8.
23 *Ibid.*, Ia IIae, q. 109, a. 3.

The axioms, "The good is to be done" and "Evil must be avoided" indeed tell us very little; the decisive thing is to show in what exactly the good and evil consist, and thus we are again and again referred to the nature of things and the nature of man himself. Murder, theft, robbery, divorce, lying, etc., are forbidden by the natural law; but we must further determine what actions are comprised under these terms and which are excluded.

To say that murder and theft were determined and fixed by the concrete moral and juridical order of some particular people is most probably true, just as it is true that the concept of theft depends on the prevailing concept of the nature of property; but this is no valid objection against the natural law. If we analyze the moral orders or the juridical systems from which the concepts of crimes received definite form, we will always arrive at those fixed and unchanging principles and norms that arise from the nature of things. Consequently we say that the natural law is not a collection of directions cut to fit every particular instance, but rather the great canon containing the fundamental commands whose violation will unsettle the basis of human society. The definiteness of the natural law is not synonymous with rigidity; the natural law contemplates all possible cases.

CHAPTER XXXV

NATURAL RIGHTS

Many Scholastics do not distinguish clearly between the natural law and natural rights. St. Thomas, too, uses the terms interchangeably,[1] but sometimes he shows that he is aware that they express different aspects of one and the same thing. "Law" is not "right" in its actual meaning; law is rather a certain plan of right (*aliqualis ratio juris*). [2] Whatever is prescribed for a thing is right for that thing. If right is that which belongs to something according to justice, then natural right is that which an individual can claim as his own according to nature; it is owed to him, *debitum,* and he can demand that his claim be recognized.[3]

Man is directed to the perfection of his being as to his end and therefore he has an inalienable relation to what is comprised under this end. Man's obligation to perfect himself corresponds to his right to this perfection and vice versa. St. Thomas did not develop a separate system of natural rights, although we are able to discern in his teaching an outline of a system of natural rights. A sketch of man's fundamental rights will correspond to the different phases of the human person.

1. **The right to physical existence.** A presupposition for all other rights is the right to physical existence, the right to corporal inviolability and physical development. This right implies the right to self-defense, the right to those things that are necessary to support life, and the right to a dignified human existence. St. Thomas makes a distinction between the minimum required for existence and the minimum for a particular station in life. Every man has a right by his

---

[1] *In IV Sent.,* 32, 1; 33, 10.
[2] *Summa theol.,* IIa IIae, q.57, a.1 ad2; q.60, a.1.
[3] *Ibid.,* Ia, q.21, a.1; Ia IIae, q.66, a.4 ad1; IIa IIae, q.50, a.11; q.66, a.3.

very nature to what is required as a minimum for his physical existence. Therefore a man who is in extreme need has a right to support,
just as it becomes an obligation for anyone who has that support to
come to his assistance. The greater a man's wealth, the greater will
be his obligation toward others. The Fathers of the Church had already declared that to withhold necessities from those in need was
theft and robbery. In cases of extreme need, especially if life itself is
in danger, the natural law permits the person in need to take another's property, or a third person to expropriate property openly or
covertly for the assistance of the needy even with the use of force.[4]
In these claims of the natural law, we may be able to detect a minimum of communism. In cases of extreme need, all the goods of the
world belong to everyone.[5] Here the concept of private property
suffers a modification since, under certain circumstances, another has
the right to make use of the property. This concession does not, however, disturb the institution of private property, and St. Thomas consistently defended it as founded on the natural law.

2. **The right to property.** The animated discussions on the subject
of private property by Aristotle, the Fathers of the Church, in Roman
and canonical law, and by other Scholastics, afforded sufficient occasion for a treatment of the subject by St. Thomas. The right to
property, according to St. Thomas, comprised, as it does today, the
right of possession, the right to earnings, the right of management,
disposal, and use.[6] St. Thomas reasoned from basic principles and
derived the right to property from the whole complexus of the world
order. The supreme lord and original owner of all property is God.
But in that order which was established by God Himself, the lower
must serve the higher, the imperfect must serve the more perfect.
External goods, by their nature, are intended to support human life
and to provide comfort and ease for man; they seem to offer themselves of their own accord to satisfy man's needs. Therefore man has
a natural right to take the life of living beings.[7] This ability and
readiness to serve man does not, however, prove that this particular
piece of land or this particular animal belongs to some individual
person. Nothing has as yet been said about the form of the use and

4 *Ibid.*, IIa IIae, q.32, a.5 f.; q.66, a.7; *In IV Sent.*, 15, 2, 1.
5 *Summa theol.*, IIa IIae, q.32, a.7 ad 3.
6 *Ibid.*, q.66, a.1 ad 1–3; q.64, a.1.
7 *Contra Gent.*, III, 112.

possession of these external goods. Common possession with use by all the individuals, common possession and common use by the community, and individual possession and individual use by individuals, are the possible forms of possession and use. St. Thomas does not consider all of these possibilities; he devotes most of his attention to a criticism and rejection of inordinate communism in the sense of common possession by all individuals.

To establish the right of private property, a subjective factor must be brought to bear in connection with the objective factor. The individual's dominion over external things is founded on man's reason inasmuch as it is a reflection of God, as expressed in Genesis, 1:26. The deepest metaphysical root and basis for private property is to be found in the fact that man is an image of God, and one of the properties of such a person is the rational disposition and free disposal of external things. The ego, in its form of *mine*, has an immediate relation to the *it*, because external possessions are the basis for the development and activity of the human personality. This is the true meaning of St. Thomas' argument that private property is founded on a well-ordered self-love, or on the psychological and ethical development of human self-interest.

But St. Thomas might have gone farther in his consideration of the personal pronouns. The ego or the *I* has also a relation to the *you*, i.e., to the neighbor, proximate and remote. The striving for a lasting possession of external things corresponds to man's natural urge to care for his own, his family, etc., as well as to that human characteristic of coming to another's assistance, as it is expressed in the virtue of liberality and in all the works of fraternal charity.[8] The sphere in which an individual lives his life will include other human beings, those he calls his own, with whom he is united by intimate bonds both physical and spiritual, and for these a man assumes responsibility. For this reason he requires private property.

Other relationships and aspects of free rational persons demand the right to private property, and in man's social life these aspects of his nature are such that the social order itself confirms his claim to private property. In the first place, a man will care more for what belongs to him alone. Common care of a thing by many people is tantamount to common neglect, as Aristotle said in his argument with Plato. Secondly, greater order will exist if every man cares for what is

[8] *Summa theol.*, IIa IIae, q.32, a.5 ad3; *Contra Gent.*, III, 131.

his own, than when each individual is concerned with whatever presents itself to his attention. Thirdly, the satisfaction of owning private property is the basis for peace, while common possession is the occasion for dissension and quarreling.[9] The preservation of the community rests on the right of private property.

The reasons underlying the right to private property, its metaphysical roots, its psychological foundation, and its socio-ethical and economic basis, are all closely related. The objection might be raised that the metaphysical deduction is not fully justified, since St. Thomas proves merely [10] that man has a natural right to the possession of external goods, but says nothing about the form of that possession or ownership. But the objection is of no force, since St. Thomas says expressly, "That which man possesses by a natural right, he may rightly designate as his own." [11] The reference in the article to the statement of St. Basil precludes any doubt that "his own" is to be taken as the lasting possession of things that a man may use.[12]

One objection at this point is, however, more telling. St. Thomas did not give sufficient consideration to the fact that communism has, or may have, several forms, such as the communism in monastic communities or certain village communities. In these a certain order is observed in defining and limiting the activities of individuals. St. Thomas' principal objections against communism are, however, valid against every form of communism.

Thus private property is firmly based on the objective relations of things. In establishing the right to private property, human reason acted entirely in accord with reality and in a way to serve human welfare in the best way possible. The question of private property belongs to the *jus gentium*. The right to private property is not one of the first principles of the natural law, but it is derived from these principles. In explaining the origin of the right of private property, St. Thomas makes an unhappy comparison when he says that private property and slavery are derived from the natural law in the same way.[13]

In patristic times and during the Middle Ages a difference of opinion existed whether private property was a disposition of human

[9] *Summa theol.*, IIa IIae, q.66, a.2.
[10] *Ibid.*, a.1.
[11] *Ibid.*
[12] *Ibid.*, a.1 obj.2.
[13] *Ibid.*, Ia IIae, q.94, a.5 ad3.

nature itself, or whether it was an arrangement of fallen human nature, i.e., a part of a deteriorated natural law. Pseudo-Clement, St. Ambrose, Gratian, William of Auxerre, and St. Bonaventure thought that communism was the paradisiacal system. Influenced by tradition, St. Thomas occasionally expressed the thought that in the state of innocence the human will was so well ordered that the common use of external goods might take place without dissension.[14]

St. Thomas' principal argument for private property, however, points to another conclusion. If this right belongs to man inasmuch as he is the image of God, then the arrangement of private property should be found in Paradise especially since then the divine image in man had not yet been distorted. If, however, the introduction of private property went apace with the introduction of slavery, it appears that sin was a presupposition. No definite decision seems possible because of the conflicting historical influences that affected the reasoning of the great doctor.

St. Thomas distinguishes between a twofold right to external things: the right of acquisition and administration, and the right of use. With respect to the right to use a thing, man may not look on it as his personal possession, but as the property of all in common, which he will readily share with those who are in need. That was the intent of St. Paul when he said, "Charge the rich of this world . . . to give easily, to communicate to others." [15]

One important matter must not be lost sight of: the Thomistic concept of private property is clearly opposed to the idea of property contained in Roman law. St. Thomas' insistence on the proper administration and use and the obligation of assisting the neighbor is not indeed socialism, but the teaching has social implications and points to the individual's obligation to the whole, to the community. This social element he found clearly expressed by Aristotle and it was emphasized by the moral code of Christianity, while the community characteristics of Teutonic law may not have been without some additional corroborating influence.[16]

Private property rests firmly on the natural law; its detailed regulation according to time and place is the concern of the positive law. St. Thomas considered the just distribution of goods and possessions

---

[14] *Ibid.*, Ia, q.98, a.1 ad3.
[15] I Tim. 6: 17 f.
[16] *Summa theol.*, IIa IIae, q.118, a.1; *De reg. princ.*, I, 13; *In IV Pol.*, 10.

as one of the most important duties of the state. Following Aristotle again and conforming to the political thinkers of his medieval world with its guild system, he stood for a decent livelihood for each one (*nullus inconvenienter vivere debet*), which differed according to one's higher or lower station in life. As the philosopher of the middle, he approved a point somewhere between want and superfluity. Those who have a surplus must give to those who are in extreme need, according to the dictates of the natural law. If the individual is forgetful of his obligation, the state may intervene and act for the common good.[17]

3. **The right of physical freedom.** St. Thomas did not recognize a universal right of physical freedom; influenced by his time, he defended the institution of slavery. The Sophists taught that God had given all men freedom, and that according to the law of nature there are no slaves. Aristotle here represented the party of the reaction and tried to justify slavery on the basis of the varied equipment which nature gives to men. A slave is a human being to whom only such a share of intellectual ability has been given that he is able to understand the orders coming from other men; he is incapable of developing his reason or his own personality, and thus his chief activity consists in the use of his physical powers.[18]

The Stoics achieved special significance in the slavery controversy. The attempts made by Euripides, Plato, and the Cynics for a recognition of the universal dignity of man were accepted by the Stoics as the groundwork for their system. The world is a uniform, harmonious whole, and every man, without exception, is a part of this whole; each man has the same origin as the others, each is endowed with the same divine reason and should therefore live according to the same natural laws of reason. Slavery, of course, was irreconcilable with such a bold recognition of man's dignity, and, although the Stoics did not demand the abolition of slavery, their doctrine of the universal respect and love that is due the dignity of man did much to bring about an amelioration of the condition of the slaves.

From these Stoics, Cicero derived his views on slavery. Later a higher state of development was reached in Seneca, who indeed ascribed the body of the slave to the master, but taught that a man's spirit is exempt from this ownership. For the treatment of slaves he

---

[17] *Summa theol.*, IIa IIae, q. 118, a. 1.
[18] *Pol.*, I, 5.

proclaimed the axiom: *Homo sacra res homini* "Every man should be sacred to every other man." He counseled the citizens of Rome: "Treat your slaves as you yourselves wish to be treated by your superiors; treat them so that they will reverence you and not fear you." Such thoughts are the noble fruit produced on the tree of Stoic humanitarianism and they suffer but slight derogation when Seneca, partly because of a strange inconsistency in his nature and partly because of the maliciousness of some slaves, descended to some revolting remarks about slavery.[19]

The Roman jurists, too, acknowledging the existence of natural rights under Stoic influence, contributed to the betterment of the lot of the slaves by proclaiming that by their nature all men are free and equal. Slavery, they said, was part of the *jus gentium* and arose in the beginning from the captivity of prisoners of war.

In the patristic era the attitude toward the question of slavery was affected by three factors: first, the actual existence of slavery; secondly, its legal recognition by the ancient state; and thirdly, the influence of philosophical ideas derived from the Christian religion. With regard to the last, the fact that Christ did not demand the overthrow of existing social relationships and that St. Paul declared that an individual's social position in this life was of no consequence in attaining his last end, was decisive. Almost all the Fathers of the Church expressed themselves on the subject of slavery. Although we find a variety of opinions, a certain unity may be discerned over a period of time.

In the first place, the Fathers agreed with the Roman law and the Stoa that slavery is not based on the natural law, but that men are created free and equal in the beginning. With respect to the origin of slavery, the Fathers say that it is a consequence of sin, either original sin or the sin of Cham (St. John Chrysostom), or the actual sins of the whole human race (Theodoret and St. Gregory Nazianzen). St. Basil merely particularizes when he traces slavery back to the capture of war prisoners, to economic destitution, or to the disposition made by some fathers whereby their retarded children were entrusted to others for training.

St. Augustine also taught that slavery had its origin in sin. Slavery appeared for the first time in human history when Noe called his son a slave in punishment for his sin. War imprisonment, one of the

---

[19] *De benef.*, III, 19–22; *Epist.*, 31, and especially 47 and 95.

causes of slavery, is itself caused by sin because every victory, even the victory of the wicked, carries out the just judgment of God by humiliating the defeated people for the punishment of their sins or for their spiritual improvement. If, therefore, slavery arises from sin as a violation of the natural moral order, St. Augustine thought that this penal servitude was a prescription of the natural law as an atonement and compensation for the violation of the moral order. The good man may, of course, be sold into slavery, but for him his servitude will be the test of virtue.

From this teaching it was not a long step to conclude that slavery was a good thing for many individuals because of their sins or their moral deficiency (St. Isidore, Theodoret, St. Basil). This conclusion conformed with the theory of many, that freedom and the power of dominion should be permitted only to the wise and able, that freedom and power were dangerous for the ignorant and weak, and that those who were incapable of self-direction should be made subject to others (St. Ambrose). Although most of the Fathers of the Church refused to admit Aristotle's view that slavery was a primary disposition of the natural law, they acknowledged it as an arrangement indirectly derived from the natural law.

In their treatment of the problem of slavery, many of the Fathers approached a condemnation, but only one, St. Gregory of Nyssa,[20] openly opposed slavery when he said, "A human person may never be treated as a thing, he may never be bought or sold." He followed the Stoa's teaching that slavery is not a disposition of the natural law but only a historical development. Although the Fathers of the Church as a whole did not rise to St. Gregory's height in this respect, the Church can point to an important contribution which she made for the betterment of the slave's lot. Within the Christian community, the slave was accorded equality in every respect, and in religion the slave knew that he was considered a human person with all rights. Before God all men are equal, and all may expect the same things from Him: just judgment, punishment for sin, and reward for a good life.

Because of Scholasticism's receptivity and its high regard for tradition, we cannot suppose that it would have disturbed existing relationships and conditions or that it would have deserted the path traced out for it by its highly prized authorities. In his judgment of

[20] *In eccl. hom. IV* (Migne, *PG,* XLIV, 664 f.).

slavery, St. Thomas, too, was entirely dependent on his predecessors.

In his description of the term "slavery," St. Thomas followed Aristotle.[21] Those who have an inferior spirit but a strong body are intended by nature to be servants. Slavery is a necessary institution in order that shelter, clothing, and other necessaries may be provided for men, and the slave is an "animated tool," *"quasi instrumentum domini in operando";* he is the property of the master. The slave is not *causa sui,* he is directed toward another.[22] St. Thomas classified the household servants and the peasantry among the slaves, who, he said, were generally members of uncivilized tribes and had been obtained as prizes of war or by purchase. A slave did not possess the full rights of a human being; like the animal, he was not a member of the civil community, and because he was easily bribed he could not be admitted in court as a witness.[23]

St. Thomas was not able to hold with Aristotle that certain individuals are by nature determined to slavery. Slavery, he said, was indeed against the first intention of nature but not against its secondary intention. In agreement with the Roman law, with the Fathers and St. Isidore, he taught that originally all men are free and equal, while slavery is a punishment for sin.[24] The violated moral order demanded a punishment in which man would be deprived of the free disposition of his own person. St. Thomas continued to justify slavery as necessary after the Fall. He found a certain propriety in the subordination of those who were inferior in mind and morals to those who were more gifted. The introduction of slavery is compared to the introduction of the right of private property; both have their origin in the *jus gentium* and both are devices instituted by man's reason for some practical purpose. One difference exists between the two: slavery alone is against the primary intent of the natural law.

Even Aristotle had begun to realize the difficulty in saying that the slave as slave was an animated tool, a thing, but that in other respects he was a man. In his *Politics* (I, 13), he proposed the question whether the slave possessed only thoroughness in his corporal

[21] *In II Sent.,* 44, 1; *Contra Gent.,* III, 81; *Summa theol.,* Ia IIae, q.105, a.1; IIa IIae, q.189, a.6 ad2; *In I Corinth.,* chap. 14, 1; *In Rom.,* chap. 1, 5.

[22] Cf. St. Augustine, *De op. Monach.,* chap. 22.

[23] *De reg. princ.,* I, 14; *Summa theol.,* Ia IIae, q.98, a.6 ad2; IIa IIae, q.70, a.3.

[24] *In II Sent.,* 44, 1, 3; *Summa theol.,* Ia, q.92, a.1 ad2; IIa IIae, q.189, a.6 ad2; q.57, a.3 ad2 f.

duties, or whether he was also capable of ethical virtues. He could not give an unqualified answer for, to say that the slave had only corporal perfections would deny the slave's humanity, and to affirm that the slave also was capable of higher virtues would erase the difference from other men. He solved the difficulty by a distinction: the slave also possesses virtues, but the measure of his virtues corresponds to the degree of his spiritual equipment. The slave has no faculty of reflection; he has only to obey and therefore he requires little virtue; he requires virtue only in so far as he does not neglect his duties through sloth or intemperance.

St. Thomas accepts this distinction with some modification. The slave, inasmuch as he is a slave, cannot reflect about his own actions because that power belongs to his master. St. Thomas, in contrast to his customary position that man's reason should influence all his vital actions, makes a distinction with respect to the slave. Inasmuch as he is a slave, he does not possess the virtue of prudence, but inasmuch as he is a man endowed with reason and will he is capable of prudence.[25] The person of the slave is not of equal value with other men. Inasmuch as he is a man, the slave has claims in justice, and therefore the law undertakes to regulate the relationship between master and slave; inasmuch as the slave is the property of his lord he has no claim to justice, he lacks *"perfecta ratio justi."* [26]

Because the slave is endowed with reason, St. Thomas drew a number of conclusions that Aristotle was unwilling to make. For these he relied on the ancient philosophers as well as on the teachings of Christianity. The slave must be treated differently from an animated, irrational being, differently from an animal that is entirely under the direction of its master. Although the slave is subordinated, his right to self-determination must be considered.[27] Because the slave possesses reason, St. Thomas places certain important restrictions on the power of the master. Thus the command of the master is worthless when it opposes the command of a higher power, e.g., God (so St. Paul and St. Augustine). Furthermore, the master cannot command the slave in those things in which he is not subject to the master; with Seneca, St. Thomas holds that it is only the body and not the soul that is subject to the master.

[25] *In I Pol.*, 10; *Summa theol.*, IIa IIae, q. 47, a. 12 ad 2; *De reg. princ.*, I, 14.
[26] *Summa theol.*, IIa IIae, q. 57, a. 4 ad 2.
[27] *Ibid.*, q. 50, a. 2.

With respect to the inner acts of the will, no man is subject to another man, but only to God. Even the body of the slave is not subject to the master in every respect, but only in those things that are done externally (*quae per exterius corpus sunt agenda*), not in those things that belong to the nature of the body.

The slave has a right to physical existence, to the integrity of his body, to the procreation of offspring, i.e., to marriage. The choice between marriage and the celibate state must be left to the slave's free choice; and St. Thomas declares that masters are obliged to take care that marriage is not made difficult for the slaves, even though it might entail financial loss. The natural moral order must be observed at all times. Masters who mutilate or murder slaves must be punished; slaves who serve their masters beyond what is required must be rewarded.[28]

The condition of slavery lasts for life and it is not removed by baptism.[29] In this matter St. Thomas follows the Fathers of the Church. Christ did not come to dissolve the order of justice by faith; He came to liberate us from the slavery of the soul, not the slavery of the body. That slavery of the body will also be terminated in the next life.

Aristotle had said that the slave was incapable of practicing virtue and that the attainment of eudaemonia was impossible for him. According to St. Thomas, the slave could attain happiness in the next life; the slave also can be raised to the dignity of a child of God. In the attainment of the happiness of heaven it is of no consequence whether a man is free or slave. In answer to the question whether a slave could enter the priesthood or become a member of a religious order, St. Thomas referred to the legal solution, which required the consent of the master.[30]

On this question of slavery, St. Thomas was able to draw opinion from many sources, but he was not successful in presenting a harmonious picture of the problem. Some students of history have said that the enlightened view leading to the abolition of slavery was beyond the intellectual horizon of even the medieval genius, and therefore the Scholastics acquiesced in slavery as they saw it in their

---

[28] *In IV Sent.*, 36, 2 ad 4; *Summa theol.*, IIa IIae, q. 10, a. 12 ad 3; q. 104, a. 5; q. 106, a. 3 f.; *In IV Sent.*, 36, 1.

[29] *Summa theol.*, IIa IIae, q. 10, a. 10 ad 3.

[30] *Ibid.*, q. 189, a. 6 ad 2.

world. But that judgment is not quite fair, since the Stoics, and even Seneca to a certain degree, and especially St. Gregory of Nyssa centuries before, had actually called for the liberation of the slaves. The medieval Scholastics were in a certain sense better prepared to adopt such an enlightened view since economic conditions in the Middle Ages were well acquainted with the free worker and servant who might have replaced the bound and bonded slave. True it is that many of the slaves of the Middle Ages belonged to uncivilized tribes, and a certain subordination was called for in the case of these people living *extra leges* and *sine regimine juris* for their own welfare.

4. **The right to work.** A man's judgment of economic conditions and problems will, by the very nature of things, depend on the circumstances in which he lives. More important than that judgment, however, are the principles that shine forth amid temporal circumstances and that are applicable to other times. Fichte designated the right to work as the most fundamental right of the individual because activity is the most fundamental function of every spiritual being. St. Thomas did not delve so deeply into the structure of human personality as to be able to assign a place to the right and obligation to work.

Because of the times in which he lived, Aristotle had no appreciation for the dignity and value of labor; he despised not only the work of slaves but also the lower crafts that were paid for with money. But this attitude did not prevent the Philosopher from commending the efforts of those who tried to support themselves rather than depend on the help of others. Only a life of free leisure, which must not be confused with idleness, is worthy of a free man.[31]

As a Christian, St. Thomas had a much higher opinion of the value of labor. In Paradise man had been engaged in the completely effortless spiritual activity by which he entered into the great harmony of the powers of nature as God had originally established them. But our question is not concerned with this activity but rather with man's vocational activity now. In the post-paradisiacal time man became engaged in the social cooperation of various vocations. Such vocational activity or labor is profitable and beneficial for a man that he may avoid the evil effects of sloth and may discipline his passions, but no outright obligation exists that a man should labor, because these two effects may be obtained by other means.

[31] *Pol.*, VIII, 2; *Rhet.*, II, 4.

An obligation to work exists only for a man when he has no other way to obtain his livelihood. Man has a right to work since he has a right to live. If a man's livelihood is secured in some other way, he has no obligation to work for his support. Still every man is obliged to engage in some occupation. St. Thomas, influenced by an ancient and respected tradition, valued spiritual activity higher than manual labor and had little appreciation for that manual labor by which a man supported himself. But he does demand that labor be rewarded by a just wage.[32]

5. **The right to marry.** Every man as a sexual being has a right to beget children or produce offspring, which in the human species is the right to marry. This right may not be denied even to slaves. The right to marry comprises a group of rights, including the right of the man as a husband and the head of the house, the right of the woman as the wife and mother, the rights of the children to nourishment and to physical, moral, and spiritual development, and the right of the master of the house as against his servants. As Aristotle before him, St. Thomas groups all these rights together under economic justice. He declares that between the two members of these relationships there is no quantitative equality but only a proportional equality.[33]

Not every right has an unconditioned obligation corresponding to it. St. Thomas distinguishes between natural inclinations which tend to the perfection of the individual, and inclinations which tend to the perfection of the species. The former are binding on all individuals, the latter are not. Not every individual is obliged to become a farmer, an artist; and not everyone is obliged to lead the contemplative or the active life. In those things that concern the whole species, the multiplicity of men must be regarded as one man. Just as the body possesses many members, each of which performs a particular task and is not intended to perform all duties, so the members of the human race are active in various vocations according to their inclinations and talents. All these occupations are necessary for the community, but the choice is left to the individual.

Analogously, not every man is obliged to enter the state of matrimony and produce offspring; the individual may forego marriage

---

[32] *Contra Gent.*, III, 132; *Summa theol.*, IIa IIae, q.187, a.3; *Quodlib.*, VII, 17.
[33] *In IV Sent.*, 32, 1, 3; *Summa theol.*, IIa IIae, q.57, a.4; q.58, a.7 ad 3; IIIa, q.85, a.3.

if he wishes to dedicate his life to the attainment of ideals that can be realized not at all or only indifferently in the married state. Thus St. Thomas justified lifelong virginity; the community is the perfect union of all vocations, and among these the contemplative life has an important place. Every right, if it is purely a personal right, has a corresponding unconditional obligation; but if the right is a specific right, i.e., a right belonging to the whole species, it is not accompanied by an unconditional obligation, even though the right is exercised only by the individual.[34]

Marriage serves the preservation of the race and the quantitative increase of individual persons, and thus it serves the nation, the state, and the Church.[35] Marriage is the origin of the family and thus it is also the origin of the natural right to all that belongs to the maintenance and activity of the family. This includes the right to security and the preservation of a certain economic stability, the right to growth, the right to have children, and the right to provide for their physical and spiritual welfare. St. Thomas emphasizes the parents' right to teach religion to their children. "As long as the child is in the womb of the mother, its body is not yet distinct from the parent. After birth, as long as the child has not attained the use of reason, it remains in the custody of the parents; it is, as it were, in the parents' spiritual womb. According to the natural right, the child is in the care of its father before the age of reason, and it would be against the natural right to take the child from the care of the parents or to do anything against their will. When the child reaches the age of reason it may follow its own decisions, it begins to belong to itself." [36]

6. The rights of man as a spiritual person. Every man has a right to the development of his spiritual and moral powers and faculties; he has a right to his own activity in this respect. Because of his direction and tendency to a supernatural end, he has both the right and the duty to religious activity and to the worship of God. The *Theological Summa* of St. Thomas is really nothing more than an explanation of these rights and duties. The exercise of these rights follows a certain inner conviction. Here we come upon freedom of

---

[34] *In IV Sent.*, 26, 1, 2; *Summa theol.*, IIa IIae, q.49, a.2; q.152, a.2 ad 1; a.5; *Contra Gent.*, III, 136; *Quodlib.*, VII, 17.

[35] *Contra Gent.*, IV, 83 ad 1; *Summa theol.*, Ia, q.98, a.1 ad 3.

[36] *Summa theol.*, IIa IIae, q.10, a.12.

conscience in religious and moral matters. Opinions have been divided for a long time about the validity and recognition of this freedom of conscience in the Middle Ages.

St. Thomas is an outspoken and determined defender of freedom
of conscience. Aristotle had taught him the autonomy of the soul,
and this doctrine he found to be entirely in accord with the Christian
view of the soul. The Founder of Christianity Himself came into
conflict with the Jewish authorities and He carried out His mission
in open opposition to the secular authority. The scene described in
the Gospel of St. John in which many disciples "went back and
walked no more with Him" (John 6:66 ff.) may be considered the
charter for religious autonomy and an unmistakable proof that Jesus
demanded that His disciples follow Him of their own free choice.

In the patristic era, practice was often at variance with the theoretical teaching of freedom of conscience, although the Fathers of
the Church, no matter how much they may have differed in other
things, firmly and clearly taught that freedom of religion was a
natural right. Chief among those who expressed themselves on this
point are Tertullian,[37] Athenagoras,[38] Origen,[39] and St. Augustine.[40]

St. Thomas is defending the highest tradition when he upholds
the autonomy of conscience as the supreme court of human actions
in the religious community, even when the individual should find
himself in conflict with ecclesiastical authority. The precepts of authority should not be obeyed if they are opposed to one's own moral
convictions. A Catholic who is commanded by ecclesiastical authority to perform an act which violates the moral law, may not obey;
he must rather die under the sentence of excommunication. Obedience in this instance would be against "the truth of life," which may
never be sacrificed. Such was St. Thomas' verdict against Peter Lombard.[41] Such too were the decisions of St. Albert the Great, St. Bonaventure, Peter of Tarantasia, and Richard of Middletown.

Even an erroneous conscience is absolutely binding. The example
which St. Thomas uses in the *Summa* is most illustrative. Faith in
Christ is indeed good and even necessary for salvation. But if a man
should labor under the erroneous conviction that this faith is some-

---

[37] *Ad Scapul.*, chap. 2; *Apolog.*, chap. 24.
[38] *Suppl.*, chap. 1.
[39] *Cont. Cels.*, V, chap. 63.
[40] *De vera relig.*, chap. 6.
[41] *Summa theol.*, IIa IIae, q. 104, a. 1 ad 1; *De verit.*, XVII, 5 ad 4.

thing evil, he would be obliged by the voice of his conscience to abhor Christianity.[42] St. Thomas is consistent in respecting the natural right of a free spiritual person. Prisoners of war who are sold into slavery may not be forced to adopt the Christian faith, and the children of pagans and Jews may not be forcibly baptized.[43] He grants toleration for the religious practices of infidels, but he knows no tolerance for heretics and apostates, those who once possessed the true faith and fell away from it. He recommends the use of physical force in the case of recalcitrant heretics who give no hope of conversion; these are to be delivered over to the secular tribunal, which may carry out the death penalty.[44]

This doctrine of St. Thomas shows the influence of a theory that had grown into a tradition and of a practice of long standing. In seeking to support such coercive measures, reference could not be made to the Founder of Christianity or to the primitive Church, and similarly, the Fathers of the Church, although they unanimously and vigorously condemned heresy, were far removed from recommending force and compulsion in the case of heretics. But the practice preceded the theory. Just as the pagan emperors had decreed severe penalties for offenses against the state religion, so Christian rulers since the time of Constantine established punishments in order to suppress paganism and heresy. Even the gentle St. Augustine tells us that in the beginning he had rejected the use of all force, but that in the course of his life he had learned from facts that the forceful return of heretics and apostates to the fold was a good thing.[45] He approves only the milder punishments, such as those in use already at his time, exile and confiscation of property; he does not approve of the death penalty.

The reasoning that led St. Augustine to adopt this position is that which influenced the other writers of the patristic age. Heresy was considered a conscious and open opposition to the teachings of Christ and thus was one of the most grievous sins. According to St. Augustine, no legal means should be left untried in order to bring back those who have fallen away.[46] We can, of course, understand his noble motives and the circumstances in which he lived and

---

[42] *Summa theol.*, Ia IIae, q. 19, a. 5.
[43] *Ibid.*, IIa IIae, q. 10, a. 8, 12 ad 2-4.
[44] *Ibid.*, q. 10-12; *In IV Sent.*, 13, 2; *Quodlib.*, III, 27 ad 2.
[45] Cf. Letter to Vincentius, *Ep.* 93, 1-10, 16-19; 185, 21.
[46] *De civ. Dei*, V, 24; *Ep.* 133 f.

thought, but in principle his attitude was unsound; for posterity it was most unfortunate since it is his authority to which men always appealed to justify the use of force in religion. Once the practice had been inaugurated, the penalties were continually increased; Theodosius introduced the death penalty, and Justinian incorporated it into the code of law.

St. Thomas found himself in the midst of a well-developed juridical practice which he felt obliged to support. His reasoning was somewhat as follows: The acceptance of the true faith is a matter to be decided by the free will, but once it has been accepted it must be preserved, just as making a promise is a matter of one's free choice, but once the promise has been made it must be kept. Anyone who counterfeits the true religion deserves the death penalty. Indeed, St. Thomas speaks of infidelity as a sin against nature [47] since the human spirit is not permitted to oppose the truth to which it has a natural inclination and which has been announced externally. St. Thomas, like the Fathers, is convinced that a man endowed with the grace of baptism cannot fall away without burdening his soul with great guilt. Therefore opposition to the faith is always a conscious act, it springs from hatred of the truth and it leads to hatred of God and inflicts great harm on the rest of the faithful.

Since infidelity is a greater sin than counterfeiting or lese majesty to which the secular authority has attached the death penalty, and since the eternal salvation of the soul is much more important than this earthly life, the obstinate heretic must be put to death lest he contaminate others and harm them.

If we review the entire Thomistic position we will find that St. Thomas understood and recognized the autonomy and freedom of conscience. This freedom ceases only when the Christian faith has once been accepted. St. Thomas says expressly that the Christian, in matters of his eternal salvation, has no liberty with respect to error and he has no liberty to endanger the salvation of his fellow men. Apart from the defect of this reasoning, St. Thomas lost sight of the fact that a man may give up a certain form of religion because of an inner conviction. When he states that a Christian always is guilty if he falls into error in matters of faith, he neglects to offer proof; but in this respect he fails as do all the thinkers of his time. Yet St. Thomas was so impressed by the idea of the autonomy of conscience

---

[47] *In IV Sent.*, 13, 2, 1.

that he demands that a man refuse obedience to ecclesiastical authority in moral matters if the command is opposed to his conscientious
conviction.

7. **The natural rights of communities.** St. Thomas acknowledged
not only the natural rights of individuals but also those of communities. As the origin of communities is conditioned by the natural
law, so their activities are also founded deep in the natural law.

We have already spoken of the natural law and right of the family, and we have pointed out that the nature, function, and rights of
the family could be best determined from a consideration of the
purpose of marriage. Similarly a definition of the nature of the state
includes a statement of its natural rights. The state has a right to
all those things that are necessary for a fulfillment of its tasks. The
field in which it is to work comprises all those things necessary for
the attainment and preservation of the common welfare. Among
these are the making of good laws, the administration of justice, the
preservation of peace and order within the community and protection and defense against external enemies, and provision for the intellectual training of good citizens, and, in a sense, also their religious
education. Aristotle taught that the civic education of citizens was
especially a duty and a right of the state. St. Thomas preferred to
speak of the individual's moral education which, as St. Augustine
had said, includes the right relation to one's fellow men and to the
state.

The Church also has natural rights for the fulfillment of its duties,
such as the right to the religious education and training of the faithful. A presupposition for this right is the right to transmit the teachings of the faith to the members of the Church. A consequence of
this right is the right to establish institutions, cultural centers, and
organizations which serve the religious education of the faithful, the
training and education of priests, and which provide an opportunity
for the cultivation of religious ideals.

Like communities, individuals possess natural rights. In view of
the rights of a multitude of individuals, the fundamental and practical question arises: Do the natural rights of the individual have an
absolute precedence over the rights of the community or are the individual's rights relative to them? Do the rights of one supersede the
other's? Or are these rights limited by each other?

St. Thomas did not treat of the relation between the rights of dif-

ferent communities or the relation between the rights of the community and those of the individual in a separate section, but sufficient
light is thrown on the basic problem by the general principles which
he enunciated elsewhere. In the first place it is clear that St. Thomas
viewed the natural rights of the individual within the framework of
the rights of the community. The individual is a member of an
organism, not indeed of a physical organism but of a moral organism.
Forgetfulness of this important distinction has given rise to far-
reaching misinterpretations of certain Thomistic texts. A violation of
the corporal integrity of an innocent individual is not within the
rights of even the civil authority, for man has an inalienable right
to his life. Of course, St. Thomas grants that the state may cut away a
diseased member of the organism, but the disease is not a physical
disease; it is a moral disease. If the community were a physical
organism, then a member might be amputated for physical reasons.
But since the human community is a moral organism, a member may
be amputated from the whole only because of moral defects.

The imposition of the death penalty by the state is based on the
state's higher authority, but this punishment may be meted out only
for some grave crime. To put the innocent to death is intrinsically
evil, *secundum se malum*. The death penalty is imposed for two
reasons: as a punishment of the criminal, and here the civil authority
acts as God's representative, and secondly as a protection of the good
and for the preservation of the common good. Both these ends unite
in the mind of the head of the state and constitute the justification
of his act.[48]

What justification is there for capital punishment? The injury
inflicted on the community is measured by the malice and depravity
in the mind of the criminal individual. A man who commits a crime,
falls from the order of reason, he casts aside his human dignity
(*decidit a dignitate humana*), he abandons the value of his human
personality and precipitates himself into an animal servitude.[49] To
put such a man to death is permitted as it is permitted to kill an
animal. Aristotle, too, had referred to an evil man as worse than an
animal.

St. Thomas permits the physical mutilation of criminals as a punishment, and he held that the castration of criminals was permissible.

[48] *Summa theol.*, IIa IIae, q.64, a.; q.63, a.3; *Contra Gent.*, III, 146.
[49] *Summa theol.*, IIa IIae, q.64, a.2 ad 3.

Castration as a preventive measure, however, is not permissible. Here again St. Thomas recalls the distinction between the physical and the moral. The well-being of the body may require the amputation of a sick member, but the welfare of the soul may be secured by other means than bodily mutilation, by influences brought to bear on the will (*et ideo in nullo casu licet membrum praescindere propter quodcumque peccatum vitandum*).[50] Further, a man may be flogged only as a punishment; man's natural right to bodily inviolability includes three things: no striking, no mutilation, and no attack on his life.

In the same way, man's right to move about and the right to the free use of his members is not unlimited. For reasons dictated by justice, either as a punishment or as protective custody, the civil authority may decree an individual's incarceration. The individual's intellectual freedom likewise is limited by the rights of the community. From Thomistic principles it is evident that the civil authority has the right and duty to proceed against anyone who by act or doctrine attacks the foundations of the community.

The Church's limitation of freedom of conscience is supported by the secular arm, the state.

The family, according to St. Thomas, does not owe its stability, at least not exclusively, to the community of the state. The family is more necessary and more fundamental than the state; but, after the state has been formed from the family by way of the village community, the family becomes subordinate. Since the Christian family and the Christian state have the same ends both in this life and in the next, the educational and penal rights of the family need not be limited by the state, but they should rather be complemented.[51]

8. The unchangeable natural law. The question of the possibility of a dispensation from the precepts of the Decalogue was frequently discussed before the days of St. Thomas. He was unable to pass over this cardinal problem since its solution would necessarily include an expression of his whole philosophy and also since this problem offered an occasion for his general principles to be tested by a particular difficulty. As was his custom, St. Thomas attempted a solution by making a distinction.

The natural law is unchangeable; everywhere and at all times it

---

[50] *Ibid.,* q.65, a.1 ad 3.
[51] *Ibid.,* Ia IIae, q.95, a.1; *In IV Sent.,* 37, 2, 1 ad 4.

has the same binding force, since it derives from the essential nature of things. The natural law may be complemented by divine and human legislation, but it can suffer no change in its inner nature. In asserting this absolute immutability, St. Thomas compares it to the immutability of the supreme theoretical principles, thus following tradition (Alexander of Hales, St. Albert); but the conclusions from the first principles of the natural law do not possess the same absolute immutability.

We must likewise remember that when St. Thomas is speaking of the first principles of the natural law he includes not only the precept that good must be done and evil avoided, but also the precepts: a man must act reasonably, a man may not be unjust to anyone, justice must be rendered to everyone according to his deserts, the commandments of the love of God and neighbor, and indeed the whole Decalogue, which are often considered as conclusions from first principles, are said to possess the same absolute immutability.

On this basis, St. Thomas approaches the question of the possibility of a dispensation from the Decalogue. When can a dispensation be made from any law? Only when the observance of the law would militate against the lawgiver's intention. The intent of the lawgiver aims at two things: (1) the common good; (2) the order of justice and virtue by which the common good is actualized and preserved. All precepts that immediately serve these ends are not subject to any dispensation. Such commands as, no one may injure the state or betray the country to the enemy, may not be dispensed.

The commandments of the Decalogue contain the intent of the divine Lawgiver. The commandments on the first table govern human society as a civic body under divine governance and direct it to God as its common and final good. The commandments of the second table express the order of justice among men and they require that everyone receive his due physically, economically, and spiritually.[52] A dispensation from these precepts is absolutely excluded, and this because of a metaphysical reason, because of the immutability of the divine essence and the immutability of the world order which is founded on that essence. God would deny Himself if He were to relinquish His order of justice. The Decalogue does not arise from arbitrariness in the divine will. God could not have given other com-

[52] *Summa theol.*, Ia IIae, q. 100, a. 8; IIa IIae, q. 122, a. 2–5; *Contra Gent.*, III, 129.

mandments because the natural essences on which they are based correspond to ideal essences, these essences are derived from the divine essence, and the divine will is always in accord with the divine essence and the divine intellect.[53] Here we see the fundamental doctrine of the universals and its far-reaching importance. Even God is obliged, by an obligation toward Himself, of course; consequently man is all the more bound by these laws.

With respect to the conclusions from the natural law, St. Thomas admitted certain modifications. In the case of conclusions drawn from the first theoretical principles, no exception is permitted; they are always valid and true. But with respect to the conclusions from the first practical principles, these are true and valid only in most instances. Here St. Thomas makes use of Rufinus' example, which says: It is generally true that a man must act in accord with his reason, and from this it follows that a man must restore stolen goods. This conclusion is valid, however, only in most instances, not always. Cases may arise when the observance of the precept would be unreasonable and injurious, e.g., when another, in a state of moral depravity or mental debility, might use the restored goods to injure his neighbor or inflict harm on his country.

Tradition (Aristotle, St. Augustine, Alexander of Hales) taught that the individual instances of life do not always permit the application of a general principle and that single instances are sometimes withdrawn from a general law. In this sense, St. Thomas speaks of an application by way of subtraction. What is the actual practical and moral reason why the application of a law is suspended in an individual instance? As soon as we look at the Thomistic illustration, the answer will no longer be in doubt. St. Thomas takes into consideration the existence of a higher value which is involved. Two values, one of which is an individual value, for instance, an individual's right to private property, comes into conflict with the demands of the common welfare, for instance, the welfare of the country. Now, it is a fundamental teaching of Thomistic sociology that, all other things being equal, the common good is to be preferred to the individual good.

But what is the real cause of such a conflict? St. Thomas replies: For those beings that have an immutable nature, the natural law is always valid; but since man's nature is variable, exceptions must be

[53] *Summa theol.*, Ia, q. 21, a. 1 ad 2; Ia IIae, q. 100, a. 8 ad 2; *De verit.*, XXIII, 6.

made. If human nature would always be in the right order, then the natural requirement that ill-gotten goods should always be restored would be valid without exception. The occasional depravity of human nature, however, requires a departure sometimes from this general principle so that the human will in its perversity may not make evil use of the restored goods.[54]

The natural law is the law decreed by nature. In the Old Testament we read of instances where God commanded the killing of the innocent, e.g., the command that Abraham kill his son in sacrifice, the taking of others' property, e.g., the Jews taking the silver and gold vessels of the Egyptians, and sexual intercourse with a prostitute (Osee). These instances led to the question whether these divine commandments violated the natural law and whether a dispensation could be given from the precepts of the Decalogue.

St. Bonaventure thought that God could not command anything against the natural law if the command dealt with duties owed to Himself, but that He could give precepts in opposition to the natural law in order to regulate the relationships among men. These latter commands of God would not be against the natural law but rather above it. Considering the possibility of a dispensation from the precepts of the natural law found on the second table of the Decalogue, St. Bonaventure concluded that a dispensation could never be given if the intention were evil. On this point he agrees with St. Albert, who also thought that a dispensation was possible if the act were purified of every evil intention and motivated by a good intention. Both St. Albert and St. Bernard looked on these events of the Old Testament as portents of the redemption through the death of Christ. But such an exegesis comes into conflict with the moral law inasmuch as God cannot make use of an immoral command in order to teach a religious truth.

St. Thomas follows another line of thought. He adopts the viewpoint that the killing of the innocent, adultery, and theft are indeed violations of the natural law, but he tries to explain the difficulties by referring to God as the supreme Lord and Lawgiver, who has peculiar relations to men and things. He finds it easiest to justify God's command to Abraham to kill his son. The fifth commandment forbids only unjust killing. Apart from the fact that God actually possesses the right over life and death, man has already forfeited his

[54] *Summa theol.*, IIa IIae, q.57, a.2 ad1.

right to life by original sin. Therefore God's command did not come into conflict with the natural law.[55] The other instances require more explanation. According to St. Thomas, every marriage is made by divine law; it is not adultery therefore if a man cohabits with a woman who has been given to him by divine ordinance. St. Thomas seems to have lost sight of the fact that marriage has a definite nature and substance according to the natural law.[56] God is furthermore the Lord of all material things, and it is therefore not theft if a man takes what belongs to another in obedience to a divine command. Every divine ordinance respecting human affairs is always right and just.

St. Thomas draws a parallel between the moral order and the order of nature. In the latter some things are found to occur which are not indeed against the order of nature, but beside it, *praeter ordinem*.[57] According to participation in the order of justice and with respect to their substance, the precepts of the Decalogue are immutable. A change is possible, however, inasmuch as the matter of these precepts is withdrawn from the field of duties prescribed by the natural law. It is not the law that undergoes a change; it is the object of the law that is changed in a particular instance.

These distinctions and explanations contribute no more to the solution of the difficulty than the simple reference to God's absolute sovereignty, and this latter explanation is an unintentional admission of moral positivism. According to St. Thomas himself, the natural law is not a merely subjective norm of the will; it is founded deep in the objective nature of things. And this objective nature or essence is permanently fixed according to the divine idea. If the natural law is an expression of the objective essential relations in things and if the essences in things express an essential relation with an identical idea in the divine mind, then any change even by the divine will is impossible.

A dispensation is possible only when the essential relations in a thing admit of several different orders under which the above-mentioned instances may be brought. Confronted with this same difficulty, Duns Scotus seems to have been aware of this truth. He does not, as some have said, fall into moral positivism, but, on the other

---

[55] *Ibid.*, Ia IIae, q.94, a.5 ad2; q.100, a.8 ad3.
[56] *Ibid.*, q.94, a.5 ad2; q.100, a.8 ad3; *De malo*, XV, 1 ad 8.
[57] *Summa theol.*, Ia, q.105, q.6, a.1.

hand, he proclaims an absolute natural law, binding on all men at all times, which even God cannot shake.[58]

Duns Scotus goes much farther than his contemporaries. He distinguishes between a natural law in the narrower and stricter sense and a natural law in a broader sense. The attribute of immutability belongs only to the natural law in the stricter sense. According to Scotus, the natural law is the practical judgment about what is to be done and what is to be omitted. Under the natural law in the narrower sense are included all those axioms which can be derived analytically from the concepts of the judgment and those conclusions that follow from these axioms with logical necessity. Only the first two commandments of the first table belong here. Scotus seems to have been in doubt about the third commandment. The commandments of the second table do not belong to the natural law in the strict sense; they are parts of the natural law in a wider sense. They do not follow necessarily from the first practical principles and they do not have that analytical character mentioned above; but they have a universal validity because of their close connection with the natural law in the strict sense.

Duns Scotus admitted the possibility of a dispensation from the natural law in the broader sense.[59] What arguments did he offer in justification of this stand? The precepts of the second table of the Decalogue do not express a relation of things that has a metaphysical necessity; they are not conceptually necessary. They are, however, in close harmony with the natural law in the strict sense as we see not only from experience but also from our reflection on the nature of man. They offer the best method for regulating human relationships and for the fulfillment of human obligations; they are the best but not the only way. In view of a higher good a dispensation may be given from the commandments of the second table in particular instances.

The validity of natural moral values is not the same as the consciousness of this validity on the part of man; the two things are, however, closely related. The validity of a moral value attains consciousness in the practical reason of a man in order that it may regulate his practical attitude. What is to be said of the knowledge of the natural moral law? Relying on his epistemological theories, St. Thomas made

---

[58] *Oxon.*, III, d. 37, q. 1, 5, 8, 14.
[59] Cf. Ephrem Longpré, *La philosophie du B. Duns Scot* (1924). pp. 80–82.

the following distinction: Like the first theoretical principles, the supreme practical principles are known to all men, and no power can tear them from the heart of a man. On the other hand, human passions may obstruct or suspend the application of these first principles in individual cases.[60] The secondary precepts of the natural law may disappear entirely from the heart of man, and the human appreciation of moral values may be disturbed or destroyed by evil persuasion, by bad habits, by evil dispositions, or by evil customs prevailing among a people. Thus theft and unnatural vices came to be permitted by some peoples although they are directly against the natural law. St. Thomas assigns this loss of the appreciation of moral values as one of the chief reasons for the necessity of an explicit divine revelation.

[60] *Summa theol.*, Ia IIae, q. 77, a. 2.

CHAPTER XXXVI

HUMAN LAW AND DIVINE LAW

1. Positive human law. Some justification seems necessary to show the need for positive legislation. If the natural law is inscribed on the heart of every man, why is a special human law required? St. Thomas pondered this question and answered it according to the tradition he found at hand.[1] Laws are made to protect the good and to restrain the wicked by the threat of punishment.

Laws are an integral part of the order of ends and purposes. Man is able to attain thoroughness and perfection in the performance of his duties only with the help of others. Those men who have good characters and dispositions, and who besides have been reared under the influence of good morals and some religious instruction, will become valuable and profitable members of the community. Other men, however, whose characters are depraved and who have come under evil influences must be forced to observe morality and order by laws and they must be kept from evil by force, that is, by the threat of punishment.

In treating of this question of the need of positive legislation, St. Thomas again has in mind the picture of the ancient city community. Like Aristotle, Plato, and Cicero before him, he recognized a legal morality, which indeed did not present any ideal of conduct, but which was necessary for the common good. He refers to the saying of Aristotle, that the man who ignored law and morality was the worst of all living beings. In trying to show the usefulness of positive legislation, St. Thomas emphasized the point that such laws tended to restrain and punish evil citizens.

He was far from conceding, however, that this was the only justification for positive laws. Laws and rights are necessary to particu-

---

[1] Cf. Isidore, *Etym.*, V, 20.

larize the natural law, to apply it, and to determine the manifold relations between private individuals (positive private law) and the relations between the state and its members (positive public law). Laws serve to make secure the benefits of tranquillity and peace and they further the common good in many ways. Finally, these laws provide a basis for a well regulated and an efficiently functioning judicial system.

The inner connection between the positive law and right, and natural law and right, is clearly and definitely set forth by St. Thomas. If all of man's activities ought to represent the expression and development of his nature, then law and right must be in harmony with that nature; at any rate, they cannot be adverse to it. In agreement with St. Augustine, St. Thomas teaches that the positive law is dependent on the natural law of which it is a derivation and a development.[2] This derivation from the natural law may proceed in one of two ways: the first way is similar to that employed in the sciences, and here the positive law is a logical conclusion derived from more general principles. Thus, when the supreme law of nature commands that good must be done and evil avoided, we conclude that we are not permitted to kill. The second way of deriving the positive law is by determining a law to apply to a particular instance. The natural law orders the punishment of evildoers, but the fixing of the penalty is left to the positive law. St. Thomas compares the lawgiver to the artist who applies the general form of art to a particular material and to particular circumstances.

The laws derived from the natural law by the first way are binding not only as positive laws but also by reason of the natural law. Those derived by the second method possess validity only because of human promulgation.

Some comment is needed on the derivation and content of human positive legislation. We recognize immediately that the direct conclusions from the natural law really belong to the natural law. The whole Decalogue is a direct and immediate derivation from the natural law. Duns Scotus made a clear distinction when he spoke of the obligating positive law and the purely positive law. The former is really positive law with respect to its promulgation, but it is natural law as to its content. St. Thomas concurred with Scotus substantially. Those laws which are made by learned and experienced jurists after

[2] *De lib. art.*, I, 6.

much study are farther removed from the principles of the natural law because they are more remote derivations.

When St. Thomas says that the binding force of the positive laws in the secondary category depends solely on the human authority that promulgates them, he does not relinquish the natural law's demand that the punishment and the measure of the punishment be in accord with justice. The purely positive validity belongs to those laws whose matter is entirely indifferent according to the natural law. Such laws are found in both the private and the public positive law. Sometimes St. Thomas designates the indifferent matter as the proper object of positive legislation.[3]

If the matter is really indifferent, we cannot say that the positive law is derived from the natural law; it is then rather a complement or an addition to the natural law.

The natural law is also the positive and negative norm for the positive law. If St. Thomas distinguishes between two kinds of justice, that which is just by the nature of the thing and that which is just by positive determination, the latter kind of justice has an inner relation to the former. The will of man cannot change the nature of things. If the written law contradicts natural law and right, it is unjust and has no binding power. Thus St. Thomas, in agreement with Aristotle, Cicero, St. Augustine, St. Bonaventure, and St. Albert, affirms the identity of justice and legality, declaring that only that is just which is in accord with the order of reason, or better, the natural order of things. If a prescription is opposed to the order of reason, it is not law but a corruption of the law. Anything that opposes the natural law, such as theft or adultery, can never be made right by positive law. The positive law can command only those things that are in accord with the natural law or those that are indifferent. Therefore St. Thomas made the following distinction: in both the divine and the human law some things are commanded because they are good and some are forbidden because they are evil, while some things are good because they are prescribed and evil because they are forbidden.[4]

Just laws are binding in conscience because the civil authority issuing the laws derives its power from God. Those laws are just that serve the end of the common good, which are issued by the rightful

---

[3] *Summa theol.*, Ia IIae, q. 95, a. 2.
[4] *Ibid.*, IIa IIae, q. 57, a. 2 ad 2 f.

authority without overstepping its competence, and which lay burdens on the individuals proportionate to the demands of the common welfare. Unjust laws do not bind in conscience, although St. Thomas taught that they must be observed occasionally in order to avoid scandal and confusion. Those prescriptions of any law which are opposed to the divine law may not be obeyed under any circumstances; "God is to be obeyed rather than men." [5]

St. Isidore enumerated a long list of attributes of the positive law: it must be honest, just, possible, according to nature, according to the customs of the country, considerate of time and place, necessary, useful, understandable, not for private gain but for the common welfare. St. Thomas reduced these properties to three: the accord with the divine law, the accord with the law of nature, and the end of the common welfare. In another connection, however, St. Thomas added a further characteristic: the positive law is always a universal prescription; the application to individual instances is left to each person.

The law is intent on the attainment of the common good and it strives to bring about the practice of justice, the community virtue. But since the common good embraces a plurality, the law also refers to a plurality of persons, things, and relationships of time and place. Because of the contingency that attaches to human relationships and conditions, the universal prescriptions of the law must be content with the truth (*verum*) as it is found in the many. If circumstances offer unusual difficulties in the application of the law, the counsel of older, experienced, and prudent citizens is to be sought.

The physical sanctions used in enforcing law and justice have some connection with the obedience due the civil authority. But this physical force is not the essential characteristic of the law as has been taught since Kant's time. The physical penalties are merely the means the state may use to enforce the law.

In agreement with St. Augustine and the Roman jurists, St. Thomas taught that laws may be changed. Indeed every product of man's reason is capable of progress and improvement, and human relationships are subject to continual change. St. Thomas said that a change in the law is imperative when such change is plainly advantageous for the community, but otherwise the legal status of a people should not be disturbed. Sometimes we must act contrary to the letter of the law in order to carry out the intention of the lawgiver

---

[5] *Ibid.*, Ia IIae, q. 97, a. 3 ad 1–3.

and prevent injustices. The civil authority may dispense from the law if a prescription intended for the many becomes injurious for an individual in a particular instance. St. Thomas approved the proposition that custom has the force of law, a question which was frequently discussed by St. Augustine and the jurists of his time: *"Consuetudo et habet vim legis et legem abolet et est legum interpretatrix."* His reasoning is interesting. The reasonable will of the lawgiver may be expressed not only in words but also in actions. Custom, however, may not be contrary to the divine or natural law.[6]

Although St. Thomas recognized the close relationship between law and morality, he was able to distinguish clearly between the moral order and the legal order. The law does not prescribe all virtues but only those which have a direct or indirect connection with the common good. Since the law contemplates the average man and seeks the performance of the possible, it prohibits only the grosser failings of mankind which are prevalent in the greater part of the community. The law seeks the elimination of those crimes which injure the fellow man and which disturb the peace of society, as murder and theft. Many other things are regulated by the divine law. The positive law does not touch the intention.[7]

The most important division of law is that of the *jus gentium,* the law of nations, and the *jus civile,* the civil law. The reason for this distinction is the manner of derivation from the natural law. The *jus gentium* comprises the conclusions drawn from the natural law, as, for instance, the statutes about purchase and sale and other regulations of man's community living. The *jus civile* comprises the more particular determinations of the natural law.

The law of nations has a long history. Originally, in the body of Roman law, the law of nations regulated the intercourse with strangers (*peregrini*), while the civil law governed the citizens of the Roman state. Later the law of nations became the expression of those legal principles that were recognized by all peoples. St. Isidore of Seville transmitted this latter definition to the Middle Ages together with several others.

While the older jurists, including Cicero, thought of the law of nations as a part of the natural law, Ulpian and St. Isidore distinguished between the law of nations and the natural law. Ulpian

---

[6] *Ibid.*
[7] *Ibid.,* q.93, a.3 ad3; q.96, a.2, a.3 ad2.

taught that the natural law was the sum of those regulations which govern the activities that are derived from natural impulses, while the law of nations comprised the legal principles that govern the relations between nations and that are everywhere accepted and recognized by men. When we recall what St. Isidore enumerated under the law of nations (treaties of peace, martial law, the law of occupation, the taking of prisoners of war, slavery, etc.), we see that he came close to the modern concept of international law. At that time, however, the idea of the natural law was so prominent that these legal principles were supposed to be active in the legal consciences of all people so that express pacts and treaties were not necessary.

In his treatment of the law of nations St. Thomas was influenced greatly by the Roman jurists, but this position was in frequent conflict with his later explanations. He distinguished between the natural law and the law of nations by saying that the former embraces everything that belongs to all living beings by nature, while the law of nations established by human reason refers only to human relationships.[8] Here he accepts a definition of the natural law which he was afterward obliged to reject.

St. Thomas' concept of the law of nations included not only the relations between nation and nation; it referred also to certain domestic national relations. Thus he speaks of the relation of the ruler to his subjects, the introduction of slavery, the forms of private property, of purchase and sale, as parts of the law of nations. He treats of these domestic national relations because a people begins with these internal affairs and by them is guided in its relations with other peoples. St. Thomas bases on the natural moral law the regulations of peaceful intercourse between nations as well as the regulations in time of war. No sphere of human life is isolated from the moral law.

The repudiation of lying and deceit, the requirement of fidelity to treaties, truthfulness, and genuine political prudence are the foundation of peaceful intercourse between nations. St. Thomas displays the consistency of his moral principles as well as the just, noble, and humane spirit of the true Christian when he discusses the immunity of ambassadors, the permissibility and even the necessity of war, the manner of carrying on a just war, the treatment of prisoners of war and neutrals, the protection of innocent children and women, and a people's right to defend itself. When St. Thomas acknowledges the

---

[8] *Ibid.*, IIa IIae, q. 57, a. 3 ad 2 f.

right to take booty and spoils and when he says that a war is fought not between army and army but between two peoples, he merely gives expression to the viewpoint of his time.

2. **The divine law.** If man had only a natural goal in his life, the law of nature and the positive law of the state would be sufficient for the ordering of his life. But since he has a supernatural end, he has a corresponding supernatural order of life, and this supernatural order is governed by the divine law. The great benefit of the divine law is that it gives man an infallible religious attitude and that it supplements human law in two ways. In the first place, the divine law regulates inner acts, the intention of a man, whereas the human law regulates only the external acts, having for its aim the preservation of tranquillity in the community of the state. Secondly, the human law is unable to punish all evil, because otherwise it would not be able to do the good things required by the common welfare. The divine law, however, is watchful that no evil goes unpunished in the world.

The divine law comprises both the Old and the New Testament. The fullness of the grace of the Holy Spirit is transmitted through Christ, but the relationship to Christ was established already by the Old Testament when it gave testimony for Christ and when it preserved the true idea of God against the evil of polytheism. The revelation was made to the Jews because of the promise that Christ would come from the Jewish people. The revelation of the divine law was made at the time of Moses to show man the helplessness of his own reason and the weakness of his will and to prevent the complete obscuring of the natural law.

St. Thomas' engrossing study of the Old Testament need not cause us any displeasure. For him the Old Testament and the Decalogue were the anteroom of the New Testament and also integral parts of the New Testament. The New Testament does not, however, lack completeness in presenting the Christian doctrine of faith and grace. In other instances, St. Thomas is not the creative philosopher of history, but on this occasion he rises to an interpretation of the course of history. He presents a philosophical explanation of the religious development of man, of that great educational process which advances in a definite order from the imperfect to the perfect. The student of history must be able to recognize the stages of the development, to understand their purpose and necessity and distinguish between what applies to all humanity and what had significance only for the needs and culture of a certain time. In spite of its imperfections (*lex puerorum*), the Old Testament had an important part to play between the law of nature and the law of grace. It served the establishment of friendship between God and man and it contained three kinds of prescriptions: moral, ceremonial, and judicial. To live in God's friendship required that a man live a life of moral rectitude; the ceremonial and judicial prescriptions were the more detailed injunctions of the law of divine worship and the law of justice in human society.

While we can easily see the inner relation between the religious and the moral phases of man's development, the question naturally arises about the relation of the moral prescriptions of the Old Testament to the natural law. All the moral prescriptions of the Old Testament belong to the natural law, although all of them do not come to man's knowledge in the same manner. Some moral laws are immediately known by the human reason, others are known only after study and reflection by wise men, while still others must be made known to us by God. Not all the moral laws can be reduced to the Decalogue; the Ten Commandments were given to the Jewish people by God Himself, while the other moral prescriptions were promulgated by Moses. The Ten Commandments are moral laws which were given to men by God, commandments which may be known from first principles after some reflection and those which we know by the light of the faith which we receive from God.

The enumeration of the Ten Commandments was made with a view to human society conceived under the goverance of God. Two things are required for the welfare of an individual in a community: first, a proper relationship to the head of the community: secondly, the right relationship to the other members of the community. Man owes the head of the community three things: fidelity, respect and reverence, and service. The obligation of fidelity demands that man shall not divide the honor of dominion with another (first commandment); the reverence he owes consists in the avoidance of any offense to the head of the community (second commandment); the service consists in the sanctification of the Sabbath in remembrance of the benefits he has received (third commandment).

The good relationship of the individual with his fellow men is sometimes of a general nature and sometimes it refers to special circumstances. These special circumstances are relations of obligation, such as that of children to their parents. Parents, however, do not have an obligating relation to their children, since the children are really a part of the parents and will be cherished by them without a special command.[9] A commandment enjoining the love of one's children was no more needed than a commandment to love oneself.

The harmonious community life of fellow citizens is jeopardized by the infliction of any injury by thought, word, or deed. Therefore any injury to the person of another is forbidden (fifth commandment), any injury to the person with whom an individual is joined for the purpose of producing posterity (sixth commandment), any injury to the possessions of another (seventh commandment), injury inflicted by speech (eighth commandment), and injuries inflicted by the mind or heart (ninth and tenth commandments).

In cases where the enjoyment of an object is permitted in itself, the inordinate desire is forbidden. The Decalogue contains no prescriptions with regard to man's attitude toward himself. But because the law of nature was obscured by sin, laws became necessary to enjoin the love of God and of the neighbor; but no law was needed to strengthen man's self-love, for in this respect the natural law lost none of its vigor. Moreover, the law of the love of God includes the right love of self.

St. Thomas was obliged to meet an objection that arose from his acceptance of the Platonic-Aristotelian division of the powers of the soul. Two lower powers are named as opposing the rule of reason: the concupiscible and the irascible appetites. The Decalogue, therefore, ought to forbid the inordinate movements of the irascible appetite as well as those of the concupiscible appetite. In reply St. Thomas said: the passions of the irascible appetite actually arise from the concupiscible appetite; therefore the Decalogue is content with forbidding the failings against the concupiscible appetite.

The arrangement of the Ten Commandments is entirely consonant with the end to be attained. The end of human life and human society is God. Therefore the first commandments must regulate the relations of man toward God, just as in an army obedience to superiors is the soldier's first law. Of the three commandments referring to God, the law of loyalty and fidelity to Him has the first place, then the law of veneration and of service. With respect to man's relations

[9] Cf. Aristotle, *Eth. Nic.*, VIII, 12.

to his fellow man, the neglect of his duty toward his parents is particularly sinful and offensive to reason. The remaining commandments are listed in the order of the grievousness of the sins they forbid. Sins of deed are more grievous than sins of speech, and the latter are more grievous than sins of thought. Among the sins committed in deed, murder is graver than adultery, and adultery is graver than theft, because the first destroys a life already in existence, the second jeopardizes the offspring, while the last injures external possessions.

The Decalogue does not contain all the moral laws. All moral laws, however, agree in one characteristic; they are based on the law of reason. The moral laws deriving their obligatory force from the law of reason may be divided into three classes. The first class includes the laws that are of a general tenor and that are so clearly and certainly apprehended as to require no further promulgation. Among these are the commandments of the love of God and of neighbor. These are, as it were, the very ends of all precepts. The second class comprises the more particular prescriptions of the Decalogue. They may be known by the average man, but because of the occasional perversity of human judgment they must be expressly promulgated. The third class of these moral laws contains those that are known only to the more learned and wise. These last form the complement to the Decalogue and were transmitted to the people through Moses and Aaron. St. Thomas discusses in detail the supplementing of the first eight commandments; the ninth and tenth commandments do not require additional precepts since they forbid every evil desire in general.

The ceremonial prescriptions are the particular regulations of the moral law with respect to the relations of man to God. They regulate external worship, which has an ordered relation to the inner worship of God and embraces three parts: sacrifice, the ministers of the sanctuary and the people, and the paraphernalia of worship (the altar, etc.). As in his three *quaestiones* on the ceremonial prescriptions St. Thomas develops a philosophy of the liturgy of the Old Testament, so in his tract on the judicial prescriptions he evolves a sociology of Israelitic society with its four relations: the ruler to the people, the subjects among themselves, the people to strangers, and the individuals who dwell in the same house among themselves. The significance of these discussions is much broader than the actual problem to be solved, since St. Thomas takes occasion to enunciate his principles with regard to moral, legal, and political matters.

In accord with the ancient tradition of the Church, St. Thomas calls the New Testament the grace of the Holy Ghost transmitted by faith in Christ.[10] The law of the New Testament has a twofold function: it prescribes what a man shall do and it supports him in the observance of that law. The most important part of the New Testament was not written down but was inscribed in our inner being. The only things written down were those that prepare men for the reception of the grace of the Holy Ghost and those that refer to the use of this grace.

In the long process of man's religious education, St. Thomas was able to discern the clear pattern of order. The New Law, which is the culmination and the immediate preparation for the kingdom of God, came relatively late in man's history, but it does not differ in its purpose from the Old Law; both aim at man's submission to God. The Old Law is, however, the law of children, while the New Law is the law of adults. The Old Law regulates external justice, the New Law regulates man's inner acts; the former "disciplines the hand, the other disciplines the spirit." The earlier law is the law of fear and it deals with penalties and external sanctions, the later law is the law of love. The Old Law was written on stone tablets, the New Law is written in man's heart as the basis of the service of the spirit; the New Law is compared to the Old Law as the perfect to the imperfect, as the fulfillment and complement of the Old Law. The New Law is indeed implied in the Old Law, out of which it grew organically. Such had been the teaching of the early Fathers, St. Augustine and St. John Chrysostom. From them St. Thomas also drew his comparison that the natural law, the law of Moses, and the law of the Gospel were like the blade of grass, the ear of corn, and the fruit.

Not the entire content of the Old Testament was received into the New Testament. The moral prescriptions were taken over without change, the temporary legal prescriptions were later subject to the discretion of men, and the ceremonial regulations were fulfilled in Christ and were consequently brought to an end.

3. **Conclusion.** Man's life is governed by several overlapping orders

[10] *Summa theol.*, Ia IIae, q.106, a.1-4; q.108, a.1-4.

of right and law, all of which lead him either to the goal of his earthly existence or his supernatural end. These various orders of law are partly dependent upon one another, but even when no dependent relationship exists between them they are not entirely unrelated. The eternal law, the natural law, and the divine law all come from God, while the positive laws are made by human authority. The eternal law, the natural law, and positive laws lie, as it were, in one continuous line since the natural law is a result of the universal law of God, and the positive laws are conclusions and particularizations of the natural law. The divine law and the natural law can never be invalidated by positive law since the higher law nullifies the lower law. The eternal law and the natural law govern divine and human relations, the divine law is concerned principally with man's relations with God, and the positive law regulates the relations of men among themselves.

CHAPTER XXXVII

THE ORDER OF SALVATION

Aristotle knew many things about the universe and about man, but he was ignorant of the most important thing. More important than the history of nature and the scientific and systematic study of nature is the history of salvation and the order of salvation. Aristotle knew indeed that man had a purposeful existence, but it was Christian revelation that first gave certitude about man's last and highest end and revealed the reason for man's existence here on earth.

Man's natural equipment corresponds to his natural end. We have thus far been speaking of man's natural endowments and his natural duties. But man has two ends or goals: a natural end to which he is directed by his nature, which is attainable by his natural powers and which corresponds to his nature, and a supernatural end, the vision of God and the union with Him by love, which is in every respect above human nature and transcends all human powers, which cannot be thought of or attained by his natural faculties, and which was promised to man only through divine generosity.

The efficient cause underlying man's supernatural end is the triune God in whose inner Trinitarian life and order man is permitted to participate through grace. Only God can make creatures like to God and He alone can grant creatures participation in the divine nature without substantial union with them. "Since grace is above human nature, it cannot be a substance or a substantial form but only the accidental form of the soul. That which is substantial in God becomes accidental in the soul that participates in the divine goodness." [1]

Grace makes man worthy of eternal life, a dignity which man could never attain by himself. Even in his original state, the original justice and the friendship of God which man possessed did not arise

---

[1] *Summa theol.*, Ia IIae, q. 110, a. 2 ad 2.

from his natural faculties and powers; they were a gift bestowed upon man by divine magnanimity. Here St. Thomas himself raises the objection whether man's nature is not sufficient for him to attain his end. He replies by saying that man was indeed perfect in his natural equipment but not in the order of grace. Sanctifying grace, which resides in the substance of the soul, gives the soul a spiritual and divine being and signifies the perfection and completion of natural being.

Because man's supernatural happiness is essentially above all of man's powers, an inner relation exists between nature and grace, and this relation is dominated by the principle that grace does not destroy nature but perfects it. Nature is the anteroom of grace (*praeambula ad gratiam*), and union with God in the next life is the ultimate end of nature. Sanctifying grace elevates nature into the order of the supernatural, it enables the soul to engage in a vital activity that far exceeds the natural in seeing, knowing, and loving God, and it effects a mysterious union between nature and the supernatural. By sanctifying grace man is received into the adoptive sonship of God.

Grace never becomes nature, but St. Thomas discerned an analogy between the order of grace and the natural order. As natural things act through their essential forms, so the soul lives its life of grace through the form of grace. As things in nature are ordered to an adequate end, so the principle of grace is ordered to the supernatural life. In the same way that God endows natural things with forms and potencies that they may the more easily carry out their natural activities, so He also grants the soul special powers and properties so that it may attain its supernatural end. As natural knowledge and the natural morality of man's actions are securely founded on unassailable first principles, so the life of grace possesses a firm foundation in faith. Supernatural love corresponds to the natural inclinations, and the supernatural virtues correspond to the natural movements to the end.[2] How St. Thomas valued the supernatural infinitely above everything natural is clear from his statement: "The good of one grace is better than the good of the nature of the whole universe." [3]

---

[2] *De verit.*, 14, 2; 24, 2; 27, 1–7; 28, 1–3; *Summa theol.*, Ia, q.23, a.1; Ia IIae, q.62, a.2; q.109, a.1–6; q.110, a.1–4; IIIa, q.8, a.1; q.23, a.1–3; q.62, a.5; *In Boeth. de Trin.*, II, 9.

[3] *Summa theol.*, Ia IIae, q.113, a.9 ad 2.

The life of grace is transmitted through Christ. From the divinity of Christ the supernatural power of grace flows through His sanctified humanity into the sacraments which the Church, the mystical body of Christ, dispenses to her faithful. The ancient Christian concept of Christ as the head and the Church as the mystical body of Christ was lovingly accepted by St. Thomas and logically developed by him.[4] In the God-man the most perfect union between God and His creation takes place.[5] Christ, the head of the supernatural order, moves God to grant grace to men and through the merits of His divine and human natures transmits the fullness of grace in the sacraments. Thus Christ becomes the supernatural progenitor of all who are redeemed and receive grace.

St. Thomas demonstrates the purposeful order in the sacraments, according to a custom of long standing with him, by referring to the analogy between the natural and supernatural occurrences in life. The spiritual life resembles the physical life. In his natural existence the individual strives for perfection either as an individual person or as a member of society. Again, the life of the individual person is fostered either directly or indirectly, *per accidens,* by the removal of obstacles. The individual's life is fostered directly by birth, growth, and nourishment. The sacraments of baptism, confirmation, and the Holy Eucharist correspond to these three stages. If man were immune from suffering and sickness both in the spiritual and physical spheres, these three stages would suffice for him. But man needs to be cured of sickness in two ways: his health must be restored and his earlier strength must return. In the spiritual realm, penance and extreme unction restore health and strength.

As a member of the community, man is perfected in two ways: he is prepared to exercise leadership and he has the power of natural propagation. In the spiritual realm the priesthood and matrimony correspond to these two activities and make their contribution to man's social nature. Matrimony represents perfection in both the physical and the spiritual respects since it is not only a sacrament but also a natural activity. All the sacraments are directed to warding off the injuries inflicted by sin.[6]

The supernatural life is perfected and brought to completion by

---

[4] *Ibid.,* IIIa, q. 8, a. 1.
[5] *Ibid.,* q. 2, a. 9.
[6] *Ibid.,* q. 65, a. 1.

the Holy Ghost, whom Christ promised to His Church. As the Being that moves rational creatures toward God and as the dispenser of the supernatural gift of grace, the Holy Ghost has most important functions to perform in the sanctification process of man.[7] The supernatural life of virtue is founded on sanctifying grace and the gifts of the Holy Ghost that flow from it, and it culminates in the supernatural virtue of charity, manifesting itself in the continual growth of Christian perfection. This life of virtue takes concrete form in the two forms of the active life and the contemplative life which fructify each other.[8] Begun during this earthly pilgrimage, this life of sanctification is concluded in that state of bliss which the Evangelist praises with such fervor and enthusiasm.

No finite being can completely comprehend the infinite content of the divine being and the divine goodness, but the immediate vision of the divine inner Trinitarian life, together with the uninterrupted love and undisturbed possession of God, is the foundation for a life of eternal happiness. Thus the circle of divine being and activity is closed. The things in the universe had their beginning with the triune God, to Him their being was directed, to Him they return, and, in so far as they are capable of happiness, they participate in the divine glory.

[7] *Contra Gent.*, IV, 20–22; *Summa theol.*, Ia IIae, q. 67–70.
[8] *Summa theol.*, IIa IIae, q. 179–82.

CHAPTER XXXVIII

COMMENTARY

Such is the Thomistic view of the universe. We have before us a picture of grand dimensions, rising from the earth to the highest heavens; a scientific organism elaborated with multitudinous detail, seeking to comprehend with one perspective the structures of being in the whole universe and all its parts. It was erected in one of those rare epochs of human history when philosophy was in universal honor. St. Thomas shared with Aristotle the conviction that the human spirit was directed and geared to the intelligible content of things, that man had a natural desire for knowledge, and that this thirst for knowledge could be satisfied.[1] Again with Aristotle, he believed that the noblest perfection of the soul consisted in this, "that on it should be inscribed the total order of the universe and its causes."[2] The order of known being in the subjective intellect corresponded to this order of real being. Not only was the foundation for a realistic theory of science and knowledge thereby given, making all science and knowledge dependent on the existence and nature of things, but the most comprehensive task was set for the human intellect that could be assigned to a finite being.

By this bold presentation of the total order of the existing cosmos and by its valiant attempt to understand the cosmos in its universalist system of thought, the Middle Ages, and especially St. Thomas, came closest to the ideal of total knowledge in the long history of Occidental thought. Because of the completeness and consistency of its philosophical concepts, Scholasticism had no separated fields of research, it saw about itself no separate structures of science and knowledge irreconcilable with itself, there was no alien spirit of

[1] *In I Met.*, 1; *In X Eth. Nic.*, 10.
[2] *De verit.*, II, 2; cf. Aristotle, *De anima*, III, 4.

knowledge abroad, and any *diversitas litterarum* was suppressed in its very origin.

Only an age with a highly articulate sense of the Infinite could erect such mighty towering Gothic cathedrals as were erected in the Middle Ages, and only those men who believed that the complete and universal truth was not a dream but an attainable reality could undertake the task of building intellectual cathedrals and writing summas that by their universality and harmony spanned the whole philosophical space. And that intellectual structure in its completeness embraced the spiritual realm as well, for it was, indeed, the ultimate aim of the Thomistic system to search out the harmony between faith and science, between the natural and the supernatural. From the Christian revelation the life of man, and indeed the whole cosmos, received its ultimate meaning and its actual valuation. For St. Thomas, the wisdom of this world, that is, the true knowledge of the structure of the universe and its origin, was neither superfluous nor foolish. Natural knowledge is not in contradiction to faith, on the contrary it supports faith as its preamble, and by that faith natural knowledge is ennobled. The order of salvation completes and perfects our knowledge and understanding of being and history.

This all-embracing and harmonious interpretation of the universe was the rational support of the believing man of the Middle Ages. St. Thomas knew nothing of an unbridled theorizing in philosophy, by which thought was estranged from reality. Even the ancient Platonic Academy was not an organization assembled for the mere acquisition of knowledge; it was deeply rooted in life, in the life of Greece. The philosophy in which Plato was engaged with his disciples was a wrestling to discover the true order of being in the universe of which man was a part. Plato sought the true order of human living and he believed that in that order reposed perfection and happiness, just as the violation of that order brought man to ruin.

Therefore Plato wished to form and fashion the life of the individual and of the political entity according to an idealistic philosophy. To look on Platonic philosophy as a flight from this real world to some world beyond is a gross misunderstanding of it. Plato wished to make this mundane world intelligible from the viewpoint of a higher sphere. Once he had indeed said that philosophy was preparation for death, but in reality it was a preparation for life, a philosophy of living, an interpretation of the fundamental values of human existence. Aristotle did not abandon this aim and tendency, but he tried to attain it in another sphere, by the proof of the total order of the cosmos and the knowledge of that order by means of universalist thought.

St. Thomas adhered with his whole mind to this universalism in his attempts to establish the forms of the order of Christian existence; but he brought to consummation Aristotle's immanent philosophy by his transcendental interpretation of the universe. St. Thomas was unable to relinquish the ancient tradition of thought and philosophy as the molder and fashioner of life; that tradition was closely bound up with the essence of Christian thought. We have already referred to St. Augustine in this respect. St. Anselm announced the program, *"Credo ut intelligam,"* and that axiom was the expression of the mental attitude of a man inspired by religion, whose knowledge and faith are rooted deep in his soul and inextricably intertwined.

The same attitude influenced the Cistercians (St. Bernard), the monks of St. Victor (Hugh and Richard of St. Victor), the Franciscans (St. Bonaventure), as well as the Dominicans. The difference between these schools was merely the different valuation they placed on the required intellectual effort. In founding his order, St. Dominic had accepted as the special task of his disciples the refutation of heretics with the weapon of reason. Quite naturally, therefore, St. Albert and St. Thomas, more than previous ages, recruited reason in their critical attacks on the enemy as well as in their positive upbuilding of the true system. In this way a great philosophical system came into being under the fire of bitter encounters with the powers of human reason. This system of thought was to serve not only those who had wrested it from the jaws of battle but all men who desire to use reason to gain an insight into the factual causes and reasons of things. Thus it came about, too, that the medieval system of thought had so few personal marks on its structure.

If the Thomistic system were nothing more than an accumulation of erudition and scientific conclusions, it would not have been accepted as an interpretation of the universe and of human life, it would not have been the center of such bitter controversy, and it would not have become the philosophical and theological background for the greatest literary product of the Middle Ages, Dante's *Divine Comedy.* The canticle that Dante intoned in praise of philosophy was intended for the system developed in the period of high

Scholasticism. This mighty system of thought produced in the thirteenth century is in itself a magnificent work of art with a design and development pointing to the extraordinary intellectual power of its author. But its significance is enhanced by the fact that it was able to supply the philosophical basis for the greatest poetical work of the Christian Middle Ages. Plato, Dante, and Goethe may be said to mark important stages on the royal road of human thought.

These observations do not, of course, represent the final word in the judging of a philosophical system. Later generations will admire the beauty of the great Gothic cathedrals, and many will attest the poetic beauty of the *Divine Comedy* without acknowledging the truth of the underlying philosophy. The real measure of any philosophical system is the truth; St. Thomas himself had declared the aim of the knowing man to be truth as known, *verum ut cognitum*. But, as the human mind went on its way in search of truth, weighty objections were arrayed against St. Thomas' system.

1. The objections. What concern have we with a scientific system of the thirteenth century? A whole world separates the modern man from St. Thomas and the Middle Ages. Shall we be reduced to the viewpoint of the Middle Ages even after our natural and theoretical sciences have made such radical and extensive changes in the physical, astronomical, political, historical, and philosophical pictures? The tendency of the Middle Ages to relate everything to the other world does not impress us today. The metaphysical dream is over; we have been awakened. Modern skeptical thought has less confidence in the ability of human reason; modern thought is positivist, it is more cautious. The medieval picture of a static world must give place to the mighty dynamics of progress and development.

The ancient transcendental system depending on God yielded to the autonomy of the self-glorifying individual. Changes have taken place in moral values, a new table with new fundamental values of human existence has been set up. Modern man has no grasp of the medieval concept of Church and state. We must liquidate the Middle Ages. Such is the cry of those who say that Christianity is a falsification of ancient culture and that we must return to the ancient way of thought and life. According to these, Christianity has depreciated the fundamental values of human existence prized so highly by the Hellenic thinkers and so greatly needed in Western culture.

These critics of the Thomistic philosophy say further that when Christianity introduced the relationship of the world and man to a personal God in place of the old Greek basing of all things in this world, it introduced a transcendental philosophy of the world and of humanity and an entirely new concept of the nature of man and of the world. By revaluating the old Greek views of human life, Christianity denied the fundamental value of life and became hostile to human life. Through Christianity, sin, despair, contrition, and redemption have become principles of human existence. History became the story of salvation. External nature became only the arena, the environment. The all-important thing in life is the process of salvation which is carried on in the realm of grace and in union with the mystical body of Christ and is completed only in another world. When the two great historical forces of Hellenic culture and Christianity met, the contrast of their basic philosophies could not remain hidden long. A union could be effected only when Christianity had appropriated the Greek ideas and concepts and transmuted them to its own purposes. Thus the Greek idea of the whole was changed into the problem of the universals, thus St. Augustine despoiled the Platonic theory of ideas.

If these reproaches are valid against the Fathers of the Church, they are equally telling against the continuation of patristic thought in medieval Scholasticism. Beside these radical opponents are others who do not draw such a sharp line of cleavage between themselves and the Middle Ages, but who adduce serious doubts about the Thomistic position. Some prefer the affective direction of the Franciscans who follow St. Augustine; others are able to discern in St. Thomas' doctrine of concepts the rank growth of hairsplitting that marked a later decadent Scholasticism. A third group offers another misgiving which is no less serious. They ask: "Was this Dominican friar, St. Thomas, a man of such intellectual stature and such broad and extended experience that he was able to know all aspects of existence, the somber and tragic sides of life, and was he able to embrace all spiritual phenomena so as to explain them faithfully? Did not St. Thomas, with his penchant for harmonizing, lack the faculty for the discordant and irrational that is found in the universe and in human life? Is there really an accord between faith and science? Is not a Christian philosophy, especially one that is under ecclesiastical tutelage, too heavily laden with religious doctrines to permit freedom of consent and thought? Is philosophy really an apt means for the speculative penetration of the teachings of faith?" This group also demands the liquidation of the Middle Ages, not because it is unfriendly to Christianity, but because it wishes to defend genuine Christianity. According to these men, philosophy has endangered Christianity by accepting the ancient pagan concept of man as applicable to the Christian man.

A long array of objections arises to assail the Thomistic system. An attempt will be made to consider the more important and weighty among them.

2. **The force of the objections.** At first sight the following objections against Thomism seem to be the most formidable. However, after closer inspection, they appear quite harmless, so that Christian science and the Thomistic system in particular are in no way endangered.

Those who reject Christianity and call for a liquidation of the Middle Ages do so because of their opposition to the teleological, transcendental basis on which the Christian interpretation of the universe rests. But it is easy to show that this viewpoint is distinctly Hellenic; it can be traced back from Hellenism to the beginnings of Greek speculation. Plotinus' thinking was theistic and transcendental; he was concerned about the welfare and the salvation of the spiritual man and he knew that man's last end was the mystical vision and union with God. Not only the theistic wing of Neo-Pythagoreanism, but Plutarch, whose origins were in the peasantry of Greece, determined the purpose and task of human life within the framework of a transcendental philosophy.

St. Augustine did not despoil or adulterate the Platonic theory of ideas. Before him, Philo, Plutarch, and the Neo-Pythagoreans accepted the Platonic ideas as thoughts in the mind of God, as the eternal prototypes in the divine mind after which the universe was formed in matter. Plato himself and the older Pythagoreans are the true fathers of such an interpretation. Whatever interpretation St. Augustine may have placed on the Platonic theory of ideas, he learned from the Neoplatonists themselves. Plato and the Pythagoreans were concerned about the forms of order in human existence —and what vital system of philosophy could do otherwise?—they sought for the ultimate explanation from the standpoint of an idealistic, transcendental philosophy. In this framework Plato developed his doctrine of the origin of the soul, of its position in the universe and its life task, of the salvation and redemption of the soul, and of its fate after death. The Platonic ideas are not so much the essences of reality and of existing things; they are rather the conceptual bases for the possibility of an actual universe and its existence. The explanation of the Platonic ideas as an autonomous immaterial world at whose head is the personal idea of the Good, cannot be gainsaid.

In the tenth book of his *Laws*, Plato presented a proof for the existence of God and ordered the banishment of atheists from his state. If Plato did not believe that man belonged to some higher spiritual realm, then no one has yet believed it. Only in this way can we explain Plato's evaluation of life and the universe. The Greeks were not blind to the somber side of human life; their epic and lyric poets, their tragedians and historians, join in the lament over the trials and difficulties and the nothingness of life. Their ultimate conclusion was that it is best not to have been born, and the next best thing is to return as soon as possible to Hades.

In the philosophical field, however, pessimism was an infrequent phenomenon. Not only the Pythagoreans, but all the intellectuals from Thales to Democritus and Socrates valued life, not every kind of life, not the life of sensual indulgence which pleased the great multitudes. These thinkers valued a rational life, a life in accord with reason, a life of the spirit and of scientific effort and discipline. Plato did not stray from this intellectual tradition. In *Gorgias, Theaetetus*, and especially in *Phaedo*, he declares that the body is a sepulcher, a prison from which the soul should be freed as soon as possible; he says that true philosophy is a "rehearsal for death," and that the flight from this world should be undertaken as soon as possible.

But even in this vehement desire to be freed from this world, Plato did not despise life absolutely. He turned away only from the life of the body with its strong tendency to the sensual and the evil; he always retained a high appreciation for the life of the soul and the mind with its treasures drawn from the realm of spiritual values. The words that Plato permits Socrates to say in his *Crito*, "Not life, but a good life, is to be chiefly valued," is the expression of Plato's lifelong conviction. He supports that view in his *Laws* when he says that the attainment and possession of virtue are more to be desired than life itself, and that a man who looks on life as the highest good, dishonors the soul.

Plato admitted that the body and external possessions were aids in the fulfillment of life's duties and he accordingly assigned them a place in his table of values. Besides this, Plato had many harsh things to say about the trials and uncertainties of this life. With reference to the transitoriness of all earthly things, to the shortness of life and especially the rapid flight of his own years, Plato compared the life of man to the May fly and declared that it was not worth while to make so much ado about our physical circumstances.

Plato has often been blamed for this sentiment of other-worldliness, and he has even been charged with the corruption of Hellenism because of this mysticism. But the question arises: "Where shall we find the true representatives of Hellenism?" Even the ancient Homeric poems, representing the viewpoint of only the aristocratic element of the Greek people, spoke of the continuation of life after death, although this continued existence in Hades was not something desirable. Achilles would rather be a servant in the house of his father than a ruler in the kingdom of shadows. We find an entirely different appreciation of the life to come in the writings of the Orphic and Demeter mysteries, although the happiness of the next life is promised only to those initiated in the mysteries. It is quite irrelevant in this connection, how the various philosophies rationally explained these mysteries, since these religious ideas had their influence on the initiated and uninitiated alike.

Even in the purely philosophical sphere, Anaxagoras and Aristotle did not abandon the transcendental viewpoint in determining the ultimate reason and cause of the universe. The Stoics indeed explained the cosmos by principles immanent in the world itself. But their Roman disciples (Seneca, Epictetus, and Marcus Aurelius) praised the divine and the spiritual so highly that we are inclined to wonder why they did not seek the answer to their philosophical problems in Platonism since they had so little regard for the mundane and such a high appreciation of the spiritual.

This transcendental philosophy and the theistic teleological interpretation of Christianity do not, therefore, represent an apostasy from Hellenism, but its continuation in the religious and philosophical fields. The Fathers of the Christian Church, trained as they were in the ancient schools of rhetoric and philosophy, were alert to adopt any trends of Hellenic thought that were intrinsically related to Christianity. The recoining and restatement that the concepts and ideas of the old Greek philosophy experienced when they were incorporated into the new organism of Christianity, were patently necessary.

The objection that a Christian philosophy, or a philosophy under the tutelage of the Church, such as Thomism is, cannot be accepted, may be answered by recalling that St. Thomas together with St. Albert and the Faculty of Arts was the actual defender of the idea that philosophy is an autonomous science. For St. Thomas, philosophy was not what it was for St. Augustine, an explanation of the universe and of man resting entirely on the basis of Christian teaching. According to St. Thomas, the system of philosophical thought and all philosophical knowledge developed by means of rational and autonomous effort into the branches of epistemology, metaphysics, ethics, natural science, and political science.

This philosophy, it is true, is reconcilable with Christianity; hence it is not atheism, materialism, pantheism, naturalism, or deism. It is a theistic teleological philosophy, founded on Greek philosophy, developed in the Greek, Arabic, and Christian cultural cycles, and finally completed when St. Thomas supplied further philosophical reasoning.

Because of the connection between the various sciences, the natural and theoretical sciences present new problems to philosophy. Thus modern philosophy receives many more stimuli than medieval philosophy received. Further, because of the relation between their fields, quite naturally philosophy received frequent and fruitful stimuli from religion. Thus the idea of personal immortality was originally a religious idea; but in his *Phaedo*, Plato attempted to solve the problem by means of philosophical arguments. Since that time this question has been one of the basic problems of metaphysical psychology. The idea of creation is an essential part of the Christian world of ideas, but it has migrated into philosophy; St. Thomas, following tradition, attempted to master the problem with philosophical reasoning.

Whenever an idea or concept is submitted for philosophical clarification and elaboration, and thus subjected to philosophical criticism, anyone, no matter what his religious belief, is permitted to investigate and test the factual basis of that concept. The origin of a philosophical thought does not guarantee its validity. So an idea, in spite of its origin, may become a problem incorporated into philosophy for its speculation and solution.

Related to St. Thomas' theory of the autonomy of philosophy, is his doctrine of the harmony between faith and science. His contemporaries, as well as succeeding ages, have expressed their thanks to him for his rejection of the "hypocritical formula of a twofold truth" which would destroy unity and truth in man's spiritual and intellectual life. Philosophy is able, of course, in its own sphere, with its own suitable methods, to make a solid contribution to truth, but it is not entirely free from error. For this reason St. Thomas announced the theology of revelation as the negative criterion of the profane sciences. He made this decision from the standpoint of his faith, and no one will find fault with that conclusion. But St. Thomas failed to delimit and determine the boundaries beyond which theology may not go when it enters the field of the profane sciences. That sphere of doctrines and problems with regard to which philosophy must submit to revision at the behest of theology does not include questions of natural science as much as the ultimate questions of philosophy, such as the ultimate causes of things. The autonomous concept of philosophy would no doubt have won out in the end, if St. Thomas had not retrenched himself behind faith and if he had relied solely on philosophical reasons in meeting the attack of philosophical criticism. The nature of the Thomistic philosophical and theological doctrinal structure, however, was the cause of this overlapping and intermingling.

How far may the so-called speculative penetration of the teachings of faith go? Is the Aristotelian universe of concepts the most fitting instrument for such rational discussion of the teachings of revelation? This question was seriously discussed during the Middle Ages, and even today opinions differ on it. Christianity existed before the patristic and Scholastic eras; and the doctrines of Christianity were taught without the help of Platonic and Aristotelian concepts. Men lead Christian lives and have Christian sentiments without the aid and support of the philosophical schools. Even today we hear the demand for an existential and factual worship and liturgy in place of Scholastic intellectualism.

The true task of the philosophy of religion and of critical theology is to mark off clearly the limits within which philosophy can be of service to religion. When a revelation is made by the divine intellect to a rational being, the believing mind is justified in its attempt to explain and elucidate the meaning of the contents of the revelation, and in the case of objections against the revelation such assistance by the human reason may even be necessary. In all instances, however, the essential mystery of the revelation may not be disturbed. If the relation of the natural reason to the supernatural revelation remains intact, if grace does not destroy nature, then natural reason must have some part to play in the total organism of man's spiritual, moral, and religious life.

St. Thomas went far in his discussion of the contents of revelation; for this reason the charge of rationalism was hurled against him. Because of his high regard for the intellect, he could not permit the individual doctrines of faith to dangle unconnected and unrelated in isolation, nor could he permit an uncritical obscurity in the mind of the believer. His love of the concept of order urged him on to show the relation between the contents of revelation to every department of this earthly life. Nevertheless St. Thomas was aware that human concepts were in no way adequate to illuminate the object of supernatural faith. He also knew that the ultimate is unknowable and ineffable, he knew what it meant when the human soul was touched by divine power, he knew the meaning of ecstasy.

3. **The Thomistic view of the universe.** Thomistic philosophy does not suffer in comparison with any other important system of philosophy produced during the course of Occidental thought. But this fact does not imply that the Thomistic system must be accepted in its entirety. The inconsiderate continuation of the Thomistic tradition could not be countenanced in either the subjective or the objective forums, and especially not in the court of the divine intellect.

The statement that the profane sciences had reached their highest point in Aristotle is so monstrous that it is a psychological riddle how respected scholars could have given expression to such a conclusion. No age and no epoch and no individual mind possesses enough intellectual energy to master the universal cosmos in one all-inclusive system. The knowledge of the universe is a task set for the whole of humanity, and mankind continually renews its attempts to press on to the realization of this goal. No philosophical system is free from error or limitations; not even the Thomistic system. St. Thomas had many physical misconceptions, and his whole astronomical picture was wrong. His concept of the origin, extent, and composition of the world, of the position of the earth, and of the function of the heavenly bodies was erroneous. The earth, which for St. Thomas was the center of the whole universe and about which the heavenly spheres were busily concerned, has become a tiny planet in the immeasurable space of the universe. The heavenly bodies have abdicated their offices to natural laws and natural forces. The crystal sky and the empyrean no longer exist.

In the same way his biological notions did not correspond to the facts. St. Thomas was not yet able to see the world in its great developmental connections and he adhered to an erroneous theory of generation, while his cultural and historical judgments were limited by the knowledge of his time.

Sometimes these errors had their effect on his philosophical conclusions. Some questions and problems are altogether ignored. Many of the universal propositions from which he was accustomed to draw conclusions rested on insufficient knowledge of nature and cannot withstand critical investigation. The Middle Ages themselves progressed farther than St. Thomas. In the Parisian Faculty of Arts of the fourteenth century the foundations were being laid for the newer natural sciences. Soon Leonardo, Galileo, Keppler, and Newton appeared on the scientific horizon and showed the way to the vast natural knowledge of modern times and also to the enrichment of philosophy with a multiplicity of new methodological and factual problems.

It is not mere accident that even in the Middle Ages criticism was directed against the methods and the contents of the Thomistic system. St. Thomas cannot, of course, be held responsible for the mental acrobatics performed on the logical and ontological horizontal bars by later Scholastics and also by certain Neothomists. In St. Thomas a keen sense of logic and a prodigious power of synthesis were united to discipline of the mind which warded off any exaggerated rationalism. The accusation that Thomism hides behind the faith against the attack of criticism, that it hides behind criticism against the attack of infidelity, and that it hides behind the mysticism of dogma against the attack of reason, arises from a misconception in the minds of those who do not understand the Thomistic method sufficiently. St. Thomas was a dialectician, it is true, but he fought on philosophical grounds with philosophical weapons.

The philosophical basis of all St. Thomas' Christian thinking was a theistic teleological system of thought, and in that system the concept of order has the dominant role. No single concept is ever adequate to give us a complete grasp of the essence of a great system of thought. But if we are looking for the concept that goes deepest into the core of Thomistic thought, the most apt and adequate concept is that of order. If the order as conceived in Thomism is at times too anthropocentric, in general St. Thomas is not far from the truth. To conceive of the universe as an order presupposes that the universe actually exists and that its purpose can be comprehended. When we speak of the universe as an order, we presuppose that we can understand the purposeful existence of the universe and its integral parts. The concept of order is indispensable to every philosophy; if the concept of order has been destroyed or has been made problematical, it becomes necessary to build up an order from the standpoint of the subject.

According to the Thomistic view, man is inseparably connected with the great cosmos which came into existence through an act of God's will. This cosmos is integrated into a magnificent order which is related to the Creator. Everything returns according to a definite plan of vital movement to the point of origin. In this relationship every single stage of existence, including man, has its own significance. Man's stage in this order determines his value, and from his being arises the requirement that he give his faculties expression, not according to his own unlimited desire, but as a duty imposed by God.

Man is possessed of the dignity of personality; he is the actualizer of moral values. Because of his social nature he is a member of a multiplicity of definite communities which have as their model the authoritarian and hierarchical structure of the universe. All things in nature have a relationship to this cosmic order and interrelationship and from it they, too, derive their value. When St. Francis addressed nature about him as "Brother" and Sister," he elevated this valuation to the point of solidarity with human nature. By this appreciation of the impersonal world about him, the medieval man was deterred from abusing the things of nature.

This order of the medieval man was primarily concerned with man's inner nature. But because of the close connection between the inner form and the outward expression, this order also affected the outward manifestations of human life. Every man lived in the shadow and under the influence of a sublime symbolism that reminded him of the subordination of the elementary things, of the subjection of the individual's appetite to spiritual forces, and of the relation of human activity to the ultimate end.

This does not mean, however, that the Middle Ages did not sin against this order or even fall away from it. No other age in history includes such opposites, no other period of man's cultural history gave rise to such violent intellectual activity. Here are servitude and freedom, asceticism and complete indulgence, troubadours of God and romanticists who sang of women, here are high sanctity and black malice. But man was always conscious that he was violating the order of things and that he was opposing the supreme principle of his existence if he disturbed this order.

The concept of order presupposes God. For this reason St. Thomas gave so much attention to the proof for the existence of God. He knew, as did St. Augustine and St. Anselm, that these proofs for God's existence do not give man his original conviction that there is a God, but that they merely add intellectual support to a conviction gained in some other way. The concept of God is originally a religious concept. Perhaps these proofs for God's existence have not yet led a single man to his original conviction that God exists; at least, no man has yet become interested in these proofs who had not been convinced of God's existence in other ways.

The "five proofs" in the *Theological Summa* have been subjected to much criticism. Religion, of course, does not need metaphysics to substantiate its position; it stands alone and it is able to come to the knowledge of its subject matter, God, by its own resources. Through metaphysics, however, religion associates itself with the complete philosophical picture of the universe. The God of religion and the supreme principle of the universe in metaphysics are really identical.

All the Thomistic proofs for God's existence are drawn from external experience. The intellectual tradition dating from St. Augustine, which with all the mystics taught that God and the soul come into immediate contact in man's inner nature, laments the fact that St. Thomas neglected this inner nature of man as a starting point in man's ascent to the knowledge of God. Undoubtedly St. Thomas underestimated the importance and significance of the religious a priori and thus lost the opportunity of incorporating into his system the indisputable force of the historical and psychological proof for the existence of God.

St. Anselm, Hugh of St. Victor, Alexander of Hales, John of
Rupella, and St. Bonaventure are representatives of the view that
the concept of God is congenital inasmuch as the soul knows God
because it is the image of God. The concept of God belongs to the
equipment and inventory of our intellectual souls. By reflecting on
itself, our mind continually discovers the striving for eternal wisdom, the desire for the highest good and for lasting peace in some
supreme unchanging being. This is the expression of the supreme
divine being which becomes ever present to our intellect. St. Thomas
reduces this thought to a minimum of significance and explains it
merely as the natural disposition to know God. He says that this
thought means no more than that man has an inborn faculty to attain to the knowledge of God by the causal route. St. Thomas did not
reason subjectively or from the matter supplied by rich experience;
he always looked at things objectively.

St. Anselm's argument that the idea of God is the concept that includes all perfection is also inadequate. If we look at this concept
from the standpoint of its origin, we see that it is merely a concept
impressed upon us from our youth that has become habitual with us.
But a psychological experience can never take over the task of supply-
ing the basis of knowledge even though it have the force of a natural
faculty. If we look at this concept as a logical structure we find it
bereft of all reality, and the transition from the order of thought to
the order of being is not permissible. The idea of God as the most
perfect being exists only in our thoughts; nothing is determined
thereby as to its reality.

In the same way, St. Augustine's proof of God's existence by the
argument of the mind's attraction to truth by which the mind ascends
to God without any use of causality, does not win the approval of
St. Thomas. His proofs for God's existence are causal proofs and they
may be referred back to this fundamental thought: something exists,
therefore God exists. For, either this something is God Himself, or
it is such that the existence of God is required to explain its existence.
The universe in its contingency, in its mere possibility, and in its
state of motion, cannot exist of itself; it requires a cause that produces
it. This is ultimately true because the existence of the things in the
universe is not immediately posited by their essences.

The validity of the Thomistic proofs for God's existence rests on
the objective force of the principle of causality. Hence every true

disciple of St. Thomas has labored to safeguard and support the
principle of causality since the time of the nominalists up to the attack of modern thinkers. In the rather limited panorama of the
medieval view of the universe it was not difficult to distinguish between God and the universe. But today metaphysics has the more
difficult task of showing how the supreme cause of the universe
transcends a universe almost unlimited in space and time and human beings whose psychological experience almost extends to the
unlimited.

As with God's existence so also the closer determinations of His
nature can be learned only from creatures. God is not the primary
object of our knowledge in whose light we learn the truth about
things. St. Thomas in his stark realism could never have entertained
a thought so contrary to all experience. Only through creatures, as in
a mirror, can God be known. The essential difference between God
and the universe forbids the univocal attribution to Him of concepts
derived from experience from created things. Certain concepts have
validity in all phases of being extending even into the transcendental
realm and therefore they may be attributed in a certain sense to God
because all concepts and predicates are attributable to God only analogically. Because of the radical and fundamental difference between
God and the universe, only a certain similarity exists between God
and the universe; and when we have said this we have said too much.
St. Thomas admits only a relation of the universe to God.

In this respect St. Thomas' use of analogy had two periods. In his
early years he inclined to the teaching of the unknown God, maintaining that all our predications about God have only equivocal
validity. During this period he feared anthropomorphism more than
agnosticism. In his later years he predicates substance, being, person,
goodness, truth, and cause, of God but in an entirely different sense
and measure than with creatures; yet he seems to be convinced that
in these fundamental concepts there is something that we can grasp
about the nature of God.

The great danger of identifying God with the universe arose also
from another side. How can a substantially different universe exist
outside of God, who contains all being? If there is a divine causality,
a divine foreknowledge and a divine plan for the universe, how can
there be another autonomous causality of creatures? How can we
account for such things as liberty, responsibility, and man's sover-

eignty? In our day serious attacks have been made upon the theistic teleological philosophy because of these problems. St. Thomas, too, had met these difficulties. Some theistic thinkers prefer to take the stand that the problem of the existence of a universe together with an all-embracing divine Being cannot be solved by the human intellect. St. Thomas, however, sought to master the difficulty by the distinction between *ens per essentiam* (being that is essentially being) and *ens per participationem* (being that is being only by participation). This distinction he derived from Platonism. God's essence is identical with His existence and it constitutes an absolutely perfect actuality of life and being that exists and acts of itself. In this realm of being in the true and actual sense there is no room for an extra-divine being. Separated from this most perfect Being by an infinite abyss is the universe created by the free act of God, the universe which is a reflection of the divine being, a reflection which is more clearly illuminated the higher things are in the plane of being.

Creatures are entirely different from God, especially those that are bound to matter. St. Thomas divides things in three ways; and each time the point of division is different. Things are composed of matter and form, of substance and accidents, and of essence and existence. These three pairs are not identical, although they have an inner relationship with each other. This threefold division expresses important elements of the Thomistic system which are not everywhere acceptable without further scrutiny.

This is especially true of the principle of form. In the individual thing St. Thomas discerned the idea, the basic type; he saw the universal in type and law that lay at the root of the individual and controlled it. At the same time this inner structure of a thing is identical with the essence, or it approaches it closely, it is the dam against a meaningless flux, and it is the firm framework which looks for and finds completion in the ebb and flow of events.

St. Thomas' doctrine of the principle of individuation remains one of the weakest points in the whole Thomistic system. All attempts to save it by later Thomists have been of no avail. We can cheerfully concede that an important philosophical thought is contained in the idea of *materia signata* and that it is quite correct to say that the soul can develop only in a proper and appropriate matter. But this means only that the individual soul requires individual material organs suited to it. Nothing has thus far been determined about the principle of individuation. Because of the factual difficulties, many admirers of St. Thomas have adopted the modified Thomistic doctrine of Suarez with respect to the principle of individuation and the distinction between essence and existence.

The concept of substance is still more fundamental. Things are substances. This means they have their own being and possess a relative, if not an absolute, autonomy. St. Thomas does not teach that all being is concentrated in one individual and that the phenomenal modes and attributes of this individual are the forms and shapes of all other things. In asserting the autonomy of the being of things, St. Thomas rejects monism and acknowledges a pluralistic universe. Every substance is a unity, an entity, a totality, something that exists for itself. But substantiality appears in various degrees. The extended material body is a substance, but it is a substance possessing similar parts and it can be separated into these similar parts. The organism is higher in the plane of substances; it lives, preserves itself, acts, and develops. The highest form of substantial being known to us is the substance that attains to the consciousness of itself. This form of substantial being is found in the person, whose characteristics are self-consciousness, reflection, and the power to rule itself. The Thomistic characterization of the various stages of life as different degrees of self-movement is proof that the metaphysics of being is a priori to all knowledge derived from the sciences that deal with reality, that the metaphysics of being reaches conclusions that cannot be disturbed by the individual sciences, and that these metaphysical findings must serve to deepen the knowledge of the various sciences.

No creature is pure act; no creature is absolute perfection as God is. Every creature is permeated with the opposition of potency and act. This relation speaks of the creature's limitations, its finiteness, and of its faculty for development and perfection. The transition from potency to act is the road to fullness of existence and to the actualization of something that has been preformed in the germ. A disposition is not a disposition to nothing but to something, and that something corresponds to the disposition. This relation of opposition is a teleological relation; according to the principle, *ens et bonum convertuntur,* it seeks to attain a state of perfection and thus it supports the optimistic philosophy of Aquinas.

This concept of being has certain consequences in the Thomistic concept of the world. Just as the world is not something resting statically on the quiet basis of being, so the world of happenings is not a mere accumulation of relations. These various relations are borne by things, they reside in things that act upon one another. Here St. Thomas found the opportunity to delimit and define the realm of secondary causes. Creatures have their own being, and corresponding to this being we find that creatures have their own activity. Therefore St. Thomas understood that creatures were obliged to strive to create a culture here on earth; and he rejected any metaphysics that showed a tendency to flee from this world.

The relation between matter and form found fruitful application to the relation of body and soul in the psychological sphere. In this way St. Thomas rejected any materialist explanation of the life of the soul as well as any dissolution of the life of the soul into a sum of associated acts. The nonsense of a "psychology without a soul" was unknown to the Middle Ages. More important than this, however, is the fact that St. Thomas, in contrast to Plato and St. Augustine, saw man as a unified, harmonious whole in which body and soul play their proportionate parts. This concept of the unity and harmony of the body and soul was presaged in the biological sphere, but when it found a place in the psychological sphere the dominion of the soul over the lower physical faculties was in no way impaired.

St. Thomas laid the foundation for an ontology of the corporeal and spiritual personal entity in which the matter was viewed with a sense for the whole. Although St. Thomas did not present an experimental psychology such as we know today, he made an analysis of the structure of the basic powers of the soul, he studied the connections between the senses and the spiritual soul, and he gave us the psychology of acts, which is in agreement with modern findings.

When we come to study man we reach a new order, the order of the spirit. Man is a member of the spirit world; he forms the lowest estate in that world. Some have taken umbrage at the Thomistic definition of man as *animal rationale*. Today this definition appears to be a rather empty formula, but for St. Thomas the phrase was rich in meaning. The *animalitas* signified man's complex connection with nature and the union of his soul with the body; the *rationalitas* signified man's membership in the spirit world and expressed man's higher spiritual self with all its judgments, desires, and needs. According to St. Thomas, the intellect is man's distinguishing mark, i.e., his thinking, understanding, knowing, which form the basis for his willing and acting. If anyone wishes to uphold man's consciousness of values as the essence of his nature, he would not find St. Thomas on the side of the opposition, for St. Thomas actually designated the practical reason as the principal faculty and organ of value. At the same time, we must admit that he exaggerated the rational element in man inasmuch as he neglected the discussion of the influence which the lower appetitive and emotional urges have on the higher stages of man's personality.

The realm of nature rises of itself into the realm of the norm and morality governed by values. Ethics is a natural growth out of the field of ontology. As a spiritual person, man has no other duty than the development of his essential nature, not in the pattern of the compulsion of the natural law or of instinct, but in the form of an obligating duty in the accomplishment of which intellect and will unite their services. The human will by its nature is filled with the urge to strive for the good, while the intellect discovers the fullness of human values and relates earthly goods and values to the highest good.

At no time did St. Thomas lose sight of the natural and human origins of virtue, at no time did he identify this earth and sin. No Christian moralist emphasized the importance of the natural moral law as did St. Thomas; yet no other moralist was able to give such a high place to the divine law of grace. Some students with only a superficial acquaintance with Thomism have attempted to sum up the position of St. Thomas as follows: He taught that the man who obeys the moral law opposes evil, but when he obeys the law of grace he surrenders to the good. The natural law is the negative pole, while the law of grace is the positive pole of the same principle. By asserting his dignity and observing morality, man satisfies his conscience and enters into an accord with himself, but when he surrenders to a higher power he receives the blessed gift of grace and enters into an accord with God and the universe. Just as the critical philosopher destroys error while the believing hero receives the truth; so the man with a moral character fights sin while the pious man receives the reward. Whoever concludes such a summary from the writings of St. Thomas has completely misread him. According to St. Thomas, the natural law is not negative, but positive, and morality does not bring man into harmony with himself alone but with God and the universe as well. The man with the moral character does not merely oppose sin, but he builds the structure of the cosmos of moral values and develops his own personality and receives the reward of happiness in this life as well as in the next. The morality of the natural law is the natural foundation for the supernatural life of grace; but in practical life the natural and supernatural laws condition and support each other.

The magnitude and excellence of St. Thomas' dissertation on natural morality has evoked the admiration of many. Werner Sombart, the great sociologist, wrote: "When we read the writings of the Scholastics, especially that wonderful and monumental work of the great St. Thomas Aquinas, with which only the creations of Dante and Michaelangelo can be compared in magnificence, we obtain the impression that these writers were trying to teach men not only how to become prosperous and loyal citizens but also how to become upright, courageous, prudent, and industrious men. At all times these medieval writers are striving to instill into life a certain buoyancy and vigor. Nothing seems to merit their condemnation as much as slovenliness, whether spiritual, intellectual, or moral." [3]

This formal advantage of Thomistic ethics is founded on its realism, its close connection with life, its references to natural dispositions and original values, and on its recognition of fundamental and immutable values. In the history of the theory of moral values St. Thomas deserves a high place. No individual and no age, it is true, was able to comprehend the whole scale and table of values in one glance, nor did St. Thomas enumerate all the moral values. His gradation of values may not find universal approval. Of course, perhaps he did not personally experience in his own inner life the conflict between moral values. Sometimes he lays so much stress on the *bonum commune* that private welfare seems to suffer. He understood little about the differences between individuals in the moral sphere, the difference between subject and subject as represented by individual men; he did not reckon that two persons will not always react and judge in the same way in the presence of the same human value.

We rejoice that St. Thomas so clearly taught the autonomy of conscience and recognized conscience as the court of last instance in human conduct, but we are chagrined to learn that he was so much

---

[3] Werner Sombart, *Der Bourgeois, zur Geistesgeschichte des modernen Wirtschaftsmenschen* (1913), p. 311.

the child of his time that he was unable to cast off the doctrine that force may be used against heretics. The reason for this teaching is, of course, the medieval concept of values, according to which the care of the soul was more important than the welfare of the body. As if the use of force could ever become a means of saving men's souls!

St. Thomas rooted the natural law in the divine essence, and he sought thereby to make human morality secure against any inroad or attack. In spite of its limitations, this most important ethical and legal system of the Middle Ages has influenced succeeding ages down to our own time. It is interesting to note that the latest development in French jurisprudence, the theory of institutions, has adopted St. Thomas' teaching on the common good and his metaphysical basis of law.

Of all the cardinal virtues, justice, the virtue of action, is given the paramount place. Justice is the virtue that refers to the neighbor; it divides things according to right reason among individuals and communities. As social justice it orders human life within the social communities, within the family, the community, and the state. The isolated individual does not actually exist, an individual in isolation is only a fiction; a human being exists only in conjunction with other human beings, and in association with others a human being comes into being, develops, and preserves himself.

St. Thomas, it is true, was not the first to reject the theory of the sinful origin of the state, but by his realistic, unartificial, honest thinking he pointed the way to a better understanding of the significance and importance of the state. Even though much of Thomistic thought bears the unmistakable limitations of the political theories of his time, nevertheless his concept of the organic community and the organic state, his delineation of the relation of the individual to the state, and his delimitation of the legal spheres of individual and community, are accepted as valid even today.

In all his political thinking St. Thomas was as careful to avoid any condemnation of the secular state as he was to point out that the state had aims and purposes beyond those of this life. Like the individual, the state is ordered to its last end in all of its religious and moral activities, and it is likewise directed to God. Since he was always faithful to reality even in his political thinking, St. Thomas was able to show that the state had an independent value, an independent sphere, and an autonomy distinct from that of the Church.

St. Thomas did not teach that the Church had absolute dominion over the state in purely secular matters; he safeguarded the sovereignty of the state within the secular realm. Logic was completely on his side when he taught the subordination of the Christian ruler to ecclesiastical authority in spiritual matters, when he taught that the Church is a higher society because of its higher purpose, and finally when he taught that both Church and state must mutually support each other and cooperate because man has only one final destiny.

Reality, however, generally has no concern about theory, and might is generally little concerned with the logic of an idea. The bitter feud between the papacy and the empire was a strife for everything except the peaceful division of power. Unlike Dante, St. Thomas did not give a legal and moral judgment of this conflict, he took no sides in the controversy. He did not publicize or approve the arguments of either the papal or the imperial representatives, although his disciple, Aegidius Romanus, the Augustinian, entered the service of the papal cause.[4] St. Thomas was not concerned about the particular points of difference between Pope and Emperor; for him the matter was one of principles.

St. Thomas sought to give the basis as provided by the natural law for the peaceful division of powers and the harmonious cooperation of the two autonomous societies, a desideratum devoutly hoped for since the time of Pope Gelasius (492-496). On one point St. Thomas remained loyal to the all-embracing idea of order as promulgated by the theistic Christian society of the Middle Ages: both Church and state are bound by the natural law and the divine law, both powers are in the service of the great Christian *Imperium,* both perfect societies are under God.

In the development of a great philosophical interpretation of the universe, the epistemological attitude is of decisive importance, i.e., the methods and means by which man approaches the world of things, the methods by which he obtains his primary and fundamental knowledge, how he proceeds in the various spheres of being, and how he determines the limits of human knowledge. The philosophy of St.

---

[4] In defense of Pope Boniface VIII, Aegidius wrote *De renuntiatione Papae* and *De ecclesiastica potestate.* While he was a tutor in Paris at the royal court, he wrote *De regimine principum.*

Thomas is the philosophy of natural reason, a philosophy that stands firmly on natural realism and tries to evaluate properly all the data of experience. Some may think that the human reason is too awkward an organ to attempt the solution of the highest scientific problems, but it is none the less true that all scientific knowledge is derived from natural reason. It is by criticism, by refinement of thought, by development, and when necessary by elimination of antiquated concepts and the introduction of newer approaches and new viewpoints, that the mind comes closer to the scientific object. But at all times the chief corrective is the data of experience.

Because of this simple and unadulterated view of actuality, St. Thomas, like Aristotle, took the middle road between two epistemological extremes, between sensualism and rationalism. Knowledge is not the same as the reception and association of the content of things, it is not an outpouring of the content of our own minds, and it is not the mere awakening of the consciousness that certain principles and ideas exist a priori within us.

All knowledge begins with the experience of the senses, but it is not the mere accumulation of the data of sense experience. Experience and thought work together in organic fashion. The data of the senses have a teleological relation and tendency toward the higher intellectual potencies. The intellect possesses the power to extract spiritual contents from the data delivered by the senses, it is able to penetrate the external sensible hull to the inner structure of things in its abstracting process. The human reason forms the supreme principles and ideas that underlie all other modifications of being, and that form the basis for all metaphysical, mathematical, and scientific research and study as well as for all the practical sciences. An important point in the system is that the human powers of cognition are in direct contact with the sensible and spiritual contents of things by reason of a teleological relation to the objects of knowledge consisting in the peculiar receptivity of these faculties of knowledge.

Thus, according to the Thomistic view, knowledge is not a process consisting merely in something that comes from the object alone, nor is it simply a creative synthesis. Knowledge begins with the reception of sensible and spiritual data, it is accelerated spontaneously by the intellect, and in the sensible and intellectual spheres it is perfected by an active process of the mind. The mere formation of ideas, judgments, and conclusions does not constitute knowledge; human knowledge reaches its completion in the relational concepts of the most varied kind and in the panoramic view of all the parts in relation to the whole. The abstractive and discursive processes of thought have an important place in the structure of Thomistic thought; but intuition, in the sense of contemplative knowledge, has its place in the lower as well as the higher planes of knowledge.

We cannot deny that St. Thomas made certain assumptions in his theory of sense knowledge with regard to the intermediary means that today seem rather primitive in the light of our knowledge of physics and psychology. It is also true that he left many difficulties unsolved. The important thing is that he was right in principle because of his natural realism and that he offered a working analysis of the complex structure of the acts that participate in perception.

The fact that St. Thomas taught that the active intellect had the power to penetrate to the inner content of things is of the utmost importance. Like is known through like. The spiritual content of things can be known only by the spirit. He unerringly rejected the Augustinian theory of illumination; he was realist enough to know that we have no illumination in our natural knowledge. At the same time, St. Thomas cast aside the theory of Nominalism with its threat to the validity of our knowledge and its destructive tendencies against ethics and law. We comprehend the essences of things in spite of the inadequacy of our knowledge.

St. Thomas is careful to emphasize the point that the cognitional forms of our mind are determined not only by the nature of the real beings which are to be represented in our minds but also by the spiritual nature of the intellect as the formative power of these intentional entities. This is true of the concepts of our mind, which are *similitudines rei existentis extra animam,* but especially of those concepts which our mind forms and which have no direct counterpart in the actual world. The mode of knowledge in our mind is not identical with the mode of being of the thing we know. Although there is a difference in the mode of knowledge and the mode of being of the thing known, yet our knowledge is not a counterfeit of reality.

The Thomistic concept of the knowledge of essences has its limitations. Not all the sciences are intent on the metaphysical essences of things in the Aristotelian-Thomistic sense, yet they form concepts and distinguish between essential and nonessential characteristics. What do these different sciences understand by essence and what is the criterion by which they distinguish between essential and non-essential properties? Modern methodology is aware that the formation of a concept is preceded by a leading and guiding viewpoint, which in turn is determined by the purpose of the particular science. Since these concepts are based in reality and since they investigate forms, structures, and laws, this new methodology is a new expression of an old thought.

St. Bonaventure merely tolerated philosophy. But for St. Thomas philosophical knowledge was the natural and preferred cognitional function in the realm of the essences of things which are to be known not only as reflections of divine ideas but in their own autonomous being and activity. In the graded structure of knowledge St. Thomas recognized the place of the contemplative life and the contemplation of the divine, but contemplation is not the basis of knowledge; it is the culmination of all knowledge. Whoever does not dare to ascend the highest battlements of knowledge to attain the mystic vision will find many other rooms in the Thomistic structure of knowledge where he will be comfortable; from the windows he may look out on the whole building and even gaze aloft to the highest pinnacle of contemplation.

Because of his natural realism and his frequent reference to the object, St. Thomas' logic avoided any exaggerated preoccupation with psychological processes and remained an objective science. Logic is not actually concerned with the physical processes that occur in the subject, but with the intentional content of thought which is constantly related to some object. Thomistic logic is an objective logic inasmuch as our thoughts are directed to the object and are said to be true or false according as they agree or disagree with the actual object. The intentional content corresponds to the content of being. All knowledge implies an adjustment of the one who knows to the thing known; when our thoughts agree with actual things, the concept of truth formally attains its fulfillment.

St. Thomas took a broad view of the science of logic. He knew that the truth of our logical contents was conditioned on the correct functioning of the positing acts. Thus, in his treatment of the subject of logic, he speaks of logic as the art and science of correct thinking. At all times, however, his logic remains dependent on the content of our thoughts. In modern times controversy raged for decades before the position of an objective logic could be made secure against the exaggerated psychological speculations of some thinkers. Nietzsche clearly understood that the concept of truth as the agreement between thought and actuality presupposes the theistic concept of God, and that it is best integrated in a theistic teleological system of philosophy. This maintenance of the objectivist concept of truth brought St. Thomas close to Kant in at least one respect. St. Thomas understood that reason itself is "the ultimate touchstone of truth" (Kant) and that truth can be successfully attained only by reflection on our acts and on the nature of our intellects.

By the austere discipline of his thinking, St. Thomas was preserved from an exaggerated rationalism and from distortion of the various sciences by allowing them to overlap and run into each other. The various sciences are clearly separated and distinguished from one another according to their formal objects. Since the Middle Ages the natural sciences have greatly increased as have also the theoretical sciences, and thus countless new problems have arisen in methodology, in scientific procedure, and in the formation of concepts, which were entirely unknown to the man of the Middle Ages.

CHAPTER XXXIX

PHILOSOPHY AFTER ST. THOMAS

No proof is required to show that through the centuries St. Thomas has had many admirers and disciples. His important place in philosophy has been attested up to the present time by many thinkers, beginning with his greatest opponent in the Paris Faculty of Arts, Siger of Brabant, who wrote: *"Praecipui viri in philosophia Albertus et Thomas."* Our present purpose would not be well served if we were to recall the many eulogies spoken about Aquinas, nor is it our intention here to outline a history of Thomism.

After a diligent study of the Thomistic commentaries, we see that an interesting light is thrown on various individual problems, but that little is gained toward an understanding of the whole philosophical system. An interesting chapter in the history of Thomism would consider the position which Thomism took in the various controversies of the later Middle Ages. In their battle with Nominalism and Occamism the religious orders chose St. Thomas as their leader. The most loyal followers of St. Thomas were the Dominicans, who in numerous general chapters proclaimed him as their guide; beside the Dominicans were the Augustinians, Benedictines, Carmelites, Jesuits, and others.

St. Thomas was fortunate in having many able commentators and interpreters, such as John Capreolus (d. 1444), Francis Sylvester of Ferrara (d. 1528), the illustrious commentator of the *Summa contra Gentes,* Cardinal Cajetan (d. 1534), the Dominican John of St. Thomas (d. 1644), Philip of the Blessed Trinity (d. 1671), a Discalced Carmelite, and finally the Jesuits of Coimbra and the Carmelites of Alcala and Salamanca.

Of special importance is the Dominican General, Cardinal Cajetan, whose brilliant philosophical mind enabled him to penetrate deep into the Thomistic doctrine of the metaphysics of being and the

Thomistic speculative theology, and whose commentaries on *De ente et essentia* and the *Summa theologica* (printed in the Leonine edition) are valuable aids toward an understanding of the Thomistic system. Among the Spanish Scholastics of the fifteenth and sixteenth centuries a notable advance was made in the development of Thomistic political ideas and theories by Francis de Vittoria, Dominic Soto, Gabriel Vasquez, and Francis Suarez (d. 1617), whom Schopenhauer rightly called the compendium of Scholasticism.

When the revival of Aristotelianism began in the nineteenth century under the leadership of Adolph Trendelenburg, the movement benefited the system of the greatest Aristotelian of the Middle Ages, and when historical research into the origins and sources of Aristotelianism in France, Germany, Italy, and other countries was made, it was seen that St. Thomas was the focal point of the Aristotelian movement.

In ecclesiastical circles the greatest impetus to the study of Thomism was given when Pope Leo XIII in 1879, in his encyclical *Aeterni Patris,* directed students of theology to an intensive study of St. Thomas' philosophical and theological system. The founding of chairs of philosophy in the Sorbonne in Paris, in Holland at the University of Amsterdam, in England at the University of London, and in the United States at Harvard University for lectures on medieval or Thomistic philosophy, are eloquent testimonials to the greatness of the Thomistic system. Neo-Thomism is represented by prominent scholars in Belgium (at Louvain University), France, and Germany.

In spite of its determination to travel a different road away from Scholasticism, modern philosophy finds itself again and again confronted with the old problems, and in many instances it has involuntarily continued the great medieval tradition. The wall that some historians tried to erect as a barrier between Scholasticism and modern thought has remained a mere fiction of the mind. Descartes, Spinoza, Leibnitz, and Wolff are proofs of the connection between medieval and modern thought. Even in England lectures on scholastic philosophy were given at Oxford University until sometime in the eighteenth century, and Locke acknowledged his debt to medieval philosophy.

Because of his liberal understanding and appreciation of the achievements of the past, the great Leibnitz was attracted to the

Thomistic theory of substantial forms in spite of his tendency to mathematics and the natural sciences. His words are noteworthy: "The doctrines of the scholastic philosophers and theologians are far more valid than we are inclined to think, especially when we know at what time and in what place they are to be applied. I am convinced that some more precise and more penetrating mind that can develop and interpret their thoughts and present them according to the form of analytical geometry will discover a treasure of important and demonstrable truths."[1]

In all its textbooks and through the conscientious efforts of its illustrious exponents, Thomism always strove for the continuation and preservation of the intellectual bequest of the great master. Correct interpretation and avoidance of faulty commentary are not sufficient, however, if the spirit of Aquinas is not to be lost. The sterility and the triteness of schoolroom philosophy of later centuries, which monotonously restates old concepts and theories, is an example of what happens when philosophy does not look about and try to answer the problems of its own time. Even in ecclesiastical circles a strong opposition has arisen against such textbook philosophy. This opposition found leadership in the eighteenth century within the Benedictine Order in Abbot Frobenius Forster of St. Emmeram in Ratisbon and in Andrew Gordon of the University of Erfurt.

St. Thomas knew well that the unchanging insistence on the individual theories of a system is a sin against the intellectual life and against the march of intellectual progress. The knowledge of truth, according to St. Thomas, is the task of generations, or rather the task of all mankind of all times, and with Aristotle he recognized that time is the great auxiliary on the road of intellectual progress. The movement toward truth began in ages past and continues on. St. Thomas demands that we be grateful to all who have increased the deposit of truth and he has high appreciation for the gain that is made when error is the occasion for renewed study and research. He knew the progressive force that comes from intellectual controversy.[2] St. Bonaventure said that the progress of knowledge depends on three factors: (1) the discovery of new objects of knowledge, (2) the ap-

---

[1] "Discours sur la metaphysique," no. 11 in *Nouvelles lettres et opuscules de Leibniz* by A. Foucher (1857), p. 341.

[2] *In II Met.*, 1; *In de coelo*, 22; *Summa theol.*, Ia, q.44, a.2; Ia IIae, q.97, a.1; q.106, a.3; *De verit.*, XI, 1; *In I Phys.*, 10.

plication of new modes of knowledge (methods), and (3) the appearance of thorough students who will enter deep into a study of
the new objects of knowledge and know how to make use of the
new methods. In the same conviction, St. Thomas taught the continuous development of knowledge and science.

Both antiquity and the Middle Ages are distinguished from modern
times by the fact that they believed themselves close to a complete
knowledge of all reality because of the limited nature of their picture of the universe. To the unaided eye and to the mind working
without modern instruments, the structure of things appeared much
simpler than it is in reality.

Every philosophical system is in a sense a detailed explanation and
a comprehensive statement of the totality of reality. This effort is
made from the viewpoint of the various problems of a particular era
and with the aid of whatever cognitional means and scientific tools
are available. Two aspects of every system must be kept in mind:
the influence of a particular historical era and the basic scientific attitude as it is expressed in established principles and methods. The
influence of a historical era will, of course, often yield to better insight and judgment. The basic scientific attitude, however, as it is
known in method and principle, must always be prepared to weather
every test of its validity. A philosophical system cannot be content
with monotonously repeating concepts, judgments, and doctrines for
which a modern era with its own problems will have no understanding. Every age has its own problems growing out of its own historical
situation. New problems arise, old truths must be furnished with
new proofs and related to new connections.

The basic principles themselves must be subjected to critical review and reinforced. The treatment of new problems and new tendencies must be vital. Aristotle's admonition is still applicable: "He
who has not fully grasped the difficulties cannot understand the
solution, even though it is placed in his hand." [3]

The more compact and closed a system is the less will it be able
to adjust itself to the march of progress. Only a system of thought
that is broadly receptive to new knowledge and new critical attitudes
will be able to keep pace with progress. Codices and summas are
never written at the beginning of an epoch but always at the close
since they are the synthesis and summation, the intellectual pinnacle

[3] *Met.*, III, 1.

from which a review is made of the achievements of a past era. Progress from this point is found generally in individual branches of knowledge, and often it bursts through the framework of the old system and calls into question the validity of the old principles and methods. The Thomistic system, however, was so all-embracing and so receptive to anything new that it flourished throughout the continuing forward movement of intellectual progress. St. Thomas himself had been a master in the art of meeting the challenge of intellectual crises and conquering them.

The search for the various Thomistic concepts that found their way into later systems would no doubt make an engrossing study, but an attempt to make a comparative study of whole groups of ideas in different systems and show thereby the great general direction and tendency in philosophical thought and solution would perhaps be more interesting. Such a study would show that philosophy is indeed perennial. Much could be learned from such a comparative study by adding new concepts and viewpoints; St. Thomas himself would no doubt have welcomed such an excursion.

Thus we would see that the theism of Nicholas of Cusa is broader and more optimistic than that of St. Thomas. The concept of God has so many aspects that new viewpoints will appear again and again in the course of progress and development. Leibnitz's ideas of God as well as his concept of the harmony of the universe would offer many new viewpoints for the theistic teleological philosophy of Thomism. And anyone filled with the spirit of Aristotelianism would have been found on the side of Copernicus, Galileo, Descartes, and Newton.

The mathematical character of the natural sciences of modern times and the monadology of Leibnitz call for a review of the Thomistic epistemology and ontology. From the English thinkers Thomism may be able to learn more psychology than philosophy, while the shock of Kant's critique would have forced St. Thomas himself to investigate the foundations of his epistemological viewpoint and attempt to reinforce them. At first sight St. Thomas seems to be at variance with German idealism more than with any other systems or movements, but after some reflection we find that an inner relationship exists between Thomism and Hegel, the great systematizer who was in substantial agreement with Aristotle. A controversial encounter with the Hegelian comparison of the idea and reality, of the totality of the organic idea and that of being, might have fructified Thomistic ontology. The age from Herder to Hegel, from Neohumanism to William von Humboldt, from the classical period to Goethe, was characterized by the conviction that purposefulness and the rational order pervade not only the universe but the forms of human life and the intellectual movements of mankind. That era is united in one respect with the spirit of the Middle Ages; both eras had an antipositivist attitude, an understanding for the rational connections in life and a rejection of the theory of irrationality in human affairs. Later when the voluntarist metaphysics of Schopenhauer and his disciples appeared with its theory of an irrational and primal instinct, the Thomistic-Aristotelian concept of entelechy combining disposition and teleological supplementation, established a harmonious union between instinct and idea.

In particular, the thinking of the humanist and idealist era about social concepts differs very little from the medieval view. Yet the solutions offered differed even as the historical situations differed. Apart from the fact that humanism was more conscious of a mundane destiny, it looked on the community and the individual in it not only as a systematic structure, but with all the relationships to the historical situation. Gradations of being were considered phases of development, and the static order of the Middle Ages was dissolved into a network of functions and phases of activity. An acquaintance with the methods of modern thought and speculation and the new view of history will richly benefit the Thomistic world of concepts, and frequent points of contact can be found with the modern theory of values, the recent theories in epistemology and metaphysics, and the theory of objectivity and phenomenology.

According to the Thomistic view, true liberty of the spirit consists in the surrender of what has become untenable and in the acceptance of what appears to be established knowledge. Such is the sublime mission of the perennial philosophy: *Vetera novis augere et perficere.*

THE WRITINGS OF
ST. THOMAS AQUINAS

The innumerable writings and admirable intellectual elasticity of the great figures of the heyday of Scholasticism still evoke our admiration. Thus St. Albert the Great, the lector and master in theology, the provincial of the German province of his order, the Bishop of Ratisbon, the papal legate and preacher of crusades and arbiter in many legal controversies, manifested an amazing activity in practical life. At the same time he was able to achieve a universalism in his scientific studies and in his literary productivity, so that his contemporaries spoke of him as, *"Nostri temporis stupor et miraculum."* Similarly the brilliant Franciscan, Duns Scotus, who did not attain his fortieth year, left behind him as his life's work a philosophical system of magnificent dimensions. In the same way we admire the astonishing versatility St. Thomas displayed in his literary products.

The important dates in the life of St. Thomas may be helpful in reviewing his literary activity.

In 1224 or 1225, St. Thomas was born in Roccasecca. At the age of five he entered the monastery of Monte Cassino. In 1239 he went to Naples to begin the study of the liberal arts, and in 1244 he entered the Dominican Order. From 1245 to 1248 he resided in Paris to study. From 1248 to 1252 he studied in Cologne. In the years from 1252 to 1259 he received the bachelor's and master's degrees in Paris.

From 1259 to 1268 he resided in Italy. The years from 1261 to 1264 of this Italian sojourn were spent as papal theologian at the court of Urban IV. In 1265 he taught in Rome in the monastery of St. Sabina on the Aventine, and in 1267 he lectured in Viterbo, where the court of Pope Clement IV was then residing.

From 1269 to 1272 he sojourned for the second time in Paris. At this period of his teaching at the University of Paris he reached the highest point in his scientific activity.

In 1272 he was recalled from the professorship in Paris, and in the same year he established a complete course in theology in Naples.

In 1274, on March 7, he died while on a journey to the Council at Lyons.

Among the complete editions of St. Thomas' works we mention the following:

1. The Parma edition by P. Fiaccadori in Parma (25 volumes, 1852–72).

2. The Paris edition by L. Vives in Paris (34 volumes, 1871–80, 1889–90).

3. The Leonine edition, under the patronage of Pope Leo XIII, which has reached the fourteenth volume.

I

THE SYSTEMATIC WORKS

1. The commentary on the Sentences of Peter Lombard, *Commentum in quattuor libros Sententiarum magistri Petri Lombardi*. It was written during the period of his first stay in Paris, from 1254 to 1256, and has been published by Lethielleux in Paris under the direction of Father Mandonnet in three volumes.

2. *Summa contra Gentes,* completed in 1264. The Leonine Edition (Vols. XIII–XV) is deserving of special mention because of its faithfulness to the original text. This edition also contains the commentary of Francis Sylvester of Ferrara. Other editions have appeared with the colophon of Forzani (Rome, 1894), of Marietti (Turin, 1920), and of Lethielleux (Paris, 1906).

3. *Summa theologica,* 1266–73. Of the available editions, the Leonine (Vols. IV–XII), with the commentary of Cardinal Cajetan, is especially recommended. Other editions have appeared with the imprint of Forzani (Rome, 1897), Marietti (Turin, 1932), Lethielleux (Paris, 1886), and Blot (1926–34).

4. *Quaestiones disputatae* and the *Quodlibeta.* The *Quaestio de veritate* was written 1256–59; the other *Quaestiones* appeared between 1263 and 1272. The *Quodlibeta* are from the first and second Parisian sojourns and the period when St. Thomas was teaching in Italy. Edi-

tions have been published by Marictti in Turin (*Quuestiones disputatae*, Vols. I–IV, *Quodlibeta*, Vol. V.), and by the Lethielleux in Paris (*Quaestiones disputatae*, Vols. I–III, *Quodlibeta*, Vol. IV).

5. *Compendium theologiae ad Fratrem Reginaldum*, written during the teaching term at Naples.

II

THE COMMENTARIES ON ARISTOTLE AND ON THE LIBER DE CAUSIS

1. *In libros perihermeneias expositio*, 1269–72. Only the explanation of the first book and the first two lectures of the second book are the work of St. Thomas. It is in the Leonine edition.

2. *In primum et secundum posteriorum Analyticorum expositio*. Written about 1268 and contained in the Leonine edition.

3. *In octo libros physicorum expositio*, written after 1268 and found also in the Leonine edition.

4. *In libros de coelo et mundo expositio*. Written about 1272. Only the first two books and part of the third book are the work of St. Thomas; the rest was written by Peter of Alvernia.

5. *In libros de generatione et corruptione expositio*. Written in 1272 and 1273. St. Thomas wrote the first seventeen lectures of the first book; the rest is the work of Thomas de Sutton. Printed in the Leonine edition.

6. *In libros Meteorologicorum expositio*, completed between 1269 and 1271. The first and second books and the tenth lecture belong to St. Thomas; the rest belongs to Peter of Alvernia.

7. *In libros de anima expositio*, written 1270–72. In the edition of P. A. M. Pirotta, O.P., Turin, Marietti, 1925.

8. *In librum de sensu et sensato expositio*, and *In librum de memoria et reminiscentia expositio*. Edited by P. A. M. Pirotta, O.P., Turin, Marietti, 1928.

9. *In duodecim libros Metaphysicorum expositio*, written after 1268. Edited by P. M. R. Cathala, O.P., Turin, Marietti, 1926.

10. *In decem libros Ethicorum expositio*, written about 1269. Edited by P. A. M. Pirotta, O.P., Turin, Marietti, 1934.

11. *In libros Politicorum expositio*. St. Thomas wrote Books I–III; the rest is the work by Peter of Alvernia.

12. *In librum de causis expositio*, about 1269–73.

III

THE GENUINE *OPUSCULA* [1]

1. *De ente et essentia.* Editions of this important work were published by Ludwig Baur, Münster, 1933; by Roland-Gosselin, O.P., Paris, 1927; by C. Boyer, S.J., Rome, 1933.

2. *Contra errores Graecorum ad Urbanum IV Pontificem Maximum.*

3. *De rationibus fidei contra Saracenos, Graecos et Armenos ad Cantorem Antiochenum.*

4. *De duobus praeceptis caritatis et decem legis praeceptis.*

5. *Devotissima expositio super symbolum apostolorum.*

6. *Devotissima expositio orationis dominicae.*

7. *Devotissima expositio super salutatione angelica.*

8. *De articulis fidei et ecclesiae sacramentis ad archiepiscopum Panormitanum.*

9. *Responsio ad Fr. Johannem Vercellensem, Generalem Magistrum ordinis, de articulis* XLII.

10. *Responsio ad lectorem Venetum de articulis* XXXVI.

11. *Responsio ad lectorem Bisuntinum de articulis* VI.

12. *De differentia verbi divini et humani.*

13. *De natura verbi intellectus.*

14. *De substantiis separatis seu de angelorum natura ad Fratrem Reginaldum socium suum carissimum.*

15. *De unitate intellectus contra Averroistas.*

16. *Contra pestiferam doctrinam retrahentium homines a religionis ingressu.*

17. *De perfectione vitae spiritualis.*

18. *Contra impugnantes Dei cultum et religionem.*

19. *De regimine principum ad regem Cypri.*

20. *De regimine Judaeorum ad ducissam Brabantiae.*

21. *De forma absolutionis ad Generalem Magistrum ordinis.*

22. *Expositio primae decretalis ad archidiaconum Tudertinum.*

23. *Expositio super secundum decretalem ad eundem.*

24. *De sortibus ad dominum Jacobum de Burgo.*

---

[1] Complete edition by Father Mandonnet, O.P., in five volumes, published by Lethielleux, Paris, 1927.

25. *De judiciis astrorum ad Fratrem Reginaldum socium suum carissimum.*

26. *De aeternitate mundi contra murmurantes.*

27. *De principio individuationis.*

28. *De principiis naturae ad Fratrem Sylvestrum.*

29. *De natura materiae et dimensionibus interminatis.*

30. *De mixtione elementorum ad magistrum Philippum.*

31. *De occultis operibus naturae ad quendam militem.*

32. *De motu cordis ad magistrum Philippum.*

33. *De instantibus.*

34. *De quattuor oppositis.*

35. *De demonstratione.*

36. *De fallaciis ad quosdam nobiles artistas.*

37. *De propositionibus modalibus.*

38. *De natura accidentis.*

39. *De natura generis.*

40. *De emptione et venditione ad tempus.*

41. *Expositio in librum Boethii de hebdomatibus.*

42. *Expositio super librum Boethii de Trinitate.*

43. *Expositio in Dionysium de divinis nominibus.*

44. *Officium de festo Corporis Christi ad mandatum Urbani Papae IV. Hymnus Adoro Te Devote. Epistola de ratione studendi.*

45. *De secreto.*

46. *Responsio ad Fratrem Johannem Vercellensem, Generalem Magistrum Ordinis Praedicatorum, de articulis* CVIII *sumptis ex opere Petri de Tarantasia.*

47. *Responsio ad Bernardum, abbatem Cassinensem.*

Besides his sermons and two newly discovered *Principia* and an unedited *Quaestio disputata de natura beatitudinis*, we list the following:

IV

COMMENTARIES ON HOLY SCRIPTURE

1. *Expositio in Job.*

2. *In psalmos Davidis expositio.*

3. *Expositio in Cantica canticorum.*

4. *Expositio in Isaiam prophetam.*

5. *Expositio in Jeremiam prophetam.*

6. *Expositio in Threnos Jeremiae prophetae.*
7. *Catena aurea super quattuor Evangelia.*
8. *Expositio in Evangelium Matthaei.*
9. *Expositio in Evangelium S. Joannis.*
10. *Expositio in S. Pauli apostoli epistolas.*

INDEX

Abelard, 34: and Augustinianism, 20; faith and reason, 5; translation of the *Organon,* 6; universals, 85
Absolute being, 370
Absolutism of Naples and Sicily, 427
Abstraction: of conceptual content, 329; metaphysical, 334; process of, 84, 187, 340; stages of, 328
Accident, 97-126
  cannot exist without substance, 103
  cessation of, 105
  classes of, 105 f.
  an entity *per accidens,* 103
  exists only in subject, 104
  inseparable, 105
  nature of, 103
  necessary, 105
  per accidens, 106
  per se, 106
  proper, 104 f.
  relation to substance, 104
  separable, 105
  of the soul, 151
Accidental being: genesis of, 260; not the object of science, 328
Achilles, 523
Act: "first," 64; identified with form, 62; priority of, 268; "second," 64
Active intellect, 187, 330-50, 540: characteristics of, 187 f.
Active qualities of physical being, 141
Activism, 314
Acts: immanent, 119; of perception, 324 f.; transient, 119
Acts, human, 369: interior, 506; morality of, 373
Actualization, principle of, 302; *see also* Existence
Adultery, 374, 502
Aegidius of Lessines, 16
Aegidius of Rome, 16, 538: on origin of the state, 423
Aeterni Patris (encyclical), 544
Aevum, 123

Alan de Lille, on God's existence, 237
Albert, St.
  the angels, 223
  the Arabians, 14
  and Averroes, 16
  creation, 275
  defense of St. Thomas, 54
  dispensation of natural law, 496
  end in morality, 370
  free elements, 145
  history, 366
  influence on St. Thomas, 24 f.
  intelligible matter, 338
  justice, 392 f.
  Maimonides, 18
  natural law, 465
  natural sciences, 32
  plurality of forms, 142
  potency of matter, 267
  principle of causality, 264
  principle of individuation, 74
  proof of creation, 278
  proof of God's existence, 237
  and Pseudo-Dionysius, 22
  successive creation, 282
  synteresis, 402
  teacher of St. Thomas, 7
  transcendentals, 134
Alcidamas the Sophist, 460
Alexander IV (pope), 53
Alexander of Aphrodisias on composite bodies, 142
Alexander of Hales, 49
  law, 456
  moral knowledge, 402
  plurality of forms, 142
  principle of individuation, 78
  and St. Thomas, 24
  on works of Aristotle, 7
Alfarabi, 14, 18
Algazel: and Aristotle, 14; indirect creation, 277; theory of causality, 257
Alger of Luettich, 34
Ambassadors, immunity of, 505

Ambrose (St.): on communism, 478; on love of parents, 381; natural moral law, 401 f.; on slavery, 481
Ammonius on logic, 362
Analogical knowledge of God, 238-42
Analogy
of art, 60, 62, 70
of being, 132 f., 247
concept of, 128 f.
of external attribution, 130 f.
between God and universe, 241
kinds of, 129
meaning of, 132 f.
of proportion, 129
of proportionality, 129 ff.
St. Thomas' use of, 531
Analytic method, 366 f.
Analytica of Aristotle, 361
Anaxagoras, 4, 295 f.: on the angels, 221; on genesis of being, 61; on origin of the universe, 271; philosophy of, 523
Anaximander, 294
Angels, 220-32
activity of, 225
choirs of, 232
complete happiness of, 232
conversion of, 231
Dionysius on, 221
emotions in, 229
existence of, 221 f.
fall of, 230
fallen, 228
freedom from error, 228
freedom of will, 229
Greek Fathers on, 222
and heavenly bodies, 224
hierarchies of, 226, 232
ideas of, 226
immateriality of, 224
impeccability of, 232
incorruptibility of, 224
individuation of, 224
intellect of, 225
intuition of, 228
knowledge of, 224 ff.
knowledge of future by, 227
knowledge of men, 227
nature of, 222-32
number of good, 232
origin of evil in, 230
perfection of knowledge in, 228

Angels (*continued*)
and place, 224
potency for the supernatural, 231
previous creation of, 222
St. Augustine on, 222
self-knowledge of, 347
simplicity of, 222
sin in, 230
species of, 224
supernatural happiness of, 230
and time, 224
will of, 229
Animal rationale, 534
Animal soul: not created, 287; subsistence of, 159
Animals, 146 f., 159-72
appetite of, 164-68
apprehension of, 164-68
cognitive equipment of, 164
consciousness of, 171
evil not possible by, 169
instinct of, 168
knowledge of, 162
memory of, 163
and moral habits, 389
no habits, 113
nourishment of, 155
practical "intelligence" of, 171
self-motion of, 171 f.
time perception of, 163
training of, 165
value judgments of, 163
voice of, 171
Anselm, St., 45
and Augustinianism, 20
concept of God, 530
existence of ideas, 359
faith and reason, 5, 37
fideists opposed by, 43
God's existence, 237 f.
ontological proof of God's existence, 237
philosophy of, 518
and St. Thomas, 24
transcendentalism, 135
Anselm the Peripatetic, 42
Anthony the Hermit, St., 420
Anthropology: differential, 207; of St. Thomas, 217; study of, 173, 214; theocentric, 216
Anthropomorphism, 309, 531
Antiphon the Sophist, 460

Apocatastasis, Origen's theory of, 230
Appetite: intellectual (see Will); rational, 165; sense (in man), 184 f.; sensitive, 164-68; stages in human, 379
Apprehension, animal, 170
Apriorism, 339
Apulejus of Madaura, 20
Arabians, the
    and Aristotle, 8
    on essence and existence, 96
    on human intellect, 187
    influence on St. Thomas, 13-17, 74
    on intelligible matter, 338
    principle of individuation, 74
    St. Thomas' criticism of, 16
Aristocracy, 429 f.
Aristotelianism: beginning of, 5; Christian, 7; Jewish, 18
Aristotle
    angels, 221
    autonomous state, 454
    causality, 258, 266
    Christianity, 35-40
    common possession, 476
    composite bodies, 142
    concept of nous, 12
    defense of personality, 439
    dignity of labor, 485
    the Eleatics, 61
    errors of, 8
    essence, 84
    essence and existence, 95
    eternal return of things, 366
    eternity of the universe, 278
    the five senses, 161
    founder of logic, 362
    the four elements, 285
    harmony in the universe, 232
    on history, 365 f.
    the human soul, 176 f.
    on the individual, 72
    influence on St. Thomas, 5-13
    influenced by Platonism, 100
    intellectualism of, 199
    kinds of causes, 259 f.
    law, 461
    manifestation of the logos, 4
    man's social nature, 417
    matter and form, 59 ff.
    monarchy, 431
    moral virtues, 406
    on new problems, 546

Aristotle (continued)
    nous in knowledge, 332
    on the object of science, 360
    order, 296
    origin of the soul, 288
    origin of the universe, 271
    perishable substances, 307
    philosophy of, 518
    place defined, 120
    potency and act, 61
    powers of the soul, 151
    prime matter, 70
    on principle, 256
    principle of individuation, 73
    the priority of the state, 423
    prohibition of works of, 6
    proof for God's existence, 237
    quoted by St. Thomas, 10
    realism of, 214 f.
    revised concept of matter and form, 70
    and St. Thomas, 9
    St. Thomas' criticism of, 12
    on science, 526
    slavery justified by, 479
    on the soul, 147 f.
    the state, 439
    substance defined, 102
    substantial form, 100
    table of values, 384
    teleologist, 262
    terminology in St. Thomas, 12
    theology of, 12
    theory of form, 138
    theory of relations, 114
    theory of substance, 98
    the transcendentals, 134
    true being, 97
    unity of the soul, 149
    value of virtue, 406
    vegetative life, 154
    virtue defined, 407
    on women, 207
Association, mechanism of, 170
Astronomy of St. Thomas, 526
Athanasius on philosophy, 42
Atheists, Plato's attitude to, 522
Athenagoras on freedom of conscience, 488
Atomism, mechanical, 294
Atomists, 61
Attributes of being, 127-40
Attributes of God, 242

Augustine, St.
analysis of consciousness, 349
angels, 222
Church and state, 449
concept of order, 293
doctrine of creation, 263
eternal law, 460 ff.
eternity of truth, 358
on evil, 383
on good of order, 489
on heresy, 489
on the hexaemeron, 282
on history, 366
on human memory, 192
the human soul, 175
idea of God, 239
influence on St. Thomas, 5, 20
inner struggles, 213
on love, 379
metaphysics of inner experience, 346
on Neoplatonism, 521
on order, 299
order of causes, 305
origin of slavery, 480 f.
origin of the human body, 284
origin of time, 278
and pagan philosophy, 5
and Platonic ideas, 521
problem of faith and reason, 36 f.
proof for God's existence, 530
religious significance of time, 213
and St. Paul, 50
and St. Thomas, 23
and the Scriptures, 37
on seat of virtues, 410
seminal theory, 284
simultaneous creation, 282 f.
theory of illumination, 337
theory of knowledge, 332
threefold good of marriage, 424
on time, 120
on virtue, 389
voluntarism of, 199
Aureolus, knowledge of the individual, 343
Authority: essential form of the community, 427; nature of, 428; as proof, 8; in the universe, 427
Authority, secular: founded on natural law, 450; independence of, 449; of the pope, 451

Authority, spiritual: independence of, 449
Autonomy of conscience, 488
Avencebrol on angels, 222 f.
Averroes
Algazel condemned by, 14
Aristotle and, 8
critical attitude of, 15
and divine providence, 310
on habit, 113
refuted by St. Thomas, 16 f.
Averroists on forms of mixed bodies, 142
Avicenna
Aristotle and, 14
denial of God's essence, 92
distinction between essence and existence, 90
on divine being, 236
on essence, 83
essence and existence, 96
indirect creation, 277
on intellectual memory, 192
Maimonides and, 18
matter and form, 63 ff.
plurality of forms, 142
powers of the soul, 151
principle of individuation, 74
series of forms, 143
simple substance, 92
the transcendentals, 134

Bacon (Roger), 31 f.: on plurality of forms, 142; on principle of individuation, 78 f.; on theory of divine illumination, 37 f.
Baptism, 514
Basil (St.), 23: simultaneous creation, 282; slavery, 481
Basis of science, Aristotelian, 40 f.
"Battle for existence," 368
Beautiful, characteristics of the, 186
Becoming, 250-70: process of, 59 ff., 266
Being, 127-40
absolute, 86, 98, 128, 370
analogy of, 127-33, 247
contingent, 128
finite, 213
formal principle of, 86
forms of, 138 ff.
generation of living, 286
genesis of, 99 f., 276

Being (*continued*)
  living, 146-248
  mental, 360
  necessary, 96
  not a substance, 101
  possible, 96
  potential, 360
  prior to thought, 106
  real, 360
  science of, 81
  specific, 86
  the substance of reality, 98
  substantial, 98
Being, concept of: above genera and species, 127; analogous validity of, 128; most extensive, 127; poorest in content, 127
Bellarmine on indirect power, 451
Benedict (St.) on degrees of humility, 397
Berengarius of Tours, 42
Bernard of Clairvaux, St.: condemnation of philosophy, 42 f.; on the fruition of God, 399
Berthold of Constance, 34
Biran (Maine de) on reality of the world, 322
Birds, social instinct of, 420
Blood relatives, love of, 381
Body, human: elements of, 182 f.; function of brain in, 183; function of heart in, 183; and the mind, 183
Boethius: Averroes and, 16; on order, 299; principle of individuation, 75; relations, 115; St. Thomas and, 22; St. Thomas on the *De Trinitate* of, 74
Bonaventure, St.
  angels, 222
  Aristotle and, 35
  defense of religious orders, 53
  faith and reason, 37
  kinds of goodness, 375
  law, 456
  matter in the angels, 223
  on philosophy, 541
  plurality of forms, 142
  potency of matter, 267
  powers of the soul, 15
  principle of individuation, 77 f.
  progress of knowledge, 34, 545

Bonaventure, St. (*continued*)
  St. Thomas and, 24
  simultaneous creation, 282
  subordinate forms, 144
  theory of the human soul, 175
  and works of Aristotle, 7
Boniface VIII (pope), 538
Boyle, Robert, 69
Brain in human body, 183
Buridan, Jean, 70, 80

Cajetan: on analogy, 133; as a commentator, 543
Capital punishment, 492
Carmelites of Alcala, 543
Categories, 106 ff.
  criticism of Thomistic, 124
  denial by Hegel, 107
  denial by Kant, 107
  division of, 107
  objective nature of, 106 f.
  order of, 108
  theory of, 102
Causa per posterius, 263
Causa per prius, 263
Causal relation, necessity of, 257
Causality
  history of theory of, 256
  objectivity of, 257
  principle of, 4, 256-70, 335, 530 f.
  a relation of order, 305
  Thomistic theory of, 265
  validity of theory of, 258 f.
Cause
  actual, 263
  analogous, 262
  assisting, 261
  counseling, 261
  disposing, 261
  distinct from effect, 257
  and effect, 242
  efficient, 260, 306
  equivocal, 261
  exemplary, 263
  extrinsic, 260
  final, 260, 262
  first, 268 f.
  formal, 260
  and the idea of order, 305
  instrumental, 263
  intrinsic, 260

Cause (*continued*)
  kinds of, 259
  knowledge of, 328
  material, 260
  per accidens, 263
  perfecting, 261
  potential, 263
  principal, 263
  priority of, 268
  proximate, 263
  remote, 263
  secondary, 268 ff., 311
  sufficient, 261
  univocal, 261 f.
Ceremonial prescriptions of Old Testament, 509
Certainty: of knowledge, 334; of truth, 322 f.
Change, 118 f., 250-55: in God, 251; kinds of, 254
Chaos, 294
Characteristics, inherited, 291
Characterology, study of, 207
Charity, 398
Charles the Bald, 21
Chastity, 414
Children and the state, 439
Choice, act of, 195
Choirs of angels, 232
Christ: and freedom of conscience, 488; the King, 453; and life of grace, 514; mystical body of, 514
Christian philosophy, 523
Christianity: Aristotle and, 35-40; Greek philosophy and, 314
Church, the
  community of, 444
  indirect power in secular things, 451
  individual and, 440
  medieval, 440
  power of civil rulers, 451
  and right of religious education, 491
  right to depose rulers, 451
  slavery and, 481
  and the state, 432, 449-54
  supremacy of, 449
  supremacy in spirituals, 452
  totalitarian claims of, 449
Cicero
  congenital knowledge, 337
  derivation of the law, 456

Cicero (*continued*)
  eternal law, 460
  his place in history of thought, 461
  influence on St. Augustine, 50
  law and reason, 457
  law of nations, 504
  man's social nature, 418
  St. Augustine and, 21
Circumstances of human act, 374
Citizen, as belonging to the state, 439
City, the medieval, 426
City of God by St. Augustine, 454
Civil rights of women, 201
Civitas, of St. Thomas, 425 f.
Clement of Alexandria, 5, 42
Cognition; *see* Knowledge
Cognitive faculty: object of, 188; as a passive potency, 186; *see also* Intellect
Cognitive form of angelic mind, 345
Commentary on Aristotle by St. Thomas, 9
Commentary on the Sentences by St. Thomas, 10, 30
Common good, the, 413, 430, 438: limitations of, 441; quantitative aspect of, 443
Common man, the, 426
Common sense, 162, 324: in animals, 166; in man, 184
Communism: forms of, 477; inordinate, 476; monastic, 477
Community, the
  an accidental relation, 435 f.
  of the blessed, 445
  central authority of, 427
  conscience of, 436
  a corporate body, 436
  a creation of God, 448
  differentiation of, 423
  Epicureanism and, 440
  eternal happiness of, 444
  formation of, 425
  grades of, 423-33
  morality of, 417
  necessity of, 419
  an organism, 421
  political, 428
  preferential position of the civil, 441
  purposes of, 420
  quantitative structure of, 443

Community, the (*continued*)
  reality of, 435
  rights of, 491 ff.
  social, 200
Concept of God, formation of, 233-36
Concepts, Thomistic, 547
Conceptual image of the intellect, 329
Concubinage, 471
Concupiscible appetite in animals, 166
Confessions of St. Augustine, 50
Conscience
  autonomy of, 404, 488, 536
  of the community, 436
  erroneous, 404, 488
  freedom of, 405, 488
  function of, 402 f.
  law of, 459
  man's, 197
  as origin of law, 459
  social, 436
  and synteresis, 402
Conscious knowledge, 355
Consciousness: in animals, 162, 171; data of, 349
Consent, act of, 195
Constantinus Africanus, 179
Contemplative life, 415, 487
Contingent being as object of science, 106, 328
Continuity, law of, 140
Continuity of philosophic thought, 28
Contract, social, 423, 428
Contradiction, principle of, 41, 127, 335
Corporeal being, 141-45
Corporeal body, divisibility of, 109
Corporeity, derived from the soul, 174
Corporis regitiva, 288
Corpus juris civilis, 456
Corruption of things, 250-55
Cosmogony, Thomistic, 281 f.
Cosmos, 294: framework of, 304; in philosophy, 138; study of, 57
Courage, 394
Creation, 255, 257, 292
  concept of, 274-78, 524
  indirect, 277
  in Mohammedan theology, 278
  proof of, 279
  simultaneous, 281-84
  successive, 281-84
  and time, 278 ff.

Creationism, 181, 288: kinds of, 289
Creatures: composed of essence and existence, 90; goodness of, 247; happiness of, 247
Criticism: of proofs for God's existence, 238; of Thomism, 519-26
Custom and law, 504
Cynics: and the natural law, 467; slavery and, 479
Cyril of Alexandria, St., 23

Dante, 22, 34, 518 f.
Darwinians, 170
Death penalty, 492
De causis, Liber, 48
De divinis nominibus, 47
De ente et essentia, 10
De natura materiae, 75
De principio individuationis, 76
De veritate, 47
Decalogue: dispensations from, 493 f.; and the natural law, 472, 501, 508
Deduction, 367
Definition, 82, 355, 362, 367
Deity, 244; *see also* God
Demiurge in creation, 272
Democracy, 429 f.
Democritus, 295: on accidental occurrence, 310; on man's social nature, 417
Demons, 230
Depository of truth, 351 ff.
Descartes, 29, 544: on animal life, 170; on extension, 109; on time, 121
Dilthy, William, 322
Dionysius (the Areopagite): the angels, 221; evil in the angels, 229; influence on St. Thomas, 21; on knowledge of God, 235; number of the angels, 232; on order, 302
Discursive knowledge, 190
Diseases, mental, 179
Disorder, 383
Dispensation: from the Decalogue, 493 f.; from law, 497, 504
Disposition, corporeal, 112
Divine Comedy by Dante, 518
Divine right of kings, 429
Divisibility, basis of, 109
Divorce, 472

Doctor Angelicus, 52
Dominic (St.), Order of, 518
Duhem (Pierre) on substantial form, 69
Duns Scotus Eriugena
  on creation, 274
  criticism of the categories, 124 f.
  faith and reason, 5
  his *haecceitas,* 79
  knowledge of the individual, 343
  principle of individuation, 79
  proofs for God's existence, 238
  rescue of the individual, 88
  superiority of the individual, 343
  theory of matter, 223
  on time, 121
  translator of Pseudo-Dionysius, 21
  on worldly knowledge, 42
Durandus on knowledge of the individual, 343
Durantel on Pseudo-Dionysius, 22

Economics, 365
Ecstasy, 202, 205, 526
Education of children, 471: by the state, 439
Effect: necessity of, 257; resemblance to cause, 265
Eleatics, the, 250: and natural philosophy, 61
Electro-dynamic theory of matter, 72
Electrons, 72
Elementary forms in a composite, 144
Elements
  in animal nourishment, 155 ff.
  the four, 141, 285
  in the human body, 182 f.
  origin of, 290
  qualities of, 113
Emanation, process of, 273 f.
Embryo, the human, 289
Empedocles: denial of genesis of substantial being, 61; on eternal law, 460; on origin of universe, 271; theory of accidents, 304
Empire, the, 426 f.
Empiricism: conflict with rationalism, 30; and law, 459
End: cause of causes, 263; of human acts, 374 f.; of moral acts, 373; ultimate, 384
Enemies, love of, 381
Enlightenment, liberalist, 440

Entelechy, 148, 366; *see also* Form, Matter and form
Entity, logical, 352
Epictetus, 523
Epicureanism, 440
Epicurus, 43
Epistemology, 313-25, 364 f.: of cultural sciences, 365; realism of Thomistic, 314; St. Thomas' knowledge of, 33
Equivocation, 128, 133
Eros of ancient man, 214
Error, 353: in angels, 228; in the intellect, 355; in man, 228; in the senses, 320 f.
Essence
  absolute, 86
  abstract, 86
  actual, 94
  according to Aristotle, 81 f.
  autonomous existence of, 84
  concrete, 86
  eternal, 87
  existing in the mind, 84
  as form of things, 83
  ideal, 94
  includes form and matter, 93
  kinds of, 86
  knowledge of, 329-34
  mathematical, 328, 333, 338
  meaning of, 81
  metaphysical, 333
  as nature of things, 83
  necessary, 87
  as object of the intellect, 189
  as object of knowledge, 326
  in potency to existence, 91, 95
  as principle of order, 82
  properties of, 86 f.
  relation to existence, 89
  of simple substances, 91
  of things, 81 ff.
  unchangeable, 87
  universal, 94
Essence and existence, 81
  compared to potency and act, 91
  criticism of theory of, 96
  in God, 235 f.
  idea of distinction between, 96
  identical in God, 90
  in immaterial things, 91
  in material things, 91
  relation to potency and act, 95

Essentia creatrix, 277
Essential relation of things, 329
Eternal happiness, 515
Eternal laws, 455-63: and human acts, 377 f.
Eternity, 123: of God, 242; of motion, 12; of truth, 358 f.; of the world, 12
Ether, in heavenly bodies, 219
Ethics, 368-87, 535: of Aristotle, 418; Nicomachean, 9; and order, 369; Thomistic, 536; *see also* Morality, Morals
Eubulia, 409
Eucharist, the, 514
Eudaemonia, 412
Euripides on slavery, 479
Evil, 406
 without autonomous reality, 382
 as contribution to perfection, 311
 existence of, 383
 of guilt, 383
 in man, 196
 in morality, 370
 origin in the angels, 230
 physical, 312
 of punishment, 383
 in the universe, 311
Excluded middle, principle of, 41, 127, 335
Existence, 87 ff.
 act of the form, 93
 first act, 89
 through the form, 64
 in God distinct from others, 92
 greatest perfection, 88
 highest of all creatures, 89
 indefinable, 88
 kinds of, 81
 limited by capacity of nature, 92
 meaning of, 81, 87 f.
 not a part of the definition, 91
 not identical with the form, 93
 participated, 91, 95
 a participation in divine goodness, 89
 perfection of things, 95
 reality conferred by, 89, 93
 relation to the essence, 89-96
 the right to, 474 f.
 united to the form, 96
Experience the basis of knowledge, 41
Extension defined, 108 f.
External act of the will, 374

External goods: purpose of, 475; value of, 385
External senses, 159 ff.
External world, reality of, 321 f.

Faculties: sense, 159-72; of the soul, 152 f., 185
Faith, 398: act of, 201; independent value of, 46
Faith and science, 4 f., 44 f., 517, 525: among the Arabians, 13; among the Jews, 18; problem of, 41 f.; and St. Thomas, 29
Fall of the angels, 231 f.
Fallen angels: conversion of, 231 f.; knowledge of, 228 f.; number of, 232
Family: integrity of, 425 f.; priority of, 423 f.
Fathers of the Church, 4
 and Greek philosophy, 36
 influence on St. Thomas, 23 ff.
 and matter and form, 62
 and pagan philosophy, 4
 on slavery, 480
Fichte, 80: on the right to work, 485
Fidelity, 396 f.: in marriage, 425
Figure as the expression of species, 112
Final cause, 69
Fire as cause of life, 154
First principles, 41, 335 f.
 and the active intellect, 335
 of knowledge, 335
 moral, 197
 no error in, 336
 validity of, 336
Florilegia of Aristotle's works, 7
Force, use of, 490
Form, 40; *see also* Matter and form
 accidental, 104, 144
 basis of species, 68
 certain quantity possessed by, 110
 of composite bodies, 142, 144
 essential cause of being, 87
 existence given by, 64
 existence of, 65
 hierarchy of, 304 f.
 identified with act, 62
 immateriality of, 347
 an important concept, 137
 intelligible, 329
 not identified with existence, 93

Form (continued)
object of knowledge, 106
origin of, 285
a part of the essence, 83
perfection of, 65
plurality of, 142, 144, 175
primary, 143
principle: of activity, 65; of actualization, 302; of existence, 64; of individuation, 77, 344; of knowability, 65; of order, 65, 68; of totality, 66
priority of, 65, 268
quantitative, 339
rational, 467
secondary, 143
substantial, 151, 254
theory of, 266
unity of, 143
as universal, 85
Forma corporeitatis, 143
Forma factiva, 277
Forster, Frobenius, 545
Fountain of Life by Avencebrol, 222 f.
Francis, St., 528
Francis de Vittoria, 544
Francis Sylvester of Ferrara, 543
Franciscan Scholasticism, 520
Franciscan school: on the angels, 223; and Averroes, 16; on the human soul, 175; on theory of ideas, 359
Freedom
of conscience, 488
intellectual, 493
right to, 479-85
rooted in reason, 195 f.
of the will, 195, 231
French jurisprudence, 537

Galen, 8, 179: idea of the soul, 147
Galileo, 70, 527
Gassendi, 69
Gelasius (pope), 538
Generation: act of, 208; influenced by heavenly bodies, 219 f.; of living beings, 286; of things, 254
Generationism, 288: and original sin, 291
Genesis: of being, 59 ff.; of substantial being, 260
Genus, 107
Geometric forms, 339

Gerard of Abbatsvilla, 53
Gerhard of Cremona, 6, 22
Gifts of the Holy Ghost, 201 f.
Gilbert de la Porrée, 90
Gilson, Etienne, 78 note
Gnome, 409
God, 233-48
the absolute individual, 79
absolute perfection of, 243
affective vision of, 202
analogical knowledge of, 238-42
analogy of proportionality in, 241
attributes of, 242
Author of order, 300
the bonum privatum, 445
cause: of all knowledge, 357; of order, 302; of substance and accidents, 104; of the universe, 262
concept of, 233-36
congenital knowledge of, 237
contemplation of, 194
cooperation of, 269 f.
creative activity of, 267
creative causality of, 257
the Creator, 270
the end of man, 201
the end of the universe, 309
esence and existence of, 243
eternity of, 242
existence distinct from others, 92
final cause, 306
first cause, 241
goodness of, 245
happiness of, 244
in hierarchy of being, 138 ff.
highest efficient cause, 306
highest end of human life, 375
His absolute being, 236
His individuation found in His goodness, 92
immanence of, 247
immutability of, 242, 245
incomprehensibility of, 235
an infinite substance, 236
infinity of, 236, 243, 245
intelligence of, 243
is deity, 244
knowledge of His essence, 233
knowledge of His existence, 235
the lawgiver, 458
love of, 382
most universal cause, 276

God (*continued*)
necessary being, 242 f.
no accidents, 245
no genus, 234
no habits, 113
in no species, 92
our imperfect knowledge of, 239
owner of all property, 475
perfection of, 236
positive idea of, 236 ff.
pre-eminence of, 240
proofs for existence of, 237, 529
pure act, 242
religious concept of, 248
St. Anselm's proof of, 237
St. Augustine's idea of, 239
and secondary causes, 268 ff.
self-knowledge of, 347
simplicity of, 236, 243, 244
substance without accidents, 86
unity of, 246
and the universe, 239
univocal ideas about, 240
unknowable, 234
vision of, 386, 512
will of, 243
Goethe, 27: on Kant's ethics, 378; and human thought, 519
"Golden middle" of virtues, 407
Gondechapur, medical school at, 13
Good, the, 185: arduous, 394; concept of, 334; in morality, 370; order of, 383-87; transcendental, 136 f.
Goodness: of act, 374; of creatures, 247; of God, 245; of moral act, 377
Goods: of enjoyment, 386; of use, 386
Gordon, Andrew, 545
Gorgias by Plato, 522
Government, citizen's interest in, 431
Grace, 201, 216, 382, 399: and nature, 513; not a substance, 512; order of, 513; sanctifying, 513
Grades of life, 146, 154-248
Gratian: definition of the natural law, 466; on law, 456
Greek philosophy: and Christianity, 3; providential significance of, 4
Gregory the Great, St.: and St. Thomas, 23; on virtue, 395
Gregory VII (pope), 538
Gregory IX (pope): decretals of, 456; and translation of Aristotle, 6

Gregory Nazianzen (St.) on origin of slavery, 480
Gregory of Nyssa, St., 23: on simultaneous creation, 282; slavery opposed by, 481; and traducianism, 288
Gregory of Rimini on the knowledge of the individual, 343
Guilds, medieval, 440
Gundissalinus, Dominicus, 6

Habit, 388 f.: in categories, 108; defined, 112; related to potency and act, 112 f.; subject of, 113
Haecceitas, principle of individuation, 79
Hand, the human, 183
Happiness: eternal, 445, 515; and morality, 387; as object of the will, 194; subject of, 386
Hartmann, Nicolai, 33
Hearing, sense of, 159
Heart, the, 287: in animals, 155; in man, 183; organ of common sense, 162; according to St. Thomas, 148
Heavenly bodies, 219: and generation, 287; without habits, 113; and substantial forms, 69
Hegel, 28, 326: denial of Aristotelian categories, 107; and reality, 547
Hellenism: its concept of man, 211; philosophy of, 523
Henry of Ghent, 53: on the categories, 125
Heraclitus, 4, 250, 295: on eternal law, 460
Heretics, 537: toleration of, 489
Hesiod, 417
Hexaemeron, 282
Hierarchy of being, 138 ff.
Hippias Major, 186
Hippocrates, 8, 179
Hispanus, Joannes, 6
Historical influences on St. Thomas, 3-23
History, 365 f.: interpretation of, 506
Hobbes, Thomas: the concept of society, 419; popular sovereignty, 428
Holy Ghost, gifts of, 201, 515
Homer, 417
Hope, 398: act of, 201; passion of, 168
Hugh of St. Victor: on the human soul, 175; and St. Thomas, 24
Hugh of Strassburg, 9
Huguccio and popular sovereignty, 429

Human nature, corruption of, 216
Humanitarianism, Stoic, 480
Humanity, solidarity of, 200
Humboldt, William, 548
Humility, 397: virtue of, 414
Husband, in domestic society, 424
Hylomorphism, 67
Hylozoism, 146, 271

"Ideal realism" of Thomistic philosophy, 357
Idealism in sense knowledge, 318
Ideas
  in the angels, 226
  congenital, 314
  in God, 300
  inborn, 337
  Plato's theory of, 20, 72, 295, 359, 460
  transcendental, 240
  univocal, 240
Identity, principle of, 127, 335
Image, cognitive, 315, 318
Imagination, 162, 184
Immanence of God, 247
Immateriality of the angels, 224
Immortality of the soul, 178, 524
Immutability of God, 242, 245
Imperative: the eternal, 460; in man, 373
Incarnation, the, 212: angelic knowledge of, 227
Incomprehensibility of God, 235
Incorruptibility of the angels, 224
Indissolubility of marriage, 471
Individual (person)
  belongs to the state, 442
  among Christian thinkers, 73
  and the community, 438-54
  destiny of, 216
  duty to the state, 438
  good of, 308
  importance of, 440
  independence of, 448
  influence on the community, 442
  and the law, 455
  obligation to the state, 442
  position in the community, 442
  preservation of, 446
  punishment of, 442
  rights of, 422
  suppression by socialism, 448

Individual (things)
  knowledge of, 342-45
  notes, 72
  object of natural science, 58
  perfection of species, 79
  structure of, 58-80
Individualism: absolute, 427; ethical, 80;
    metaphysical, 80; origin of, 440; of
    Sophists, 438
Individuality: of the human soul, 180; of
    the human person, 206
Individuation: of angels, 224; through
    matter and form, 78; principle of,
    72-80, 532
Indivisibility of matter, 64
Induction, 41, 367
Infidelity, sin of, 490
Infidels, good acts of, 376
Infinity: of act, 66; of God, 245; of mat-
    ter, 64
Inner sense, 162
Innocent III (pope), 538
Instinct, 163, 165, 168
Intellect
  active, 330-50
  activity of, 331
  dependence on the will, 193
  human, 186-92
  illumination of, 405
  limitations of, 333
  the possible, 329-50
  practical, 191, 379, 390
  precedence of, 199
  reflection on itself, 342
  subject of virtues, 410
  theoretical, 191, 390
Intellectual knowledge, 326-50: object of,
    326-29
Intellectual life, 147
Intellectualism in Thomism, 41
Intellectus agens, 30, 39, 187, 330, 332,
    339, 364
Intellectus complexus, 190, 353
Intellectus incomplexus, 190
Intellectus possibilis, 187, 329, 364
Intelligible species, 331
Interest, payment of, 450
Internal act of the will, 374
Intuition, 336, 540
Intuitive knowledge in man, 190
Inviolability, corporal, 474
Irascible appetite in animals, 166

Isidore, St.: definition of natural law, 464; on law, 456; on law of nations, 504 f.; on positive law, 503; and St. Thomas, 23; on slavery, 481
Islam, philosophers of, 13
Ivo of Chartres, 34

Jacobi, Friedrich, 80
James I (of England), legitimism of, 429
Jehring, Rudolph von, 33
Jerome, St.: on divine being, 236; on natural moral law, 401
Jewish philosophy: influence on St. Thomas, 17 ff.
John Capreolus, 543
John Chrysostom, St.: on origin of law, 459; on origin of slavery, 480
John Damascene, St., 23: on divine being, 236; on fall of the angels, 231; on successive creation, 282
John of St. Thomas, 543
John of Salisbury, and the state, 422
John Teutonicus, 24
John the Baptist, solitary life of, 420
Joy, 185
Judgment, 334, 353: act of, 190; in animal knowledge, 162
Julian the Apostate, 451
Jus civile, 504
Jus gentium, 477, 504
Justice, 392, 537
  commutative, 393
  distributive, 393
  essence of, 396
  forms of, 393
  legal, 393, 413
  and legality, 502
  objective aspect of, 393
  original, 394
  particular, 413
  in positive law, 502
  state of, 199
  and the Ten Commandments, 397
Justinian, and the natural law, 464

Kant, Immanuel, 29
  analytical judgment, 341
  Aristotelian categories, 107
  autonomy of conscience, 404
  dogmatic knowledge, 341
  ethics of, 378
  morality and happiness, 387

Kant, Immanuel (*continued*)
  powers of the soul, 185
  sanction of law, 503
  truth, 353, 542
Keppler, 527
Kiekegaard, 214
Kilwardby, Robert, 39
Kindi (Arabian philosopher), 14
Kingdom: of God, 200, 445; medieval, 445
Kings, divine right of, 429
Knowledge
  of the angels, 224 ff.
  in animals, 162
  based on experience, 41
  causal, 363
  a causal relation, 314
  certainty of, 334
  conscious, 355
  desire of, 516
  discursive, 190
  extent of human, 189
  first principles of, 335
  of God, analogical, 133, **238-42**
  of the individual, 342-45
  intellectual, 326-50
  intuitive, 190
  moral, 402
  per negationem, 234
  of non-being, 358
  non-sense in animals, 163
  objectivity of, 314
  objects of, 314
  order of, 315
  in plants, 161
  progress of, 28, 34, 329, 545
  reflective, 343
  sense (in man), 184 f.
  sociological character of, 28
  standard of, 256
  of subjective states, 314
  a teleological process, 315
  theory of, 540
  of truth, 351-59
  of the universe, 526
Koran, and Aristotelian philosophy, 14

Labor, division of, 420
Language and man's social nature, 420
Law
  acts of, 458
  concept of, 456-59

Law (*continued*)
cosmic, 460 f.
definition of, 458
derivation of, 456
divine, 459, 500-11
of the Gospel, 510
of grace, 506
human, 459, 500-11
international, 505
kinds of, 459
moral, 535
of nations, 504
penal, 459
philosophy of, 455
private, 501
promulgation of, 458, 501
public, 501
relation to reason, 457
relation to the will, 457
and right, 501
Roman, 456
sanction of, 458, 503
unjust, 503
Law, eternal, 455-63
creatures' participation in, 464
and human acts, 377
man's participation in, 466
and the moral law, 462
and order, 462
and Providence, 310
St. Thomas' definition of, 462 f.
universality of, 463
Law, natural, 459, 464-73
and animals, 168
contents of, 468
definition of, 464
and the eternal law, 465
first principles of, 494
in man, 197
and natural morality, 468
prescriptions of, 469
and reason, 467
Law, positive, 500-6
attributes of, 503
binding force in conscience, 502
changing of, 503
dependence on natural law, 501
dispensation from, 504
human, 459
justice of, 502
need of, 500
Laws, Plato's, 439, 522

Legality and justice, 502
Leibnitz, 27, 544 f.: idea of God, 547;
monad theory, 80; and Thomistic
theory of individualism, 77; and
truth, 353
Leo XIII (pope), 544
Liberality, 397
Life, 146-248
essential characteristics of, 146
grades of, 154-248
intellectual, 147
on the land, 426
modes of, 151
principle of, 154 f.
problem of, 154 f.
sensitive, 147
vegetative, 149
Light of the intellect, 331 f.
Literary form of St. Thomas' writings,
33 ff.
Liturgy of the Old Testament, 509
Local motion, faculty of, 159
Locke, 544
Logic, 361: Thomistic, 541
Logos
angelic knowledge of, 229
in man, 211
as principle of being, 295
in St. John's Gospel, 3
spermatikos, 296
Love: the form of all virtues, 412; of
neighbor, 380; and the passions, 379
Luther, Martin, 214

Macrobius, 22
Magnanimity, 397
Maimonides, 18, 96
on creation, 275, 278
on God's existence, 237
Guide for the Perplexed by, 18 f.
idea of God, 239
the knowledge of God, 234
the number of angels, 232
providence, 310
relations in God, 118
Man, 146, 173-218
angels' knowledge of, 227
bodily equipment of, 182-85
conscience of, 197
common sense of, 184
cultural activities of, 200 f.
dignity of, 446

Man (*continued*)
    direct creation of, 283
    and ecstasy, 202
    equipment of, 182-203
    erect position of, 183
    evil in, 196
    free will of, 216
    function of, 288
    and God's grace, 201
    the image of God, 212, 215 f.
    inferiority to animals, 183
    knowledge of, 185-92
    last end of, 512
    meaning of his existence, 211-18
    metaphysical position of, 211-18
    metaphysical structure of, 214
    the middle being, 212, 217, 291
    moral development of, 197
    most perfect of natural things, 212
    original state of, 465, 512 f.
    in Paradise, 201
    a person, 204 f., 372 f.
    and prophecy, 202
    relationship to God, 201, 216
    religious aptitude, 200-3
    religious development of, 506
    religious position of, 211-18
    St. Thomas' study of, 182
    sensitive equipment of, 184 f.
    sensitive soul of, 178
    social aptitude of, 200-3
    a social being, 200, 422
    social nature of, 417-54
    spiritual equipment of, 185-203
    a spiritual person, 446
    subject to suffering, 181
    supernatural life of, 201
    technical achievements of, 217 f.
    ultimate end of, 216
    union with God, 386
    vision of God, 202
    will of, 185, 192-200
Manegold of Lautenbach, 42
Manichaeans, 273: dualism of, 278; and evil, 382
Manual labor, 486
Marcus Aurelius: and death, 215; and the spiritual, 523
Mare, William de la, 54: on the knowledge of the individual, 343; and the principle of individuation, 77
Marital intercourse, 209

Marriage, 415, 423 ff., 487
    of blood relatives, 471
    Christian, 424
    indissolubility of, 471
    monogamic form of, 425
    natural inclination to, 470
    purposes of, 470
    right to, 486 f.
    threefold purpose of, 424
Married life, duties of, 209
Marsilius of Padua, 429
Mas occasionatus, 207
Materia primo prima, 223
Materia signata, 30, 74 f., 92, 532
Material object, 360
Mathematical body, divisibility of, 109
Mathematical essences, 328, 338
Mathematical ideas, suprasensible origin of, 340
Mathematical procedure, 340
Mathematical structure of things, 338
Mathematics, 361, 363: analytical character of, 341; science of, 340; subject matter of, 40, 364
Matrimony, sacrament of, 514; *see also* Marriage
Matter
    the basis of change, 105
    condition of individuation, 78
    corporeality and, 223
    created by God, 62
    disposition to form, 66
    distinct from privation, 62
    divisibility of, 74
    Duns Scotus' theory of, 223
    electro-dynamic theory of, 72
    indifference of, 66
    indivisibility of, 64
    infinity of, 64
    the "informing" of, 267
    intelligible, 328, 338
    lowest in hierarchy of being, 140
    metaphysical, 62
    numerical differentiation excluded by, 62
    numerical unity of, 64
    passive potency rooted in, 119
    potency of, 64
    potentiality of, 266 f.
    prime, 272
    principle of imperfection, 312
    principle of individuation, 72-80

Matter (*continued*)
  priority of, 268
  proper, 66
  "signed," 74, 92, 532
  the substance of possibility, 97
  transitoriness of, 181
  uniformity of, 62
Matter and form, 40, 59-80
  basis of being, 62
  of the community, 433
  definition of, 59-65
  derivation of, 59-65
  evaluation of, 67
  intrinsic principle of being, 62
  and the predicaments, 66
  relation between, 65, 534
  Thomistic view of, 62-80
  and the universals, 66
Matthew of Aquasparta, 456: and the
  knowledge of the individual, 343;
  and the knowledge of the soul,
  349
Mechanistic theory of animal life, 170
Medicine, 365
Memory, 163: intellectual, 192; in man,
  184; in prudence, 408
Metaphysical abstraction, 334
Metaphysics, 361 f., 367: objects of, 363;
  subject matter of, 40
Metaphysics of Aristotle, 244
Method, scientific, 366 f.
Methods, Thomistic, 527
Middle Ages: culture of, 528 f.; philoso-
  phy of, 215; sciences of, 361
Mixed bodies, 141, 286
Modern science and plurality of forms,
  145
Modern thought, 519
Mohammedan theology on creation, 278
Monad theory of Leibnitz, 80
Monadology of Leibnitz, 547
Monarchy, 429 f.
Monism, 533
Monogamy, 425, 472
Monte Cassino, St. Thomas at, 7
Moral act, the, 373
Moral attitude and bodily disposition, 179
Moral order, the, 368-415
Moral philosophy, division of, 40 f.
Moral prescriptions of Old Testament,
  507
Moral values, 372-78

Morality, 368-415: and freedom of the
  will, 369; and order, 369; and pov-
  erty, 385; *see also* Ethics
Morals, science of, 365; *see also* Ethics
Moreh, the, 19
Morphology, historical, 366
Moslems, 13-17
Movement, 251: continuity of, 253; kinds
  of, 252; process of, 158; succession
  in, 253
Mover, unmoved, 237
Mutilation, physical, 492
Mystical body of Christ, 217, 444, 514
Mysticism, 529: not hostile to science, 43

Name of God, 235
Naples and Sicily, absolutism of, 427
Nativism, 337
Natural law, 464-73: immutability of,
  493, 498
Natural reason, 44
Natural rights, 474-99
Natural sciences, 363: St. Thomas'
  knowledge of, 31 ff.; subject mat-
  ter of, 363
Necessary being, 96
Negative knowledge of God, 234 f.
Negative theology, 235
Neoplatonism, 36: its negative idea of
  God, 239; among the Syrians, 13;
  and time, 213; and universals, 72
Neothomism, 527, 544
Nestorians and Greek philosophy, 13
New Testament: and man's social nature,
  418; and natural law, 466
Newton, 70, 527
Nicholas of Amiens, 264
Nicholas of Cusa, 35: and the individual,
  80; theism of, 547
Nicholas of Lisieux, 53
Nicomachean ethics, 9, 439
Nietzsche on truth, 542
Nihilism, 215 f.
Nominalism, 80, 540: and form, 70;
  knowledge of the individual, 343
Non-being, 156, 371: knowledge of, 358
Non-life, 156
Nourishment of animals, 155: and vege-
  tative soul, 155
Nous, 288, 295, 364: of Aristotle, 332;
  in man, 178, 185, 199; of Plotinus,
  359

Now, the, 122
Number: kinds of, 110; a species of quantity, 110

Obedience, virtue of, 414
Object: formal, 360; of the intellect, 188; material, 360; of moral act, 373
Objections: to Thomism, 519-26; to the Thomistic theory of individuation, 76 f.
Objective correlative of the universals, 85
Objects common to the senses, 160
Occupational groups, 426: medieval, 440
Ochlocracy, 430
Officials in the state, 431
Old Testament and the law of grace, 507
Oligarchy, 430
Ontological truth, 356 ff.
Ontology; see Being
Order
  of accidents to substance, 303
  in activity, 305 ff.
  actualization of, 301 f.
  author of, 300
  authoritarian, 427
  and beauty, 299
  in becoming, 305 ff.
  of causes, 306
  of cognitive powers, 315
  comprehended by the intellect, 260 f.
  concept of, 528
  of cooperation, 313
  of the cosmos, 516
  definition of, 298
  as divine providence, 301
  dynamic, 305
  of effects, 306
  among the elements, 304
  and the eternal law, 462
  and ethics, 369
  of generation, 301
  good of, 307
  of good, 383-87
  of grace, 513
  and the individual, 302 ff., 307
  kinds of, 298 f.
  of knowledge, 313 ff.
  legal, 504
  of love, 380
  in the mind of God, 300
  moral, 368-415, 504
  in nature, 361

Order (continued)
  of objects of knowledge, 315
  of origin, 313
  partial, 301 f.
  of perfection, 313
  a perfection of being, 299
  place in philosophy, 298
  among powers of the soul, 313
  principles of, 304
  and providence, 309
  of purposes, 369
  of reason, 378-83
  of salvation, 512-15, 517
  among the sciences, 360-67
  and sin, 312
  social, 365
  static, 305
  supernatural, 444, 506
  total, 306 f.
  and the transcendentals, 137
  in the Trinity, 301
  unity of, 299 f.
  in the universe, 293-312
  and virtue, 388-415
  of the will, 378-83
Oresme, Nicolas, 70
Organism: growth of, 154; life of, 157; structure of, 154
Organon by Aristotle, 6, 361
Organs: corporeal, 150; number of, 148
Origen
  defense of philosophy by, 42
  equality of spirits, 177
  on love of relatives, 381
  origin of human body, 284
  and St. Thomas, 23
  theory of guilt, 304
  theory of universal apocatastasis, 230
Origin: of things, 250-55; of the universe, 271-74, 283
Original sin, 216: and generationism, 291
Originality of St. Thomas, 28
Orphic mysteries, 523

Paganism, suppression of, 489
Pantheism, 246 f.
Papal States, 427
Parallelism between thought and being, 60, 70, 79, 95, 100, 326
Parents: influence on children's souls, 180 f.; love of, 508; their right to teach religion, 487

Pascal, 138, 217
Passions
  abnormal, 179
  in animals, 166
  control of, 199
  corporeal, 167
  and freedom of the will, 198
  influenced by the will, 198
  in man, 198
  moral indifference of the, 394
  seat of, 167
  spiritual, 167
Passive potency rooted in matter, 119
Passive qualities of corporeal being, 141
Patience, virtue of, 415
Patriarchal idea in sociology, 424
Patriotism, virtue of, 394
Paul, St.
  ecstasy of, 202
  influence on St. Augustine, 50
  influence on St. Thomas, 50
  man's social nature, 418
  mystical body of Christ, 444
  natural law, 401
  order, 293
  private property, 478
Peckham, 51: principle of individuation,
  77; St. Thomas opposed by, 53
Perception, meanings of, 317
Perfection of things, 371
Peripatetics and the seat of virtues, 410
Perseitas, 98
Person, the human, 204-18
  differences of, 206
  individuality of, 206 f.
  meaning of, 204
  ontology of, 185
  a substance, 98
  unity of, 204 f.
Personality, 206: attribute of, 175; concept of, 205; moving principle of,
  209; rights of, 439
Pessimism among the Greeks, 522
Peter, St. (apostle), 429: spiritual primacy of, 449
Peter Damian, St.: and worldly knowledge, 42
Peter Lombard, 49: and Augustinianism,
  20; on law, 456; and St. Thomas,
  24; on successive creation, 282
Peter of Hibernia, 7
Peter of Tarantasia, 206

Phaedo by Plato, 20, 522
Phantasm, instrumental in knowledge,
  329
Phantasy in animals, 162 f.
Phenomenologists, 326
Phenomenology of Peripatetics, 69
Philip of Greve, 6
Philip of the Blessed Trinity, 543
Philip the Chancellor, 392 f.
Philiponus, 142
Philo, 4, 36, 46
  on creation, 273
  on ecstasy, 202
  interpreter of the Pentateuch, 273
  and Jewish philosophy, 18
  on knowledge of God, 233
  on simultaneous creation, 282
Philosophia perennis, 28
Philosophy
  abuse of, 44
  autonomy of, 524 f.
  and Christianity, 4
  of culture, 365
  defined by Plato, 82
  fundamental problem of, 57
  "handmaid" of theology, 46
  of history, 366
  independent of theology, 36, 38
  of law, 455
  modern, 544
  moral, 361
  natural, 40, 361
  and the natural sciences, 173, 524
  opposition to, 42
  practical, 365
  rational, 361
  in service of religion, 525
  subject matter of, 39
  and supernatural revelation, 45
  and teachings of faith, 45-50
  and theology, 41-49
  threefold task of, 44 f.
Physical perfection, 385
Place: category of, 119 f.; modern definition of, 120; potency to, 219; reality
  of, 120
Plants, 146 f.
  appetite of, 164
  without habits, 113
  knowledge of, 161
  nourishment of, 155
  sense perception in, 156

Plato
active principles, 119
atheists, 522
cardinal virtues, 390
causality, 258
the common good, 413
concept of God, 272 f.
concept of the soul, 148
creation, 272, 276
eternal ideas of, 20
human soul, 175 f.
human thought, 519
idea of the individual, 332
as a manifestation of the logos, 4
mathematical forms, 339
matter, 63
movement, 251
the next life, 522
number of angels, 232
philosophy of, 517
and the politician, 438
pure spirits, 222
slavery, 479
socialistic views of, 439
society, 417
Sophists opposed by, 460
the state, 438
table of values, 384
teleology, 295
theory of essences, 82
theory of ideas, 82, 100, 138, 150, 276, 295, 359, 460, 521 f.
theory of intuition, 354
theory of the origin of the soul, 288
theory of participation, 95 f.
theory of universals, 83 f.
true being, 97
unity of the soul, 149 f.
the universals, 326
world of ideas, 72
the world soul, 146
worldly goods, 523
Platonism and St. Thomas, 19-23
Platonists: on angels, 230; and extension, 109; and logic, 362; and matter and form, 62
Plotinus
on angels, 222
criticism of the categories, 125
essential form, 84
on God the Creator, 273
influence on St. Thomas, 21

Plotinus (continued)
on the knowledge of God, 233, 235, 238 f.
theism of, 521
on time, 121
Plurality of souls, 150
Plutarch, philosophy of, 521
Pneuma: divine, 460; primal, 461
Point as principle of quantity, 64
Polis: of Aristotle, 425, 438; religion in the, 452
Politics by Aristotle, 418
Polyandry, 471
Polygamy, 470
Polytheism, 506
Pope, the: authority of, 453; secular power of, 451
Popular sovereignty, 428
Porphyry: on potency of matter, 267; principle of individuation, 75
Poseidonius and causality, 305
Positive idea of God, 238 f.
Positivism: atomistic, 68; legal, 457, 459; modern, 68; in modern philosophy, 238
Possession, forms of, 476
Possible, the: as identified with matter, 61
Possible being, 96
Possible intellect, 187, 329-50
Posture, 425
Potency: to act, 533; of matter, 64; to place, 219; see also Matter and form, Potency and act
Potency and act: applied to substance and accidents, 103 f.; compared to essence and existence, 91; compared to matter and form, 60
Poverty and morality, 385
Powers of the soul, 150-53
Powers of the vegetative soul, 157
Practical "intelligence" of animals, 171
Practical sciences, 365
Praedicabilia, 107
Praemotio physica, 269
Praepositinus of Cremona, 24
Prayer and providence, 311
Predicaments, 107: and matter and form, 66
Predicate in judgment, 354
Preservation of species, 158
Preservation of the universe, 284-92

Pre-Socratics on creation, 276
Pride, sin of, 414
Priesthood: Christian, 453, 514; pagan, 452
Primary form, 143
Prime matter: according to Aristotle, 70; *see also* Matter and form
Principle: concept of, 256; of continuity, 212; of individuation, 72-80; of separability of matter, 363
Principles: first, 41, 335; first moral, 468; of science, 367
Priority of form, 65
Prisoners of war, 489
Private property, modification of right of, 475
Privation: and matter, 62; the principle of becoming, 260 f.
Proclus, 20, 22: and geometric forms, 339; on universals, 85
Procreation, theory of, 381
Professions in the community, 420
Progress of knowledge, 28, 34
Prohibition of Aristotle's works, 6
Promulgation of law, 501
Proof: from causality, 237; ontological, 237
Proofs for God's existence, 237 f.
Proper object of senses, 316
Properties, accidental, 105
Property, private
  basis of right of, 476
  origin of, 477
  in Paradise, 478
  reasons for, 476
  right to, 475-79
  in Roman law, 478
  social implications of, 478
Prophecy in man, 202
Proportion, concept of, 128
Proportionality: actual, 131; analogy of, 129 ff.; figurative, 131
Prostitution and the natural law, 471
Protagoras and man's social nature, 417
Protestant theology, 214
Providence of God, 446
  and the eternal law, 310
  extent of, 310
  and order, 306
  and prayer, 311
  and prudence, 408
Province, the medieval, 426

Prudence, 372
  commanding function of, 407
  element of moral virtue, 405
  function of, 405
  importance of, 405
  integral parts of, 408
  norm of moral action, 405
  potential parts of, 408
  social, 441
  subjective parts of, 408 f.
  subordinate virtues of, 409
  twofold task of, 402
Pseudo-Clement on communism, 478
Psychology, 363: differential, 207; experimental, 364; sense, 317-25; Thomistic, 364
Psychopathic types, 179
Punishment: kinds of, 387; by the state, 442
Purpose in morality, 369
Pythagoreans
  on eternal law, 460
  and extension, 109
  matter and form, 62
  order, 295
  the soul, 147
  true being, 97

Quaestio de potentia, 47
Quaestiones: de anima, 47; *de bono,* 47; *disputatae,* 9, 47; *quodlibetales,* 550
Quality, 110-14
  accidental, 110 f.
  in the categories, 107
  of corporeal being, 141
  defined by Aristotle, 110
  defined by St. Thomas, 111
  division of, 111
  dynamic, 112
  kinds of, 110 f.
  passive, 111
  quantitative, 111
  sensitive, 112
  static, 112
  substantial, 110
Quantitative forms, 339
Quantitative relations, 339
Quantity, 108 ff.
  basis of divisibility, 109
  basis of relation, 108
  in the categories, 107
  continuous, 108

Quantity (*continued*)
   contributing factor of individuation, 76
   defined, 108
   discrete, 108
   idea of, 340
   and mathematical essences, 338
   and the object of the intellect, 328
   and the object of the senses, 316
   three-dimensional, 109
Qui est, 236
Quidditas; *see* Essence

Rational soul, the, 151 f.
Rationalism, 526: conflict with empiricism, 30
Raymond of Pennafort, St., 48
Read (C.H.V.) on political theories, 454
   note
Realism: of Aristotle, 214 f.; of St.
   Thomas, 58, 214, 531
Reality: of the external world, 322; of a
   thing, 95
Reason
   dependence on the body, 179
   and faith, 4
   in man, 191
   practical, 399 f.
   speculative, 192
   and the supernatural, 46
Redemption, the, 216, 368
Reginald of Piperno, 51
Regnum, the German, 427
Relation, 114-18
   accidental, 118
   of *actio-passio,* 118
   of analogy, 128
   basis of, 115
   of body to soul, 176 f.
   in the categories, 108
   causal, 242
   definition of, 114
   divine, 234
   of effect to cause, 117
   between essence and existence, 89
   essential, 118
   in God, 114
   between God and creatures, 116 f.
   of identity, 116
   importance of, 114
   logical, 116, 118
   mixed, 116 f.

Relation (*continued*)
   place in the universe, 115
   predicamental, 118
   quantitative, 117 f., 339
   real, 115 ff.
   reality of, 115
   secundum dici, 117
   secundum esse, 117
   of time, 118
   transcendental, 117
   in the Trinity, 118
Religion: subject to the state, 452; virtue
   of, 414
Religious aptitude of man, 200-3
Religious concept of God, 248
Religious development of man, 506
Religious toleration, 489
Renaissance and individualism, 440
Reproduction, process of, 154, 156
Republic by Plato, 418
Rest, 251
Return of all things, 230 f.: eternal, 366
Revelation: and philosophy, 45 f.; teach-
   ings of, 525
Rhetoric, 361
Richard of Middletown, 206
Richard of St. Victor, 43
Right
   to inviolability, 493
   to marry, 486 f.
   to physical existence, 474 f.
   to physical freedom, 479-85
   to property, 475-79
   to religious worship, 487
   to work, 485 f.
Rights: of communities, 491 ff.; natural,
   474-99; popular, 427; of a spiritual
   person, 487-91
Rigorism in morals, 404
Robert of Kilwardby, 54
Roger Bacon; *see* Bacon
Rousseau and popular sovereignty, 428
Rufinus, 429: and the natural law, 465
Ruler: duties of, 431; obedience to an infidel, 451

Sacra doctrina, 365
Sacraments, order of, 514
Sacred science, 361
Sacrilege, 374
Sanctions of the law, 503

Scheler, Max, 322
Scholasticism's lack of historical appreciation, 9
Schopenhauer, voluntarism of, 548
Sciences
  division of, 360-66
  differentiation of, 360
  liberal, 365
  order among, 360-67
  the practical, 365
  productive, 365
  theoretical, 362-65
Scientific method, 366 f.
Scotus, Michael, 6, 14
Scotus Eriugena; see Duns
Seed, formation of, 155
Self-consciousness: in animals, 164; in man, 189
Self-control, 394
Self-defense, 474
Self-determination of the animal, 165
Self-formation, 146
Self-knowledge, 345-50: of angels, 347; of God, 347; infallibility of, 347; man's, 189
Self-love, 380
Self-movement, 157, 171 f.: characteristic of life, 146
Seminal theory, 284
Sempiternity, 123
Seneca: and congenital knowledge, 337; on slavery, 479 f.; and the spiritual, 523
Sensation, 161 f.
Sense, common, 162, 324
Sense, organ of, 319
Sense appetite, 184 f.
Sense judgment, 324
Sense knowledge, 38, 184 f., 320 f.
Sense of touch in man, 184, 315, 322
Sense perception, 162, 317-25, 327
Sense psychology, 317-25
Sense species, 318, 321
Senses, 159 ff.
  accidental object of, 316
  adequate object of, 317
  common object of, 316 f.
  external, 159 ff.
  inner, 162
  of man, 184
  objects of, 315 ff.
  organs of, 316

Senses (continued)
  proper object of, 316
  truth in the, 355
Sensibile per accidens, 316
Sensitive life, 147
Sensitive soul, 152, 159, 178
Sensualism, 339
Sentences, St. Thomas' Commentary on the, 10
Separability of matter, 363
Sex and physical characteristics, 207
Sexual generation, 287
Shaftesbury, personalist theory of, 80
Shape, 120
Siger of Brabant, 54: on indirect creation, 277; and St. Thomas, 543; supports Averroes, 16
Sight, sense of, 159
Simplicius: on composite bodies, 142; on quality, 111
Sin, 388
  of the angels, 230
  essence of, 382
  harmony of soul disturbed by, 465
  nature of, 383
  against nature, 472
  original, 395
  violation of order, 312
Skepticism, 346
Slavery, 471, 477, 479-85: necessity of, 482; origin of, 480; in the patristic era, 480
Slaves
  baptism of, 484
  and eudaimonia, 484
  right to existence, 484
  right to marriage, 484
  rights of, 483
  treatment of, 483
  and virtue, 483
Sleep, physiological basis of, 179
Smell, sense of, 160, 183
Social aptitude of man, 200-3
Social contract, 423, 428: and the Sophists, 438
Social implication of private property, 478
Social justice, 537
Social life of man, 417-54
Social nature of man, 417-54
Social order, 365
Social problems, 385
Socialism, 448: of Plato, 439

Society
  atomic mechanistic concept of, 420
  biological background of, 419
  disposition to, 422
  domestic, 424 f.
  natural origin of, 422
  nature of, 417-54
Sociology: of Israelitic society, 509; Thomistic, 417-54
Socrates: on life, 522; as a manifestation of the logos, 4
Sombart, Werner, 536
Sophists: opposed to slavery, 479; and rights of the individual, 438
Sophocles, 460
Soto, Dominic, 544
Soul
  actions of, 151
  age of, 176
  and corporeity, 174
  of the deceased, 180
  definition of, 147 f.
  dependence on the body, 176 f., 290
  direct creation of, 283, 288
  as essential form, 151
  as first act, 151
  goods of, 384
  immortality of, 178
  independence of the body, 177 f.
  individuality of, 180 f.━
  intuitive knowledge of, 349
  kinds of, 151 f.
  knowledge of itself, 346
  localization of, 150
  materialist concept of, 147
  a microcosm, 313
  origin of, 178, 288
  in Plato's world of ideas, 176
  powers of, 150 ff.
  properties of, 151
  relation to the body, 174
  salvation of, 444
  the seat of grace, 201
  sensitive, 159
  separation from the body, 176
  and sleep, 179
  subsistence of, 177 f.
  unity of, 149-54
  vegetative, 154-58, 289
Space, 108, 120
Species, 107
  God is in no, 92

Species (continued)
  good of, 308
  intelligible, 329
  intentional, 331
  preservation of, 156, 158, 169
  sense, 318 ff.
Species depurata, 331
Species expressa, 319, 331
Species impressa, 318 f.
Spinoza, 27, 544: on time, 129
Spiritual equipment of man, 185-203
Spiritual substance, 92, 308 f.
Spoils, the right to, 505 f.
Spouse, love of, 381 f.
Stagirite, the; see Aristotle
State, the, 417
  autonomy of, 433, 435, 454
  basis of, 424
  children in, 439
  Christian, 453
  and the Church, 449-54
  the creation of man, 422
  and education, 491
  establishment of, 431
  formation of, 425
  forms of, 430
  government of, 431
  hostile to human nature, 438
  importance of, 417
  a juridical person, 436 f.
  necessity of, 420
  an organism, 423
  origin of, 537
  the perfect community, 425
  priority of, 421, 423
  and public morals, 432
  and religion, 432, 452
  right of punishment by, 442
  rulers of, 421
  total, 417
States of life, 415, 426
Stephen of Tournai, 429
Stoics
  and the cosmos, 523
  first principles, 337
  logic, 362
  matter and form, 62
  optimism of, 215
  pantheism of, 461
  and the passions, 394
  and slavery, 479
Strategy, 365

Structure of things, 338
"Struggle for existence," 368
Suarez
  democracy, 429
  essence and existence, 94
  and the individual, 80
  popular sovereignty, 428
  prime matter, 72
  principle of individuation, 77, 533
Subjectivism in modern philosophy, 238
Subsistence: of first substance, 98; of human soul, 177 f.
Substance, 97-126
  and accidents, 97-126
  change of, 99
  concept of, 533
  the constant factor, 99
  distinct from accident, 104
  efficient cause of accidents, 104
  extension of, 108
  final cause of accidents, 104
  first, 98, 101
  first object of knowledge, 102
  first of categories, 102
  foundation for other being, 100
  imperishable, 306
  individual, 99
  kinds of, 97-101
  material cause of accidents, 104
  as object of knowledge, 101
  ontological self-sufficiency of, 102
  and order, 303
  perishable, 307
  principles of, 100
  resemblance to matter, 102
  second, 100 f.
  spiritual, 103
  subject of accidents, 99
  and substratum, 99
  and time, 99
Substantial being, genesis of, 260
Substantial form, 289: unity of, 143; see also Form, Matter and form
Substratum in genesis of being, 59 f.
Suicide, 442
Sulzer on soul's powers, 185
Summa aurea of William of Auxerre, 456
Summa contra Gentes, 48: theology of, 242 ff.
Summa de creaturis of St. Albert, 7
Summa theologica, 48 f., 487
Supernatural acts, 202

Supernatural happiness in angels, 230
Support, right to, 475
Supremacy, spiritual, 449
Syllogism, 35, 361
Synesis, 409
Synteresis, 197, 337, 400-10
Synthesis in judgment, 353
Synthetic method, 366 f.
Syrians and philosophy, 13

Taste, sense of, 161
Teleology, 182
Temperance, 394, 414
Tempier, Stephen, 53
Temporal goods, love of, 382
Tertullian, 4: freedom of conscience, 488; natural moral law, 401; traducianism, 288
Thales, 294
Theaetetus by Plato, 522
Themistius, 17
Theodicy, 383
Theodoret on origin of slavery, 480
Theology, 361, 365: negative, 235, 237; and philosophy, 41-49; subject matter of, 40; of the two summas, 242-48
Theophany, 274, 279 f.
Theophrastus, 17
Theoretical material sciences, 362-65
Theory of values, 365
Thomas Aquinas, St.
  abuse of language, 420
  angelic knowledge according to, 227
  on animal soul, 159
  anthropology, 217
  and the Arabians, 12 ff.
  and Aristotle, 9, 35
  Aristotle's terminology, 12
  astronomy, 526
  Augustinianism opposed by, 53
  authority, 31
  and Averroes, 14
  Averroism opposed by, 17, 153
  biology, 208
  and Boethius, 22, 74
  canonization of, 54
  the Christian Aristotle, 8
  commentaries on Aristotle, 10
  condemnation of, 54: revoked, 54
  creation, 271

Thomas Aquinas, St. (*continued*)
  critical attitude toward Aristotle, 12
  criticism of the Arabians, 16
  death of, 54
  defense of profane sciences, 52
  definition of the eternal law, 462 f.
  description of the human body, 183 f.
  distinction between essence and exist-
    ence, 94
  Doctor Angelicus, 52
  on ecstasy, 203
  epistemology of, 313 ff.
  essence and existence, 90
  ethical system of, 31
  existence of essence, 84
  and external goods, 385
  faith and science, 38
  the Fathers of the Church, 22 ff.
  founder of modern philosophy, 39
  on goods of life, 158
  instinct, 169
  intellectualism of, 51 f.
  Jewish philosophy, 17 ff.
  knowledge of Aristotle's writings, 10
  knowledge of the individual, 342
  life of, 549
  literary form of writings of, 33 ff.
  love of prayer, 51
  love of truth, 51
  the man, 50-54
  master of theology, 53
  matter and form, 62-80
  matter in angels, 223
  medical knowledge of, 179 f.
  method of commentaries, 11
  mildness of, 52
  the *Moreh,* 19
  the natural sciences, 31 f.
  Neoplatonism, 20
  ontology of the person, 185
  opinion about labor, 485
  origin of time, 278
  originality of, 28
  and the passions, 167
  the philosopher, 52
  philosophy of, 217
  philosophy of law, 455
  and Platonism, 19-23
  plurality of forms, 144
  popular sovereignty, 428 ff.
  praise of the intellect, 189
  the predicaments, 107

Thomas Aquinas, St. (*continued*)
  program of, 51
  proofs for God's existence, 237
  public life of, 52
  the *Quaestiones disputatae,* 47
  realism, 214
  relationship to St. Albert, 24 f.
  revised concept of matter, 71
  second sojourn in Paris, 17
  secular clergy in opposition to, 52
  sense knowledge, 38
  the simple friar, 51
  on slavery, 481 f.
  on the stars, 228
  study of man, 182
  substance, 98
  the systemizer, 28
  the teacher, 51
  the teachings of faith, 45
  the theologian, 29 f.
  theologians in opposition to, 53
  theory of eternal law, 460
  and tradition, 27 f.
  on unity of the soul, 150
  University of Paris in opposition to,
    53 f.
  on woman, 207
  writings of, 549-54
  youth of, 50
Thomas of York, 6
Thomism: criticism of, 519-26; origin of,
  30
Timaeus by Plato, 258, 272
Time, 108
  animals' perception of, 163
  category of, 120-24
  existential form of creatures, 213
  a mode of being, 121
  and movement, 121
  objectivity of, 122
  origin of, 278
  religious significance of, 213
  St. Augustine on, 120
  subjectivity of, 122
  unity of, 123
Topica by Aristotle, 361
Touch, sense of, 161, 183 f., 315, 322
Tradition, St. Thomas and, 27 f.
Traducianism, 288
Training of animals, 164
Transcendental relation of man to the
  community, 445

Transcendental truth, 135, 357
Transcendentals, the, 133-37
  convertibility of, 136
  and form, 68
  founded on divine ideas, 137
  ideas, 240
  importance of, 136 f.
  properties of, 136
Transitoriness of matter, 181
Trendelenburg, Adolph, 544
Trinity, order in, 301
Truth
  concept of, 467
  depositary of, 351 ff.
  and the divine intellect, 3
  eternity of, 358 f.
  knowledge of, 351-59
  logical, 353
  and man, 185
  ontological, 356 ff.
  in the senses, 355
  transcendental, 135, 357
  unchangeableness of, 358 ff.
Truthfulness, 397
Two powers of Christendom, 449
Tyranny, 430

Ulpian: the law of nations, 504; and
    natural law, 464
Ulrich of Strassburg, 49: on history, 366
Unchangeableness of truth, 358 f.
Undetermined dimensions, theory of, 75
Unity
  of body and soul, 173-76
  of God, 246
  of human person, 204 f.
  of matter, 64
  numerical, 72
  the principle of number, 110
  in Scholasticism, 26
Universal, the
  and the animal, 171
  compared to spirits, 208 f.
  according to Duns Scotus, 79
  existing in the individual, 84
  and matter and form, 66
  in the mind, 84
  in the mind of God, 85
  object of intellectual knowledge, 326
  objective correlative of, 85, 328
  pre-eminence of, 326
  as the principle of form, 40

Universal, the (continued)
  the problem of, 83-86
  according to Proclus, 85
  reality of, 328
  relation to the phantasm, 342
  theory of, 72
  value of, 73, 308
Universe, the
  authority in, 427
  anthropocentric view of, 306
  beauty of, 311
  beginning of, 278
  the best, 309
  and the categories, 125 f.
  the center of, 219
  eternity of, 278
  evil in, 311
  fourfold purpose of, 307
  knowledge of, 526
  necessity of, 272
  order in, 293-312
  an ordered structure, 294
  an organic whole, 308
  origin of, 281-92
  passing of, 281-92
  preservation of, 254-92
  purpose of, 309
  structural law of, 140
  structure of, 221
  the study of, 57
  a unity of order, 301
Univocation, 128: leads to pantheism, 133
Unum, the transcendental, 134
Urges in man, 209
Use, the right of, 478

Value
  absolute, 370
  concept of, 371
  fundamental moral, 405
  imperative, 369
  moral, 372-78
  theory of, 365
  of virtue, 406
Vasquez, Gabriel, 544
Vegetative life, 147, 155
Vincent of Beauvais, 27, 33
Vinci, Leonardo da, 70
Virginity, 414, 487
Virtues
  Aristotelian definition of, 407
  cardinal, 390, 392, 413

Virtues (continued)
definition of, 388
disposition for, 388 f.
divine, 398
division of, 390
"golden middle" in, 407
grades of, 415
the highest earthly good, 386
infused, 416
integral parts of, 396
intellectual, 390 f., 412
moral, 390 f., 409 f., 412
order among, 384
and order, 388-415
and practical reason, 399
rank of, 411
right middle of, 406
subject of, 410 f.
supernatural, 390, 398
theological, 407, 412
value of, 406, 411
Vision, beatific, 226, 386
Voice in animals, 171
Voluntarism, legal, 457

War, necessity of, 505
Warmth in the vegetative soul, 157
Wealth: dangers of, 385; obligation of,
475
"When," category of, 119 f.
"Where," category of, 119 f.
Whole, its superiority to the part, 307
Will
in the angels, 229
capable of good and evil, 196
dependent on the intellect, 193
external act of, 374
free causality of, 257
freedom of, 195, 231

Will (continued)
the human, 192-200
internal act of, 374
knowledge of, 348
object of, 165
and the passions, 198
precedence of, 199
threefold order of, 382
William of Auvergne, 96: and the works
of Aristotle, 6; and the natural moral
law, 402
William of Auxerre
on communism, 478
on law, 456
on natural law, 465
on prudence, 407
and the writings of Aristotle, 6
William of Champeaux on universals, 85
William of Moerbeke, 11, 20
William of Occam: and the individual,
80; and the knowledge of the individual, 343; legal voluntarism, 457
William of St. Amour, 53
William of Tocco, 30
Wisdom, order according to Book of, 303
Wisdom, virtue of, 391
Wolff, 544
Woman
in the Church, 208
civil rights of, 209
different from man, 207 ff.
formation of, 284
function of, 288
in the home, 208
inferiority of, 207
St. Thomas on, 207
Work: obligation to, 485; the right to,
485 f.
World soul, 146, 295
Writings of St. Thomas, 549-54